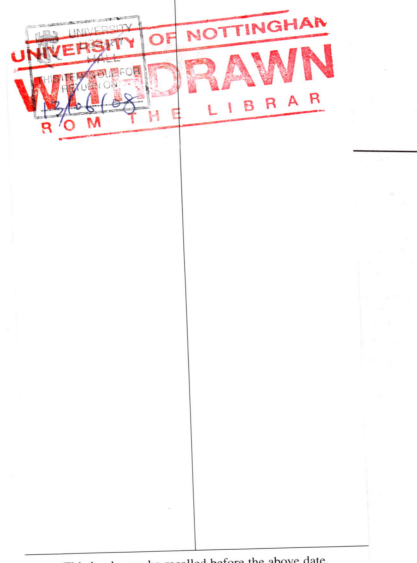

This book may be recalled before the above date.

LONGMAN

LONDON AND NEW YORK

Addison Wesley Longman Limited
Edinburgh Gate, Harlow,
Essex CM20 2JE, England
and Associated Companies throughout the world.

Published in the United States of America
by Addison Wesley Longman, New York

First Edition © Little, Brown and Company (Inc.) 1978
Second Edition © Longman Group Limited 1995

First published 1978
Tenth impression 1992
Second Edition 1995
Second impression 1996
Third impression 1996

ISBN 0 582 05071 5 CSD
ISBN 0 582 05070 7 PPR

British Library Cataloguing-in-Publication Data

A catalogue record for this book is
available from the British Library

Library of Congress Cataloging-in-Publication Data
African history / Philip Curtin . . . [et al.]. - 2nd ed.
    p. cm.
  Includes bibliographical references and index.
  ISBN 0-582-05071-5
  1. Africa - History.   I. Curtin, Philip D.
 DT20.A619   1994
 960 - dc20   93-47290
                                                         CIP

Set by 3 in 9½/12pt Ehrhardt

Produced by Longman Singapore Publishers (Pte) Ltd.
Printed in Singapore

CONTENTS

LIST OF MAPS

PREFACE

Before 1960, African history was barely recognized as a regular field of historical study. By the time the first edition of this book appeared in 1978, it had come of age as an established area of historical specialization. It reached a new level of maturity with the publication of two eight-volume reference histories of Africa, the *Cambridge History of Africa* and the UNESCO, *General History of Africa*. The last of these sixteen volumes appeared in 1993.

The present volume is also a general history of Africa, though much shorter. It is designed partly for the general reader and partly as a textbook for university-level courses in African history. When we set out to write a text, we also wanted to create a new synthesis, different from the main lines of African history as they were understood in the past, and even from the usual pattern of texts designed for university-level students. We were less interested in events and more interested in patterns of historical change. We were less interested in the deeds of the great than we were in the culture and behavior of ordinary people. With this in mind, we have intentionally given less than the usual emphasis to political history and more to social, economic, and intellectual trends. Because we would like to say something significant about peoples' changing ways of life, we have introduced more than the usual concern for the kinds of problems and solutions dealt with by anthropologists. Two of us, Steven Feierman and Jan Vansina, are anthropologists as well as historians.

Historians of Africa, in Africa and elsewhere, have been trying in the past four decades to get away from the older, Europe-centered view of the African past. But an African point of view is not easy to come by, even for historians of Africa who were born and raised there. In Africa itself, there are many different points of view toward African history. Most of the existing textbooks written by Africans for African schools and universities are, as perhaps they should be, centered on a particular country or region. The African history normally taught in Egypt barely extends beyond the Sudan and Ethiopia. African history in South Africa rarely reached north of Zimbabwe. The African history taught in francophone and anglophone tropical Africa carries strong vestiges of the educational system that formed the intellectual elite. Each of these "African histories" is different because each asks the implicit question: "How did our particular African society come to be as it is today?" That is a proper question. As historians from outside Africa, our implicit question is somewhat different. It is partly this: "How did the societies on the African continent come to be as they are today?" But it is broader still. We would like to use African history as a way of getting at part of a more general question: "How do human societies change through time?" This implies a conscious effort on our parts to avoid all ethnocentricity – African or Western.

The first three quarters of this book are organized by regions – North Africa including the Nilotic Sudan, East Africa from Ethiopia to Madagascar, Africa south of the Zambezi, Equatorial Africa from Angola and Zambia north through the Congo basin to the edge of the Sahara in Chad, and the conventional West Africa between the Sahara and the Gulf of Guinea. These regions are far from equal in either size or importance. The recorded information for the history of North Africa exceeds that for the rest of the continent several times over, especially for early millennia. West Africa is far more populous than any of the other four regions. Southern Africa has had the most rapid recent economic growth, hence the greatest weight of wealth and power. Contemporary challenges to the gross economic and political inequities in the region might warrant more emphasis on South Africa's recent past. We have nevertheless given these regions approximately equal attention in most time periods, in order to benefit from the variety of historical experience. A lightly populated and comparatively poor region like Equatorial Africa, for example, contains many societies whose historical experience was markedly different from that found elsewhere. It is therefore especially valuable for our understandng of the human experience at large.

This regional organization, however, may suggest that the regions were internally more homogeneous and more sharply divided from one another than they were in fact. This is one reason why precise regional boundaries are not always carried over from one chapter to the next.

North Africa is a special case and a long-standing problem for the organization of historical knowledge. Since the eighth century, it has been part of a broader Islamic society, whose main centers lay in western Asia. But it is also part of the African continent, illuminating similarities and contrasts among African countries, especially in the period of the colonial impact. Other aspects of sub-Saharan history – like the rise and penetration of Islam – require knowledge of North Africa and even of Arabia, if they are to be clearly understood. The problem is that North Africa belongs to two cultural worlds, one related to the Sudanic belt across the Sahara, the other reaching out to the broader world of Islam. The approach we have chosen is a compromise. Space limitations make it impossible to treat North Africa within the full context of Muslim civilization, yet North Africa was an essential stepping-stone between sub-Saharan Africa and the broader intercommunicating world. We have therefore dealt with North Africa as part of the African world, realizing that we may well have slighted the perspective of North Africa within the world of Islam.

Periodization is another organizational problem without guidelines. The old sequence of ancient, medieval, and modern is obvious nonsense for Africa. Yet historians of Europe and Africa alike have spent a good deal of effort locating and quarreling over the watersheds of history, where the style of change seems to alter sharply – as it did with the beginning of agriculture, the coming of the Iron Age, or of industrialization. No such changes took place all over Africa at the same time. We have divided our book arbitrarily at about 1500, 1780, 1880, and 1960. These divisions help to mark off a pattern, assigning more space to the recent than to the more remote past. Starting with an index of 1 for the ratio of pages to centuries before 1500, the index rises to about 10 for the period 1500 to 1780, 25 for the pre-colonial century, and 30 for the colonial period.

It is arguable that the progression should be steeper still, with more space assigned to the colonial period and still more to the post-colonial. We have chosen instead to give special attention to the pre-colonial century. That is the last time period in which independent African societies can be studied with their own dynamics for change intact. They were already overshadowed by Europe, but the European factor was not the overwhelming influence it was to become under colonial rule.

One price of this decision was to abandon the regional divisions after 1880. Instead, we present the colonial period in a series of chapters that deal with the whole continent. To present the economic, social, and political history of the colonial era on a region-by-region basis would require another book the size of this one. A continent-wide synthesis also follows from our original intention to look for patterns rather than events, and the patterns that can be distinguished in the colonial period are continent-wide.

We have omitted post-colonial Africa for reasons that are both pragmatic and intellectual. On the pragmatic side, this book is already long. To deal with the intense social and economic changes of the past thirty-five to forty years would require another book. On the intellectual side, African history after 1950 or so cannot be understood in the context of that single continent. The major themes in world history were truly worldwide. It would be impossible, for example, to deal with African international relations and political history without serious attention to the shadow of the Cold War. The great-power rivalries had an influence all over Africa, from the rise of Mobutu to the fall of Haile Selassie. In the late 1980s and early 1990s, the disappearance of the Soviet Union from the world scene was again an important factor in the weakening of apartheid in South Africa, as it was in the general shift away from broadly socialist forms of development planning in tropical Africa.

Nor was the Cold War alone among the major world influences of these decades. In economic change, the oil shocks of 1974 and after made a profound difference to the oil-rich like Nigeria and Libya and to the oil-poor everywhere. In international relations, the rise of Israel was a profound influence on the whole northwest corner of Africa from Morocco to Ethiopia – and considerable influence elsewhere. In social history, the explosion of African population was not simply an African phenomenon, but one that has to be understood in its whole, worldwide setting. The same is true of the African aspects of the worldwide AIDS epidemic.

Given the complexity and the worldwide nature of these changes, most teachers of African history will want to send students to a variety of readings that can give the emphasis required to lead them through these themes of worldwide importance.

Although all authors contributed something to most chapters of the first edition, the final responsibility for the chapters of the present edition is indicated in the table of contents.

We have avoided detailed recognition of our authorities in footnotes, but this book is only possible because of the heritage we, the authors, have received from the painstaking research of the scholars in Africa and abroad who have created a new African history in the past forty years.

THE ROOTS OF AFRICAN CULTURES

Veiled figures on the glistening terraces of a *kasbah* in Tunisia, a forlorn little group in the eternity of the Kalahari, chatting away around a smouldering fire. These two ways of spending an evening in very different surroundings are symbolic of the great variety of cultures that flourished in Africa until recent times – hundreds of cultures in endless variations, like so many flowers in the same bed. Yet, despite the differences, all have grown from humble and very similar origins, and underneath all the variation common themes can still be discerned, themes and patterns that stretch back into the hallowed past. The unity, then, derives from the roots, for these African cultures have grown up in the surroundings where they flourished for thousands and thousands of years ever since the first of our direct ancestors, *Homo sapiens*. *Sapiens* emerged there between 200,000 and 120,000 years ago in Africa. Africa has been inhabited ever since, and ever since cultures have developed there.

Yet the *history* of Africa does not go back through the hoary ages of the first developments. The timescales are so immense that the chronology of Stone Age archaeology is not really the chronology of historians. In practice, African historians seem to have agreed that their most meaningful starting point is the food-producing revolution, the period when agriculture, stock raising, and later, iron-working were introduced. These changes in people's livelihood made them much more independent from their environment than before. Earlier, when the population lived from hunting and gathering, the nomadic way of life and the need to keep each community down to a size related to the availability of game and wild plants had stunted the possibilities for further growth. In many surroundings these early foragers found their food without too strenuous an effort, so that the desire to augment the food supply was a major reason for a gradual switch to agriculture at first only in marginal environments. But even earlier, perhaps 20,000 years ago, and in very favorable environments some people stopped roaming about, became sedentarized and began to live in larger communities, villages. In many cases they obtained much of their food from fishing, but in some others they began to care for the wild plants, grasses or yams or oil palm trees, which they had been gathering, increased their yields and eventually turned them into crops.

Once people became sedentary in large numbers, the communities grew and food had to be produced rather than gathered. As environment gradually became less of a dictating agency, cultural and social change could increase, leading to greater and greater variety in cultures. A history of society and a history of culture now become meaningful.

We shall begin with the tale of how the major African ways of life unfolded. Here is a sketch of the roving life of foragers and how people shifted to agriculture and husbandry, how metallurgy was introduced, and how the Bantu-speaking peoples came as a spring tide that swept over almost half the continent. The story runs from *c.*8000 BC to 1000 AD, a period eight times longer than that covered in all the other chapters of this book.

The Late Stone Age way of life

By 8000 BC all Africa still lived in the Stone Age, but had entered the most refined period of that age, the Late Stone Age. Hunters and gatherers, also known as foragers, had interacted to the environments in which they lived and to an as yet unknown extent altered them.

Direct evidence about life in this period can still be found on the rare sites that have preserved not just stones but also organic material. One example is the remains of a camp that flourished around 2300 BC at Gwisho near the Kafue River in Zambia. The inhabitants belonged to the so-called Wilton stone culture. Like the other Late Stone Age cultures, the Wilton is characterized by a greater number of tool types than its predecessors. This variety indicates that artefacts were increasingly specialized for particular uses. In addition the Wilton people had a developed bone industry with items such as awls, rubbing tools, spoonlike instruments, ornaments and composite arrows. The dog had been domesticated, bows and arrows were used for the chase, and large bone points may have served as spearheads. These people also made wooden tools, such as digging sticks to uproot edible roots, and they used shells as implements. They worked skins and used natural pigments. Gwisho does not show it, but other Wilton people were responsible for much magnificent rock art in southern Africa.

The living on the Kafue flats was good. Wildlife thronged the grassy plains as it did in the nineteenth century, when the environment was exactly the same as we know from pollen analysis. The Gwisho foragers balanced their meat diet by foraging for roots, seeds, nuts, and berries as they came in season. At the site the archaeologists did not easily recognize some of these vegetable remains. But it is a remarkable testimony to the continuity of cultural knowledge that a foreign twentieth-century San or Bushman hunter, brought to the place, was still able to recognize all these without exception, to describe their uses and the seasons when they could be found and to convincingly describe the presumed function of all the tools found in the excavation. The people in this camp used baskets, built wind screens for housing and perhaps made mats to sleep on. Evidence of lean-tos or houses was not found there, but because the seasonal rains were (and still are) heavy at times, shelters must have been available.

It seems fair to assume that Gwisho was the focal point of a corporately owned hunting territory of relatively large size. There are in fact four sites at Gwisho that may reflect individual household lodgings of the same social group at the same time. The evidence confirms a truth that had already been assumed: foraging groups must remain small to exist. Ethnographic evidence from recent times indicates that although they sometimes numbered as many as one hundred people in wetter areas and even three hundred in some wet season camps, usually a group of foragers included from twenty to fifty people. With such small numbers, leadership posed a problem. Obviously there could be no organized role of chieftainship, for the chief would soon have quarreled with all his followers in turn. Face-to-face relationships of so few people for a whole lifetime imply that people know each other too well to obey the same person always. In addition, a leader could not arbitrate because his decision would first hurt one member, then another, and soon he would find himself at odds with all of them and ostracized. It is likely therefore that then, as now with almost all modern foragers in the world, decision making was communal, offenders were punished by banishment or by beating and mutual help was the cardinal value of the camp.

Anthropologists speculate that the people of Gwisho all belonged to a single family or *kinship group*, that is a collection of people related to each other by descent in a variety of ways, a group called a *kindred* or a *bilateral group*. They might find wives to marry by a straight exchange of one of their girls for a girl of another group. But one must be somewhat wary of such a model. Short lifespans intervened and the hazards of childbirth as well as of hunting and other accidents made for unequal lifespans as well. There probably were people who had lost all of their relatives or who had quarreled with their own kin and now had joined an unrelated group. As to marriage, some women might have followed a man they liked or had been adopted as little children or came into the group as the result of some other vagary of life. All one can say is that, given the presence of households it is quite likely that notions of kinship and marriage were used to *justify* why people lived in this small community, even if they were not truly kin at all.

At Gwisho the hunting itself may have been communal, because the animals were all big mammals such as zebra, buffalo, antelope, and occasionally even a rhinoceros. Fully grown elephants, however, seem to have been avoided and smaller animals were not very important in the diet. Despite the proximity of an excellent river and marshes, few fish or marsh antelopes were eaten and then only in one of the four sites. But big game must have been plentiful and close to the camps, because the hunters carried whole carcases of the animals home for butchering. From the remaining tools we can infer that these hunters must have been a bit bigger and stronger than the San of today, perhaps because their diet was richer. Yet despite their prowess at the hunt most of the food supply may have come from gathering edible matter.

By the nineteenth century AD, foragers could still be found in Africa but almost all of these were closely linked as inferior partners to farmers or pastoralists, and their way of life cannot be directly used as testimony to the way of life of people in the Late Stone Age in any part of Africa. Living fossils may occur in the animal kingdom where heredity rules, but not in the human kingdom, where heredity plays second fiddle to culture. It is the very nature of humans to reflect, to communicate their thoughts and feelings and to learn from experience. Because people live in groups (society) such reflections and experience become common to all the members of a group (culture) and inform their desires and motivation which then lead to action. Hence the way in which ethnographic studies about recent hunters and gatherers can be used to understand the ways of life millenia ago is very limited. Such studies reveal the practical constraints and requirements of foraging and living in small groups. These insights can be used in reconstructing *the requirements* that faced early foragers. But they tell us nothing about the *solutions* these people found to meet such requirements.

Fishermen and sedentary life in the Late Stone Age

A picture of Africa as peopled only by foragers around 8000 BC or 10,000 years ago would not be quite correct. Even then there were some sedentary populations. Early stable settlements of fishermen, at Ishango south of Lake Albert (Lake Mobutu), date to some 25,000 years ago and perhaps thousands of years earlier, while early settlements of fishermen who took care of stands of wild but edible reeds were found at Wadi Kubbaniya in southern Egypt and are nearly as old (c. 18,500 BC). But such settlements remained very rare until about 7000 BC. The finds at Ishango and at Baringo on Lake Turkana which date to c. 8000 BC include beautiful, efficiently barbed, harpoons, and also net weights. Nets evoke dugouts, paddles, weirs and most of the later fishing gear. With such equipment and the resources of lakes, oceans, and rivers settled life became possible and desirable. It allowed for a mostly sedentary life even though, along the rivers at least, the fishermen would abandon their village for several months in the dry season to make the most of the favorable conditions for fishing, especially on broad rivers with low banks such as the Zaire and many of its affluents or the upper Zambezi, or parts of the Nile and the Niger.

The fishing settlements could grow much larger than those of the foragers without danger of falling short of food and could have permanent houses, to be improved as the generations went by. Sedentary villages grouping from 100 to 1000 people came into being and with them village life. Obviously a social structure based on an informal collection of a few households, presumably held together by the ideology of a kindred, was no longer suited to groups of this size and even households were no longer functioning in the same way as before. Fishing probably required a greater division of labor by gender than had hitherto existed. The equipment required for fishing led to the development of notions of property, both common and personal, and hence to the practice of inheritance, certainly for equipment, such as dugouts, that had been fashioned with a great labor input and could be used for many years. Notions of property and inheritance provided a new focus for the household. Meanwhile communal activities continued, but may have involved smaller groups than a collective hunt for big game did. Fishing with nets required the cooperation of a few adults only. That, too, affected the overall spirit of solidarity in the community. Under such circumstances, it is likely that public authority began to be formalized and that an ideology to justify leadership developed. But one cannot even guess at the sort of social institutions and ideologies that were developing in such settlements, because the ingenuity of social imagination in inventing such devices defies second guessing.

Furthermore the development of formal authority, and the necessity of maintaining a balance between an *esprit de corps* within households and settlements and peaceful relations between such groups, as well as the growth of notions of property, must have found expression in beliefs and rituals that sanctioned group cohesion. Fear of sanctions for non-cooperation may well have been the force that underlay the group's solidarity. In more recent times such sanctions derived from beliefs in witchcraft and sorcery. People attributed witchcraft and sorcery to persons who were loners or of whose conduct public opinion disapproved. Whether the powers of such people were innate or acquired from charms, they allowed them to kill or harm others. As it was believed that witchcraft or sorcery grew out of envy, leaders and more wealthy people were more vulnerable than others while the poorer and weaker people were often suspected of being witches or sorcerers. The fear of being accused, and perhaps killed as a result, strongly contributed to group solidarity, and conversely, so did the fear of being hurt by witchcraft or sorcery. Accusations of witchcraft or sorcery in a community signaled unusual social tensions and often broke out when there was competition for leadership.

Whatever the precise institutions, values, beliefs and rituals that developed in such settlements they must have taken generations and generations to reach maturity. No one has recorded the many trials and errors that preceded the evolution of successful patterns of social structure and culture which finally emerged. When sedentary life later became common as people turned to agriculture, the experience gained by the earlier fishing communities was available, a fact which eased the transition to sedentarization.

Later, when most people had become agricultural, the fishing folk continued to play a major role in African history. They moved up and down the streams and rivers according to the seasons and traded with inland groups, exchanging fish and pottery for crops. Later again they began to buy other products from one inland group and to sell them to another. As commercial intermediaries they also carried news of the outside world to each of their customers, breaking down cultural isolation. They carried the information and the goods that led to much diffusion of ideas, behavior, and artefacts and thus stimulated the growth of different civilizations.

The most crucial groups known among early fishermen were those of Wadi Kubbaniya along the Nile in southernmost Egypt. They began to nurture the reeds whose seeds they ate, a food which their descendants in Pharaonic Egypt still appreciated nearly 15,000 years later. These early fishermen along the Nile were the first communities known to experiment with agriculture and perhaps they were also the first to herd cattle as well.

The spread of food production to 2000 BC

Ceramics are a good indicator of a sedentary life style because their weight and their fragility makes them unsuitable for a nomadic life. Hence their appearance, especially in larger sizes, indicates a settled way of life. Before 7500 BC pottery was invented in Africa and it was then being made from the banks of the Nile near Khartoum to Air, a mountainous region in Niger. This area was much less arid than today's Sahara but still not very humid. So far, however, no firm evidence for any domesticated animal other than the dog, or for crops has been found on these sites. The earliest secure presence of domestic livestock dates from the fifth millennium BC when goats, sheep and bovine cattle were present in the whole Nile valley from the Delta to upstream Khartoum, as well as over most of North Africa. Whether these bovines were imported from Asia, domesticated from wild local cattle, or a type that was the product of breeding imports with local cattle, we do not know. Goats and sheep were imported from western Asia. As to crops, wheat was an Asiatic import, but barley may have been domesticated in Egypt.

By 4000 BC, then, pottery, pastoralism and agriculture based on wheat and barley were well established in northern Africa. A millennium later the crops and the domestic animals had reached the highlands of Ethiopia and northern Nigeria, but neither had yet reached Africa, west of the meridian of Greenwich.

Given the timescale in thousands of years, sedentary life and pastoral nomadism obviously spread at a snail's pace. In most cases environmental barriers prevented a faster spread. To overcome these major innovations were needed. Barley and wheat do not grow in tropical savannas and hence the domestication of other cereals was needed. By 6000 BC millet and sorghum were beginning to be domesticated in Upper Egypt. Between *c.*3500 and *c.*2500 BC domesticated millets, sorghums and sesame were cultivated in Ethiopia and probably all along the southern fringes of the Sahara from the Nile to north and west of Lake Chad. Indeed African sorghum has been found at Hili, a site in the Persian Gulf area where it dates to earlier than 3000 BC while sesame, diffusing from Africa, reached Sumer before 2350 BC. Moreover, the farmers in the highlands of Ethiopia developed totally new local crops such as the cow pea or the *ensete*, a relative of the banana, in addition to cereals, and they also began to integrate cattle into farming activities. A farmer would keep a few heads of cattle, feed on their milk and meat, while fertilizing his fields with their manure, and using the stubble left after the harvest of the cereals as fodder for the cattle. This integration of husbandry and farming was a major technological breakthrough.

Once millets and sorghums had been domesticated farming and cattle keeping began again to spread further. Herders colonized the lowlands of the Horn from about 2000 BC onwards while farmers and herders practicing integrated farming spread southwards in East Africa and reached the northern shores of Lake Victoria by the same date. By 1500 BC herders had begun to exploit the excellent grasslands of northern Tanzania and pottery related to the early farmers has been found even further south in east central Tanzania where it has been dated to *c.*1000 BC. But then the spread of farming and herding came apparently to a full stop.

In West Africa herders and farmers with the new cereals did not move very far southwards before they met people who practiced a very different kind of food production, *vegeculture*. In the moister lands where forests alternated with grasslands (savanna/forest mosaic) between the ninth parallel North and the deep rainforests far to the south, a variety of wild yams and palm trees flourished. The inhabitants there had discovered that certain roots and trees would grow again on the same spots, provided they put slips in the ground or buried nuts and weeded a little when necessary afterwards. In this way they gradually domesticated several types of yams, all sorts of gourds and calabashes as well as the oil and raphia palms. At first these merely supplemented gathered plant food, fish and game. The practice of vegeculture leaves

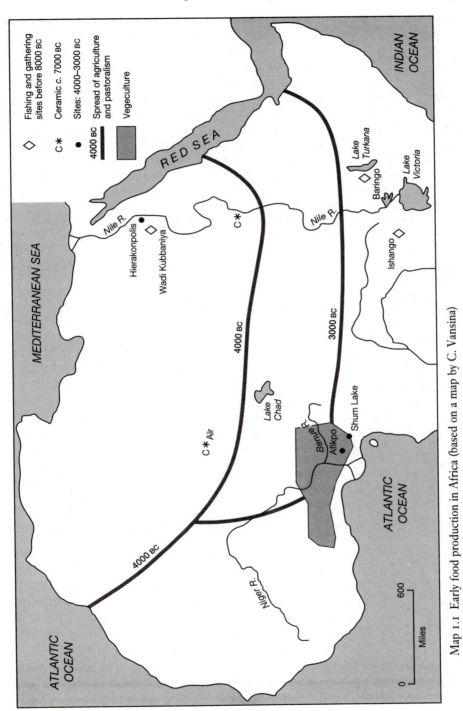

Map 1.1 Early food production in Africa (based on a map by C. Vansina)

no permanent traces, and hence archaeologists cannot directly date the domestication processes, but the practice was evidently well established in the fourth millennium BC.

At that time pottery appears on the site of Shum Laka in western Cameroon, and on Nigerian sites near Afikpo, all located at the time in deep rainforests. The use of ceramics once again points to a fairly sedentary way of life, probably made possible by vegeculture. Whether the people in this area were inspired by the agriculture of their northern neighbors to intensify their practices, for instance, to borrow at least the notion of regular fields from them rather than to grow their crop in bunches here or there, we do not know. The people living in the rainforests found that cereals would not grow there nor would livestock flourish except for goats. Around 3000 BC, or in the following centuries, they perfected a new type of economy there based on root crops and their weeds, on the vegeculture of trees (especially oil palms), and on the products of trapping, gathering and fishing.

The evidence adduced here points to the conclusion that the most momentous achievement was not the early introduction of agriculture in the northeast, but the invention of forms of agriculture adapted to various tropical environments. Thus the most crucial period in the history of food production in Africa falls in the millennium after *c.*3500 BC.

Meanwhile, however, in the lands where agriculture dated from 4000 BC, further developments were occurring. From about 4000 BC onwards the Egyptians raced ahead. Technical improvements in pottery making, stone carving, leatherwork, basketry and the weaving of linen occurred at an astonishing rate. Soon copper and then bronze tools appeared. Then, before 3500 BC, the first known city in Africa emerged in upper Egypt. This was Hierakonpolis where some two hundred years later a practical form of writing appeared. Around the same time the whole Nile valley in Egypt came to be incorporated into two rival kingdoms, one in upper and one in lower Egypt. By 3150 BC the Pharaoh of Hierakonpolis then unified the whole country. Thus Egypt became the earliest large-scale centralized state known anywhere in the world. This rapid pace of change has been attributed to constant communication with the developing centers of the Middle East. Yet this can only be a partial explanation, for in some ways Egypt was ahead of the Middle East. Among the local factors involved one must stress the extraordinary fertility of the Nile valley and the ease of communication along the river because the almost constant winds from the north pushed sailing boats along against the current southwards, while the current facilitated movement northwards. The ease of communication, allied to the developing technologies, fostered a division of labor between riverine settlements with specialization of skills and produce, which in turn facilitated the rise of towns and larger political entities.

Life in the central Sahara and along the Mediterranean coast meanwhile retained strong nomadic features. Even though the population there grew cereals and used pottery, they were mainly pastoral nomads. Numerous rock paintings all over the Sahara, dating from *c.*4500 BC onwards, inform us about this way of life. They show huge herds of cattle being herded, or milked, they portray the game that was hunted and they illustrate a few features of domestic and religious life. The most ambiguous feature about this Saharan art unfortunately concerns the evidence for the cultivation of domestic plants. Some authors interpret a few rare scenes as the reaping of the harvest, where others see only the gathering of wild grasses. After *c.*4000 BC developments in Northwest Africa began clearly to diverge from those in the Central Sahara perhaps because of connections with the Iberian peninsula. By 3000 BC farming played a greater role there than in the Sahara, and a local Bronze Age is attested by 2000 BC.

Languages

Languages and groups of languages are said to belong to a single *family* when their resemblance to one another is so strong that it cannot be ascribed to chance, but must be the result of common origin. When languages are grouped in a family, it means that at some distant time in the past the ancestor of them all – a proto-language – existed as a living, changing language, spoken by people with a culture and a history of their own. Language changes over time as it passes on from parents to children. When groups speaking the proto-language separate from one another their languages diverge. Successive divergences of the groups descended from a proto-group can lead to large numbers of languages within a family, so that the pattern of descent looks like a family tree.

Linguists are agreed on the classification of African language first proposed by J. Greenberg. There are only five independent language families in Africa. The whole of North Africa, the Horn and the area around Lake Chad speak *Afro-Asiatic* languages. This family has six coordinate branches. Semitic in Asia, Ancient Egyptian, Berber in northern Africa, Cushitic in Ethiopia, Omotic in western Ethiopia and Chadic around Lake Chad. The most widely spoken Semitic language in Africa nowadays is Arabic which was brought by various waves of immigrants mainly between the seventh and the eleventh century. The ancestral language from which all these branches descended was spoken millenia before 4000 BC, the date at which linguists think ancestral Semitic began to diverge and when Ancient Egyptian was in use in the Nile valley. Further westwards Berber-speakers made up much of the nomad populations in northern Africa and portions of the Sahara when the Sahara was still good pasture land. By 2000 BC at the latest Omotic and Cushitic were spoken in Ethiopia. Of the language families in Africa Afro-Asiatic has the longest association with both pastoralism and agriculture and the expansion of these languages may well be linked to the early spread of food production.

The foragers of southern Africa as well as the Sandawe and Hadza of Tanzania spoke *Khoisan* languages. This may well be the oldest language family of all. Indeed it is possible that this does not constitute a single language family but that a few of the languages now grouped together as Khoisan belong to other independent families which have not yet been recognized.

The third major stock is called *Congo-Kordofonian* with two branches, *Niger-Congo* and *Kordofonian*, although it may turn out that Kordofonian constitutes only a subunit within Niger-Congo. The ancestral language of this stock is probably as old as the ancestor of the Afro-Asiatic languages, because the ancestral language of one of its sub-sub branches dates itself to about 3000 BC. Niger-Congo is subdivided into a number of branches but there is no linguistic consensus about their number and composition. At the most there are seven branches of which six cover West Africa and

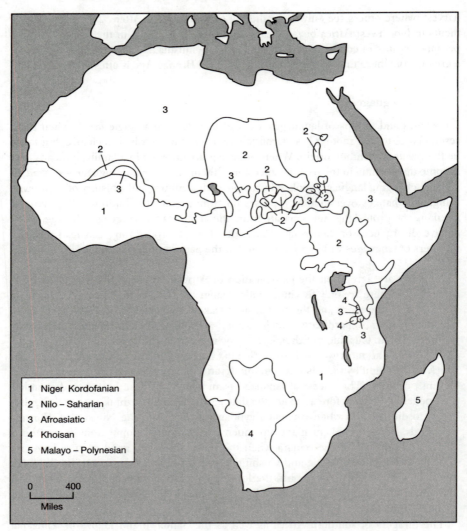

Map 1.2 The languages of Africa *c.*1900 (based on a map by C. Vansina, using data from Greenberg, J.H., *The Languages of Africa*, The Hague: Mouton, 1963)

one the grasslands of Cameroon and the Central African Republic. A single offshoot of one of the West African branches, called *Bantu*, covers most of the southern half of Africa.

The last of these families is *Nilo-Saharan*. It is divided into six branches of which only one, *Chari-Nile*, comprises a great many languages; the five others are isolated and found in small regions south of the Sahara or in the desert itself northeast of Lake Chad. The ancestral tongue of this stock was spoken, many thousands of years ago, in the eastern sahel and the adjoining portions of the Sahara between Chad and the Nile. The people who retreated from this portion of the Sahara, when it dried up, were probably speakers of this stock. More than any other in Africa, the speech of these people is linked to a culture emphasizing cattle, even though in later times many groups among them became intensive farmers.

One more family, not to be reckoned among the language families of African origin however, is *Austronesian*. It is centered on Southeast Asia and is represented in Africa by Malagasy, the national language of Madagascar, where speakers of Austronesian immigrated in the first centuries AD. Intrusive European settlers carried Dutch into southern Africa, where it was transformed during the eighteenth century into Afrikaans, as it became the home language of the so-called Coloured people of the Cape province. Gradually it was also adopted by most Dutch speakers in South Africa and became an official language in this century. Elsewhere Portuguese, English, and French are languages of international communication and in many countries also used internally, so that many Africans speak and write in one of these as a fully mastered second language. In addition, these originally alien languages, especially Portuguese and English, have blended here and there with African tongues to produce mixed languages called *creoles* and have become the first languages for scattered but significant elements of the population.

Race

All humans belong to a single species – they can all mate among themselves and produce fertile offspring. Today there exists a single human race; the genetic differences between humans are minute. There has been a time when several humanoid races lived alongside each other, but the last surviving group other than humans, the Neanderthalers, died out more than 30,000 years ago. However, in so far as human groups have lived for centuries in comparative isolation, so that a particular group mates only with people nearby whose genes are similar, distinctions between such groups can and do arise. People sharing a particular collection of genes or gene pool are properly labeled a *population* in genetics, and should not be called a *race*. Each recognizable different population is constantly changing, however, and for that matter no gene pool was ever so isolated as to be unmixed with others. To talk about different races at all is therefore only a dangerous inaccuracy. At the latest when agriculture and husbandry were introduced contacts between populations increased over long distances, and relative genetic barriers weakened. Over time, then, Africans have exchanged more and more genes.

The literature has made much of many external physical characteristics such as muscular strength, stature, or the shape of nose or lips. These most often result from a slow genetic adaptation to a given environment or from a more rapid response to different patterns of nutrition. The sturdy size of fishermen stems from a better diet containing protein, while the very black skin of the thin tall Nilotes may be a genetic adaptation to the great heat and dry climate in which they live. Human biologists have been exploring such questions for years but only very recently has it become possible to study genetic inheritance directly from an examination of human genetic material, its

DNA. Eventually such studies will tell us a great deal about the vagaries of biological evolution among Africans.

Meanwhile it is evident that the existing classifications of the people of Africa by their appearances are superficial – in the literal sense of the word – and worthless. There are no "Caucasians," "Khoisans," "pygmies," "negroes," "Nilotics," "Erythroids" or "Mongoloids." Such terms are merely labels that survived from a totally discredited and erroneous approach to human biology. They are literally "nonsense" because nothing biological corresponds to them.

Historians must therefore reject all such summary classifications and the conclusions drawn from them. They should be suspicious of statements made in the past with reference to mere bodily appearance, such as for example that the Caucasoids brought husbandry or agriculture to East Africa. They should distrust the evidence of a few skulls or even skeletons, because the characteristics of a population can only be established from statistical measurements for a full *range* of the people that participated in a single gene pool. And they should be patient and wait for the promise of DNA studies to be fulfilled.

In contrast to linguistics then, little can be said about the genetic make up or even about the appearance of Africans around 2000 BC. Rock art shows us that people in the Sahara were frequently depicted as tall people, brown as well as white, while in southern Africa rock art suggests that people there looked like today's San only taller and stronger. But even this evidence is dubious because colors and sizes may be dictated more by the requirements of artistic convention rather than by any attempt to portray actual appearance. That is precisely what happened to the paintings in Ancient Egypt. There overseers are always taller than mere navvies and white, reddish, yellow, brown or black, refer to occupation, ethnicity and social class. The paintings do not tell us much about the actual appearance of real people, a point directly made by comparing them to contemporary mummies.

The spread of food production in West Africa after c.2000 BC

Two major dynamics have affected the spread of food production from the third millennium onwards: the desiccation of the Sahara and a huge migration of farmers, known as the Bantu expansion. The vast expanses of the Sahara had been fertile and blessed with grasslands, large lakes, and rivers between 4500 and 2500 BC. But then 1500 years of drought set in. There soon was no more reliable rainfall; gradually the waters evaporated, the vegetation died, and the soils turned to dust and desert. This process was well underway by 2300 BC and around 2000 BC most of the present desert was established in the eastern and central Sahara where it had acquired its familiar landscapes of bare rocks and moving mountains of sand. The climatic change forced many people to gradually retreat before the advance of the barren sands had imposed a major readaptation of life style for those who chose to remain in the desert. They either clung to farming and retreated into the oases that survived, or they became nomads abandoning cattle for sheep and goats who could survive better on the remaining scraps of vegetation. Large tracts of land that were too far away from water were totally lost only to be recovered with the introduction of the camel from the last centuries BC onwards. Such a momentous change over such a vast area, even if it occurred ever so slowly by the yardstick of the duration of human life, was to have a profound impact on the societies of cultures not only of those who continued to live in what was now a desert, but also on the adjacent peoples of northern and western Africa.

First we look at what happened to those who stayed. Many of these were Berber speaking and they stayed on mostly in the northern Sahara where they adapted to the new conditions. When the climate changed again to become slightly more humid after 1000 BC these Berbers ventured further south in the desert. By the seventh century BC they occupied portions of northern Niger and northern Mali where the Tuareg, a Berber speaking people, still live today.

To adapt to the rigors of a desert environment, it became necessary to spread the livestock and the herdsmen out over every last square mile of the huge expanses of land during the short annual periods when there was rain, for after every rain shower grasses rapidly sprout up, but dry out almost as quickly. At the height of the dry season, however, hundreds of people and all their flocks had to be concentrated around a waterhole. These necessities of life required a form of rule that would function well to govern people when they were spread out in small groups of ten or fewer and yet function equally well when they were crowding around the wells.

New social systems were invented to cope with this dual way of life. One of these, the *deep segmentary kinship* system, eventually became universal in the Sahara. It is reported from the first centuries AD but must be much older. The population was organized in very large groups who believed that they were descended from one ancestor, and who were linked by a commonly accepted official genealogy in the male line. In the literature such groups are called "tribes," by analogy to the "tribes of Israel". Within this genealogy subgroups can be recognized, the supposed descendants from lesser ancestors, and then again subgroups of those and so on down to the level of a group of sons of the same father. Therefore this organization allowed a very large group to be subdivided into smaller and smaller groups as the need arose. The community to which an individual person was to belong at different times of the year was thereby codifed. So efficient has this system been that pastoral nomads in the horn of Africa, in East Africa and in Central Asia all have invented it independently over and over again as the need arose. Thus pastoral nomadism became a new way of life, a distinctly original accommodation to environment. Yet a side-effect of the system was that it contained a principle of inequality. Not only did real or presumed heredity determine the status of everyone but a genealogy that distinguishes between "elder" and "younger" creates inequality. The eldest sons in the eldest line of the genealogy soon claimed preeminence and privilege and their descent groups formed governing "dynasties." Moreover the acceptance of such a segmentary kinship system was a choice which, once made, was never undone. As the subsequent developments in the Sahara show all later social innovations have complemented this system rather than supplanted it.

Furthermore, as the desiccation grew worse sheep and goats became predominant in the flocks because these animals could eke out a subsistence long after increasing aridity made the land unsuitable for cattle, even though their grazing accelerated erosion and further desertification. This trend as well as the worsening climate meant that cereals and other domesticated plants cultivated in the oases became more and more vital for the survival of the nomads. The increasing drought also forced innovations in the oases. The most spectacular of these was the establishment of a system of underground channels for irrigation at the cost of a huge investment in labor. As a result the farmers there were not only forced to live closer together in larger settlements but also had to accept a strong communal authority to supervise an equable distribution of water. The greatly increased labor requirements probably led to the rise of large numbers of servile workers.

Meanwhile the survival of the nomads required an accommodation between oasis dwellers and pastoralists. The struggle over control must have worked first to the advantage of the oases dwellers. From the last centuries BC when camel herding began to be adopted, however, the balance shifted in favor of the nomads. Camels greatly increased the mobility of the nomads and gave them military superiority. They now could concentrate forces many miles away undetected, and suddenly swoop on the oases to raid them. By successive raids they gradually forced the oases dwellers into submission, and by the early centuries AD the farmers of many oases began to accept the "protection" of a "tribe" of nomads in return for payment of fixed amounts of cereals, dates, and a supply of water. Every one of these processes increased the inequality in these societies. The menial workers in the oases were inferior to the farmers, who were inferior to the nomads, most of whom were inferior to the members of their leading or "dynastic" lineage. No wonder that a "caste" system became common in the area not many centuries later!

The desertification of the Sahara proceeded from east to west. Even at the best of times the western part of Egypt, Libya and the Sudan had been a semi-desert, and from 2500 BC onwards the incipient drought forced some cattle herders out of it in every direction including westwards to the still well-watered massifs of the central Sahara. Later rainfall there faltered also and forced herders into northwest Africa, southwards towards the Niger and westwards into southern Mauretania, an area that retained good grazing and farming land until the onset of our era. Thus the process of migration or rather drift was very slow, and often hesitant: whenever a few years of higher rainfall occurred, the nomads retraced their steps backwards. Hence immigration in West or North Africa never caused population pressure. The great longevity of the process is indicated by the spread of the known dates for arrival of Saharan technology in central West Africa. The Kintampo industry which has Saharan affinities appeared by the eighteenth century BC in the north of modern Ghana, yet 1,500 years later (c. 250 BC) ceramics in the inner Niger Delta still show new arrivals from the Sahara!

This more than 1,500 year-long retreat produced lasting consequences. The emptying of the Sahara so lessened the intensity of interaction between northern Africa and the lands south of the Sahara that West Africa and northwest Africa became different cultural areas. Berber speakers eventually occupied most of the Sahara itself. The thousand year long trickle of the Saharans southwards first carried the tropical cereals to the West African savanna where rice was added to them, probably in the Niger valley. Rice in turn became the agricultural basis in the southwesternmost parts of West Africa. Later the trickle also brought specialized herders southwards where they met fishermen, foragers, and farmers. A division of labor then developed in which each of these groups remained specialized. But they all bought products from each other so that the resources of the West African savanna came to be exploited in more efficient ways. Moreover, each of these specialized groups retained or acquired a sense of their own ethnicity as opposed to others. Yet as they all had to cooperate to develop common institutions of governance they acquired a second sense of identity on that basis as well. Thus arose original systems of government, especially along the Senegal and in the inner Delta of the Niger.

Bantu expansion before the Iron Age

The Kongo on the Atlantic Ocean call a person *muntu*, plural *bantu*: "people." On the Indian Ocean the Swahili say *mtu* (singular), *watu* (pl.). The Duala of Cameroon say *moto* (sg.), *bato* (pl.), the Mongo in the Equatorial forests *bonto* (sg.), *banto* (pl.), the Shona of Zimbabwe *munhu* (sg.), *vanhu* (pl.) and the Xhosa of the Eastern Cape *umntu* (sg.), *abantu* (pl.). The similarity in all these words is clear and it is not only there in the root -*ntu*, that is, in the vocabulary, but in prefixes denoting singular and plural as well, that is in the grammar (morphology). Linguists recognized this similarity as soon as they began to study these languages and called this group of languages *Bantu* after the term the ancestral language used to designate "people." The ancestral language is called Proto-Bantu.

Most of the people living in Africa south of a line running roughly from the Bight of Biafra to the Indian Ocean near the Kenya–Somali border speak Bantu languages, some six hundred of them, all closely related to each other. In this huge area, a subcontinent, the only non-Bantu languages now remaining can be found in Kenya and an adjoining portion of Tanzania, and in southwestern Africa.

This linguistic situation raises major questions. From where, when and how did the Bantu languages spread? Did they spread by themselves, perhaps as people in one community after another abandoned their ancient tongue to adopt Bantu speech? Or did immigrants carry these languages all over the area?. The closest relatives of the Bantu languages all happen to lie in a small area on the grasslands of Cameroon and in adjacent parts of Nigeria and all linguists agree that this situation betrays the fact that in the beginning the first Bantu language, or Proto-Bantu, was just another language in that area in close proximity to these near relatives. So the Bantu languages spread from this area. All linguists also accept that it was population movement which disseminated the Bantu languages over the subcontinent, because that seems to be the simplest explanation of the linguistic situation. After all Bantu languages are no more attractive than any other, so they would not spread by themselves. Comparable and well-known cases indicate that most languages spread either by the migration of a large number of people who imposed their speech on the minority they overran, or by the migration of a small number of people whose language became dominant because they were con- sidered by both the local people and themselves as vastly superior in "civilization." Most of the Germanic languages spread in the first way; the Romance languages diffused in the second fashion. Either case presupposes some migration. In the case of Bantu the immigrants enjoyed a superior technology. The original inhabitants were foragers and fishermen, but the newcomers farmed, kept goats, had ceramics, and may have been weavers. We know about this superior technology because Proto-Bantu had a vocabulary relating to ceramics, to the cultivation of both cereal and root crops, as well as a term for "goat." And much of the vocabulary of Proto-Bantu is known to linguists who can establish this from a comparison between the languages which are its descendants. These findings also show that the Bantu language expansion must have begun *after* agriculture had spread to their area of origin. According to archaeological evidence this could not be earlier than 3000 BC.

By which routes and when did these immigrants then spread over the subcontinent? A linguist can answer this question if she or he succeeds in establishing the family tree within the Bantu language family. For instance we know that Rwanda is more closely related to Rundi (the language of Burundi) than it is to any of the languages in western Uganda, but it is in turn more closely related to those than to any language in Cameroon. Hence we know that a sub-family split off from the languages of Cameroon, then later split internally so that Rwanda and Rundi were separated from the languages of western Uganda and finally Rwanda and Rundi became different. We have now a relative timescale and by placing languages on a map we can roughly trace the diffusion: in this case from Cameroon eastwards to Uganda.

For almost a century linguists have attempted to discover the exact family relationship of each Bantu language to all of the others. But only in 1992 has it been possible to establish a reliable overall genealogy by lexicostatistics, which has yielded a reliable overall genealogy including nearly all Bantu languages. Lexicostatistics is a technique which consists of comparing the same basic vocabulary in the languages involved and establishing the degree to which they are related. To a certain degree the same technique allows one to propose a very approximate absolute chronology as well.

The linguistic results tell us the following. There have been three successive Bantu expansions. During the third part of the second millennium BC people speaking Proto-Bantu, a single language, slowly expanded mostly eastwards from the present southern Nigerian–Cameroon border all the way to the western great lakes, partly north of the rainforests and partly within them. Within the rainforests these people arrived as far southwards as the Ogowe delta in the west and as far as the Equator just west of the Great Lakes. These immigrants introduced two systems of food production, one adapted to the rainforests and one adapted to the savanna. In the rainforests an integrated system of food production combined the farming of root and tree crops (the oil palm was the main one of these), with trapping, gathering and fishing in the rainforests. In the savannas they combined the cultivation of cereals and yams mainly with hunting and trapping. These people were also the first in the region to settle in villages and to group each handful of villages together in a larger unit, the district, which is estimated to have, on average, encompassed about five hundred people. This expansion can be called North Bantu.

Only after this expansion was well underway and because people were moving further and further apart, did they begin to have more and more difficulty in understanding each other's dialects, which were slowly changing as all speech does over time. Thus Proto-Bantu spawned a number of new languages in this North Bantu area (see map 1.3). Two dialects among these were the cradle for later further large-scale

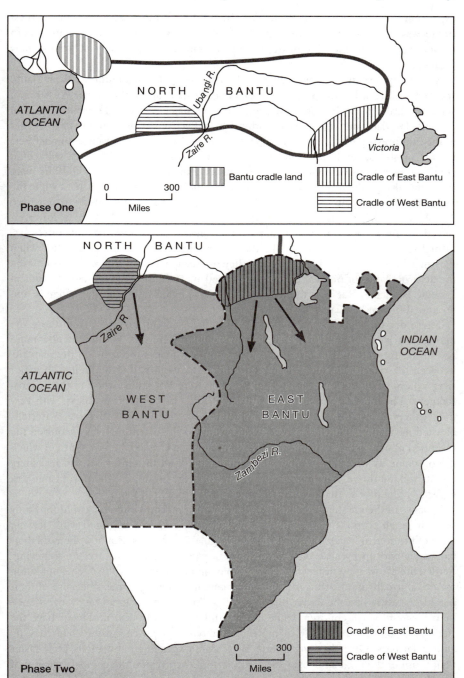

Map 1.3 Bantu expansion (based on a map by C. Vansina)

expansion and can be named Proto-West Bantu and Proto-East Bantu. Proto-West Bantu was first spoken in what is now a small area in northern Congo and eastern Gabon while Proto-East Bantu developed in a small area just west of what is now Uganda.

As the first expansion was ending in the later second millennium BC West Bantu speakers and East Bantu speakers began a major expansion of their own. West Bantu speakers, used to live in rainforests, followed the major rivers in the central basin of present-day Zaire but also moved southwards and arrived at the southwestern border of the rainforests perhaps as early as 900 BC. There they found the rich savanna/forest mosaic of the lower Zaire/Congo area, an environment in which they still could continue their accustomed way of life by exploiting the gallery forests around the main rivers but also gradually learn how to farm and hunt in savanna lands. After a while the expansion began again. Some West Bantu speakers moved due south to northern Angola where they soon met a new environment: the dry woodlands. Others, however, stayed in the by now familiar savanna/forest mosaic and, following the waterways, turned eastwards towards the middle Kasai river, where their advance was halted when they met East Bantu speakers there. So they too turned southwards and thus entered the dry woodlands of Angola. Up to this point all West Bantu speakers had still spoken a single language. But now the dialects were once again mutually unintelligible and became different languages.

These dry woodlands were a very different environment, however, from those the immigrants were used to. Droughts were common here and became all the more severe the further south the migrants went. In most places the soils on the plateaux between the rivers were too poor for farming. Settlement had to be limited to major river valleys while the vast expanses in between were left undisturbed to the original foragers. The altitude was higher and the rivers ran in steep, deep valleys, with very little gallery forest. Moreover the waterways themselves were different. Waterfalls blocked navigation, and the currents were swifter to the extent that they required the invention of new fishing techniques. The migrants also crossed the line south of which the oil palm, as well as a number of other plants found in rainforests and in gallery forests will not thrive. Also trapping was no longer very productive there, yet game was especially plentiful so that hunting became a major source of food.

Because of their system of food production the West Bantu migrants could thus only settle in small portions of the lands into which they had now migrated while leaving most of the area in which they settled to the original inhabitants. But how then did their languages end up by absorbing all others? The probable reasons are the following. Settled life allows for a faster increase of population than nomadic life does. Population control is usually more stringent among foragers than among farmers because of their need to be always on the move: this means that their women cannot be overburdened by babies and small children, while elderly and sick people who no longer have the stamina or indeed the ability to move also impose a heavier burden than they do among farmers. Over the longer term West Bantu speaking populations grew faster than those of the original people. Secondly within each region the compact villages of the Bantu speakers became the social focus for all people, foragers or not. While the total number of foragers in the hinterland of a village would be much higher at first

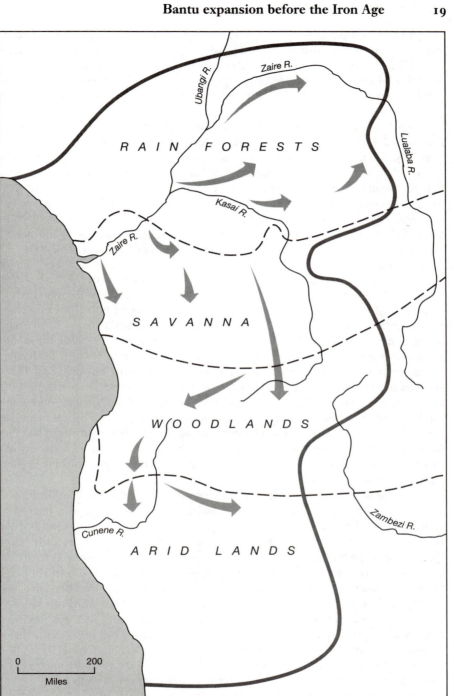

Map 1.4 West Bantu expansion (based on a map by C. Vansina)

than the one hundred or so Bantu speaking villagers, the size of a village was three to four times larger than that of the camps of foragers. In addition, each district, the largest community for West Bantu speakers was perhaps ten times bigger in population than that of any camp, the largest foraging community. For these reasons Bantu speakers, even if a minority in a given region at first, were well placed to eventually impose their speech on others.

Meanwhile speakers of the original East Bantu language also moved southwards from the rainforests in what is now eastern Zaire into the forest/savanna mosaic and later they, like the West Bantu speakers, also overcame the difficulties of entering the dry woodlands of southeastern Zaire and Zambia. From the woodlands they expanded both into southeastern Africa and into eastern Africa proper. Although the chronology of this dispersal remains murky, it occurred before any East Bantu speakers had acquired any knowledge of metallurgy. A portion of them entered the highlands of the Great Lakes area where they met populations who farmed grain crops and herded some cattle and were at least their technological equals. The Bantu speakers slowly and gradually learned from the earlier settlers how to farm grain crops and they adopted cattle. They also created a new social organization under the influence of these people. They abandoned settlement in compact villages to adopt a pattern of dispersed settlement each inhabited by a large household and spread all over the hills. They reinforced the internal cohesion of each household by introducing new patterns of marriage alliances, an innovation perhaps induced by the necessity to better regulate the inheritance and transfer of cattle. And they developed a new form of stronger leadership. Given the influence of other farmers and herders in the area on early East Bantu speakers it is not at all evident how these people managed to preserve their language in such a situation, for East Bantu seems to have remained a single language during this whole period. It comes as an even greater surprise to find that these people eventually succeeded in imposing their Bantu language on others. In what, if anything, had they become superior to others? The answer may well be that they achieved a mastery of a totally new technology: metallurgy. For around 800 BC traces of iron smelting begin to appear in the area.

This reconstruction is based entirely on linguistic data, with some consideration of the natural environments involved. Such findings are however of great interest to archaeologists. After all the population movements inferred from the spread of the Bantu languages must have left material and recoverable traces. Because early Bantu speakers were potters and sedentary (unlike others, in Central Africa at least) the earliest sites where pottery and some evidence for farming occur have been attributed to Bantu speakers.This assumption seems more reasonable than any alternative, and the archaeological data uncovered so far seem to fit well. Yet a word of caution is necessary: the area is huge and compared to its size the number of sites that have been found still remains minute; most excavations were somewhat small scale, rather than a systematic unearthing of whole sites; and most research in western Central Africa is of such recent vintage that a comparative in-depth analysis of the ceramics uncovered is only beginning. Only further research will tell us how good the fit really is.

The Iron Age

Most of Africa never knew the Bronze Age. North Africa did. Bronze was worked in Egypt since early Pharaonic times and metallurgy reached the Maghrib (northwestern Africa) around 2000 BC. The working of pure copper spread south to northern Niger by about 1000 BC. By 500 BC bronze objects were made in Mauretania and Senegal using a technique which derives from the Maghrib.

By the Bronze Age, the Mediterranean was becoming a well-traveled sea, and eastern influences continued to spread west. Eventually after 1000 BC settlers from Phoenicia arrived in the western Mediterranean and founded colonies in North Africa. These activities culminated with the rise of Carthage. Thus northwestern Africa found itself heavily influenced by the technologies, social patterns, and religious ideas of the Middle East. Among the new techniques brought by the Phoenicians was the knowledge of how to smelt iron.

Iron-smelting is such a complex process that it is thought to have been invented independently only two or three times in world history. The difficulty of smelting is the following. At very high temperatures iron will melt and become a liquid, just as the copper in a copper ore melts but at a much lower temperature. The high temperatures needed to melt iron, however, could not be reached in an ordinary furnace. The secret was to produce iron at lower temperatures, by taking advantage of a chemical change. When charcoal is mixed with iron ore and burned in an enclosed space, one combustion product is carbon monoxide, which picks up an oxygen molecule from the hot ore and turns it from ferrous oxide into iron, while the gas turns from carbon monoxide to carbon dioxide. Once this has happened in a furnace hot slag can be drawn off and the product left at the bottom of the furnace is bloom, a mass of iron and steel mixed with slag and other impurities. When it is reheated and then hammered, slag can be removed and a usable piece of iron remains. This product can be highly variable, depending on the mixture of other elements with iron, especially carbon. This depends on the chemical nature of the ore, the type of furnace, and the temperature reached during smelting. Carbon content is crucial. If too little carbon is absorbed by the hot iron, the iron will be soft, malleable, and not likely to hold an edge. Just a little more carbon yields steel, which is malleable, yet can be tempered by heating and sudden cooling. Still more carbon, and the product becomes cast iron, brittle as glass and impossible to shape on an anvil.

Most Africans used shaft furnaces of various shapes. They were a more efficient device than the bowl furnace, which had been used in the Nile valley since the Bronze Age, and were still reported in northern Kordofan in the early nineteenth century and even later in the northern part of East Africa. Smelting ore in a shaft furnace means placing alternating layers of carefully milled (by hand) and dried ore and charcoal in the furnace, sometimes on a bed of reeds or grasses to provide carbon. Oxygen is then admitted during the firing by means either of bellows (pot bellows for most of Africa south of the Sahara, bag bellows in northern Africa, and pump bellows of Indonesian origin in southeastern Africa), which forces air through a series of *tuyères* (long earthenware tubes) through the wall of the furnace to the base of the fire. Some furnaces are so built as to create a natural draft of air and could be worked without bellows. The crucial skill during firing is proper control of the air admitted. Further ramifications of African iron technology are highly varied responses to the nature and iron content of the ore as well as to the nature of the charcoal. A shaft furnace typically produces about five kilograms of iron in one smelting, while a bowl furnace would yield only one kilogram or so at best.

Iron ore was available in most parts of tropical Africa, although the iron content of ores was quite variable: from as low as 25 per cent to well over 75 per cent. Most ore was dug from surface deposits, often from hillsides by open pit methods, but underground mining was practiced at times as in southeastern Nigeria, at Phalaborwa in Transvaal, in southern Ghana, or at Télénougar in southern Chad, where shafts and galleries were dug. Mining and smelting involved considerable labor and were delicate and chancy operations that required a single overall manager, a master founder, who was credited with esoteric knowledge. No wonder that the "masters of the fire" held such a special status – either very prestigious, or, as in Ethiopia, the eastern and western Sudan and generally in North Africa, despised but feared and casted persons.

It has been believed that the technology of iron smelting everywhere in Africa derived from the Middle East: West Africans would have learned the craft indirectly from the Phoenician colonies in North Africa after 1000 BC, and East Africans would have learned it from the Egyptians and the people of Merowe in the Nilotic Sudan. But this belief has not been substantiated. The problem is that existing carbon 14 measurements which yield dates corresponding to any time between 800 BC and 300 BC are presently not good enough to tell us more than "sometime between 800 and 300 BC." Unfortunately, most early sites in tropical Africa north of the Equator fall in this chronological window. Hence it is not yet possible to establish their true chronological sequence and to trace the paths by which this technology diffused into the area.

In northwest Africa, and in Niger, copper was smelted after about 1000 BC. The oldest sites for iron smelting known so far from the sites of Taruga and Nsukka fall in the 800/300 BC range. Studies of the Taruga furnaces show that their technology was not simply borrowed from that in use along the Mediterranean. Considerable innovations had been made which led to the production of high quality steel and iron. Was there any input from North Africa? We do not know. Again sites in southern Cameroon, Gabon and Congo have yielded dates in the 800/300 BC range. Was the technology here borrowed from Nigeria? Again we do not know.

In Egypt a few imported iron objects had been buried with Pharaoh Tutankhamen c.1352 BC, but iron-smelting was practiced there only after the Assyrian invasion of 671 BC. Archaeological evidence from Ethiopia, Merowe and the upper White Nile all falls in the accursed 800/300 BC range, so again we do not know what the chronological connections are between these sites, if any. This brings us to a consideration of sites in the area of the Great Lakes, more precisely between lakes Tanganyika, Kivu and Victoria. Again the earliest sites fall in the 800/300 BC range. Once more the technology is original, although claims that it allowed for the production of liquid iron, produced at very high temperatures, have so far not been accepted by all. And once again we cannot establish what, if any, connections exist with Sudan, Ethiopia or Egypt. Yet it is known that all Bantu speakers, even those in Gabon and Cameroon share part of their terminology for the process of smithing (not smelting!) including such terms as

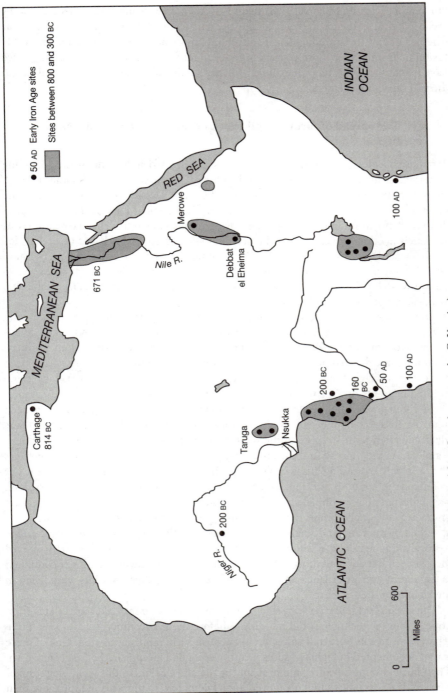

Map 1.5 The earliest Iron Age in Africa (based on a map by C. Vansina)

"to smithe," "smith," "anvil," "hammer." But so far we cannot link this fact to any archaeological evidence. Hence in the present state of knowledge we cannot say whether or not the introduction of metallurgy into tropical Africa resulted from diffusion or from one or more centers of independent invention. The only certainty we have is that the diffusion of metallurgy further south came from the Great Lakes and the Gabon-Congo centers.

The spread of farming and iron working in eastern and southern Africa

A rich archaeological record in eastern and southern Africa documents the spreading of ceramics, herding, grain farming and iron working in eastern and southern Africa from *c.*200 BC onwards to the sixth century AD. Until recently it was thought that the dispersal of these technologies accompanied the expansion of East Bantu speakers, but this position can no longer be held because the linguistic and archaeological records are totally at odds with each other. Hence the following account is based on archaeological data and in particular on the results of comparisons of the styles of pottery found on different sites. This allows one to establish groups of sites with similar styles and to show how styles changed over time, so that "family trees" of pottery can be established just as one does in the case of languages.

Around 200 BC the herding of cattle and the use of pottery appeared in a region encompassing much of central and western Zimbabwe, northeast Botswana and adjacent sites on the upper Zambezi in Zambia. These techniques stem from northern Tanzania, but the manner in which they diffused is unknown. They may have been borrowed from community to community or they may have been carried by cattle herding migrants or a mixture of both. One thing though is certain. Near the Zambezi or in Zimbabwe, Khoi, a sub-group of Khoisan speakers, who had hitherto been nomadic foragers now began to herd cattle and sheep as well, a life style that was ideally adapted to the steppes of the Kalahari of Botswana and as far west as northern Namibia. As they spread in these areas they met the vanguard of West Bantu speakers who were still expanding but now with great difficulty. They were now south of the dry woodlands in lands so arid that they could only farm on irrigated land and irrigation was only possible in the deltas of the seasonal rivers. Khoi and Bantu speakers interacted as equals. Some Bantu speaking groups, now called the Bergdama, were absorbed by the Khoi and abandoned their language. Others in southern Angola added pastoralism to agriculture while still others in Namibia, now called Herero, preserved their speech but adopted most of the Khoi way of life. Meanwhile the Khoi continued to expand in ever drier lands and by AD 1 Khoi speaking sheep herders were living in the vicinity of the Cape.

The earliest evidence for iron smelting in the western Great Lakes area dates from *c.*800 BC but the technology did not diffuse before the first century AD. But then three separate dispersals occurred either simultaneously or in rapid succession. One of these is first documented in highland spots near the coast of Tanzania in the first century AD. Then in a lightning advance, and probably by sea, the carriers of this technology and of a new style of ceramics suddenly moved 2000 kilometers southwards in little more than

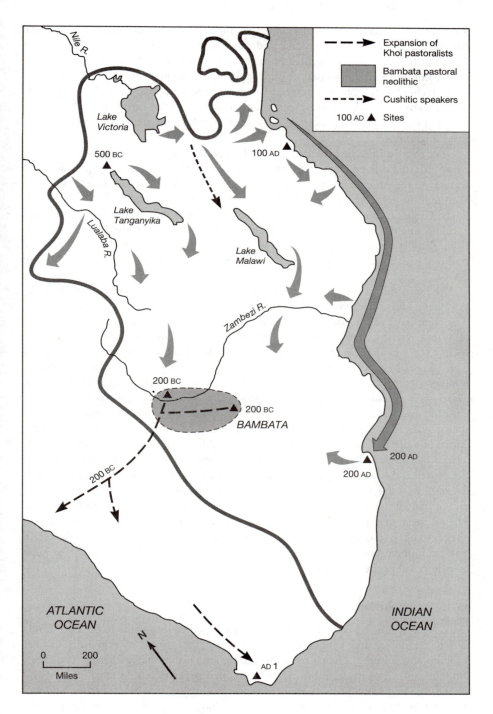

Map 1.6 The spreading of farming and iron working in eastern and southern Africa (based on a map by C. Vansina)

The labels and legend within the map:

- Expansion of Khoi pastoralists
- Bambata pastoral neolithic
- Cushitic speakers
- 100 AD ▲ Sites

Nile R.

Lake Victoria

500 BC

Lualaba R.

Lake Tanganyika

Lake Malawi

Zambezi R.

100 AD

200 BC

200 BC   200 BC

BAMBATA

200 AD

200 AD

200 BC

ATLANTIC OCEAN

INDIAN OCEAN

N

0   200

Miles

AD 1

a century. By 250 AD they had reached southern Mozambique and northern Natal where they also introduced herding and grain farming. A second movement, known from northern Malawi, brought iron metallurgy and cereal farming to central Zimbabwe not much later than that. A third and perhaps slightly later movement brought these technologies from southernmost Tanzania into Zambia. East Bantu speakers were involved in all these movements, but according to the linguistic evidence they were not the first Bantu speakers in these areas and the movements may not have been mass migrations.

Once they had reached Zambia and Shaba small groups of immigrants went further westwards and carried grain crop farming, and where possible the herding of cattle, all the way to the Atlantic into territory already settled by West Bantu speakers. We have seen that the rootcrop agriculture of the latter was quite inadequate in the dry woodlands. Grain farming was far superior in both woodlands and savanna and West Bantu speakers adopted grain crops with enthusiasm even as they absorbed the immigrants from Zambia and Shaba. The result was the emergence of a new specific regional tradition which can be called Central Bantu and which also encompasses Zambia and Shaba.

The net result of these complex population movements was an expansion of food-producing and iron-using societies throughout central, eastern and southern Africa. The complexity of the process also led to other major consequences, due to the fusion of several groups, Bantu speaking and others. Several new and different types of society arose in all these areas around c. 500 AD. One was the village and district based type of social organization in Zambia, in which both West Bantu and East Bantu traditions merged. Another was the development on the coast of a type of society, based on a complex economy and an innovative social system, derived from both Cushitic and East Bantu roots, but including some inputs from overseas that soon spawned the urban Swahili life style. A third one was the appearance in southeastern Africa of a distinct new social organization, called the Central Cattle Pattern, characterized by circular villages in which the houses surrounded a common cattle corral in the center and where the participating family heads exercised collective rule. And in the southwest the merger between West Bantu and Khoi produced a nomadic pastoral way of life with its own characteristics. We cannot as yet say much about the reasons why all these migrations occurred between c. 200 BC and 500 AD nor why Bantu languages so often (but not always) became dominant over others. Much more research in historical linguistics and in archaeology is needed before firm answers to such questions will begin to emerge.

Conclusions

Once food-producing economies had taken root, populations came to be more firmly tied to territories and a foundation was laid for the growth of regionally distinct societies and cultures. The choice of producing food rather than gathering it has been fundamental. Once made, it was never questioned again, except by small groups who even then saw foraging as a specialized niche in a regional division of labor, and still required foodstuffs cultivated by others. Once food was produced population could

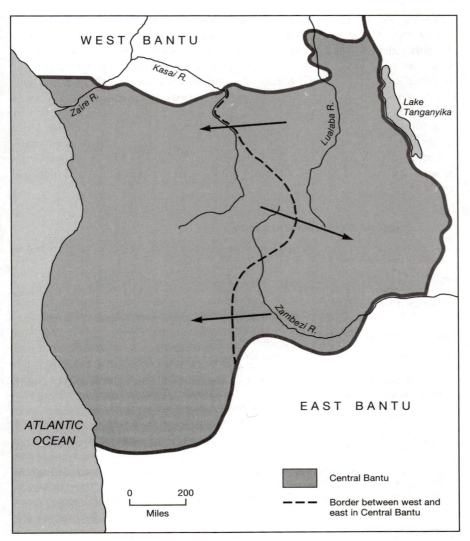

Map 1.7 Central Bantu: a fusion of east and west (based on a map by C. Vansina)

grow more rapidly than before, even if the rates of growth remained highly irregular. Once communities were settled further technological processes in agriculture, husbandry, metallurgy, or other industries could be perfected. At the same time interaction between settled communities for mutual advantage (trade, intermarriage, medicine, mutual security) could from now on proceed in more predictable ways. Thus the foundations for the various types of African societies and cultures of later times were laid in the centuries following the acquisition of food production.

Stressing such continuities in social and cultural history, helps us to understand Africa's present as well as its history. Each African society represents literally millenia of experimentation and that experience explains why social systems, values, and cultures were not completely swept away when European norms were forced into the continent during the colonial period. Yet paradoxically such continuities can only survive over thousands of years if they are accompanied by constant change. Otherwise they soon become irrelevant. Thus while African ways of life do indeed rest on very powerful and deep traditions, the picture of a "traditional" and unchanging Africa merely reflects ignorance about the continual changes that occurred at all times. Indeed, apparently African societies changed at much the same rate as other societies in better documented parts of the world did between the agricultural and industrial revolutions.

Suggestions for further reading

Three general reference works surveying the whole sweep of African History can be consulted on specific issues. They are:

Ajayi, J. and Crowder, M. (eds), *Historical Atlas of Africa*, London: Longman, 1985.
Fage, J. and Oliver, R. (eds), *The Cambridge History of Africa*, Vols I–VIII, Cambridge: Cambridge University Press, 1975–86.
UNESCO, *General History of Africa*, Vols I–VIII, Berkeley: University of California Press, 1981–93.

Suggested reading for this chapter are:

The African Archaeological Review, Cambridge: Cambridge University Press, 1983– .
Clark, J.D. and Brandt, S.A. (eds), *From Hunters to Farmers*, Berkeley: University of California, 1984.
Journal of African History, Cambridge: Cambridge University Press, 1960– . (The journal regularly carries articles bringing the archaeological situation up to date.)
Greenberg, J.H., *The Languages of Africa*, The Hague: Mouton, 1963.
Kryzaniak, L.H. and Kobusiewicz, M. (eds), *Late Prehistory of the Nile Basin and the Sahara*, Poznan: Poznan Archaeological Museum, 1989.
Lewis-Williams, J. David, *The Rock Art of Southern Africa*, Cambridge: Cambridge University Press, 1983.
Muzzolini, A., *L'art rupestre préhistorique des massifs centraux Sahariens*, Oxford: Cambridge Monographs in African Archaeology, 16 BAR 318, 1986.
Phillipson, D.W., *African Archaeology*, Cambridge: Cambridge University Press, 1985.

2

NORTHERN AFRICA IN A WIDER WORLD

Africa north of the Sahara is so different from sub-Saharan Africa that some treatments of African history exclude it altogether. They do so partly because North Africa has been part of a Muslim, Middle Eastern culture-area since the eighth century. Egypt also belonged for several millennia before that to a small group of urban, literate societies with relatively intense intercommunication and relatively rapid technological progress. Other parts of Africa no further away than Nubia, Ethiopia, or the western Sudan had some contact with this zone of intense intercommunication, but they and the rest of sub-Saharan Africa were only on the fringes until the nineteenth century AD. North Africa meanwhile played a role in the history of the whole of the Mediterranean basin – and in that of a wider world that stretched off to the east.

But the rest of African history was not played out in isolation. The Sahara was not as uncrossable or uncrossed as the pre-Columbian Atlantic; the Red Sea was even less of a barrier. Even if the history of sub-Saharan Africa were the only concern of this book, it would still be essential to fill in something of the history of its neighbors and points of contact with other people. This book therefore takes its northern limit to be the Mediterranean and the Red Sea, with occasional notice of events in Arabia or even further afield.

To put the relationship another way, North Africa was long in the core area of intercommunication, and it was customary to write its history with little or no reference to the world south of the Sahara. We would have had a better perspective on the human experience if that older history had not confined itself to the history of what it conceived of as "civilization," but the history of sub-Saharan Africa is even less comprehensible without reference to its neighboring regions across the Sahara and the Red Sea.

The geographical framework

The physical environment of northern Africa was far more than a backdrop against which history was to be played out. Even more starkly than in many other parts of the world, environment set the limits of what was likely or even possible. The fundamental

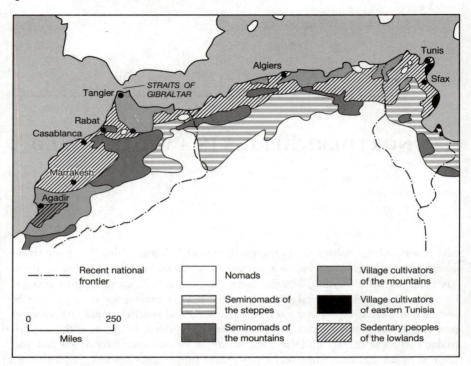

Map 2.1 The setting of North African history

feature was aridity. The Sahara is the largest and driest desert in the world, and the problem of insufficient rainfall shades off from the desert itself to the *sahel* (Arabic for the "fringe" or "shore" of the desert), and on to the better-watered lands along the North African coast or the Nile valley. It was not simply a crude question of whether or not there was enough rain to grow crops. Oasis conditions made agriculture possible wherever the natural setting supplied surface or underground water, which may have fallen hundreds if not thousands of miles away – and centuries or millennia ago. Different kinds of society came into existence to deal with different environments, and the interactions of these societies over time form one of the major themes in African history as a whole.

Nor were these interactions peculiar to Africa. Africa is a continent, but it also forms a part of the great Afro-Eurasian landmass. The Sahara is merely the westward extension of the great Afro-Eurasian dry belt that begins at the Sea of Okhotsk and stretches westward across the Gobi Desert, across central Asia, Afghanistan, Iran, and Arabia, to cross the Red Sea and the African continent to the Atlantic coast of Mauritania. This belt cuts off sub-Saharan Africa from the sedentary farmers of northern Africa far more effectively than the Mediterranean Sea separates those sedentary societies from southern Europe. This same desert in Arabia cuts off south-ern Arabia and Africa from the fertile crescent of the Middle East far more effectively than the Red Sea separates Arabia from the neighboring African coast. For that matter, another arid zone to the south of the Ethiopian highlands strikes the Indian Ocean coast along the present frontier of Kenya and Somalia and constitutes a second line of defense, isolating central and southern Africa from the north – and incidentally making the high and relatively well-watered plateaus of Ethiopia and southern Arabia a kind of mountainous island in the desert sea.

In fact, northern Africa is divided into a series of different regions, each separated from the others by zones of comparative aridity. The westernmost is the region now known as the Maghrib, from its Arabic name meaning "the West." It was so separated that the Arabs sometimes called it "the western island," thinking of the desert to the south and east as equivalent to the sea to the north and west. The region includes parts of Morocco, Algeria, and Tunisia, although the present-day boundaries of those countries include much more than the true western island, a strip of cultivable land some 2000 miles long east-to-west but only seventy to two hundred miles from north to south. Even within this cultivated zone, the sharply accented relief of the various ranges of the Atlas Mountains makes for a great variety of smaller sub-regions. The large stretches of fairly flat land are found at either end – the Moroccan coastal plains on the west, northern Tunisia and northeastern Algeria on the east.

The climate of the Maghrib, like that of the far south around Cape Town, is "Mediterranean" in type with winter rains and a long drought in midsummer, not unlike southern California. As a result, the land is productive in the same crops that grow on the European side of the sea – wheat, wine, and olives, and sometimes barley in the drier regions. As in California, differences in altitude make for great differences in rainfall within a small space, so that many crops have to be grown on irrigated land that receives little actual rainfall. This kind of agriculture was especially important historically on the desert side of the Atlas, where rainfall from the high mountains runs off in streams, some of them underground, until they finally disappear into the sand. This source of water makes possible a strip of intense cultivation, a ribbon oasis.

Moving east from Tunisia, the Gulf of Syrte indents North Africa, carrying the shore south into desert latitudes – too far south for continuous cultivation all along the coast. Only in the vicinity of Tripoli, and again where the coast bends north to form the bulge of Cyrenaica east of Benghazi, is there enough rainfall for regular cultivation. Otherwise the region that is now Libya and western Egypt is steppe and desert broken by occasional oases. Some of these oases are important, especially in the region south of Tripoli called Fezzan and centering on Murzuk, and another south of Cyrenaica. They have figured in history out of all proportion to their size or wealth, for they have served as stepping stones for crossing the desert – either in an east-west direction from Egypt to the Maghrib, or north and south from the Mediterranean to the well watered lands south of the Sahara.

In fact, Egypt itself is an oasis in a region that would be desert if it were not for the water from the Nile, provided by rain that originally fell thousands of miles away in the East African highlands or in Ethiopia. The rest of Egypt has only enough rainfall to support sparse nomadic pastoralism. Historical Egypt is a very long ribbon-like oasis stretching down from the southern mountains. This oasis is not uniform through all its length. In the lower Nile valley of Egypt proper, the river brings water for irrigation of the flood plain on either side. From Aswan to Cairo, usually called Upper Egypt, the valley is truly ribbon-like; in Lower Egypt, below Cairo, the river splits into the many branches of the delta, flowing through low-lying and often swampy country until it reaches the sea.

Above Aswan, the character of the river valley is again different. Easy and continuous navigation by sailing vessels ends here at the first cataract, the lowest of a series of six rock shelves that force the water through rapids or over low falls between that point and Khartoum, where the Blue and White Niles come together. This stretch is the Nubian Nile, which flows through the desert with the stream bed often cut more deeply into the countryside than in Egypt itself, limiting the area of flood-plain irrigation. The natural frontier at the first cataract was the historical frontier between Egyptian and Nubian cultures. It was also to some degree a racial line, with people to the north looking like modern Egyptians or Middle Easterners and those upstream looking more like other people in sub-Saharan Africa. It also became a language line; the ancient language above Aswan was ancestral to modern Nubian and belongs to the Eastern Sudanic branch of the Nilo-Saharan language stock (and is thus related only to sub-Saharan languages), whereas Coptic or Ancient Egyptian belonged to the Afro-Asiatic language family, related to Berber, Arabic, and Hebrew – though most Ethiopian languages and the Hausa of northern Nigeria also belong to that family. Many linguists believe the Afro-Asiatic language family originated south of the Sahara near the present-day frontier between Ethiopia and Sudan, but that was long before ancient Egypt emerged as an historic entity.

The Nubian Nile, however, was not uniform as a natural region. Some parts were comparatively rich for agricultural purposes. Others had such bad soils that they were left uninhabited for long periods. The conventional terminology identifies a series of "reaches" between Aswan and Khartoum. Three of these were historically important. The lowest is Lower Nubia, now covered by the waters of Lake Nasser backed up by the Aswan high dam. This was the part in closest contact with Egypt and with the most significant Egyptian cultural influences. The second is the Dongola reach, where the Nile makes a bow to the south and then bends north again. This was to be the core region for Napata, one of the earliest Nubian kingdoms. The third was the Shendi reach, from Khartoum to Atbara, which was to be the core region for Merowe.

South of Nubia was the savanna country of sub-Saharan Africa, where rainfall agriculture was again possible. This was also the Sudan, in Arabic *bilād al-Sūdān*, "the land of the blacks" (though the people in this part of the Sudan are no blacker than the Nubians). Along the Nile, the sedentary populations of the Sudan could use irrigation, but that was not common until the twentieth century AD. The older base here was rainfall agriculture, as it was along the whole east–west belt of savanna country stretching from the Red Sea to the mouth of the Senegal, and the Arabs called all of it the Sudan – not just the part that falls within the present-day republic of that name.

Within this belt, the northernmost region usable for agriculture has twenty to twenty-four inches of rainfall, and rainfall increases steadily as one moves south toward the equatorial forest. But this did not mean that populations were denser further south. Desert-side conditions were often just as favorable for agriculture. In the Nilotic Sudan, in particular, the natural environment became more difficult away from the sahel. Further south, the Nile became choked with vegetation and spread out across the neighboring grassland each high-water season. Rather than favoring agriculture as similar floods did in Egypt, this environment was far more friendly to pastoralism than to tilling the soil. The vegetation-choked reaches of the Nile, called the *sudd*, were also a barrier to further navigation up river, and the annual flooding made travel to the south difficult by land as well. As a result, the dense agricultural populations along the Nile in the northern Sudan were not a threshold of contact, leading easily to the rest of tropical Africa; they themselves had no intense and continuous contact with other peoples further south. The Nile Valley was therefore less than adequate as a transportation route leading from the East African highlands to Egypt.

On the other hand, the lower Nile provided superb transportation at early stages of maritime technology. All during the season of low water from November through the following August, sailing vessels could easily move upstream by using the prevailing northerly winds. The return to Cairo or the delta was equally easy, with the current helping. Above Aswan, the cataracts were not an insuperable barrier, but they made water transportation more difficult.

As a transportation route, the Red Sea is more deceptive. It was not a good route from north to south until the nineteenth-century invention of steamships and the construction of the Suez Canal. The main difficulty was not the land bridge at Suez; it was a navigational problem on the sea itself. The same northerlies that help navigation on the Nile also blow over the northern Red Sea, but they blow all year with no river current to help on the return trip.

In the southern half of the Red Sea, the wind direction alternated with the Indian Ocean monsoons. In winter, winds on the Red Sea blow from the southeast as far north as Jiddah and Mecca, where the northerlies take over. With the southwest monsoon of the summer months, northerlies prevail along the whole length of the sea, making it easy for Indian-Ocean ships to return home. This made for easy sea communication in the southern half of the sea, but sailing ships rarely made the whole voyage from one end to the other. It was more efficient to off-load the southern cargoes at some convenient port about midway along either shore. On the western side, it was convenient to trans-ship from a port like Suakin to the Nile below Aswan for the final trip down the river to Cairo or a Mediterranean port. To the east, it was convenient to trans-ship at a port like Jiddah for overland caravan by way of Mecca and Medina to Syria or other parts of the fertile crescent. The Red Sea was thus usable in connection with camel caravans, but it never played the same historical role as the Mediterranean in uniting peoples and cultures around its fringes.

The final region of early sedentary population and good rainfall is the combined highlands of Ethiopia and south Arabia. These two regions are on different continents, but the Red Sea has not divided them historically. They are not merely geologically and climatically similar; their cultures also have much in common, with the Amharic and Tigrinya languages of Ethiopia closely related to the Arabic of southern Arabia. The very fact that both sides of the straits have long practiced sedentary agriculture separates them from the surrounding nomads. South Arabia is also somewhat cut off from the east by the "empty quarter" of pure desert that occupies the southeast interior of the Arabian peninsula. In much the same way, Ethiopia was cut off from the south by the arid belt of the present-day Kenya-Ethiopian border, and from the west by the

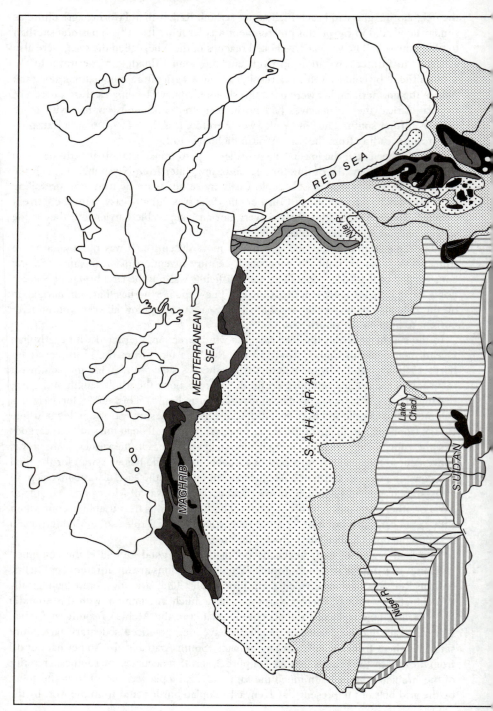

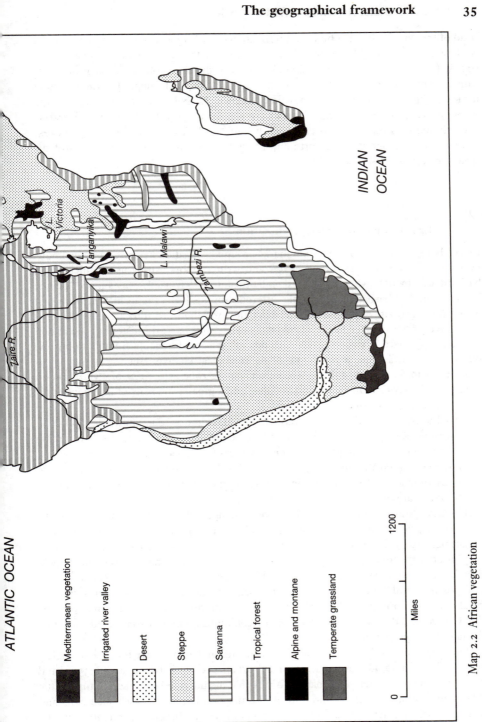

Map 2.2 African vegetation

sudd of the Nile Valley. Yet both southern Arabia and Ethiopia enjoy easy access to the Red Sea, since the highlands drop off precipitously to the seacoast on either side of the straits. Both have their easiest overland contact to the north – in Arabia, through the caravan route along the eastern shore of the Red Sea, in Ethiopia by way of routes northwest to the Nilotic Sudan and thence down the Nile through Nubia to Egypt. Although Ethiopia and southern Arabia are clearly south of the great Afro-Eurasian dry belt, both regions were closer to the style of North African history, partly because of their easy contact with the north and partly because they were even more isolated from the rest of sub-Saharan Africa.

Egypt: the first African civilization

In this book, we often put quotation marks around civilization because of its invidious overtones. Westerners have long talked and written about Africa as an uncivilized, barbaric continent – when what they really meant by "civilized" was simply "people like us," and by "barbarians," "people different from us." But the term *civilization* first meant the way of life of people who lived in cities, and the word still can be used in that sense. We prefer to refer to the *intercommunicating zone* in world history as the region where people were in easiest touch with one another, and hence were able to borrow innovations and achieve a rapid rate of technological change. But we might just as easily refer to the origin of this intercommunicating zone as the rise of civilization, in the sense that civilization means life in cities, and a greater intensity of intercommunication began with city life.

Afro-Eurasian agriculture appeared for the first time to our knowledge either in southwest Asia or northeast Africa about 10,000 BC, and the agricultural revolution spread out from there with profound consequences for human society. This new phase is sometimes called the neolithic, or New Stone Age, to separate it from the period when the rougher tools of the hunting and gathering peoples were used, and from the metal tools that followed.

The next threshold of human technological change was a combination known as the Bronze Age, even though metallurgy was not its greatest achievement. The true secret of Bronze-Age achievement was efficient agriculture – efficient enough to leave a surplus after the food needs of the farmers themselves had been met. Some food could then be diverted to pay specialized and skilled craftworkers. Denser populations were also possible, and concentrations of people began to gather around a point of trade, a royal court, or an important temple. These concentrations were in fact embryo cities. They increased the intensity and variety of communication and stimulated invention through the exchange of ideas.

The first Bronze-Age society was Sumer in Mesopotamia, where the archaeological record shows a rapid development of an urban society between about 3500 and 3000 BC. The technology that made this possible included irrigated agriculture in the Tigris and Euphrates valleys and improved transportation, such as wheeled carts and sailing vessels; refinements in metallurgy and pottery; and finally, in about 3000 BC, the

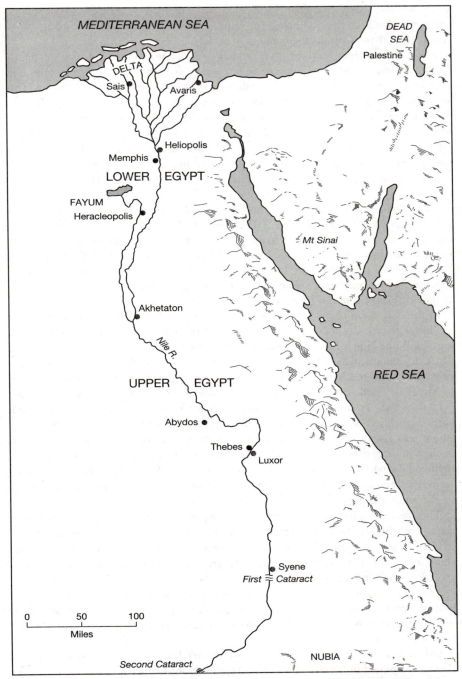

Map 2.3 Early Egypt (based on William H. McNeill, *A World History*, Second
Edition, London: Oxford University Press, 1971)

art of writing. Early Sumerian civilization was confined to irrigable river valleys, apparently because the technology of rainfall agriculture was still not adequate to support a non-food-producing segment of society.

It is also possible, however, that irrigation agriculture made for a more tightly controlled society, where whatever the farmers or fishermen might produce beyond their own needs could be drawn off for the support of priests, rulers, or a nobility. This supposition rests on the reasoning that irrigation works often require a larger scale of work-organization than either hunting or rainfall farming. Having learned to organize the masses to build irrigation works, the rulers could go on to manipulate the people for their own benefit. Rainfall farmers, on the other hand, normally worked the land in family-sized units, which were more nearly self-sufficient, hence harder for the rulers to manipulate and less prone to contribute their resources to the cities, temples, or courts.

Other urban societies appeared a little before 3000 BC, often in distant river valleys where irrigation was also possible, rather than nearby places that lacked that crucial environment. Another center of irrigation agriculture and urban life was the Indus valley in northwest India; still another was the Nile in Egypt. The desiccation of the Sahara had not yet begun, and the Nile was a reliable source of irrigation water, while the neighboring lands were suitable for some rainfall agriculture and for raising sheep, goats, cattle, and donkeys. (Horses and camels were not yet available.)

In the Nile flood plain, early irrigation was comparatively simple. The behavior of the lower river today follows from the fact that the flow from Lake Victoria-Nyanza into the White Nile is fairly constant throughout the year. But the Blue Nile from Lake Tana in Ethiopia, which contributes twice as much water each year, does so sporadically. The water reaching Egypt in August and September is about forty times the flow in March or April, toward the end of the Ethiopian dry season. For Egypt this meant (as it does today) that the Nile flowed over its banks in the summer months. The silt it carried provided renewed fertility for annual cropping, and the earliest form of irrigation was simply to plant the crops as the water receded. Residual moisture was enough to carry these crops through to the harvest. The first artificial irrigation simply modified the natural order by building levees and channels to control the flow from the main river, and earth banks to impound it to a depth of one or two meters long enough to guarantee adequate deposits of moisture and silt.

This system, called basin irrigation, could be supplemented by devices for raising water from the Nile to the flood plain even in seasons of low water. One possibility was to build canals to carry water from further upstream. Others used animal power, and some used human strength alone. The total area in perennial irrigation in early times was very small indeed, but it contributed to the wealth of the valley by allowing a second or even a third crop on the same land. Today the great majority of cultivated land in Egypt is under perennial irrigation, but the dams to store the water, the canals to carry it, and the powered pumps to lift it came only with the nineteenth and twentieth centuries.

Urban society using basin irrigation arose remarkably fast in Egypt, compared to its slow development in Mesopotamia. Shortly after 4000 BC, copper came into use. After 3600 BC, technological change came even faster, with borrowing from Mesopotamia in agricultural and craft production, and perhaps in some aspects of social organization. The early cities of sun-dried brick emerged at this time, along with long-distance trade at sea and on the Nile, and innovations in the art of writing. Egypt began to develop its own style and character. Writing, for example, took the form of hieroglyphs or picture writing, as opposed to the Mesopotamian cuneiform, which worked on an altogether different principle. (A third system, Phoenician writing with symbols that stood for sounds, not ideas, was different again. It was, of course, the ancestor of the alphabet later adopted by the Greeks, Romans, and the Western world generally.) Authorities generally assume that writing grew out of interactions between Mesopotamia and Egypt by stimulus diffusion, in which the ideas about writing passed back and forth but the particular techniques were invented locally.

In other respects, Egypt moved rapidly past the point reached in Mesopotamia. From about 3600 BC to about 3000 BC, Egypt's long-term cultural forms took shape. The most notable achievement was in political organization. The earliest urban society in the Nile valley was divided into a number of small states. After 3400 BC, these states grew in size and in social complexity. By 3200 BC, they had merged into only three, two in Egypt proper and one in Nubia; by 3100 BC, the whole country was united under the first pharaohs. The initial political unity lasted during most of the next thousand years, in spite of periods of disorder and changing dynasties. It was built in part on the natural unity of the Nile valley from the first cataract to the sea, reinforced by excellent water transportation – and by lack of neighbors. The narrow flood plain of the Nubian Nile could not sustain a large population, and potential enemies had to come from across the sea or across the desert from the east or west. Only the nomads of the Red Sea hills or the western desert posed a constant threat, but their land was too poor to give them real power unless the Egyptian state was weak or disunited.

Egyptologists use the label *Pharaonic* for the whole period from the first united kingdom of 3100 BC to 332 BC, when Alexander the Great of Macedonia conquered Egypt. The period before that is called *Predynastic*. The period of Alexander's successors is called *Ptolemaic*, after the Graeco-Egyptian Ptolemies who ruled until Egypt was absorbed into the Roman Empire just before the birth of Christ. Specialists also subdivide the Pharaonic period, beginning with the Old Kingdom (3100–1640 BC), the original united Egyptian state under the pharaohs. A period of disorder followed in about 2180–2080. Then came the Middle Kingdom (2080–1640), then a second intermediate period, and finally a New Kingdom (1570–1090 BC). The remaining Pharaonic period is often categorized as the period of the invasions or the era of foreign dynasties, because Libyans, Assyrians, and Persians controlled the country – sometimes with supreme control exercised from their homeland, sometimes merely as dynasties of foreign origin naturalized in Egypt. A further convention divides the Pharaonic period into thirty dynasties labeled in Roman numerals from I to XXX.

It is important to recognize that these separate periods and sub-periods are conventions imposed by historians, not a reality that ancient Egyptians themselves would have known. Although these conventions are useful to help make order out of nearly three thousand years of confused history, they can also suggest the misconception that historical change is properly summarized in the political shifts of rulers or ruling dynasties. When art is ascribed to a particular dynasty, for example, all we really know is that it was created when that dynasty ruled – not that the pharaohs were actually responsible for it, directly or indirectly.

Some historical developments seem to mature slowly, but Egyptian culture of the Pharaonic period rose to a remarkable flowering in the Old Kingdom and then retained much of its characteristic style for millennia. It was not changeless, but many Egyptologists believe that established traditions stifled further innovation. Monumental building, for example, reached a kind of peak in about 2600–2500 BC (dynasty IV), when some of the most impressive pyramids were constructed, and it continued over the next millennia. Other art styles that first emerged at the beginning of the Old Kingdom can still be traced in art produced 2000 years later.

Egyptian religion, however, is an exception to this impression of monolithic uniformity and stability over time. The earliest pharaohs of the Old Kingdom were regarded as incarnations of the raven god, Horus. Without quite giving up this claim, later pharaohs were also recognized as god-descendants of Re, the sun god, or of Osiris, the god-ruler of the underworld. The accepted explanation is that the original pharaohs came to rule over a country with a great deal of religious diversity, with each of the small original kingdoms having its own gods and local priesthoods. One way to reconcile them all might have been to establish an authoritative account that would show them as members of a common pantheon, where one god was supreme but all found an honored place – and some Egyptian theologians tried this without long-term success. Another solution that worked better for the central authorities was not to worry about primacy among the gods, but to allow each group of priests to go its own way so long as all recognized that the pharaoh himself was a god-king incarnate on earth.

As we have seen, Pharaonic Egypt was one of the many African states with institutions that used to be classified as divine kingship. The god-king was not merely a deity; his personal physical health and well-being were peculiarly and intimately associated with the land, the harvest, and especially with the supply of water by the Nile flood. While anthropologists and historians once postulated that this kind of kingship may have originated in Egypt and passed from there to the rest of Africa, the best present hypothesis suggests that many aspects of sacred kingship were independently invented in several places to justify an accepted structure of authority over society. Other aspects may have been diffused up or down the Nile valley in the distant past, but there is no reason to suppose that they went from Egypt upstream rather than downstream from the Sudan toward Egypt. Indeed, these ideas about kingship were probably accepted at a time before the desiccation of the Sahara, when Egypt had more numerous neighbors where deserts now exist.

Early representations in Egyptian art show pharaohs with some symbols of pastoralism like the shepherd's crook, and several authorities believe that their later religious position as god-kings is traceable to an earlier role as magicians and rainmakers among pastoral nomads or semi-nomads. All of this suggests that the original unification of the Nile valley may have been achieved through conquest by a pastoral nomadic community from the not-yet-desiccated Sahara. If a nomadic confederation had been formed under religious leadership (as often happened among nomads in more recent history), and if it conquered the sedentary states of the Nile valley (as often happened to other sedentary societies), the resulting administration might well have been similar to that of the early pharaohs – a political structure that was essentially an extension of the god-king's household, imposed from above on localized peasant communities, each with its own local gods and beliefs.

In any event, peasant communities formed the base of Egyptian society. Most peasants were freemen, though a small class of slaves also existed. At least during the Old Kingdom, no important social groups stood between the peasantry and the royal household – no merchants, for example, and only the bare beginnings of a local gentry. The entire organization of the country, including foreign trade and irrigation works, was in the hands of the royal household. The peasantry either had their labor taxed or were conscripted to work on levees, dykes, irrigation channels, and monumental architecture like the pyramids. Tens of thousands of people must have been mobilized each year to create public works on the scale of those that remain, though they may not have worked in such terrible conditions as our mental pictures of "Egyptian bondage" suggest. Before the coming of perennial irrigation, little or no farm work was possible for a few months. Historians now believe that pyramids and irrigation works alike were built by mobilizing labor during this slack season, rather than by keeping thousands of slaves at work on a year-round basis.

After the first millennium of pharaonic rule, the royal household became less efficient. Perhaps it grew too big and unwieldy, or perhaps officials began to make their offices hereditary. In any case, the centralized kingdom broke down after about 2180 BC, creating the first Intermediate Period in which political authority was fragmented. Several local leaders claimed to be the god-king of all Egypt, though none of them could make the claim stand.

Then, after 2080 BC, centralized authority returned with the foundation of the Middle Kingdom, but the consequences of recent localization remained. Landlords and local priests became an important intermediate group between the peasantry and the royal household. Egypt also began to lose some of its previous isolation behind the surrounding deserts. Toward the end of the Old Kingdom, Egyptian expeditions sailed down the Red Sea to southern Arabia, Ethiopia, and the horn of Africa. With the Middle Kingdom, they became more systematic and regular. More intense trade by sea reached out to the Levant and across the Mediterranean, while overland contact brought systematic and regular relations with the fertile crescent.

Up the Nile, parts of Lower Nubia probably fell under Egyptian domination even before 2000 BC. Shadowy early kingdoms may have appeared further south during the second millennium BC, but the substantial and lasting kingdom of Napata (sometimes called the Kingdom of Kush) flourished on the Dongola reach between the ninth and the fourth century BC. Later on, Merowe took its place as the principal Nubian kingdom, from the fourth century BC to the fourth century AD. Sailing vessels could use the Nile between the cataracts. Thus, the Nubian Nile was an important trade route carrying Nubian products like dates along with others from the Sudan. Cultural exchange between Egypt and Nubia was important, but Nubia was not simply another part of a greater-Egyptian culture area. Merowe, for example, used Egyptian hieroglyphics but it also had its own alphabet, which scholars have not deciphered completely.

Egypt's increasing contact with the outer world shot forward decisively in the Second Intermediate Period (1640–1570 BC), bringing new rulers from Asia, called the Hyksos. Historians are uncertain who these Hyksos may have been. One possibility is that they were chariot-riding warriors who swept down and conquered Egypt, as similar charioteers had recently conquered Mesopotamia. But they could have been less powerful immigrants from Asia who infiltrated and then rose more slowly to power. In any event, they founded a Hyksos principality that ruled most of the delta while a native dynasty continued to rule over Upper Egypt. Whatever their political role, the Hyksos brought new modes of Asian technology, from military chariots to bronze metallurgy, new textile manufactures, and new musical instruments, even new agriculture (for example, olive trees and new breeds of cattle).

After 1570 BC, an Egyptian dynasty united the entire country; the phase of Egyptian history called the New Kingdom began. The Hyksos disappeared or were assimilated into the Egyptian population, but the impact of increased foreign contact remained. Egyptian military power and political influence reached into Asia; several Egyptian armies invaded the fertile crescent. For a time after 1500 BC, it looked as though Egypt might unite all the urban societies of the Middle East under its rule, much as Rome later united the Mediterranean world. During the early centuries of the New Kingdom, Egypt ruled parts of northern Nubia, but the Egyptian threat was overtaken by the rise of Nubian states to the south. In the late eighth and early seventh century BC, Nubians conquered Egypt and ruled there as the twenty-fifth dynasty.

Especially after about 1400 BC, a series of Asian powers came in turn to a position of dominance – first Hittites from Anatolia, then Assyrians, and finally the Persians, just before the Macedonian conquest swept over them all. While Egyptian armies still sometimes marched in Asia, Asian armies also now marched in Egypt. Both Assyrians and Persians ruled Egypt for a time. Other foreigners founded Egyptian dynasties, including Libyans from the west (people ancestral to the present-day Tuaregs of the Sahara), and Egyptianized Nubians from the south. Egyptian cultural influence was important throughout the eastern Mediterranean, just as foreign elements had a strong impact on Egyptian life and art. Iron metallurgy came in from Anatolia. Even before 332 BC when the Ptolemies brought a period of Greek overrule, interaction between Egypt and its neighbors had already paved the way for the Hellenistic synthesis that was to pull Egypt more firmly than ever into the intercommunicating world of the Mediterranean and the Middle East.

Nomads and sedentaries

Historians generally believe that pastoralism without agriculture was a late specialization that followed the rise of mixed farming in Asia, as it did in Africa. Some early pastoralists were pure nomads without a fixed base where crops could be raised. Others were semi-nomads who practiced transhumance – sending their stock off seasonally to the high mountains or into the desert during the rainy season. In either case, they were specialist producers. As such, they needed commercial outlets among farmers who would exchange grain, wine, and oil for meat and milk – farmers whose sedentary life made it easier for them to produce the tools and textiles that the nomads also needed. This specialization tended to make early nomads dependent on sedentary society, all the more so before the nomads had horses or camels to give them wide mobility.

This situation gave the sedentary farmers a better bargaining position than the nomads. The less-specialized farmers did not need nomad products as much as the nomads needed their grain, cloth, and tools, and the farmers must have taken advantage of that fact in bargaining the terms of trade. Nomads, on the other hand, had a chance to redress the balance through force. They were usually organized in bands a good deal larger than a single family, while the single household was often the basic unit of sedentary work organization. Nomads were mobile; sedentaries were fixed to their plots of ground and their stores of grain for the next planting. The nomads' wandering life of herding and hunting also developed skills that could be turned to military ends. The final product was mutual dependence, tempered by the fact that either side might try to push its advantage over the other.

Nor was the balance of advantage constant through time; it changed with changing technology. Before about 1700 BC, none of the nomadic groups living in the shadows of the great urban societies was a serious military threat. Even though horses were first domesticated about 3000 BC, the usual beast of burden was the donkey, and men went into battle on foot. The nomads' big advantage – mobility to assemble and strike fast with a large force – came only with the effective military use of horses, and that was slow in coming.

To use horses for mounted fighting required bits, bridles, saddles, and stirrups so that a rider could control his horse and fight at the same time. The first military use of horses came with chariotry, not cavalry. A two-wheeled chariot provided a mobile platform and some protection for an archer and a driver, but even that was slow to evolve. The first horses were raised for meat. After a time in Mesopotamia, they were used to pull four-wheeled carts, but these had fixed axles and the cart had to be dragged around turns. The real shift to military importance came only a little after 1700 BC, when horses began to be attached to a pole leading forward from the chariot. They could then carry part of the weight and turn the two-wheeled vehicle with ease. About the same time, reins were invented for steering the horses from the chariot. Short and light compound bows made the archers more effective in battle, and spoked wheels increased the chariot's speed without sacrificing strength.

By the time chariots were effective, the intercommunicating world of the Bronze Age "civilizations" had expanded from Egypt and Mesopotamia to include the fertile crescent and the Iranian plateau. Further afield, similar centers existed in China and the Indus valley. In northwestern Africa and Europe, the agricultural revolution had already come, but with only embryo cities, in spite of the impressive temple sites of standing stones like Stonehenge in Britain and other similar sites in Malta and North Africa. More significant was the spread of bronze metallurgy into the steppe lands that stretched across the whole of Asia from the Black Sea to Manchuria. It was there that chariot warfare was first perfected.

Between about 1700 and 1400 BC, charioteers from the steppe attacked and conquered most of the urban "civilizations" from Mesopotamia to China. Some of them, speaking Indo-European languages, moved into the north Indian plain, while others moved into Europe. In both places their languages are still dominant. The Hyksos who brought an end to the Middle Kingdom in Egypt were also charioteers, whatever their other role may have been. Further west in Africa, the Berber-speaking peoples, whom the Egyptians called Libyans, were using chariots for their raids on the Nile Valley as early as 1235 BC. By that time, chariots must have been commonly used by all the nomadic peoples on the fringes of the Maghrib as far as the Atlantic coast.

Chariots must have brought even more drastic changes to the Sahara, which was then well on its way to desiccation. The most plausible hypothesis holds that the chariot revolution was seized by the Berber-speaking peoples of northern Africa. Their monopoly over this military innovation made it possible for them to drive the desert people off to the south along the whole stretch from Lake Chad to the Atlantic. Whatever languages may have been spoken in northwestern Africa before this time, Berber languages became dominant north of the desert from Libya to Morocco, south to the Senegal and the Niger bend, and out to the Canary Islands in the Atlantic, while Nilo-Saharan languages related to Nubian were spoken by desert people from the Nubian Nile westward to the Tibesti mountain range in mid-Sahara north of Lake Chad and all along the sedentary fringe of savanna country to the south. In the western Sahara, a sequence of rock engravings of chariots is found along a route that extends southward from Morocco to the Niger bend, then back to the north by way of the Saharan highlands to end in Tunisia. It is possible that chariots had some role in trans-Saharan communication from as early as 1300 BC. People of the Fezzan in Libya were famous charioteers in Roman times, so the chariot phase in the western Sahara may have lasted as long as a thousand years. It is unlikely, however, that the chariots were ever important transport vehicles. In a region without roads, pack animals are far more efficient than carts. The chariots were more likely used as military protection for the slower caravans – though caravan trade across the western Sahara was not extensive until camels became available about 300 AD.

Meanwhile, the steppe peoples in Asia far to the northeast had been riding horses in an experimental way even before chariots were perfected. Riding techniques improved gradually, but the regular use of cavalry in battle is recorded no earlier than 900 BC. Then, it came as part of a horse revolution associated with a whole set of social changes on the steppe that made possible a new kind of nomadic mobility. In a military sense, it called for special techniques for guiding a horse in battle and shooting arrows from its back. It also called for new breeds of horses strong enough to carry a man and his supplies over a long distance. Other patterns of nomadism shifted as well, as people could move more stock faster and further with horses to help with the herding.

War chariots gave way to cavalry very rapidly after about 900 BC, and most rapidly in places where pastoralism encouraged other uses for the mounted horse. It was especially fast, therefore, throughout the Eurasian steppe and again in the Maghrib and the deserts to the south, but slower in Egypt. A little before 700 BC, for example, Libyans from the west, using mounted horses, conquered northern Nubia against Egyptian forces still using chariots. To the west of the Nile, the cavalry revolution followed the chariot revolution by a delay of about six hundred years; cavalry, in short, spread into that region much faster than chariots had done, an index of the way northwestern Africa was gradually being pulled into the spreading intercommunicating zone.

The last millennium BC was also the period when camels finally arrived in Africa, coming first to the region east of the Nile. They were never the principal military animal, but they could carry heavier loads than donkeys, and over longer distances without water. Because the load per animal was greater, a single drover could control a larger carrying capacity, so that the manpower requirements per ton of freight were less. Camels could also graze on more arid land than that usable by cattle, sheep, or even goats.

The camel made its first significant impact on Africa before 1000 BC, because they made possible improved communications between northern and southern Arabia. About that time, a series of kingdoms appeared in the highlands of what was now Yemen, across the straits from Ethiopia, linked by commercial caravan to the "civilized" world of the Middle East. In the Ethiopian highlands near the Red Sea coast, a ruined palace dating from about the fourth century BC also shows strong south Arabian architectural influences along with a number of inscriptions in a south Arabian language. With camels, the arid belt became less of a barrier. Toward the end of the Pharaonic period, camels began to be used on the Egyptian side of the Red Sea as well, but they were not used intensively elsewhere in Africa until after the birth of Christ.

The westward movement of camels into the Sahara proper followed a different route from that taken by horses. Instead of moving along the North African coast and then out into the desert, in the first century AD, camels first diffused along the southern desert edge from the Nile valley to Borku and Tibesti, north of Lake Chad. By the fourth century, they were common in the Sahara between Chad and Tripoli and had spread even further west. The desert people now gained an edge against the sedentary peoples of the Maghrib, who were then more or less unified under imperial Rome. The Romans were weakening in any case, and they were forced to fall back – trying merely to hold the nomads outside an elaborate set of fortified lines stretching from Tunisia to Morocco.

Looking back from about the fourth century AD, the nomads had gained steadily in power through technological increments of chariots, cavalry, and then camels. At that point, the balance of technology against sedentary societies reached a plateau of relative stability, which was to last until the seventeenth-century invention of good field artillery – and even that was not much used in the Sahara until the nineteenth century. But a pattern of nomad-sedentary relations had developed much earlier. Nomads had been raiding sedentary peoples even before the era of the chariot; tensions growing out of complementary production and exchange were equally old; sedentary and nomadic peoples were rivals for the land marginal to either group, even before Cain and Abel came to represent the two ways of life for the Old Testament. At least by the time cavalry arrived on the scene, nomadic-sedentary relations had fallen into a pattern that became a major theme in world history between the agricultural and industrial revolutions. It was noticed in the Bible, and again by Ibn Khaldun, the great historian of Tunis in the late fourteenth century. More recently, Owen Lattimore developed it further with his study of *The Inner Asian Frontiers of China*.

These authorities noticed, first of all, the rivalry and complementarity of the nomadic and sedentary ways of life, especially along the natural frontier between the steppe and the sown. Both Lattimore and Ibn Khaldun wrote about recent periods when technological advantage had been relatively constant, yet history seems to have passed from phases of nomadic to phases of sedentary dominance. This alternation took place because either side could capitalize on its natural advantage with good organization. Once organized to act in concert, either could control the marginal lands and thus weaken the other. Lack of organization for common effort was disastrous. The sedentary village was helpless in the face of surprise attack from the steppe so long as each village had only its own resources for defense. But an organized sedentary state could pool the resources of many villages, defend the frontiers, seize the marginal lands, and, if necessary, police the steppe itself. If the state became weakened or disorganized, however, nomads could raid at will, regain the marginal land, build their own organization, and finally carry their forays into the heart of the sedentary empire.

Nomads under purely nomadic leadership might envy the wealth of their sedentary neighbors without understanding how that wealth could be exploited. In that case, their raids tended to be destructive, but that was all. When nomads fell under the leadership of men who understood both nomadic and sedentary cultures, another possibility appeared. If marginal leaders could command a nomadic following, yet understand how a sedentary society might be controlled to their own advantage, these raids could turn into conquest. Nomadic leaders often founded new dynasties ruling over a sedentary society, but once in command of a sedentary empire, the nomad leaders soon found themselves on the other side of the ancient rivalry. Their interests became those of sedentary society from which they drew their wealth. They then had to deal with nomads beyond the frontiers – either those who had lost the spoils of conquest or others who had come to take their place on the steppe. At that point, the struggle began again, with a new victory promised to those who could organize most effectively.

This style of history is a theme that runs along all the fringes of the great Afro-Eurasian arid belt during the past three thousand years and more, with men like Genghis Khan and Tamurlane as examples of the marginal leader of nomads who built a great empire. Some historians see the Hyksos in Egypt as essentially chariot-riding barbarians who destroyed the Middle Kingdom and rebuilt it under their own control. Ibn Khaldun interpreted the history of North Africa from the ninth to the fourteenth century as a series of nomad-founded dynasties that rose to power and then fell to new nomadic leaders from the steppe. The Saharan fringes of the West African savanna can be used to illustrate a similar process. Changing technology in the last millennium BC thus set the scene for a new style of history that was to last nearly to the present.

Hellenism and the rise of Rome

One of the myths of African history, only recently dissipated, stressed as a main theme that the isolated and "primitive" continent had been gradually enlightened by the successive spread of "civilization" by increments – each new phase being a greater intensity of contact with the West. The interpretation is vastly oversimplified. It also carries a false suggestion that African history was made in Europe, not in Africa, and the overtones of European racism and cultural arrogance are obvious. Yet there is some validity to a similar interpretation of world history – one that is equally broad, but less value-laden and centered on Europe. This view stresses the gradual formation and spread of a series of intercommunicating zones, beginning from small points in the river valleys and spreading gradually to larger and larger parts of the Afro-Eurasian land mass.

The lower Nile valley was obviously one of the earliest of these points. The most significant next steps for northern Africa were the incorporation of Egypt in the greater Hellenic world, politically articulated by Alexander of Macedonia's conquests after about 320 BC. The conquest was not so important as the spread of Hellenic culture, to which Egypt itself had contributed greatly in past centuries. During the next centuries Hellenism spread west in the Mediterranean basin, now unified politically by the new Roman Empire, which included all of North Africa in the first century BC. All this was not the spread of "civilization" into Africa; it was the incorporation of northern Africa, along with other newcomers, into a new and more intense intercommunicating zone.

Greek culture had begun to expand into neighboring parts of Asia, Africa, and Europe long before the formation of the Macedonian Empire in the 330s BC. Greek commerce based on the export of wine and olive oil reached into the western Mediterranean, Asia, and Egypt. The Greek way of fighting in disciplined and armored infantry units – the famous Greek phalanx – was another export. Along with this military technique went Greek mercenary soldiers – and other Greeks seeking employment in commerce, government, and many other fields. Greeks of this stamp were active in Egypt from the late seventh century BC, and Egypt gradually merged culturally into the Hellenistic world in the centuries that followed, down to Alexander's conquest. Even though Macedonian political control disappeared after about 280 BC, the Greek-dominated kingdom of the Ptolemies was one of the most powerful states of the early Hellenistic world, along with a Seleucid kingdom ruling much of western Asia and a Macedonian state that was now reduced in size (though larger than the original Macedonia).

As Greek culture spread into the Middle East, it also changed. Some well-springs of its own originality in the homeland dried up; Greece itself continued to absorb cultural elements from abroad, as well as exporting them to others. Exported elements tended to change and adjust to their new environment. In sum, the Greek culture of the fifth century BC turned into the Hellenistic culture of the second, a culture that was common to the whole of the Middle East – especially in the cities and in international communication. Older cultures survived in part as a substratum. In Egypt, for example, the city of Alexandria became one of the great centers of the Hellenistic world, perhaps its greatest urban center. But the countryside and the older cities up the Nile were less changed. The new government administration was probably more efficient in extracting tax revenue from the peasants than the last pharaohs had been, but that revenue went to pay for life in Alexandria. The cultural mix may not have been very different from that of modern Africa, where Western education and Western institutions dominate the centers of power while aspects of the pre-colonial way of life survive in the countryside with much less change.

Neither the Maghrib nor Western Europe were affected by the first phase of Hellenism. Macedonia itself was a frontier territory of the "civilized" world, and its

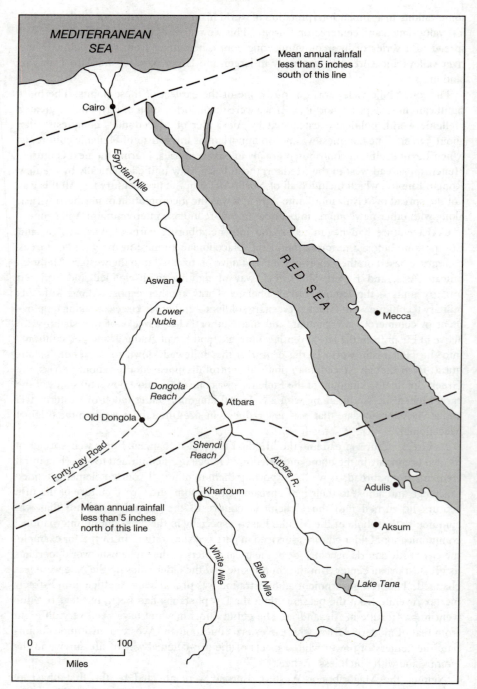

Map 2.4 Nubia

military conquests took it back to the core area of southwestern Asia. The western Mediterranean was a distant fringe, but one that already had commercial contact with the core. This spread of cultural influence from east to west was carried principally by trade diasporas of Greek or Levantine origin. In early phases of cross-cultural trade, some kind of mediation was needed to help open commerce between people of differing cultures. Usually agents were sent out to establish a small trading post or colony in alien society. There they could learn about the local ways of doing business and mediate between the local people and merchants from their own homeland who might follow. The Greeks established many trade outposts of this kind on the shores of the Mediterranean. Many grew into enclaves under Greek control, and these often grew on into Greek city-states populated by colonists from a home city on the Aegean. As far west as southern Italy and eastern Sicily the shores were ringed with trade enclaves and cities of Greek origin. The Greeks were not only traders but also unofficial cultural missionaries from the intercommunicating zone.

In North Africa, Phoenicians played a similar role. The original Phoenicians were Canaanites from the coastal towns of what is now Syria, Lebanon, and northern Israel. These cities were sometimes dominated by Egypt, Persia, or Assyria during the last millennium BC, but they kept their separate identity as specialized urban centers oriented toward maritime trade. Their trade diaspora to the West began about 1000 BC. By 800 BC, the main lines of the network were complete – one line of trading posts in coastal Egypt and thence up the Nile as far as Memphis; a major western base at Carthage in Tunisia; and a second at Cadiz, in Spain beyond Gibraltar. Smaller bases and trading posts were scattered along the North African coast from Tunisia to Morocco, on Sardinia and Sicily, and at Ibiza in the Balearic Islands.

In the 330s BC, Macedonia conquered the Levant and pulled it into the broader Hellenic world, leaving Carthage in the west as the main Phoenician base and center of Punic identity for a few centuries more. Carthaginian influence in the Maghrib, however, was much like Hellenistic influence in Egypt of the Ptolemies. It was concentrated in the cities, with only a triangle of Punic-speaking countryside bounded by the Mediterranean and a line connecting Annaba in eastern Algeria with Sfax in central Tunisia. Elsewhere, the hinterland was controlled by a number of Berber-speaking states. Their institutions are somewhat shadowy to us, but one large state the Romans called Mauritania lay in the far west of Morocco and western Algeria. Present-day eastern Algeria, which the Romans called Numidia, was divided between two other sedentary Berber kingdoms. Carthage seems to have stayed clear of deep involvement with its hinterland as a matter of policy; it was essentially a maritime power and its prime strategic interests lay overseas in its control of trade routes and seaports. The great struggle between Rome and Carthage for dominance of the western Mediterranean in the second century BC began when they clashed over which was to dominate Sicily.

Both Rome and Carthage grew to importance as part of a broader process in which the "civilization" of the eastern Mediterranean spread to the west. Just as the Phoenicians carried the culture of the Levant, Greek and Hellenistic culture spread westward along the trade routes, expanding first to Greek settlements in southern Italy and then north through the rest of the peninsula, parallel in timing to the spread of Hellenism

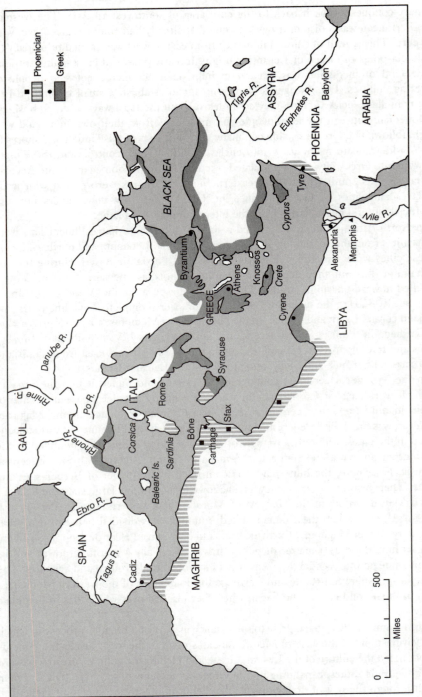

Map 2.5 The Greek and Phoenician push to the West (based on McNeill, *A World History*)

into the older urban societies of the Middle East. In Italy, however, Hellenism met a culture that was only just emerging into the pattern of literate, urban societies. Compared to Greece, Italy had some of the advantages of a new country. Wine, wheat, and olive oil could be grown on a larger scale than in Greece itself. Italy was also open to a larger scale of political organization, in contrast to the quarreling city-states of the Greek heartland. Once the Roman city-state began to expand in Italy, it took on some of the advantages of a frontier territory in relation to its metropolitan society, the kind of advantage that helped Macedonia build its empire to the east.

In the third century BC, Rome had advantages of scale, manpower, and economic resources that no Greek city-state could muster. By the 260s BC, it had united central and southern Italy and moved on to challenge Carthage for Sicily. By 200 BC, it had completed the destruction of Carthaginian power, with help from the Numidian Berbers. Shortly after 150 BC, Rome had gone on to conquer Greece as well. From then on, the fringe Hellenization of early commercial contacts turned into a much more thorough and conscious effort to imitate the Greek way, though the Roman form of the Hellenistic synthesis kept some characteristic Latin overtones. The Romans were concerned with some matters (law, for instance) that had not deeply interested the Greeks. The fundamental character of Roman society was nevertheless Hellenic, and the growth of the Roman Empire provided an articulating framework for that cultural synthesis.

But Rome stopped short in one very important way. It did not unite the "civilized world" in the way Macedonia had once done from a similar position on the frontiers of Hellenic culture. Rome captured the Greek heartland, Anatolia, Egypt, and the Levant, but its conquests stopped short at the upper waters of the Tigris and Euphrates rivers. Mesopotamia, home of the oldest urban societies, was left out, along with the Iranian plateau. By the third century AD, a new Sassanian dynasty in Persia united the most ancient Middle East and gave that region a degree of stability and security superior even to the Roman achievements in the west. Thus, while the Roman Empire pushed Hellenism into new lands in the west, it lost control of the east.

Roman North Africa

All of northern Africa fell into the Roman sphere, although with different consequences for Egypt than for the Punic and Berber territories to the west. Egypt was agriculturally rich, and it could now be exploited for the benefit of the Romans, rather than the local ruling class. Alexandria continued to be one of the really great cities of the Roman empire, while the hinterland became a principal supplier of wheat for Rome (and later for the new capital at Constantinople). The culture of the countryside was as unchanged as the ancient cycle of the Nile flood.

In the Maghrib, on the other hand, Roman conquest and administration led to new developments in the countryside. In the *tell*, the relatively well-watered coastal plains and inland valleys of Algeria, and in the former Punic region of northern Tunisia, Roman rule led to the Romanization, of at least the upper classes and the townspeople. Roman towns served as administrative centers, surrounded by Roman estates, with large-scale agriculture worked by slave labor. A second kind of change came to the high plateaus that lay behind the plains. This high country was more arid than the tell, and much of it lacked the twenty to twenty-four inches of annual rainfall needed to grow a successful grain crop in that climate. During the first century or so of Roman occupation, the high plains were still used only for sparse seasonal grazing. Then, about 100 AD, Romans introduced olive trees, and dry-farming techniques made it possible to grow barley on favored sites on the high plateau. Olive trees could survive the hot summer dry season, and they could grow on ground too steep and rocky to be tilled. Unlike the richer plains of the tell, the land here remained in the hands of Berber smallholders, who profited greatly from the Roman connection that gave them a distant market for their oil. The tell peoples lived largely on the export of grains to the Roman world as a whole, but their prosperity passed its peak after the second century AD, whereas the high plateaus were still climbing toward their peak of prosperity about the middle of the third.

The gold trade across the Sahara also began a little before 300 AD and rose to significant proportions in the century that followed. This is easily connected to the introduction of camels in the western Sahara. The Roman mints in Carthage began at this time to strike gold coins made from sub-Saharan gold, and the practice was to continue with the Tunisian mints of their Muslim successors in that part of Africa. The strengthening of the gold trade in the fifth century no doubt brought other changes on both sides of the Sahara, but late Roman records are sparse in this period of Roman decline; and written records of sub-Saharan Africa only begin to appear in the eighth century – but now in Arabic, not Latin.

The Roman state promoted a new commerce in ideas as well as goods, and not necessarily from Rome itself. In religion, for example, the old paganism with combined Roman and Hellenistic roots began to decline during the civil wars of the third century. A variety of new, alternative religions appeared. Christianity was one of these, coming from the Levantine Judaic tradition, with a message more attractive for its emotional and moral appeal than for the complexity of its theology.

During the first three centuries of the Christian Era, the new religion was far more important in the eastern Mediterranean than it was in the west. Rome was the only western site among the four original episcopal sees, the others being at Antioch, Constantinople, and Alexandria. Alexandria was, in fact, the most important early center for the development of Christian doctrine and Christian education. When the empire was divided for administrative convenience in the late fourth century AD into a western half (based on Rome) and an eastern half (based on Constantinople), Alexandria lost some of its primacy to the two capitals, especially to Constantinople. Constantinople's new eminence led to a rivalry among bishoprics and ultimately to the division of Christianity into an Orthodox and a Roman Catholic branch, but that issue was hardly raised before 324 AD, when Christianity became the favored religion for the empire as a whole.

The Maghrib had meanwhile kept to its old ways and retained ancient Berber and Punic religions until after about 200 AD, when Christianity began to penetrate the urban centers and the tell, especially the former Carthaginian territories. Its spread to the Berber-speaking peoples of the high plains and the semi-nomadic fringes was somewhat slower, though North Africa was to be the home of some of the most important of the church fathers, including Tertullian (d. *c.*230), the first important Christian theologian to write in Latin, and Augustine (d. 430), whose writings did more than any other to set the theological traditions of the Roman church.

As Christianity moved up from its early position of one among many oriental religions current in Rome, it encountered new problems. Especially after it became the official church of the empire, the question of tolerance or intolerance became serious. An official and approved Christian view of things began to appear, and those who disagreed with the principal bishops and church councils were branded as heretics – those who had chosen to follow error even where the truth was known and proclaimed. It is hardly surprising that all kinds of social and ethnic differences within the Roman Empire tended to encourage heresies in opposition to the dominant forces in Rome and Constantinople.

Sometimes it was almost pure chance that particular heresies became the preferred religion of certain minorities. One early view of the relations between God the Son and God the Father held that the sanctity of Christ was derived from the divinity of God the Father. In the early fourth century, missionaries carried this view to the Germans north of the Danube. It was called Arianism, and it was later condemned as heretical, but the Germans had already begun to accept it. It therefore continued, and it grew to be their principal variant of the Christian faith, a variant they kept even after they entered the imperial territory. Arianism finally reached the Maghrib with the Vandals, after moving more than a thousand miles in space and a century in time from the point where missionaries had first begun preaching it beyond the frontiers.

In much the same way, the Donatist heresy became the doctrinal variant peculiar to the Maghrib. The issue in this case was partly the proper form of church government and partly the question of whether a lapsed sinner could be saved without undergoing martyrdom. The issue itself was not so important as the fact that the Roman government supported the Catholic position, while the dominant Romanized classes in urban Africa, as well as the Berber countrymen, became Donatists. The original schism, indeed, began only shortly after about 300 AD, just as Christianity was coming to be tolerated in the empire. It became serious in the North African provinces nearly a century later, when the Donatist church was officially banned. But Donatism lasted in the rural areas until the end of Roman rule and beyond. About 430 AD the Vandals arrived to become the new masters, setting Arianism in competition with Donatism and Catholicism alike. Donatism continued as the version of Christianity peculiar to Berbers, just as Arianism was peculiar to Germans.

Egypt also acquired its own Christian variant. When the political division between Rome and Constantinople was separating the Latin-speaking from the Greek-speaking parts of the empire, eastern Christianity itself was being divided between the Greek core with its center in Constantinople and the Syrian and Egyptian fringes, where Hellenism had always been something of an overlay on the non-Hellenic popular culture. This time the local view, ultimately proclaimed heretical, was the Monophysite doctrine that Christ had one nature, wholly divine, that his human appearance was only the appearance of humanity, not the reality. The opposing Orthodox and Catholic view held that Christ had two natures, one human and one divine. Even after Monophysitism was declared heretical in 451 AD, it continued in Egypt and Syria in spite of occasional persecution by the government in Constantinople.

In spite of internal strains, Christianity became an important cement holding together the various peoples united politically by Roman rule. Beyond the frontiers, the spread of Christianity was an extension of Roman influence and of the intercommunicating zone. And Christianity did expand beyond the frontiers, to the Celts in Ireland, to the Germans as Arianism, south of the Sahara into Nubia and Ethiopia in the Monophysite version.

Nubia and Ethiopia

Roman influence and Roman trade spread up the Nile and along the sea routes. About 150 BC, shippers on the Indian Ocean began to sail directly across the Gulf of Arabia to India, rather than following the coastlines as they had done in the past. The voyage to India was comparatively easy for stout ships, because mariners could use the wind of the southwest monsoon blowing in the hot months, while the prevailing northeast winds blew during the remainder of the year. Hellenized Egyptians carried Roman trade on these routes, not only to India but south down the African coast at least as far as the present Tanzania. For the northern half of the Red Sea, trade was carried by camel caravans on the Arabian side or by a combination of caravan and Nile shipping on the Egyptian.

The southern regions within reach of Roman influence, but without Roman rule, could react in several ways. In Nubia, for example, the local culture had often assimilated some aspects of the Egyptian way while rejecting others. Even after a superficial Egyptianization under the New Kingdom, Nubia began to drift off in its own directions from about 600 BC, taking new gods from sub-Saharan Africa and making the Queen Mother into an important constitutional figure. When Roman Egypt became an early center of Christianity, Nubia remained as the last stronghold for many Egyptian religious ideas. Though Monophysite and Orthodox missionaries visited the upper Nile, they failed to convert the rulers of Nubia until nearly 600 AD. But Nubia then turned to Christianity, and remained Christian until the fifteenth century, sometimes united as a single kingdom, sometimes separated into two or more kingdoms – one centered on lower Nubia, one on the Dongola reach, and one further south on the Shendi reach, sometimes controlling territory into the region of rainfall agriculture.

Ethiopia and southern Arabia were subject to Roman cultural penetration even earlier than Nubia. Commercial contact with Egypt had been at least sporadic since about 2000 BC, and was reasonably continuous during the last millennium BC. South Arabia and the horn of Africa were commercially attractive because the trees of the region extruded two aromatic gums. Frankincense, the gum of *Boswellia carteri* and *Boswellia frereana*, was especially important for Roman funeral pyres, and myrrh from *Commiphora myrrha* was used mainly for cosmetics and perfumes. The increasing prosperity of the Hellenistic and then of the Roman elite increased the demand for these products.

These commercial currents carried both Christianity and Judaism into Ethiopia and southern Arabia in the first centuries AD. The main political force in the region at that

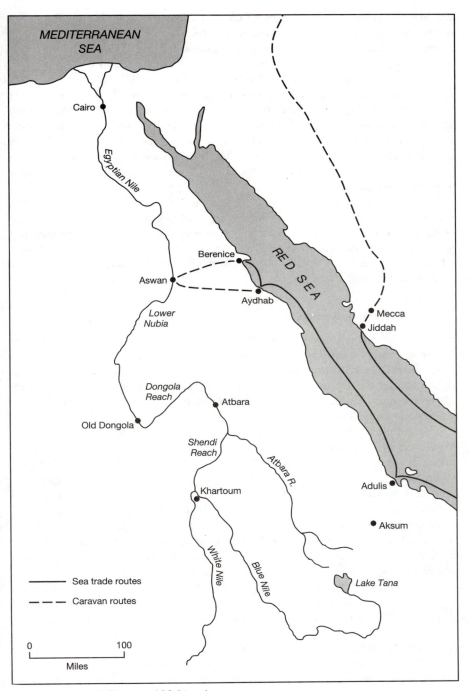

Map 2.6 Egypt and Nubia *c.*600 AD

time was the kingdom of Aksum, based on the Ethiopian side of the strait but having occasional control over Yemen as well. Aksum was never under Roman control, but its commercial interests prompted a policy of alliance with Rome. This may be one reason why Aksum adopted Christianity as its official religion in about 350 AD, only a generation after Christianity became the official faith of Rome itself. Ethiopian Christianity, however, followed the Egyptian or Monophysite version, and the Ethiopian church remained attached to the Patriarch of Alexandria even after the rise of Islam in Arabia and the Islamization of Egypt itself made the Christian position precarious. Contact was not always easy, but Ethiopia and Nubia remained faithful to Christianity, even after Islam began to replace it in parts of the Mediterranean Basin. Much the same thing had happened earlier, when Nubia had held on to the ancient Egyptian religion after Egypt turned to Christianity.

Just as Nubia had earlier Nubianized Egyptian beliefs, both Nubia and Ethiopia changed Christianity slightly to accommodate local culture. From a Mediterranean point of view, this was a shift away from orthodoxy, but it also gave Christianity new strength of attachment to local traditions. In the long run, this helped to preserve Christianity in Nubia for seven centuries and more, while Christianity and Judaism in Ethiopia lasted down to the present.

The end of Roman unity

The "Fall of Rome" was such a complex process that historians shy away from assigning simple causes. In one sense, indeed, 'Rome" did not fall. West Rome may have fallen as a political structure, but the other Rome based in Constantinople evolved by stages into the Byzantine Empire and lasted in one form or another until the fifteenth century. By then, Latin Christendom had recovered and was giving new form and content to the Roman heritage.

The decline of west Rome in the fourth and fifth centuries AD was undoubted. Weakened by epidemic disease, economic decline, political instability, and social unrest, it was unable to hold the frontier against the pressure of German "barbarians," who wanted to enter the empire, whether as peaceful migrants, forceful migrants, or mere hit-and-run raiders. The German migrations can be traced through layers of indirect pressure of one people on another across the Eurasian steppe to the frontiers of China. But the Huns who terrorized Europe from the Hungarian plain in the late fourth and early fifth centuries were the only nomadic peoples to attack Rome from the north or east. The Germans were farmers, not nomads, though they sometimes came organized in war bands that resembled the nomads' military formations.

Throughout the fifth century, Rome still maintained a theoretical claim to rule over the whole of western Europe, but a number of German kingdoms actually held power. The chief spillover into Africa was the movement of the Vandals into the Maghrib by way of Gibraltar in 429 AD, after migrating across France and Spain. Once in Africa they settled down, but theirs was hardly a mass movement. Their total numbers (probably exaggerated at that) were no more than eighty thousand, or less than the population of Roman Carthage. Nor were they any more given to vandalism than other military groups of their time. Our word *vandalism* comes from their Roman enemies, who especially disliked them because they were Arians, not Catholics. They nevertheless established their control over the cities and eastern coastal plains that had once been Carthaginian and Numidian. The rest of the Maghrib fell back into the control of the kind of Berber leaders who had been the real rulers ever since the Donatist struggle against the Roman government.

Vandal rule tended to follow the Carthaginian rather than the Roman pattern. Vandal strength lay with their navy, which dominated the west basin of the Mediterranean from about 440 to 480 AD. Like the Carthaginians, they neglected the hinterland and concentrated on seaborne control over the Balearic Islands, Sardinia, and Corsica; and they contested Latin control of Sicily just as the Carthaginians had done a half millennium earlier. This pattern of control centered on the port towns and the sea lanes was to recur in the history of the Maghrib, as other conquerors seized the ports and paid little attention to the sedentary populations in the hinterland.

The Byzantine Empire that replaced Vandal dominance in the Maghrib had a similar source of power at sea and a similar lack of control over the hinterland. While the western part of the Roman Empire was overrun by Germans, the Greek-speaking east held its frontiers by borrowing the Persian manner of fighting with heavily armored cavalry. The Byzantines called these troops "cataphracts," and they were similar to the armored knights that were to emerge later in medieval western Europe. After a successful holding action through the fifth century, the emperor Justinian set out in the 530s to build his naval power so as to reconquer the Italian peninsula and Rome itself. This move required a preliminary victory over Vandal naval power, which succeeded even though the final assault on Italy failed. The Vandal part of the Maghrib remained under Byzantine control for another century and a half – down to the Muslim conquest shortly after 700 AD, although the far western Maghrib remained independent, as it had been in fact since about 400 AD.

The rise of Islam

The sixth-century Byzantine failure to reunite the Roman world was final. From then on, the Christian world was to be divided, and Islam emerged from Arabia in the middle of the seventh century as a third heir to the Hellenic synthesis. Arabia was beyond the formal frontiers of Rome, but it was economically and culturally associated with the Roman world. The caravan route down the east coast of the Red Sea was a key link in Rome's commercial tie to Aksum and the Indian Ocean. Communities of Christians and Jews lived along the trade route in cities like Mecca and Medina, just as similar communities from the Roman world lived in Yemen, Ethiopia, and the port towns of south India. These Arabian cities were also in touch with Sassanian Persia to the northeast.

When the Hellenistic culture area split into two, Rome controlled one half, while Persia controlled the other. A little before 600 AD, Sassanian Persia began to extend its control westward from southern Iraq and eastern Arabia. It drove the Aksumites out of Yemen, and set up their own control over the eastern side of the straits. In a long-term competition between the Red Sea and the Persian Gulf as alternate routes from the

Mediterranean to the Indian Ocean, the Persians now tilted the advantage toward the Persian Gulf.

Arabia in the seventh century AD had its trading cities, but it was also a country of nomads, who were especially numerous in the better-watered lands along the Red Sea coast, near the highlands of the south, and along the southern fringes of the fertile crescent stretching from Palestine and Syria to Iraq. Like other borders between the desert and the sown, the ancient style of history here featured competitive reciprocity between nomads and sedentary peoples. In the past, nomads and semi-nomads from the steppe, the ancient Hebrews among them, had often moved north to found king-doms in the better-watered lands of the fertile crescent – or in the highlands to the south. In the early seventh century, the sedentary kingdoms were especially weak. Monophysite Syria and Egypt were disaffected with Greek rule from Constantinople. Sassanian Persia had similar problems trying to control Iraq. To make matters worse, Persia and the Byzantine Empire had been locked in a long and expensive war for a quarter-century ending in about 630 AD.

The sedentary empires, in short, were in disarray and ripe for a new nomadic attack, if only the nomads and the marginal people could find effective leadership and organ-ization. A little before 620 AD, Muhammad appeared in Mecca with a message from God. This was not a new god but the God of the Christians and Jews. He made no claim to found a new religion (though a new religion was to be the result), but rather to complete the divine revelation already given humankind by earlier prophets in the Jewish tradition – Abraham, Isaac, Jacob, and by Jesus as well. He saw himself as the last of the line, "the seal of the prophets." His message also contained elements of the local Arabian polytheism, such as its reverence for a great black rock, the *kaba*, at the center of Mecca. Both the kaba and the city of Mecca itself, as a holy city, became a central focus of the new faith, and pilgrimage to Mecca became a religious duty for Muslims.

The Koran, which contains the corpus of Muhammad's own words, was not com-posed as a single volume. It brings together various shorter pieces released in varying circumstances throughout his life, and it is supplemented by oral traditions about his sayings, which were later written down. The whole message was not theologically complex or especially new, and it was congruent with the existing religious traditions of the Middle East. Muhammad held that each individual had a personal relationship with a single God who could guide his way in this life to good fortune or bad and would see to it that he entered paradise after death, if he believed in God and performed a set of fairly simple prescriptions for conduct and ritual behavior. The message also held a millennial element, in that God would bring the world to an end in the imminent future. With that final event, all would be judged as ready for paradise or not, accord-ing to their actions in life. Among the principal actions enjoined on those who accepted Islam were daily prayer at set times, obedience to the Prophet and the laws He had received from God, giving alms to the poor, pilgrimage to Mecca at least once in a lifetime, and struggle (*jihad*) against the forces of error and disbelief.

The first installments of the message were directed at townsmen and sedentary farmers in the oases along the Red Sea coast, not at the nomads of the desert, and even there Muhammad met opposition in the early years. In 622 AD, the town authorities of

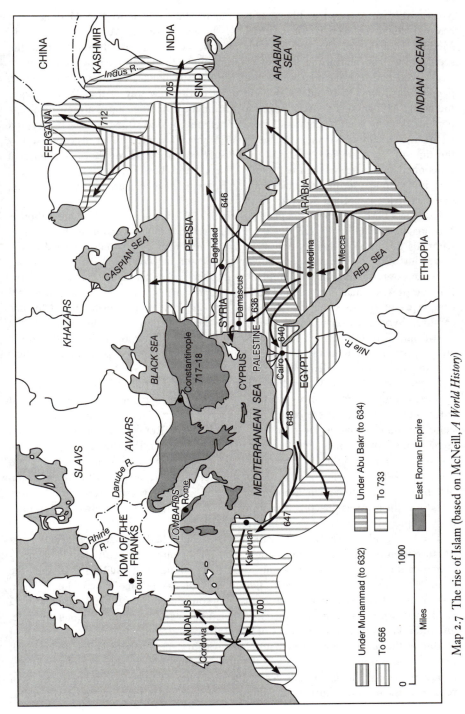

Map 2.7 The rise of Islam (based on McNeill, *A World History*)

Mecca were so opposed to him that he and his followers moved to Medina. This removal, flight, or *hejra* is still taken as the beginning of the Muslim era. Once in Medina, Muhammad changed from his old role as a mere preacher to become the secular as well as the spiritual head of a community of the faithful. Many converts were Arabs who had left the nomadic way of life for a sedentary existence in the oases, people who found their old religion unsuited to the new way of life. With a larger following, Muhammad's forces began to win military victories against their local opponents. Victory itself brought still more adherents. By 630 AD, Mecca itself accepted Islam and Muhammad's rule, and the rest of Arabia was united under his command by the time of his death in 632 AD. In these early Islamic years, in short, Muhammad functioned as a marginal man between the steppe and the sown, a city man by origin, with initial appeal to the sedentary society, but with an increasing nomadic following that succeeded in uniting the Arabian steppe.

Conquest beyond Arabia was mainly the work of Muhammad's successors, though Muslims had raided north into Byzantine and Sassanian lands even during his lifetime. After his death, his followers first struggled briefly over who should succeed to the leadership of the new community. The first successor, or *khalifa*, was Abu Bakr, whose main task was to rebuild the Arabian unity that had faltered on the death of the Prophet. It was Umar, the second khalifa ("caliph" in English) who led the successful campaigns of conquest against the sedentary empires to the north. The Muslims captured Syria in 636. By 651, they had completed the conquest of the whole Middle East from Egypt through the fertile crescent to Persia. These operations fell into the ancient pattern of nomadic conquest under marginal leadership, founding a new dynasty to rule over a sedentary empire.

By the 660s, the new Arab rulers, whom historians call the Umayyads after Umar, the first conqueror, were firmly established with a new capital at Damascus. The first rulers were Arabian, but the center of the empire was no longer Arabia, and the new cultural synthesis that began to be formed took on the Roman heritage of Egypt and Syria along with the Sassanian heritage of Iraq and Persia. But this union was not so much the joining together of disparate elements as it was the reunion of cultures and territory that had once been the center of the Hellenistic synthesis. With the exception of Greece and Anatolia, which remained Byzantine, the new core area of the Muslim world was the same as the core area of the "civilized" Middle Eastern world Alexander had conquered more than a thousand years earlier.

The Umayyad dynasty lasted only until 750 AD, but it had a special significance, first because it united all Muslims in a single state for the only time in all Islamic history – although the dream of Muslim unity was to continue as a political goal into the twentieth century. The Umayyad period was also the time when the Arabian conquerors of two sedentary civilizations first confronted the problems of creating a viable new synthesis from their ancient Arabian heritage, their new religious message, and their borrowings from the ways of life of the conquered.

One of the most important new problems was to decide what relations to establish between the Arabian conquerors and the new Muslims who converted to Islam in the conquered lands. The Umayyads decided against forced conversion and persecution of religious dissent. Jews, Christians, and even Zoroastrians in Persia were considered to be "people of the book" whose religion was partly true, though it lacked the full revelation God gave to Muhammad. These people were merely called on to pay higher taxes than Muslims paid, but many, if not most, of the new subjects did convert to Islam within the first century of Muslim rule.

The early Umayyad rulers based their power on the Arabian tribal organization that had supported them from the beginning. The Prophet, however, had proclaimed the equality of all male believers. This set up a tension between the ancient Arabian emphasis on kinship ties and the new Muslim emphasis on a community of believers. The new converts resented their position as second-class citizens, and that resentment was one foundation of the revolution that dethroned the Umayyad caliphs in 750 and brought to power the new Abbasid dynasty. From then on the question was partly settled. Arabs were no longer to have an exclusive position of power in the Muslim world, and the descendants of the original Arabian conquerors became a comparatively small element in the population of Islamic states. The Arabic language nevertheless remained as the official language of Islam, largely because it was the holy language in which God had given his final message to Muhammad.

A second division occurred among the Arabs themselves: some settled down in the conquered territory and began to assimilate the sedentary values and way of life, while others sought to preserve the nomadic way and the values of their early training. Some of these simply took the booty of the conquest period and faded back into the steppe. Others stated their opposition in religious terms and tried to halt the tendencies they saw as laxity among the higher leadership. One manifestation of this religious opposition was an open revolt in the 650s along the nomadic fringes of Iraq. The rebels were called Kharijites, or "seceders," because they chose the direction of heresy against the judgment or consensus of the Muslim community as a whole. In the immediate situation, the revolt failed, but the authorities in Damascus or Baghdad gradually lost control of the Arabian steppe and its nomadic peoples. In the old relationship between nomads and sedentaries, the successors of Muhammad had now crossed to the sedentary side. Kharijism, however, was to continue on the fringes of the sedentary empires with a special importance in Berber North Africa.

A third division separated those who saw the khalifa as mainly a religious leader and those who wanted him to be a successful politician and military leader. This difference of opinion took many forms in later Islamic history, but one early dispute of continuing importance was over eligibility for the caliphate. The religious purists thought the caliph should be a blood descendant of Muhammad through his daughter, Fatima, and her husband, ʿAli (who was also Muhammad's cousin). This claim to office was then joined by a second proposition, that the full word of God was not there for all to see in the Koran. Instead, an esoteric body of knowledge and interpretation was preserved and passed down through the line of ʿAli. This view, with many later variants, came to be known as *shiʿa*. Its opposite, the main line of *sunni* Islam, held that the correct interpretation of God's revelation could be found only through the consensus of the community, not through the special powers of a particular lineage.

It is possible to see the split between shiʿa and sunni as a Muslim variant of the Christian division between Catholic and Protestant, but that parallel has serious limitations. Sunni Islam allowed far more tolerance for differences of belief than any version of Christianity did. The shiʿa belief tended to be narrower and less tolerant. With time, however, many different offshoots of shiʿism came into existence, and many wandered still further from the beliefs and practices of the sunni majority.

Early Islam in Africa

The Maghrib was only partly involved in these early divisions. The first phase of Muslim expansion to the west stopped after 641 AD with the conquest of Egypt. The Muslims were not strong enough for a frontal assault on the Byzantine Empire, and the Byzantine fleet still dominated the Mediterranean. The Arabs, however, were quick to incorporate the conquered peoples and use their skills. By the 660s, the Umayyad empire had built a fleet to threaten Byzantium by sea. The real target was Constantinople, but the Muslims began – as Justinian had begun in his sea campaigns against Rome – with a move on Tunisia. By 670 AD, they had established their hold on the corner of Africa opposite Sicily. (The Romans had called that part of Tunisia "Africa," and the name spread to the whole continent only later. The Umayyads now Arabized it to "Ifrīqiyah.") The Umayyad empire found itself in the same strategic position as the Romans, Vandals, and Byzantines before them. The attack on Constantinople failed, but the Muslims moved inland in Tunisia and established a key base at Kairouan, which could serve as a strong point against the non-Muslim Berbers of the hills and a point of safety against the Christians, who necessarily had to come by sea. There the Muslim advance stabilized until after 700 AD, with Berbers holding most of the Maghrib, Byzantine garrisons in many of the North African port towns, and the Umayyad empire holding central Tunisia from their base at Kairouan.

By 711 AD, the Umayyad armies had marched back and forth through most of the Maghrib, but no single controlling authority could surrender in a way that would allow the Arabs to rule through an existing administrative framework, as they had done in Egypt or Syria. The sedentary Berber region, the future Algeria and Morocco, was controlled by a vast number of different Berber authorities. Whatever power might claim to rule the region – whether Roman, Vandal, Byzantine, or Muslim – the Berbers had enjoyed de facto independence for more than three centuries. Neither the sedentary Berber authorities nor the Berber nomads of the hinterland were willing to give up the reality of power. They might accept a theoretical Umayyad sovereignty, they might even convert to Islam, but the full impact of Islam, of Muslim rule and Muslim culture, came only slowly over several centuries.

The Muslim advance in Spain was actually more impressive than that in Africa itself. By the early eighth century, Roman rule had long since passed over to Visigoths, who had followed the Vandals across France and the Pyrenees. The Muslim invaders in this case were mainly Berbers from North Africa who had accepted Islam, rather than Arabs from Arabia, although the Umayyads sent reinforcements after their first military successes in 711 AD. By 720 AD, they had acquired at least a formal claim to everything south of the Pyrenees and to parts of southern France. (The further advance into western Europe, stopped by the Franks at Poitiers in 732 AD was more nearly a raid-in-force than a real invasion.) The hold on Spain was consolidated by the middle of the eighth century – so much so that, when the Abbasid dynasty replaced the

Umayyads in Damascus, a member of the Umayyad dynasty managed to retain control over Spain. That act broke the formal unity of the Muslim world, but the aggressive first phase of Muslim conquest was then over in any case. The date 720 is therefore a convenient mark of a new phase in Mediterranean history, when Islam had completed its early gains and joined western and eastern Christendom in a three-way partition of the Roman world.

The Muslim drive across North Africa, however weak their actual political dominance over the Maghrib, changed Africa's relation to the intercommunicating world from then onward. Most obviously, it joined all of North Africa to the Muslim world. Since Muslims and Christians were to be chronic enemies for the next thousand years or so, it implied that neither of the Christian heirs of Rome would have much influence on Africa by overland routes. But Christian influence was already established south of the desert in Nubia and Ethiopia, and neither was strongly threatened at first. The very fact that the original Arab outburst went north of the desert meant that nomadic pressure on the southern fringes was relieved for the time being. Yet the capacity of Ethiopia or the Nubian kingdoms to mediate between the intercommunicating zone and the rest of Africa was slight. On the other hand, the Muslim world began as the most dynamic and creative of Rome's three heirs. Between 750 and 1500 AD, sub-Saharan Africa was to be far more deeply and permanently influenced by the Islamic world than it had been by Christian Rome in the first seven hundred and fifty years of the Christian Era.

Suggestions for further reading

Abun-Nasr, Jamil M., *A History of the Maghrib in the Islamic Period*, Cambridge: Cambridge University Press, 1987.

Connah, Graham, *African Civilizations. Precolonial Cities and States in Tropical Africa: An Archaeological Perspective*. Cambridge: Cambridge University Press, 1987.

David, A.R., *The Pyramid Builders of Ancient Egypt: A Modern Investigation of Pharaoh's Workforce*. Boston: Routledge and Kegan Paul, 1986.

Fage, J.D. and Roland Oliver (eds) *The Cambridge History of Africa*, Vol. I, Cambridge: Cambridge University Press, 1975.

Fairservis, Walter A., *The Ancient Kingdoms of the Nile*, New York: Mentor, 1962.

Gibb, H.A.G., *Mohammedanism: An Historical Survey*. 2nd edn, London: Oxford University Press, 1953.

Holt, P.M., Ann K.S. Lambton, and Bernard Lewis (eds), *The Cambridge History of Islam*, Vols 1 and 2, Cambridge: Cambridge University Press, 1970.

Julien, Charles-André, *History of North Africa from the Arab Conquest to 1830*, London: Routledge and Kegan Paul, 1970.

Lewis, Bernard, *The Arabs in History*, rev. edn, London: Arrow Books, 1958.

McNeill, William, *The Rise of the West*, London and Chicago: University of Chicago Press, 1963.

Montet, Pierre, *Eternal Egypt*, London: Weidenfeld and Nicolson, 1961.

Moscati, Sabatino, *The World of the Phoenicians*. London: Cardinal, 1973.

Mokhtar, G. (ed.), *A General History of Africa*, Vol. 2, Paris, UNESCO, 1981.

Wilson, John Albert, *The Burden of Egypt: An Interpretation of Ancient Egyptian Culture*, new edn, Chicago: University of Chicago Press, 1967.

3

AFRICA NORTH OF THE FOREST IN THE EARLY ISLAMIC AGE

Historians deal with North African history from a number of perspectives, each with its own conventions and terms of reference. At one level, they write about the rise and fall of dynasties named for the founding leader, like the Umayyads, who ruled from Damascus until 750 AD, followed by the ʿAbbasids with their capital at Baghdad until nearly the year 1000. But the name of the dynasty refers to more than the actual rulers. It also stands for a period of time, like the dynastic chronology used by Egyptologists. A dynastic name is a generalization covering a multitude of events. It is useful, even essential, as a way to cut through masses of detailed political history, but exceptions always exist behind the general façade of a dynastic name and style, and any reference to dynasties always loses a little in accuracy for the sake of generalization.

At a higher level of generalization, historians talk about periods that take in a number of dynasties. The Middle Kingdom or the Old Kingdom in ancient Egypt, for instance, were groups of dynasties. In Western history, we have the sequence of ancient, medieval, and modern, with the Middle Ages conceived as falling between ancient and modern and usually given dates of approximately 800 to 1500 AD. When historians in the West first began writing about Africa, they tended to carry over their European terms and write about "Africa in the Middle Ages." This is obvious nonsense, because in Africa this period is not a middle between any clearly detectable phases. Yet historians of Africa still lack generally accepted terms to designate periods of time.

The Islamic world is a clearer entity, and a set of terms has been suggested that seem to mark off the main phases after the brief Umayyad period. The first of these is the classical age of ʿAbbasid rule (750–1000 AD), a period of enormous creativity when Islamic civilization took on its main features. The next period, roughly 1000 to 1500, can be called the Islamic Middle Ages, roughly coterminous with the European Middle Ages, but it was "middle" in this case between the ʿAbbasid period and the Age of Three Empires that followed. In political terms, this Islamic Middle Age was a time of political fragmentation after the relative unity imposed by the ʿAbbasids, and it was followed between 1500 and 1750 by a new phase of Muslim unity. But this time it was unity in three separate parts; the Ottoman Empire dominated in the west, the Saffavid

Empire in Persia dominated the center, and the Mogul Empire held the east from the plains of northern India. This chapter deals with the ʿAbbasid period and the Islamic Middle Ages.

We can also consider Islamic Africa from the broader perspective of world history as a whole. Beginning a few centuries before our era and extending on to the time of Muhammad in the seventh century AD the scattered parts of the intercommunicating zone began to form clusters with increasingly homogeneous cultures. In east Asia, the result was a Chinese culture area that became unified by the Han empire a little before the time of Christ. In the Middle East the process began with the Hellenistic synthesis, which then split politically between the Roman empire centered on the Mediterranean and the Sassanian empire centered on Iran.

The next period in world history, roughly 750 to 1750, is sometimes called the Islamic Age. It was a time when Muslim civilization was the most successful heir of Rome and also heir of the Sassanian civilization. In the early part of this thousand years the Muslim world was the most creative of the major "civilizations." It was so located that it bordered on the rest, and it soon became the intermediary through which the others were able to communicate. Chinese inventions like the compass and gunpowder, Indian inventions like positional notation in mathematics, and the Hellenistic heritage, particularly Aristotle's philosophy, all passed to western Europe by way of Islamic intermediaries. Still other ideas and inventions passed in the other direction or were borrowed from Islamic originals.

In this same perspective of world history, the period that followed was the European Age, when Europe replaced Islam as the central turntable of world history. Historians differ as to the best date for the transition. In fact, it was gradual. The balance had clearly swung to Europe by 1800, yet the beginnings of the shift can be traced to the European maritime breakthrough of the late fifteenth century. As a shift in technology, the maritime revolution was not so important as the scientific revolution of the seventeenth century or the beginnings of industrialization in the nineteenth, but it gave Europeans the capability of reaching every continent by sea. For parts of the world beyond the reach of Islamic culture, the maritime breakthrough was itself the beginning of the European Age, in the sense that European mariners were the first direct link to the intercommunicating zone. This was the case for the whole west coast of Africa south of the equatorial forest – just as it was for the Americas. But for Africa north of the forest and down the east coast to the Mozambique Channel and beyond, the Islamic world remained the vital link with the intercommunicating zone well into the nineteenth century.

Neither label – Islamic Age or European Age – should be misunderstood. Both imply for Africa the possibility of cultural borrowing, not complete dominance from abroad. Africans continued to invent new ways of doing things and to modify their old ways for reasons having nothing to do with outside influence. When they borrowed from another culture, they borrowed selectively and fitted the borrowed feature into their own framework.

Some parts of Africa, however, came into the sphere of Islamic culture at a much earlier date, notably Egypt and the core area of Tunisia around Kairouan even before 750. Between that date and about 1500, the rest of Africa north of the desert had become Muslim; so too had much of the Nilotic Sudan, the nomadic fringe to the Ethiopian highlands, and the desert-edge region south of the Sahara. This chapter will cover all of Africa north of the forest belt, not just Africa north of the Sahara.

The geographical base of West African history

Just as the Maghrib has some of the characteristics of an island, with a sea of water to the north, east, and west and a sea of desert to the south, West Africa is like a peninsula, attached to the mass of sub-Saharan Africa at the Cameroon mountains and stretching westward between the Gulf of Guinea and the Sahara. The Arabs called everything they knew of south of the desert "the Sudan," but it now means the belt of open savanna country south of the desert and north of the forest. It is one of those longitudinal layers of climate and vegetation zones whose orderly progression from north to south is typical of the west coast of a continental land mass. Beginning with the Mediterranean climate of Morocco, the rest of the sequence is desert, savanna, forest – then, moving south of the equator, savanna again, desert again (the Namib and Kalahari of southern Africa), and finally a climate like Morocco's at the Cape of Good Hope.

West Africa has only two of these zones, savanna and forest, and geographers discriminate carefully between the vegetation and climatic subdivisions within each of these. Savanna, for example, can be divided into two or three main types of vegetation, with still finer distinctions within each. But insects could sometimes influence the course of history more than vegetation did. Tsetse flies made a fundamental difference in what human societies could do. They were the carriers of trypanosomiasis to humans and animals alike. The human form is sleeping sickness, which causes lethargy and finally death for those who are infected, although many people escape infection even in a tsetse fly zone. The cattle variant of the same infection is called *nagana*. Where tsetse flies are dense, it is virtually impossible to raise cattle or horses. In general, the northern savanna is safer, but human occupation keeps down high brush, and the flies flourish only in the shade.

It is all too easy to think of the sequence of zones – desert, savanna, forest – as a set of stereotypes. Tropical rain forest can be imagined as steaming jungle, and some of it is. But the geographical category comes from the "natural vegetation." People can change that; the forest zone today supports some of the densest agricultural populations in Africa, and it has done so for centuries. The stereotyped savanna is even more of a problem. Technically, savanna grasses predominate over other vegetation, but it is far from being open prairie. Trees and bushes dot the savanna almost everywhere, right to the edge of the desert. In some places savanna woodland is so thick, even in the dry season with no leaves on the trees, that it is hard to see more than a hundred yards. Curiously enough, the most open and treeless part of the savanna is the part near the forest, the "derived savanna," or man-made grasslands that were once forest.

The physical explanation for differing natural vegetation is the difference in annual rainfall. In West Africa, it varies from more than 160 inches at a few places along the coast to less than fifteen inches at the edge of the desert. Beyond that point, with less than ten to fifteen inches, rainfall agriculture is impossible. In the West African tropics rainfall seems to follow the sun. As the sun moves north in summer, a tropical air mass moves inland from the Gulf of Guinea, bringing rainfall further and further north until it reaches the southern Sahara in July. Then, as the sun returns to the south of the equator, the maritime air is replaced by a dry continental air mass. By January, this dry air reaches the Guinea coast, and even the forest region has a brief, comparatively dry season.

The more northerly regions not only receive less rainfall; what rain they do get is concentrated in time. At the desert edge, it might be only fifteen inches a year, but that rain would all come in two months of midsummer. Crops that need more rain or a longer growing season can only be grown further south. Forest requires nearly year-round rainfall, whereas grasses can die back, leaving seeds to wait for the rain to come back. Savanna tree species are those able to survive a long dry season, and then only if they are widely spaced.

Human beings also had to adjust to the short growing season and the long arid period. Much of the savanna belt has annual rainfall roughly equal to that of the American Middle West – thirty to forty inches a year. But when this rainfall comes in four or five months, not distributed through the year, and when it is very hot, special problems turn up. Some soil types common in West Africa tend to form a permanent rocky crust if they are cleared of vegetation for tillage. This crust is called laterite, and laterization has gone further in West Africa than anywhere else in the world. Many sections that once must have been productive are now barren rocky plains, virtually useless except for sparse grazing. Even where laterization is no danger, the pattern of intense rainfall and heat tends to dissolve and carry off the nutrients in the soil. The traditional solution is to practice shifting cultivation, using a field for only a few years followed by a long period of fallow.

Further north, where tsetse flies are less common and cattle more so, the seasonal problem takes another twist. Livestock have to be kept alive all year on the grass that only grows during three months or less. Many places have no water for people or animals in the dry season, although they have plenty of pasture and water in the rains. The obvious solution is to have a base with year-round water during the dry season, feeding the cattle elsewhere during the rains. The result is *transhumant pastoralism*, a pattern of seasonal movement with the herds, sometimes combined with cereal culti-vation around the base village. This pattern is also common in North Africa, where flocks could be taken to the high mountains in summer. In West Africa, transhumant pastoralism is practiced near the desert edge but also further south, where there is enough rainfall for agriculture, but with large tracts of fallow land as well.

Differences in rainfall from year to year can also have a profound influence on history. In some years the rain zone extends far out into the Sahara. In others, the rain is normal in amount but irregular in distribution, producing too short a growing season. In some years no rain at all falls over the northern savanna. These variations produce hunger and sometimes famine, as they did all along the sahel in the early 1970s and again in the 1980s when the rainfall was insufficient for several years running.

Our knowledge of climate history in the distant past is based on indirect records like pollen deposits in lakes, but African chronicles composed in Timbuktu on the Niger bend provide a written record for the sixteenth century onward. These records suggest fairly reliable rainfall in the northern savanna during the sixteenth century, followed by a failed harvest every seven to ten years in the seventeenth century, and every five years or so in the eighteenth. In addition, the consecutive failure of the rains for a series of years led to two major disasters. One centered on the years 1639–43 and the second on the late 1740s and early 1750s. Estimates (inevitably very uncertain for lack of hard evidence) suggest that at least half the population of the northern savanna region died or fled on each of these occasions. Some desert-edge cities, like Walata, had to be abandoned for a time. A disaster on this scale was averted in the 1970s and 1980s only because food could be sent in from the outside, but many people and many cattle died.

Certain north-flowing rivers like the Senegal, the upper Niger, and the Shari, which flows into Lake Chad, provide a kind of safety valve. Each is fed by water that falls far to the south, creating a crest fifty to a hundred feet higher than average low water. At high water, these rivers overflow their banks and carry both silt and moisture to the surrounding fields. Crops, which are planted on the wet fields as the water recedes, grow and ripen during the early dry season, as they did with the basin irrigation in ancient Egypt. The height of the flood varied from year to year, according to the amount of rainfall further south. Along the Senegal, a high-flood year will irrigate an area twice the size of a low-flood year, but the water does rise every year whether it rains locally or not. The riverine populations thus had two chances for a reasonable harvest, one based on local rainfall and one based on rainfall upstream.

Most people in West Africa were farmers, but centers of specialized production existed long before the beginning of historical records. Fishing along the coasts and rivers was an intensive and specialized occupation, so that many fisherfolk farmed only as a sideline. Dry-season hunting was a major source of meat in savanna and forest alike. People mined rock salt in the Sahara and evaporated sea salt along the coast; some extracted it from salt-concentrating plants like the mangrove. Iron ore is found almost everywhere in West Africa, but some regions with the best ore and the most plentiful charcoal became iron centers and sold their iron to other regions less well endowed. Still other regions concentrated on cotton and cotton textiles, or on sheep raising and woolen cloth. As a result, regular patterns of internal trade helped to exchange the surplus of one region with others. The vegetation zones stretching east and west for thousands of miles – savanna, desert, and forest – encouraged extensive north-south trade between them. Trade, in turn, encouraged the growth of cities – some near the desert-edge to profit from the trans-Sahara trade, others well back from the desert, like Jenne-Jenno on the inland Niger delta in Mali. Jenne-Jenno flourished as long ago as the third century BC, and it was located so as to profit from the transfer between riverborne trade on the Niger and the overland routes reaching on toward the forest.

Peoples and cultures of the Sudanic belt

The three different environments of forest, savanna, and desert demanded three distinct systems of human ecology. We might expect to find three different cultures –

one for the Sahara, one for the Sudanic zone, and one for the rain forest. For material culture this outcome is obvious, but other aspects of culture are by no means uniform within each vegetation zone. Nor do they change sharply on crossing an ecological frontier to the north or south. Instead, each aspect of culture seems to be distributed in its own particular way. If we were to map these distributions we would need a base map of northern Africa with a series of overlays – several hundred of them. These overlays could map each important aspect of culture – language, political structure, religion, art, family life, kinship systems and much more. Very few of the overlays would show an identical pattern, and few would correspond closely to the pattern of the physical environment. The total pattern would show a remarkable degree of homogeneity, but with diversity, too, as widely shared cultural features were mixed in different ways.

Even the frontier often drawn between the Sahara and sub-Saharan Africa, one of the sharpest cultural lines anywhere in Africa, is only one step along a continuum. An older view, that the Sahara fringe was a sort of cultural divide, was largely based on racist assumptions: Saharan peoples were generally considered to be "white." It was assumed that they must therefore be culturally different from the "blacks" to the south. This view is mistaken on two counts. First, race has nothing to do with culture; and second the racial frontier between "black" and "white" is only roughly coterminous with the ecological frontier. In the west, many "white" and sedentary Moorish farmers live in the Senegal valley today, though they and the desert nomads to the north are very much a mixed race. In the central Sahara, to the north of Lake Chad, the desert nomads are negroid peoples speaking languages in the same Teda-Daza family as those spoken in the savanna to the south. The people of Nubia, the desert reaches of the Nile, are also "black" and so are the sub-Saharan "Arabs" of the Republic of the Sudan. Many people of southwestern Arabia, for that matter, look very much like Ethiopians or Somalis on the African side of the straits.

Language families not only straddle the desert-savanna frontier; they also cross the racial line. Hausa is one of the most widely spoken of all sub-Saharan languages, and its speakers are overwhelmingly both "black" and sedentary. It is nevertheless related linguistically to Arabic, Berber, and Hebrew, not to the nearby languages of the savanna belt. Again, the Fula language, spoken by the people who are variously called Fulbe, Fulani, or Tukulor, is closely related to Wolof and Serer and other languages of Senegal, though many of the Fulbe are somewhat European in appearance – just as many negroid people from Mauritania to the Nilotic Sudan have Arabic as their home language.

In the far west, from Morocco south across the desert and into the western Sudan, pre-Islamic kinship systems appear to have been matrilineal. This block of peoples was contiguous; but it included both sedentary and nomadic Berbers and sedentary peoples south of the desert, and it included both "blacks" and "whites." Then, after a thousand years of Islamic influence, these people have all turned to patrilineal reckoning of kinship ties, again regardless of language, race, or ecology.

Other culture traits can be found from the desert edge south to the Gulf of Guinea. The Hausa, for example, had a pre-Islamic religion of a distinctive West African type. They worshipped many of the same deities found far to the south among the Aja of the Benin Republic and Yoruba and southwestern Nigeria. But other traits of Hausa culture, like the language itself, are far more closely associated with the Tuareg of the Sahara. Similar patterns are found in the horn of Africa, where many culture traits are common to both Ethiopia and south Arabia, while others stretch far beyond the highland area to people whose physical appearance is not at all Ethiopian.

No simple hypothesis can account for all these cultural patterns, and no true explanation is likely to be simple. The horizon of written and oral history combined hardly goes back more than a thousand years anywhere along the sahel, except in the Nile valley. Add another 3000 years for the Nile Valley itself and we still cover only a tiny fraction of human experience. Within the time period we know about, however, we have evidence of dramatic changes over a few centuries. Whole regions can and sometimes did change their "mother tongue" without significant influence from mass migration. The Egyptians, for example, went from Coptic to Arabic largely because of the religious prestige of a language associated with Islam. Other people moved in mass migrations that took them thousands of miles before they settled down again and began to exchange culture traits with new neighbors. Small-scale, selective borrowing takes place continuously along all cultural frontiers. We can only assume that something similar happened in the past as well.

Large and durable political units can also encourage the cultural homogeneity of their people. France is a European example, creating a remarkable degree of cultural unity among people who originally spoke languages as different as French, Breton, Basque, German, Flemish, Occitan, and Provençal. Similar tendencies can be seen in parts of the Sudanic belt. On the upper Niger, the pattern of Mande languages is indicative. Some are fairly closely related; others are more distant – roughly equivalent to the Romance languages of Europe – but the language variously known as Mande, Mandinka, Malinké, or Bambara occupies a greater territory and has many tens of thousands more speakers than any other. The Mande-language area is very nearly the same as the core region of the ancient empire of Mali. Malinké means the language of Mali, and its geographical spread suggests that Malian control encouraged the unification or merger of a number of pre-existing regional dialects. Relatively isolated communities that were not brought into the empire also speak Mande languages, and these have tended to grow more distinct with time.

But empires do not necessarily spread their language over a wide region. Gao, on the Niger near its northern bend, had a home language called Songhai, and it grew to be the heart of a Songhai empire, but the language spread very little beyond its original homeland on the banks of the Niger downstream from Timbuktu. Hausa, on the other hand, was never associated with a large state until the nineteenth century, but it had already spread over an area equivalent to Mali and became a prominent trade language even further afield. It would appear, then, that some large empires furthered cultural homogenization, whereas others did not, and wide cultural homogeneity could appear without help from a large state.

States and stateless societies

One striking difference between African and Western history is that Western history is almost always set within the framework of the state. Even during the disturbances after the fall of Rome, the state remained the aspiration, whatever the reality. Partly for this reason, when Europeans first began to consider African history, they took the existence of states as a mark of political achievement – the bigger the state, the bigger the achievement. Recent authorities, however, suggest that this view is far from accurate. At some levels of technology, state administration may only draw off part of the social product for officials and courtiers who contributed little or nothing to create it in the first place. Many Africans apparently reached this conclusion; states and stateless societies have existed side by side over nearly two millennia, without the stateless people feeling a need to copy the institutions of their more organized neighbors. Whether statelessness should have been preferable or not, it was clearly preferred.

This fact has left some difficult gaps for historians of Africa. Stateless societies leave few records. Their political operations are far too subtle and complex to be described accurately by early travelers from abroad, whether Arab or European. Oral traditions find no "great men" to celebrate. Genealogies are crucial to the operations of these societies, but people tend to remember everybody's genealogy for two to five generations rather than that of the ruling family for thirty. As a result, our only information on the way stateless societies changed is that gathered in the nineteenth and twentieth centuries. Yet as many as a quarter of all the people in West Africa belonged to stateless societies at the beginning of the colonial period. Historians of earlier periods simply have to leave them out. The only remedy is to look at statelessness in the recent past for hints as to what it might have been like earlier.

Political anthropologists, the scholars principally concerned with statelessness, do not always agree as to what characteristics mark a state. In reality, political institutions shade off from complex political structures toward other structures that were clearly stateless. At one extreme, full-time rulers claimed authority over every individual within a defined territory. These were clearly states. At the other, authority was so dispersed that no permanent rulers could be identified. Those who exercised authority did so part-time, temporarily, over small groups of people, and over only a limited sector of their affairs. Whatever the finer distinctions, this dispersal of authority is a mark of statelessness. In recent centuries it has been most clearly epitomized by the Tiv and most Ibo of Nigeria, and by many Berber societies in North Africa.

One common misconception is to confuse the kind of political organization with the scale of organization. Some African states were very small, and some stateless societies were very large. A few hundred people living together in a village or group of villages could have a full-time ruler drawn from a royal lineage, exercising authority over a territorially defined state, and completely independent of other such states. In contrast to a microstate of this kind, some stateless societies settled conflicts between individuals as the Tiv did, by letting each antagonist call on the support of his kin. Thus, one kinship group was balanced against another, and the matter was settled by agreement, arrived at by representatives of the two groups. The size of the kin group called into play varied according to the antagonists' place in the kinship system, each conflict therefore called for a different *ad hoc* alliance and different representatives for each occasion. But thousands of people could be involved in a conflict between distant kin, and the Tiv system extended to nearly a million people at the beginning of the colonial period.

Stateless societies could work in many different ways, but the key building block in Africa was usually the lineage, whether matrilineal or patrilineal. Lineages often settled their own internal quarrels, even where the state existed. The crucial problem was to resolve conflicts between lineages. The Tiv system of balancing kinship segments was one way. Another was to assign control over one aspect of life, such as landholdings, to the leadership of one lineage, while other lineages dominated in other spheres. Still other societies worked through cross-cutting social divisions, such as age grades, which had their own solidarity, separate from that of lineages. In other places, secret societies held both religious and judicial functions. Many forms of organization cutting across lineages were also common in regions of microstates. A secret society sometimes had influence within an area far larger than any state, and could use its influence to reduce the dangers of interstate conflict.

In spite of the many advantages of a stateless society, some things were hard to do without a more elaborate political structure. Warfare on a large scale called for military command. Defense against a numerous enemy called for the mobilization of resources from a large area. Stateless societies could concentrate for attack or for a short war, as stateless nomadic societies have shown again and again in their raiding operations. But a permanent mobilization for defense – the kind of defense, say, that a sedentary society would require along a steppe frontier – called for permanent officials.

Trade was a second problem. Only a well-organized state could easily regulate and protect trade over a large area. Traders need a way to protect goods in transit, a system of law allowing aliens to come and go in peace, and laws that make it easy to borrow and to collect debts. Finally, only a state with its permanent officials and central direction could easily mobilize the wealth of society for special purposes such as temple building or the support of a priesthood, a nobility, or a royal lineage.

None of these functions was completely beyond the capacity of stateless societies, but some were hard to carry out. Sedentary societies living along a frontier with nomads had little choice: either set up permanent states or become tributary to the nomads. Defense in other situations, however, could often work well enough. The British, for example, found the Tiv far harder to conquer than any of the large states that finally made up Nigeria. But the problem in that case was simply that the Tiv had no one in authority, capable of surrendering for the entire group. The British had, in effect, to force the surrender of each individual kinship segment. Commerce could also be organized without a state. The Ibo of Nigeria had a lively commercial system with periodic local markets linked by long-distance commercial specialists traveling under religious protection. Fictitious kinship ties could be used to increase security. The state's ability to tax and spend for public purposes is obvious, but wealth can be spent voluntarily for such purposes in a stateless society as well. Some social patterns, like deep social stratification with important differences between wealth and status for different groups or people, were not likely to be voluntary, and here a state structure was necessary to enforce inequality.

Early states south of the Sahara

Africa north of the Sahara had a long tradition of political life under a variety of states later annexed by the Roman Empire. But the Berbers of North Africa also had their own tradition of segmentary society. We know almost nothing about the way it operated in the distant past, only that it survived as a living tradition and reappeared alongside states at the very eve of the European conquests. Other regions with a long history of contact with the Hellenistic and then the Roman worlds also developed their own individual political traditions. This was the case with the Christian Nubian kingdoms of the desert and the Nilotic Sudan, as it was of the Christian states that succeeded Aksum in the Ethiopian highlands. It was also true of the states that were to emerge south of the Sahara.

The location of these earliest states in West Africa suggests that they arose, as states have done elsewhere, to meet the needs of trade and the problems of defense. The ecological frontier between nomads and sedentaries was a source of friction but it also held the possibility of cooperation through trade. The savanna country was badly supplied with salt of any kind, while several deposits of excellent rock salt lay in the Sahara. The steppe people could also supply cattle and horses, which were hard to breed in the humid savanna. The sedentary farmers, in turn, could supply millet and sorghum and other food products. As trade developed, it drew products from further afield – kola nuts and gold from the south, North African and European manufactures and metals from the north.

The earliest Sudanic states we know of appeared at nearly the same time, in a row along the northern fringe of the savanna. Early urban centers like Jenne-Jenno, which was well to the south of the desert, may have had states attached, but the history of their earliest centuries is known from archaeology alone, and this tells little about political forms. By the tenth century, one or more states existed along the middle Senegal, where Takrūr (or Fuuta Tooro) was to be in later centuries. Ghana, a Soninke-speaking state, occupied the desert edge between the northward bends of the Niger and the Senegal. Gao, a Songhai state, had already organized the territory around the northern bend of the Niger. Another state emerged near Lake Chad under the shadowy and probably mythical leadership of the Sefawa dynasty, which ruled parts of the region down to 1846. The Kanuri people formed the nucleus of this state and went on to rule over the successive empires of Kanem to the east of the lake and Borno to the west.

The earliest reports of these states date from the seventh century, but this is merely an accident of North African history and of the fact that camel caravans began to cross the western Sahara after about 300 AD, bringing vastly increased trade. The Islamization of the north meant that North Africans could compile detailed records in Arabic, and many of these accounts have survived. The earliest sub-Saharan states were certainly much earlier, to judge from the number and variety present by the eighth century – and from the archaeological evidence of Jenne-Jaro. Some may have been there from the beginning of our era.

Little is known about any of these states before the eleventh century, but the geographical setting tells something. In the far west, Takrūr on the middle Senegal had

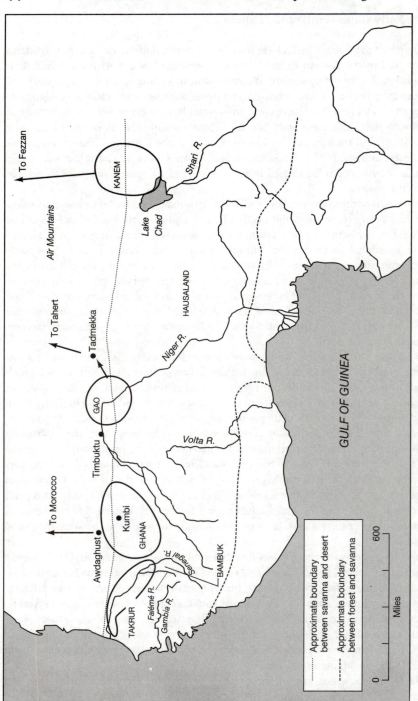

Map 3.1   The earliest recorded states in West Africa c.1000 AD

the natural advantage of a river flowing from the south, making dense population near the desert possible. Some of the Fulbe Takrūri lived still further north than they do today, as rainfall farmers to the north of the river. In the desert, Berbers operated the caravan trade to Morocco, exporting some gold, which undoubtedly came from Bambuk, the gold-bearing region between the upper Senegal and its tributary, the Falémé. Takrūr also grew millet and cotton and manufactured cotton textiles, which were sold to the nomads. Desert salt was not so important here as it was on the Niger bend, because salt could also come from coastal evaporating ponds at the mouth of the Senegal River.

In geographical terms, Ghana seems to have been less well placed than Takrūr, though its reputation was greater to the north of the Sahara. The capital at Kumbi was at roughly the same latitude as the two river bends, where rainfall agriculture is now marginal. The population must have been sparse. Awdaghust, the main desert port for the trans-Saharan trade, was more an oasis than a sedentary town – a setting that must have posed serious security problems for the state. North Africans knew Ghana as the country of gold, though the gold actually came from Bambuk, and Ghana did not rule directly over this region. Soninke merchants, however, may have had some way to control the supply at its source, to prevent its diversion to Takrūr or elsewhere.

Early Gao was in a different position. As in riverine Takrūr, the Niger provided Gao with fish, irrigation water, and silt to renew the fertility of the land. But Gao had no gold trade until the fourteenth century. Before that time, its line of communications toward the south ran southeast down the Niger toward Hausaland, not upriver toward the gold fields. While Takrūr and Ghana both had their principal trans-Saharan contacts with southern Morocco, Gao in the ninth and tenth centuries dealt mainly with the Kharijite state of Tahert (now in eastern Algeria) using the desert out-port of Tadmekka in much the same way Ghana used Awdaghust.

Between the Niger bend and Lake Chad, the largest ethnic group were the Hausa, many of whom lived a good deal further north than they do today. This region, however, was slower to develop states or to feel the direct influence of the trans-Saharan trade than either Songrai to the west or Kanem to the east. Even Kanem passed through a process of state-building different from that of the western Sudan. The nucleus was a nomadic confederation of peoples speaking separate languages of the Teda-Daza group, probably formed in the ninth century. Nomadic confederations of this kind are common enough in history; the unusual thing is that this one held together. Sometime before the early twelfth century, it overran the sedentary lands in Kanem to their south. By the thirteenth century it had become sedentary itself, with Njimi as its permanent capital. It was deeply involved in the trans-Saharan trade, but Kanem had nothing to offer to outsiders so attractive as the gold of the western Sudan. Its advantage lay in its location at the southern terminus of a very favorable route to the north along a sequence of well-spaced wells leading to the Fezzan, now in central Libya.

Of the region between the Kanuri and the Nubian kingdoms on the Nile, historians know very little beyond the fact that states came into existence at some points before about 1000 AD in a pattern similar to that of states further west. That is, in the circumstances of growing trade between the desert and the sown, a focus of political authority was likely to turn up wherever trade was especially intense, as at the southern end of the easy desert crossing from Lake Chad to the Fezzan – or whenever the geography made possible a denser population or offered a more secure rainfall. These conditions were fulfilled by north-flowing rivers such as the Niger, the Senegal, or the Shari emptying into Lake Chad. They were also fulfilled where altitude both improved the chance of rainfall and made defense against desert raiders easier. The best example is the Marra mountains in the western part of the Republic of the Sudan, almost halfway between the Nile and Lake Chad. There, in the plateau and mountainous region of Darfur, with a peak rising to more than 10,000 feet, a series of kingdoms flourished over the centuries. Whatever Darfurian kingdom might exist at a particular time was an important way-station in the east–west diffusion of culture across Africa. These kingdoms were in contact with Christian Nubia, for example, as well as with Kanem to the west; they also had direct contact with Egypt by way of an ancient caravan route that ran northwest from the Marra mountains to join the Nile at the Dongola reach – a route known historically as the "forty-day road."

The coming of Islam

Islam came differently to different peoples. Some of those conquered early in the Umayyad period, like Egypt and Tunisia, converted quickly to Islam. The rest of the Berber Maghrib also became Muslim early, but less completely. Beyond the Sahara – along the Sudanic belt, in Ethiopia, or down the East African coast, Islam came later through missionary work and voluntary conversion. But even in the core area, the picture of a homogeneous Muslim civilization can be overdrawn. Some parts of Muhammad's message went everywhere and took root with extraordinary uniformity given the fact that Islam had no specific institutions for enforcing orthodoxy. Other aspects of pre-Muslim culture withstood a millennium of Muslim influence with remarkable tenacity.

The ideal of the Muslim state itself owed more to historical experience than it did to the prescriptions of the Koran. Muhammad's followers had founded a universal empire, but it differed from the Roman Empire it replaced. At its head, the caliph was theoretically Muhammad's successor on earth. The Muslim world thus began with a basic trust in the state's capacity to create a good society on earth – not a paradise, but the kind of society in which men could do God's will and earn their salvation – and in which God's law would be enforced as nearly as possible. Christian Rome and its successor states, on the other hand, looked back to the time when the state had persecuted Christians. A Christian state deserved the allegiance of its subjects, but good Christians still had to choose between what was Caesar's and what was God's. A Muslim caliph, in theory at least, had the responsibility to make sure within his sphere that what was God's and what was Caesar's were the same.

Ideals of this sort are rarely realized, of course, but they tend to give direction to the way institutions develop. With Islam, that influence was especially strong in law, which was more closely integrated with religion than it was in the Christian tradition. Since Muhammad had begun as head of a religious community, his message from God was legal as well as theological, even though the law set forth in the Koran was neither systematic nor clear on every point. One of the first tasks of Muhammad's successors was to study, elaborate, and systematize the legal framework he had left them, and this task fell to the clerics or learned men, the *'ulamā* (singular *'alīm*), who dealt with faith and law alike. Over the early Muslim centuries from about 730 to 930, the 'ulamā of the Muslim world worked out a kind of legal synthesis known as the *sharīa*. In fact, they worked out four different and equally authoritative versions, but the Malikite view was the one that came to be most respected in Muslim Africa.

In this as in other interpretations of the Koran and the traditions, the 'ulamā had to settle differences of opinion. In theory, differences could only be settled by a consensus of the community of believers; but someone had to decide what the consensus was, and the 'ulamā, as an informal corporation of learned men and judges, took this duty on themselves. They were not a priesthood, ordained with special powers other men lacked, but their ability to speak in the name of religion and law gave them an important political role in most Muslim societies.

During the 'Abbasid period, Islam was very much an urban religion. The bedouin, the pastoral nomads from Arabia, became insignificant. The dominant voice spoke from the key cities of Damascus, Baghdad and Cairo. The 'ulamā reflected and reinforced this urban character as the caliphate itself became the key institution organizing and supporting religious life. The Muslim message took on a dry and legalistic character, which appealed to the Muslim urban elite but not to the people in the countryside, who conformed when necessary but made their own mixture of new religion and the old.

Shīa offered a more emotional kind of religion, but *sunni*, or orthodox, Islam had only a few spokesmen along these lines until the time of al-Ghazāli (d. 1111 AD), who found a way to open up a more personal and emotional kind of religious experience while still meeting the demands of orthodox theology. This new mysticism was called *sufi*, and it emerged at a time when the state was weak and people had reason to doubt that all was well with the world. Many different kinds of sufism appeared. Some prescribed specific rituals or actions that would bring the believer into closer contact with God; others incorporated aspects of pre-Islamic belief. Though many of these beliefs and practices were far from orthodox, they were tolerated, if not supported, by the 'ulamā.

The organizational form of sufi Islam was the religious brotherhood (Arabic *tarīqa*, pl. *turuq*). In Arabic, *tarīqa* means "path," and each brotherhood had its own different path to a more personal and satisfying religious experience. At first, the *turuq* were simply groups of followers who gathered around a leader whose name and ideas were associated with the order. In time, the brotherhoods tended to form branches in other cities and in the countryside. Like Protestant Christian sects, they could divide and divide again, although several orders have a continuous history from the early centuries of sufism down to the present. Several grew to have branches throughout the Muslim world, like the most famous of all, the Qadiriya, founded in Baghdad by 'Abd al-Qādir al-Jīlāni (d. 1166). Others had a more regional following, like the Shādhiliyya whose founder, al-Shādhili (d. 1258), studied at Fez in Morocco but settled in Alexandria. The Shādhiliyya was especially strong in North Africa, though it also reached south-east into Arabia. The most important Maghribine sufi theologian, however, was Ibn al-

'Arabi (d. 1240) of Spain, whose influence was very strong in the later sufi movement. After the thirteenth century, when the turuq began to rival the state as the main articulating institution of Islamic life, the office of *shaykh*, or leader of a brotherhood, rose in importance as that of the urban 'ulamā declined. The sufis orders became the main missionary influence carrying Islam beyond the frontiers of the Muslim empires.

Even earlier, less orthodox versions of Islam had spread into unadministered or lightly administered territory such as Berber North Africa. In the eighth century, when sunni Islam was confined to the plains of Tunisia, the followers of the Kharijite heresy began to make converts in the mountains and desert fringes to the west and south. Before the end of that century, two Muslim Kharijite kingdoms had already emerged in the oasis country north of the Sahara, one at Tahert in southern Algeria and the other at Sijilmasa in Morocco. Later, about 900 AD, the shi'ite doctrine also appeared, with special success among the Berbers of the Kabylia mountains of northern Algeria. In time, it was to spread from that new base eastward into Tunisia and Egypt.

The Berbers, who had earlier preferred Donatism to orthodox Christianity, kept their habit of choosing heretical versions of foreign religions. With Islam they began with Kharajism, then shi'ism. Even after sunni Islam had won out in the North African cities, the Berber country people conceded a wide area in human affairs for the action of supernatural forces other than God. These supernatural forces were mainly survivals of ancient nature spirits, reinterpreted in Islamic terms as *jinn* or genies. Berber Islam also emphasized the personal power of a saintly man or his descendants, a cult of living saints whose quality of holiness, or *baraka*, gave them the power to see the future and perform miracles. Combined with sufi Islam, it was a short step to ascribe magical powers to the shaykh of a tarīqa and to venerate the tomb of a notable saint after his death.

Islam south of the desert

Merchants carried Islam across the desert to the western Sudan even before the Maghrib itself was fully converted. The Kharijite center at Sijilmasa was a main northern terminus of the caravan trade. Townspeople and traders were generally Muslim before most of the rural population had been converted. Some people in sub-Saharan Africa converted even before 800 AD, and the knowledge of Islam spread in the southern desert edge during the next century. The first reported conversion of a royal court followed in 985, when the rulers of Gao accepted Islam.

Rulers on the desert edge received Islam in different ways. In Gao, the rulers became Muslim, but they made no effort to force or encourage the conversion of their subjects. In Takrūr, the rulers became Muslim in the 1030s with more enthusiasm. Further east, the *Mai* (or king) of Kanem became Muslim before the end of the century, even before the Kanuri became sedentary. Here too, the ruler tried to do what he could to spread the new religion, with special encouragement for the 'ulamā. In Ghana, the rulers rejected Islam for themselves, but they welcomed Muslim merchants.

Islam offered clear advantages to sub-Saharan merchants. It was the religion of their trading partners from the north, and it brought the invaluable technique of literacy. The Soninke merchant class of Ghana were among the first West African converts to Islam, and they spread the religion as their trade networks spread out to the south.

Early Islam in West Africa followed the patterns of the Maghrib, with a strong Kharijite influence followed by shi'ism. It also picked up the continued influence of local religions, much as it did in the north. All West African religions before the colonial period were monotheistic in the sense that they contained the belief that the world was created by a single God. They differed from Christianity and Islam in holding that the creator God was no longer in active charge – nor was he ever a moral force for good or evil; he simply set the stage and then retired into neutrality. The supernatural forces that counted in day-to-day affairs were themselves part of the created world. They, too, were morally neutral, subject to influences that could make them act for good or for evil. But they also had their own interests, responsibilities and even personalities.

One group included the spirits of the ancestors, the personal guardians of specific lineages or ethnic groups. These spirits watched over their descendants, but they were not always beneficent; they required handling through prayer, sacrifice and ritual. A second group of spirits included the members of a general pantheon, without ties to a particular lineage, but with occupational specialties, like the pagan gods of Greece and Rome. One had special powers over thunder and lightning, another over smallpox; still another was a trickster with certain evil proclivities suggesting the Christian devil. The number of deities recognized in a particular African society differed widely, from fifteen or twenty to sixty or more. But the individual believer was not called on to perform rituals for all of them. He might participate actively in the worship of only one or two, working under the supervision of semi-professional cult leaders.

The individual used ritual to communicate with a particular deity which often included a sacrifice, sometimes that of an animal that was later cooked and eaten by the congregation. Music and dance helped the spirit to enter the worshipper's body. Individual worshippers could sometimes enter a trance-like state, possessed by the spirit that had been invoked. He or she could then communicate with the rest of the congregation in the spirit's name. Prayer was a crucial part of ritual and private devotion, as it is with Islam and Christianity. In special circumstances, some African religions called for human sacrifice, but such sacrifice was almost always associated with the particular or family gods, not with the general pantheon.

Alongside the ritual of the cults, most West African societies also practiced some form of divination. Diviners were usually a separate group from the cult leaders and were, like them, at least semi-professional. Their main task was to give advice, to help the individual deal with the spirit world. A diviner would be consulted, for example, in deciding which cult or deity should be most honored. He or she could be asked to foretell the future or deal with misfortune – whether human or supernatural in origin. When witchcraft or sorcery was suspected, a diviner could help to identify the witch and recommend appropriate countermeasures. The diviner did all this by using a battery of supernatural charms and techniques, although one suspects that common sense and non-Western psychiatry were the real secrets of success.

It is obvious that many of these religious ideas – ritual sacrifice, for example – occur also in Middle Eastern religions like Judaism and Christianity. It is generally believed that these resemblances go back to an ancient substratum of religious thought that was common to much of the Old World before cultures diverged. Detailed resemblances between the religious ideas of the Maghrib and West Africa, furthermore, suggest that these two regions were closer to one another in religious culture than either was to the Middle East before the rise of Islam. In both the Maghrib and West Africa, animal sacrifices were the main way to placate the spirits. In both, the blood of the sacrificed animal was the crux of the ritual. Spirits both north and south of the Sahara were thought to live in particular species of trees; wooden objects and living trees were often important objects of veneration.

These parallels could have originated from close contact before the desiccation of the Sahara, or from more recent diffusion across the desert in either direction. Perhaps we shall never know, but the fact remains that Maghribine Islam was the version that came into West Africa, which was already predisposed to receive it.

Islam advanced into the Nilotic Sudan and the horn of Africa with nearly the same timing as its advance into the Western Sudan – that is, with a delay of two centuries or more after its initial success in Arabia and the Middle East. This is surprising, given the fact that the Nubian kingdoms on the upper Nile are less than 500 miles from Mecca, while Morocco lay thousands of miles to the west. After the seizure of Egypt in the 650s, the Muslim caliphate turned away from Nubia. It wanted to move in other directions, and it therefore arranged a treaty with the Nubian kingdoms, which provided for open trade up and down the Nile and tribute payments in the form of Nubian slaves but otherwise left the frontier where it was. In one form or another, a treaty-like arrangement with similar provisions lasted during the next six centuries, until the 1260s and 1270s, when a Muslim Egyptian government once more took up the military advance toward the Sudan. In the intervening period, Islam had advanced without military support, mainly passing around Christian Nubia. Bedouin Arabs from Arabia had been moving into the desert regions on either side of the Nile. The Nubian Christian kingdoms held to their old religion until the fourteenth century, and individual Nubian Christians still made the pilgrimage to Jerusalem for several centuries more.

The Islamization of the Red Sea region was similar – no open conquest but a slow infiltration of Islamic ideas. These penetrated fairly rapidly among nomadic peoples along the fringes of the Ethiopian highlands, generally by about 1000 AD. Muslim infiltration of the highlands was slower. So long as the ʿAbbasid caliphate was strong and had its capital near the Persian Gulf, most trade from the Muslim Mediterranean to the Indian Ocean went through Baghdad, and the Red Sea remained a backwater. Then in the eleventh and twelfth centuries, ʿAbbasid rule weakened under Turkish and Mongol attack. The Persian Gulf route was no longer as safe as it had been, and the Red Sea route from Egypt to India revived. Muslim merchants began to penetrate the hinterland of Ethiopia, sometimes passing through the Christian kingdom when political conditions permitted, but going around through the eastern highlands when they did not. By about 1250, the eastern highlands of Ethiopia and all the territory to the east and north of the Christian kingdom were already Muslim or strongly influenced by Islam. From the point of view of the sedentary, mountain Christians, however, Islam was not only an alien religion; it was also the special faith of nomads and merchants, just as it was in West Africa.

Merchants in long-distance trade were to be the principal carriers of Islam into all parts of sub-Saharan Africa, just as Greek and Phoenician merchants in long-distance trade had carried the Hellenistic synthesis into the western Mediterranean. This role of culture-bearer was common to merchants precisely because they were forced by their occupation to remove themselves, to go and live among aliens. And yet they also had to keep in touch with the culture of their homeland.

As trade increased in the western Sudan from the eleventh century onward, sub-Saharan African merchants who had converted to Islam pushed their commercial networks southward from the desert edge. They formed trade diasporas, sending out emigrants to settle at all the principal points of trade to assure trustworthy business contacts. The Arabic sources refer to all these traders as "Wangara." Some of the earliest networks were organized by the Soninke of the desert edge, connected to ancient Ghana. Others were run by Songhai boatmen on the Niger River. Still other offshoots were run by Hausa to the east and Mande people in the west. A little after 1000 AD, these routes had continued all through the savanna country and down to the coast from the Gold Coast through to the Cameroon highlands.

Migrations

The most significant migrations in the known history of Africa – the Bantu migrations, the southward movement of savanna peoples into the West African forest, the empty-ing of the Sahara following its desiccation – had all taken place long before the eighth century AD. The main lines of cultural and linguistic geography in northern Africa were set by then. Yet people still moved from place to place in small numbers, as refugees from local drought or political oppression, in search of better land or new opportunities. As they moved, they carried their culture with them. As they settled down among aliens, they created plural societies, with small enclaves of foreign culture that could sometimes last for a century or more before they were absorbed in the culture of their neighbors. Meanwhile, their presence created a source of cross-cultural borrowing.

This kind of individual and small-group movement ran parallel to a similar but involuntary movement of the internal slave trade. Slaves were captured in warfare, but they were rarely kept by their captors because they might easily escape and might be dangerous. They were sold into the trade, taken hundreds of miles from home, and then sold to the people who intended to use their services – if, indeed, they managed to avoid the export trade to North Africa – or later on to the Americas. The early slave trade within Africa has not been studied in detail, and the evidence may be too thin to yield a secure picture when it *is* studied. It is known, nevertheless, that slavery and a slave trade existed in sub-Saharan Africa at a very early time.

The more recent pattern of slavery in sub-Saharan Africa also provides some hints. It was quite different from the economically oriented slavery of the New World – and from the slave plantations that were to grow in importance in nineteenth-century West Africa. In most places, slavery was an assimilative institution, designed to serve as an

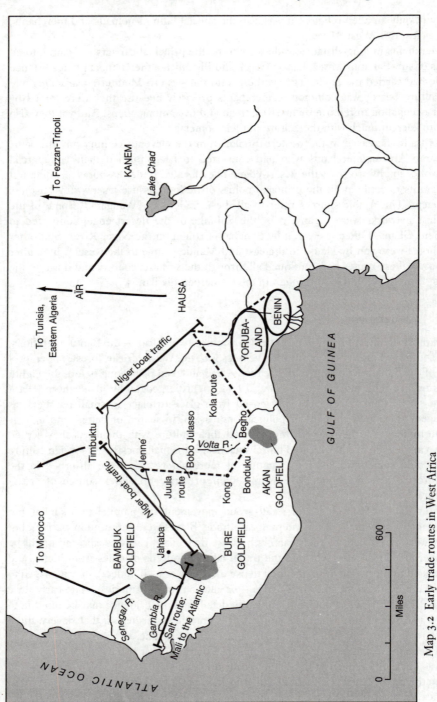

Map 3.2 Early trade routes in West Africa

artificial kinship tie permitting the addition of members to one's group, village, or society. Newly purchased slaves gradually acquired rights as they became members of the new society. In time they or their descendants settled down as fully-fledged members of that society, though usually with a subordinate social status. Second generation slaves could rarely be sold after the first generation, so that, in the Western sense of chattel slavery, they were not slaves at all. Although it is clear that the newly purchased slaves usually assimilated the culture of the master's community, what we know about acculturation suggests that the very process of absorbing aliens must also have changed that community's way of life. The influence of this process in building a common West African culture may have been considerable, especially when we remember that in many West African societies half or more of the population was in "slave" status at the beginning of the colonial period.

Larger migrations took place along or near the desert edge. Nomads tended to be more numerous near the desert edge than they were in the central Sahara. Rainfall was better and they had the opportunity to trade with the sedentary farmers. On the sedentary side of the line, transhumant pastoralists took their cattle north each wet season. Transhumant and nomadic pastoralists had to move at least twice each year in any case. They could therefore move more often and in larger numbers than their sedentary neighbors could. Beginning in the eleventh century, four important population movements took place along the desert edge, both north and south of the Sahara. These migrations – not the original Muslim conquests – began the Arabization of the Maghrib, the western Sahara, and the Nilotic Sudan.

Several thousand Arabs had settled in Egypt after the first Muslim conquest of the eighth century, but Arabic speech and culture penetrated further west only in the cities and through the religious prestige of Arabic as a holy language. Berber Muslims of the first Islamic centuries spoke Berber, just as most Spanish Muslims at the same period spoke an early form of Spanish.

In origin, these population movements were a continuation of the movement of people out of Arabia into the Middle East, a movement that had begun long before the rise of Islam and continued whenever the sedentary authorities to the north were weak. The Egyptian desert to the east of the Nile was Arabized before the time of Muhammad, and bedouins continued afterward to push into Egypt along the fringes of the Nile Valley, sometimes crossing to the western desert, sometimes pushing southward toward the Sudan. The nomadic Beja of the Red Sea hills held their own, though they gradually turned to Islam. The Arab immigrants found it easier to move south or west and ultimately to set up a new pattern of life near the Sudanic savanna country or in the far west.

In the first stages, these migrating Arabs had to deal with the governments of sedentary Egypt, sometimes in cooperation or even in alliance against third parties, sometimes as enemies in the ancient pattern of sedentary-nomadic rivalry. In the tenth century, as ʿAbbasid power weakened, the nomadic side became more daring. A little before 1000 AD, the Banu Hilal and the Banu Sulaym, tribes from the central Arabian plateau, moved into the Egyptian desert east of the Nile; then, beginning about 1050, they moved west in force for a major attack on Tunisia – perhaps at the urging of the Egyptians who wanted to be rid of them, but at least without Egyptian resistance to their crossing the Nile and moving off. In the next centuries, some of these people and their descendants kept moving until they reached the Atlantic coast of Morocco and Mauritania.

Historians disagree about their long-term impact on the Maghrib. One view held the Hilalians responsible for the destruction of classical "civilization" that had survived since Roman times. It pointed to the destruction of irrigation works and the turning of plowed fields into mere pasture for Arab herds, driving the native Berbers into the mountains. A more moderate revision holds that the nomads were sometimes destructive but not without redeeming contributions to Maghribine civilization. They sometimes cooperated with sedentary regimes, and they were not alone as a nomadic threat to the sedentary Maghrib; Berber nomads had also been destructive in the past and would be so in the future. Whatever else, the Arabs were a politically unsettling force in Maghribine politics for centuries to come; and they also accomplished the linguistic Arabization of Tunisia, the plains in Algeria and Morocco, and a great deal of steppe and desert off to the south as far as the western Sudan.

A second movement from Arabia into Egypt branched southward parallel to the Nile in a massive but badly documented migration. Some migrants also crossed the Red Sea directly into the Nilotic Sudan, but the main movement by-passed the Christian states along the Nubian Nile and the Beja of the Red Sea hills. When they reached the southern edge of the desert, the Arabs dispersed. Some kept to their old role as camel nomads and pushed west along the desert edge to occupy the northern plains of Kordofan, Darfur, Wadai, and into present-day Chad. Others pushed south into regions of sedentary agriculture and mixed with the original inhabitants to create the population that is still there, a stable mixture that is mainly African in descent but Arabic in language and many other aspects of culture. Later arrivals from Arabia found the land that was suited to camels and sheep already occupied, so they crossed into the savanna side of the desert fringe and became cattle nomads called *baqarra*, practicing transhumant pastoralism in a country that could also be used for agriculture. Some of them moved west, living among many other peoples until, in time, they reached the longitude of Lake Chad, where their descendants, the Shuwa Arabs, are still to be found.

Meanwhile, in the Nile Valley itself, in the century from 1250 to 1350, Egypt stepped up military pressure to the Nubian kingdoms, which were gradually going Muslim by peaceful conversion in any case. Those in lower Nubia and the Dongola reach fell to Islam, leaving only the kingdom of Alwa controlling part of the Shendi reach and the savanna country to the south to continue a token (and partly Islamized) existence into the sixteenth century.

While the Arabs were moving along the desert edge from east to west, the Fulbe (or Fulani) were moving from west to east. They were cattle people like the baqarra, keeping south of the desert and practicing transhumance rather than true nomadism (that is, they stayed near permanent sources of water in the dry season, moving out with the rains only to return when the pastures and water holes dried up). As a result, they had to be away from home when their farmer neighbors were planting and harvesting. Theirs was therefore a specialized occupation of their particular ethnic group. Fulbe pastoralists are found today scattered through the western Sudan from the Atlantic to

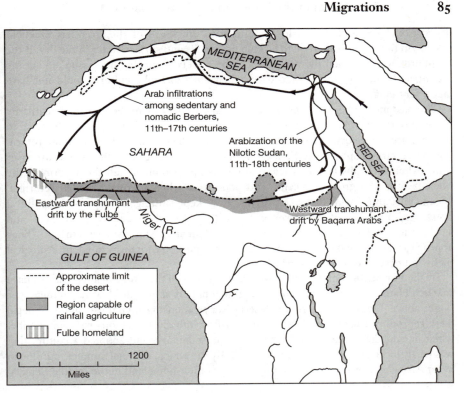

Map 3.3 The Arab and Fulbe migrations

Lake Chad, speaking a common language with comparatively small dialectal variation over great distances. Many also have a physical appearance suggesting a European or North African strain somewhere in the background. But all people speaking their language are not pastoral. Sedentary Fulbe are the dominant population along the middle reaches of the Senegal on the Senegal-Mauritania border.

Ethnographers who encountered the Fulbe in Senegal decided that the pastoral Fulbe were a separate "tribe," whom they called Peuhl, while they called the sedentary speakers of the same language Tukolor. Europeans who met the Fulbe in Nigeria called them all Fulani, regardless of occupation. To avoid confusion, they will all be called Fulbe here, that being their most common name for themselves.

The most plausible hypothesis to explain the different appearance of sedentary and pastoral Fulbe recalls that sedentary Fulbe have long been the dominant population in the state of Takrūr and its successor, Fuuta Tooro, on the middle Senegal. They look like their Wolof and Serer neighbors, whose languages are also similar. The pastoral Fulbe often have distinctly different facial features, suggesting a genetic mixture between sedentary Fulbe and some of the Berbers from the near-by desert. The Berbers of the desert have been neighbors of the sedentary Fulbe since at least the beginning of our era. The logical assumption is that some of the Berbers moved over and joined Fulbe society as pastoral specialists. The Senegal River made an excellent dry-season base, and the Ferlo wilderness to the south of the river has excellent pasture in the wet season, though lacking both wells and surface water in the dry. If the shepherds who attached themselves to Fulbe society spent the dry season among the sedentary Fulbe and took Fulbe wives, their shift to Fulbe culture would not have taken very long.

The pastoral Fulbe, however, were especially vulnerable to the climatic irregularity of the desert edge. A series of dry years would force pastoralists along the Senegal to seek a more secure dry-season base further south. Once shifted, they might not return. The sedentary people of the Senegal Valley could stay, because they could use river water when the rains failed. A few pastoralists might remain with them, forming the nucleus of a new growth of cattle and population when adequate rainfall returned. Meanwhile, those who had been driven away kept shifting in response to political pressures, or the lure of still newer pastures. They drifted off, generally to the east and staying more or less in the latitudes where transhumant pastoralism was efficient. They appear to have been welcomed, because their type of pastoralism filled an ecological niche not occupied by the savanna farmers.

By the thirteenth century, the most advanced edge of the Fulbe drift appears to have reached Hausa country. Along the way, large numbers settled in Maasina on the upper Niger above Timbuktu, where the desert-river relationships like those on the Senegal were reproduced with variations. Others drifted into close relations with non-Fulbe, which meant that many settled down, became sedentary, and adopted a culture that was partly local and partly from the Senegal. By the 1990s, the total number of Fulbe in West Africa was several times the population of their homeland in the middle Senegal valley.

Climatic irregularity caused the dispersion of sedentary farmers as well. The Soninke or Sarakolé, for example, had an early homeland in the region between the middle Senegal and the Niger bend in the heartland of ancient Ghana. It was an area of light rainfall at the best of times, but very well placed for trade across the desert. Soninke oral traditions tell of a time when all Soninke lived together in a place they remember as "Wagadu," but the displeasure of the gods stopped the rain for seven full years. "Wagadu" turned to desert, and the people had to flee to the south. The climatic disaster resembled those of the seventeenth and eighteenth centuries or the 1970s and 1980s in the same region, but this one took place well before 1500. It scattered the Soninke far and wide. Some still live near "Wagadu," but the majority are dispersed through the western Sudan from the Gambia to Burkina Faso. Some live in large communities that were able to maintain Soninke-speaking states for centuries. Villages isolated among aliens, however, often took on the culture of their neighbors, though with a Soninke input that is still detectable. The dispersion of the Fulbe is therefore only one of several cases of dispersion caused by climate, but the Fulbe were specialists who moved together in a tight community. They therefore preserved their language and culture over a longer period than was possible for sedentary farmers who settled among new neighbors.

Political change in North Africa

For most of the Islamic world, the period from about 1000 to 1500 was marked by a breakdown of 'Abbasid unity and a rise in the importance of the turuq as a key institution guiding religious, and sometimes secular life. In spite of political weakness it was also a key period for the expansion for Islam beyond the old frontiers into Southeast Asia, sub-Saharan Africa, and down the East African coast.

The Maghrib was different; it was never in the 'Abbasid empire to begin with. For North Africa, these five centuries can be divided in the middle. Before about 1270, North African political affairs were dominated by three successive attempts to create a new, universal, Muslim empire: a shi'ite effort based on eastern Algeria and Tunisia; a nomadic empire-building invasion by the Almoravids of the western Sahara; and a final effort by the mountain Berber Almohad movement of central Morocco. After 1270 and the collapse of the Almohad empire, political life became still more fragmented, as each region fell under the control of local forces. In Egypt and the Maghrib alike, secular-minded dynasties rose and fell without claiming the caliphate or universal rule over all Muslims.

The three earlier efforts at unification also had a good deal in common. Each had a home base and source of major support in a region that was geographically and culturally marginal to the Muslim civilization it sought to conquer. Each called for a purification of Islam and a return to the first principles of religion, though they disagreed about what those principles were. Each wanted to create a good society by breaking the social and political mold to create greater justice based on Islam. Each helped generate a creative phase in the history of art and letters. And each achieved a measure of economic success within its territory, though none was able to create a state with enough unity and administrative continuity to last more than a couple of centuries.

The first of the three empire-building attempts began in the 890s with the following of an itinerant shi'ite preacher among Berber mountaineers in the eastern Kabylia mountains of Algeria, and it ended with the establishment of the Fatimid sultanate, controlling the eastern Maghrib but centered on Egypt. The founder belonged to a branch of shi'ite Islam which believed in an imminent Mahdi or savior who would come to root out injustice and perfect the shar'ia by showing the hidden meanings in God's message to Muhammad. The result would be a new order on earth, where the state would no longer be needed because Muslim law would be followed automatically from the internal convictions of the faithful.

The rise of the Fatimids began when the movement came out of its mountain base and seized Tunisia in 909 AD. It then consolidated its position in the eastern Maghrib, capturing the Kharijite kingdoms of the south in the 950s. By the 960s, it was ready for an advance on the Middle East. It captured Egypt easily enough and campaigned briefly in Syria, but the conquests stopped there. The Fatimids moved the capital to Cairo in the 970s and settled down for two centuries as a mainly Egyptian regime with uncertain control over their former base in the Maghrib.

Their descent on Egypt gave the Fatimids a role in the dissolution of the 'Abbasid caliphate, but their real importance in Islamic affairs was their reorientation of Mediterranean and Indian Ocean trade. From their base in Egypt, they developed the Red

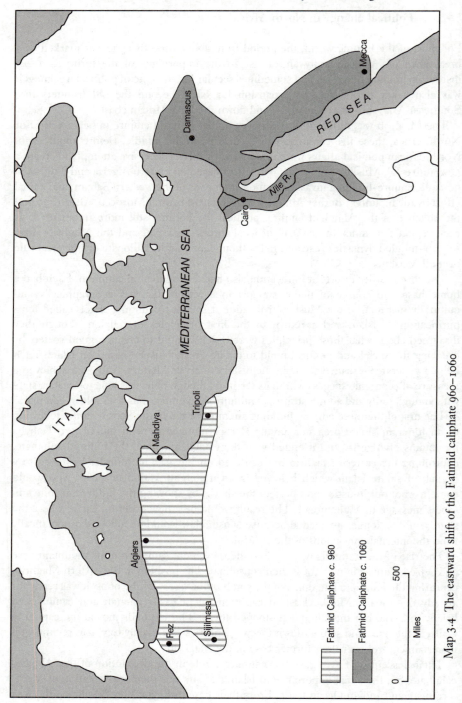

Map 3.4 The eastward shift of the Fatimid caliphate 960–1060

Sea route, providing naval patrols at sea and secure control over the desert caravans from Aswan to the port of ʿAydhab, opposite Jiddah and Mecca. This not only diverted trade from the Persian Gulf; it also increased total trade between the Mediterranean and India. Even Christian powers like Genoa and Venice began to profit by coming to Alexandria for goods from as far away as Southeast Asia.

When the Fatimid dynasty fell in the 1170s, Egypt's position in international commerce was not affected. Tunisia was already lost to the Hilalian Arabs in the 1050s. The loss of Egypt was a blow to shiʿite Islam, because the next dynasty returned to sunni orthodoxy; and the original Berber ruling class had long since lost real control. Their power came originally from their position as military leaders over soldiers from the Maghrib. Once established in Egypt, the Fatimids phased out the Maghribine armies in favor of slave soldiers from Asia or the Sudan. After a brief intervening dynasty, control of Egypt passed to these slave soldiers called Mamluks. They were recruited in childhood by purchase beyond the fringes of Islam and brought up to be professional soldiers. With their monopoly of physical force, it was easy for them to become masters of the state, and new generations of soldiers could be recruited in the same way to carry on. The Mamluks were to continue as rulers of Egypt down to its conquest by the Ottoman Empire in the early sixteenth century.

The Almoravid empire, second of the three Maghribine empires, began in the eleventh century at the opposite end of North Africa. The Almoravids were nomads, like the Hilalians who were moving into the Maghrib from the west at the same time. The combined movement created a nomadic crisis for the sedentary Maghrib in the second half of that century, but the crisis also suggests that the sedentary societies had fallen into a period of weak organization and inadequate defense.

The Almoravid movement first began among the Lamtuna, a nomadic, Muslim, and Berber tribe which controlled one of the caravan routes from southern Morocco to the western Sudan. In the 1040s, they attracted a Muslim preacher from southern Morocco to serve as their spiritual guide. With his leadership, they put together a nomadic confederation that mobilized the military power of the western Sahara in much the same way the original Muslims had mobilized the nomadic power of Arabia. On the intellectual side, the movement called for a return to the primitive purity of Islam, with a strong emphasis on the role of the sharʿia and especially the Malikite version. It was thus at the opposite end of the spectrum of Islamic thought from the sufi movement that was to blossom in the following century. The name, Almoravid, however, comes from the Arabic *murābitun*, meaning men of the *ribāt*, a holy retreat or fortified place for the defense of Islam.

Whatever the religious drive of the Almoravids, their early moves reflected their interest in trans-Saharan commerce. In the 1050s, they turned both north and south, first capturing Awdaghust, the chief desert port for the empire of Ghana, then turning north to capture Sijilmasa in southern Morocco. This gave them the two main termini of the gold route across the desert. In the late 1050s, however, they failed in another southward move against Takrūr, but their further northward movement took them far into the sedentary parts of southern Morocco. By the mid-1090s they went on to capture all of Morocco, western Algeria, and Muslim Spain, establishing a new nomadic dynasty in control of the Muslim far west.

The Almoravid empire was the most ephemeral of the three, lasting a bare half-century from its conquest of Spain to its dissolution. But the Almoravids made an important contribution to the culture of the Maghrib, up to now a rustic frontier district of the Muslim world. The union of Spain with the Maghrib opened the way to new influences from the north, especially in art and architecture. Urban life became important as never before. By the 1140s, however, most of Spain and much of the western Maghrib was already lost to local princes or to the growing power of the Almohad movement in the Atlas. Historians tend to explain this quick failure by pointing to the legalistic aridity of the Almoravid doctrine, which lacked appeal in the Maghrib, or to the small number of nomads compared with the size of the military and administrative task (and combined with their failure to co-opt others into positions of power).

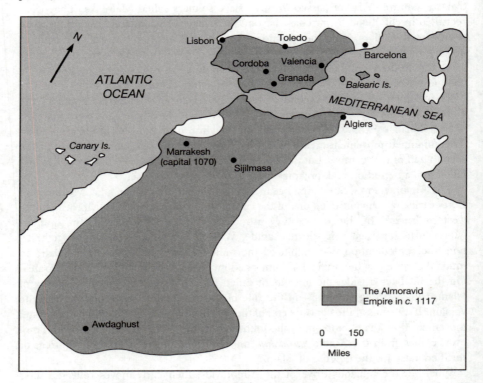

Map 3.5 Expansion of the Almoravids to 1117 AD

The Almohad movement that superseded the Almoravids over much of the same territory completed and extended the cultural consequences of the Almoravid empire, but the religious message was quite different, with overtones of shi'a Islam and of the sufism that was just then beginning in the Middle East. The religious leader was 'Abd Allah Ibn Tumert, a native of the southern Atlas, where the movement first caught on among his own Masmuda people. Ibn Tumert went east in his youth for an education

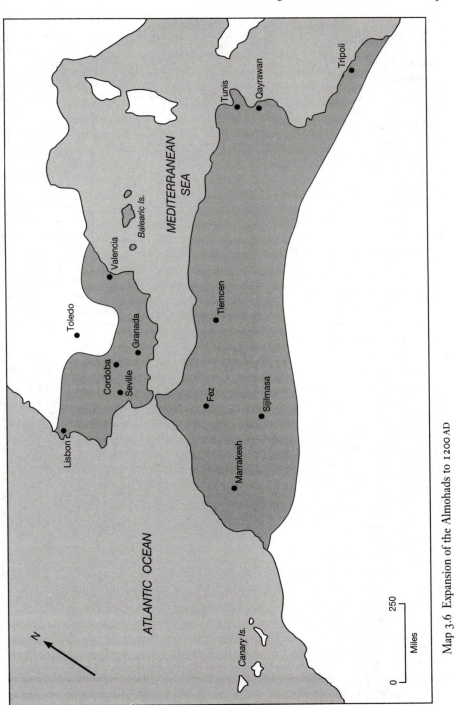

Map 3.6 Expansion of the Almohads to 1200 AD

and a period of wandering in the holy cities, returning in 1118 when he was nearly forty. His doctrine was a form of fundamentalism, laying special emphasis on the oneness of God. The Almohad name is itself a corruption of the Arabic *al-muwahhidūn* meaning the movement of the unitarians. Ibn Tumert also introduced the shi'ite notion of an infallible Mahdi, and in time he claimed to be that Mahdi. He also preached opposition to the Almoravid overlords, a common enemy whose presence helped him to unite the segmentary societies of the Atlas in a common purpose.

Ibn Tumert died in 1130, before the movement had advanced beyond the mountains. His successor and the real founder of the empire was 'Abd al-Mu'min ibn 'Ali, who defeated the Almoravids and annexed all Morocco before 1148, adding Spain in 1150 and the rest of the Maghrib as far as Tunis and Tripoli by 1160. In the process he had to take on the local Berber powers, the Hilalian Arabs who then controlled most of Tunisia, and the Christian government of Sicily which controlled the Tunisian ports. He also played down Ibn Tumert's religious message and made the government a personal domination for his own family. He and his successors sought new support by compromising with the Hilalian Arabs, inviting them into the empire as allies. That move may have solved some short-run problems, but it brought a long-term source of instability into the political life of the Maghrib. By the early thirteenth century, the empire was already in decline, with severe military losses to the Christians in Spain. By 1250, Almohad rule was effectively finished, and Berber nomads came over the sedentary frontier in 1269 to capture the old capital at Marrakesh and establish themselves as a new dynasty over the Moroccan part of the empire.

The Almohad movement was thus also ephemeral; even the complete Almoravid-Almohad sequence was shorter than the two centuries of Fatimid rule in Egypt. Yet the movement had wider significance. It brought about a general revival of commerce, just as the Fatimids had done in the east. At its height it had the best fleet in the western Mediterranean, and it opened the sea to Christian as well as to Muslim traffic. Urban life continued the development begun under the Almoravids, with a new burst of creativity represented by figures such as Ibn Tufayl (d. 1185) in Spain, among the most important of medieval Islamic philosophers and theologians. Ibn Rushd (d. 1198), whom the Christians called Averroes, was even more important for his commentaries on Greek philosophy; his works in translation were to bring new knowledge of Greek philosophy into Europe. The last decades of the twelfth century also witnessed a flowering – some say the finest flowering – of western Muslim architecture in Morocco and Spain alike.

The second half of the Muslim Middle Ages, from the end of the Almohads in about 1270 to about 1500, brought political fragmentation but was not necessarily a general decline. Local political authorities worked with the informal but significant understanding that all belonged to the larger community of Islam. Economic growth in both Egypt and the Maghrib continued until the mid-fourteenth century, still later in some areas. Art and letters may have lost the outstanding creativity of the recent past, but the courtly arts of polished upper-class life continued in local centers like Granada, the only remaining Muslim state in Spain, and with the Merinids, who ruled much of Morocco from Fez in the fourteenth century.

This was also a classic period for the interplay of nomadic and sedentary pressures, observed and recorded by Ibn Khaldun (d. 1406) of Tunis, an outstanding philosopher and historian who used the past few centuries in the Maghrib to illustrate his theme, which was a form of environmentalism: nomads were tough because nomadic life was hard; sedentary life made for the dissipation and weakness of the ruling class. Nomadic life encouraged collective effort for a common goal; sedentary life allowed the selfish pursuit of personal or family interests. Sedentary kingdoms were therefore liable to become increasingly weak, and so to encourage conquest from the steppes. But a new nomadic dynasty ruling over sedentary society would weaken in its turn. The whole cycle passed through five stages and occupied about one hundred and twenty years.

Historians today honor Ibn Khaldun for his insight but do not accept his entire set of beliefs. They recognize the nomadic-sedentary conflict as one major theme among several, but they also see a complex web of cooperation as well as rivalry between the two ecological systems. Many would also stress the change from the early to the late Middle Ages, from a phase in which political leaders were trying to create a new empire in conscious imitation of the first caliphs, to a new phase of limited ambitions and limited power in which the rulers represented a particular ethnic group, tribe, fraction, or social class (in the case of Mamluk Egypt). Islamic states, in short, no longer claimed religious as well as secular leadership. The leaders of the sufi turuq had begun to replace them, and secular leaders acquiesced by acting mainly on behalf of their own class and extended family. By the late fifteenth and early sixteenth centuries, these changes contributed to a real weakening of the Maghribine powers and a basic shift of power from Muslims to the Christians north of the Mediterranean.

Trade and politics south of the Sahara: Ghana

Written sources for the political history of sub-Saharan Africa, are hard to come by, so that West Africa emerges slowly through time as information becomes available. Before the tenth century, we have only archaeology, linguistics, and a range of indirect evidence. From the tenth century to the fourteenth, we have the added element of reporting from North Africa in Arabic, combined with the earliest oral traditions. Then, from the fourteenth century, European written records from the coast are added, followed in about the seventeenth by more and more detailed oral traditions and the survival of written records compiled by Africans at the time.

The period from about 1000 to 1500 is one of intermittent and partial reporting. Some of the best travelers' accounts of this period, like Ibn Battuta's marvellously detailed report of his trip across the Sahara and south to Mali in 1352–3, tells much more than we know about most later periods up to the eighteenth century. But aliens encountered severe health problems in West Africa, and merchants tended to turn back at the desert's edge. Information reaching North Africa was therefore often at second or third hand, with nothing but silence about some regions for a century or more at a time.

Even if it were desirable to give a consecutive political narrative, it would not be possible. It is possible, however, to see something of the style of international relations – and, behind the recurrent pattern of events, some of the factors that influenced the rise and fall of states. One of the problems facing any sub-Saharan state in this period was implicit in the economic geography of its situation. The point of contact with the trans-Saharan trade was the desert's edge. A sedentary state near the desert would seek to control the desert ports and to control as long a section of the desert-savanna frontier as possible. With an exchange like that of gold for salt, bargaining was open, without a multiplicity of buyers and sellers to establish a market price. Salt could be monopolized because the Saharan deposits were few and easily controlled. Gold could also be monopolized, at least in theory. But, so far as our meager evidence goes, no sub-Saharan state ever came to control the three principal goldfields in West Africa – Bambuk between the Senegal and the Falémé, Buré to the southeast near the upper Niger, and the Akan goldfield in the forest and savanna of present-day Ghana. It was rare, indeed, for one of the larger states to control any of these gold-producing areas for long. They could seek the same result by controlling the desert-savanna frontier, blocking off the Saharan traders from access to the gold. The result would then be a monopoly on each side. If the Sudanese could exercise some control out into the desert itself, they might even break the monopoly on that side and create a decisive shift of the terms of trade in their favor. These considerations are reflected in a recurrent pattern of expansion by strong states on the desert fringe – first east and west from the core area, then out into and across the desert if possible. They rarely tried to build an empire in their hinterland to the south, away from the desert.

If control of the desert edge was a way to control trade, the desert edge was also dangerous; it was open to nomadic attack and subject to irregular rainfall. Both of these dangers played a role in the fall of Ghana. At the Ghanaian peak of power in the eleventh century, Bambuk was the only one of the three goldfields already drawn into the Saharan gold trade. Therefore, Ghana's stretch of sahel from the northward bend of the Niger to the upper Senegal may well have been enough to blanket access to the gold; it would certainly have been enough if Ghana could have found a way to prevent leakage through Takrūr. But then, in the middle of the eleventh century, both Awdaghust and Sijilmasa fell to the Almoravids. That ended Ghana's power as a great incorporative trade empire, but not its existence as a state. It held on to the original Soninke core area until perhaps the thirteenth century, and the final blow was the climatic disaster and the Soninke dispersal from "Wagadu."

Mali, Kanem, and Songhai

For two centuries after Ghana's first decline, no successor state established equivalent control over the desert edge. A Songhai state held the Niger bend, and a Fulbe state held the middle valley of the Senegal. Another state rose to control some of the desert edge between the two rivers, but only briefly and on a smaller scale. Then, in the second half of the thirteenth century a new incorporative empire began to form around the kingdom of Mali, lying well back from the desert. The legendary first leader of Malian expansion was Sunjaata (*Soundiata* in French), whose position in the oral literature of the western Sudan is equivalent to that of Charlemagne in western Europe. The peak of Malian success, however, came later, in the reign of Mansa Musa (1312–37 AD).

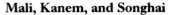

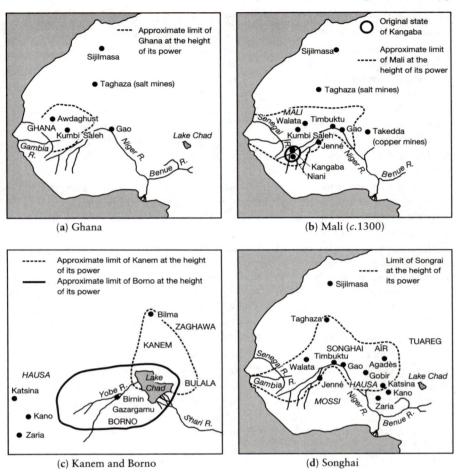

(a) Ghana

(b) Mali (*c.*1300)

(c) Kanem and Borno

(d) Songhai

Map 3.7 Ancient kingdoms of the Western Sudan (based on Margaret Shinnie, *Ancient African Kingdoms*, London: Edward Arnold, 1965)

The precise causes of Mali's success are unclear, but a growing trade network within the Sudan was one of them. Where Ghana had drawn gold from Bambuk alone, the trade routes now reached the Buré goldfields, which Mali was able to control. Most Malian expansion, however, was northward to the desert edge. In time, Mali controlled virtually all that ancient Ghana had controlled, but with some new twists. It combined domination of the desert edge with extension of trade routes to the south, leaving the Niger at Jenné to reach the Akan goldfields. Still another direction of Mande expansion was westward to the Atlantic by way of the Gambia River. This westward empire-building left a belt of Mande-speaking peoples, who still live along the line between the old heartland and the mouth of the Gambia, remnants of an ancient need for salt independent of the desert. These developments not only built the power of Mali, they left a permanent change in the geography of commerce; people at the Niger bend could tap the trade of all three goldfields, and Timbuktu became the principal desert port of the western Sudan, even after the decline of Mali.

The rise of Mali was crucial to the Islamization of the western Sudan. It brought a southward movement of Islam into new territory beyond the normal reach of North African traders, and full acceptance of Islam as the court religion spread the new belief very widely through the empire. Mali apparently accepted Islam just as the state was expanding. Sunjaata is remembered as a Muslim ruler, but nothing in the traditions from that period suggests that Islam was anything but a formality. By the middle of the fourteenth century, however, the Malian court and urban life were described by Ibn Battuta in terms that suggest an ordinary Muslim country of a type the famous traveler had visited many times before. It seems doubtful that Islam had as yet penetrated to the outer provinces or among the rural masses, but that process was beginning.

By the time of Sunjaata, the Kanuri far to the east had moved in from the desert, settled in Kanem, and from that base had begun a military expansion of their own. Their outstanding leader was Mai Dunama Dibbalemi (who ruled $c.$ 1221–59 AD), nearly an exact contemporary of Sunjaata. The two empires, however, were quite different. Whereas Mali began well back in the savanna and expanded to the desert fringe, Kanem began on the desert fringe and expanded still further out into the desert. The Kanuri nation had for some time been assimilating kindred people in the region. The inhabitants of Kawar oasis, nearly halfway across the Sahara, had become Kanuri during the course of the twelfth century. Before the end of the thirteenth, Kanem conquered the Fezzan, an outlier of North Africa, and ruled it directly for a half century, while an offshoot Kanuri dynasty ruled it for another century. A second direction of Kanuri expansion, under Dunama Dibbalemi, was to the northeast. A trade route ran eastward along the desert-savanna fringe and then across a corner of desert to reach the Nile and Egypt. Kanuri trade of the thirteenth century reached out this way as far as the Nile and probably to the Red Sea, connecting to the sphere of Mamluk Egypt.

Only partial explanations of Kanuri success emerge from the evidence we now have. One interpretation stresses the role of Islam in the Kanembu state, pointing out that the Mai (kings) had become Muslim, though their authority still depended on many of the pre-Muslim sanctions of Sefawa rule. Dunama Dibbalemi shifted to Muslim sanctions for his rule, destroying the pagan regalian symbols. This move could have been a bid for Muslim support, or simply a sign that he felt strong enough to dispense with pagan support. If so, it may have backfired; the Mai lost power in succeeding reigns, and an anti-Muslim reaction may have been one cause.

Dunama Dibbalemi also made some political innovations. About this time, the Kanuri developed a system of delegated military command, the successful commander being rewarded by a grant of authority over a section of the empire. Throughout world history this is a common way to govern newly conquered territory, but it always carries the danger that the military become a hereditary nobility by turning their public office into private property.

In any event, Kanem did not succeed in governing a vast empire for long. Some territory and people near the home base remained independent – the Lake Chad islands, for example, and the peoples immediately to the south of Kanem, who were culturally similar but lived under their own rulers, the Bulala.

Through the maze of political history, some themes emerged after the thirteenth century that were common to both Mali and Kanem – and almost certainly to other states whose political history is less well known. One problem was succession to office: how to find procedures flexible enough to exclude incompetents, but fixed enough to allow the new ruler to take office without a civil war? The problem was not specific to Africa, though polygyny tended to complicate it by increasing the number of possible heirs. In Mali, the problem of succession was solved (to the extent that it *was* solved) by the royal officials. On a number of occasions, after the death of a Mansa, they were able to choose between several branches of the royal Keita lineage, depriving incompetents of office but keeping power in the hands of the dynasty. These shifts at appropriate moments appear to be one reason Mali lasted into the nineteenth century as a state, though it was vastly reduced from its former imperial size.

Kanem was far less successful in escaping dynastic quarrels. Over time, many different branches of the Sefawa came into existence. Lacking royal officials who could balance one against another, each branch tried to make its own arrangements for a military following among the nobility. As a result, civil war became endemic over long periods, to the advantage of the Bulala. In the late fourteenth century, just as Mali was reaching its peak of power and well-being, the Bulala drove the Sefawa and their following out of Kanem. After a century or so in exile and division, the Sefawa finally re-established their own capital at Gazargamo, this time in Borno to the west of Lake Chad. The local inhabitants assimilated Kanuri language and culture, and, by the first part of the sixteenth century, Borno was able to re-establish a degree of control over the old homeland in Kanem, but the center of control was now in Borno.

Further west, Mali had declined in area and power, but a new empire began to expand toward the middle of the fifteenth century. This new empire had its core area on the Niger bend, with its capital at Gao, though the main commercial city was Timbuktu. As Malian power shrank in the fifteenth century, Timbuktu's economic advantage remained. Three contestants emerged, seeking to control the strategic Niger bend: the Mossi states within the bend south of Timbuktu; the riverine Songhai downstream from Gao, and the Tuareg nomads to the north. The Songhai won militarily, and this began the formation of a great empire based on the Niger bend. Unlike Mali, which had a Mande ethnic core, the Songhai were only a small minority in a multi-ethnic state that included many Mande, Fulbe, and Tuareg from the desert edge. The new empire expanded to become the largest ever of the Sudanese empires. It conquered up the Niger to Jenné and beyond, took control of part of the Mossi country to the immediate south, and, in the first decade of the sixteenth century, extended its lateral control westward to the Senegal, thus blanketing Mali's access to the Saharan trade and establishing once more the dominance of the desert-savanna fringe, to last nearly to the end of the sixteenth century.

Trade and politics: the Nilotic Sudan and Ethiopia

In the Nilotic Sudan and the Red Sea region, a different geographical environment produced a different pattern of commercial strategy, but trade and politics were nevertheless linked as clearly as they were in the western Sudan. One strategic link was the desert Nile between the first cataract above Aswan and the junction of the Blue and White Niles near present-day Khartoum. Whoever held this stretch of the Nile could control trade and collect tolls, not only on trade bound for the Nilotic Sudan but also caravan traffic along the forty-day road from the third cataract southwest to Darfur.

But the Nile was not the only route to the Nilotic Sudan. Caravans could reach the upper Nile from Red Sea ports like Suakin or across a corner of the Ethiopian highlands from mainland points opposite the Dahlak Archipelago. The commercial strategy of the Nilotic Sudan was thus tied to the Red Sea as well as the Nile. The Red Sea trade was tied, in turn, to the competitive struggle between Iraq and Egypt for control over trade from the Mediterranean to India.

During the 'Abbasid downswing in Red Sea trade from about 750 to 970, the Christian society in the Ethiopian highlands turned away from the sea. Some people who spoke Semitic languages ancestral to Tigrinya and Amharic migrated south along the backbone of the mountain ranges. Christian missionaries also began to work their way south into the regions that were then Cushitic-speaking and neither Christian nor Muslim in religion, including the plateau of Showa where Addis Ababa now stands. The rise of Fatimid Egypt in the eleventh century brought a new commercial prosperity to all those who depended on Red Sea trade, and this included the Ethiopian highlands.

The coast was now lost to Islam; Ethiopians no longer had their own ships on the Indian Ocean or the Red Sea. Christian Ethiopians could, however, reach Egypt, and they continued and strengthened their contact with Coptic Christianity. In the late twelfth century, when the Frankish Christian invaders had been cleared from Palestine, Ethiopians again began to visit Jerusalem as pilgrims. The inspiration of these visits can still be seen in the monumental churches carved from solid rock at Lalibela.

About 1270, a new dynasty – the Solomonids – came to power and moved the political center southwards into Amhara. The more able monarchs of the new series, like Amada Syon (ruled 1314–54), pursued a self-conscious strategy of trade, first trying to dominate the coast (which failed), then trying to control the main north–south trade routes down the backbone of the western highlands from shore points opposite the Dahlak archipelago to the regions south and west of Showa. This route, incidentally, ran through the core of the Christian highlands, but the merchants were mainly Muslims from the coast. Their missionary work helped to create a small Muslim minority at an early date.

The strategy of conversion was linked to the strategy of trade. A competing all-Muslim route from the Gulf of Aden to Showa began at Zeila and ran along the axis of the present-day railroad from Djibouti to Addis Ababa. Its western anchor was the small sultanate of Ifat in Showa itself. The competition in trade set the stage for

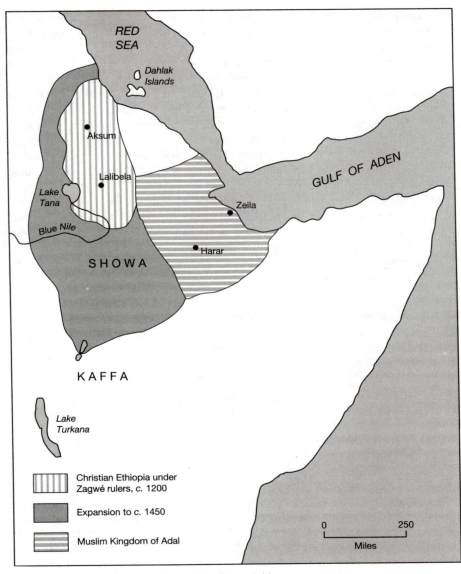

Map 3.8 Christian Ethiopia and its neighbors *c.*1200–1450

political competition which was to reach its peak in the sixteenth century, and which was then to shape the political map of Ethiopia for centuries to come.

A word of warning about the history of northern Africa through this period may be appropriate. The nature of the evidence makes unintended distortion inevitable. Political change in Egypt and the Maghrib can be traced in detail, and the trends of intellectual and social change are far clearer than for any region south of the Sahara.

Once south of the desert, the great empires of the sahel receive most attention because travelers from North Africa wrote about them, but these travelers stopped there. Further south, our knowledge is limited to shadowy outlines. The Hausa-speaking region of northern Nigeria, for example, had already begun to develop extensive towns that served as marketing and craft centers. These towns came into existence as early as 1000 to 1300 AD, apparently without much direct influence from the patterns of urbanization in North Africa. But Hausa emerged into the light of recorded history only in the fifteenth century, when Muslim influence first began to be important. In this case, Islam came indirectly from the Niger bend to the northwest, or from Borno to the northeast. By the fifteenth century, Hausa was divided into a series of walled towns, each ruling over the surrounding countryside; Katsina, Kano, Zazzau (or Zaria), and Gobir were already important.

Other centers of state-building existed still further south. On the Benue, a state had already emerged among the Jukun people, alongside the resolutely stateless Tiv. Still further south, both the Yoruba states and Benin had been founded before the fourteenth century. Their bronze sculpture demonstrates great art and technical proficiency in metallurgy, but the lack of other evidence forces us to overemphasize the savanna as against the forest.

Suggestions for further reading

Ajayi, J.F.A. and Michael Crowder, *History of West Africa*, Vol. 1, 3rd edn, London: Longman, 1985.

Oliver, Roland, and J.D. Fage, *The Cambridge History of Africa*, Vols II and III, Cambridge: Cambridge University Press, 1977.

Hasan, Yusaf Fadl, *The Arabs and the Sudan from the Seventh to the Early Sixteenth Century*, Edinburgh: Edinburgh University Press, 1967.

Hourani, Albert, *A History of the Arab Peoples*, Cambridge: Harvard University Press, 1991.

Le Tourneau, Roger, *Fez in the Age of the Merinids*, Oklahoma City: University of Oklahoma Press, 1961.

Levtzion, Nehemia, *Ancient Ghana and Mali*, London: Methuen, 1973.

Lewis, Archibald, *Nomads and Crusaders, A.D. 1000–1368*, Bloomington: Indiana University Press, 1988.

Mauny, Raymond, *Tableau géographique de l'ouest africain au moyen âge*, Dakar: IFAN, 1961.

Mohammed Hassen, *The Oromo of Ethiopia: A History 1570–1860*. Cambridge: Cambridge University Press, 1990.

Tamrat, Taddesse, *Church and State in Ethiopia, 1270–1527*. London: Oxford University Press, 1972.

Watson, Andrew M., *Agricultural Innovation in the Early Islamic World: The Diffusion of Crops and Farming Techniques, 700–1100*, Cambridge: Cambridge University Press, 1983.

4

ECONOMY, SOCIETY AND LANGUAGE IN EARLY EAST AFRICA

Many characteristic elements of East African life, including the distribution of languages, the ways people earn their livelihoods, and the forms of local social organization, took shape in a time without written documentation. Arabic documents, so important for the early history of the West African savanna and for towns on the East African coast, are almost entirely absent for the eastern interior. Historians have therefore had to turn to archaeology, linguistics, and the study of oral traditions to piece together an account of the formative centuries in East Africa.

Linguistics, archaeology, and history

Well over a hundred languages are spoken in East Africa. This presents a challenge to historians (even those born in East Africa) who wish to hear the voices of East Africans within their diverse local societies, speaking about their own histories. But it also provides scholars with a rich body of linguistic evidence about the region's history. Historians examine languages that are closely related to learn the circumstances under which ancient speech communities separated from one another. They are able to discover which words were likely to have been spoken in the distant past – words for ritual leaders or crops, for example – and thus to learn about ancient cultures. They are able also to uncover the way ancient speech communities borrowed these words from one another.

The languages of East Africa are divided among four language families. We have seen that languages belong to a single family when they resemble one another so closely that we can think of them as descended from a single ancestral language, or proto-language. Linguists examine the similarities among living languages so as to reason about what the proto-language must have been like. They understand that when speakers of an ancestral language began to live apart from one another, speech in each locality took on unique characteristics, and separate local dialects emerged. Later, the dialects became so different that they were no longer mutually intelligible; they became separate languages. These new languages, in their turn, continued the process of local differentiation. Each early language thus developed into a cluster of related languages or a branch of a language family.

Each of the language families is spread over a large part of the African continent, and, in some cases, beyond the borders of the continent itself. For this reason, when historians refer to linguistic groupings of the people of East Africa, they usually refer to subgroups of the larger language families. Dozens of Bantu languages are spoken across East Africa, from southern Uganda and southern Kenya southward. Other chapters show the importance of Bantu-speaking peoples in Equatorial and southern Africa. Yet the Bantu languages are merely a part of one subgroup within a larger grouping (Benue-Congo), itself a sub-branch within the Niger-Congo language family which includes many of the languages of West Africa. A second major group of East Africans speak Nilotic languages, one small sub-branch of the Nilo-Saharan language family. A very large majority of present-day East Africans speak either Nilotic or Bantu languages.

Historical linguists make a careful examination of relations among groups of languages to learn about the histories of the people who spoke them and who spoke the ancestral languages that preceded them. By locating the languages of a present-day language family on the map, and then constructing a history of how these separated from one another in the past, they are able to get some sense of the geographic spread of related languages at different stages in history. By studying the degree of difference among related languages, they can talk about how long it took for the separations to emerge. The more different related languages are, the longer ago they separated from one another. Historians and linguists examine also which of the branches of a language family has a word for a particular thing or practice: for cows, or sheep, or milking, for example. By placing those branches within the family's larger history, they are able to point to the period when these things were first introduced – when people first kept cattle, for example. Historians of language are also able to identify words that people in one language family or branch learned from people in another, and thus to talk about the way cultural or economic practices spread from one group to another after they were introduced.

While historical linguists study today's languages to learn things about speech in the past, archaeologists study material remains to learn about similar historical periods, but from a different angle. Just as linguists study relations among many words and many languages to imagine what life was like in a particular speech community, archaeologists study relations among many kinds of remains to construct a picture of society and culture in the past. They may find, for example, that wherever iron working is found in a particular region, a specific kind of pottery is also found, and these always occur in places where the forest has been cleared and grain crops planted. They identify a way of life through its material remains.

A community identified through its assemblage of material remains may, however, be quite different from a speech community of the kind studied by historical linguists. This should be clear to us from our experience of today's world. A car factory in Japan has a lot in common with one in the United States or France, but each one exists in a very separate speech community, where different languages are spoken. To understand how we construct a picture of early East African society we must imagine a world in which we have one body of knowledge about the material remains of car factories (or of iron-smelting and pot-making), and another body of knowledge about the development of the Japanese, English, and French languages (or Bantu and Nilotic languages), and we must then bring together the different kinds of knowledge to create a single coherent picture.

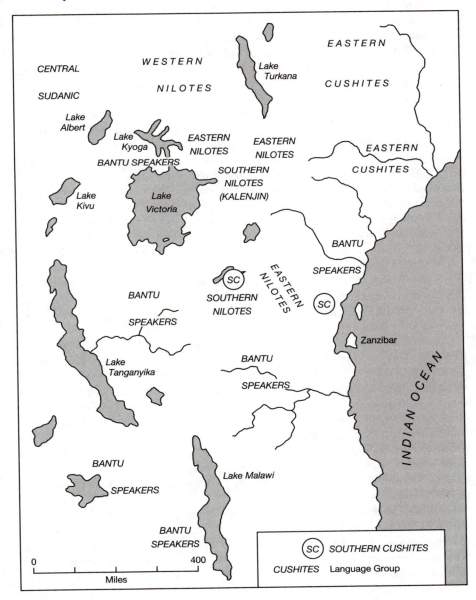

Map 4.1 Major language groups of East Africa *c.*1880 AD

Nilotes and Cushites

A large majority of East Africa's people at the start of the twentieth century spoke Bantu languages or Nilotic ones, lived by farming mixed with livestock keeping, and used iron tools made by blacksmiths who knew how to create iron from local ores. These patterns of language, livelihood, and tool-making took shape over the preceding four thousand years. The whole landscape of peoples, their economy, language, and culture, would have looked radically different in 2000 BC, a time when iron tools did not exist and when most people relied on hunting, fishing, and gathering for their livelihood.

The shift from hunting wild animals to the breeding and rearing of animals and from collecting wild plants to cultivating domesticated ones was long and complex. In each generation, and in each locality, people created new economic forms, drawing on the full range of economic possibilities that had come before. The unfolding of this history in East Africa was not marked by a succession of clear stages – hunting and gathering, then pastoralism, then farming – but rather evolved when local people created new possibilities, which they added to the wide range of practical knowledge that had come before. After farming emerged, people did not reject the earlier activities. Farmers continued to collect wild plants; some also supplemented their crops by hunting to win the meat of wild animals. In some places pastoralists (or farmers) lived side by side with hunter-gatherers, together creating a regional economy based on the interdependence of domestication and other forms of food production. Farmers and hunters came to rely on trade with one another; no group planned its economic activities in isolation.

The pattern of change in the economy was, therefore, one in which new possibilities were explored, but old ones were not always abandoned. People of each generation, in each locality, created their own syntheses, their own ways of combining economic activities, using the inherited expertise of earlier generations, creating new knowledge, and borrowing knowledge and practices from their neighbors.

Domesticated cattle were first introduced in and near the Rift Valley of what is now Kenya in about 2000 BC. The archaeological record indicates that this new form of activity – the raising of animals rather than the hunting of animals – was not the radical break then that it sometimes seems to us now. The first cattle keepers made the same sorts of stone tools that their hunting and gathering ancestors had made; their skeletons look the same, supporting the idea that the earliest cattle keepers were people with local roots. Most important, they did not simply shift from hunting to domestication. For the first thousand years of cattle rearing, and longer, the bones of domesticated animals (cattle, sheep, and goats) were found alongside the bones of wild animals. Indeed, the bones of wild animals predominated, and livestock were only gradually introduced.

Some time after 1000 BC a very different sort of economy emerged around the Rift Valley, in which livestock played a much more central role. This economy was more like the economies of pastoralists who live in the region today, people for whom hunting is marginally important, at best. One possible explanation for this pastoralist shift away from hunting is that it took place after the introduction of a new breed of cattle (the Zebu) that thrived more easily than earlier breeds in the region's conditions of heat stress, periodic drought, and periodic food shortages.

The earliest pastoralists were probably Southern Cushites, speaking languages forming a sub-branch of the Afro-Asiatic language family. Calculations about the timing of the spread of Southern Cushitic languages show that they are likely to have entered northern Kenya in about 2000 BC, the time when domesticated livestock were first introduced. The hypothesis identifying the earliest cattle keepers with the Cushites, despite the relative absence of Cushites today, is based on the survival of isolated groups of Southern Cushitic speakers in Tanzania's Rift Valley, as remnants of what must once have been a more widespread community. That Cushites must have been more numerous in the past is indicated by the survival of Southern Cushitic words in Nilotic and Bantu languages, which are more common in the region today. These words must have been learned by Nilotes or Bantu-speakers at a time when Southern Cushitic languages were spoken widely. The historical reconstruction of early vocabularies shows that the Southern Cushites grew grain crops, although the archaeologists have not yet found supporting evidence for grain agriculture among the earliest generations of livestock keepers.

The recognition of the importance of Cushites is mildly embarrassing to African historians who have spent years trying to slay the dragon of the Hamitic myth. "Hamitic myth" is the term writers have used for a racist set of historical ideas, which attributed the great achievements of Africa to light-skinned outsiders who came down from the north. In the words of C. G. Seligman, a major proponent of the idea, "the incoming Hamites were pastoral Caucasians – arriving wave after wave – better armed as well as quicker-witted than the dark agricultural Negroes."* This is maddening; it breaks a basic rule of method by mixing race (Caucasian), language ("Hamitic"), and culture (weapons, economy), and further makes the assumption that lighter skinned is quicker witted. Joseph Greenberg was among the first to point out the one-hundred per cent negative correlation between "Hamitic" languages and pastoralism in West Africa.** He succeeded in having the word "Hamitic" dropped from respectable use by discrediting the linguistic analysis on which the grouping was based.

Although the Hamitic myth has been abandoned, the importance that recent authorities give to the Cushites is so strongly reminiscent of it that the two hypotheses must be compared directly. The Cushites did indeed enter East Africa from the north (although the language might then have spread to other people long-resident in East Africa), and they *do* speak languages of the same large family as Hebrew and Arabic (Afro-Asiatic). The evidence, however, roots the Cushites firmly in African soil. Of the seven branches of the Afro-Asiatic language family, all except Semitic are found only in Africa, from Berber of the far northwest across to Ancient Egyptian in the northeast. This makes it virtually certain that the family's ancestral language was first spoken on the African continent. The importance of the Cushites points to the creative role of movement and communication among Africans; it does not support the idea that creative ideas came from outside Africa.

Within East Africa, the "Hamites" had been described as bringing the civilized arts

---

* C.G. Seligman, *Races of Africa*, rev. edn, London: Thornton Butterworth, 1939, p. 156.
** Joseph H. Greenberg, *The Languages of Africa*, Publication No. 25. Bloomington, Indiana: Indiana University Research Center in Anthropology, Folklore and Linguistics, 1963, p. 51.

to a pre-existing substratum of cultivators. In reality, the Cushites are among the early populations that were later absorbed and pushed aside, although they contributed institutions, words, ideas, and knowledge of the local environment that survived in the languages and cultures of those who supplanted them.

In about 500 BC a new group, speakers of Nilotic languages, began to move into the western part of what is now Kenya. This began a process which was to continue over the next 2000 years in which the domain of the Cushites and of the other early populations of East Africa began to contract as the Nilotes intermingled with and ultimately supplanted the more northerly of these early peoples, while Bantu-speakers occupied the south. The Nilotes spread from their homeland, between Lake Turkana in northern Kenya and the Nile River to the west and northwest. This is an arid belt which supports pastoralism and only the most marginal agriculture. Quite early, the ancestors of the Southern Nilotes began to separate from other Nilotes, and went on to occupy the highlands to the west of the Rift Valley of Kenya.

The Southern Nilotes, as identified through the history of their language, appeared in western Kenya in times and places known to archaeologists for the particular assemblage of material objects which they call Elmenteitan. The archaeological record tells us that the people who occupied these sites relied heavily on herding, and gave up the emphasis on hunting shown by earlier people in this part of Kenya. The expansion of the Nilotic languages appears to have been part of a larger process by which hunters and gatherers were assimilated or pushed aside by herders and farmers. Some of the earlier hunter-gatherers now being supplanted may have spoken Cushitic languages (while other Cushites herded and farmed), and others probably spoke Khoisan languages, of which there are few speakers left in East Africa today.

The western highlands of Kenya, where most of the Southern Nilotes settled, enjoyed much higher rainfall than the Nilotic homeland in the north, and grain agriculture became more important in their economy, along with raising cattle, sheep, and goats. The people who practiced mixed farming and herding lived alongside hunter-gatherers, the people of the high forests, some of whom came to speak Southern Nilotic languages also. The newer economic forms – grain agriculture and herding – did not supplant the older ones as stages in a succession. Each new generation created its own synthesis of inherited economic and cultural forms, and each generation added its own innovations to the inheritance for those who would come later.

One possible reason why the Southern Nilotes proved able to supplant earlier populations in the area was their reliance on the social institution of the age-set. Christopher Ehret, whose research on Southern Nilotic language history is the basis of our knowledge of the period, has shown that age-set organization was a comparatively early development. The Southern Nilotes and their early neighbors lived in scattered villages without chiefs. Age-set organization made it possible for the Kalenjin (the Kenya branch of the Southern Nilotes) to organize men on a fairly large scale, extending far beyond the single village. This was useful for defense, but also for absorbing strangers, whatever their origins, and in providing a structure for cooperation over a wide area.

As the institution has existed in more recent times, an age-set formed when a group of adolescent boys were initiated together. This set would then have its own name, some common rights and obligations, and a sense of unity. A single set was supposed to move through the different grades together. Members of the *Kimnyekeu* age-set, for example, were initiated together, immediately entering the grade of young initiates. When the appropriate time came, the whole of the set moved on to the next grade together, becoming warriors but keeping their set name, while the *Kaplelach*, the next older group, went from the grade of warriors to that of elders. When successive sets had used up each of the seven or eight age-set names (after somewhat more than a hundred years), the cycle would begin again with the first name.

Because similar sets existed among a number of neighboring Kalenjin Southern Nilotes, individuals or small groups who moved from one place to another could easily become part of local village life simply by entering the appropriate age-sets. This meant, furthermore, that aliens could be integrated more easily into Kalenjin society than they could be into a society organized on narrow lineage principles. Because members of an age-set had to treat one another as equals, the sets made attractive points of entry for strangers.

The historical reconstruction of this process of absorption is based on the existence of age-sets by the time of the early Southern Nilotic spread, perhaps in the first millennium AD, and on examples from more recent periods. Beginning in the seventeenth or eighteenth century, the Terik, a subgroup of the Kalenjin, offered asylum to neighboring Bantu-speakers on condition that they join the Terik age-sets. In the end, the Bantu were numerically superior to the Terik, but they called themselves Tiriki after their hosts.

Bantu-speakers

To the west of the Southern Nilotes, in the regions to the north and west and south of Lake Victoria, a somewhat different set of institutions and syntheses emerged between 3000 BC and 1000 AD. In this case speakers of Bantu languages, especially those of the Great Lakes branch of Bantu, came to emerge as central actors.

The ancestors of the Great Lakes Bantu-speakers lived in wet forest environments. Their economy was particularly well-suited to this kind of environment. They grew root crops, including yams, along with beans, gourds, a variety of peanut, and oil palms. They also raised goats.

Two very different kinds of evidence, explored by the historian David Schoenbrun, point to related long-term processes: one by which the environment was transformed as farming spread, and the other by which Bantu languages of the Great Lakes branch grew in importance and in the breadth of their distribution.* The first kind of evidence, from the historical study of the environment, suggests that medium and low altitude forests began to shrink at the extreme west of the East African region, in Kigezi and Central Burundi, by 3000 BC. This process, which may have been initiated by reductions in rainfall, became more intense in later millennia, when farmers and

---

* David L. Schoenbrun, "Eastern Africa's Great Lakes Region: Linguistic, Ecological, and Archaeological Approaches, *c.*500 BC to AD 1000." Ph.D. dissertation, University of California at Los Angeles, 1990.

herders worked to clear forest land. The area was particularly well-suited to the early Bantu economy based on moist-forest crops. The second kind of evidence, from the historical study of language, points to a part of this region – the area between Lakes Kivu and Edward (Rweru) – as the place from which Great Lakes Bantu languages began to spread. This was happening by 500 BC.

The spread of these languages was to unfold in a region that takes in the north-western part of Tanzania, the southern part of Uganda, the whole of Rwanda and Burundi, and the adjacent parts of Zaire. In this region, when the process of Bantu expansion was just beginning, the languages of several different language families were widely spoken. Each set of people, each group speaking related languages, occupied a separate niche within the region. We have already seen that Bantu-speakers occupied the humid forest, where their agriculture centered around root crops.

The long-term process of the spread of people who spoke Great Lakes Bantu languages was one by which they learned from the economies of their neighbors, created new agricultural and economic syntheses, and thus were able to break out of their particular niche in the low, wet, humid forests. Many diverse economies of Bantu-speakers emerged, each one suited to the environment of one part or another of this region.

As this process unfolded, Bantu-speakers spread until they occupied the greatest part of the western zone of East Africa. We do not know exactly how they did this – the moments at which the process might have involved warfare, or intermarriage, or the peaceful negotiation by which speakers of different languages came to live together in economic interdependence. We do know that speakers of Bantu languages created a number of radically new economic syntheses, each one adapted to the particular environment of one small part of the Great Lakes region. They continued to develop their own moist-forest agriculture. Where appropriate they took on cattle-keeping, so as to be able to make full use of the grasslands. In some places they adopted grain agriculture.

One possible cause of this movement towards diversification was the decline of the moist forest in which the early Bantu-speakers lived – a decline that became more serious as their numbers grew. Quite likely, also, these farmers saw that each movement towards greater economic diversity increased food security. When crops fail, people who have access to cattle as well as farm land, or to both root crops and grain crops, are more likely to survive than those dependent on a narrow economic base. If the decline of moist forest pushed people to try new crops and new techniques, the advantages of diversification pulled them at the same time. The two processes may well have unfolded together. The advantages of improved food security would have appealed to people who saw their forest base declining.

The pressure on forest land became very much greater from the first century AD, when more of the Bantu-speakers began to produce iron and to use iron implements. The iron tools contributed to the transformation of the forest because they made it easier for people to clear forest land and to plant and weed root crops. The development of iron technology increased the pressure on forest land for a second reason: because workers cleared large areas of wooded land to make the charcoal needed for iron production.

The introduction of iron technology did not mean that people necessarily gave up their earlier tools; it meant that they worked out new combinations of tools. For some jobs digging sticks were superior to iron, and for others stone tools were preferred. Iron, once introduced, did not replace everything that had come before; instead, it added an important new set of tools to the ones that already existed.

The smelting of iron was a technical process of great complexity. The master-smelters had to consider the heat-resisting qualities of the materials they used to build furnaces, for these operated at very high temperatures. In addition, the smelter needed to master a process by which the oxygen in iron ore would be removed chemically. African technologists of iron created their own methods; their innovations followed a unique course, one of great complexity, and one different from the course of techno-logical evolution in Europe.

The iron-smelting and -forging technologies, and the complex farming strategies of the same period, were embedded in rituals and in religious conceptions about which we know too little at this moment. Smelters in the region in more recent times have shaped their rituals so as to respond to what they see as the female fertility of the furnace that gives birth to a child of iron. In addition, the sophisticated chemical and physical process could succeed, as they saw it, only if the god controlling earth and iron were honored.

By 1000 AD the Bantu-speakers, using iron, had changed the landscape of this region of East Africa. They had transformed large areas of virgin forest, making them into the kind of forest in which human intervention is visible. They had created many new economic syntheses, adapted to the region's varying environments. Some took advantage of the combination of grassland and forest to combine farming and herding; some created new combinations of root crops, or of root and grain crops. By the beginning of the present millennium, the people of the Great Lakes zone had begun to adopt new varieties of bananas and other crops originating in Southeast Asia. These too opened new possibilities for forest agriculture. The ecological evidence shows that by 1000 AD some of the lakes region's people were living in very dense populations, and managing their land intensively, in much the way that land has been managed in more recent times.

The spread of Bantu-speaking peoples, and the creation of new, diversified econ-omic forms, took place also beyond the Great Lakes area, in many parts of East Africa. Bantu speakers appear to have concentrated especially in those wooded areas where rainfall was high, and where a yam-based agriculture was possible. This was the case in the mountain areas of central Kenya and of northeastern Tanzania. It was the case also in the highlands of southern Tanzania.

As in the lakes region, however, the Bantu speakers continued to adapt and improve their economies. In the highland areas the new patterns made use of crops from southeast Asia introduced by late in the first millennium AD – Asian yams, taro, and new varieties of banana. These were well-suited to the moist forest environment. In the mountains of northeastern Tanzania a complex agricultural system emerged combin-ing the newly introduced bananas, widespread irrigation, and manuring.

In the same period, Bantu-speakers created new economic forms as they moved into new environments in the drier parts of western and of east-central Tanzania. Bantu-speakers in the wet regions relied heavily on vegetative reproduction in which they did not plant seeds, but rather parts of the plant itself – parts of the edible root in yams, for example, or a single stem taken with its roots from a cluster of banana plants. In the drier regions, grain crops grown from seed became much more important, as did cattle-rearing. The process by which the speakers of Bantu languages spread to occupy much of East Africa was related to their capacity to adapt to new environments, and to borrow and make use of the technological and agricultural heritages of all their neighbors.

Traditions of movement and the environment

The cultures of Bantu-speaking peoples in East Africa were closely related to one another at first, and then diverged. Each small area developed its particular local culture. This happened in the early centuries of the second millennium AD. The change can be seen archaeologically in the emergence of numerous local pottery styles in place of the broadly similar styles of earlier centuries.

For this new period, oral traditions become considerably more relevant. They are a rich source of knowledge on the past thousand years, although in rare cases they shed light on historical processes as early as 500 BC. Oral traditions often describe the movements of groups or individuals from one place to another, the creation of cultural and social forms, and the way relations unfolded among social groups. For historians, the availability of oral traditions changes the whole style of description. It becomes possible, in a richer way, to place other kinds of knowledge – archaeological and linguistic – within the context of local ideas. When we try to imagine what life must have been like in past centuries we have the help of local historians who have expressed their ideas about the relationship between past and present, the way in which societies came to be what they are.

Two sorts of traditions of movement are important for the processes discussed here. First, many small lineage and clan groups recount where their ancestors came from, why they moved, and under what circumstances. Second, people who today identify themselves as members of a single ethnic group speak about the historical sources of their common identity. Each kind of tradition has its own historical uses. The traditions of a small lineage tell only about that group, and sometimes only about local events or details of land ownership. But tens of traditions, or hundreds, can be fitted together to form general patterns of history – as they do when we learn that many lineage groups moved after a particular nineteenth-century famine or war, or that people who moved tended to seek out particular environmental settings for their new homes.

The traditions of the highland peoples who live on either side of the eastern Kenya–Tanzania border, for example, tell of the movements of many small groups from one highland region to another, passing across lowlands, even for some distance. Each lineage or clan tells of its own movement, unconscious of the larger pattern which informs us of the way particular sets of people adapted their cultures to the highland environment.

The scattered masses of mountains are wetter than the lowlands, because the moisture-laden air blown in by the Indian Ocean winds passes over the lowlands, rises in the mountains, cools, then deposits rainfall. The technological knowledge and agricultural skills of highland peoples came to be adapted specifically to the highlands. Parents taught their children the properties of plants, how to use wild vegetation as indicators of when and where to plant, and how to identify and use different soil types. Learned medicine men of the highland zone today know the names and characteristics of thousands of highland plants. They know the taste of the leaves, roots, and bark of most plants, and which berries and leaves are eaten by birds or animals, which are not. Local plants were often the central symbols of complex rituals, so that a religious event strengthened an individual's sense of belonging in that particular part of the environment. When people were forced to move, therefore, they sought out other places where they could apply their knowledge, avoiding the lowlands.

Although in some rare cases highland peoples moved to the lowlands, this sort of move was more difficult, involving the development of new skills. The Kamba from the area southeast of Mount Kenya, for example, expanded from their highland home to the neighboring dry lowlands. As they did so they were forced to become less reliant on agriculture and more so on cattle herding and hunting.

Special adaptation to a particular environment could take biological as well as cultural forms. Epidemiologists now recognize that over the long run of history humans and the diseases that prey on them work out a kind of mutual adaptation. Even in comparatively short periods some special adaptations have been important in African history. Through most of tropical Africa, for example, people tend to have an inherited blood characteristic called sickle-cell trait from the shape of certain cells under the microscope. Some who have the sickle-cell trait die of anemia before they reach the age of reproduction. Over a long time, the trait therefore tends to disappear from the population. But the sickle-cell trait has another characteristic; it provides protection from falciparum malaria, the characteristic African form especially dangerous to infants and to people who first encounter the disease as adults. Where falciparum malaria is unimportant, the higher death rate for people with the sickle cell trait leads to a long-term decline in its frequency in a population. Where falciparum malaria is a threat, people with the sickle cell trait are more likely to survive than those without it, and their numbers increase to a high level.

In East Africa, to a greater extent than in any other part of the continent, the local populations developed optimum incidence of the sickle-cell trait so that, until recently, in many places tested the frequency of the trait varied in direct relation to the danger of malaria. In the non-malarial highlands of Mount Kenya or Kilimanjaro, populations had almost no sickle-cell trait, whereas those who lived along the infested southern shores of Lake Victoria had extremely high levels, and intermediate intensities of malaria were matched by intermediate frequencies of the trait. This distribution meant that migration from the non-malarial highlands to the wet lowlands would inevitably increase the death rate. Because it takes about seven hundred years for the slow attrition of excess deaths to bring sickle-cell frequencies to optimum levels, it also means that the people of East Africa must have been relatively stable in their choice of environments.

The traditions preserved by large groups – often all of the people who speak a single

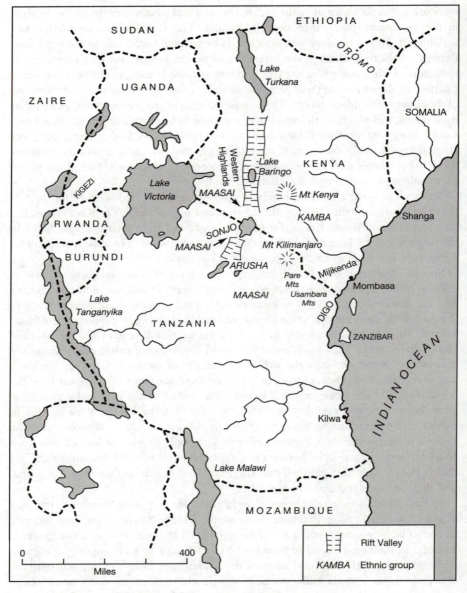

Map 4.2 East Africa with modern national boundaries

language – contain a very different set of characteristics from those preserved by clans and lineages, although the two sets of traditions usually exist side by side. Local historians usually tell both at one time or another – the stories of their particular lineage groups and of the larger language group with which they identify. Indeed, the large group traditions are instrumental in creating a sense of ethnic identity. The traditions of the larger groups often explain a group's cultural unity; they show which institutions are thought to be central, which local groups are closely related to one another and which are thought to be strangers or enemies. They are usually rich in literary value and symbolic content, and for this reason can be called myths. The power of a myth in shaping perceptions sweeps people along in agreement, so that alternative visions of history become hard to find. The myth seems all-encompassing. Where small-group traditions are usually poor in content and rich in variety, large-group traditions are rich in content but lack variants for critical analysis. Oral historians reconstruct the past by comparing divergent accounts; the more powerful the myth, the more restricted the divergence.

Maasai traditions and history

The pastoral Maasai of the Rift Valley have shaped their oral traditions to accord with the perception of themselves as the only pure pastoralists. They explain how they came to be different from the surrounding peoples who lower themselves by digging the soil or by subsisting on meat from the hunt. For example, a Maasai story about the hunting people they call the Dorobo begins when a Maasai elder came upon the first Dorobo. The Maasai, as yet unseen, overhears God telling the Dorobo to come the next day to receive God's gift. The next morning the Maasai goes to see what God will give, but the Dorobo does not appear. According to one recorded version of the tradition,

> God then let down a bark-rope . . . from the sky and began to let cattle down, until there were so many that they intermingled with those of the Dorobo. Then the Dorobo came, and when he could no longer recognize his cattle among those of the Maasai, he was angry and shot away the bark-rope with an arrow. . . God caused the cattle to stop descending and he moved up into the sky, and was never seen on the ground again. Thus all the cattle which Maasai now own were first given to them by God, and it is because the Dorobo lost his cattle by not listening to God that he must hunt wild animals for his food.

According to the myth the division between hunters and cattle keepers originates in the relationship between humans and God. Maasai claim a God-given right to all cattle and therefore speak of themselves as the "people of cattle," and of their leaders as "leaders of the cattle" rather than leaders of people.

In another Maasai myth the first man, at the beginning of time, divided his goods among his three sons. The ancestor of the Maasai chose his father's herding stick; the ancestor of hunting-peoples chose the bow; and the ancestor of all farmers took his father's hoe. In either myth, the listener is told that economic specialization began in the time of origins and is therefore permanent and unchanging.

Maasai strongly preferred to subsist entirely on the products of cattle, but this was very difficult. A household needed a very large herd if they were to live off the milk, meat, and blood of cattle, without other sources of nutrition. People had difficulty doing this when disease reduced the size of herds, or when drought reduced milk production. In these times Maasai sometimes purchased agricultural products from their neighbors. Maasai women were the main traders. In the nineteenth century they traveled to the territory of neighboring Bantu-speaking farmers to exchange animal products for the fruits of the soil. Trade with small groups of hunter-gatherers was also important.

Difficult times revealed divisions between rich and poor Maasai. Wealthy households had herds large enough to survive periodic setbacks while sustaining a pastoral way of life. Poor households were forced, at times, to take up farming or hunting, hoping for the day when they could return to cattle-rearing. When seen in the light of these divisions, the myth of permanent Maasai pastoralism can be seen as a selective and partial representation of experience, one that reinforced the prestige of those Maasai wealthy enough to remain pastoralists in times of distress.

A study of one village, Pagasi, shows the interplay between the experience of everyday life and the values of the myth. The village, as described in the 1960s, was located on the lower part of the escarpment separating Sonjo (agricultural Bantu-speakers) at the top from Maasai in the plains at the bottom. The people of the village all spoke Maasai but subsisted on farming. They were unable to raise cattle because of the tsetse flies which carry cattle disease, but some village members owned cattle, which were kept by Maasai relatives in the plains. Of the men in the village, about half were born Sonjo, half Maasai; they learned the language, joined Maasai clans, and had brothers, sisters, sons, and daughters living as Maasai in the plains. The village was thus a school for Sonjo who wished to become Maasai. When Maasailand was experiencing good times, young women from farming communities like Sonjo joined the Maasai as wives and young men came as herders. In this process of becoming Maasai, Pagasi served as a half-way house. In bad times Maasai went to their farming in-laws and friends for food and safety. The process by which Sonjo and Maasai learned one another's cultures was not new in the 1960s. The village existed in the same form and with the same effect in the nineteenth century.

The Pagasi pattern was one in which language change preceded full economic change, in which a Sonjo who wished to become a pastoralist needed first to become a Maasai. The linking of ethnic identity and economic activity was reflected in the myth on the origin of economic divisions. The myth, as a statement of fundamental values, was one of the ways each new generation learned about the importance of the divisions, which they then recreated by bringing their economic practice into line with their ethnic identity.

The Pagasi pattern was not the only way of reconciling contradictions between pastoral ideals and agricultural practice. The Arusha and the people of Nkuruman were farmers who spoke the language of the Maasai, and who continued to treasure pastoral ideals, but who practiced irrigation agriculture in well-watered oases in or near Maasailand. They were Maasai in language and in cultural ideals, but they practiced irrigation agriculture. They, together with pastoral Maasai, with hunter-gatherers and Bantu-speaking farmers, joined in creating a varied and interdependent regional economy. Within this region each set of economic practices, each language, and each myth (like the myth of the origin of pastoralism) was a contribution to a rich stock of inherited culture on which all peoples in the region could ultimately draw in creating new syntheses.

For historians, each myth is also a historical text which can be interpreted by comparing it with other oral traditions, in the light of evidence from archaeology and historical linguistics. Historians of the pastoral Maasai begin by studying the history of each separate Maasai clan-cluster. These are the largest political units in Maasailand. At any one time there have been twenty or more of them. Each clan-cluster has its separate oral traditions, as do the lineages of the religio-political prophets who provide leadership within many of the clan-clusters. By comparing many detailed local traditions, historians have been able to see that a few dominant clan-clusters were taking control of large parts of the Rift Valley in the nineteenth century. That is the time when the Maasai political system, as it is known, took shape. The dominant political units took control of grazing land and watering places, leaving defeated groups to scatter, to be absorbed by their conquerors, or to move off to terrain where pure pastoralism was more difficult to sustain. In light of these events, the myth of original Maasai pastoralism can be seen as making a political statement. It glorifies the dominant clan-clusters that took over the Rift Valley in order to sustain a pastoral way of life.

The movement by Maasai-related peoples into the region had taken shape a thousand years earlier. Historical linguists tell us that by about the eighth century speakers of Maa-Ongamo languages (the group that now includes Maasai) were moving into the area near Laikipya and Lake Baringo. They then spread southwards in the Rift Valley, occupying land where Southern Nilotes and Southern Cushites lived up until that time. These earlier peoples left their mark on Maasai language, and a few groups of Southern Nilotic or Southern Cushitic hunter-gatherers continued to live in separate settlements amongst the Maasai.

The linguistic and archaeological evidence points to the probability that the ancestors of the Maasai, in the Rift Valley, practiced some agriculture along with their herding. Pure pastoralism emerged late in this process, perhaps as late as 1800. Historians are not certain why people of the Rift Valley narrowed their economies to exclude agriculture. Perhaps political changes among clan-clusters played a role; perhaps the key was a shift towards drier weather, so that agriculture became more difficult to sustain. The progression from mixed herding and farming to "pure" pastoralism shows, once again, that it would be incorrect to treat pastoralism as an earlier stage which was then superseded by farming. Cattle-rearing is always part of a complex set of interrelated economic activities. Pastoralism in its "pure" form always existed as part of a larger economic system in which hunting, collecting, fishing, and farming were practiced by neighboring peoples. Even if the Maasai did not hunt or till the soil themselves, they relied on exchange and interaction with people who practiced these other economic activities.

The Luo

Over a huge area of East Africa people who speak Luo languages tell traditions that describe the movements of their ancestors. Luo-speakers are centered in Uganda, but live also in the Sudan, Kenya, Zaire, Tanzania, and Ethiopia. The oral traditions are enormously diverse, and yet they seem to fit together. Some of the traditions describe movements within sub-regions of the large Luo area. Others speak of ultimate origins.

Many of the traditions point to movements from north to south, and some speak of Luo origins in the southern Sudan.

Within the large Luo-speaking area, people in each locality build on a rich shared heritage of ritual, culture, and language. In many places, for example, people use the word *jok*, or some closely related word, to refer to "spirit." Among the Shilluk of the Sudan, for example, *jok mal* is the creator God. Among the Alur of Uganda, each small chiefdom comes into relation with its own special chiefdom jok. Alur chiefs might have many wives, but jok possesses only one wife of the chief. She is expected to serve jok through her husband's reign. In Acholiland, in Uganda, the jok priestess is entirely separate from the chiefship. In recent times, at the annual Acholi feast of jok each clan head would report on the state of affairs in his area: the sicknesses that people suffered, and the distress or prosperity of the farmers in his area. It was the priestess who then decided on the causes of misfortune, and on the measures to be taken to cure it. In the same area "the hut of jok" is the shrine at which people honor their ancestors. Witchcraft and divination also involve entering a relationship with particular forms of jok. The cluster of meanings might seem unusual to Americans or to Western Europeans, to whom the conception is an alien one, but within Luo-speaking areas the cluster of meanings would seem familiar. People in each locality develop their own set of usages, but within an accepted range, so that shared cultural forms, while diverse and varied, have a kind of coherence and translatability from one local culture to another. The same sort of clustering and variation would be characteristic of other Luo terms – of *reth* or *ruoth*, for example, the term that refers to authority within a lineage, and to kingship, among many meanings.

Shared language and meaning are a consequence of shared historical experience over the very long term. Oral historians within Luo societies reflect on elements in that shared experience. Academic historians have also been concerned with this process, ever since the pioneering work of B.A. Ogot.* Many of the local Luo traditions interpret the sense that neighbors share related culture by saying that in the past we were one people with our neighbors, and now we have become two. They do this by telling of how small groups of people separated from others with whom they once lived together.

Among the things that many Luo-speaking societies share is a set of stories told in different ways in different places, each of them about a spear and a bead. These are symbols that oral historians use to talk about events in which people who once shared a common identity came to be separate from one another. One version of the story, told in Alurland, begins with two brothers who lived together – Nyipiir and Nyabongo. One day Nyipiir was tending his field near the Nile, to the north of Pubungu, when an elephant broke into the field. Nyipiir grabbed the nearest spear, which happened to belong to his brother, and hurled it at the elephant. The animal ran off wounded, with the spear hanging from its side. Nyipiir offered to pay his brother for the lost spear, but Nyabongo insisted on having it back. Nyipiir therefore set off through the wilderness to hunt for the spear. He finally found it at the legendary home of the elephants together with some beautiful beads that became the royal beads.

* Bethwell A. Ogot, *A History of the Southern Luo*, Nairobi: East African Publishing House, 1967.

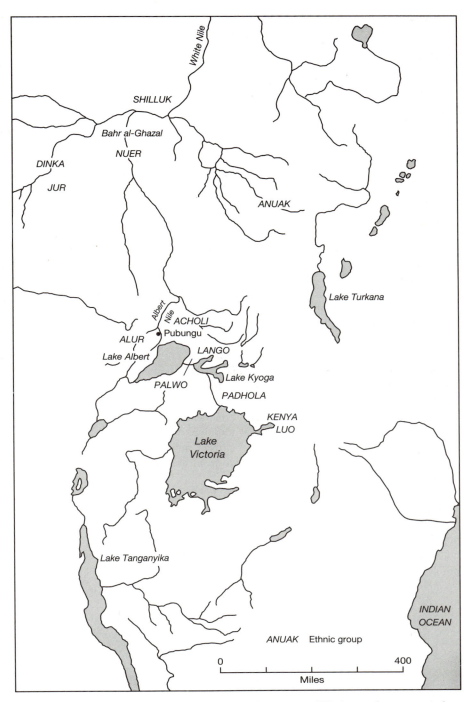

Map 4.3 Luo-speaking peoples and other western Nilotic-speakers: twentieth-century locations

After Nyipiir returned, a second episode tells how Nyabongo's baby swallowed one of the royal beads from the land of the elephants. Nyipiir first demanded his bead back, then cut open the baby's stomach to get it. Nyabongo, his baby dead, left with all his dependents, and the other Luo families also left, driven on by the impact of the tragedy. Some traveled east of the Nile, some west. They sank an axe in the Nile as a symbol of this separation. The axe remains today at a sacrificial shrine, looked after by the headman of Pubungu, whose lineage remained behind to serve as guardians.

The story of the spear and the bead is not, of course, an account of actual historical events, for it is told over a vast area and in each place it is given as the reason for groups separating. Nevertheless, each particular version may preserve locally specific information about the past – about the names of particular individuals and the direction in which small family groups moved. At the same time, it is a way of conveying wisdom about humanity and society. The story explores relations between brothers, and what happens when extreme, unreasonable demands are made in the name of kinship.

The spear and bead stories, and other traditions of separation and movement, fall into three sets: a northern, a central, and a southern one. The first tells about the way northern Luo (Anuak, Jur, and Shilluk) separated from one another in a cradleland of Luo origins. The second and third are enormously diverse sets of traditions, told mainly in Uganda, in which people in hundreds of local groups try to explain how they came to be separate from other Luo groups with whom they were once unified. Central and southern Luo do not have detailed or circumstantial accounts of their origins in the Sudan, but their overall trend of movement is from north to south.

The oral traditions are reflections of a very long process by which Luo-speaking peoples came to occupy the large area that is their home. According to historical linguists, ancestral Luo came to be separate from closely related languages by about 1000 AD. This separation happened to the south and east of the place where the Bahr-al-Ghazal river runs into the Nile. What is remarkable about this process is that this is very close to the place identified in oral traditions as the Luo cradleland. In later periods, probably in the first half of the current millennium, the languages of the central and southern Luo began to separate from the northern languages and then from one another.

The population movements which led to the current distributions of northern, central, and southern Luo languages, and which continued over many centuries, were not massive migrations in which thousands of Luo marched southwards. Instead, large population patterns emerged from thousands of decisions by lineage leaders and household elders who wished to move in search of better lives. These decisions unfolded in the normal course of events. Among many of the Luo who kept cattle, for example, it was often necessary for one group to move off from a collective cattle camp, to settle somewhere new in search of fresh pasture or more adequate water sources. In other cases family quarrels led to separation. Over a very long period Luo speakers came to occupy an area which extended nine hundred miles from north to south.

The Luo who entered this large area came to interact with, to live alongside, to learn from and to teach, people who spoke many different languages. These other peoples had created their own economic, cultural, and political syntheses before the Luo arrival. The Luo languages were Western Nilotic ones. The central and southern Luo ultimately lived alongside Eastern Nilotes in some areas (of the group that included Maasai), Central Sudanic speakers in others, and Bantu-speakers in still others.

Luo patterns of interaction were substantially different from those characteristic in many other parts of East Africa. We have seen that the Maasai abhorred any change in their ecology, or in the way they won their livelihood. Highland Bantu clung to a familiar environment. The Luo peoples, by contrast, lived across a wide range of territories with considerable variation in topography and rainfall. They adapted to many different environmental settings, and adopted many different forms of economic activity. Most Luo-speakers of central and northern Uganda practice a varied economy, including cattle keeping, fishing, and seed agriculture based on millet. But the Alur, the Padhola of southeastern Uganda, and the Kenya Luo all occupied some areas of higher land where they relied less on seed agriculture or fishing than other Luo, less also (except for the Alur) on cattle keeping, and more on growing bananas and root crops.

In some areas, such as the lands of the Luo-speaking Acholi and Lango of northern Uganda, the environment lacked such dramatic contrasts as the high margins and low bottom of the Rift Valley, where the Maasai lived. It was difficult, therefore, for Luo-speakers and their neighbors to create sharp boundaries of economic practice, and therefore unlikely that they would use economic activities as a way of defining ethnic identity.

Wherever the Luo-speakers went they lived alongside, and came to interact intimately with, people who spoke other languages and practiced other cultural forms. We must therefore picture each place where Luo lived as a frontier zone in which diverse peoples were meeting and creating a new society. The Luo-speakers of Uganda, Kenya, and Zaire, were not practicing a pure variant of an ancestral Luo culture: they were building new cultures, creating new syntheses, based on many elements including the Luo language. Aidan Southall, the most important scholar to study Alur society, argues that when people refer to their ethnic identity as Alur they are not saying that they are Luo; they are referring to a new synthesis of diverse peoples, of whom ancestral Luo were only one element.

The Luo element in each of these syntheses was itself the product of many previous interactions. The concept of jok, for example, as it existed in Padhola, in southeastern Uganda, was the product of a long history in northern Uganda – in Acholiland and other Luo-speaking areas. In these places people did not simply transmit unchanging jok rituals in a passive way from one generation to the next. They shaped their understanding of jok and gave it new meanings in the process of passing it on. The Luo culture inherited by the Padhola was not the culture of the Luo cradleland in the Sudan; it was a product of all Luo history. The Padhola themselves added to that history of change, for example by borrowing the Bura shrines of their Bantu-speaking neighbors.

In each place some of the elements of everyday culture among Luo speakers came from earlier generations of Luo; some came from non-Luo neighbors; some were created by the diverse set of people who came to live together in a single location. People found ways to create new cultures drawing on diverse sources. For example, if we examine the material objects in everyday use among the Luo-speaking Padhola early in this century, we see that they were part of a larger regional system of the creation and transmission of culture. Some of their stools resembled those of particular Bantu-speaking neighboring peoples, and also those of Luo-speaking Acholi and Lango. Their head ornaments, which they used when dancing, were the horns, hippo-tusks, and feather ornaments used by some of their Bantu-speaking neighbors. But their bracelets were blue beads, of a kind used by Luo and not by Bantu-speakers.

In each place where Luo languages were introduced people created new identities, drawing on all the diverse cultures of that place. It is for this reason that historians of the process speak of the creation of Luo encampments as a "rehearsal" for twentieth century identity formation on a wider scale.

In many places Luo appear to have had an influence out of proportion to their numbers. In Alurland and Acholiland, for example, the great majority of people speak Luo languages today in areas where, according to oral traditions, only a minority of immigrants were Luo-speakers. This happened in situations where Luo emerged as a separate stratum of chiefs. In Alurland, for example, the Nyalwo emerged as an aristocratic stratum, governing populations which included Central Sudanic Okebo, Lendu, and Madi. Some historians have suggested that where Luo were prestigious and powerful, other people learned their language, but it is difficult to see how power and prestige alone lead people living in their own villages to learn a new language and switch over to it.

A more specific possibility is that Luo men, as polygynous cattle owners and as wealthy chiefs, were able to take many non-Luo wives, whereas non-Luo were less likely to marry Luo women. This would have led to language shift, however, only if the women had chosen to teach their children the language and culture of their fathers. This would have happened only under very special conditions – at times when there was a great disparity of power between husband and wife. This was not the case at most times in these parts of Uganda, where women played a central role in transmitting culture, and in some cases had considerable authority of their own.

The time when Luo chiefs and husbands had the greatest power over non-Luo wives in Alurland was in the most recent period before conquest – in the late nine-teenth century, after oceanic slave trading came to this part of East Africa (see Chapter 19). Once the slave trade came, Luo chiefs were able to take as wives captives who might otherwise have been sold, or who were looking for safety in very insecure times. These wives would have had little choice if their husbands wished for children to be raised speaking Luo, and the wives would in any event have wanted their children to be members of the dominant class. According to this scenario, the time when Luo speakers first entered the region was not the time of greatest language spread, which came much later under slave trading conditions that were completely new to the region.

The coast

At first glance the history of the East African coast seems very different from that of the interior. While men and women of the interior traveled short distances overland to trade, coastal traders traveled hundreds of miles across the ocean. While men and women in the interior passed on their knowledge to the next generation by means of oral tradition, some coastal people were transmitting knowledge in written form from early times. While people of the interior practiced local religions, some coast dwellers had begun to practice Islam by the start of the second millennium AD. While people of the interior built with wood and grass and earth, some coastal people began to use stone in their buildings before 1000 AD.

Careful study by a generation of historians has shown that despite these differences, coastal society grew up out of local African roots, with a deep history in the African interior. Swahili, the most commonly spoken language of the coast, is a Bantu language with roots in the lakes region and beyond, across the heart of the continent to the western side of Equatorial Africa. A rich world of oral tradition, still alive, tells us about coastal history. In addition, when we look behind the written chronicles of the coast we find that many are based originally on oral tradition much as medieval European chronicles would have been. The agriculture, the domestic pottery, and many of the house-building styles of the coast are rooted in the wider cultures of Bantu-speaking East Africa.

Swahili is one language within a subgroup of Bantu languages that are spoken today in a wide zone extending from the interior of Kenya and Tanzania to the coast. The ancestors of this subgroup (the northeast coast Bantu) were probably centered in an area running down from the high mountains of Usambara and Pare to the coast. Their farming patterns, knowledge of nature, and ideas about leadership all drew on the broad heritage of the Bantu-speaking world. Each particular community of Bantu-speakers created its own local synthesis, while drawing on the common heritage. First a small group of coastal languages broke off from the regional grouping, and then Swahili differentiated itself from those others. The emergence of Swahili probably began to take place during the middle centuries of the first millennium AD.

The grammar of Swahili and its system of sounds show clear signs of its origin among the Bantu languages. Later in the life of Swahili its speakers adopted words drawn from the speech of people with whom they came into contact. At various times, especially after 1500 AD, Swahili speakers added many Arabic words to their language. In more recent times Swahili has added English words like *redio* (radio), *kondakta* (conductor), *edita* (editor), and *chifu* (chief).

The archaeological record, like the linguistic one, points to the presence of iron-using farmers in the region behind the coast from early in the first millennium AD. Early Iron Age remains have been found at Kwale, near Mombasa, dating to the second or third century AD. Related pottery has been found as far south as southern Mozambique.

At first the region's Bantu speakers lived across a broad strip of the mainland, and not on the coastal strip where many of the Swahili towns were later to emerge. Historians and archaeologists try to understand the process by which people moved from the hinterland to the coast, changed from building in mud and timber to building in stone, and left scattered villages or homesteads to live in towns. This process began in about the eighth century AD.

All the evidence points to a gradual process by which Swahili speakers moved coastwards, began building houses of mud on a framework of wood, and then gradually

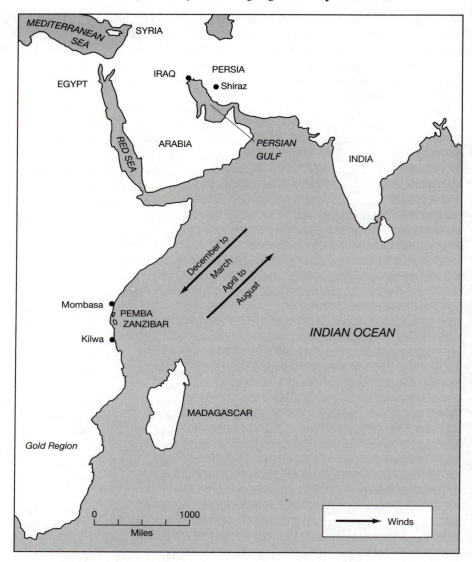

Map 4.4 The Indian Ocean

shifted to stone. At Shanga for example (one of the early towns on the Kenya coast), the earliest layer of building, from about the ninth century, was done in mud. Then came a period in the twelfth and thirteenth centuries when people used blocks of coral – a locally available building material – held together with mud mortar. Finally in the latest period, beginning in about 1250, they used coral with lime mortar. Even after the introduction of coral and lime as building materials, the towns of the Swahili coast held large areas of housing made of wood and mud. The fact that stone ruins survive over time, while wood and mud ones disappear, has led historians to put too great an emphasis on the stone towns and to ignore houses that would have resembled the ones in the interior.

When the ancestors of the Swahili moved to the coast they began to do what other Bantu-speakers were doing across East Africa: creating a new culture to adapt to a unique environment. We have already seen that at about the end of the first millennium AD Bantu-speaking societies in many parts of the region were developing specialized skills to deal with local environments. They were becoming more different from one another by learning how to make the best use of their local landscapes. Bantu-speakers of the highlands, for example, were learning the plants and weather patterns and soils of the highlands, and basing their rituals and songs on this local knowledge. In just this way the Swahili were creating a new set of local adaptations, but theirs were geared to the coast and its islands.

The ancestors of the Swahili had mastered the technologies characteristic of Bantu speakers in many parts of East Africa. They knew how to make iron implements; they cultivated sorghum and other grain plants as well as yams; they grew beans and peas. They raised dogs and cats, goats and chickens, sheep and cattle. They made canoes, caught fish using lines and nets and baskets, and their tools included hoes, machetes, knives, axes, mortars, and pestles.

The movement to the coast and islands called for a new set of skills. One of the most important was the construction of wells, since the water on most islands was salty, and communities depended on scarce fresh water for survival. People in the coastal communities learned how to make shell beads for trade with the interior, to build boats adequate for the ocean, and to catch the fish and turtles and mammals of the sea. They also learned to work with coral, which was one of the most abundant local building materials. Increasing specialization implies increasing exchange. The people of the coastal towns often relied on the hinterland peoples to supply agricultural products grown on the more abundant soils of inland areas, and also to supply cattle products.

The Swahili were the creators of a new synthesis, one that drew on the cultures of their region and combined them in a unique way. In this they were very much like the Luo speakers of the interior. The Alur, for example, relied on multiple sources for their synthesis: they drew on the Luo language to talk about jok as "spirit," but drew also on the skills of non-Luo highlanders who had mastered the art of raising bananas and root crops. The Swahili similarly drew on the knowledge of all the participants in their cultural region, but this region was significantly different from the cultural regions of inland communities.

The region of the Swahili, the zone within which they communicated with others, had a dual character. First, each town kept in touch with the people of the nearby hinterland. On the northern coast, in what is now Somalia and northern Kenya, Swahili traded with Cushitic-speaking herders and formed political links with them. Further south, Swahili interacted continuously with the Bantu-speaking farmers of the hinterland. All of these hinterland contacts, north and south, were characterized by difficult communications. In most places direct contacts extended only tens of miles into the interior. In contrast with the hinterland zone of communication, the second zone was a maritime one, its boundaries extending many hundreds of miles. Traders moved regularly and rapidly among the coastal towns and also to distant ports of the Indian Ocean. The Swahili towns assumed a dual identity: their overland ties developed through the slow movement of populations and the arduous transfer of trade goods over short distances; their maritime links spanned thousands of miles.

The great contrast between sea and land travel lasted into the era of caravan trade between the coast and the interior in the nineteenth century. The accounts of European explorers document the difference. In 1848 and 1850 Johann Krapf, the missionary explorer, traveled first on land, then in a small coasting boat, and then in a ship sailing overseas. He made about six miles a day on land, twenty-five miles a day along the coast, stopping at small ports along the way, and over one hundred miles a day on the long-distance voyage. Krapf found it easier to travel 1600 miles to Arabia than to visit his neighbors in the not very distant coastal hinterland.

The small boats that moved up and down the coast, carrying goods between East African ports, also moved people who carried with them language, ideas, and technologies. It is because of the ease of coastal transport that a single language – Swahili – came to extend 1000 miles from north to south along the coast. It is because of the ease of transport that pottery and building styles quickly moved long distances, so that distant Swahili towns came to resemble one another. The coasting boats of the Swahili towns served local trade among East Africans, and they also helped traders to collect large quantities of goods in a few trading towns to await the arrival of overseas traders, who then carried them to Arabia, the Persian Gulf, or other regions.

The intercontinental trade was ancient, older than the Swahili towns themselves, and very much older than the trade down West Africa's Atlantic coast. It was under way early in the first millennium AD. Long distance sailing was made possible by the regular alternation of prevailing northeasterlies and the southwest monsoon. Northeasterlies blow from November to March, carrying ships south from India, Arabia, and the Persian Gulf. In April, the wind starts blowing from the southwest for the journey northwards.

Seen from the viewpoint of the Bantu-speaking Swahili of the coast, ocean travel and land travel brought many different sets of strangers from whom to learn skills for survival and for the enrichment of life. The Swahili towns could draw for enrichment on the people of their hinterlands – outsiders to Swahili culture, yet neighbors. Each region of the coast adopted cultural terminologies from nearby hinterland peoples: words for agricultural techniques and innovations, words also for forms of religious expression. In each region a separate dialect of Swahili developed, drawing on the cultural terminology and the style of a different set of hinterland peoples. In addition, people from ports all around the Indian Ocean contributed to the Swahili synthesis. The Arab contribution to Swahili has long been known, but ocean travel opened Swahili to contributions from all directions. For example Madagascar, to the south, was a major contributor to the culture of the East African coast.

Madagascar brought into the Swahili synthesis contributions from distant overseas regions. That large island, to the south and east of the Swahili coast, was settled by people from Indonesia about 2000 years ago. At about the same time, or soon afterwards, a number of Asian crops were introduced into East Africa and became important in a wide range of Bantu societies, including Swahili ones. Sugar cane, coconuts,

Asian rice, and new varieties of root plants and bananas all came from Asia to Africa. By the time the Swahili towns were developing, between the ninth and twelfth centuries, trade goods from the north were reaching Madagascar. This island was clearly part of the wider Swahili world.

The Islamic contribution to the Swahili synthesis is much more widely known. Ocean travel between East Africa and the Muslim world – especially Arabia and the Persian Gulf – brought Africans into regular contact with overseas Muslims. The earliest small timber mosques were built at Shanga on the Kenya coast by the ninth century AD. Islam then expanded broadly on the coast in the twelfth century. The Muslim religion ultimately became one of the central elements in Swahili identity. To be a Swahili, in later centuries, meant to be a Muslim. With the influence of Islam came also the growing importance of the Arabic language, seen from Arabic inscriptions on coins and carved into the stone of mosques. The importance of the language is seen (especially in a later period) in the growing number of Arabic words in Swahili – words for such basic things as the breath of life (*roho*) and for intention or purpose (*nia*), but also for religious conceptions. Some Swahili numbers are of Bantu derivation; others come from Arabic.

Within Swahili culture itself, it is possible to differentiate elements with roots in the wider Bantu-speaking world from others with roots in the wider Islamic world. The division is clear with regard to forms of religious expression. Prayers said in the mosque are classically Islamic, but then people in Muslim families sometimes take part in rituals meant to control *pepo* – local spirits that bring illness and other forms of personal misfortune. Families differ from one another in the weight they give to pepo, and neighborhoods also vary in religious practice. In general, women are much more likely to recognize pepo in rituals than are men.

Some scholars have observed that women are more likely than men to make claims under customary law, which has deep local roots, and men are more likely to resort to *sharʿia* – the law of Islam. At times, women's rights to property or position are much more substantial under customary law. This certainly was the case when it came to political office. Women served as the top leaders in a number of Swahili societies. On the island of Zanzibar in the seventeenth century, for example, the Swahili as described by the Portuguese were governed by a queen, possibly the one remembered in traditions as Mwana Mwema. She and other queens drew their authority from their position within the ancient Muslim Swahili-speaking families of the coast.

The greatest stone towns along the Swahili coast were built between 1200 and 1500 AD. It is to this period that the largest buildings at Kilwa are dated. Husuni Kubwa, the palace complex, extends for over a hundred and fifty yards, with a large audience hall, a pool, and domed roofs. The great mosque at Kilwa also dates to this period, as do many stone buildings up and down the coast. Duarte Barbosa the Portuguese commercial agent described Kilwa at the end of the period. Kilwa, he wrote, was "built of handsome houses of stone and lime, and very lofty, with their windows like those of the Christians; in the same way it has streets, and these houses have got their terraces, and the wood worked in with the masonry, with plenty of gardens, in which there are many fruit trees and much water. This island has got a king over it, and from hence there is trade with Sofala with ships, which carry much gold."

It was the gold that drew overseas traders as far south as Kilwa. Without it they would have preferred to visit only the northern coast from which they could return with the shift in the annual winds, avoiding the need to wait months for a good sailing time. Kilwa's gold came from southern Africa, from the region between the Zambezi and the Limpopo Rivers. It was brought overland to the southern portion of the coast, then taken north by sea.

In the great age of the stone towns maritime merchants carried East Africa's ivory up to the Red Sea, and from there to the Mediterranean world. The ivory went also to Indian buyers, who preferred the soft and workable tusks that originated in East Africa. It was used for the bangles worn by Indian brides. When either the woman or her husband died the bangles were destroyed, thus insuring continuous demand. Substantial quantities of ivory were also shipped around India to China.

East Africa's trade linked the coast and the interior. The gold and ivory (and other products like rock crystal) were carried from the interior to the coast before being shipped. Some goods produced at the coast – iron, for example, produced by East African technology – probably went in both directions: they were carried overseas and overland.

The double heritage of coastal culture is reflected in the area's oral traditions. Speakers of Swahili and other Bantu languages of the coast tell one set of traditions in which they claim origins on the African mainland, and another in which they claim origins overseas.

Many traditions of mainland origin point to a homeland in the north, at a place called Shungwaya. Academic historians say that it was located in the hinterland of the southern Somali coast. The traditions begin with a period when a number of different peoples lived together at Shungwaya. Then conflict arose between these Bantu-speaking peoples and their Cushitic-speaking neighbors, the Oromo. The people of Shungwaya were driven out and began to move southwards until they came to their homes in what are now Kenya and northern Tanzania. Those who remember Shungwaya include the Mijikenda – nine related peoples who live in the strip of land paralleling the coast of southern Kenya and northern Tanzania; they include also Taita, Pokomo, and many local Swahili-speaking groups.

The stories of Shungwaya origins carry two different messages. One is that some elements of local culture are so central that they were brought from a single cultural source as a fully developed set of ideas and practices. These practices are too central to think of as developing slowly over a period of time, or as drawing on many different sources. They came, fully formed, as a cultural "Old Testament." The Mijikenda, for example, say that their most important clans all originated at Shungwaya, their age-sets originated at Shungwaya, and their protective village medicines all originated there.

The second message of these stories is that each of the Shungwaya peoples shares roots with each of the others: the Swahili Shungwaya clans of Mombasa share roots with the Mijikenda of their hinterland; Swahili-speakers of Vumba have a common origin with the Digo of their hinterland.

Historians have taken the Shungwaya story as a description of actual historical events. They find supporting evidence in the historical relationships among the languages of the Shungwaya peoples and in documentary sources. The linguistic evidence points to a common origin for many of the Shungwaya peoples: Swahili, Mijikenda, and Pokomo are all related to one another within the Sabaki subgroup of northeast coast Bantu languages. Documents written by Portuguese of the sixteenth and seventeenth centuries show that conflict between Bantu-speakers and Oromo, described in Shungwaya traditions, was an actual set of events, not an imagined one.

It would be a mistake, however, to take the Shungwaya traditions too literally. The traditions say that Bantu-speakers arrived in the Mombasa hinterland as a result of events that we know happened in the sixteenth century. People speaking Bantu languages had actually begun to occupy this area more than a thousand years earlier. Migrants driven from the north by Oromo found thriving Bantu-speaking societies already in place. They merged with the established population, formed a common identity with them, and were open to further settlers who came from many different places. People of the region recognize the diversity of their origins. Separate lineages maintain separate traditions of origin, often having little to do with Shungwaya, but then they also say "We all came from Shungwaya." In much the same way some Americans remember their origins in Scandinavia or Eastern Europe but say that their cultural heritage comes from Ancient Greece. The people of the East African coast formed a local cultural synthesis including, as one element, stories about origins in Shungwaya. A Mijikenda elder put it well in his own oral tradition. "The water and soil of a place determine a people's language," he said. "But we are all related and we all came from Shungwaya."

The Shungwaya story and other traditions of mainland origin tell us about one half of the coastal region's double heritage. We hear about the other half in traditions of overseas origin like those of the Shirazi. In most of the old coastal towns the Swahili-speaking families which seem to be the most deeply rooted, the most ancient in each locality, tell traditions about origins in Shiraz, in Persia. These people, the Shirazi, have typically been the fishermen, farmers, artisans, and small traders.

The claims of these traditions are not supported by the evidence for early coastal history. Early Arab travelers' accounts do not mention Persian settlers on the coast, nor does the Swahili language show the degree of Persian influence that would have come from substantial early immigration. When Shirazi tell traditions of Persian origin they do so as a way of emphasizing sharp differences between themselves and two sets of outsiders. On the one hand they explain how different Shirazi are from mainland Africans. They make the point that Shirazi are Muslim townspeople; mainlanders are non-Muslim rural folk. On the other hand they differentiate Shirazi as established local people from Arabs who have no local roots and who come in from the outside. While there may have been a few immigrants from Persia over the centuries, the vast majority of Shirazi ancestors were Africans. The Shirazi, when put down by visiting Arabs for their lack of Arabian pedigrees, have responded by claiming Persian ones.

One historian who has reviewed the evidence on the Shirazi has described them as "prototypical Swahili;" another has called them "primordial Swahili." The Shirazi are descendants of the very earliest Swahili – people who found themselves living at the intersection of Bantu-speaking East Africa and the overseas world of the Indian Ocean. They tell traditions of Shirazi origin so as to distinguish themselves from Arabs overseas and from non-Muslims on the mainland. They, like the people who migrated from Shungwaya, tell oral traditions which define their cultural identities. In fact, they combine identities to express the dual character of coastal culture. We can see this from the fact that many Shirazi have, in the past, also told Shungwaya stories. They defined themselves as "Shirazi from Shungwaya," people who feel deep roots of shared heritage with Muslims around the Indian Ocean, and similarly deep roots of shared heritage with the other Bantu-speaking people who came from Shungwaya.

Suggestions for further reading

Ehret, Christopher, "The East African Interior," in M. el-Fasi (ed.) and I. Hrbek (asst. ed.), *Africa from the Seventh to the Eleventh Century*, UNESCO *General History of Africa*, vol. 3, Paris: UNESCO, 1988, pp. 616–42.

Pouwels, R., *Horn and Crescent: Cultural Change and Traditional Islam on the East African Coast, 800–1900*, Cambridge: Cambridge University Press, 1987.

Robertshaw, Peter (ed.), *Early Pastoralists of South-western Kenya*, Memoir number 11, Nairobi: British Institute in Eastern Africa, 1990.

Schoenbrun, David L., "We Are What We Eat: Ancient Agriculture Between the Great Lakes," *Journal of African History*, 34/1 (1993), pp. 1–31.

Southall, Aidan, "Power, Sanctity, and Symbolism in the Political Economy of the Nilotes," pp. 183–222 in W. Arens and I. Karp (eds), *Creativity of Power: Cosmology and Action in African Societies*, Washington: Smithsonian Institution Press, 1989.

Spear, Thomas, and Richard Waller (eds), *Being Maasai: Ethnicity and Identity in East Africa*, London: James Currey, 1993.

Waller, Richard, "Ecology, Migration, and Expansion in East Africa," *African Affairs*, 23 (1985), pp. 347–70.

5

POLITICAL CULTURE AND POLITICAL ECONOMY IN EARLY EAST AFRICA

In the two thousand years before colonial conquest East Africans developed an enormously diverse range of political institutions. Large kingdoms grew up in Ethiopia and near the great equatorial lakes. Age sets performed major political functions near the Rift Valley of Kenya. Independent self-governing kin groups, which did not recognize any king or chief, were important in many parts of the region, as were minor chiefdoms. Yet despite this diversity, the boundaries of political systems did not restrict the exchange of goods or of political ideas. People in self-governing villages exchanged salt, iron, grain, and cattle with one another and with villagers in large kingdoms. The rituals people performed in these kingdoms were similar to those performed in autonomous villages, and people in diverse societies spoke in similar terms about the nature of prosperity, of hunger, and of political values.

Political authority in early East Africa

Historians learn about political leadership among East Africa's early Bantu speakers by examining material remains and by studying words in reconstructed languages, from two thousand years ago or longer. The earliest Bantu languages had a number of words that tied together leadership and a settled place. The root -*banja* for example, and the words related to it, had a fan of meanings. It referred to a place where people built their houses, and also to a place where prominent people discussed public affairs. Other words show that at a time when people who spoke other languages usually lived in scattered homesteads, Bantu speakers spoke about, lived in, and organized their public life around villages.

The word for ancestor existed back then, and it is probable that leadership and the ancestors were tied together. In more recent times, the leaders of villages in Bantu-speaking societies around the Great Lakes have most often been older men who made names for themselves by accumulating wealth and having many children. These prominent men hope to be remembered after their deaths as important ancestors. As they grow older and approach death they are relied on to make connections on behalf of the living with the world of ancestors. In other parts of eastern Africa it is women who live on in memory after their deaths to become important ancestors.

A few words for political leaders have existed from very early times. Ancient words related to *mwami*, for example, were already in use in East Africa two thousand years ago. Mwami is the king's title in Rwanda, and the title of the chief in the Kimbu chiefdoms of western Tanzania. The antiquity of this royal title, however, does not mean that kingship like Rwanda's or chiefship of the Kimbu kind necessarily existed two millennia ago. The mwami was certainly a notable person back then, but it is difficult to be certain about the exact kind of notability. Even more recently the word has been used for minor village headmen (among the Nyanga, west of Lake Kivu), and for any person initiated into a ritual secret society (among the Lega of eastern Zaire). The word could have had any of these meanings among early Bantu speakers: king, chief, village headman, or ritual officer. We know that the word's meanings had to do with authority and that people could use it, could shape a meaning for it, when they created political institutions. Some people used the word in the process of creating kingdoms, others in the process of creating ritual secret societies. The existence of a common store of words and of the associated ideas made for easy communication between people who lived in very different types of societies – in kingdoms and independent village societies, for example.

Eastern African Bantu speakers were able to draw, over long periods of time, on a shared cultural heritage while building new kingdoms, or chiefdoms, or ritual societies, or other social forms. The shared heritage extended not only to words, like mwami and -*dimo* (the root of the words for "ancestor"), but also to ritual practices, and to images in oral traditions. In many of the region's societies, for example, there is a close association in traditions and rituals between male authority and hunting. In some places a man who plays a prominent role in initiation rituals acts the part of a hunter. In others, a hunter is invoked as the first male ancestor from whom all lineages are descended. In northeastern Tanzania this person is remembered as Sheuta, "father of the bow." In still other places, it is the first king who is remembered as a great hunter, usually one who came from the wilderness to found a kingdom. This is the case among the Shambaa of northeastern Tanzania, who tell of a heroic wandering hunter named Mbegha, who killed the wild pigs that destroyed crops and was made king by the grateful people he had helped. The tellers of this tradition emphasize Mbegha's skill as a hunter because hunting is an appropriate image for male authority in general and kingship in particular, with its connections to war and to ritual power. "The hunter," like the word mwami, was then a part of the regional heritage on which people could draw to build institutions of many kinds, whether these were kingdoms or groups that performed initiation rituals. In fact, there is strong evidence that eighteenth-century Shambaa kings drew on the cultural heritage of their region by borrowing the earlier myth of Sheuta the ancestor-hunter, and transforming him into Mbegha, the founding hunter-king.

Many centuries before, among East Africa's early Bantu speakers, people already respected ritual authorities who engaged in healing and in divination. Many pieces of evidence support this conclusion. The root word -*kumu*, for example, had shifted in eastern Africa by 2000 years ago from its early meaning of a leader or big man in the western Bantu languages, and became *-fumu*, meaning "diviner." This is someone who has special skills at finding the moral causes of practical events. East Africans of that period also had the root word *-ganga*, meaning "healer."

Another kind of leadership in early Bantu-speaking East Africa, alongside the mwami, the elder, the healer, and the diviner, was the smelter of iron. The master smelter coordinated the work of a number of men, because iron production required charcoal preparation, furnace-building, and the collection and preparation of ore and other raw materials, as well as furnace feeding and other tasks during the actual process of smelting. Smelters must have been prominent economic leaders; the iron they produced was one of the most valuable commodities of the time. Master smelters were also ritual authorities – men who had mastered the occult process of transforming one substance into another, ore into iron. Hints of the ritual authority that existed more than two thousand years ago have been found by archaeologists, who discovered the remains of early iron working beneath important religious shrines in the Great Lakes region. Further hints from more recent centuries include iron implements buried along with kings in royal graves.

Bantu speakers were, of course, not the only creators of authority structures in eastern Africa. In Chapter 4 we saw the importance of age sets among the speakers of southern Nilotic who lived near Kenya's Rift Valley. They drew together men from many scattered homesteads into groups organized by age, thus helping to develop a sense of unity, integrating strangers into local communities, and serving as decentralized authority structures. The age-set system ultimately came to be adopted by neighboring Bantu speakers. This was part of a wider process. Institutions created by people speaking a language in one language family could ultimately be adopted by others. The Luo Nilotes of southern Uganda, for example, learned about local shrines from their Bantu-speaking neighbors, and ultimately came to build similar shrines of their own. The cultural resources on which East Africa drew were not limited to any one language family.

The political institutions that emerged near the coasts of the Indian Ocean and the Red Sea also drew on their regional cultural heritages, but in these places an additional set of factors was important: intercontinental trade and travel. We saw in the last chapter that towns on East Africa's Indian Ocean coast began to emerge very early, and that they participated in intercontinental trade while building on the heritage of Bantu-speaking cultures. The result, over the long term, was the emergence of Swahili society, in which city-states played a central role.

Early authority and its economic setting

The strongest case for the early importance of long-distance trade in East African state formation has been made for the kingdom of Aksum in Ethiopia, which emerged in the highlands rising from the Red Sea by the end of the first century AD. Aksum is known for its rich remains of monumental stone architecture, and for the early presence of writing in its local language. As we saw in Chapter 2, Ethiopia had long been involved by this time in commercial contact with Egypt. The king of Aksum controlled trade in gold from southern Ethiopia to the Red Sea coast, and also trade from the interior to the coast in ivory. Trade routes from Aksum extended to the Nile Valley and in many other directions.

Intercontinental trade was not, however, the sole relevant factor in the creation of the kingdom. Aksum's location in the interior enabled it to tap the maritime trade only from a distance – through the port of Adulis. A caravan moving from Adulis to Aksum's main town needed to spend several days climbing, for the town was at 6800 feet above sea level. Its core region included large areas of rich and well-watered agricultural land, suggesting that agriculture was important to the kingdom's political economy. Aksumite kings enjoyed a strategic location for controlling peoples from whom they collected tribute, often in cattle. Inscriptions at Aksum enumerated tens of thousands of head of tribute cattle in the royal herds.

From the very start, this early Ethiopian kingdom was rooted in a culture that spread across continental boundaries. Aksum, and the pre-Aksumite societies of the northern highlands, shared in a regional culture that grew up on both sides of the Red Sea. Its religion was similar in a number of respects to that of pre-Islamic South Arabia. The first stone monuments and the first evidence of writing, in about the fifth century BC, emerged in both Ethiopia and South Arabia at about the same time. We have seen that it was Aksumites who introduced Christianity into the horn of Africa in the fourth century AD. From the seventeenth century onwards, Aksum's power began to fade; the kingdom's center shifted southwards. Historians and archaeologists have given many reasons for this decline: that the soil lost its fertility with time so that the land near the town was no longer able to carry large numbers of people; that Beja herders from the west expanded into the plains below Aksum; and that the new religion of Islam, important along the Red Sea coast, made the northern region seem less hospitable to the Aksumites. One result, in any event, was that conversions to Christianity began to occur in the highlands further south, and continued even after the dynasty's end in the ninth century.

In the interior of East Africa to the south of Ethiopia, it is difficult to know the times at which different forms of authority first appeared. Many small chiefdoms rose up and disappeared, leaving slim traces of their existence, or no traces. Historians do know, however, about a number of major kingdoms that grew up near the great equatorial lakes after the middle of the present millennium, and that survived to face the colonial challenge at the end of the nineteenth century. Scholars of the Great Lakes region also have some knowledge of ancient ritual authority – of the activities of specialists who mediated between the world of the living and the world of the spirits, and in so doing instructed people in how to order their lives. In this part of East Africa, the economic changes that set the stage for religious change, for stratification, and for state formation had more to do with innovations in agriculture and herding than with long-distance trade.

Two sets of economic innovations, both of them after about 1000 AD, set the stage for major changes in ritual and political authority in the Great Lakes region.* The first

---

* The following argument draws on David Schoenbrun, "Cattle herds and banana gardens: the historical geography of the western Great Lakes region, *ca* AD 800–1500," *African Archaeological Review*, 11 (1993), pp. 39–72.

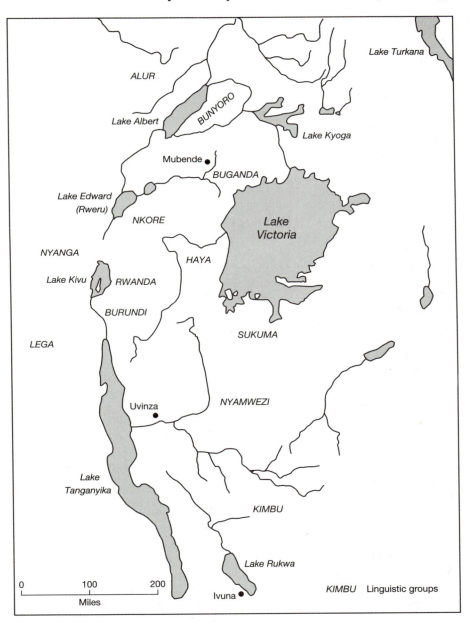

Map 5.1   Linguistic and political groupings of the late precolonial Great Lakes zone

was the emergence, in some places, of a division between specialized farmers and specialized herders. The earlier economy in these places had been based on mixed farming; each farmer raised some crops and kept some livestock. Over time some of these farmers devoted their time increasingly to herding, others increasingly to farming. When specialized herders or farmers emerged in a local area they continued to share the same language and they developed new forms of interdependence based on separate identities and on joint participation in the area's economy.

Historians have several reasons for thinking that the new economic forms began to develop early in the second millennium AD. First, recent archaeological evidence indicates that the grasslands of western Uganda, where specialized pastoralists have lived in recent centuries, were not occupied before 1000 AD. Second, the landscape in a number of parts of the Great Lakes region had been going through important changes during the centuries leading up to this period. Intensifying agriculture, and the use of wood to make charcoal for iron smelting, both led to forest clearing and to the opening up of grasslands suitable for herding. Third, the evidence of historical linguistics shows that many specialized terms for cattle colors and for the shapes of cattle horns appeared in some Great Lakes societies in about the same period.

Some of the Great Lakes kingdoms that grew up later on, in the centuries after 1500 AD, became known for rule by pastoral aristocracies. The leaders who created these kingdoms built a system of political domination on the base of the economic specializations. In the kingdom of Nkore, for example, in southern Uganda, the rulers and the high status lineages were cattle keepers, and subordinate subjects farmed the land. Similarly, in the kingdom of Rwanda cattle keepers have formed an upper class governing over farmers. In creating their kingdoms, the rulers of Rwanda and of Nkore made very special use of the political potential inherent in the system of economic specialization. Pastoral rule over agriculturalists was not the invariable outcome. In Buganda, for example, the kings identified with the agricultural majority of their subjects, but gave their cattle into the care of herdsmen who occupied a weak and insignificant position in Ganda society. In Bunyoro, the herders enjoyed high prestige but were completely separate from the kings and princes. Perhaps the emergence of pastoral domination resulted from intense interaction in areas with fairly dense populations of herders.

Just as the increasing specialization of herders in the Great Lakes region opened the way for state forms based on pastoral domination, a second innovation opened the way for domination based on control over land. This was the emergence of increasingly specialized banana farming. Some varieties of bananas had long been cultivated in East Africa; others, which originated in India or southeast Asia, were introduced into the region. In the first millennium AD bananas appear to have been merely one among many varieties of food plants grown by mixed farmers. An important change came later, in southern Uganda and northwestern Tanzania, with the development of special farm plots devoted to bananas. Words for permanent banana plantations and for banana groves as property in land appeared only in the second millennium AD, and in most cases after 1400.

In modern Buganda, over the past two centuries, banana gardens have been the key to the economic, and therefore political, value of land. The climate of Buganda is unusually well-suited for the cultivation of these plants, which are not only eaten as fruit but form the starchy staple of the diet and are even the main ingredient in brewing beer. Banana gardens require a considerable initial labor investment: the soil must be cleared and usually another, preparatory crop planted before the young banana plants can be put in and grown. In Buganda, once a stand is producing, however, it goes on for decades with relatively little attention, and it produces yields of up to five tons per acre. Ordinary cultivators in Buganda therefore had a substantial investment in their land; moving to new land meant losing that investment. The fact that banana groves required a comparatively large investment and gave large yields meant in turn that the population was comparatively dense and stable. It was then worthwhile to make a further investment in infrastructure such as communications. Thus, in nineteenth-century Buganda, each important chief used the labor owed by his subjects to construct footpaths four feet wide between his own seat and the capital.

By the eighteenth and nineteenth centuries, and probably several centuries earlier, land in Buganda took on a symbolic value, and it became an instrument of political control. The most ancient and honored clans of Buganda had land of their own, although over the centuries the king came to control an increasingly large proportion of the land. In later centuries, the king came to "own" almost all the land, and controlled the people through control of the land. When he assigned an administrative territory to one of his chiefs, the appointment implied control over land used by ordinary cultivators. The farmers, for their part, owed their chief loyal service and tribute. One of the greatest rewards a king could bestow on a chief was an estate exempt from royal taxes. This was then an independent power base, for a chief could grant land to minor chiefs, and they to ordinary cultivators, in return for their material and political support.

The creation of specialized banana gardens in Buganda after 1400, like the emergence of cattle keeping in Nkore, did not lead automatically to political centralization. The change in land use simply made it possible for people to assign a new kind of value to pieces of land. Then at some point, possibly long after the period of economic innovation, political leaders in Buganda and in other places found ways to create political hierarchies by exploiting farmers' dependence on their valuable banana plantations.

Some historians of the Great Lakes have been fascinated by the possibility that the growth of trade played an important part in state formation. The evidence from this sub-region suggests that trade was indeed important very early, but that in the area north of the Zambezi Valley and south of Ethiopia it was not a major factor in state formation, nor was state formation necessary in order for trade to emerge.

Regional trade networks existed through the whole of the Iron Age in this large part of eastern Africa. Iron, salt, pottery, and grain were exchanged for one another and carried from market to market. Goods exchanged in this way could travel quite far, even when individual traders did not. Copper arrived from central Africa, and by the seventeenth century, beads from the coast reached the Great Lakes. In the archaeological record and the record of traditions for the period before 1750, the nodes of the network, the most important centers of commercial production and trade, were not located on a political basis – at the courts of kings – but rather on the basis of production and transportation. Trade centers sometimes formed at lake ports for canoe traffic, or at the juncture between two climatic zones where growers of different food crops met, or where farmers in a hungry season could buy food from their neighbors whose crops had already been harvested.

Unlike the western Sudan, where large empires were closely related to trade, many of the richest trading networks in early East Africa thrived amid very small chiefdoms and in the border areas between kingdoms, where no one authority held supreme control. Evidence for early trade networks has been found, for example, at points where exploitable concentrations of salt or iron ore were located, often far from the major states. The archaeological excavation of Ivuna and Uvinza, two salt-producing sites in western Tanzania, shows evidence of extensive local trade from the thirteenth century, with no hint of state growth. Uvinza's political organization is known only for the nineteenth century, hundreds of years after the trade began. The salt springs were located where the borders of three chiefdoms converged, beyond the exclusive control of any one leader. In Uganda, two sites seem especially important for the salt trade. One is far from the center of any kingdom, at Katwe on Lake Edward (Rweru); the other is at the edge of the kingdom of Bunyoro, at Kibiro on Lake Albert (Rwitanzige). Some of the salt of Kibiro was consumed in Bunyoro, but some was also shipped across the lake to areas not under the king's control. Examples of trade within a kingdom, as in Bunyoro's salt trade or the fish for farm-produce trade of Buganda, have been taken incorrectly to show that political centralization makes commerce easier. Trade like this was, in fact, carried on all across East Africa wherever local specialities were found, whether within political boundaries or across them.

The Chwezi

Scholars have been working to recover lost chapters in the history of authority in the Great Lakes region. They are especially interested in the period between the introduction of specialized pastoralism and the time of formation of the well-known kingdoms of Buganda, Bunyoro, Nkore, and Rwanda. Pastoralism began to appear after about 1000 AD; the kingdoms did not begin to emerge until at least five hundred years later. What was the picture of authority between those times?

One way of approaching this question is through the study of oral traditions about heroes called Chwezi, who are said to have lived in the region before the currently known dynasties. Historians who listen closely to the Chwezi traditions have learned a great deal about the character of ritual authority during the period before the emergence of the great kingdoms. The traditions encode evidence on a wide range of subjects: the place of early iron working, the role of religious shrines in the centuries before 1500, the place of religious authorities within the later kingdom, the character of women's authority, the history of healing, and the histories of local clans. Because of their richness they are worth recounting briefly and then exploring for what they contribute to historical understanding.

The legends of ancient Chwezi heroes are told in kingdoms across a wide expanse of southwestern Uganda, northwestern Tanzania, and beyond. According to a version of the legend, as told in Bunyoro, the last legitimate king from the days before the Chwezi was named Isaza. He had the bad fortune to anger the king of Okuzimu, the place beneath the earth where the ancestral spirits live. The king of Okuzimu, the World Beneath, then sent his daughter as a spy to learn about Isaza and report back. Isaza married her without knowing that she had come from Okuzimu. She became pregnant and then returned to the World Beneath, to report on Isaza's secret: that he loved cattle beyond anything. This was his weakness. The king of Okuzimu then sent him two magnificent head of cattle, which became his favorites. One day the cattle wandered off, and Isaza followed them into a deep pit. When he tried to get them out the earth swallowed him up, and forever after Isaza was a captive of the World Beneath. His gatekeeper took over his kingdom.

Isaza never returned, but his son Isimbwa (who had been born below in Okuzimu) went hunting on earth. He learned that the gatekeeper-king, who had taken Isaza's kingdom, had a daughter named Nyinamwiru. The king kept her hidden away because his diviners predicted that if she married, her son would overthrow the king. Isimbwa, the hunter from the World Beneath, managed to enter Nyinamwiru's house and impregnated her. Nyinamwiru gave birth to a son. This infant was connected through his father Isimbwa to the old line of kings; he was connected through his mother to the gatekeeper-king, for she was the king's daughter. The gatekeeper-king, fearing that Nyinamwiru's son would ultimately overthrow him, had the baby thrown into the river. The baby was saved, and ultimately he did overthrow his grandfather and, with his mother's support, he took the throne. He became known as Ndahura, the first of the Chwezi kings. Legend has it that the Chwezi ruled until local strife and evil omens convinced the last Chwezi king to leave. When the Chwezi disappeared, their place was taken by the founders of the Bito dynasty that held power until the time of colonial conquest in the 1890s.

The Chwezi have been the subject of a rich body of historical writing. Early European administrators and missionaries whose view of the world was shaped by their racial prejudices decided that Africans were not sophisticated enough to have created the region's kingdoms. They therefore described the Chwezi as racially separate from the rest of the region's population – a lighter-skinned people who had originated in the north. There is no good evidence for this racial argument.

From the 1920s onwards African intellectuals from the region, who were employed by the surviving dynasties (and one of whom was a member of the Bito dynasty), wrote histories based on the Chwezi legends. They described the Chwezi as early kings and used the stories to glorify the long tradition of kingship that underlay more recent rule.

Skeptical historians began to emerge in the 1960s. They found it impossible to accept the legends of the Chwezi as history. In the skeptical view these legends are statements about the order of the world, about fundamental issues of life and death, and about the relationship between humans and spirits; they are not about people who had ever actually lived. In this skeptical interpretation stories about the last Chwezi are about the origin of death for all humankind; they are not about the misfortunes and disappearance of a particular king.

More recently, historians have realized that in order to make sense of oral traditions like the Chwezi legends it is necessary first to understand all the ways that Chwezi fit into the lives of people in the region. The Chwezi are indeed described in oral tradition as ancient kings, but local people also see them as spirits that enter people's bodies, spirits that people honor in rituals meant to heal the sick or to bring fertility to the childless. Every extended family in Bunyoro had a patron spirit, and most of these were drawn from among the characters of the Chwezi legends; each family formed a regular relationship with one or more mediums (usually women) who would give them access to the spirit. The Chwezi spirit was believed to enter the body of the medium and climb onto her head, so that family members could consult the spirit through the medium. There were many other kinds of mediums in addition to the ones who served families. There were bands of traveling mediums who lived permanently at shrines dedicated to the Chwezi. Some of these shrines served the whole region, such as the shrine for Ndahura at Mubende Hill. At the royal court there were also mediums who advised the king on affairs of concern to the whole kingdom.

The importance of the Chwezi in everyday life means that the historian who wants to collect the fullest possible range of information about the Chwezi, to create a rich history, can explore a multitude of sources. The historical legends told about the Chwezi serve as only one type of source among many. There are also songs used to address or call the spirits at possession ceremonies, and praise names for each of the Chwezi heroes or gods. In some places the Chwezi are subjects of epic poetry. The keepers of Chwezi shrines told their own local stories. Other kinds of memories were preserved in association with places where the Chwezi were supposed to have lived or rested, so that people living near a lake or rock that played a role in Chwezi history might have special stories to tell. Additional traditions were preserved by individual families who recalled the ways in which their ancestors had cooperated with particular Chwezi, or lived near them, or developed some special connection to them. The Chwezi traditions have been part of a living tradition. This makes the job of the historian daunting. The body of songs, proverbs, and legends is so extensive that it is impossible to know them all. But their existence makes possible the creation of rich, culturally informed historical analysis.

An awareness of the range of traditions and cultural associations makes it possible to read (or to hear) the Chwezi stories at many different levels.* At one level, the story of how Nyinamwiru was impregnated by Isimbwa was a story of infertility and reproduction. Nyinamwiru, like many women who seek the help of mediums, was childless. Isimbwa, like the spirit mediums themselves, moved back and forth between the world of people and the world of spirits. A person hearing the story of Nyinamwiru and Isimbwa, who had these associations in mind, might well have understood it as the tale of a childless woman who became a mother after a medium had cured her. With the medium's assistance she asked a spirit to help her conceive and her wish was granted.

The story of Chwezi origins could also be taken as a straightforward political tale, about a process by which one set of leaders came to replace another. The story tells how the dynasty before the Chwezi disappeared and how kingship was taken over by the gatekeeper who had served the last of the old kings. Isimbwa, a descendant of the

---

* The following analysis owes much to the unpublished work of Renee Tantala, "The Early History of Kitara in Western Uganda." Ph.D. dissertation, University of Wisconsin-Madison, 1989. See also the important work of Iris Berger and Peter Schmidt (see Suggestions for Further Reading at the end of this chapter).

old dynasty, was born in the World Beneath but came to earth, where he found the gatekeeper's daughter. He made her pregnant, and so became the father of Ndahura. Since Ndahura was the founder of the Chwezi dynasty, his descent from Isimbwa connects the Chwezi to an earlier dynasty. The story of Isimbwa establishes the claim that the ancient ruling line achieved continuity despite its disappearance. The story of Ndahura's rise to power and his creation of a new dynasty also gives a central place to Nyinamwiru as the archetype of the ambitious political mother, the woman who manages her son's political campaign and thus defines the fate of the kingdom. Senior women in the region's dynasties were able to choose and define the political battles their sons fought.

In a very different way, Nyinamwiru's story could be taken as an account of the transition from one period in the religious history of the region to another. Chwezi ritual is probably not the oldest form of spirit mediumship in the region. An earlier form probably involved rituals honoring the spirits of living creatures: pythons, leopards, lions, and so on. The title of "gatekeeper," in at least one neighboring society, was given to an official at an ancient shrine honoring a python god. Nyinamwiru and her father the gatekeeper lived in an area where a python god was honored. The transition from a religious form in which this python god was central, to one involving the Chwezi, came about when Isimbwa the hunter entered Nyinamwiru's house. That Isimbwa came as a hunter is significant because "hunting" is one of the ways to describe what a spirit does when he afflicts someone. A spirit captures a woman by making her ill, so that she will seek healing through the mediumship ritual. If we see the story in this light, Isimbwa's visit from the World Beneath was a time when a prominent priestess of the python god first learned about Chwezi mediumship and helped to introduce these new rituals into her home area.

A number of historians have been asking about changes that actually took place in the early history of the region and that are reflected or reported in the cycle of traditions. The existence of a rich range of traditions, songs, proverbs, and shrines, along with the evidence of archaeology and historical linguistics, makes it possible to explore forms of change in the distant past. The traditions then can be interpreted as commentaries about actual historical processes.

In the days before the Chwezi period, authority in southwestern Uganda was very localized, although there are hints in the traditions of some large polities. In many places, small self-governing areas were bounded by lakes, swamps, rivers, or other natural features. Historians know this from the place names listed in the Chwezi legends, and from the local oral histories of many small groups that claim to have been important before the Chwezi. There seems to be little basis to the claims that a great empire existed in this region before Chwezi times.

Within the small political units authority was divided, for alongside the political leaders were the keepers of local shrines in honor of spirits manifest as animals or snakes. The introduction of Chwezi ritual appears to have been a significant change. Many of the new mediums spent their time traveling from place to place, although some served at shrines, the way earlier mediums had done.

The archaeological evidence and the evidence of the traditions tie the central concerns of the Chwezi legends to a period when specialized pastoralism had already emerged. Ndahura's shrine at Mubende Hill, and other archaeological sites in the core area of the Chwezi legends, date back to the periods between the eleventh and sixteenth centuries. We have already seen that this was a time when specialized herding and farming were practiced in this sub-region. The traditions themselves point over and over again to the importance of cattle, and to pastoralist values. Isaza, for example, was drawn to Okuzimu, the world of the spirits, because of his excessive love for cattle.

The archaeological evidence also points to the emergence of a new kind of production and trade during this same period. Major salt-producing areas grew up on the western border of Bunyoro after 1200 AD, contributing to a regional trade in salt. There is some evidence that traveling Chwezi mediums were also, at the same time, traders, because they moved from place to place with relative ease. This points to the possibility that the mediums took part in the salt trade.

The archaeological record also points to one of the great mysteries of the Chwezi record, surrounding the history of iron making. At some of the Chwezi shrines, remains of very early iron making have been found, dating to a period much more ancient than the time of the most substantial settlement. Most estimates of the timing of the main settlement at Chwezi sites, whether based on genealogies or on archaeological evidence, point to the middle centuries of the present millennium. The early Iron Age remains at some of these sites point to a period a thousand years earlier, or more. The most dramatic of these remains was found by Peter Schmidt, who dug at a Chwezi shrine in Buhaya and found evidence of iron working with a probable date of 500 BC. The existence of very early remains raises the question of whether some of the shrine sites have been in use for more than two thousand years. We cannot be sure.

The history of this region is one in which each successive group of leaders took over some of the symbols and some of the ritual power of earlier leaders. The most important shrine of the Chwezi Ndahura at Mubende, for example, is very probably located at a place that had earlier been the shrine of a python god. In a similar way, kings and shrine mediums appear to have taken on some of the religious authority of groups that controlled the ritual of iron production. The continuity made sense in symbolic terms. Just as fertility was a central concern of Chwezi mediums, so it was also central to the process of iron production. Smiths in Buhaya, for example, perform rituals that treat the smelting furnace as a female womb: the clay pipes that bring air into the furnace are masculine. In some cases, the medicines placed in the furnace to make the production of iron a success are identical to medicines used for women's fertility.

In the history of this region, each generation of political and ritual leaders took over and built on the imagery, traditions, and religious rituals of previous generations. Each ritual, therefore, and each tradition, draws together the historical product of many centuries of creativity. Each set of actions has evidence of innumerable historical periods crystallized within it. This sense of historical richness makes Chwezi legends and Chwezi rituals powerfully evocative, even when it is not possible to know the precise time in which each of the details came into existence.

The process by which each generation built on the creativity of earlier ones changed only in the colonial period. Colonial rulers in some parts of the Chwezi region saw mediumship as dangerous, and worked to suppress it. They did not suppress kingship or chiefship in the same way. One consequence of this was that women's ritual authority which found expression in mediumship declined or was transformed while men's political authority survived.

Political culture in Ethiopia

The culture of royal rule in Ethiopia seems, at first glance, radically different from political culture in the Chwezi region. In studying the Chwezi, historians must rely almost entirely on unwritten sources of knowledge, and kingship is built on local religious practices. In Ethiopia there are written records that go back for more than two thousand years. Christianity and Islam have been important for most of that time. Nevertheless, in Ethiopia as in the kingdoms of Uganda, kingship was a core mythological subject: it was presented in terms that tied it to the culture of people at many social levels, and that led the kingdom's subjects to identify in important personal ways with their rulers.

The growth of the Ethiopian state in the form known from more recent times took a major step forward with the founding of the Solomonid dynasty in about 1270 AD. The dynasty is called "Solomonid" because the oral and written traditions of the period claimed that its members were descended from King Solomon in Jerusalem. Zara Ya'qob, a Solomonid king of the fifteenth century (1434–68), is reported to have been asked, during his installation ceremony, about his origins. He replied, "I am the son of David, the son of Solomon, the son of Menelik."

The many written and oral traditions about Solomonid origins were written down in a definitive form in the thirteenth or fourteenth century, in a document called the Kebra Nagast, the "Glory of Kings." The document claims to include a much earlier book that had never been translated or brought into general use, about the origins of the kingdom. At the heart of the book is an attempt to answer the question, "In what does the greatness of kings consist? Is it in the multitude of soldiers, or in the splendor of worldly possession, or in the extent of rule over cities and towns?" The answer appears to have been that the greatness of kings comes out of two things: possession of the sacred Tabernacle of Zion, and descent from an ancestor with whom the Lord made a holy covenant. The tradition then explains how both the Tabernacle and the line of chosen descent through King Solomon came to Ethiopia.

The document as written in the years of the Solomonid dynasty arranges the traditions of the period into an explanation of these origins. According to the story, a merchant returned from Jerusalem to tell Makeda, the Queen of Sheba, about Solomon's great wisdom and justice. She then traveled to Jerusalem, where she decided that her own religion needed to be left behind, and that her people ought to follow the religion of the God of Israel. Before she left Jerusalem she became pregnant by Solomon, returned to Ethiopia, and gave birth to a son who was remembered in the oral traditions as Menelik. After the young man grew up he traveled to Jerusalem in his turn, where he was crowned king of Ethiopia. According to the legend, his traveling companions stole the Tabernacle of Zion and took it with them to the ancient kingdom of Aksum, in Ethiopia, which was established as the new Zion. The Ethiopians became God's chosen people.

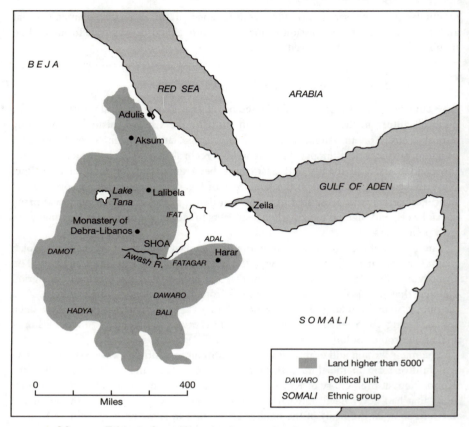

Map 5.2 Ethiopia from Aksumite times to the sixteenth century

This legend, parts of which had entered popular culture before the Solomonid centuries, imbued Ethiopian politics with a rich set of meanings. Some of the Solomonid kings traveled to Aksum to be crowned, because they were convinced that Solomon's dynastic line ran from Jerusalem to Aksum and then to themselves. Lalibela, the town that became the political center after the decline of Aksum and before the rise of the Solomonids, was the location of remarkable churches cut out of solid rock. Some historians think that the great efforts taken at Lalibela were meant as a way of rebuilding Zion in the highlands of Ethiopia. The story of Solomonid descent had the effect of defining Ethiopians as God's chosen people, and of defining the relationship between kings and Ethiopian Christian leaders as central to the fate of the kingdom.

As in the case of traditions about the Chwezi, the history of Ethiopia as receiving the heritage of Solomon and of David is meaningful, true in some important senses, but not supported by academic histories in a literal sense. We have seen, for example, that early Aksum had not practiced the religion of Solomon, as the Kebra Nagast claimed.

It was a town that practiced a local religion, shared with people on both sides of the Red Sea, until the first conversions to Christianity in the fourth century.

Today's historians should not be surprised that the story of Aksum as told in the Kebra Nagast is different from the story as told by the archaeologists. Each generation, each set of historians, finds meaning in its own special way. People who reflect on history try to understand the world in which they live. As that world changes, the relevant meanings change. This is true of oral history, of written history (as in the Kebra Nagast), and of academic history, which has come increasingly to accept in recent years that the creativity underlying Ethiopia's kingdom had roots on the African continent.

The Kebra Nagast came to enjoy wide popularity in the lands of the Solomonid kings. People who could not read knew the story. Central elements were passed on from generation to generation orally, by tellers of tales. The history of Solomon, of Queen Makeda, and of Menelik was represented also in paintings. In the early Solomonid era the emphasis on Christianity must have been important to the way the kingdom's people defined themselves in relation to their neighbors. To the northwest of the kingdom were Ethiopian Jews with their own forms of political organization, probably small states. To the south of Lake Tana was the kingdom of Damot, where the rulers practiced local religion. To the east were the Muslim states of Shoa, Ifat, Fetegar, Dawaro, Hadya, Bale, and Adal. The coasts were controlled mostly by Muslims. Aksum's conversion to Christianity, its move southwards after the rise of Islam, and the further southward moves of successive Christian dynasties meant that the Solomonid Christian state was isolated in a world populated by rulers who followed Jewish, Muslim, and local African religions. In this world the Kebra Nagast defined Ethiopian identity.

The spread of the Christian religion and the spread of Solomonid political control went hand in hand. Small colonies of Christians moved out beyond the borders of the state and established a presence which made conquest easier. In newly conquered non-Christian areas the dynasty encouraged the establishment of Christian monasteries. The monks worked to convert the local people, who relied on them to drive out demons, to perform rituals of protection against wild beasts and illness, and to settle disputes between neighbors and between relatives. The monks also performed divination to predict royal success in war, and prayed for victory. The expansion of the kingdom as a political entity could not be separated from the expansion of the Christian religion. The relationship between local ritual practice and the religion of the state, which was important in the Chwezi areas, was important here too, with the monks playing an important role in the spread of Christianity as a popular religion.

Alongside Christianity, local cultural forms survived to become part of both monastic and royal culture. The healing practices of the monks were built on local forms. The Solomonid kings, similarly, built on local political culture. In the coronation ceremony at Aksum the king was brought a lion and a buffalo to kill, to begin his reign well. The kings of Ethiopia were Christian kings, heirs to Solomon and to David, but they were also African hunter kings.

Patrons and clients

The boundaries of East African kingdoms expanded in some periods and shrank in others. Kings pulled back from old boundaries because of internal dissension, or when powerful neighbors expanded. Territories shifted often from one kingdom to another, and more frequently still from kingdoms to small chiefdoms, or to societies that governed themselves through communal consensus.

One of the central tasks of those who governed was to bind their subjects ever more tightly to the center of government; a close relationship between subjects and rulers was the best defense against a kingdom's disintegration. Every subject lineage was expected to give loyal service to its chief, but lineages were more likely to support a chief in practice if the lineage head had established a personal tie of patronage and clientship with his ruler. The tie could also be used to bind powerful non-royals to weaker ones. The patron–client relationship was variable. It bound the king or chief to some men from the subordinate classes but not others. To know about these relationships is to begin to understand how chiefs and subjects, each of whose interests opposed the other's, could act in concert, how powerful people and powerless ones came to cooperate. It is important also for an understanding of how the weak worked to insure their own security.

The patron–client relationship has been most extensively described for a number of kingdoms west of Lake Victoria, and especially for Rwanda. In that kingdom specialized farmers and herders were tied to one another through relationships of patronage and clientship. Rwanda's rulers were drawn from a stratum of society called Tutsi; the majority of subjects were called Hutu. The Tutsi of central Rwanda thought of themselves as pastoralists who governed Hutu agriculturalists. As so often when identity is based on economic activity, reality was much more complex than the accepted image. The boundaries between farming and herding did not precisely match the boundaries between the two Rwandan social categories: some Hutu were quite wealthy in cattle. But the image of Tutsi pastoralist rulers had ideological power and was true in many cases. As in many stratified societies, the social separation of Hutu and Tutsi was heightened by barriers to intermarriage.

Rwandans created patron–client ties and a wide variety of other relationships by making payments in cattle. One Rwandan man might give another a cow to create a special friendship, or to seal a contractual obligation between equals. In the relationship called *umuheto*, an army chief would select a lineage which would then send him a gift once every year or two; in return, the chief would protect the lineage from other powerful people who might want to take away their wealth. Tutsi clients paid cows as umuheto; Hutu clients often paid in goods made by craftspeople, like hoes, fiber bracelets, or sleeping mats.

Whereas umuheto was a payment by an inferior client to a powerful patron, in *ubuhake* clientship it was the powerful person who made the symbolic payment to his inferior. "Ubuhake" was derived from the verb meaning "to pay one's respects to a superior in his court." A person created the tie by approaching a richer, more powerful man to beg for "milk" and protection. "Be my father," he would say, "and I will be your son." The superior, if he wished to accept his client, could give the man a cow as a mark of the relationship. When a Hutu was client and a Tutsi chief his patron, he was expected to give service and loyal support. In return he gained protection from other powerful Tutsi. A Rwanda proverb says, "A dog is feared not for his fangs but for his master."

The threads of patronage and clientship wove a tight social fabric to bind together Rwanda's diverse social groups. The king, for example, would make a Tutsi army chief into his client by awarding him the right to establish umuheto ties. The army chief would establish ties, in turn, with his own umuheto client lineages. By binding king to chief, and chief to lineage, umuheto (and other institutions like it) tied the kingdom together, joining Tutsi to Tutsi, Tutsi to Hutu, and Hutu to one another.

For much of the twentieth century it seemed to outside observers that Rwanda's elaborate tapestry of Hutu and Tutsi, patrons and clients, had existed for many centuries. Historians have slowly come to understand, however, that this social fabric has been created over the past two centuries. At the start of the nineteenth century, herders and farmers in many parts of what is now Rwanda saw themselves as relative equals – as neighbors with economies that fitted together well, not as ruler and ruled, superior and inferior. Farmers lived on hilltops, where they held independent rights to their land; herders controlled their own pasture land on hillsides and in valley bottoms. The kingdom, at that time, had not yet grown to the full extent of its later borders, and areas outside royal control did not exhibit the sharp social divisions of a later period.

Throughout the nineteenth century the kingdom expanded its boundaries by conquest. The Tutsi kings were concerned to guarantee the loyalty of army leaders who governed the newly conquered territories. The king would give an army chief the right to allocate land in a part of the conquered area, or the right to collect umuheto cattle from a specified group of lineages. Farmers and herders who had been conquered suddenly found themselves making payments in produce or in cattle in return for the right to stay on the land their ancestors had occupied for generations. Wealthy herders from among the conquered people could escape from tribute requirements by forming special relationships with the king's Tutsi and doing jobs for them. By doing this they were "becoming" Tutsi, in the sense that they were joining the stratum of privileged and politically powerful herders.

The greater the number of herders who participated in the king's network, the heavier the exactions on agriculturalists who were being transformed into a servile class. When the herders became Tutsi, the farmers became Hutu, in the sense that they became members of an inferior social stratum. It was in the reign of King Rwabugiri, who ruled from about 1860 to 1895, that the heaviest demands on Hutu began to emerge. Under his rule conquered territory was divided into provinces and the provinces were divided into hills. At each level, the chief collected cattle and goods from the people who lived there. Alongside the provincial chiefs and hill chiefs were other chiefs who could demand special kinds of payments (like umuheto).

Seen from the point of view of Hutu, this was a very difficult period. Only decades earlier they had been in control of their own lands, living as equals with their pastoralist neighbors. Now they found themselves losing status and power. One of the most hated signs of this new status was a new form of taxation that required them to work for their Tutsi superiors.

It was in this new context that ubuhake emerged. This was the form of clientship in which the weaker partner approached his superior to beg for "milk" and protection, to ask the superior to become his "father." The advantage to the weaker client was that his stronger patron would help to protect him from subjection to labor dues. Ubuhake emerged fully in the colonial period, at a time when the colonial rulers supported Tutsi dominance, leaving Hutu with little protection. A Hutu who received an ubuhake cow from a Tutsi chief gave service and loyal support in return for protection as well as exemption from some of the dues he would have owed the chief who was now his patron. The cow he received was a personal pledge of protection, very different from the impersonal provisions of defense by a chief in a territorial tribute relationship.

At one time anthropologists thought that the peasant gave loyalty, service, and tribute in return for the cow and the dairy products it provided. But studies of Rwanda diet show that milk and beef have had minimal importance in the farmers' subsistence. Nor could the cow be seen as an exchange for tribute, because the subjects who paid the most tribute were the ones who received nothing from their chief. The farmers without patrons were worst off because they had to do without protection and also without exemption from arbitrary demands for service.

Earlier historians of Africa speculated about the origins of rule by cattle keepers in Rwanda. They thought that pastoralists were superior to agriculturalists. They imagined a history in which Tutsi, as an entirely separate people with their own language and culture, invaded the region, conquered the tillers of the soil, and imposed their political institutions. In fact, this view is simply another misconception about African history that was heavily influenced by the Hamite myth. It is now thoroughly rejected.

The myth of Hamitic conquest assumes that Bantu-speaking farmers were early occupants who had lived in the region for a long time when cattle-keeping conquerors arrived from the north, speaking "Hamitic" languages and bringing with them the idea of the state. All the evidence on language and settlement patterns points to a very different process. As we saw in Chapter 4 and the earlier part of this chapter it was the Bantu speakers who entered the region after the earliest period of settlement, intruding into an area where people already spoke southern Cushitic languages among others. Bantu speakers became the majority population by creating diversified economic forms. They practiced moist forest agriculture and appear to have learned livestock-rearing and grain agriculture from the people who were already there when they arrived. The genius of the Bantu speakers consisted in their ability to diversify their economies. In each locality they created a broad synthesis, drawing on as many possibilities as they could from among the different varieties of farming and herding. We have seen that it was only later, at the beginning of the second millennium AD, that the Bantu speakers in Rwanda and Nkore moved towards a form of specialization that depended on the separation of farming and herding, which were then practiced by separate sectors of the population.

Linguistic evidence shows that the specialized separation of herding and farming developed as an internal process within Bantu-speaking societies, not through the introduction of herding from the outside. The rich and complex terminology for cattle colors and horn shapes that emerged in Rwanda at the time of economic specialization, were innovations internal to the language, not terms introduced from the outside.

Alongside forms of clientage like Rwanda's, based on payments in cattle, were others in which the patron gave land to a client in return for support and allegiance. We have already seen that this was the case in the kingdom of Buganda, where the king awarded independent estates to favored chiefs, and where chiefs in turn granted land to their own clients.

It was the case also in Solomonid Ethiopia where, as we have seen, the kingdom spread to areas where Christians did not form a majority of the population. Small colonies of Christians who lived beyond the kingdom's borders served as the advance guard of royal expansion. They stayed on after conquest, and were joined by additional colonies of the king's soldiers. In the first stages of conquest a defeated ruler, a non-Christian who had been independent, might remain in office, but now as a subject of the king and now ruling over Christian settlements that were in touch with the king. There were many royal strategies for keeping control of this territory. The king often required the tributary chief to send a number of his children and other relatives to live at his court. They served as hostages in case of rebellion, and they also came to learn how to behave as Solomonid courtiers.

The king created patron–client relations by awarding land grants, called *gult*, to the colonies of Christian soldiers and settlers who helped him to govern new territories. Kings continued to reward their administrators with gult during later periods. The gult-holding client was not entitled to cultivate the land. His were rights in the peasants who cultivated the land. He could collect tribute from them in kind – in livestock or grain, for example. In some senses this was an institutionalization of a pattern by which the king allowed a part of his army to requisition needed food from the people among whom they lived. It was a way of dividing up the people of the land into small convenient units for the support of the king's agents. The king's award of gult served to bond administrators to him as clients. The system of awarding gult, of creating royal clients, survived for over half a millennium, right into the twentieth century.

The award of gult land opened up a long term process of negotiation between king and gult-holders. The king tried to keep land awards temporary, so that he could choose new clients as it pleased him. The holders, for their part, tried to find a way to make their temporary authority permanent, and to transform their rights in peasants into rights in cultivable land. They were interested in acquiring the sorts of rights that were called *rest*. This was land owned by a group of people who shared common descent through both males and females. A person was a member of the same rest-holding group as his mother's brother, father's brother, mother's mother's descendants, and so on. This was a group of people that was essentially unbounded: it was everyone to whom one was related, in every way. In theory, all members of a group shared equal rights in the land, but in practice it became difficult for a member to assert a claim if land was scarce. What emerged was a flexible system for allocating land, one in which prominent and powerful people had a somewhat greater ability than others to stake their claims.

Gult-holders could enter the local system of land holding by intermarrying with their neighbors in the countryside. By doing this, they acquired rest rights – to cultivate the land on the basis of shared kinship. They tended, however, to be very special members of the kinship association: they were powerful people who had the authority to judge local disputes, and so they could enforce their own rights to rest-land more effectively than others. They might even succeed in putting together big pieces of kinship land, whereas ordinary rest-holders had to make do with small and divided holdings. The long-term results of this process were that gult-holders who had been given the right to collect tribute sometimes became wealthy in land. They became locally powerful people whose positions did not entirely depend on the whim of the king or of his agents. As they became more independent, the king's local power weakened. In general, the king's control of a region strengthened or weakened over time, as his agents became more or less independent, as they built their own landhold-ings within a locality. The king's power grew or declined also in cases where he awarded pieces of land to prominent followers – in these cases not as gult but directly as awards of land. Even in these cases, which were rarer than gult awards, the king usually gave the land on a temporary basis, and the holders struggled to convert them into permanent family estates. During any one reign the king's power was subject to the outcome of thousands of local struggles over land, and over the capacity of royal clients to defend their positions and to make their land-rights into inheritable property.

Christians, Muslims and Oromo in Ethiopia

The Solomonid kings of Ethiopia engaged in two sets of struggles at the same time. The first was a struggle with gult-holders over whether they were to become hereditary land-holders or remain subject to the will of the king. The second was the struggle to expand the kingdom, and by doing so to extend the area under Christian control. We have already seen, in Chapter 3, that Christian kings and Muslim merchants competed to control the trade to the Red Sea. The kings depended on trade along north-south routes down the backbone of the western highlands, and the Muslims developed the route up the Awash Valley to Shoa. But trade was not all that was at stake. As the period of Solomonid rule unfolded, Christians and Muslims fought also for control over territory.

The most important conflicts crystallized in the Awash Valley and the surrounding highlands. In this area, political leaders within one or another of three traditions competed to control territory and people. At one corner of the religious and political triangle was the Christian kingdom, which expanded towards the Awash Valley through its classic process of informal colonization followed by formal conquest. By the first half of the thirteenth century large numbers of Christian families had moved into the mountain area of Shoa, to the west of the upper Awash Valley. They prepared the ground for the expansion of the kingdom, which then made western Shoa into part of its core territory.

The Muslims, for their part, had begun to control territory in the interior by the early twelfth century, when Muslim traders from abroad succeeded in converting some local rulers. A number of small Islamic states grew up. They participated in the trade with southern Ethiopia and with other parts of the region. These emerged in eastern Shoa and other peripheral parts of Shoa, and also across the Awash Valley in Harar and in Dawaro, in Bale further southwards, and in scattered places along the trade routes. In the first half of the fourteenth century the Christian kingdom took control of a number of these Muslim states and forced them to pay tribute. The most important of the Muslim states, Adal, on the Harar plateau, quickly reasserted its independence. Religious authorities, some of them based in Adal, worked to convert the Somali herders of the surrounding lowlands to Islam.

The third corner in the competitive triangle was occupied by political leaders who practiced local religions and who adopted neither Christianity nor Islam. In the twelfth and early thirteenth centuries the kingdom of Damot, which was based on local religious practices, was a key power in the region until its defeat by the Christian kingdom. In the fourteenth century the areas to the south of the Christian and Muslim states were treated by traders and raiders as sources of gold and ivory, but especially as sources of slaves who practiced neither religion, for export to the Middle East. The competition between Christian and Muslim states was, in part, a competition to control this trade. When the Solomonids conquered a number of small Muslim states they imposed import and export taxes on this trade, and they introduced Christian caravans. The kings of Adal, the Muslim state on the Harar plateau, fought in the last decades of the fifteenth century to challenge Christian control of the trade.

The destruction of Christian control in this region came after the rise to power of Ahmad ibn Ibrahīm al-Ghazi as the leader of Adal in the late 1520s. He was also called Ahmad Gran – "Ahmad the Left-handed." Ahmad built a powerful coalition of Muslim forces. He won the support of religious leaders in Adal and took care to build alliances with powerful Somali leaders of the lowlands. He gave his sister in marriage to one of the most powerful Somali leaders, and concluded alliances with other key Somalis. He made contact with the Ottoman Turks, who had recently expanded their power into Egypt, and who helped him to procure firearms. In 1527 and 1528 Ahmad's forces attacked border areas under loose Solomonid control and then penetrated deep into Christian territory, burning churches and taking captives and booty.

One of the great turning points in Ethiopian history came in the battle of Shimbra-Kure in 1529 between Ahmad's forces and a huge army assembled by the Christian king. The Muslim forces had by this time defined their war as a *jihad*, a religious war for the propagation of Islam. They invaded the highlands of Shoa, fought against superior numbers, and shattered the Christian army decisively. From this point on, Ahmad's forces were unstoppable. He took back the Muslim states of Fatagar and Dawaro that had been controlled by the Christians. By 1531 he was nominating Muslim governors in what had been Christian Shoa. His forces burned down the famous monastery of Debra-Libanos, and continued on northwards into the ancient heartland of the Christian kingdom. In 1535 his forces occupied Tigre, far to the north. By the time they were done they had destroyed the church at Aksum that was the coronation site of the Solomonid kings.

The final result of the religious wars, however, was the decline of both Muslim and Christian power in this region. The great beneficiaries were the Oromo people of the south, whose social and religious institutions proved flexible enough to allow them to take and to hold the territory of their enemies.

The Oromo, sometimes called Galla, speak an Eastern Cushitic language. Some branches of Oromo are sedentary and live primarily by agriculture; others place more emphasis on herding. In the period before Ahmad's wars there were pockets of Oromo in a number of areas near the Awash Valley. Their core homelands were further south, in parts of Bale. The widely dispersed Oromo maintained their unity in a number of ways. They all respected the high priests of Waqa, the sky god. They joined together once every eight years for ceremonies at which they prayed for peace, fertility, and rain. Pilgrims went to one of a few sites where these ceremonies were held. Oromo men were organized in age sets, each one taking in men born over an eight year period. As the men of an age set grew older they moved up through the grades of seniority until their own set was senior enough to take over the leadership of their people.

Oromo institutions proved to be a source of stability in the period of insecurity following the devastating warfare between Muslims and Christians. At a time when people who had lived under Christians or Muslims were desperate, cut loose from the protection of any political leader, Oromo moved in and provided a governmental structure. They practiced a form of adoption so that the homeless could find a new home within an Oromo clan. The head of an Oromo age set would say a prayer blessing new members, who would repeat after him the oath binding themselves to an Oromo clan. They would say, "I hate what you hate, I like what you like, I fight whom you fight, I go where you go, I chase whom you chase," and they would continue with further statements in the same spirit.

The Oromo fought to extend their boundaries: they did not limit themselves to providing a refuge for people cut loose in the wars between Christians and Muslims. They worked to destroy security in areas just beyond Oromo borders so that they could then move in and establish control. For the most part the Oromo avoided the large-scale set battles favored by the Christian royal armies. Instead, they engaged in regular night raiding, always retreating to a safe area, until the place they had been raiding was so beset by insecurity that its people were willing to accept Oromo protection. But raiding alone could not have produced the greatest Oromo advances; these were helped along by the religious wars between Christians and Muslims.

The Muslims, after Ahmad ibn Ibrahīm's victories, proved incapable of consolidating their gains. When Ahmad was killed in battle by the Christians in 1543 his army fell apart; many of his soldiers went over to the other side. The Christians also proved incapable of picking up the pieces and reestablishing control in the regions adjoining the Awash Valley. After 1559 the Christians moved their capital away from Shoa, northwestwards across the Blue Nile, leaving the eastern provinces to the Oromo. By the end of the period of warfare the Muslims at Harar were similarly weakened. To people in the south who were neither Muslim nor Christian the Oromo offered some possibility of security and of protection from their slave-raiding northern neighbors. By the time the wars of the sixteenth century had ended Christian power was much reduced. Muslim power had not taken its place, and the Oromo had occupied a huge area of southern Ethiopia.

The story of the Oromo expansion demonstrates, once again, that large kingdoms did not enjoy any definitive superiority over smaller or more decentralized political systems. The area under Oromo control expanded because their society was able to absorb rootless people and the dispossessed. Institutions at the local level, like Chwezi mediumship in Uganda, and like the network of clientage ties in Rwanda, were central in defining the character of a political system for those who lived within it. It was institutions at the local level that gave comfort and protection to ordinary people, or that sometimes exploited them and left them vulnerable. The value and stability of a political system were defined as effectively by the network of intimate ties at the local level as they were by the size and prestige of its largest structures.

Suggestions for further reading

Berger, Iris, *Religion and Resistance: East African Kingdoms in the Precolonial Period*, Tervuren: Musée Royal de l'Afrique Centrale, série in 80, sciences humaines, no. 105, 1981.

Hassen, Mohammed, *The Oromo of Ethiopia: A History 1570–1860*, Cambridge: Cambridge University Press, 1990.

Munro-Hay, Stuart, *Aksum: An African Civilisation of Late Antiquity*, Edinburgh: Edinburgh University Press, 1991.

Newbury, Catharine, *The Cohesion of Oppression: Clientship and Ethnicity in Rwanda, 1860–1950*, New York: Columbia University Press, 1988.

Schmidt, Peter, *Historical Archaeology: A Structural Approach to an African Culture*, Westport, Conn.: Greenwood Press, 1978.

Schoenbrun, David, "Cattle herds and banana gardens: the historical geography of the western Great Lakes region, *ca* AD 800–1500," *African Archaeological Review*, 11 (1993), pp. 39–72.

Tamrat, Tadesse, *Church and State in Ethiopia, 1270–1527*, Oxford: Clarendon Press, 1972.

6

AFRICA NORTH OF THE FOREST
(1500–1880)

The fifteenth and sixteenth centuries witnessed a new phase in the history of northern Africa, marked principally by the rise of powerful and forceful neighbors. The year 1500 has no particular significance. It is simply a convenient date that will serve as a marker for trends that began far earlier but took on weight and importance about this time. The most spectacular change was the emergence of the Ottoman Empire as one of the three empires that were to dominate the Muslim world in the sixteenth and seventeenth centuries. Turkish nomads from central Asia had captured Baghdad in the eleventh century. A Turkish state under the Ottoman dynasty appeared in Anatolia in the fourteenth century, crossed over into Europe, and began the conquests that ultimately gave it control of the territory that had once been Byzantine. The conquest ended in 1453, when the Ottomans captured Istanbul, the former Constantinople. New Turkish naval power in the Mediterranean, the Turkish seizure of the Levant and then of Mamluk Egypt brought them into Africa. By 1550, they had become dominant across North Africa to the frontiers of Morocco.

In these same centuries, Western Europe also became important for Africa, with a new position of importance in the world based on technological advances going back to the eleventh century. These advances were matched by scholarly work in the sciences, as Europe appropriated all the mathematical and scientific knowledge available from anywhere in the intercommunicating zone. The fact that much of this knowledge came through Islamic transmitters is a small irony in the major transition from an Islamic Age to a European Age in world history. That transition was not complete until the mid-eighteenth century, but it began for the Maghrib in the fifteenth century with Spanish and Portuguese military pressure on the coasts.

Meanwhile, political power in the Maghrib was fragmented in the face of the Turkish and Iberian threats. The successor states of the Almohad Empire were in full decline by the fifteenth century. Central government almost everywhere became a legal fiction, as real political power slipped into the hands of Muslim holy men, Arab lineage authorities, Berber segmentary societies, or small Muslim states.

Seen from across the Sahara, these political changes in North Africa foreshadowed an important shift in Africa's relation to the world. A great Muslim empire, whose heartland was far away in southeastern Europe and Anatolia, now commanded the northern coast of the continent from Suez to the Atlas. In sixteenth-century Morocco, a new dynasty consolidated its power in reaction to the Turkish and Christian threats. Furthermore, the Ottomans and the Moroccans were armed with fire-arms, which were all but unknown south of the Sahara. Both Morocco and Istanbul had diplomatic relations and chronic military conflict with the states of western Europe. During the sixteenth century, Ottoman and Moroccan diplomacy and force reached across the desert. States to the south of the Sahara – from Ethiopia in the east to Jolof and Fuuta Tooro in the west – were pulled, at least indirectly, into the fringes of a web of international relations that linked them distantly to Europe.

In the longer run of history, these changes spelled the beginning of the end of Africa's isolation. But the longer run of history needed several more centuries to be played out. Fire-arms in the service of alien conquerors would bring an end to African independence – but only after 1880. Sixteenth-century fire-arms were not yet dominant on the battlefield. The Ottomans, the Moroccans, and the Europeans, were all armed in the same manner, but sixteenth-century battles in Europe were won by highly trained and disciplined infantry whose key weapon was the pike, not the musket; and the Turks' most effective unit was unarmored cavalry. Artillery was decisive only as a siege weapon until at least the 1630s when light and numerous field artillery began to be available.

Christians, Turks and naval power in the Mediterranean

The Christian threat from the north and the Turkish threat from the northeast were based on naval power. Non-nomad invaders of the Maghrib had always come by sea. It was so of the Phoenicians, the Vandals, the Byzantines, and the first Muslim caliphate. The Maghrib's island-like situation made it hard to reach any other way – except out of the desert. The sea had become even more of a frontier when the Christians held the northern shores and the Muslims the southern. Organization was the key to defense on that frontier as it was against the nomads. When Maghribine society was well organized, and the ports were linked to a productive economy in their hinterland, they could be strong at sea with the combined resources of the whole society. When political authority was fragmented, the ports were on their own, prey to the superior mobility of a seaborne enemy. This jeopardy was also true for the Christian coasts to the north, which were equally subject to raids from the sea when the Muslim powers were strong.

Partly as a result, the coastal Maghrib passed back and forth between relative safety and prosperity on one hand and instability and danger on the other. The theater of action, however, was not the Mediterranean as a whole but smaller regions within it. The Almoravids successfully built their empire and captured Muslim Spain at the same time the Christian Crusaders were capturing Jerusalem at the other end of the sea. To some degree, the Mediterranean basin west of Italy was a single unit, but the strategic places there were the narrow seas – the straits between Sicily and Tunisia and the straits of Gibraltar. From the twelfth century onward, control alternated between Christians and Muslims.

On the Sicilian channel, the Fatimids once controlled Sicily, but in the twelfth

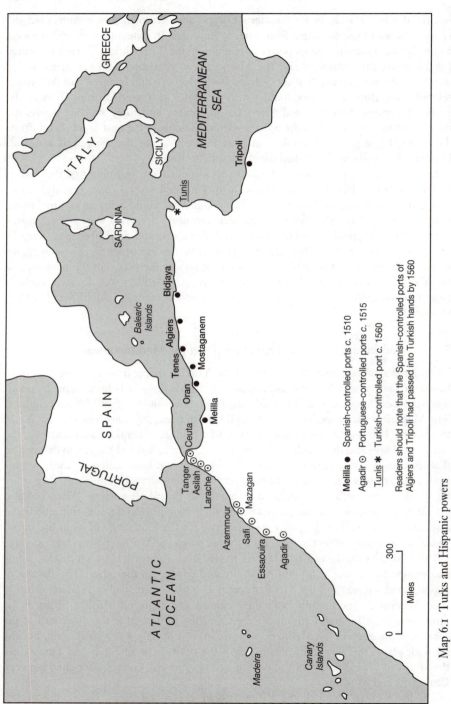

Map 6.1 Turks and Hispanic powers

century as the dynasty weakened, Sicilians captured most of the Tunisian coastline. By 1160, with the rise of the Almohad empire, the Sicilians were again expelled, only to return a century later with French support (it was then that a French king who was also a Christian saint, Saint Louis, was killed trying unsuccessfully to capture Tunis). After that, Tunisia held its own until nearly 1490, though Christians and Muslims continued to raid one another's seaborne commerce and the opposing coasts, in spite of increasing peaceful trade as well.

At the end of the fifteenth century, Christians again returned to the attack. Ferdinand and Isabella, monarchs of Aragon and Castile respectively, married and united Spain. They captured Granada, the one remaining Spanish Muslim kingdom, and Sicily. Spain could now threaten the Maghrib from Gibraltar to Tripoli. From the late 1590s to about 1610, the Spanish descended on the Barbary Coast in a series of raids and captures that gave them Melilla in the west, Mers-el-Kébir near Oran at the center, Bidjaya (formerly Bougie) in Tunisia, and Tripoli still further east. For a time, it looked as though the Spanish monarchs would repeat the Vandal success of a thousand years earlier and conquer the Maghrib from the sea.

Spain's ambitions, however, lay in Italy, and its most serious naval rival in the Mediterranean was the Ottoman empire, which emerged as a naval power in the first decade after 1500. The Ottomans then moved into the Levant and conquered Mamluk Egypt in 1517. By that time, private Ottoman commerce raiders had already appeared in the western basin of the Mediterranean. The most famous were Aruj and Kair-ed-Din, two brothers whom the Christians called the Barbarossas for their red beards. They began harassing the Spanish from about 1510, privately at first but with increasing support from Istanbul. They and the Turkish navy that came to their aid began to capture the North African ports one after another. At first, they simply replaced the Spanish overlordship of the port towns, but after the 1570s they turned to the hinterland as well. It was the Ottomans, not the Spanish, who became suzerain over the Maghrib from Tripoli to western Algeria. The coastline once conquered by the Byzantine Empire from Constantinople was once again conquered from the same capital, now called Istanbul.

A similar struggle was played out west of Gibraltar, where public and private ships of the opposing religions raided each other's coasts and shipping. Muslim Moroccan forces were seriously divided, and the Christians gradually pulled ahead with the seizure of Moroccan port towns. Portugal picked up Ceuta opposite Gibraltar in 1415, adding Tanger, Asilah, and Larache, mainly in the 1470s, and Safi, Agadir, and Azemmour in the early sixteenth century. In time, Morocco would retrieve most of these, but simultaneous with this short-term rise of Portuguese power was a far more significant period of experimentation off the African coasts that led to the major breakthrough of the maritime revolution.

Portugal and the maritime revolution

The maritime revolution of the fifteenth century affected all of Africa. Over the short period between 1430 and 1490, Portuguese mariners opened direct access to the western coast from Tanger to the Cape of Good Hope. A dozen years later, rounding the Cape gave them access to the eastern coast as well. The change was revolutionary; Europeans could now reach almost any coast of Africa, but Europeans were still far too weak to conquer.

In 1444, the first European mariner to reach beyond the Sahara sailed back to Europe. The achievement was greater than may appear at first. It was a coastal voyage, like many Europeans made in the Mediterranean or around the coasts of northwest Europe. The problem was that, while sailing ships could tack back and forth to make progress against a contrary wind, they could rarely get anywhere against both wind and current. On the Saharan coast, the wind blows from the northeast all year round, and it creates a strong current in the same direction. That is why European sailors in the European Middle Ages told about ships that had set out to the southwest down the coast of Africa and had dropped off the edge of the world. In the fifteenth century, however, Portuguese sailors learned that it was possible to sail back against wind and current if they took advantage of the fact that the winds veered inshore in daylight hours and offshore at night. By sailing in a series of long tacks to take advantage of these changes, it was possible to return against wind and current.

That first discovery led on to another that was to be still more important. Sometime between 1444 and the 1470s, Portuguese mariners now unknown found that by sailing on a single long tack to the northwest, keeping as close as possible into the trade winds, one would soon arrive at the latitude of the Azores, where the winds were variable but generally westerly and fair for the Portuguese coast. This discovery not only made it possible to sail easily to Cape Verde and back but was the first recognition that the ocean winds followed a circular pattern. From a little north of the equator to about 30° North or South latitude winds generally blow strongly and uniformly from the northeast or southeast. In the 40s and 50s north or south latitude, prevailing winds blow from the west.

In the 1470s and 1480s, the Portuguese exploited the first phase of this breakthrough by reaching into the south Atlantic. Before 1470, no European ship had sailed beyond Sierra Leone. By 1481, the Portuguese began constructing an expensive castle at Elmina on the Gold Coast, now Ghana – more for protection against European interlopers than against the Africans. By the end of the 1480s, they had explored the equatorial coasts and those of the southern savannas and had reached the Cape of Good Hope. These voyages taught them how to use the wind system south of the equator. Along the east-west coast of the Gulf of Guinea, the winds and currents often tend to the east. They learned that they could escape a difficult return by dropping south across the equatorial calms to catch the southeast trade winds south of the equator. From this, they learned that the north Atlantic pattern was repeated south of the equator.

It was these discoveries off the African coast that made possible the later explorations of Columbus and his successors across the Atlantic and those of Da Gama and his successors around the Cape of Good Hope into the Indian Ocean. This phase of discovery that began about 1430 ended in 1522, when Sebastian del Cano brought Magellan's fleet back to Spain, having discovered that trade winds are uniform and tend to blow in the same direction in similar latitudes all over the world. Once that was known, Europeans could go almost anywhere.

The Portuguese in West Africa

The Portuguese were the first to achieve this maritime breakthrough, and theirs was the first move, the first chance to experiment, to innovate in search of national or personal advantage in sub-Saharan Africa. Especially over the decades before about 1505, when Portuguese interest was diverted to the richer promise of Asian trade, they learned what was and was not possible in the African trade. In the first years, they sometimes practiced coastal raiding, as they did on the coasts of Morocco and as the Moroccans did against their own coast. They soon learned that peaceful trade was more profitable. They learned to leave the inland trade to African merchants whose developed commercial networks were already at hand. They also learned that trade forts were useful in some places, but only if they had the cooperation of the African authorities. It was therefore customary to pay these authorities an annual fee, which Africans and Europeans variously interpreted as tribute, rent, or license fee.

The Portuguese also learned in these first decades that they suffered enormously high death rates from disease in West Africa; 25 to 50 per cent died within a year. They nevertheless tried several different experiments with the African trade, and these served as precedents for other Europeans who were to follow.

Gold was the commodity that had lured them down the African coast in the first place. Europeans had long known that North Africans imported large quantities of gold from sub-Saharan Africa. Well before 1500, the Portuguese had learned the main lines of West African geography. They knew precisely where the gold came from, and Portuguese travelers whose accounts have since been lost visited all three of the important goldfields as well as the court of Mali.

The Portuguese began by offering European products in return for gold and other African exports, but they soon learned that they could also sell their shipping services from one part of Africa to another. West Africans were ready to buy woolen cloth and cavalry remounts from Morocco as well as copper and brass from Europe. The Portuguese were able to supply both by sea in competition with the caravan trade. Once on the Guinea coast, they could sell the metals at a place like Benin in return for beads, pepper, and slaves. The pepper went to Europe, but the beads and slaves were exchanged for gold on the Gold Coast. This trade in slaves from one part of Africa to another died down after the Atlantic slave trade became important, but a European carrying trade from one part of Africa to another remained. Europeans carried African cotton cloth from one part of the coast to another. They brought cowrie shells from the Maldive Islands in the Indian Ocean, which served as a major West African currency. They imported Indian cotton textiles, which were more important than European cottons far into the nineteenth century.

Map 6.2 illustrates a major change in the strategy of trade. Peoples who had been furthest from possible contact with the intercommunicating zone now became among the closest, because relatively cheap maritime shipping was now available. Trade possibilities opened up all along the coast.

Further inland, a balance had to be struck between the old routes across the Sahara and the new routes by sea. Long-distance trade from North Africa to the Gulf of Guinea existed before 1500 from at least two points. One was the Gold Coast, where

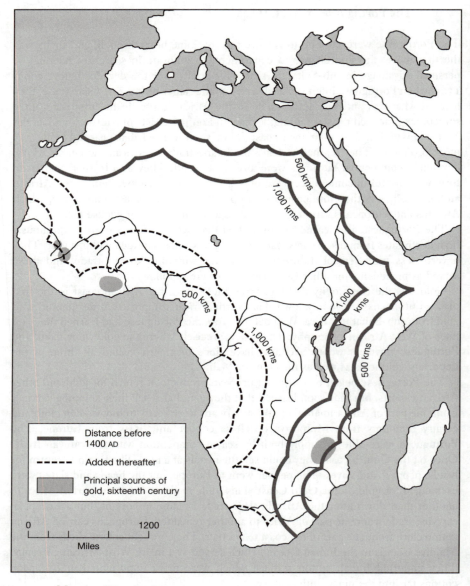

Map 6.2 Distance from ocean ports

the Juula trade route from the Niger at Jenné reached through the Akan goldfield and on to the sea. Another route led south from Hausaland to the Yoruba cities, which in turn had commercial relations with the coast at Dahomey and Benin. From coastal points like these, the maritime revolution could reverse the flow along north–south overland routes, attracting gold toward the seacoast rather than the desert fringe.

When this happened, inland states that lived by the gold trade could be seriously affected. During the sixteenth century, for example, Songhai may well have been weakened by the loss of the gold trade. The ruler, Sonni ʿAli (ruled 1464–92) and his immediate followers built their empire westward along the desert fringe as far as the Senegal, following the old formula for controlling the flow of goods across the Sahara. To the extent that the Portuguese could divert Akan gold to the sea route, Songhai would have less foreign exchange with which to buy northern imports like cavalry remounts.

The Portuguese carried away nearly 700 kilograms of gold in a peak year of the late fifteenth century, and they averaged around 410 kilograms yearly between 1500 and 1520. This was a great deal of gold for its time, perhaps a quarter of the West African annual production. Judging by production levels of the late pre-colonial period, West Africa could probably produce about four metric tons of gold a year. The Portuguese diversion would therefore have been damaging to the revenues of a country like Songhai, but not disastrous.

The reversal of trade flows may have been more serious elsewhere. In the Senegal valley, the dominant state was Jolof, which ruled the whole of Senegambia at the end of the fifteenth century. Because the gold of Bambuk could be brought through Jolof to the mouth of the Senegal or Gambia River, Jolof was a natural setting for Portuguese intervention. About 1590, the Portuguese decided to make a serious effort, sending a fleet of twenty caravels to support the cause of a pretender to the office of *Buurba* or king of Jolof. The effort failed, partly on account of disease and partly because the Portuguese commander quarreled with Jeleen, the African pretender. The Portuguese still had to buy gold on the banks of the Senegal and Gambia through ordinary trade channels.

This coastal trade, however, may well have strengthened coastal Jolof at the expense of the metropolitan province in the interior. About the middle of the sixteenth century, greater Jolof began to break up, and the first provinces to secede were those like Kajoor (Cayor in French) that lay directly on the coast. Within a few decades the Jolof empire had divided into the smaller Wolof-speaking and Serer-speaking states of Waalo, Kajoor, Bawol, Siin, Saalum, and Jolof; of these, only the shrunken Jolof lacked sea or river ports for trade with Europeans.

This Portuguese effort in West Africa had political as well as commercial implications. From a Mediterranean-centered view, the Portuguese and others saw the major struggle of their time as one between the forces of a beleaguered Christendom and those of an advancing Islam, represented most forcefully by the Ottoman Turks. They hoped that maritime advance might find Christian allies somewhere beyond the encircling Muslims – or, failing Christians, allies of any kind who might become Christian.

This particular chimera was inspired by the stories of Prester John, a Christian prince somewhere in the East. By the 1480s, Portuguese agents had already visited the Ethiopian court and discovered that a Christian prince did in fact rule to the east, beyond Islamic lands, and the effort to find African allies was especially strong in the 1490s. Portuguese military support for Jeleen's effort to seize power in Jolof was just such an attempt to put a Christian king on an African throne.

In the kingdom of Kongo south of the lower Congo or Zaire river, a more peaceful approach had greater success. Christian missionaries arrived there in 1491 and soon converted a candidate for the throne. In 1506, he actually took office as Affonso I, the first of a line of Christian monarchs who were to lead an interesting effort at modernization. The early promise of that effort prompted a favorable Portuguese response to another diplomatic initiative from the African side. In 1514, the Oba of Benin sent a mission to Lisbon, hoping to arrange to buy firearms. The Portuguese answered by sending missionaries, who made a few converts but failed to convert the Oba. He, in turn, got no firearms, the missionaries died, and the effort was apparently abandoned on both sides. Meanwhile, the Portuguese continued their missionary work in Kongo, but West Africa was not to receive serious missionary attention until the nineteenth century.

Turkish rule in sixteenth-century North Africa

When the Turks first began to challenge the Spanish hold on Maghribine ports, the people of the hinterland were hardly affected. They were far too divided among themselves to resist the Turks, even if they had wanted to do so. The only strong resistance came from the Spanish masters of the ports, the only people who were actually threatened at first. For the rest, Turks were no worse masters than the Spanish, and they had the advantage of being Muslim. They also took pains to cultivate the 'ulamā in the urban centers, sometimes asking their collective advice about matters of state. In the interior, Turkish authorities tended to work through rural religious leaders like the heads of the sufi brotherhoods, and a broad current of collaboration between the Turks and the brotherhoods lasted through the sixteenth century. Such collaboration was easy enough to maintain, since the Turkish strategy was directed toward maritime affairs, with no serious effort to control the hinterland until the last quarter of the sixteenth century. It was only then that the Ottomans organized three provinces, or regencies, ruled from capitals at Algiers, Tunis, and Tripoli respectively. They apppointed as head of each a *pasha*, directly responsible to Istanbul. This territorial division was the ultimate origin of the present Algeria, Tunisia, and Libya.

The first pashas were Turks sent out for relatively brief terms of office so that they would represent Istanbul's interests in these distant outposts of empire. But the Maghrib was too far away for close control, and each regency soon began to go its own way. The pashas were still dependent on Turkish military support, especially against the Europeans across the sea, but they began to extend their terms of office. After about 1610, they began to act like independent monarchs, though recognizing the theoretical authority of Istanbul.

As the pashas became more independent of the distant sultan, they were obliged to compromise with local sources of power. Each regency had a local council called a *diwan*, intended at first to represent the officers of the garrison and other important Turkish residents. With time, however, others had to be taken into the circle of power, either informally or formally as members of the council. In Algiers and Tripoli, and to some extent in other port towns, the most powerful voice came to be that of the commerce raiders, who were organized in regular guilds.

The Christian–Muslim rivalry at sea is what brought the Turks to the Maghrib in the first place. As time passed, the Europeans dominated peaceful commerce, which left raids against that commerce as a viable alternative for the Maghribine ports. This was the beginning of the "Barbary pirates," as the Europeans called them, though Christian pirates from Malta and elsewhere also lived by raiding Muslims. The Barbary raiders' guilds became the dominant voice in the regency governments of Algeria and Tripoli in all matters having to do with commerce, captured Christian slaves, or diplomatic relations with Europe. They were less important in Tunis, however, because that capital had a more fertile hinterland within easy reach of the port and hence a more powerful voice for the hinterland in setting Tunisian policies.

Elsewhere, the pashas tried to govern through local strong men. They appointed a *ca'id*, or judge, for each important town, leaving the rural areas under existing and diverse local leadership, roughly supervised by Turkish clerks. The ca'ids themselves bought the office, collecting what taxes they could and passing a stipulated amount to the pasha at the port, who was usually more concerned with milking inland sources of revenue than he was with what actually went on in the inland regions. His control was therefore real enough in the towns but minimal in the countryside, which felt his authority only when the ca'id borrowed troops from the port for a systematic tax-gathering expedition. These expeditions were partly a show of Turkish strength to overawe the populace, partly institutionalized robbery that kept the countryside in chronic revolt through the middle decades of the seventeenth century. After a time and especially in Algeria, these raids became so important that their military leaders, bearing the title of *bey*, became more important for internal government than the ca'ids themselves. The whole Algerian hinterland was divided into administrative territories called *beyliks*, each marking off the raiding territory assigned a particular bey.

After the 1660s, the link between the pashas and Istanbul weakened still more. In Algiers, the Turkish garrison revolted against the pasha, and the commerce raiders in turn revolted against the garrison. They still acknowledged formal allegiance to the Ottoman state, but they insisted on electing their own ruler with the title of *dey*. By the eighteenth century, Istanbul recognized this situation, confirmed the elected deys, and granted them the powers of a pasha; but effective control had passed to the dey – and to the three beys, who had meanwhile managed to make their offices hereditary, reducing the tie to Algiers even as Algiers cut the tie to Istanbul. In Tunisia and Tripolitania, the course of events was similar. Commerce raiding was less important, but deys and beys of local origin replaced pashas appointed by Istanbul. But here the dominant oligarchy included more local landlords and heads of Arab lineages.

Egypt was immensely more important to the Ottoman Empire than the Maghrib was, but Ottoman rule became localized there as well. The first administrative expedient was to keep Egypt under tight control through a viceroy with more prestige than an ordinary pasha, though he was assisted and occasionally checked by a diwan representing other officials and military officers. Each important source of wealth was also assigned to an official whose job it was to supervise that aspect of the economy as well as to keep the revenue flowing in.

In the first instance, Turkish rule seems to have improved Egyptian administration and strengthened the economy. In any event, Egypt became a more efficient source of government revenue than it had been in the last years of Mamluk rule. On the other hand, most of the early officials and tax farmers were Turkish Janissaries, that is, they were slave-soldiers or slave-administrators like the Mamluks themselves. Over time, they tended to seize the reality of local power as the Mamluks had done in the past. By the end of the sixteenth century, these new Mamluks controlled local government and dominated the viceroy's diwan. The tax farmers gradually turned themselves into landlords, so that less of the revenue passed on to the central government and more of it went to the local gentry.

By the early seventeenth century, Istanbul recognized the new Mamluk order, at least informally, though it kept better control over the viceroys than it did over the Maghribine pashas. These officials were still appointed from Istanbul. They might face a council with an independent source of power, but they still kept some room for political maneuver. Egypt also remained an important source of Ottoman revenue, and it carried out important functions for the Ottoman Empire as a whole. It was charged, for example, with controlling the Red Sea, garrisoning the Red Sea ports, governing the holy cities of Mecca and Medina, and suppressing any piracy that might affect the pilgrim trade. It was only in the nineteenth century that Egypt became free of actual Ottoman control, in the way the Maghrib had done by the early eighteenth.

Moroccan recovery

At the beginning of the sixteenth century, political disintegration had gone further in Morocco than it had elsewhere in the former Almohad Empire. Yet the Moroccans managed to keep their independence from the Turks on their eastern frontier and from the Spanish and Portuguese to the north. Part of the explanation lies in the structure of Maghribine government. Large states like that of the Almohads were not a monolithic whole whose collapse meant the collapse of all government. They were a form of overrule that left the constituent parts intact. A governing dynasty might be too weak to defend the ports against the Iberians, but the hinterland had its own resources for defense, with or without a strong central government.

Morocco needed *some* central authority to defend against the Turks in Algeria, and a new dynasty arose in the course of the sixteenth century to provide that organization. This new dynasty, the Sa'dians, came to power through a special configuration of nomadic pressure and religious politics. The infidel Spanish and Portuguese were a clear religious danger, but the Moroccan 'ulamā of the late fifteenth century were too closely tied to the failing power of the old regime to rally a mass movement of any kind. The Muslim sufi brotherhoods were another source of religious authority, but they were divided among themselves. This left an opening for a new force in Moroccan politics, the *shurafā* (sing. *sharīf*, plural often written shorfa in English) – the direct descendants of Muhammad.

By this time in Islamic history, whole tribes of Arabs traced their ancestry back to 'Ali and Fatima through the male line, and these people were held in a kind of esteem that made them automatic specialists in religious knowledge and law. The most prominent lineage of this kind in sixteenth-century Morocco was the Sa'di, who had migrated westward across North Africa to settle during the twelfth century in the Dra

Valley on the Saharan side of the Atlas. Shorfa were not just religious leaders; the Sa'di had a military force of their own as well as the ability to rally others to the defense of Islam. About the middle of the fifteenth century, they had begun active military pressure against the Portuguese on the south coast. About 1515, they began to move north in Morocco, conquering the country by force and persuasion. By 1534, they had captured Marrakesh and unified the south. They could then expel the Portuguese from the southern ports and enter maritime contact with the outside world, especially with England. By mid-century, the Sa'dians had conquered all Morocco. This is not to say that they had day-to-day administrative control everywhere – no Moroccan regime had that kind of power before the twentieth century – but they were recognized everywhere as nominal rulers and as actual rulers in the more accessible parts of the country.

Nor did their victory over the infidels give them a monopoly of religious authority within Morocco. The sufi brotherhoods were still strong, especially the Qadiriya with its headquarters for the Maghrib in Algiers and very close links with the Turkish authorities there. The most important rival order was the Jazūli, which supported the Sa'dians. Once in power, the Sa'dians needed money and it was only natural for them to tax their opponents, especially if these opponents claimed religious authority of a different kind from their own. They therefore set out systematically to expropriate the great wealth of the rival brotherhoods and to reduce the authority of reputed holy men. They succeeded to a degree, but they also won a reputation for anti-sufi tendencies that was to come back to haunt them reign after reign. In the longer run, they had to compromise with one after another of the strong brotherhoods in order to gain their support against the Turks and the Iberians. The result was a Sherifian dynasty, but one that had to tolerate a great variety of religious authority and practice.

Military weakness forced the Sa'dians to compromise, unless they could point to a serious external threat. They were a small lineage in a kinship-dominated political system, chronically arrayed against other and larger family interests. When the infidels threatened, however, they could call up far more support from the whole country. In 1578, when Portugal invaded northern Morocco, the Moroccans defeated them decisively at the battle of al-Ksar al-Kebir (Alcazarquivir in English, sometimes called the battle of the three kings). King Sebastian of Portugal and the Sa'dian sultan were both killed. Ahmad al-Mansur (1578–1603), who was credited with the victory, came to the Moroccan throne. Portugal was weakened and the Portuguese crown passed to the Spanish monarch until 1640.

Even after his victory, the new sultan had to face the fact that the central government could not count on a regular and faithful military force. He therefore tried a number of expedients. One was to hire Turkish and European mercenaries as a standing army. Another was to use slave soldiers imported from sub-Saharan Africa, on the model of the Janissaries of Turkey or the Mamluks of Egypt. In the short run, this policy strengthened the regime at home and abroad, though it courted the long-range danger that a standing army might take power into its own hands.

Al-Mansur's greatest military and political achievement was to preserve Moroccan independence. That may seem to be no more than other sultans had done, but this was the period when the Spain of Philip II nearly dominated the whole of western Europe. It was also the period when the Ottoman Turks were still strong in the Mediterranean, when the reality of their power in Algeria was nearly at its peak. In fact, Morocco would probably not have been defensible if either the Spanish or the Ottomans had decided on an all-out attack. What saved the country, as it was to do many times in the future, was the rivalry of its opponents. Most of the time, al-Mansur could count on some English support against Spain, on Spanish support against the Turkish threat, and on Turkish support against a potential Spanish invasion.

Al-Mansur was also involved in the western Sudan. His great adventure in foreign policy was a cross-desert attack on Songhai in 1591. It was not really a major invasion, though it ended the Songhai empire. The Moroccans never even tried to conquer all that Songhai had once controlled. A Moroccan force held the Niger bend for a time, but the Arma, the local Moroccan force based in Timbuktu, no longer obeyed orders from the north. The Moroccan government made some short-term gains in improved gold trade, but the main importance of the trans-Saharan strike was that it marked the beginning of nearly two centuries in which sub-Saharan Africa was to be a serious concern in Moroccan international relations – not least because it was the most convenient source of the slave soldiers that were an increasingly important element in the standing army.

Al-Mansur's successors could not maintain the degree of control he had created. For a time, the country was divided between rival Sa'dian princes, and the religious brotherhoods again became informal rulers over much of the countryside. It was, indeed, the beginning of the end of power for the Sa'dian dynasty, though not for the shorfa as a ruling group. The next dynasty, the Alawī, were also shorfa and also Arabs from the Hilalian invasions, who had settled in the oasis region of Tafilelt beyond the Atlas to the south of Fez. After a slow buildup of power there on the fringes during the mid-seventeenth century, the Alawī emerged under Mawlay ar-Rachid to capture Fez and found a new dynasty.

Like the Sa'dians before them, the Alawite dynasty rose rapidly to a pinnacle of power represented in this case by the reign of Mawlay (or Prince) Isma'il (ruled 1672–1727), followed by several decades of political fragmentation and dynastic rivalry. Like al-Mansur before him, he built a slave army, mainly recruited in the western Sudan. This meant that he too became involved in sub-Saharan affairs. He led one expedition across the desert in person in 1689, married into the Sudanese aristocracy, and established at least a nominal Moroccan control over the whole of the western Sahara. After his death in 1727, however, real power passed to the sub-Saharan soldiers of the royal guard, just as it passed to the equivalent body of Mamluks in Egypt. The guard made and unmade sultans at will for the next three decades, and central power returned only gradually, with the rise of new power under able Alawī sultans in the second half of the eighteenth century.

The central Sudan

African states south of the desert were, like Morocco, forced to react to the rise of Ottoman power. In the central Sudan, states along the desert fringe on either side of Lake Chad and as far west as the upper Senegal had their main contact with the outside world across the desert, with little influence from the Atlantic trade. The region was dominated in the early sixteenth century by two powers – Borno just west of Lake Chad and Songhai centered on the Niger bend. They were not in direct conflict with each other, but they were rivals to control the trans-Saharan trade and to influence other states that lay between them. To the south, in what is now northern Nigeria, political and military power lay with the Hausa states, a group of a dozen or so states centered on a walled capital city.

The rivalry between the Sa'dians of Morocco and the Ottomans elsewhere in North Africa had important repercussions south of the Sahara, where Borno and Songhai were the principal players. Each of these four – Morocco, Ottomans, Songhai and Borno – sought to control as much of the trans-Saharan trade as possible, especially the gold trade and the sources of salt in the desert. For Borno, the rise of Ottoman power was both a threat and an opportunity. Borno had long-term diplomatic contact with North African states. When the Ottomans seized Tripoli in 1549, Borno hastened to establish relations with the new masters of Libya. Such relations were important for the health of the trans-Saharan trade, because the Ottomans had established their control over the central Saharan oases of Fezzan even before they seized Tripoli. Borno was wary, but it used the Ottoman contact to further its own power. The Ottomans had access to muskets, and Borno became the first state to bring firearms south of the Sahara, along with Turkish mercenaries to instruct local soldiers. At the same time, Borno also made diplomatic contact with the Morocco of the Sa'dians, ready to call on the North African rivals in case the Ottomans threatened to send a military expedition across the desert.

By the 1570s, Borno was moving toward a second peak of power and success in the world, equivalent to an earlier peak in the reign of Dunama Dibbalemi in the thirteenth century. The early reign of Mai Idris Alauma (ruled 1564–99) is chronicled in a contemporary account in greater detail than that of any other Sudanese ruler. This account, by Ahmad ibn Furtu, pictures a pious Muslim monarch much concerned to improve the mosques and extend the judicial system. It also pictures an endless round of military activity against recalcitrant minorities within the kingdom and against foreign enemies in all directions. The kindest interpretation is to see this constant raiding as the necessary path toward political consolidation and the creation of a Kanuri nation. Another view suggests that this was Borno's response to the Turkish challenge. Guns and powder had to come from the north; but here in the Chadic region, without gold to pay for imports, slaves had to serve instead. It may also have been easy to capture slaves in this period, when Borno had guns and its neighbors did not.

The region east of Kanem barely began to emerge into the light of historical knowledge in the sixteenth century. One or more states had existed even earlier in the Marra mountains of Darfur, but between there and Borno we can only guess that some small states may have shared the territory with a variety of stateless societies and kin-based political organizations of pastoral people. Islam had begun to come in by way of Borno, which served as a transmitter of influences from North Africa to the east as well as toward Hausaland to the west. About 1600, a new state of Bagirmi emerged east of Lake Chad, occasionally absorbed by Borno but mainly independent. A decade or so into the seventeenth century, Wadai appeared as a newly Islamicized state further east,

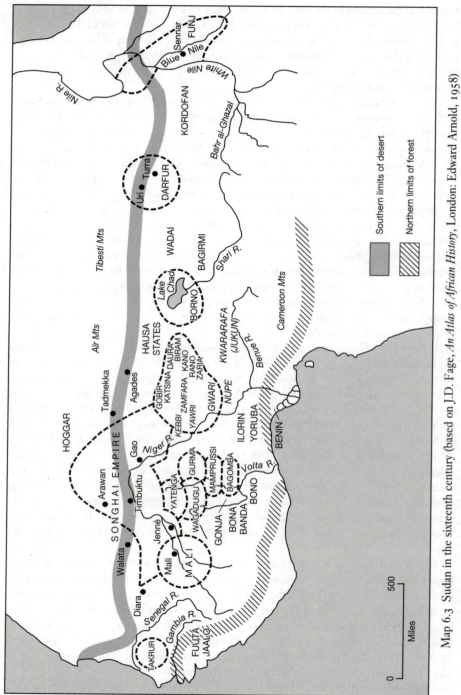

Map 6.3 Sudan in the sixteenth century (based on J.D. Fage, *An Atlas of African History*, London: Edward Arnold, 1958)

under a dynasty that maintained itself in power until 1911. A new Islamic state also emerged or reemerged in Darfur about the 1630s. All three of these states had some contact across the Sahara with North Africa, but they tended to operate even more on a commercial and diplomatic axis that ran east toward the Nile Valley and west toward Borno. When Borno was strong, they were pulled that way, only to be attracted in the opposite direction when there was a strong power in the Nilotic Sudan.

The fall of Songhai

Songhai's position in the trans-Saharan trade was similar to that of Borno. The important trade partner to the north was Morocco, with the Ottomans in southern Algeria as a potential alternate. It is hard to avoid being struck by the contrast between Songhai and Borno in the late sixteenth century. Each increased its contact with a new power to the north of the desert. For Borno, the result was to reinforce its political and military influence. For Songhai, it was military defeat of disastrous consequence for much of the western Sudan.

Songhai of the early sixteenth century was the largest empire to be assembled in tropical Africa before the European conquest. Its core area to the south of Gao was small, and the Songhai ethnic group was one of the smallest in the whole empire. The first conquests assembled a kind of nuclear Songhai centered on the Niger bend and the Niger valley upstream toward the goldfields. This control was consolidated during the spectacular reign of Sunni ʿAli Ber (1464–92). His rivals claimed that he was not a true Muslim, and a Muslim coalition drove him from power and stressed the need to use the power of the state to further the word of God. The first important ruler of the new dynasty was Askia Muhammad (ruled c.1493–1528). He not only stood firm against the pagan practices of the countryside; he also began the push of conquest over the desert edge to the west. Some have suggested a possible ambition to make himself ruler of a united and Islamic western Sudan. If so, he failed; he was finally deposed by his own sons, and his legacy was a long period of religious strife.

Economic pressures also appeared. The Portuguese effort to reverse the trade routes and export gold by sea may have made some difference, but Songhai's long reach along the desert edge seems to have helped to reestablish the trans-Saharan gold export. Portuguese exports from the coast declined after about 1520. In the early sixteenth century, Songhai also gained control of the salt-mining areas in the Sahara and directed at least one long-distance raid across the desert into southern Morocco. But military activities on this scale were very expensive, and contestants for the title of Askia spent most of their effort fighting one another. By the 1580s, Songhai was large but internally divided, and Morocco was strong after the victory over the infidels in 1578. Morocco began in the 1580s with moves against the salt mines, then in 1591 mounted an invasion across the desert.

The Moroccan army sent across the desert was small by Sudanese standards, only about 4000 men, but it was enough to defeat a Songhai army many times its size. The victory, however, was not a conquest of Songhai. The Songhai state was so disunited that it simply fell apart. All the Moroccan force won was control of the Niger bend, and especially of the trading city of Timbuktu. The Moroccan victory is sometimes credited to the use of firearms, which were loud and spectacular; and the Moroccan forces came to be called *Arma*, from the Arabic *ruma*, meaning musketeer. But the key to success was more likely the tactic of using disciplined mercenaries and slave-soldiers against the uncoordinated mass of the Songhai army. The recent economic pinch in Songhai could also have caused a serious remount problem since horses large enough for serious use as cavalry had to be imported from the north.

In any event, the Moroccan success was limited. The Arma were strong enough to seize and keep the desert ports like Timbuktu and Gao, but they were not strong enough to recreate the Songhai empire. The Songhai homeland on the Niger below Timbuktu was rarely under Arma control. Their strategic interest was to move upstream toward the goldfields, but their power to expand within the Sudan was limited. Moroccan power to control them from across the desert was even more limited. The local commander soon became an independent sovereign in all but name. By the 1610s, the Arma had taken local wives and made themselves into an independent ruling class, receiving no support from, and accepting no orders from Morocco. They and their descendants stayed on as rulers of Timbuktu and its vicinity until 1737, sometimes controlling a little of the surrounding country. The whole episode is reminiscent of Kanem's trans-Saharan conquest of Fezzan in the thirteenth century; Kanem also lost control after a few decades but left a Kenembu dynasty ruling Fezzan for about a century and a half.

Some authorities have seen the fall of Songhai as a calamity for West Africa, the beginning of disorder and decline that lasted well into the nineteenth century. It is true that no great empire rose in the place of Ghana, Mali, or Songhai. That may have weakened sub-Saharan control over the desert trade and opened the way to nomadic attack, but ordinary people back from the desert fringe may have been as well or better off than they had been under a "great empire." The more serious problem was the return of long periods of drought like those of the 1970s and 1980s. The whole of the desert fringe experienced severe drought and famine combined with epidemic disease in the 1590s, from 1639 to 1643, and again from 1738 to 1756.

But the desert edge was not all of West Africa, nor even all of the western Sudan. We have no evidence of a similar time of troubles among the second-tier states south of the desert-savanna frontier. The Hausa states appear to have prospered in the seventeenth and eighteenth centuries, though also affected by the periods of drought. They may even have gained some of the trans-Saharan trade diverted from the Niger bend. Upstream from Timbuktu, in the first half of the eighteenth century, a new state rose to power in the Niger valley, based on the city of Segu. It was ethnically Bambara and non-Muslim by religion. It encroached on the declining power of Mali to the south, established its dominance over the Fulbe herdsmen in the internal delta of the Niger, and expanded toward the desert edge. Segu in short, seized the length of the Niger from Timbuktu to Jenné – the crucial center of the nuclear Songhai empire and the territory the Arma had tried to control as well – and that gave control over the flow of trade from the forest toward the desert. In the last decades of the century, Kaarta, a second Bambara offshoot of Segu, rose to power along the desert edge between the Niger and the Senegal and began a career of expansion westward toward the Senegal valley, following the ancient strategy of seeking to control as long a section of the desert edge as possible.

The key military institution in both Segu and Kaarta was the *tõ jõ* (literally slave association), a standing army of slave-soldiers that began as an association of slave raiders who gradually built their power into permanent rule over the region. In this respect they were not very different from the Arma. Their rise to a position of military dominance paralleled the decline of the Arma, and Kaarta, alone of the desert-edge states, was successful in putting up a united defense against the Moroccans operating to the north of the Senegal.

Elsewhere, we often know only the outlines of political history – too little for confident generalizations about the health and well-being of society. At times, a military offensive may indicate strength, though military power can hardly be taken as an index of social health. The territory within the Niger bend, in present-day Burkina Faso and northern Ghana, for example, was the homeland of seven states that made up the Mossi complex. In the fifteenth century, at the time when the leader was Yatenga, they emerged briefly into the international forum of the northern tier with a bid to seize control of the desert edge and the Niger bend. As it turned out, Songhai won that position; the Mossi lost and dropped back to their old homeland.

Turks and Christians in eastern Africa

When the Ottomans conquered Egypt in 1517, they made little effort to reach up the Nile into the Sudan. Their furthest stretch in that direction was northern Nubia, which they controlled briefly, only to see their own officials transform themselves into independent rulers. Further south, the Funj kingdom of Sennar came into existence at the beginning of the sixteenth century, quite independent of Turkish moves in Egypt or the Red Sea. Very little is known of this state or its history other than that the Funj seem to have originated along the White Nile just below the *sudd* region. They first made themselves a ruling aristocracy in the *gezira* (the long peninsula separating the White and Blue Niles just above their confluence), ruling over subjects who were partly Arabian and partly of local Sudanese origin. At some time, probably quite early in their rule, they converted to Islam, and at their seventeenth-century peak of power they controlled the whole region from the Red Sea west to Kordofan.

The Turks were far more interested in the Red Sea and the valuable trade of the Indian Ocean than they were in the upper Nile, but the Indian Ocean was already contested by the Europeans. In 1505, the Portuguese arrived in strength and established bases on the East African coast. In the decade that followed, they made good their naval supremacy and tested it against the best fleets the Egyptians and other Muslim naval powers could muster. They also learned the limitations of their sea power: they were unable to secure a base capable of blocking the straits of Bab el Mandeb and closing off the Red Sea. Once in control of Egypt, the Turks built ships on the Red Sea and soon established their naval supremacy there, but they could not extend that power into the Indian Ocean.

This standoff between Portuguese and Turkish sea power had immediate consequences for the Ethiopian highlands. In the early decades of the sixteenth century, the

Christian monarchy of the western highlands was still the strongest state in the region. Adal was a Muslim rival, but it was only a minor power confined to the eastern highlands. By the 1520s, the Portuguese-Ottoman conflict at sea cut heavily into the trade and prosperity of the whole region. The Turkish presence may also have acted as a new encouragement to Muslim aggression.

As we saw in the previous chapter, the Sultan of Adal, Ahmad ibn Ibrahīm al-Ghazi, began to rebuild his power in this period. When he declared holy war against the Christians, he used some firearms acquired from the Turks but relied mainly on the nomads' response to the call of Islam and the lure of booty. The Portuguese countered by sending musketeers of their own, but the Muslim cause was generally successful. We have seen that Ahmad ibn Ibrahīm conquered the Christian highlands, but then died in battle. His coalition fell apart, opening the region to the expanding power of the Oromo, who were neither Christian nor Muslim.

Meanwhile, the Portuguese military intervention had opened the country to more extensive contacts with the West. The Jesuit order sent a mission to convert the Coptic Ethiopians to Catholicism. In time, the Emperor Susenyos (ruled 1607–32) did become a Catholic, and he embarked on a program of modernization coupled with doctrinal reformation. He made some gains, but he ran into bitter opposition from the Ethiopian clergy and the people at large. The result was civil war leading to his defeat and abdication and finally the expulsion of the missionaries. Ethiopia was then more isolated than ever, faced with the problem of continuing Oromo migration and infiltration through the seventeenth and eighteenth centuries, as provincial power grew at the expense of the monarch. By 1770, Christian Ethiopia was a single kingdom in name only.

The twilight of Turkish rule in North Africa

Ottoman rule over North Africa weakened slowly over the seventeenth century, but the decade centered on 1710 brought changes that made Turkish overrule little more than a fiction. The Bey of Tunis made his regime hereditary, founding a new dynasty that was to last two and a half centuries, though he recognized the theoretical Turkish claim to ultimate sovereignty. The Dey of Tripoli did much the same with the consent of his diwan, founding the Karamanli dynasty that lasted until the Turks reconquered Tripoli in 1835. The oligarchy of Algiers expelled the Turkish pasha at about the same time but failed to achieve the kind of stability a hereditary monarchy might have brought in its place. The office of dey passed from hand to hand with the play of local political forces. Of the thirty-odd deys who ruled between 1671 and 1818, fourteen gained office by killing his predecessor.

The old cross-Mediterranean rivalry with the Christians continued, but the regencies were now independent enough to fight one another. Tunisia's greatest threat came from Algiers, which tried several times to make Tunis tributary. Tunis meanwhile threatened Tripoli in much the same way.

All three regencies nevertheless kept a shadow of Turkish rule. The Karamanli of Tripoli were themselves of Turkish origin, though they had intermarried for several generations with the local Arab ruling families. The Turkish garrison in Algiers continued as an important force, with soldiers recruited from Anatolia as late as the early nineteenth century. Tunisia alone took on the appearance of a fairly homogeneous state with a centralized monarchy having a semblance of control over the countryside. The explanation is geographical; the agriculturally rich Tunisian plains were the immediate hinterland of the port. Tripoli, by contrast, was little more than a port city with a narrow hinterland backed up against the steppe and desert. Algiers had a mosaic-like hinterland of Arabs and Berbers in the good agricultural land near the coast, Berbers in the mountains, still more Arab and Berber nomads in the far hinterland, and the Turkish oligarchy in the capital.

Egypt also entered a new political phase with a civil war in 1711. The Mamluks were once more victorious over the Turkish garrison, which greatly weakened the viceroy's powers. But here the Ottomans could still exercise power on occasion. Istanbul's acquiescence, if not its prior consent, was needed for major policy changes. The Mamluk oligarchy shrank through time to a total of twenty-four officers with the title of bey. Each of these officeholders competed with the others for imperial favor, and the viceroy kept a measure of real power from his ability to play off one against others. From time to time, one or another combination of Mamluk political forces tried for more effective independence on the order of the Maghribine regencies, but the Ottomans still had the power to send an expeditionary force from Turkey and restore the old equilibrium.

Toward the end of the eighteenth century, the broader international situation began to change. Europe was stronger and the Muslim powers weaker. In the sixteenth century, the Ottomans had been a serious threat to eastern and southern Europe. In the seventeenth, Ottoman armies could still march on occasion to the walls of Vienna, but not in the eighteenth. By the 1760s, the British East India Company had already replaced the Mogul Empire as the strongest power on the Indian subcontinent, and the Dutch East India Company was stronger than any one of the Muslim sultanates of Southeast Asia. In 1798, Napoleon successfully invaded Egypt. Though other Europeans soon forced him to give up his dreams of North African empire, and colonial rule was still some decades away, European military superiority was an implicit threat of conquest sometime in the future.

Religion and reform in North Africa

Historians today explain the growth of European military power in the eighteenth century by the early development of industrial technology, taking the form of light and cheap field artillery or superior sailing warships. Thinking Muslims of the eighteenth century had to find their own explanations – and suggestions for future action. One response was technological, borrowing what the Europeans had invented. Another, and the dominant answer in the eighteenth century, was religious. It was religion that defined membership in Christendom or Islam. Christians often credited Christianity for their successes, and Muslims credited Islam. More to the point, if Muslims seemed to be slipping behind, it must be that something had gone wrong with the kind of Islam they practiced. For most devout Muslims in the eighteenth century the fault was failure to follow exactly the way set out by the Prophet. Details varied, but one recurrent theme was to blame the tolerance of semi-pagan practices, especially practices that had grown and spread with expansion of the sufi brotherhoods.

By the eighteenth century, the sufi turuq were both numerous and various. They were especially strong in the Berber west, in the northern parts of the Ottoman Empire, and in India – in precisely those parts of the Muslim world that were newest to the faith, beyond the range of everyday Arabic speech, beyond the core area of Islam represented by the 'Abbasid Empire. But sufi orders were also common in the Arabic-speaking core areas. World religions often made a place for earlier religious beliefs, as the Muslims adopted the sacred ka'ba in Mecca, or the Christians of northern Europe adopted the pagan Christmas tree.

But sufi thought also followed trends common to much of the Muslim world. Almost all the sufi brotherhoods had been affected by the teachings of Ibn al-'Arabi in thirteenth-century Spain. Orthodox Muslims had accounted for the existence of evil in the world by accepting the idea that an omnipotent and merciful God allowed evil to exist for his own reasons, which humans could not know, though evil acts would be punished in the life hereafter. Al-'Arabi and his followers sought an intense and emotional love of God; they could not reconcile that emotional state with the notion that a perfect God would allow any evil at all. Their solution was to deny that the apparent evil people experience *is* evil. Because of God's essential goodness, they argued, what appears to be evil must be good in some ultimate way that mere mortals cannot understand.

Doctrines that shared this tendency could lead some to reject the earthly world and spend their time in study, prayer, and contemplation of God's greatness. Some sufi doctrines took that direction, but others began with al-'Arabi's teachings only to adopt a kind of fatalism with the conviction that whatever happens must ultimately be for the best. Still another possibility was open amorality, arguing that, because people act as God wills, God will not punish them in the next life for doing what He himself has ordained, however much it might seem contrary to common morality. The more extreme versions went beyond any reasonable definition of Muslim orthodoxy, but these sufi teachings were nevertheless tolerated in the Ottoman empire alongside those of the urban 'ulamā.

The sufi brotherhoods also became more elaborate institutions as time passed. From their beginnings as informal groups which happened to follow and propagate the teachings of a particular mystic, they became societies with formal membership and rules of behavior as well as ritual. Sometimes the members lived together in a special retreat house or monastery called *ribāt* or *zāwiya* in Arabic. Those who did not reside together were often expected to pay calls at these religious centers from time to time, if only to maintain their personal contact with the head of the order or his regional representatives.

The turuq officials were not simply recognized men of learning, 'ulamā, they had a kind of institutional authority over their followers, and they were thought to possess special powers others lacked – powers passed down from the original founder of the order through a mystical chain of benediction called a *silsila*. An important sufi leader could recite his silsila as a chain of transmitters of learning and holiness back to the head of his order and beyond to someone who had known and learned from

Muhammad himself – usually ʿAli, as the person closest to the Prophet. The sufi clerics, or *marabouts*, of North Africa often had secular power, as well as religious authority based on the chain of transmission. They had a permanent organization with a permanent headquarters and often a set of regional headquarters under subordinate marabouts. Because their followers owed them obedience, they had some of the kind of authority most often exercised by a state. On occasion, they could step forward and claim to replace the state.

Some historians have argued that sufism met a genuine and felt need for religious experience; others claim that it also encouraged religious charlatanism, saint worship, and fatalism, all of which corrupted the morals and body politic of the Ottoman Empire and Morocco alike during the eighteenth century. Whether this charge is justified or not, several religious reformers of that century saw the broad currents of sufism as a cancerous growth that had to be removed from the body of Islamic belief.

The most important reform movements of this kind began in central Arabia about 1744 with the teachings of Muhammad ibn ʿAbd al-Wahāb. He wanted to return to the original Islam. This program included strong elements of puritanism and anti-sufism, and it gained the military support of the Arabian house of Saʾud. The Wahabis conquered most of Arabia including the holy cities and then moved north against the Ottoman Empire. As they moved forward on the battlefield, their doctrine also changed. The original criticism of sufi excesses went on to attack the orthodox ʿulamā for their tolerance of those excesses.

The Wahabis failed in battle in 1818 and never recovered their former military power, but the doctrine spread far more widely. The demand for religious reform spread more widely still. These broader ripples reached the core area of the Ottoman world, including Egypt, and they were to merge in the nineteenth century with other varieties of Islamic reformism. In the Maghrib, however, sufism was and remained far stronger than it was in the Middle East, and a new sufi order, the *Tijaniyya*, was founded by Ahmad al-Tijāni in southern Algeria as late as 1781. But even there the reform movement gained some adherents, including at least one ʿAlawi sultan of Morocco, though the Moroccan situation was complicated by the fact that the sultans claimed one kind of baraka through descent from Muhammad, while the sufi leaders claimed another through the silsila of their orders.

Religion and society south of the desert

The demand for religious reform took still another direction south of the Sahara. There, Islam had been introduced by informal missionary work, not by conquest or state action. West African Islam was sufi from the beginning and it has remained so ever since. It was also more than a religious message promising salvation to those who would do God's will. Islam meant literacy for serious Muslims, and this opened a small window onto the literatures of the intercommunicating zone. It also carried ethical standards, injunctions, and a body of law that was (or should have been) enforced by the state on believers and unbelievers alike. Acceptance of the new religion therefore meant an acceptance of social change. Islam thus began to change West African society, but West African society also changed Islam. This is not to say that Islam in the western Sudan became less "pure" than the Islam of North Africa or the Middle East; its purity is beside the point for historical analysis. The point is that people adjusted to the new religion, not by splitting the difference between the new orthodoxy and the traditional gods, but by changing their beliefs and actions in several areas of thought and life. The new religion fitted into its new setting by shaping society to some degree and by adjusting to it as well.

Islam came to West Africa as a merchants' religion identified with commerce from the start. It was only natural that West African merchants would be among the first to convert. It was they who had the closest contact with Muslim merchants from North Africa, and their own travels through West Africa carried them beyond the effective range of local deities who were associated with particular places or particular lineages. A more universal message suited their widening range of experience. Rulers also had close contact with the alien merchants, and they too were among the early converts – they and the people of the towns and the court.

But a ruler could not change his religion as a private act, either as a whim or from deep personal conviction. Where the masses were still non-Muslim, his conversion was a political act simply because of the long association between religion and kingship. Just as the head of a lineage was often the oldest male member and was seen as the natural intermediary between the ancestral spirits and the living members of that lineage, so too it was common in African states to conceive of the ruler as having a special ritual position in relation to the gods, especially the gods of particular peoples and places – those below the universal pantheon. A king who became a Muslim could compromise, of course, and carry out his ritual functions in regard to the old gods alongside his obligations to the One God. He could even encourage Islam, support scholarship and learning, but still fall short of the full enforcement of Muslim law. Many Muslim rulers were forced into this position, where their private beliefs might be most orthodox yet their public acts were not. Whatever his private convictions, a West African ruler was caught in a position where actions measuring up to the highest standards of Islam were very difficult.

Not so for the merchants as a class. They were under no such pressure to compromise. They might even see an advantage in the status of religious specialist. The best kind of Muslim education carried literacy, of undoubted use in commerce. Religious prestige, or the reputation of having power to manipulate the spirit world, had obvious uses in non-Muslim as well as in Muslim territory. Like some of the commercial specialists in nineteenth-century Iboland who used their religious reputation to pass back and forth through a stateless society, Muslim merchants sometimes encouraged a belief that Islamic learning brought them secret powers over the spirit world. In 1625, Richard Jobson, an English merchant, reported of his Jahaanke fellow merchants whose route ran inland from the upper Gambia: ". . . they have free recourse through all places, so that howsoever the Kings and Countries are at warres and Up in arms, the one against the other, yet still the Marybucke [Marabout] is a privileged person, and may follow his trade or course of traveling, without any let or interruption of either side."

It was also in the merchants' interests to insulate themselves from the society through which they traveled. People connected with trade diasporas had tended to do

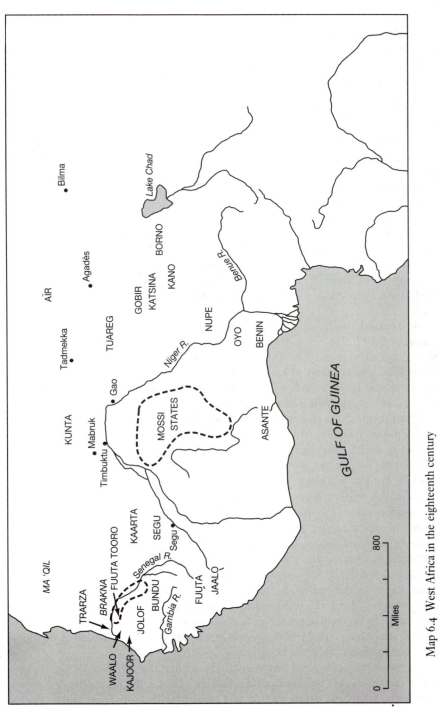

Map 6.4 West Africa in the eighteenth century

this from ancient times by setting up autonomous enclaves whenever possible. Within these enclaves, they enjoyed the right to live under their own laws and to have a representative to deal with the host government on their behalf. The western Sudan had a similar practice from a very early date. The capitals of Ghana and Gao were double cities as early as the eleventh century – one city for the king and court, the other for the merchants. Since the merchants were often Muslim, the separation was sometimes drawn on religious lines, as it was in Ghana before the court converted to Islam. Later towns with a strong reputation for Muslim piety and learning were sometimes granted autonomy by the state. Jakhaba (in French, Diakha-Ba) on the Bafing near the Bambuk goldfields was a Jahaanke town that had such a grant from the government of Mali.

Long before the eighteenth century, this division between the political and religious elites, each with its own sphere of activity, became widespread in the western Sudan. On the religious side, it was often accompanied by the ideal of pacifism and a suspicion that political rule was unworthy of a truly religious person. Although the distinction between the two elites may have originated in the need of the clerical and commercial group to protect itself in its minority position, the ideal may also be associated with certain aspects of North African sufism, with Kharijite overtones. Whatever its origin, it made for a deep division between secular and religious leadership in the western Sudan.

As time passed, this division became a source of conflict. In the first instance, fervent Muslims urged Muslim rulers to enforce Muslim law more thoroughly and on all their subjects, regardless of religion. This placed a Muslim ruler on the horns of a dilemma. If he took the prescriptions of his religion seriously, he was obliged to try to impose Islam on all the people. Such a course, however, was likely to alienate many of his subjects, and it might well destroy whatever pre-Islamic religious ideology had supported and justified his rule in the first place. If, on the other hand, he ignored or tolerated pagan practices, Muslim clerics might consider him an enemy of the faith. Even though the Muslim community in most of West Africa was small, it was powerful; it included the literate, the merchants, and those with closest ties to the greater world beyond the borders of a single state.

Signs of this tension appear early in history. Dunama Dibbalemi, the great thirteenth-century ruler of Kanem, chose one horn of the dilemma and opened the *mune*, a container of sacred regalia that was supposed to protect the dynasty only so long as it remained closed and hidden. Symbolically, he thus denied his sacred role as a ruler – and the justification of that rule in the eyes of his pagan subjects. There is some evidence that this denial seriously weakened the Sefawa dynasty and ended the rise of Kanem. Later, at the end of the fifteenth century, Sonni 'Ali of Songhai took the opposite course. Though he was formally a Muslim, he capitalized on his prestige as a sacred figure in the traditional religion, at the price of serious opposition from the clerics of Timbuktu. This Muslim opposition was one reason for the fall of the Sonni dynasty and its replacement by the Askias.

These two instances suggest that the outright seizure of either horn of the dilemma could be disastrous. Yet the Muslim ruler had little choice: the most delicate compromise between Islam and paganism was, to a pious Muslim, a decision against the full teachings of the Prophet. The orthodox view of sunni Islam held that the ruler had an obligation to see that Muslim law was fully enforced. Yet most Muslim rulers were tolerant of pagan practices, and the cry for religious reform demanded state action, not just personal action. It was an easy step from the cry for reform to the cry for revolution – from the demand that rulers should do as the 'ulamā said, to the demand that the 'ulamā themselves should rule.

The revolutionary force of Islamic reform grew with the passage of time. It was implicit in the change of dynasties in sixteenth-century Songhai. It became explicit in the seventeenth century with the idea that tolerance of paganism was tantamount to paganism itself. Jihad could then be declared against rulers who were actually Muslim, and a sequence of jihads on that basis began and continued far into the nineteenth century. Before the movement had run its course, scores of governments were overthrown, their secular rulers replaced by Muslim clerics. The clerics often emphasized the religious nature of their new office by taking the title of *Imam* or its derivatives in African languages, like the Poular *Almaami*. In normal usage, Imam is simply the title of the leader of prayer at the Friday mosque, hence its suggestion of religious guidance. In Africa it was often coupled with the title *amir al-Mu'minīn*, commander of the faithful, the title used by the Umayyad caliphate when all Muslims were united in a single state, suggesting a militant and united Islam.

Just as Islam itself came to the western Sudan by way of the Sahara, the reform movement also came across the desert – and was transformed in the process by the imprint of Saharan social and religious patterns. In the distant past, the Sahara had been occupied by the camel-using Berbers. Beginning in the fifteenth century, the western Sahara changed once more with the arrival of Arabs of the banū Maqʿīl, a tribe that had drifted across the northern fringe of the Sahara at the time of the Hilalian invasion of the Maghrib and now began drifting south into the desert. During the fifteenth and sixteenth centuries, they gradually replaced the Berbers as the dominant nomadic people in the Sahara west of the Niger bend, reducing most Berbers to a status of respectable subordination. Though not quite tributaries, the Berbers were nevertheless forced to pay a form of protection money to the victors.

During the obscure centuries of this shift in nomadic populations, a crucial change took place in the social and political relations of the desert tribes. The Berber nomads had a strong religious tradition going back to the Almoravid movement, and they began to lay special emphasis on their function as Islamic teachers and religious specialists, at the same time rejecting political and military roles as inappropriate to their clerical status. The Arab immigrants meanwhile claimed political dominance and the military role for themselves. By the early part of the seventeenth century, nomads of the western Sahara were divided into two groups. One, called *zwāya*, was clerical, normally of Berber extraction but even then beginning to shift to Arabic speech and some aspects of Arabic culture. The other was the military group descended from the banū Maqʿīl. A similar division in the Sahara may have existed even earlier, because it clearly reflects the ancient West African tendency to separate the clerical, mercantile, and religious roles from the political and military. Tuareg society, for example, was divided into a warrior group called *Imazegen* and a clerical group called *Ineslemen* (literally, "Muslim").

In the 1660s, a new Islamic reform movement sprang up in the far southwestern Sahara, just to the north of the Senegal river in what is now Mauritania. A zwāya cleric who took the name Nasīr al-Dīn began preaching personal reform and purification, asking his followers to make a complete personal submission to God and His law. Nasīr al-Dīn built a substantial following both in the desert and among the sedentary Wolof and Tukulor farmers to the south. In 1673, he shifted his movement from religious reform to religious revolution, demanding that the secular rulers in the region surrender their powers to him as Imam and Amīr al-Mu'minīn. He set out, in short, to found a new theocratic Muslim state, and he called for a jihad against any who refused to surrender. At first, his success was spectacular. The movement swept through the zwāya of southern Mauritania and overturned the rulers of the sedentary states to the south. The secular rulers soon rallied, however. Nasīr al-Dīn himself died in battle in 1674, and the movement faded away, but not without leaving a legacy for the future.

A generation later, in the 1690s, a Futaanke cleric named Malik Si took the title of Imam and established his rule over Bundu, a region just beyond the southeastern frontier of Fuuta Tooro. He recruited followers where he could and declared a jihad that was partly an effort to found a new state and partly an attempt to dispossess the Mande (and partly non-Muslim) inhabitants in favor of Fulbe immigrants. He won, and the dynasty he founded ruled Bundu under the title of Almaami until late in the nineteenth century.

A third revolt under Fulbe leadership followed in the 1720s, in the pattern set by Malik Si. The Fuuta Jaalo highlands were occupied at that period by large numbers of emigrant Fulbe living among an older population of Yalunka (French Djallonké), who were mainly non-Muslim. Two Fulbe leaders, Karamoko Alfa and Ibrahima Sori, issued the call for a jihad and founded the Almaamate of Fuuta Jaalo, ruled thereafter by their two lineages, alternating in the title of Almaami. Bundu and Fuuta Jaalo kept the ideology of Islamic reform, but genuine dedication to religion was far below that proclaimed by Nasīr al-Dīn. Fuuta Jaalo turned into a slave exporting oligarchy where religious reform was only a front for control over the non-Muslim populace. Some historians think that the cry for reform was never more than a façade for state-building by emigrant Fulbe who happened to find themselves as a Muslim minority in a non-Fulbe society. A similar drive for power was to accompany the drive for religious reform in many of the later jihads.

The nomadic frontier

In the seventeenth and eighteenth centuries, nomads from the steppe country north of the desert fringe became more aggressive, and the sedentary societies of the western Sudan were not able to respond effectively. Nomadic raids carried deep into the savanna country, and nomads occupied much of the marginal land along the desert edge. Beginning with Mawlay Isma'il, whose mother was Sudanese, Moroccan rulers again intervened in Sudanese affairs, but Isma'il turned from the Niger bend to the desert edge further west and especially to the Senegal valley. This time the Moroccans stopped short of conquest and rule over sedentary societies and contented themselves with "informal empire." By the early eighteenth century, leaders of the Maq'il, whose ancestors had defeated Nasīr al-Dīn, recognized a vague Moroccan suzerainty down to the Senegal River, and Morocco kept a military force permanently stationed on the southern fringe of the desert, raiding at will along the desert edge from the Atlantic coast to Kaarta, a distance of some five hundred miles. Called *orma* (plural *ormankobe*) on the Senegal, these Moroccan troops were as hard to control from home as their predecessors, the Arma, had been. The ca'id in command nevertheless intervened in local politics, and for many years the Moroccans virtually controlled the office of the Saatigi, the ruler of Fuuta Tooro.

Over the decades of insecurity, the frontiers of sedentary control gradually contracted to the south. By the late eighteenth century, Fuuta Tooro, which had once extended fifty to a hundred miles north of the Senegal, was confined to the south bank of the river. In its place on the north bank stood new emirates founded by Maq'īl, the Trarza opposite the lower Senegal, and Brakna opposite the northern bend. Both recognized Moroccan overrule at first, but when the Alawites weakened in the late eighteenth century, they became independent.

A similar nomadic encroachment took place at the Niger bend. The Arma there had, at first, been successful in keeping some measure of control over the neighboring Tuareg, as Songhai had done even more forcefully in the past. In the Adrar uplands, out in the desert, removal of sedentary control made room for a prolonged struggle over the grazing land between two Tuareg tribes, the Kel Aulimadan and the Kel Tadmakka. In the 1650s, the Tadmakka lost and retired southward, where they took up new lands in the steppe country inside the Niger bend. Tuareg nomads also seized control of Aïr early in the seventeenth century. Their Sultanate of Aïr reached a peak of independent power late in that century, when the Tuareg drove the northernmost of the Hausa southward into Gobir. Before the end of the century, the Kel Aulimadan also moved south, taking up land north of the Niger and downstream from Gao. There they pastured their flocks and extorted protection money from the riverine Songhai, much as the ormankobe were doing on the Senegal to the west. Finally, in 1737, the Kel Aulimadan defeated the Arma for one last time and took control of Timbuktu itself, introducing almost a century of nomadic control over the Niger bend.

This southward movement of the nomads is clearly associated with climatic change. We know, for example, that the desert fringe had generally favorable rainfall in the sixteenth century; this was followed by recurrent drought and famine in the seventeenth and eighteenth. Estimates of the extent of these changes indicate that, in the sixteenth century, the ecological borders between camel herding and cattle herding, or between rainfall agriculture and pastoralism were as much as one hundred and fifty miles further north than they were in the early twentieth century. These changes are associated with a cool phase in European climate history between 1600 and 1750, just as the great sahelian drought of the 1970s was associated with a cool phase in the northern hemisphere. Although we know little in detail, it seems clear that the southward push of the nomads in the eighteenth century was not so much a return to the ancient pattern of nomad response to sedentary weakness as it was a southward movement of the natural frontier between sedentary and nomadic occupation.

The background of religious revolution

The jihad of Nasīr al-Dīn in the 1670s began with no apparent stimulus from the Muslim world at large. No general demand for religious reform existed in North Africa or the Middle East. The reformers simply drew on local traditions of piety, some of which may well have gone back to the period of the Almoravids. By the 1770s, all this had changed. Reform movements were alive in many parts of the Muslim world, sometimes anti-sufi, sometimes led by the more conservative sufi brotherhoods. The Qadiriya in particular was active in North Africa, and it began a new phase of growth in the second half of the eighteenth century. Its North African growth also carried across the Sahara, where it was associated with the Arab zwaya tribe, whose principal base was then at Mabruk, about a hundred miles north of Timbuktu. Qādiri reformist preaching began in the 1750s. By the 1770s the order had a broad following in the desert and the savanna alike. Much of its appeal was the personal magnetism of Sidi Mukhtar al-Kunti, who reorganized and reformed the order and gained extensive political influence as religious adviser to many of the nomadic tribes. By the nineteenth century, his teaching was to provide the background for a new generation of Fulbe jihads in Maasina and Hausaland.

Meanwhile, in the 1770s, a new revolt in the Senegal Valley combined the influence of the Qadiriya with the century-old legacy of Nasīr al-Dīn. It began in Fuuta Tooro as a reformist religious movement led first by Suleiman Bal and then by Abdul Kader. They won at first, replacing the secular-minded Denianke dynasty of Fuuta Tooro with a new Almaamate. When the Futaanke reformers tried to expand, however, their invasion of Kajoor failed, and the first Almaami was killed fighting Bundu. After its first burst of expansion, Fuuta Tooro settled down as a third Almaamate, controlled by an electoral council of five or six important figures who had more real power than the Almaami they appointed and frequently removed.

This religious movement, and the earlier Fulbe jihads of the seventeenth and eighteenth centuries, foreshadow the great religious revolutions to come, but they represent a much smaller scale of political change. Measured by their early demands for religious and social reform, they were failures. The most significant success of Islam in the Sudan of the sixteenth, seventeenth, and eighteenth centuries was quiet conversion combined with the spread of new organizations like Qadiriya, and this quieter kind of expansion was an important precondition of the empire-building movements of the nineteenth century.

Suggestions for further reading

Abir, Mordechai, *Ethiopia: The Era of the Princes*, New York: Praeger, 1968.

Abun-Nasr, Jamil M., *A History of the Maghrib in the Islamic Period*, Cambridge: Cambridge University Press, 1987.

Holt, P.M. and M.W. Daly, *A History of the Sudan from the Coming of Islam to the Present Day*, 4th edn, London: Longman, 1988.

Hopkins, A.G., *An Economic History of West Africa*, London: Longman, 1973.

Lange, Dierk, *A Sudanic Chronicle: The Bornu Expeditions of Idris Alauma (1546–1576) According to the Account of Ahmad b. Furtu*. Stuttgart: Franz Steiner, 1988.

Lapidus, Ira M., *A History of Islamic Societies*, New York: Cambridge University Press, 1988.

Saad, Elias N., *The Social History of Timbuktu: The Role of Muslim Scholars and Notables, 1400–1900*, Cambridge: Cambridge University Press, 1983.

Shaw, Stanford J., *The Financial and Administrative Organization and Development of Ottoman Egypt 1517–1798*, Princeton: Princeton University Press, 1962.

Webb, James L.A., Jr., *Desert Frontier: Ecological and Economic Change along the Western Sahel, 1600–1850*, Madison: University of Wisconsin Press, 1994.

7

THE WEST AFRICAN COAST IN THE ERA OF THE SLAVE TRADE

From the broadest perspective, the slave trade was part of a more general exchange of plants, diseases, and people that followed the worldwide maritime revolution of the fifteenth and early sixteenth centuries. The process, however, was slow to unfold. The great discoveries began with Portuguese experiments off the Saharan coast, but the full consequences took centuries to make themselves felt. In the sixteenth century, for example, Africa had little part in the new patterns of maritime trade. European interest in African gold was soon overshadowed by the gold and silver of the Americas. India and China were economically the most developed regions of the world at that time. Economic opportunities for European traders were more important there than they were in Africa.

Many of the most significant consequences for Africa were indirect, growing out of the general redistribution of people, crops, and diseases within the Atlantic basin. New crops from the Americas made it possible for tropical Africa, and especially the forest regions, to sustain populations several times larger than those of the past. Maize, peanuts, and manioc – to name only three – permanently altered the way Africans could deal with their environment. But it took time before these crops were known on the coast, and still more before farmers in the interior found out how to adapt them to local conditions of soil and climate. Some of the most important changes were not complete until the nineteenth century, or even later.

The movement of people and diseases brought about changes that were equally basic, and equally time consuming. When Europeans and Africans began to move to the New World in the early sixteenth century, they took with them diseases that were unknown in the Americas. Within a century, these new diseases had wiped out most of the Indian communities of the tropical lowlands and reduced highland populations to less than half their pre-Columbian levels. This was of great importance for Africa, because, in the longer run, Africa was to supply most of the new population of the tropical American lowlands.

Africa had a peculiar and important place in the history of human diseases. Both humans and their non-human ancestors lived there for hundreds of thousands of years. During these millennia, humans and their parasites passed through a complex process of mutual adaptation. New species of parasites evolved; humans developed the ability to respond through their immune system. Each human community tended to develop countervailing immunities against the prevalent diseases of the region. Some of these immunities could be passed from one generation to the next. Others were acquired in childhood, like the immunities almost all adults have against the common "childhood diseases" such as measles or mumps or chickenpox. Many of these diseases are also less serious for children than they are for adults. All adults, in any event, are protected to some degree against the diseases of their childhood environment.

Most of Africa had close enough contact with the rest of the Afro-Eurasian world to have acquired the same diseases – including the common childhood diseases of Europe and Asia. Africans of the tropical belt had less immunity than Europeans to tuberculosis and pneumonia, but they were far safer than the American Indians from most of the world's diseases. Africa was also the place of origin of a number of diseases that were uncommon elsewhere before the sixteenth century – including yellow fever and the most fatal species of malaria. These diseases made it dangerous for outsiders to visit Africa. They were also the principal causes of death to the American Indians of the tropical lowlands.

An unfamiliar disease might occasionally be imported, followed by an epidemic that would seriously injure the population in that generation, without impairing its ability to recover in the next. The cholera epidemics of the nineteenth century did this kind of damage, and similar epidemics may well have followed the early European voyages to western Africa. Some African peoples, however, were so isolated from the rest of humankind that they were susceptible to the same kind of devastation that occurred in the Americas. The Khoikhoi peoples of South Africa, for example, had been so isolated from the smallpox prevalent in tropical Africa that they endured a series of smallpox epidemics in the eighteenth century – epidemics that practically destroyed them as a community separate from the European settlers and the slaves they had imported.

In West Africa, the epidemiological weakness lay on the other side; Europeans shared most of the African disease environment, but not the diseases peculiar to a tropical climate. Yellow fever and falciparum malaria were especially serious. Yellow fever is rarely fatal when contracted as a child, and an attack brings lifelong immunity; but it is often fatal when contracted as an adult. Falciparum malaria is the most fatal species of malaria, and the anopheles mosquitos of tropical Africa are the most effective vectors found anywhere in the world.

In the past, these conditions made for extremely high death rates among new arrivals from Europe – death rates that could often run to more than 25 per cent a year before efficient tropical medicine was known. Similar death rates were prevalent at the beginning of European trade on the West African coast, and North African merchants sustained high death rates when they crossed the Sahara. African mosquitos were not swamp or forest breeders. The open savanna country north and south of the tropical forest was even more dangerous than the forest itself. These disease conditions help to explain why the maritime revolution had so little impact on the West African coast for such a long time. Any European activity there exacted an enormous price in European mortality, but the indirect impact of Europe was nevertheless very important.

The Atlantic plantation complex

In the 1480s, the Portuguese seized the uninhabited island of São Tomé in the Gulf of Guinea, almost on the equator some two hundred miles west of Gabon. There, they set up plantations to produce sugar for the European market, under European direction but using the labor of slaves imported from the adjacent coasts of Africa. This form of production was not entirely new; it was modeled after similar plantations on Madeira and in southern Portugal, and it served in turn as a model for still other plantations run in the same way – first in Brazil in the late sixteenth century and then in the Caribbean during the seventeenth and eighteenth centuries. These plantations created the economic demand for slaves from Africa, a demand that was to make the African slave trade of later centuries the largest intercontinental migration in human history up to that point.

The whole system of plantation agriculture is sometimes called the plantation complex or the Atlantic system. Its productive centers were mainly in the Americas, and used slave labor from Africa and managerial staff from Europe, to produce tropical staples for the European market. Its origins go back to the Mediterranean in the period of the Crusades, when the Europeans first encountered cane sugar, which was already grown in the Levant and North Africa. After the Muslims expelled the Europeans from the Levantine mainland, Europeans continued to produce sugar on Cyprus. Later plantations based on eastern models were established in Sicily, southern Spain, and Portugal. The overseas production of exotic crops was an important economic innovation, based largely on improving maritime technology and the early capitalism of the Italian cities, especially Genoa, which supplied much of the capital and managerial skill.

Sugar production was a business that posed unusual problems. It was partly agriculture in the form of cane cultivation, and partly manufacturing, to reduce the cane juice to semi-refined sugar. The whole process was very labor-intensive, which meant that large concentrations of people had to work a small piece of land. No ordinary agricultural population was dense enough to provide such a concentration of manpower. Massive labor migration was always called for wherever the sugar industry was introduced. In the Mediterranean Middle Ages, the institution for forced labor migration was slavery. Unlike northern Europe, where slavery had given way to various forms of serfdom, it survived in the Mediterranean basin among Christians and Muslims alike. A small-scale slave trade carried war prisoners and other unfortunates for sale as domestic servants, as rowers in the galleys that still dominated maritime warfare, or as laborers in mines and plantations. Most agricultural labor was controlled in other ways, but its workers, secured through the slave trade, often continued in slavery.

Slavery also gave the early plantation owners a degree of control over their workers that was rare for medieval agriculture. The ordinary village in Mediterranean Europe required very little detailed management. Custom controlled the sequence of operations and the distribution of the product. New plantations, on the other hand, called for careful supervision simply because they were new and because the operations were unfamiliar to the workers. Sugar plantations also needed precise timing in the delivery of cane to the mill. As a result, organization on Mediterranean sugar plantations took the form of gang labor working under constant supervision day after day, hour by hour. The unskilled workers were easily thought of as interchangeable labor units, and this dehumanizing element of supervised gang work distinguished plantation slavery from other forms of social subordination and forced labor.

At first, the slaves on Mediterranean plantations were mainly war prisoners taken within the region, principally in wars between Christians and Muslims. In time, however, the demand for mobile labor exceeded the local supply, and slaves were drawn from a distance, especially from the seaports of the northern and eastern coasts of the Black Sea. By the fourteenth and fifteenth centuries, Africans derived from the trans-Saharan trade also began to be sold to southern Europe.

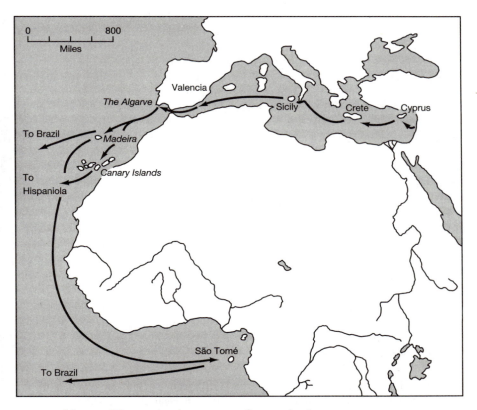

Map 7.1 The westward movement of sugar planting

As Europeans moved out onto the Atlantic, the plantation complex moved with them. The Spanish set up sugar plantations in the Canary Islands. In 1455, the Portuguese began to plant sugar on Madeira – with Genoese capital and Sicilian technicians – and the next step carried them on to São Tomé. In the sixteenth century the plantation complex moved on from the Canaries to Hispaniola in the Caribbean, and from Madeira to Brazil.

Each onward movement raised new problems of labor supply. Europeans often enslaved non-Christian war prisoners, but these were too few to solve the labor problem. The Portuguese voyages down the African coast, however, opened an alternate supply. Just as it was possible to short-circuit the trans-Saharan gold trade, it was possible to short-circuit the trans-Saharan slave trade and purchase slaves on the Guinea coast. During the second half of the fifteenth century, even before an American demand for slaves appeared, Africa appears to have exported about 500 to 1000 slaves a year to Portugal and the Atlantic islands.

Each forward move of the sugar industry led to larger plantations, with the latest technology. These plantations were farther from the European market, but their "clean-slate advantage" over smaller plantations with outmoded technology more than made up for the longer voyage to market. In the second half of the sixteenth century, sugar from the old centers on Madeira and São Tomé gave way to new production from Brazil. Growth forced Brazilian planters to turn from enslaving American Indians to importing labor from Africa. By 1600, the fully formed plantation complex was in place, not yet with the scale or geographical extension it would assume over the next two centuries, but with all the main elements present.

The next move onward from Brazil to the Caribbean was largely the work of the Dutch. By the 1630s, they had the most efficient shipping in Europe. and they mounted a sustained attack on the Portuguese in the East and West Indies alike. They occupied northeast Brazil for nearly a quarter-century and mastered the technology of the plantation complex. They captured some of the Portuguese posts on the African coast, including Elmina. Even after 1654, when the Portuguese finally drove them from Brazil, they could offer their knowledge and slaves for sale to the newly founded English and French colonies in the Caribbean. The Dutch were content with the profits of the carrying trade, leaving the actual planting to others. The result was a "sugar revolution" in the Lesser Antilles from the 1640s, extending to the larger islands Jamaica and Saint Domingue, toward the end of the century. As Dutch supremacy passed, the English and French began to carry their own trade, including the trade in slaves from Africa.

With the forward movement of the plantation complex and its increasing weight in the economies of tropical America, slaves became common outside the plantation complex itself. In the eighteenth century, after the Brazilian sugar boom was over, African labor was set to mining gold and diamonds, as it was on the mainland of Spanish America. In North America, many institutions of the plantation complex, including slavery, were imported from the Caribbean, so that an offshoot of the plantation complex grew up alongside European settler agriculture, where farmers of European origin did their own work. All of these fringe areas absorbed some of the export of people from Africa, but over the whole history of the slave trade at least 80 per cent of the total went to the tropical plantations.

The historical demography of plantation slavery

The forward movement of the slave plantations was not so much a leapfrog as a process of continuous growth behind moving frontiers. The older, outmoded plantation areas

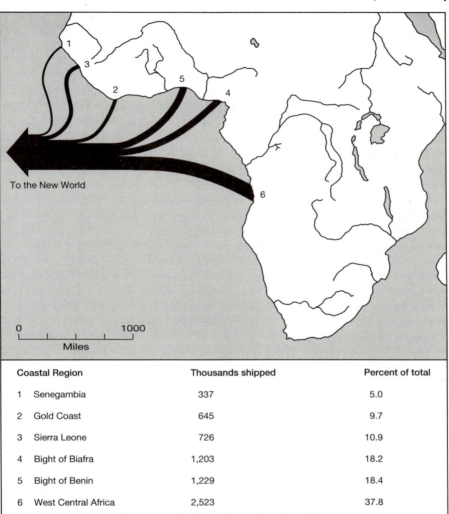

Coastal Region	Thousands shipped	Percent of total
1 Senegambia	337	5.0
2 Gold Coast	645	9.7
3 Sierra Leone	726	10.9
4 Bight of Biafra	1,203	18.2
5 Bight of Benin	1,229	18.4
6 West Central Africa	2,523	37.8

Map 7.2 Origins of the eighteenth-century slave trade

were sometimes left behind with diminished production, but the system as a whole continued to expand. The growth in the slave trade tells part of the story. From an estimated annual average import of about 2000 slaves to the Americas in the sixteenth century, the figure rose to an annual average of more than 80,000 in the 1780s, the peak decade of the trade. After 1808, one European country after another outlawed the trade, but slaves were still the most important export from tropical West Africa through the decade of the 1840s. The trade then declined sharply and ended by the 1860s.

One of the most peculiar aspects of the plantation complex in the period of the slave trade was the fact that neither the African nor the European population of the plantation colonies could sustain itself by natural increase. Both populations had to be supported by continuous immigration from Europe or Africa. This was not the case for the American south, or for backwaters outside the main plantation zone – like Cuba or Spanish Santo Domingo in the eighteenth century – but net natural decrease of the population was the rule at the economic core of the system.

The explanation is partly disease and partly sex ratio. Movement from one disease environment to another normally exacted some price in higher morbidity and mortality from those who moved. Planters saw this fact as a "seasoning" process to accustom newcomers to the "climate." Young Africans newly arrived in the American tropics died at about twice the rate expected for their age group in Africa itself. Europeans, with less resistance to yellow fever and malaria, died at ten times the expected death rate in Europe – with deaths as high as one hundred and fifty per thousand, compared to thirty to forty per thousand among recently imported slaves. These figures explain why planters preferred African to European workers. The numbers also explain why a slave population with a high proportion of African-born tended to have high rates of net natural decrease. The native-born (or "creole" in West-Indian English) were comparatively safe. Creole populations, whether Afro-American or Euro-American, could grow from net natural increase, but the usual pattern for slave populations was net natural decline, sustained only by a continuous stream of forced immigrants from Africa. In this way, the plantation complex consumed people, just as other industries consume raw materials. It used up slaves from Africa, and it used up managers from Europe at an even higher rate.

The slave trade carried about two men for each woman. European plantation workers, merchants, or soldiers had an even more unbalanced ratio of men to women. The number of women of child-bearing age was low in both racial groups, and the fertility rates were necessarily low as well – at least during the first generation in America. The American-born were, of course, roughly balanced between the two sexes. Which meant that populations receiving few new immigrants, like eighteenth-century Cuba, could have a self-sustaining population of both races. These demographic patterns are related in curious ways to economic development or the lack of it. When an immigrant population from Europe or Africa was set down in the New World, its first response to the new environment was a sharp decline in numbers as a result of "seasoning." After a few generations, however, it would level off and then begin to rise slowly. But one-shot immigration of this kind was a sign of comparative economic stagnation. Wherever the plantation economy grew vigorously, more population was added so rapidly that the stage of net natural growth was constantly put off, in most cases until after the effective end of the slave trade. Barbados, however, was a small island where the plantations soon occupied all available land. The slave population, which began to grow about 1640, ended its first phase of rapid growth in the 1680s and stabilized after about 1750. Thereafter, slaves were imported only to supply the difference between births and deaths. By about 1805, the slave population had become self-sustaining and largely creole, and few new slaves were brought from Africa.

This Barbadian demographic pattern was repeated with variations in other colonies. Everywhere in the plantation zone, the volume of the slave trade was tied to the rate of economic growth, but with a multiplier if production was to rise faster than the natural growth of the population. Sugar production, for example, could increase at the same rate as natural population growth without any additional slave trade, once a creole slave population had been established. A greater rate of growth, however, required new labor, and the new populations were those with low fertility and high death rates. Thus each economic boom in the Americas multiplied the cost to Africa in human suffering, while economic backwaters in the New World had little or no demand for immigration.

The economics of the Atlantic slave trade

In retrospect, the Atlantic slave trade seems irrational as well as immoral. It is hard to imagine why Europeans of the seventeenth and eighteenth centuries were willing to send young men to the African coast, where their life expectancy was hardly more than a year. About a quarter of the crew of each slave ship died on the voyage. The life expectancy of a young immigrant from Europe to the West Indies was only five to ten years. The explanation, of course, lies in the fact that the decision to build and run the plantation complex was not made by a whole society; it was made by individuals filling a limited number of roles, and these individuals responded, decade after decade, to an array of conditions that made the system appear profitable – at least to themselves.

One apparent irrationality of the system was to locate the plantations in America. It would seem more profitable to put the plantations where the labor was – in Africa. But Europeans died in Africa even more rapidly than they did in the West Indies; little African land was suitable for sugar; and good sugar land lay unpopulated in the New World. The decision therefore favored the Americas as soon as the comparative values of Brazil and São Tomé were known. Though Europeans tried several times in later centuries to set up plantations on the African coast, most failed until the twentieth century.

The American tropics required population from somewhere. The Indians were dying; Europeans died too; but Africans had some degree of immunity to the common Afro-Eurasian diseases, and to tropical diseases as well. Africa was obviously the most desirable source of people for the New World, but costs had to be taken into account. If voluntary emigrants from Europe had been available, cheap but inferior European labor might well have been preferred, but voluntary emigrants were not available from either Europe or Africa. Most Europeans sent overseas to work the plantations were political prisoners, convicts, and other unfortunates. They were expensive and supplies were limited. Most of the labor force came, at low cost, from Africa.

The low real cost of a slave purchased on the African coast was a crucial factor in the slave trade. West Indian planters of the early eighteenth century believed the price of slaves was so low in Africa that it actually cost less to buy a newly imported field hand than it did to raise a slave child from birth to working age at about fourteen. It now appears that they were generally correct in early decades, in spite of the high death rate of the newcomers. About the middle of the eighteenth century, however, the rising price of slaves began to change the calculation. Especially from the 1770s, planters began to encourage the natural growth of their slave gangs. They tried to have a more balanced sex ratio. Some began to give time off for pregnancy and prizes for mother-hood.

Such policies may have been common enough toward the end of the eighteenth century to affect the demand for slaves from Africa. The long-term trend in slave exports first turned downward in the 1790s. Even without the planters' new concern about natural growth, it would have come with the passage of time and the increased numbers, but the planters' concern accelerated the tendency.

The eighteenth-century increase of slave prices was important to the African side as well. The real price of slaves rose steadily from about 1680 to the 1840s, a fivefold increase over the century and a half. Few of the people sold into the trade were working slaves sold by their African masters. Most were war captives; with a mixture of condemned criminals, political prisoners, kidnap victims, relatives sold for debt or for food in time of famine. The economy of the slave trade called for a decision to sell on the African side, just as it involved a decision to buy on the American.

An abstract model can illustrate the economic forces at play. The total purchase price paid for a slave delivered to an American plantation had to be divided among those who participated along the way. Part went to the African merchants who bought slaves at the point of capture and took them to the coast for sale. Part went to the European merchants who brought them across the ocean. Part went to the men who performed the act of enslavement. The African and European slave merchants were in business, buying and selling for profit. Their decisions were market decisions. That was not necessarily the case for the original captor. He might have acted for a variety of motives. At one extreme, he might have acted for purely political reasons. A ruler or military commander might make war for reasons having nothing to do with the slave trade. In that case, his supply of captives would simply be a by-product of the war; they would have no assignable costs. In an extreme case, he might prefer to kill them rather than sell them into the trade. Where this political model was prevalent, the supply of slaves could not be expected to respond to price but only to political and military considerations.

At the opposite pole is an economic model. The commander or ruler in this case is assumed to be in the business of enslaving people as an economic enterprise. If he made war only to capture prisoners for sale, then the costs of warfare were the costs he had to cover to make a profit. In Africa, wherever this model was dominant, the supply of slaves would increase when the price rose, and decrease when the prices fell.

But this leaves the merchants out of the picture. They, both African and European, also received a share of the selling price of a landed slave. As men of business, they would tend toward the economic model. In Africa, rising prices would make it possible to travel further into the interior in search of slaves for sale. Thus, even where the political model might dominate the decision to make war, the supply of slaves would rise somewhat with rising prices.

Rising prices would influence the political decision. As the price of slaves rose, even the politically motivated commander might well try to maximize the number of pris-oners so as to pay some of the costs of the war, treating prisoners as a kind of war dividend. As the price of slaves rose, political commanders would feel this temptation all the more strongly. In theory, then, rising prices would be expected to bring in slaves from the far interior and to increase the incidence of slave raiding as opposed to by-product enslavement following military action begun for other reasons.

Life and decision-making in the era of the slave trade were far more complex than these simple abstractions suggest, but they help to explain some changes in the course of the slave trade. One of the clearest of these was the inland penetration of the slave traders during the second half of the eighteenth century and in response to increasing real prices. Where the slave trade of the sixteenth century had drawn its victims almost entirely from a band within a few miles of the coast, the trade of the late eighteenth and early nineteenth centuries drew slaves from the western Sudan and some from the southern savanna in the heart of Central Africa.

The early supply to the slave trade was also marked by a tendency to jump erratically from one place to another in response to periods of warfare or political upheaval. This pattern, combined with the very low real price paid for slaves, suggests that the political model of enslavement was dominant at the beginning of the slave trade and for some time afterward. It is impossible to say when or to what degree the rising price of slaves made the economic model a possibility. It may never have been a possibility in the full sense that the sale of slaves could pay the full cost of warfare, but by the 1730s or so some African societies began to behave in ways that suggest enslavement had become at least partly an economic enterprise. The kingdom of Dahomey is a possible example. The organized extraction of slaves from Iboland may be another. The Bambara states of Segu and Kaarta may be a third, and still other possibilities are found in Central Africa.

The second half of the eighteenth century was thus marked by a rising price, an increasing flow of slaves from Africa, a further reach into the interior, and a greater incidence of enslavement approaching the economic model. It was, of course, this same price rise that simultaneously encouraged planters in Brazil and the Caribbean to try to encourage the natural growth of their slave property.

The institutional pattern of the slave trade

Until the end of the sixteenth century, the Portuguese dominated West African maritime trade in spite of sporadic rivalry from other European powers. During this period, a body of Afro-European commercial custom came into existence, with patterns of exchange and cross-cultural behavior that were to be remarkably stable until the second half of the nineteenth century. By 1600, the Portuguese had given up the prospect of controlling any West African territory beyond their forts – a precedent their competitors and successors followed as well.

By common consent, Europeans gave up the kind of massive intervention in African military and political affairs that was represented by the Portuguese Jolof expedition of 1490, though the Portuguese continued to play a more modest military role to the south of the Congo and in the Zambezi valley. They and their successors also abandoned the early effort to support Christian missions and provide technical assistance, as they had done at first in the Congo. Except for isolated efforts in scattered places, the Christian missionary effort in West Africa stopped from the second half of the sixteenth century to the early part of the nineteenth. São Tomé became a failed plantation society; neither the Portuguese nor any other Europeans were to attempt agricultural management on a similar scale until the nineteenth century. Where the Portuguese had begun with an emphasis on the gold trade, after about 1700 they and their successors thought first of the slave trade.

Certain patterns of trade laid down before 1600 became fixed. One was the convention in West Africa (though not for Angola or Mozambique) that European traders should stop at the waterside and not move into the interior. The Africans insisted on this to protect their position as middlemen; Europeans had to accept it because they already had enough trouble manning the waterside posts in the face of fantastic death rates among the newly arrived. Their only long-term inland penetration in West Africa was to the head of navigation on the Senegal and Gambia rivers.

Governments, both African and European, tried to exercise as much control over trade as they could. Many tried to monopolize some part of the coastal trade, but they rarely succeeded in the face of opposition from private traders, both African and European. African governments most often wanted to monopolize the trade passing through to the sea. European governments tried at first to control the whole national sector of their trade to Africa, mainly to improve their competitive position against other Europeans. The African trade was rarely an important part of total trade, but the sugar colonies were dependent on a steady supply of slaves. Many policy-makers believed, probably mistakenly, that sugar colonies were the most valuable part of any European empire overseas. Each European state thought it important to supply its own colonies with slaves, for fear a foreign supplier might cut off the trade at some later date. Spain alone was content to leave the slave trade to others most of the time, though it controlled the importation of slaves into Spanish America through a system of permits, or *asientos*. The other powers also surrounded the slave trade with their own cloud of laws and regulations. Many granted a monopoly over the national sector of the trade to a single, chartered, joint-stock company, endowed with certain governmental powers. The companies were expected to use their monopoly profits as a subsidy to repay the cost of maintaining fortified trading posts in Africa. The burden of defending the slave trade in wartime was thus passed over to a private firm – at least in theory.

In fact, it was impossible to enforce the monopoly rights. Planters were always willing to buy slaves from foreigners rather than pay a monopoly price. Private shippers were always willing to enter the African trade as "interlopers" infringing the legal monopoly. With 6000 miles of coastline open to trade, all the interlopers had to do was to stay clear of the official fortified trading posts. Against such competition, the chartered companies found their profits were insufficient to pay for the upkeep of the forts. That was the probable outcome, even if the company's employees in Africa had been honest, which they rarely were. The employees, after all, went to Africa with less than a fifty-fifty chance of returning home; few were willing to take such risks for the sake of a small salary. In the end, all of the principal monopolistic companies failed financially. Some received state subsidies, but the great bulk of the slave trade after the seventeenth century was carried by independent shippers in fierce competition with one another. This competition, in turn, caused the Europeans to bid up the real price of slaves, in spite of occasional half-hearted attempts to keep it low by joint action.

The mode of trade between the seaborne Europeans and the African merchants was remarkably uniform over long stretches of coastline, perhaps because the Europeans picked up the customs of one trade area and spread them more broadly. All along the coast, bargains were struck in a currency of account that was neither a European currency nor the usual African currency of the region. One such currency was the "bar", originally a bar of iron weighing about twelve to thirteen kilograms. These bars were about three meters long, but they were usually notched for subdivision into smaller units of twenty-five to thirty centimeters each, a size corresponding to an ancient form of iron currency used on certain parts of the upper Guinea coast before maritime contact. Bars became the currency of account from the Senegal River south and east to the present-day Côte d'Ivoire.

The next currency area centered on the Gold Coast, and here the local currency and the trade currency were both gold dust for large transactions. In the course of the seventeenth century, a new fictitious currency came into use – the "trade ounce" with half the value of a measured ounce of gold dust. In the eighteenth century, the "trade ounce" spread further east until it reached into present-day Nigeria, displacing earlier currencies of brass and copper and a currency of account that represented the value of a slave. The Bight of Biafra used a great variety of different currencies, changing through time and including a horseshoe-shaped object of brass called a "manila," cowrie shells from the Indian Ocean, and a form of cloth currency based on the value of a standard piece of handwoven African cotton. Two or more currencies were sometimes used in the same place, and cowrie shells were often used for minor purchases where the currency of account had an inconveniently large value.

Whatever the trade currency, it rarely played the same role as a modern all-purpose currency. One of the main problems was the inflexibility of certain prices. The prices of African exports varied according to market conditions, but those of African imports tended to be set by custom at an early date and remained fixed for long periods – up to a century or more. A "bar" or an "ounce" worth of slaves or ivory depended on a bargain struck between buyer and seller, but a "bar" or "ounce" worth of guns or iron or textiles was a fixed quantity. At some time, perhaps in the early seventeenth century, the bar values of these products must have corresponded to their actual cost in Europe, but this was no longer the case in the late seventeenth or eighteenth centuries. One bar worth of blue bafts, an Indian textile, might represent a prime cost several times that of a bar worth of brandy. In effect, no single exchange rate expressed the relationship between "bars" and any European currency. Instead, a separate exchange rate prevailed for each of the commodities imported into Africa.

This system of multiple exchange rates complicated the process of striking a bargain. Buyers and sellers had to agree first on the price to be paid for the export products – gold, wax, slaves, and so on. Then they bargained once more about the "sorting" or actual makeup of the bundle of goods to be taken in payment. The African merchant would try to be paid as much as possible in "heavy bars", such as blue bafts, while the European would try to pay as much as possible in "light bars", such as rum.

In addition, European visitors to the coast paid a variety of fees, duties, and other charges. The African state where trade took place normally charged for the privilege and imposed additional fees for anchorage, wood and water, African authorities required ceremonial gifts at the opening and closing of a bargaining session, and a variety of brokers, interpreters, and other service personnel had to be paid. These charges varied greatly from place to place, depending on the local commercial culture and the kind of control the African authorities exercised over trade. This, in turn, depended on the political circumstances in each region along the coast.

Senegambia

The first region to the south of the Sahara was Senegambia, traditionally the shores of the Senegal and Gambia rivers and the country between them. It was the first sub-Saharan region to enter into maritime contact with Europe, and it was especially important in the first centuries of the slave trade – furnishing perhaps a third of all the slaves exported from Africa before 1600. This temporary boom in the Senegambian slave trade followed the mid-sixteenth-century break-up of the Jolof empire into a reduced Jolof and a number of successor states. Once the new political situation

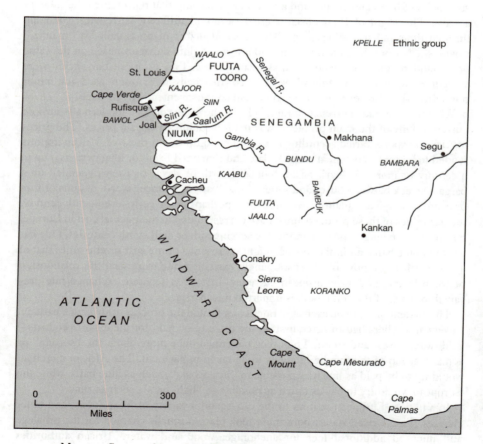

Map 7.3 Senegambia and the Windward Coast

stabilized toward the end of the sixteenth century, Senegambia took on new importance as the closest maritime approach to the Bambuk goldfields. The Gambia River
was navigable by ocean-going ships for some two hundred miles and river shipping on
the Senegal could reach four hundred miles into the interior. These rivers contributed
to Senegambia's prominence in a mixed trade, where gold and slaves were often
second in importance to cotton textiles, hides, beeswax, ivory, and gum. After the
seventeenth century, most of the slave exports from this region originated in the far
interior, beyond the head of navigation on the two rivers.

Portuguese neglected the Senegal in favor of trade along the coast from Cape Verde
to the Gambia and up the Gambia River. On the open coast, they traded at a series of
small ports. On the Gambia, the country was also divided politically into a number of
small states, the successors of the great empire of Mali, just as the Senegalese states
were successors of Jolof. A series of small Mande-speaking states lined the banks of
the river, and at least one of these, Kaabu, was still a functioning province of Mali at
the earliest period of Portuguese trade.

Rather than having a fortified factory on the coast itself, the Portuguese tried to
organize their trade with Senegambia from their base on the Cape Verde Islands, but
many individual Portuguese, contrary to official policy, went to live on the mainland. By
the end of the sixteenth century, all the principal port towns had an Afro-Portuguese
community descended from these early traders and identifying themselves as Portuguese and Catholic, though their appearance was African and their way of life was a
Luso-African mixture. By the early seventeenth century, the Afro-Portuguese constituted the main trade community on the coast and up the Gambia, willing to trade with
any ship, regardless of nationality. Their trade network reached to the head of navigation on the Gambia and all its tributary creeks.

Long-distance trade from the far interior, however, lay outside their sphere. Overland caravans required another kind of specialization, and the caravan leaders sometimes came right through from the upper Niger to the coast at Rufisque or Joal. More
often, they stopped at a convenient point on the middle or upper Gambia, where their
goods were transferred to the waterborne transport of the Afro-Portuguese. In addition to the slaves and ivory for export overseas, these caravans brought down iron,
cotton textiles, and kola nuts for Senegambia in return for Senegambian mats, textiles,
and salt for distribution to the interior. This long-distance trade therefore represented
regional exchanges within Africa as well as overseas trade, and this regional trade had
been going on before the Europeans ever arrived on the coast.

The trade route eastward from Gambia to the upper Niger was dominated in the
seventeenth and eighteenth centuries by the Jahaanke (French Diakhanké). These
people were never part of a single state: they were, instead, a people whose sense of
nationality was born of a trade diaspora that had originated, according to tradition, in Ja
near the Niger bend. By the seventeenth century, they lived in separate villages that
were semi-autonomous from the local political authorities and linked by ties of
nationality and kinship to other Jahaanke villages, no matter how distant. In many
respects, they resembled the Juula of northern Ghana, the Côte d'Ivoire, and Upper
Volta, who claimed Soninke ancestry, spoke a Mande dialect, and were traders living in
scattered towns who traced their origins to Ja. The Jahaanke cultivated the role of the

clerical, pacifist, politically neutral, and commercially oriented mercantile community. The remains of their former trade network can be seen today in a string of Jahaanke towns running in a line eastward from the Gambia to Segu on the Niger, and north and south through Bundu connecting the desert edge with the kola forests of Fuuta Jaalo.

The middle decades of the seventeenth century were a period of commercial uncertainty for Senegambia, with the Afro-Portuguese serving all comers, while the Dutch, French, English, and even such unlikely contenders as the Duke of Kurland (in later Latvia) tried to tighten their grip on part of the trade. It was only at the end of the century that a relatively stable situation emerged. The British were usually dominant on the Gambia, trying to control the trade of the river from James Island, a few miles upstream from the river's mouth; the French held a similar position on the Senegal, which they controlled from the island of Saint Louis. In fact, neither post was very strong; both fell at various times to European enemies, or even to mere pirates, though they were always reoccupied by their usual owners.

The Gambia was tidal to the normal head of navigation. The British sometimes dealt with the Afro-Portuguese, who sailed the river in large vessels called pirogues, capable of carrying ten to twenty tons, but the British also maintained a series of unfortified factories upriver, served by sloops that carried the goods back and forth from their main post at James Island. The island lay within the territory of the north-bank state of Nyumi or Barra, and it had no independent supply of fresh water. Most of the time, Nyumi was content to milk the trade by taxing passing ships, exacting payments from the British and from the French who often kept an unfortified post at Albreda, also in Nyumi, a little below James Island. The result was constant bickering between the Europeans and the African authorities, largely because the Europeans were never strong enough to overawe the Africans, while no single African state was strong enough to control the passing trade.

The Senegal, on the other hand, was not tidal and it was consequently less useful as a transportation route. Sea-going ships could hardly go beyond Saint Louis; even river craft could reach the upper river only during the few months of high water – though they could then go some four hundred miles toward the heart of the western Sudan. In the 1690s, the French placed a fortified post at Makhana, not far from the present city of Kayes in the Republic of Mali. With a permanent store of trade goods on the upper river and annual expeditions to maintain contact with the coast, they had a viable alternative to the British position on the Gambia. African merchants coming down from the interior had a choice of trading partners. Competition between the two river routes affected African states as well, because no single state could cut off both routes. Thus, while all states charged tolls on passing caravans or boats, the amount they could exact was limited by the fear of driving traffic to the other route.

The Senegal route also lacked an Afro-Portuguese community to serve as middle-men. Partly as a result, an Afro-French community grew up at Saint Louis. Even when the Compagnie des Indes tried to exercise its monopoly over the river trade, it used African boatmen and commercial agents. By the second half of the eighteenth century, the "French" trade on the Senegal had fallen completely into the hands of the merchants of Saint Louis – who were generally Wolof in language and culture, at least formally Muslim by religion, and African in appearance. A few were racially Afro-

European, but the whole community blended more European traits into its culture with the passage of time. The Afro-Portuguese of the Gambia, by contrast, were originally of European descent, but they gradually became more African in culture as well as descent.

The Senegambia was never a major source of slaves after the sixteenth century, and the Senegambian slave trade reached a peak in absolute numbers about the beginning of the eighteenth century. As it declined thereafter, it became an even smaller fraction of the whole. The Wolof states, the main source of slaves in the mid-sixteenth century, now sent as few as fifty or a hundred a year from each state, normally sold by the king as a royal monopoly. Fuuta Tooro generally tried to prevent the sale of its own people into the slave trade; and the policy was successful for the Atlantic trade. From the north, however, the anarchy of Moroccan military operations must have meant a fairly large drain of captives across the Sahara. The only eighteenth-century slave trade of real consequence was *through* Senegambia, not *from* it. The victims came from the far interior and were largely Mande in culture, captives taken during the rise and expansion of the new Bambara states.

Upper Guinea and Sierra Leone

To the south of the Gambia, the open savanna gives way first to thicker woodland and then to high forest. The coast is deeply indented by a series of drowned river mouths and numerous offshore islands. Political organization was also different; lacking the legacy of former empires such as Jolof or Mali or of persistent state structures like Fuuta Tooro. Instead, the region was one of micro-kingdoms intermixed with small stateless societies. Nor was Islam the major religious force it was in Senegambia, though Muslim-controlled trade routes reached down into the forest in search of local products like kola nuts.

During the period of Portuguese dominance, this coastal region was one of the most important for the slave trade. Perhaps a third of the slaves exported by sea during the sixteenth century came from here, even though the Portuguese had no fortified posts on the coast itself until nearly the end of the century, when they built a fort at Cacheu. Their trade was organized from the entrepôt of the Cape Verde Islands, and much of it was carried by individual Portuguese who went to live on the mainland under African jurisdiction, collecting slaves and bulked local produce for sale to passing ships. In time, they too became a separate Afro-Portuguese community, similar to those on the Gambia further north.

Although the southern part of this region, the present Republic of Sierra Leone, was only on the fringe of the Portuguese trade zone, it was briefly a large contributor to the slave trade in the mid-sixteenth century. In the early part of that century, this was a region of micro-kingdoms inhabited by culturally similar people whom the Europeans called Sape. They were, in fact, the ancestors of the present-day Bullom, Temne, Limba, Baga, Nalu, and Landuma. About the middle of the century, the region was swept by a series of invasions by people called Mane, now recognized to have been an offshoot of the Mande people of the savanna. It was not so much a military conquest as a migration by the Mane and their allies, some of whom were related to the Kru of present-day Liberia. The warfare as usual produced slaves for sale until relative peace returned early in the seventeenth century, leaving a new configuration of small states, many of them ruled by descendants of the invaders. A new pattern of culture also appeared, as Mane and Sape merged to form ethnic groups ancestral to the present-day Loko and Mende.

Once the Mane invasions had stopped, the region dropped from the mainstream of the slave trade. During the seventeenth century and into the eighteenth, it depended partly on the sale of local products like beeswax, camwood, and ivory and partly on transshipping inland products like the gold of Buré and Bambuk. Some slave trade continued, but at less than half the value of the total exports. It recovered briefly at two points in the eighteenth century – in the 1720s through the 1740s, reflecting the fighting associated with the Fulbe jihad in Fuuta Jaalo, and again in the 1780s and 1790s – but the region's contribution to the total slave trade of the century was small.

This may be one reason why Upper Guinea and Sierra Leone attracted little attention from the major slave trading companies. Instead, private traders of several nationalities came to settle on the coast, as the Afro-Portuguese had done in the past. Some of them married into important local families, which made it possible for their children to inherit chiefdoms. In the vicinity of Sierra Leone, the dominant politico-mercantile figure of the early eighteenth century was the Afro-Portuguese, Jose Lopez de Maura, but in the second half of the century he was joined by a number of powerful Afro-English families – the Rogers, Caulkers, Clevelands, and Tuckers. Trading forts began to appear in the Sierra Leone estuary only late in the century, with the French on Gambia Island and the English on Bunce Island.

The Windward Coast

Further east, beyond Cape Mount, was the region the English called the Windward Coast – to the windward, that is, of the permanent fortified posts on the Gold Coast, though it was sometimes called the Grain Coast (for its malagueta pepper, sometimes called "grains of paradise") in its western section and the Ivory Coast in the east. Its principal distinguishing characteristic is the absence of natural harbors or even of good landing spots in the lee of rocky promontories, so common along the Gold Coast. Instead, the beach is characteristically very steep, with heavy surf close to shore and poor anchorages further out. Maritime trade was mainly what the Europeans called a "ship trade," without resident Europeans on shore. Instead, a ship would call here and there along the coast, or simply sail along watching for a signal that Africans on shore had something to trade.

One result of this kind of contact was that Europeans rarely stayed long enough to find out much about the country or people, and historical sources are more meager here than they are for any other part of the African coast. If there had been large African states in the area, oral traditions might fill the gap; but traditions carrying back two hundred years or more are rarely preserved unless they serve some political function, usually connected with a state or a royal lineage. Nothing recorded so far among the maze of stateless societies and micro-kingdoms backing the Windward Coast goes back as far as 1700, though oral traditions preserved to the north of the forest belt make it possible to fill in the outlines of historical change in the western Sudan.

For lack of natural harbors, trade along this coast was fragmented, divided among many small ports or shipping points. One French survey of 1783 listed thirty-five ports of call in this region, none of them evaluated as normally supplying more than a few hundred slaves a year. It can be assumed that most of these ports drew on their immediate hinterland within the forest. Yet a few also drew slaves from the savanna country, especially during two particular periods in the eighteenth century.

A heavy export from the region of Cape Mount and Cape Mesurado (the neighborhood of the present Monrovia) occurred from the 1720s through the 1740s. This spurt may be associated with the warfare that accompanied the Fulbe jihad in Fuuta Jaalo in the 1720s and afterward, but the natural outlet for Fuuta Jaalo would have been further west at Sierra Leone. It may also be associated with important commercial changes still further in the interior. Kola nuts had long been exported from the forest regions northward to the savanna country, especially along the north–south trade routes from the Akan goldfields to Jenné. In the seventeenth and eighteenth centuries, similar trade routes carried south into the forests of Sierra Leone, Guinea-Conakry, and northwest Liberia. By the eighteenth century, they penetrated through the forest to the coast, so that European goods entered the flow of trade to and along the Niger.

One political reflection of these commercial changes was a set of movements sometimes called the "juula revolution" – that is, a political revolution organized by merchants. Just as the traders already controlled many of the towns along the routes southward from Jenné, traders now began to establish their own control over political units south of the upper Niger. One of the most important crossroads was the town of Kankan in upper Guinea-Conakry. In the late seventeenth century, the juula, or merchants, who worked that region were dominantly Muslims of Soninke origin but now Mande in speech and other aspects of culture. That is, they were very similar to the Juula of the Jenné-to-Akan route, or to the Jahaanke who worked the trade of the Gambia. Sometime in the late seventeenth century, they seized control of Kankan and its region and set up the independent city-state of Bate – an important stepping-stone for the trade headed toward the kola region or the coast, and an example to other juula who had trouble dealing with the non-Muslim and non-mercantile micro-kingdoms through which they had to pass.

A second spurt of trade from the Windward Coast took place in the 1770s and centered on the export of slaves from the port of Grand Lahou at the mouth of the Bandama River in the present-day Côte d'Ivoire. This increase was again associated with a new trade route through the forest along the line of the Bandama River. It was, in effect, a new branch of the main north–south route from the Akan region to Jenné. Increased slave exports of the late eighteenth century seem to be associated with the westward expansion of Asante, but the hinterland of the Bandama route had already experienced its own "juula revolution" earlier in the century. About 1700, juula forces under a certain Seku Watara began to create a new state based on the trading city of Kong. By the 1730s, it had become the largest kingdom created so far in Africa south of the Niger River, with control stretching to the fringes of Asante, north nearly to Jenné, and westward to the Bambara kingdoms. Some of Kong's military operations carried as far as Bamako on the Niger, but the polity was fundamentally weak, a domination by juula over ethnically diverse populations spread over a large area. It was also divided between juula Muslims and the mass of the population who were not Muslim. Asante and the Bambara kingdom of Segu finally defeated it in battle, and it fell back into its constituent units after about 1740.

It is not clear what role the fall of Kong may have played in the flow of trade through the forest to the coast, but that trade declined abruptly after the end of the eighteenth century. The Windward Coast as a whole simply dropped out of the slave trade, even though the illegal slave trade continued to flourish elsewhere. It is likely, however, that the trade that once passed through to Cape Mesurado went to Sierra Leone instead, while that of the Bandama route was diverted to Asante and then down to the Gold Coast.

The Gold Coast

The Gold Coast had the greatest density of European military architecture and trading posts anywhere on the coast of Africa. It was the gold trade, however, and not the slave trade that made for all these forts. At least in West Africa, European trading posts were rarely fortified unless they traded in gold, and they were designed for defense against Europeans, not Africans. (The African authorities had the easy option of simply cutting off trade if their guests became too demanding.) Slaves were an inconvenient mark for raiders, and other African products were hardly better, but gold was easy to carry off and easy to dispose of. This is one reason why the first Portuguese fortification, begun in 1481, was called simply Elmina, "the castle of the mine." Rival trade forts began to rise in the neighborhood only in the seventeenth century, but, by the eighteenth, the coast was dotted with twenty-five major stone forts, separated from one another by an average of only ten miles – and even less if the numerous lightly fortified or unfortified factories and out-stations are taken into account. There was, of course, no real need for that many forts, but each European power felt that it had to have its own set, as the Dutch, English, Danes, Swedes, and Brandenburgers all tried to follow in the footsteps of the Portuguese.

The goldfields also influenced the pace and character of political change in African society. Gold was a magnet that attracted traders from the north, and Juula had reached as far as the coast by the fifteenth century. In addition, kola from the Gold Coast forest was especially choice, and the value of the kola exports to the north may have been even greater than that of the gold trade. The new commerce made a larger scale of political organization desirable. The forest had been mainly organized in tiny states, while stateless societies were more common in the savanna immediately to the north. One of the first Akan states to reach a larger order of magnitude was Bono, which grew up in the early fifteenth century in the gold-producing area. It lay near the frontier between forest and savanna, and it was closely associated with the Juula town of Begho, then the principal commercial center serving the Akan goldfield.

Other state formation just north of the forest was even more closely associated with the pull of the goldfields. Gonja was founded in the early sixteenth century by the commanding officer of a cavalry force sent into the region from Mali. He broke away

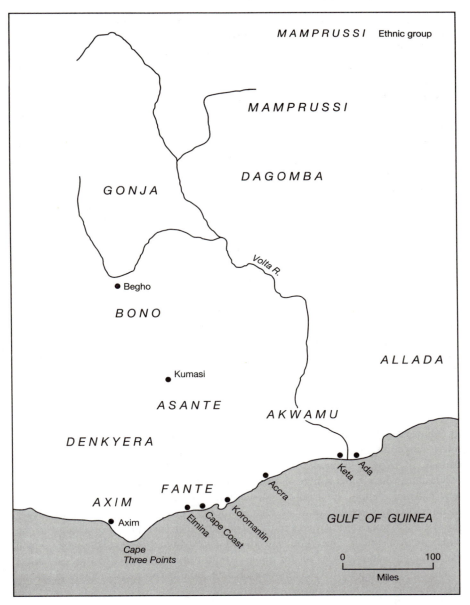

Map 7.4 The Gold Coast in the eighteenth century

with some of the troops and set himself up as an independent ruler. Later, in the mid-seventeenth century, Gonja expanded further, conquering nearby micro-kingdoms and stateless peoples until it became a major force in the region between the Akan states of the south and the Mossi complex to the north.

On the coast itself, the gold trade drew the Europeans, so that the Gold Coast became one of the first African territories to use crops from America. Maize and manioc quickly became important food crops in the Akan forest. These new crops made denser population possible throughout the forest in the course of the sixteenth and seventeenth centuries.

New trade to the coast during the seventeenth century also encouraged a larger scale of political organization. Akwamu appeared about 1600 in the hinterland of Accra, founded by Akan people. At first, they were clients of the Ga-speaking rulers of Accra; but their territory lay across the trade route from the interior, and they were able to combine military and commercial pressures to force trade through their own territory. By the late 1670s, Akwamu had become wealthy enough to begin conquering its neighbors. By the 1690s, its dominance extended over most of the coastal region from Cape Coast in the west to the frontiers of Dahomey in the east. Only the core area around Accra, however, was closely integrated with the state. The outlying conquests were autonomous regions that could break away again at the first sign of military weakness. Akwamu's control of these peripheral territories was, indeed, too weak to prevent ambitious local magnates from taking slaves within the empire itself. At a period when the gold trade was giving way to a larger trade in slaves, Akwamu weakened and disappeared about 1730.

The rise of Akwamu represented a general pattern of first controlling trade and then moving on to military conquest. Denkyera, lying behind the western Gold Coast, and Allada in the present-day Republic of Bénin, rose to power with similar timing, and Asante followed only a little later.

The Asante state was founded about 1680 with the election of a certain Osei Tutu to the leadership of a number of matrilineages around the present city of Kumasi and the region immediately to the south. By 1700, after Osei Tutu defeated Denkyera, Asante became a major power. More important still, Osei Tutu (or his advisers) made a series of creative innovations to help build political integration among the kinship-oriented micro-kingdoms of the Akan forest. One change was to set up a new, all-Asante, council, the Kotoko council, as the ruling body. Another was to create new judicial institutions, with a wider sphere of jurisdiction than ever before. A third was to found a new national identity. Each of the formerly independent divisions of the kingdom, including Kumasi itself, had a ceremonial stool of office, which was far more than a throne; each stool represented the ties of kinship that gave ultimate sanction to the authority of the ruler. Osei Tutu introduced a new stool, "the golden stool," which stood for the national unity of the whole Asante people. In effect, it was a fictitious extension of kinship so that a temporary alliance could become a permanent kingdom, incorporating some of the territory it conquered.

One continuing theme of Asante history in the eighteenth and nineteenth centuries was the struggle to consolidate the larger unit, and Asante territorial expansion compounded the problem. In practice, the Asante rulers tried to incorporate only those conquered states that were Akan in culture, but even these were sometimes reluctant to join. Several provinces in the Akan culture-area tried to secede and had to be rean-nexed by force. Non-Akan states, like Gonja and Dagomba in the north, were left their separate identities but had to pay tribute. Others, like the Ga states and a few outlying

Akan states, were under Asante domination but were not invited to join the Asante union.

The period just before 1700 was also one of crucial change for the Gold Coast economy. Ever since the opening of maritime trade in 1481, this region had been a source of gold, but only rarely of slaves. In the second half of the fifteenth century and far into the sixteenth, the Portuguese had sold slaves on the Gold Coast from the kingdoms of Benin and Kongo. Later on, the Portuguese, and then the Dutch, had discouraged and even prohibited the export of slaves for fear of interfering with the gold trade. By the 1660s, however, the slave trade began to grow in importance, first from Accra and associated with the rise of Akwamu. By the 1680s, slave exports had risen to 75 per cent of total export value. By the 1720s, the Gold Coast sometimes imported gold in exchange for slaves, though the main pattern of the eighteenth century was to export both, as the volume of the slave trade rose and fell with the rhythm of the Asante military activity in the hinterland.

Meanwhile, the long contact between European and African merchants near the coastal trade castles produced a network of personal relations and cultural interchange. Western education, at least to the level of literacy and commercial arithmetic, was important for traders, and many Africans were able to use their business connections to secure hospitality for a few years' residence in Europe. One African, Philip Quaque of Cape Coast, went to England for his education, was ordained as an Anglican priest, and returned with an English wife to become the official chaplain of Cape Coast Castle. From the European side, Richard Brew of Anomabu spent thirty years on the Gold Coast and founded an Anglo-African family that became an important part of the local elite down to the present. The process as a whole was not so much "Westerniz-ation" as the creation of a culturally mixed community that could mediate between the two parent societies.

The Bight of Benin

The Bight of Benin is the open bay east of the Volta River as far as the Kingdom of Benin in present-day Nigeria. It was sometimes called the slave coast and it takes in what is now the coastal part of Togo, the Benin Republic, and western Nigeria. It was part of a cultural continuum that reached from the Gold Coast to eastern Nigeria. Recent language reclassification considers the dividing line between Kwa languages, spoken along most of the Gold Coast, and the Benue-Congo languages spoken further east lies between the Aja of the Benin Republic and the Yoruba of southeastern Nigeria. The Ewe and associated peoples of Togo and eastern Ghana are thus similar in many respects to their Akan neighbors, and in others to the Aja peoples of southern Dahomey. In spite of linguistic difference, these Aja had even more in common with the Yoruba of southwestern Nigeria, including centuries of historical interaction. The most important recent Aja state, the kingdom of Dahomey, was an outlying part of the Yoruba Oyo empire during much of its history. To the east of the Yoruba states, the Edo kingdom of Benin has been ruled for most of the past four centuries by a dynasty claiming Yoruba origin. Benin also fits into the pattern of urbanization that was common to the Yoruba and Aja alike, though in other respects Edo culture seems

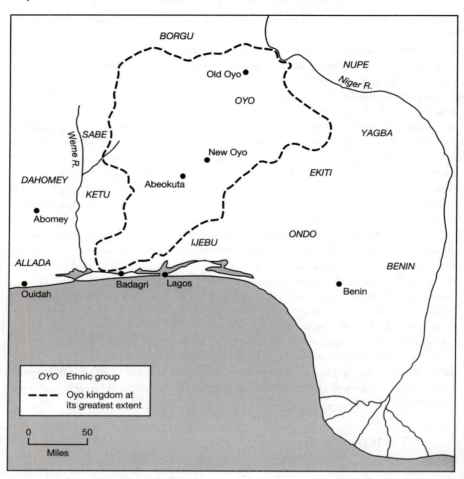

Map 7.5 Yorubaland and Oyo

closer to that of the Ibo to the east or the Igala to the northeast. Authorities may differ
in pointing out the important discontinuities in this sequence, but contact over thousands of years has produced a marked cultural continuity.

This continuity also stretches into the interior. The sharp environmental change
from forest to savanna has no counterpart in most aspects of culture. All of the
language families now found in this part of the forest zone are also found in the
savanna north of the forest. It is usually assumed that they were originally spoken by
savanna people, some of whom moved into the forest after the coming of agriculture.
Other aspects of culture also suggest ancient ties to the north. Yoruba sculpture, for
example, has strong stylistic similarities to the Nok figurines made to the north of the
Benue River before the birth of Christ. Some deities of the Aja religion are strikingly
similar to those worshipped among the non-Muslim Hausa. These and other traits

found both north and south of the forest-savanna frontier may reflect an ancient southward movement of settlers, or they may simply be the result of cultural diffusion along the trade routes. A developed flow of trade connecting the coastal region with the Hausa states and the Songhai portion of the Niger valley was already present when the Portuguese arrived in the fifteenth century. It was certainly much older, if only because the distinct resource endowment on either side of the line between forest and savanna created natural conditions for trade.

This coastal region had larger and more elaborate states, and at an earlier date, than any other coastal region short of Senegambia in one direction and the kingdom of Kongo in the other. For the Yoruba and Edo, states may go back to the eleventh century or earlier, and the elaborate technology necessary for the Ife and Benin bronze statuary suggests an even earlier date for the introduction of advanced metallurgy into the forest zone. The older view that the savanna peoples were somehow "more advanced" than those of the forest cannot be sustained, even though the existence of states was not necessarily a sign of advancement, and this is one part of Africa where large states, small states, micro-kingdoms, and stateless societies have existed side by side for centuries.

Our best historical information nevertheless concerns the larger states, and three of them – Benin, Dahomey, and Oyo – illustrate part of the range of options available to an African state responding to European trade. The lack of correspondence between the former and present names for these countries is a serious problem. The African kingdom of Dahomey gave its name first to the French colony and then to the independent republic of Dahomey, but in 1975 the republic changed its name to Benin – after the Bight of Benin, not the kingdom further east. To avoid confusion, we will use the terms Benin and Dahomey for the long-standing kingdoms, and the Benin Republic for the state that took that name in 1975.

Benin was the first to attract serious attention in Europe, partly because it reached a peak of military power in the sixteenth century and attracted Portuguese missionary efforts. Edo relations with the Europeans were not especially close. Benin was not really a coastal state at all, though its port of Ughoton on the Benin River could be reached by sailing inland through the territory of the Itsekiri and western Ijo. Benin at one time made itself overlord of the coast as far west as Lagos, but the Edo were normally far more concerned with the north – with Nupe, Igala, and the Yoruba states.

Benin also stayed out of the large-scale slave trade. In 1516, the *Oba* (or king) began to restrict the export of male slaves, and the restriction soon became a complete embargo on exporting males – an embargo that lasted until nearly the end of the seventeenth century. Because the Europeans wanted mainly male workers for the American plantations, the embargo confined Benin's maritime trade to the export of pepper, cotton textiles, beads, and ivory. Even this trade was a royal monopoly, which may have made Benin less attractive to Europeans than other ports were, though the monopoly became harder to enforce as the power of the Oba declined during the seventeenth century. By that period, the royal officials appointed to trade with the Europeans had come to be more like brokers, who helped the European traders (for a fee) in the conduct of their business.

In the eighteenth century, the embargo on male slaves was lifted, but the slave trade nevertheless remained a minor current. Slave prices were high in Benin, and the Europeans had cheaper sources elsewhere. From time to time, the Oba forced the Europeans to buy a batch of prisoners of war or political prisoners as a condition for being allowed to trade in other goods, but the total exports over the years were very low. In the late eighteenth century, when the slave trade as a whole reached its peak, exports from the whole region of the Benin River reached only about a thousand slaves a year, and most of these were supplied by the Itsekiri. In the early nineteenth century, Benin dropped out of the slave trade altogether. It nevertheless survived as a major state until almost the end of the century. Benin's experience over four centuries suggests that a major African state could decide whether or not to participate in the slave trade at all. Firearms were important in inter-state competition, but they could be paid for by selling other goods.

Dahomey, on the other hand, apparently tried to make the slave trade pay, even to make it the principal support of the state. The formation of large states was comparatively late with the Aja, the first trading state, Allada, being founded only about 1575. The Dutch began to trade there toward the end of the century, and Allada soon became the chief center for European trade to the Bight of Benin. In the second half of the seventeenth century, however, Ouidah began to compete for trade while Dahomey rose in the hinterland with a position equivalent to that of Akwamu in regard to Accra. In this location it was only natural for Dahomey to consider the possibility of controlling trade for the profit of the state.

The original Dahomean constitution was similar to those of the Yoruba states. That is, the *oba*, or ruler, was the supreme official, but his powers were circumscribed by a set of councils, some representing lineages, others professional groups. One council normally chose the oba from among the eligible members of the royal lineage. Another usually had the power to order the oba to commit suicide. Once in office, an oba could appoint some officials and councilors, but these royal appointees were always balanced by others who represented particular interests or particular lineages. The personal ties that counted most in this society were first of all the ties of kinship, and secondly the ties to fellow members of a professional or occupational group. Only then was the individual bound to give loyalty and obedience to the oba.

The Dahomean constitution began to depart from this pattern early in the eighteenth century, intentionally subverted by a succession of rulers who used their control over firearms to convert the state into a despotism. By the 1730s or so, they had created a new political order in which each individual was directly and personally subordinate to an all-powerful ruler. This new regime was not originally designed to serve the slave trade. But, in the 1720s, Agaja, the oba, led Dahomey in its most successful drive toward the coast, capturing Allada and Ouidah and giving Dahomey its first direct contact with the European slave dealers. For a time, the slave exports from Dahomey were a royal monopoly.

Just when Agaja had succeeded in dominating the coast, Oyo began to threaten the independence of Dahomey itself. Oyo had a strong cavalry force, which turned out to be superior to the Dahomean musketeers. In 1730, Oyo forced Dahomey into a tributary relationship, though Dahomey kept its political integrity and Agaja remained in power. Dahomey was even allowed to keep some of its coastal conquests, although

Oyo took others away and organized them as a new tributary state of Ajashe, or Porto Novo, which then became Oyo's principal outlet to the sea.

The continuing threat of Oyo posed a problem that might have been dealt with successfully in one of several different ways. One option was to continue along the lines of centralized government and tighter administration, waiting until Oyo might weaken. Another would have been to use state power to secure slaves by force and to sell them through the royal monopoly. This was tried for a time, but under Tegbesu (ruled 1740–74), the Dahomean state played down the alternative of using its military power to capture slaves and turned instead to a policy of building up its position as middle-man between the northern suppliers and the European merchants on the coast. The royal monopoly became a theoretical claim only, or a way of regulating the trade carried mainly by private merchants. The Dahomean merchant community became rich on the trade passing through to the coast and Dahomean government revenue also came to depend on the slave trade. This was in marked contrast to the usual Asante policy of selling only the slaves that came as a by-product of their military expansion – still more so to the Benin policy of selling few or no slaves at all.

Oyo's position was quite different from that of the kingdoms nearer the coast, and the problem of responding to the opportunities of the slave trade came with a different timing and consequence. The metropolitan province of Oyo was well out in the savanna, where its connections lay mainly to the north and with states along the Niger River. It was one of the most northerly of the Yoruba states, and not the most important until the seventeenth century. It was then that the Oyo cavalry was perfected. This army required a supply of horses from the northern savanna, strengthening Oyo's ties to the north. Oyo then began to expand, generally toward the south and among the other Yoruba kingdoms. In time, it annexed thirteen other kingdoms, which then became provinces of the Oyo empire, stretching into the Egba forest to the south and west of the present city of Ibadan. Coastal Yoruba states like Ijebu remained indepen-dent, and Oyo had only indirect commercial contact with the coast until her descent on Dahomey. Even then, coastal trade was comparatively unimportant, and Oyo's major trade lay either with the Hausa states or northwest along the Niger toward the bend. These were the strategic sources of remounts, and Oyo still depended on cavalry well into the nineteenth century.

One can only speculate about the motives and directions of Oyo aggression. As the southernmost cavalry-using power, its advantage lay in moving still further south against states whose archers could often be overwhelmed. Movement into the forest, to a place like Ijebu, would have been very dangerous to the horses on account of the tsetse fly, but the "Benin gap," a corridor of savanna breaking through the forest belt to the sea in Togo and Dahomey, opened the way to the use of cavalry against Dahomey. Oyo military activities in the Benin gap began in 1698 with an attack on Allada, and the next half century saw not only Oyo's triumph over Dahomey, but a similar hegemony extending as far west as the frontiers of Asante.

With the eighteenth century, the first slaves captured by Oyo began to find their way into the Atlantic slave trade, and Oyo began to face the possibilities and dangers of getting caught up in the trade. Oral traditions reflect some of the tensions between the military and the merchant's council – one arguing for still more military expansion, the other wanting to pursue peace for the sake of trade. In fact, neither of these possibilities seems to have been pursued consistently. For several decades before 1774, the *bashorun*, or supreme military commander, became more important than the *alafin*, whose powers were so circumscribed by councils he was in danger of becoming a mere figurehead. Then, in 1774, the Alafin Abiodun won a brief civil war and built new power for his office. Abiodun had once been a merchant and he apparently sought to develop his power on the basis of the slave trade, which increased enormously in the 1780s, while Oyo's military power declined. By the late 1780s and early 1790s, some frontier provinces began to break away. In 1796, following a series of military failures, a council required Alafin Awole to commit suicide, as the constitution provided. This time, however, they were unable to agree on a new alafin, and a long interregnum followed, with increasing military weakness and decreasing power over the subject provinces, lasting far into the nineteenth century.

With Oyo, imperial expansion began and continued for many decades before military aggression came to be linked to the slave trade, but once the link was made, the decade of the 1780s was both the peak decade for Oyo's export of slaves and the beginning of its internal crisis. The slave trade was at least one element contributing to decline, but it was not alone.

Comparisons with the political development of Dahomey and Asante suggest that other causes were more fundamental. During the eighteenth century, both Asante and Dahomey were struggling in their own ways to adapt old political institutions to the new challenge posed by European trade. The Asante choice was to create a new and larger national unit and to articulate that nationality through a newly developed political structure. In Dahomey, the first change of direction was a constitutional revolution abolishing the old way of balancing lineages through councils. This, in turn, cleared the way for a second set of moves integrating Dahomean economic policy into its position as middle-man for the slave trade. The evidence is less firm for eighteenth-century Oyo than it is for Dahomey or Asante. Oyo appears to have first built an empire and then to have begun the large-scale export of slaves without first changing its forms of government. As a result, the checks and balances of the traditional Oyo constitution failed to work, and Oyo was unable to respond adequately to the new commerce, to the rebellious provinces, or (in the longer run) to the threat of militant Islam beyond the northern frontiers. Where Asante and Dahomey were to continue as viable states until the European conquest at the end of the nineteenth century, Oyo collapsed so completely in the early nineteenth-century that the slave trade drew more heavily on Yoruba than on any other nationality, though Yoruba slaves had been practically unheard of in the Americas before 1750.

The Niger delta and the Cameroons

East of the Benin River lies the delta of the Niger, a land of myriad channels, creeks, and mangrove swamps. At the seaward fringe, the delta forms a sand ridge, high enough for villages of fishermen and salt gatherers. In the upper delta, inland beyond the salt water and mangrove swamps, is a region of freshwater swamp with some higher land suitable for agriculture. Long before the beginning of European trade, conditions

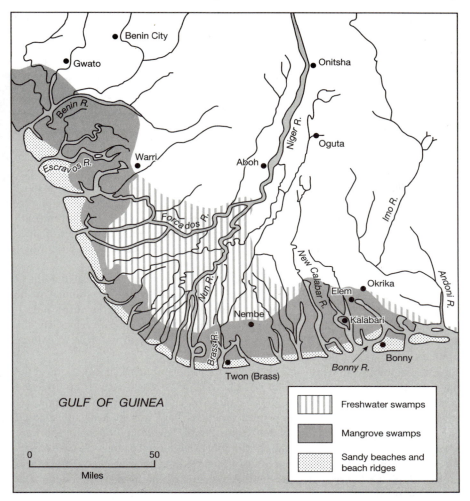

Map 7.6 The Niger Delta

in the delta itself encouraged trade between the seaward settlements and the agricultural areas of the upper delta and its hinterland. By 1500, one of the towns at the lower fringe of the delta had a population of 2000 people and an active commerce through the system of creeks and lagoons. (Two thousand people would hardly count as a big town today, but Oporto, the second largest city in Portugal, had only 8000 people at that time.) Similar conditions existed further east, where the estuary of the Cross River provided a similar opportunity to trade coastal products with the hinterland. In spite of ethnic differences between the Ijo of the Niger Delta proper and the Ibibio, Efik, and others to the east, political and historical circumstances were similar as far east as Mount Cameroon.

People along this coast had been trading with the interior in their large boats having up to fifty paddlers, even before the Europeans appeared on the coast. They traded occasionally with the Europeans in the sixteenth century, though the Europeans had no regular shore establishments, and the slave trade here was very small indeed until the second half of the seventeenth century. The coastal societies then changed radically, adapted to the demands of the slave trade, and made contact with others in the hinterland who were making similar adjustments. The result was a commercial organization that supplied far more slaves per mile of coast or square mile of economic hinterland than any other part of eighteenth-century Africa.

Some of these adaptations were political. At the beginning of maritime contact, the eastern Ijo of the delta were divided into a series of lineages, each bearing the name of an eponymous ancestor. Members of a lineage lived in a series of interrelated villages, but each village was independent of the rest with its own council and one or more headmen exercising minimal executive powers. Growing trade required a more powerful organization, capable of defending the routes to the interior. By the late seventeenth century, these formerly independent villages had regrouped to form a series of small monarchies, each under a royal lineage and centered on a principal trading town – Bonny, Nembe or Brass, Kalabari or New Calabar, among others.

The Efik of the lower Cross River also turned to a more consolidated form of government, but in a different way. There, the separate villages continued to be independent, each ruled by a chief and council and constituting so many micro-kingdoms. But they also had a common government in the form of a secret society, the *ekpe*, or leopard society, which reached into all the villages and was able to enforce common action when common action was needed.

New economic institutions came along with these constitutional changes. One of the sub-units in the older political order was the *wari*, or "house," actually an extended family made up of a man, his wives, some relatives, and their slaves. This corporate kinship unit at first performed only political functions, but it was gradually transformed into a military and economic unit, the "canoe house," made up of people who were responsible for supplying an armed boat with fifty to a hundred paddlers in time of war. They obviously had the same boat available for trade in time of peace. Trade was carried on by the house under the general direction of the head of the house, who distributed the profits to the members. In time, the element of kinship became less and less important. New members of the house were normally recruited by purchase, but, once a member of the house, a slave could rise within the organization and might even become its head if he were especially skilled in trade and war.

Neither the Ijo nor the Efik trade, however, could reach beyond the maze of creeks that ran along the coast. Both peoples were specialized navigators, like the Afro-French of Saint Louis or Afro-Portuguese of the Senegambia; they depended on other traders to bring slaves from the further interior. On the Niger River itself, other river traders brought goods down the river to markets a little above the delta, along the stretch of river between present-day Onitsha and Aboh. The trade of the densely populated Iboland to the east of the Niger was more important still. This region was almost entirely stateless, with the village group serving as the largest political unit, yet lacking the central authority that justified calling it a micro-state. Local trade took place within the village group, but long-distance trade was left to outside specialists.

One such group of long-distance traders were the people of Awka, who began traveling as priests and diviners connected with their Agbala deity. Their religious role made it easier for them to pass safely through a variety of jurisdictions, and they later developed a network of fictitious kinship ties with a host in each of the village groups they visited.

Another Ibo group, the Aro, worked with similar religious protection from Ebinokpabi, their great oracle. And theirs was a closely coordinated network of Aro colonies stretched out as a trade diaspora along the trade routes. Some of these Aro settlements go back to the seventeenth century, and by the nineteenth they had grown to be almost a hundred separate trading-post colonies. These were linked together by Aro who moved along the trade routes, and they were further linked by four-day trade fairs, alternately held at two central points every twenty-four days.

Both the Aro and the Awka trade networks were beyond the range of European observation during the period of the slave trade, and Ibo oral traditions are too shallow to be of much help. It may therefore be impossible to explore the detailed history of Ibo trade. The Ijo and Efik dealers on the coast, and their suppliers from the interior, were exceptional in their ability to maintain a numerous and steady supply of slaves to the Atlantic trade one decade after another. The supply from most other regions fluctuated widely in response to political or military changes in the hinterland. Somewhat scattered evidence suggests that the dominant form of slave catching in this region was not warfare but kidnapping combined with the manipulation of oracles, so that human sacrifices could be called for and the victims then quietly shipped off to the Americas.

The slave trade in African history

One of the ironies of African history is the fact that maritime contact, which ended Africa's long isolation and brought all coasts of the continent into contact with the intercommunicating part of the world, should also have led so rapidly to a situation in which Africa's main export was its people. The full impact of the slave trade on African history remains hard to assess. It is obvious that enslavement and exile to the New World were terrible experiences, and that the dehumanizing institutions of plantation slavery were worse still. The violence of capture and the dangers along the way surely meant that at least as many were killed as were delivered to the plantations, and the waste in human life continued as the plantations failed to achieve an excess of births over deaths. But terrible as these consequences were for the people who were enslaved, they tell little about the impact of the slave trade on African societies themselves.

That assessment is even harder to make, because the incidence of the trade was so uneven. Some small ethnic groups were completely wiped out. Others suffered heavily for a time – a few decades of political instability – but were otherwise untouched by the trade: most Yoruba and most Wolof had this kind of experience. Other societies, like Benin, were very lightly involved for centuries on end, but too lightly for the trade to have made a really serious impact. Still others, like Dahomey, may have profited from the slave trade, at the expense of its African neighbors. Elsewhere on the continent, large regions, like most of the present-day Republic of South Africa, were simply not involved in the Atlantic trade at all. With these differences, it is virtually impossible to strike a balance. But some things appear to be clear. The sheer physical destructiveness of the trade was not significant enough to produce a general and striking difference in social health and progress between areas where the slave trade was prevalent and those where people suffered only from the usual run of war, plague, and famine. Its most serious damage to African society was probably not physical destruction and loss of life, nor the drain of population but rather a warping of social purposes to serve destructive ends. The total impact of the trade therefore has to be measured not by what actually happened, but against the might-have-been if Africa's creative energy had been turned instead to some other end than that of building a commercial system capable of capturing and exporting as many as eighty thousand people a year.

Suggestions for further reading

Curtin, Philip D. (ed.), *Africa Remembered. Narratives by West Africans from the Era of the Slave Trade*, Madison: University of Wisconsin Press, 1968.

Curtin, Philip D., *The Atlantic Slave Trade: A Census*, Madison: University of Wisconsin Press, 1969.

Curtin, Philip D., *Economic Change in Pre-Colonial Africa: Senegambia in the Era of the Slave Trade*, Madison: University of Wisconsin Press, 1975.

Curtin, Philip D., *The Rise and Fall of the Plantation Complex*, New York: Cambridge University Press, 1990.

Daaku, Kwame Yeboa, *Trade and Politics on The Gold Coast 1600 to 1720*, Oxford: Oxford University Press, Clarendon Press, 1970.

Davies, K.G., *The Royal African Company*, London: Longman, 1957.

Latham, A.J.H., *Old Calabar 1600–1891*, London: Oxford University Press, 1973.

Law, Robin, *The Slave Coast of West Africa, 1550–1750: The Impact of the Atlantic Slave Trade on an African Society*, Oxford, 1991.

Lovejoy, Paul E., *Transformations in Slavery: A History of Slavery in Africa*, Cambridge: Cambridge University Press, 1983.

Manning, Patrick, *Slavery and African Life: Occidental, Oriental, and African Slave Trades*, Cambridge; Cambridge University Press, 1990.

Northrup, David, *Trade Without Rulers: Pre-Colonial Economic Development in South-Eastern Nigeria*, Oxford, Oxford University Press, 1978.

Ryder, Alan F.C., *Benin and The Europeans, 1485–1897*, London: Longman, 1969.

8

EQUATORIAL AFRICA BEFORE THE NINETEENTH CENTURY

Equatorial Africa, a portion of the world far larger than Europe, comprises the lands between the Atlantic ocean and the Great Lakes and between the *sahel* of Chad and the dry lands running from northern Namibia to the middle Zambezi. This vast area contains several major climatic and ecological regions. Its heart, between roughly the fourth degree north and south of the Equator, is occupied by a variety of rainforests, which form very complex and quite diverse environments. In many places a canopy of the giant trees towers over two levels of lower canopies and the sunlight reaches the ground only in small golden specks, as hungry leaves above drink it up. Flora and fauna are adapted to the ever-humid shadows or to the various canopies. In other places the forests are broken up in patches of open savanna (*esobe*) on poorer soils, especially in the western two thirds of the area. Many animals and plants are adapted to the forest edges there and some villagers also prefer to live there. But most people prefer to dwell near the placid, meandering rivers that cut a majestic swath through the forest, ultimately to rejoin the father of them all, the mighty Zaire (Congo), for these provide not only fish and a specially rich environment near their banks but also easy transportation. Similar advantages are found along the beaches facing the Atlantic ocean. Yet, in the past, other major landscapes were not very amenable to human settlement. Such were large marshes near the Equator, the wild relief of some mountainous lands in Gabon and Congo, the mountain forest of eastern Zaire, and tracts of land without permanent surface waters.

North and south of the forests savannas take over. From the hills or plateaus, as far as the eye can see, an ocean of grasses bends with the wind, but then most of the year, the eye does not see far, for the grasses are too high. Rainforests in the valleys hide the rivers from view and nearer the Equator copses crown the ridges. The savannas were rich environments for animals and people whose flourishing villages were dotted all over the landscape and linked to each other by a myriad of paths.

Traveling south through the grasslands yet another major set of environments occurs: dry woodlands. Woods first appear on the heights and then fill the whole land. They cover all of Central Africa between the ninth and sixteenth degree south. Here the landscape is cluttered by relatively low trees. Yet there are gaps and in a blur

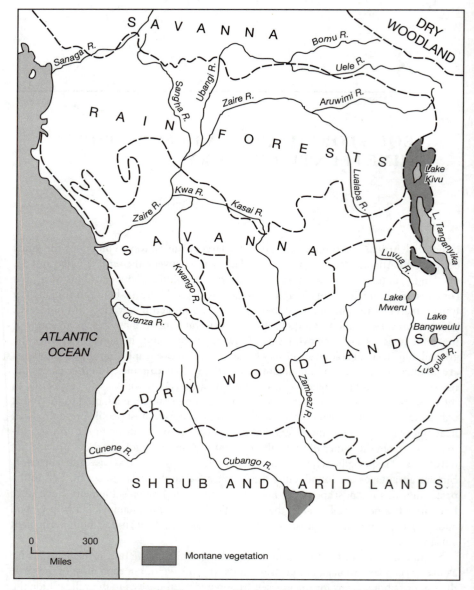

Map 8.1 Equatorial Africa: vegetation (based on a map by C. Vansina)

between leaves and stems the eye reaches the horizon. But the untrained eye is so disoriented that even a giraffe fifty feet away remains invisible. In the past, the dry woodlands and the smaller savannas within it supported sometimes very large herds of herbivores and harbored many other mammals but they were not very good for settlement. Poor soils, lack of surface water or an unreliable supply of rain led most people to settle in the river valleys. Moreover, on the whole, the landscape impeded communications more than further north or south, although it never constituted a genuine barrier to the movement of people.

In the north of equatorial Africa there are no dry forests. There the savannas gradually give way to steppe. The fingers of the gallery forests thin out and disappear, the grasses grow to a lesser height, bushes and low tree clumps appear. The landscape turns to parkland, steppe, and finally into the Sahara desert. The same succession of landscapes is also found in the far southwest where the vegetation eventually turns into the Kalahari steppe of Botswana and the deserts of Namibia.

Settlement

By the onset of our era Bantu-speaking farmers and trappers were settled in the whole of equatorial Africa. The use of metals was still spreading, although many populations in the rainforests had acquired it. South of the rainforests metallurgy was practiced in the area of Luanda round 100 AD and in what is now Zambia by 300 AD (although it is possible that metallurgy was practiced on the upper Zambezi by 200 BC). The diffusion of the technology over the whole area was certainly completed before 700 AD as is attested by sites in northern Botswana (Divuyu) and on the Benguela highlands (Feti) where a great diversity of metal objects have been found. Still the available evidence does not allow us to say how the knowledge of metallurgy diffused and whether this diffusion was accompanied by population movements or not.

Major population movements were still occurring south of the rainforests until about the middle of the first millennium AD. Most of these lands were better suited to grain crops than to the root and tree crops. The west Bantu settlers did not use the open grasslands to any extent, which allowed East Bantu speakers to move westwards beyond the Kasai and the upper Zambezi rivers and farm these with grain crops. Where the tsetse fly would allow it, they also introduced cattle. The West Bantu farmers welcomed these immigrants, absorbed them in their own communities, and enthusiastically adopted the new cereals, along with the relevant techniques and tools as is shown by their borrowing of the relevant East Bantu vocabulary (over twenty-five terms). Thus grain crops spread to the limits of the rainforests while further south cattle herding spread to the limit of tsetse fly infestation. Cattle bones, dating to c.800 AD have been found near Luanda. East Bantu speakers also influenced the ancestral West Bantu social structures. Changes in kinship terminology, for instance, reflect innovation in the structure of the West Bantu House.

Meanwhile, however, West Bantu speakers were also moving into East Bantu speaking territory eastwards as far as Lake Tanganyika in eastern Zambia. They found those lands thinly occupied by farmers, were warmly welcomed and fused with the East Bantu speakers there. They also left traces of their influence on the social organization of these people attested by the shapes of settlements and houses and the decoration and pottery in this area.

Moreover, the area was so vast that farming settlements were still thinly spread as islands in a sea where foragers roamed. By 500 AD many lands between the major rivers in Zambia and Shaba and the whole of Angola south of 10°S, with the exception of the

Benguela Highlands and the lower Cubango River, were still completely occupied only by foragers and would remain so until late into the present millennium. These foragers, especially in eastern Angola, influenced the farming populations to a significant extent. Well before the end of the first millennium AD the societies and cultures of the farming populations living in different parts of the area were becoming quite varied as a result of different inputs of West Bantu, East Bantu and aboriginal legacies. Yet because of the input everywhere of East Bantu influences all of these contrasted with the ways of life in the rainforests.

The original West Bantu heritage was well-preserved in most of the rainforests, except in its northeastern quadrant where the original Bantu district and village structure was abandoned, while every House founded its own small village, under the influence of new immigrants from the savanna beyond. Elsewhere along the northern rim of the rainforests Bantu speakers maintained their way of life, while many of their non-Bantu speaking neighbors adopted their way of life.

The crucial development in this region was the introduction of a new staple crop: plantains (AAB bananas). Plantains are large bananas which are not edible unless they are reduced to flour and processed or cooked whole. Unfortunately the introduction of these plantains cannot be dated. All we know is that it occurred at a very early date, probably after the settlement of the North Bantu and before c. 500 AD. Unlike yams or palm trees which are adapted to forest margins, plantains are a forest crop and allow those who rely on them to practice agriculture anywhere in deep forests. The yield of plantains or bananas per acre is much higher than that of yams, while the labor input required per acre is much lower. The effects of this innovation were that farmers could now settle anywhere in the forests and easily produced surpluses for exchange. Plantains, along with metal objects, later became so common in exchanges between farmers and the original foragers, that the latter could no longer do without them and became very dependent on the farmers so that eventually most of them were absorbed into the farming communities.

Population dynamics after settlement

By the middle of the first millennium AD Bantu speakers had settled everywhere in Central Africa. Major migrations ended as people realized that all the most desirable lands were now settled. Because emigration on a large scale ceased the density of population began to grow, especially in the most favorable locales. In many cases that in turn became an engine for considerable innovation, for two major reasons. First growing numbers of people required innovations in the food producing system. Agriculture became more important than before and farmers had either to increase yields per acre on good lands or bring more but poorer land under cultivation. Secondly, the fundamental political dynamic of early Bantu social organization had been competition between Big Men which presupposed that the losing leaders could emigrate and find good lands elsewhere. Such leaders encouraged rising populations in their settlements and Houses, but at the same time it was no longer a good option for losers to pack up and move away. Hence profound innovations in social organizations occurred in order to cope with this problem.

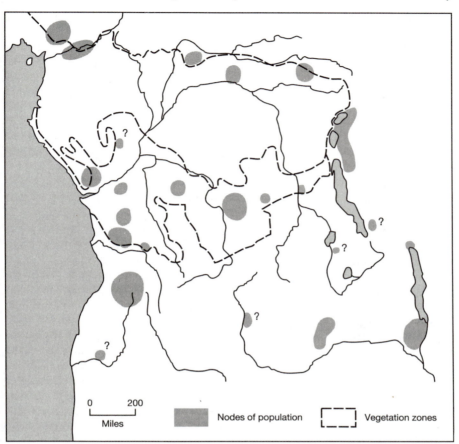

Map 8.2 Population nodes before 1500 AD (based on a map by C. Vansina)

The new dynamics of population movement can be nicely illustrated by known developments in southwestern Zambia. The first settled villages there were founded by immigrants from Zimbabwe by *c.*500 AD, who settled in discrete districts of small villages in the Zambezi valley. When the farmers had exhausted the land around the village they moved to another location in the vicinity, never to return to the land that had been cultivated earlier. A few generations later the tactics changed. Whole populations now settled along *dambos*, or places that were flooded in the wet season and thus naturally fertilized. The soils gave higher yields, the villages became larger, and the same tracts of land were repeatedly occupied in a cyclical fashion. But some time later again the local farmers chose to move onto higher, sandy, less fertile, but much larger tracts of land, where they now spread out into more numerous but smaller and less permanent villages: they had traded a small quantity of very good farmland for a larger surface of inferior land. By the ninth century AD however, the sandy soils could no longer accommodate the whole population and the surplus population returned to the richer *dambo* sites.

As a result of the stabilization of population and its distribution in clusters of settlements separated from each other by unoccupied territory, cultural diversity in the area increased at first because mutual borrowing between the now sedentary clusters decreased. Moreover, the new islands of higher population densities became cradles for innovation, because the earlier types of social organization had presupposed low population densities. High densities mean more contact between more people and hence a higher incidence of quarrels between them. Such increasing tensions could be relieved either by a population flow away from such pockets of high density to surrounding unoccupied areas or by a transformation of the original social systems.

Most lands in the rainforests were adequate for a food-producing system based on growing plantains, foraging and trapping, and the rainfall was more than adequate. Only marshlands and some sandy tracts were less desirable. Therefore the settlement of hitherto "empty lands" remained frequent. Populations built up only in a few exceptionally favored areas near the northern rim of the rainforests. In the savannas there were more undesirable lands but they were interspersed with localities where excellent conditions obtained. Hence a patchwork of nodes of higher population densities sprang up here. Further south in the dry woodlands most soils were poor and rainfall was often erratic. But the Bantu-speaking population here had been much sparser than further north. Nevertheless, three large areas of higher population densities developed here, in the Benguela Highlands, in southern Zambia, and south of Lake Malawi where environmental conditions were excellent, while in a few other localities higher densities developed along the floodplains of major rivers.

While it would be an exaggeration to state that all changes in Central Africa began in the pockets of high population and flowed from there to the surrounding areas, it nevertheless remains true that the uneven distribution of settlement over the area strongly affected the nature and rate of social and cultural change.

Economic history from c.800 AD to c.1500 AD

The major features in the economic history of equatorial Africa after settlement to 1500 AD and later were (i) great continuity in the processes, tools, and techniques of production, (ii) an increasingly developed division of labor, and (iii) in part interrelated with this, the establishment of intensive long-distance trade.

Continuity first: a few archaeological sites yield useful data on the kit of tools in use. The rich sites of the Lualaba depression show that from about 800 AD onwards ceramics for kitchen use, funerary use, or for use in canoes already represented the various types that remained in use right up to 1900. The same holds for necklets, axes, hoes, baskets and perhaps even dolls. Even the shapes remained constant, except for the ceramics which show a continuous elaboration from a set of basic choices already available since the beginning. Many of these classes of objects and shapes are directly comparable to those found at nearby contemporary sites in the southern province of Zambia, and northern Botswana, or at the site of Feti (between *c.*800 and 1300 AD) on the Benguela highlands. They are also quite similar to the kit of tools used in the hinterland of Luanda in the seventeenth century which in turn is not very different from the objects made and used there as late as 1900.

Yes the continuity is overwhelming, but nevertheless there were some changes too. The quality of the products was not always the same: sometimes later work was better made than earlier work, but sometimes it was the reverse. This process was dictated by changing costs of production as well as by technological innovation. New crops, stemming from the Indian Ocean, began to be adopted after *c.*800 AD. These included taro, sugarcane, wateryams, new varieties of bananas, eggplants, perhaps hemp, or ginger, and perhaps citrus fruits. Still these plants all remained minor crops in the cycle of food production. By *c.*1000 AD domestic fowl also began to be kept. Cotton and cotton weaving were introduced from the east coast along the Zambezi *c.*1000–1200 AD but the craft became a major industry only in southern Malawi and in isolated spots between Malawi and central Angola. In the north where the raphia palm tree grew, raphia weaving prevailed. Elsewhere cotton did not always oust barkcloth or fur.

Continuity in the techniques of food production is also more remarkable than change. The original system in the rainforests relied on a mix of farming, foraging, trapping, fishing and a little hunting. Once south of the rainforests though hunting greatly increased in importance while trapping declined. The basic operations in farming consisted of clearing a field of vegetation, burning the vegetation to fertilize the soil. Then after planting or sowing crops, and weeding, one harvested. After several cycles of cultivation, the field was allowed to lie fallow in order to restore the fertility of the soils. Once these basic technical choices had been made they were never questioned again. Still there were problems caused by rapid soil exhaustion (crops need food, provided by fertilizers or fertile soils) or inadequate amounts of water (rain), and all farming systems had to cope with these needs.

The first settlers in the rainforests farmed a single major field per House on which they planted several crops at once (crop association) and then let the land lie fallow. That remained the rule there, while in the savanna further south it became the practice to plant two major fields at once, one in forest gallery and one in savanna, and to grow a succession of crops (crop rotation) on the same field before leaving it to lie fallow, rather than to associate crops. Meanwhile in the savannas north of the rainforests a single major field was worked by crop association and crop rotation until the soils were totally exhausted.

Later experiments with specific environments produced new practices, especially in less favorable locations. Thus in the infertile woodlands with adequate rainfall in Zambia *citimene* was developed. The problem was to adduce more fertilizer to the field. The solution was to cut trees over an area six to ten times the surface of the field and burn them on the site of the field. The drawback to this solution was that it required much more labor in clearing the bush than any other, and also rapidly used up large amounts of land. Other systems became even more labor intensive. In order to obtain higher yields per acre they relied on mounding, and on various ways of fertilizing by burying vegetation under the mounds, or by building up the soil of the field by making use of river silt adduced by a major river (Zambezi, Luapula, Lualaba) and in southern and central Angola by systematic irrigation.

Meanwhile in parts of the rainforests systems which required very little labor (labor extensive) were developed. Usually these combined the cultivation of plantains with fishing or trapping. The precise proportion of the time spent in farming as opposed to other food-producing activities and the relations between these activities varied from one system to another. The allocation of time was affected by expectations concerning the quality, the diversity, the taste, and the perceived nutritional value of foodstuffs, by the advisability of buying food from elsewhere rather than to produce it oneself, and by the requirements of time needed for a host of other activities.

Efficiency depended not just on the amount of labour inputs but on a division of labor, whether by gender, by skill, or by area. This changed over time under economic influences such as the relative abundance of a given resource in one area and not in others, or the amount of technical knowledge required for the production of a given activity (e.g. iron-smelting) or the need to cope with a bewildering host of activities (the often arbitrary division of labor by gender). But the division of labor also varied and changed over time as the result of social policies (e.g. servile labor, gender). Moreover the specialization of labor in a given society could be limited and rather vague or become very pronounced. Changes in the allocation of labor by region, gender and specialty are known for Central Africa from archaeological and linguistic evidence but research on this subject is still so incomplete that the general picture remains obscure.

All these continuities and changes were in turn interrelated to the growth of trade. Local exchange, based on the uneven supply of resources and talent, had always existed ever since sedentary settlements had been built. But often the distances over which goods were traded grew rapidly thereafter. One sees this best in Shaba and Zambia. Before 800 or 900 AD there is little or no evidence of foreign objects on archaeological sites. But by 900 AD miners on the copperbelt began to produce much more copper than they needed and ingots (probably from Zimbabwe) appear in southern Zambia. At about the same time the first isolated cowries or beads from the Indian Ocean begin to appear in Zambia or Shaba also, no doubt, after having traveled from relay to relay.

In the following centuries this trade grew. Indirect communication and exchange were beginning to take place over long distances as is attested by the spread of specific political emblems: iron clapperless bells from the lands near the Atlantic coast as far as Lake Tanganyika and beads, cowries and conus shells from the Indian Ocean as far as south central Africa. But these goods were not carried by traders traveling all the way say from the Indian Ocean to Shaba. Goods such as cowries or shells were bought in one district by a trader who brought them to the next district for sale. The goods themselves changed hands many times on their journey from the coast to the interior. Thus trade remained indirect.

By 1300, however, a major expansion in trade occurred. A genuine currency, the copper cross of various denominations (sizes) appeared in the area and foreign goods became more plentiful on the major sites in Shaba and Zambia. This indicates that the frequency of trade and the numbers of items that could be bought and sold was now such that the use of a currency, rather than barter, became necessary. It is also likely that traders began to travel over much longer distances between markets hundreds of miles from each other. Less than a century later a huge trading network had been put in place. It linked most of Zambia and eastern Shaba, to the coast of the Indian Ocean, the capital of Zimbabwe, the fringes of the rainforests to the north of Shaba and probably as far westwards as the river Kasai. Many goods, ranging from iron products and salt, to cosmetics, edible oils, cloth, and copper were exchanged over shorter segments of the network, while ivory and copper were exported to the Indian Ocean and Zimbabwe in return for cotton cloth and beads. By 1400 southeastern equatorial Africa had fused with southeastern Africa in a single economic spatial sphere with outlets all along the Indian Ocean. The development of such a far-flung network must in turn have affected production and the social life of most populations of this vast area.

Archaeological and other evidence is still too scarce elsewhere in Central Africa to tell us when and how trading networks developed. But it is clear from the known trade in pottery that the coastal lands on either side of the mouth of the Zaire were linked by 1400 with Malebo Pool and a riverain trade upstream from there over a total distance of some four hundred miles. And the area stretching from southern Congo to the lower Cuanza River in Angola made use of common currencies and a uniform system of markets to trade such goods as salt, iron, copper, raphia cloth, cosmetics, furs, ceramics, mats, baskets and dried fish or seafood. Whether or not there were more than occasional or indirect contacts between this area and southeastern Central Africa remains still unclear however, nor is the extent of the coastal trade northwards or the trade up the river Zaire and its affluents known.

In most of the cases the process began as follows. The various political units within a discrete area – Houses, villages and districts in most places – were roughly of equal size and strength. This balance of power guaranteed great political stability and security, despite the continual competition between the Big Men who were their leaders. But once one of these units became much stronger than its neighbors it destabilized the whole system. Such a decisive differential of power could occur only when a leader succeeded in attracting significantly more people, especially young men, than any other. People could be attracted by a higher standard of living at the leader's settlement, or by his prestige as an arbitrator, a person with exceptional relations to the supernatural, a wealthy person, or simply as an orator. But given the perpetual competition a situation of decisive superiority was difficult to achieve, and very unlikely to occur. But the unlikely comes to pass. Thus there may be a one in a million chance that two equally talented individuals succeed each other as heads of an expanding unit. And yet it happened two or three times that we know of. There is a small chance indeed that an innovative leader would live long enough for his reforms to become "customary" and yet it happened: the founder of the kingdom of Bioko lived to be almost a hundred.

Once the balance of power was broken, with it went the stability of political relations within a cluster of settlements. Other leaders and followers felt insecure and tried to restore the balance of power by adopting the decisive innovation which had brought success to their competitors. In this fashion the leaders of the whole cluster were soon affected. But that in turn threatened neighboring clusters within striking distance of the innovating one. Whether or not they were actually attacked by military forces from the original cluster was less important than their own feeling of the danger that they could be. Their leaders reacted by copying the original innovation or by innovating on their own, so as to make their unit equally strong or stronger than the threatening ones. The result of innovations breaking the balance of power then was a chain reaction which spread over space until an area was reached where the distance to the next cluster of denser populations was so great that people there did not feel threatened. Then the overall situation became stable again.

But in many instances the balance of power was not restored and an escalation of innovations followed, often within the original cluster where the process had started. Here one leader would have overcome others and incorporated their units into his own. Often a few others in this cluster succeeded in doing the same. Competition between these large units then continued unabated. In many instances this led to further elaboration of the innovative principles which had brought success in the first place and the whole chain reaction began again, until a new stable balance of power was eventually reached. In some cases this never happened completely and the process ran on for centuries.

Sometimes, the process led to an explosive expansion. The competing leaders in a cluster sometimes succeeded in building up their military power to a much higher level than existed anywhere else in a large area around them. At first they were so focused on their immediate rivalry that they were scarcely aware of this. But in time they realized their superiority over other neighbors, whereupon they then set out to dominate whole population clusters far and wide. Such an explosive expansion occurred in central and eastern Zambia around 1200 when a new political system based on linked matrilineal clans and territorial chiefdoms swept over the whole area. The sudden appearance of a new type of ceramic, Luangwa ware, which is the forerunner of the modern types of pottery in the area, is an indicator which allows archaeologists to date the event. Another example of explosive expansion occurred in western Shaba during the fifteenth century and gave birth to the Lunda kingdom.

The principles used by leaders to create innovative ideologies in order to legitimize new institutions were infinitely varied. One could appeal to a wide range of fictions based on kinship for instance. In equatorial Africa one finds cases where leaders were fathers of a "family" that encompassed a whole country, or big men of an equally large "household", or the eldest descendants of an ancestor counting through men only (patrilineal) or through women only (matrilineal), whose other descendants constituted whole populations (lineages, segmentary and others), or they were wife givers who should be respected by other elders, considered to be the progenitor (usually called "sister's sons") of these wives, or they were senior brother-in-law whose juniors owed them obeisance as if it were matrimonial compensation.

Other principles and institutions were used as well, such as common age with command over younger age grades, or the model of patron and clients, or that of a village council of "elders", or new hierarchies into older associations of healers, or diviners, or traders, or the exploitation of the fame of the shrine of a powerful territorial spirit so that its resident priest became the highest authority in the land, or a claim of the uniqueness conferred by sacred blood, a superior charm, or rainmaking abilities. All of these principles and institutions could form the framework for forms of government, and most of these forms are very unfamiliar to westerners. In consequence they have misunderstood the whole political history in Central Africa and juggled away its fascinating idiosyncracies. Westerners have classified the resulting forms of government either as chiefdoms and kingdoms, when authority seemed to be based on territory, or as "lineages" when they seemed to be based on descent.

Each of the sixteen or so major processes of political innovation in Central Africa spawned many types of government and no two processes were identical to one another. For example, one process which began before 1200 north of the great bend of the Zaire had produced the following eight major types of government there by the middle of the nineteenth century: a kingdom, principalities, village government, segmentary lineage, an urban government with rotating leadership, chiefdoms based on matrilinearity and territory, chiefdoms based on territory, and chiefdoms based on patrilineages and territory! Nor did any of the resulting types of government always appear as the result of the same processes. Kingdoms for instance were born directly from the ideology of a house, or as the highest step in the development of hierarchical associations, through the fusion of principalities, or even when districts directly coalesced. Given such complexities the reader will appreciate that it is not possible to even sketch the political history of the whole area. There is too much to tell and the resulting systems of government are too unfamiliar.

But one feature is common to all the processes and the resulting systems. Not only were all these systems ultimately derived from the single western Bantu ancestral model, but the essential elements of that model: the House, the village or the district and the original ideology of leadership were usually preserved as well. The continuity in political thought and practice is therefore as striking as it is in the economic realm, even though it coexisted with an immense variety of later change. Furthermore, the ideal of local autonomy as a cherished value was preserved in every resulting system. They all succeeded in the task of efficiently coordinating efforts in a few domains such as common defense or trade when required, but at the same time to limit centralization to the few domains where cooperation was essential. Everywhere a fierce spirit of egalitarianism (for adult married men) was paradoxically allied to elitist notions of leadership, both tendencies being backed up by separate sets of religious beliefs and rituals. When cooperation was essential elitism momentarily prevailed but in most situations egalitarianism was dominant.

Kingdoms do appear among the various social formations that result, but the emergence of kingdoms should not be privileged over any of the other outcomes. Yet historians of Central Africa have singled them out to the virtual exclusion of all other forms of government, probably because they were familiar with kingdoms. They thought that kingdoms were larger in area or population than other polities, which would justify the practice. Yet most kingdoms were not bigger than many among the other systems. It used to be thought that all kingdoms were more centralized than any other system: that they were states. Hence the birth of a kingdom dramatically altered the scale of political systems. But this was not true in equatorial Africa. Most kingdoms there were merely societies in which everyone accepted the superior position of a king on the grounds that one or another supernatural agency had decreed it. Kings and courts were the fount of prestige and legitimacy for all. They also set the tone of culture and fashion. Nevertheless, local autonomy was fully preserved in almost all kingdoms. Most kings and their courts administered only their capitals and the surrounding villages. There was no centralization in administration, justice, economics, or anything else. Indeed there was no standing army and hence the coercive powers of the kings remained very limited. Therefore, decision making remained collective, even at court, and even when the affairs of the inhabitants of the capital itself were concerned. Most of these kingdoms then were not centralized. They were not states and their history should not be singled out over that of other social formations.

Yet some kingdoms deserve to be singled out because their courts created common socio-political cultures over territories far larger than any other type of government did. True, some of the latter, for instance, the chiefdoms in central and eastern Zambia or the segmentary lineage systems of southern Cameroon and northern Gabon, had succeeded in spreading a common socio-political culture over large territories. Yet these areas are dwarfed in size by the two common cultures that came to dominate the whole northern half of southern equatorial Africa by the eighteenth century. They were originally the cultures of the Luba and Lunda kingdoms in the east and the Kongo kingdom in the west. The sheer scale of this development justifies that special attention be paid to the history of these kingdoms, and that is why they are singled out here.

The emergence of Luba and related kingdoms

Vast cemeteries have been found in the region of the depression of the Lualaba in Shaba. They contained rich and varied grave offerings and became the most intensively studied sites of equatorial Africa. These finds enable the historian to trace the social change that took place there all the way from the appearance of the first well-populated community down to the emergence of a major kingdom more than six hundred years later. Leaving the earliest and more humble sites aside, the story begins around 800 AD at Sanga, a district in the depression. It was occupied by fishing people and farmers and already was a well-populated area where individual leaders were buried with special emblems of authority and richer grave goods. But there was as yet no sharp divide in wealth between the graves of such men and others. Indeed some clues point to the social importance of a form of association and perhaps collective government.

Shortly after 1000 AD the population rose, the material culture became quite refined, imported copper became abundant, more intensive longer-distance trade was practiced, and differences in wealth by gender and by social status became more pronounced as both jewelry and funerary goods show. The power of the leaders had grown compared to earlier times as is clear from the occasional human sacrifice, and the collective graves containing a man, accompanied by women and children. The occasional richly endowed graves of small children point to the development of regular patterns of succession to office, but whether office within an association or to the chieftaincy only, one cannot say. Slight differences in style and in prestige goods between the downstream portion of the area (Sanga) and the upstream portion (Katoto) show that two different fashion centers had arisen in the area (perhaps the capitals of two larger chiefdoms?), while the presence of ceramics typical for the time on the plateau north of the depression indicates that a large area there had come under the influence of the centers in the valley of the Lualaba. Towards the end of this period violence, probably warfare, may have become more common than before because one finds human teeth used as pendentives by women and human jawbones worn by men.

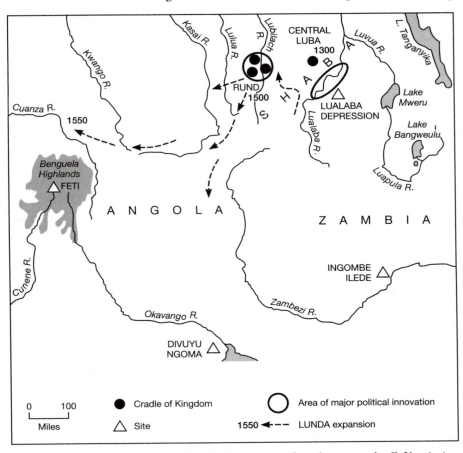

Map 8.3 South central Africa before 1550 AD (based on a map by C. Vansina)

By the fourteenth century, a new style of ceramics called the Kabambian, began to appear, starting from the northeast of the depression. By 1400 it had totally replaced the older styles. The Kabambian lasted until c.1625. Its funerary practices and the associated symbolism were quite different from previous practice. Most graves contained fewer goods while a few graves were very richly appointed indeed, indicating that social stratification had become much more pronounced. Yet the density of population remained what it had been before and long-distance trade reached new heights. Moreover, the local diversity between sites became greater than before. This picture is consistent with the incorporation of the area into a larger political whole whose center of gravity lay outside of the depression. This was certainly the case later, for after the Kabambian ended c.1625 graves were furnished even more sparsely. By now the area had been sucked into the orbit of the central Luba kingdom whose core area lay far to the north of the depression. Secure oral traditions then take up the story.

The impressive continuity of all features in the depression from the late 700s to modern Luba objects and practices leaves no doubt that the people in the depression were culturally among the ancestors of the later Luba, an assertion supported by the examination of the physical remains. Central Luba traditions of origin refer to the Kabambian period, and help us understand how the shift to the Kabambian took place. The Luba claim that their kingdom began when the ideology of *bulopwe* was adopted by their ancestors. This ideology claimed that certain people had the potential right to rule because sacred blood flowed in their veins. The complex initiation of a chosen ruler then activated this quality and turned him into a king or *mulopwe*. But kings were not autocrats. They ruled with the help of a set of titled and ranked officials who were leaders of the *bambudye* political association. Although the king was its patron, the association was not just an agent of the king which strengthened royal authority away from the capital, but it also checked royal abuse and acted as a counterforce to kingship.

The bulopwe ideology, not the association, was the innovation in Kabambian times. Similar associations linked to various forms of rule had existed before in an area far wider than the later Luba kingdom. But bulopwe now enhanced the office of a single leader and thus laid the foundation for the Luba kingdom. This became the lodestar for the development of a political title system, whether or not the titles themselves harked back to the earlier associations. Kingship added immensely to the already considerable prestige of the Luba among their southern neighbors. Their reputation was such that the oral traditions of all the peoples of central and eastern Zambia, indeed as far away as southern Malawi, claim that the chiefs of their own dynasties had originated in "Luba land". Such claims need not be taken literally, because they exist only to strengthen and legitimize local authority. Yet they testify to how great Luba prestige was at the time when they were created probably in the fifteenth century. Moreover, the adoption of a few terms and a few emblems of Luba origin in these regions also document the far-flung influence of Luba royal institutions there.

The central Luba kingdom however was only among several that took shape in Shaba during the fifteenth and sixteenth centuries. In the river valleys to the west of this kingdom a typical process of competition and escalation was pitting over half a dozen smaller chiefdoms against each other. Eventually this led to the emergence of three major kingdoms. The earliest to emerge, closest to the central Luba kingdom, was in the Luba mold. The youngest and weakest emerged to the north of the cluster *c.*1600. It was modeled partly on the central Luba model, but partly also on an earlier form of government. The third one was the Rund kingdom founded *c.*1500.

The Rund kingdom adopted neither bulopwe nor political associations. It consisted of a coalition of a number of district headmen and retained an earlier political ideology. This had been one of "family" rule. The ruler was thought of as a father and his subordinates and allies were perceived as his relatives: mothers, sons, mothers' brothers, grandparents, and so on exactly as if the polity was just a House. Now each of the subordinate leaders was expected to behave toward the main leader as if they really were uncles or sons or brothers-in-law. This behavioral model was then turned into a permanent constitution by the institution of positional succession. Any successor to one of these positions pretended to become his predecessor. He even took the name and the identity of his predecessor. Thus the successor to a leader called Chinguri was now himself Chinguri and the brothers, sisters, sons, and so on of the first Chinguri now became the brothers, sisters, sons, and so on of the second Chinguri as well. Kinship relations between leaders thus became perpetual and kinship terms among them became the equivalent of titles. By the time the Rund kingdom was fashioned some form of positional succession and perpetual kingship was probably already widespread between western Angola and eastern and southern Zambia, but the Rund invention consisted in the systematic application of these institutions.

During the century-long struggle, in western Shaba exchanges of political innovations occurred between the various rivals. As a result the Rund contributed to the political institutions of the Luba, and vice-versa. Thus the Rund adopted many Luba political titles, and some emblems, while the Luba kingdoms, including the central one, adopted a Rund myth of origin and some Rund emblems. The third party borrowed freely from the two others and contributed some features of their own to the Rund system. Thus was fashioned a common political culture. Later the expansion of Luba and Lunda kingdoms carried this common culture eventually over a huge area between the Kwango and Luapula rivers.

The fifteenth-century struggle in western Shaba is a good example of explosive expansion. By 1500 the main contenders had become militarily much more powerful than their neighbors, especially to the southwest. Some of the rival leaders who were vying for leadership in the emerging Rund kingdom realized this. As they lost out to the faction that was founding the Rund kingdom they emigrated. Leading the armed bands of their followers they began to plunder far away lands. One war band raided the lands south of the uppermost Kasai and settled there, another settled further west where the river has its source, while a third moved even further to the west. By 1550 its war leaders were camping between the Kwango and Cuanza rivers, poised to burst into the highland of Benguela. Historians use the label Lunda, rather than Rund to designate the whole area affected by these military operations as well as the commonwealth that was to result from these activities.

The kingdom of Kongo to *c.*1700

When the first Portuguese navigators arrived in the area from the north in 1483 they found an impressive kingdom south of the mouth of the Zaire. This was Kongo, a territory that contained over half a million inhabitants and covered an area of roughly 250 miles inland from the ocean and 250 miles from north to south. The country was ruled by an aristocratic elite grouped in Houses. Close relatives of the king were appointed to govern most of the provinces and dismissed by him and his ruling council at will. That provided a significant degree of centralization, unusual for equatorial Africa. Kongo then was still relatively young. It emerged shortly before 1400 in part as the result of alliances between neighboring principalities and in part as the result of long drawn-out conquest.

Kongo emerged along with the two neighboring and rival kingdoms of Loango and of the Tio. They were all part of the same regional political processes, and yet they developed very different governing institutions. The largest of them, the Tio kingdom,

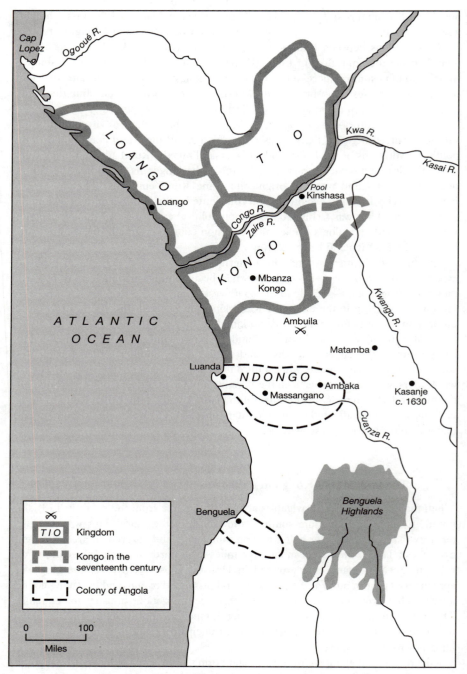

Map 8.4 Kongo and Angola: sixteenth–seventeenth centuries (based on a map
by C. Vansina)

was the most decentralized. Its autonomous territorial lords were united only by their recognition of a common kingship. In Loango the provincial rulers were close kin of the king in the female line, but they were appointed for life and enjoyed a good deal of autonomy. Kongo was the most centralized of the three and only Kongo was to become a state.

The three kingdoms had emerged from a welter of principalities occupying an area stretching from the shores of the Atlantic ocean to those of the Zaire river above Malebo Pool and to the Kwango river. Among these principalities some had institutions that later led to the Kongo and Loango kingdoms, while others prefigured the Tio kingdom. Later a third group of smaller chiefdoms took shape in the Kwango basin and later again spread between the Kwango and Cuanza rivers. Their organization borrowed from both the older types of principalities, but their ideology rested on positional succession. One among these succeeded by 1500 in creating yet another type of kingdom: Ndongo in Angola, which was formed directly through the fusion of many small territories into a single kingdom without any internal provincial organization at all.

The principalities of the Kongo and Tio types took shape probably well before 1200, out of a single type of smaller territorial unit, whose leaders were called *nkani*. Nkani based their authority on their success as arbitrators between competing Big Men. The first nkani chiefdoms themselves probably appeared in the second half of the first millennium. Thus the political culture and practice in the various kingdoms was the result of more than five hundred years of experience.

Relations between Portugal and Kongo started well. Soon the king was baptized and the Portuguese assisted in a military expedition. Later on, possibly as a result of persistent slave raids by Portuguese settlers based on the island of São Tomé, or possibly because Christianity was undermining the ideological foundation of kingship, the king returned to his former faith. But a faction in the aristocracy led by his younger son Affonso, then a provincial governor, remained Catholic. When the king died in 1506, Affonso came to power. He was to rule for thirty-seven years and strengthened the central institutions of the kingdom to such an extent that later traditions often perceive him as the founder of the kingdom and that all later claimants to the throne had to prove that they were descended from him. Kongo under Affonso became a state with central control of coercion, the administration, the judiciary, and economic policy.

A period of troubled collaboration between Portugal and Kongo followed Affonso's accession to the throne. He asked for technicians and King Manuel of Portugal obliged, but required payment in ivory, copper, and slaves. Affonso resisted Portuguese attempts to introduce their code of law or take control of the copper mines, but the Portuguese in turn resisted his attempts to establish his own fleet to trade directly with Europe. By the early 1520s, Affonso realized that the unregulated slave trade was undermining his authority and had led to general insecurity, as people at random were kidnapped and enslaved by the Portuguese or their agents. He regained control over the situation by successfully enforcing restrictions on the sale of Kongo people, while allowing the sale of foreign slaves bought at the markets on Malebo Pool near present day Kinshasa. Meanwhile he also succeeded in establishing Catholicism as the official royal religion, and he even managed to convince the Vatican to establish a bishopric in

Kongo. One of his sons was consecrated a bishop, but this prince bishop died soon after his accession and the king lost control over the See.

In his old age Affonso became less and less able to control interference in the affairs of state by the Portuguese established at his court. Diogo I, his successor, gradually managed to curtail such Portuguese interference but at the price of distancing himself from the missionaries as well and he alienated the Portuguese traders of São Tomé. These now backed the kingdom of Ndongo, especially after Diogo's army had been defeated there in 1556. By the 1560s Kongo was becoming isolated from the Atlantic trade and from Europe and its people became xenophobic. When the resident Portuguese attempted to impose a successor to Diogo the common people rose in revolt and chased them away.

Yet at the same time Kongo peasants resented the aristocracy. From the 1520s onwards arbitrary taxes and levees had steadily increased as the aristocrats sought increasing revenues to pay for foreign luxury goods. By the 1560s mutiny was in the air. Then two Kongo kings one after another died in battles near Malebo Pool, whereupon in 1658 the Jaga, a Kongo label for foreign warriors, invaded the kingdom. Many among the peasantry joined them in open war against their lords. The kingdom collapsed like a house of cards and the court fled to an island in the estuary of the Zaire river from where the king appealed to Portugal for help.

Portugal sent an army which after seven years of war, managed to re-establish royal authority. The defeated Jaga gradually left Kongo to settle north of the Zaire river, and in a part of the Kwango valley.

The Portuguese in Angola

The court of Lisbon took advantage of Kongo's weakness to proclaim the conquest of Angola and to authorize a settlement at Luanda in 1575. Within a year of founding Luanda the Portuguese started a war against Ndongo in the hope of conquering lands where silver mines were rumoured to abound. There was no silver, but the war lasted a hundred years and in the process Angola became a major exporter of slaves to the New World. The Portuguese *conquista* soon floundered when a coalition of African powers defeated them. But that coalition could not capture the new fortified towns of Luanda and Massangano. The stalemate was only broken c. 1614 because the Portuguese allied to "Jaga". These were not the Jaga of Kongo but others, for "Jaga" in Portuguese now designated any marauding military force. These Jaga were the successors of the military bands, ultimately of Lunda origin, which had been camped near the upper Cuanza by 1550. Since then they had roamed the Benguela Highlands, plundering as they went, and incorporating large numbers of local people into their bands. By 1600 the major band called itself Imbangala. These attacked Ndongo and later allied with Portugal. Thanks to their intervention the king of Ndongo was driven into hiding, and the Kongolese forces who supported him were defeated.

In 1623 the king of Ndongo died and was succeeded by his sister Anna Njinga who renewed the war and allied herself with yet other Jaga troops from the south of the Cuanza river. During the next round of fighting the Imbangala withdrew inland towards the Kwango while Njinga was forced to evacuate most of Ndongo but conquered the kingdom of Matamba to the northeast. The later 1620s and the early 1630s are a crucial decade in the history of Angola. During that period the territorial structure of the Portuguese colony took shape, Njinga established a novel form of government in her lands, and the Imbangala created the kingdom of Kasanje in the Kwango valley. All three systems of government were to last without major change until well into the nineteenth century.

After a few years of relative peace, the Dutch invaded Angola in 1641. All the African powers allied with the Dutch. Njinga with the assistance of a Dutch contingent, almost overran the last Portuguese stronghold at Massangano in 1648. At this juncture, however, a fresh Portuguese force from Brazil recaptured Luanda. The Dutch left and the African powers had to come to terms with the victorious Portuguese. The ruler of Kasanje, whose capital Cassange, had become the single most important emporium for trade far inland, allied himself immediately with Portugal, while the kings of Kongo and Njinga remained aloof but sued for peace. Even then war flared up between Portugal and Njinga's territory in Matamba. Lasting peace was only achieved by 1683.

Meanwhile the Portuguese settlers in Angola still believed that there were gold mines in Kongo and they were determined to conquer them. They invaded Kongo in 1665 and won the battle of Ambuila in which the king of Kongo died, but a few years later they were heavily defeated and had to evacuate the country. The battle of Ambuila, however, marked the start of long-lasting civil wars in Kongo between pretenders for the crown. At their conclusion in 1710 both the capital and the centralized political structure of the kingdom had been destroyed. There remained a king of Kongo, but no Kongo state. A dozen or more autonomous powers had taken over the realm. An early effect of the civil wars was the appearance of a major millennarian movement launched by a young woman who claimed to be St Anthony. She announced that she had come to teach the true religion: priests were impostors, God and his angels were black, the kingdom of heaven was especially close to Kongo, because Christ had really lived and died there, not in Palestine, and finally her divine mission was to restore the kingdom and anoint the true king. The movement shows not merely the anguish caused by the civil war, but the deep impact of Christianity on Kongo and the intensity of the clash of European and African cultures. When its founder was burned at the stake, Antonianism faded away, but official Catholicism never regained its dominant position. The church was unable to retain its centralized structure now that the state had disappeared. Moreover the supply of missionaries soon dwindled to nothing, the Christian royal cult merged with older Kongo religious convictions and practices to form a new religion whose cults changed along with the new conditions of life in the kingdom.

Meanwhile the political and economic expansion of the colony of Angola also ground to a halt. By 1700 the Portuguese in the lands north of Luanda lost control of the slave trade to the benefit of their Dutch, French and English rivals. To the east, the colony was now contained by Matamba and Kasanje who also jointly controlled the supply of slaves from this direction. In the colony itself Luso-African communities became more and more influential at the expense of the metropolitan Portuguese. The label Luso-African applies to persons who perceived themselves as permanent inhabitants of Angola and who had mixed Portuguese and African elements in their way of life. They included many Portuguese born in Central Africa, half-caste persons and some Portuguese who had been born overseas but were long-time residents in the bush. They also included African communities who had adopted many aspects of Portuguese culture including literacy and an indigenized Catholicism. The label thus designates two different groups, who were united only in their attitudes towards the metropolitan Portuguese and towards African rulers.

By 1700 Luso-African communities were old. Portuguese settlers lived at first in the capital of Kongo and intermarried with Africans already in Affonso's reign. A little later they also lived in the area which was to become Luanda. When the colony of Angola took shape many emigrated to Benguela and later in the century to highlands in the interior of that port. By 1700 Luso-Africans had captured most administrative and economic positions in the colony, except for the city of Luanda itself. All these communities lived from the slave trade and they were all strongly imbued by local African practices and religious beliefs. As to Luso-Africans of African origin, they had begun as trusted trading agents for Portuguese firms, since the days of Affonso. After *c.*1650 communities of these Luso-Africans freed themselves of outside control, whether by African rulers or by agents of the Portuguese Crown and were trading on their own account. The first of these communities were located on the major slave trading routes in the hinterland of Luanda but by 1700 they too began to settle on the Benguela highlands.

Economic transformation: the northern network

The most striking feature about eighteenth century history in equatorial Africa is the huge growth of the slave trade, both in intensity and in the size of the areas affected. This trade transformed local economics over almost half of the whole area. Given the unparalleled magnitude of this phenomenon it should be presented first.

A well-organized slave trade developed as European relations with Kongo grew. When the Portuguese arrived trade in Kongo was well-established. The kingdom had a common currency, a system of rotating markets, based on a week of four days, and clear regulations affecting trading practices. The first steady supply of slaves in these markets appeared by *c.*1525 when early Luso-African buyers for the Portuguese traders reached Malebo Pool on the Zaire river where slaves from areas far upstream were on offer. A second major market developed at Luanda even before its official foundation. Later the wars of conquest yielded larger numbers of captives for export and, when the fighting abated somewhat by the 1630s, markets in the new realms of Matamba and at Cassange became outlets for slaves from the lands beyond the Kwango.

By the later seventeenth century two different networks for trading slaves had appeared, one centered on the lower Zaire and harbors further north, and one centered on Luanda and later Benguela in Angola. During the century, both expanded in intensity and size according to demand in the Americas. Greater demand meant higher prices and that stimulated supply. Slavers traveled further, so that the area affected by the trade grew and the slaving frontier moved further away from the coast. The heart of

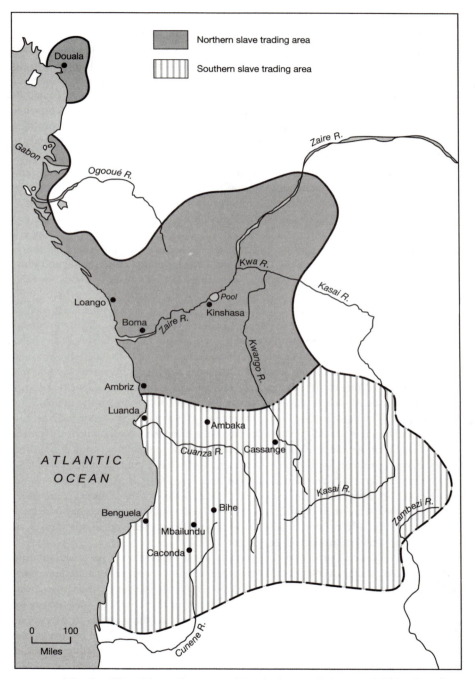

Map 8.5 The eighteenth-century Atlantic slave trade in central Africa (based on a map by C. Vansina)

each network were the coastal towns where slaves were sold. The roads led to market-places far inland where sizeable numbers of slaves could be bought. All along the road caravans acted like a traveling fair buying foodstuffs, local products, and some enslaved criminals or debtors, while selling European or African commodities. At the end of the trading routes lay the slaving frontier, a region of turmoil in which chaotic kidnapping and war were the major sources of procurement. Some local populations reacted by fleeing away from such areas, others turned to raiding and piracy on the rivers, while others still migrated towards markets that collected slaves there in the hope of profiting from the trade. By 1800 both network systems had expanded by leaps and bounds to encompass all the lands between the Atlantic, the upper Zambezi, the middle Kasai and the great bend of the Zaire river in the east. A major trade route even ran right across Africa between Luanda and the lower Zambezi. In West Central Africa only parts of southern Cameroon and adjacent territories still lay outside these networks.

Apart from these general dynamics there existed major differences between the two networks and they are therefore best described separately. In the north Europeans were confined to the coast and could not set up permanent establishments there. During the eighteenth century the French and British dominated the trade and most often practiced the triangular trade: the same ships left Europe with goods for sale, bought slaves, sold their human cargo in the New World for commodities there (often sugar) and then sold these on their home markets. African groups on the coast such as the Vili in Loango, the Mpongwe in the estuary of the Gaboon, the Duala in the coastal Cameroons or similar groups in the interior such as the Tio at Malebo Pool or the Bobangi on the Zaire river had developed business firms, which financed the caravans (ultimately often on credit from European captains) and were the carriers, while the local populations along the routes produced commodities required by the network such as food or canoes, as well as slaves and ivory for export. Even though the demand for slaves was the final input in the system, the extension of the network was equally fed by the ever-increasing demand for exotic and prestige European goods, which the chiefs and the Big Men needed to compete with each other, for prestige was power. As time passed former prestige goods such as European textiles and guns became necessities, rather than luxury goods and this intensified trade even further. African traders were not mercantilist capitalists in the sense that their goal was not to accumulate currency. Their goal was to use their profits to acquire more dependents, just as they had used goods before the advent of the slave trade. Even if they behaved in some ways as capitalists they had not absorbed the spirit of capitalism.

The slave trade had a profound effect on the overall economics of the area. Not only did it promote further development of commercial institutions such as markets, currencies, currency exchanges, or commercial law everywhere, but it also led to more organic economic integration. As most of the trade in these regions was carried by water the labor costs were low. This allowed for cabotage, that is trade in all sorts of local commodities bought and sold on markets, all along the way. That in turn gave a continuing impulse to an ever-increasing economic rationalization of production in the whole area. Every locality began to specialize in goods on which the highest profit could be made. This resulted in an increasing spatial division of labor, which in turn raised total output significantly. For instance, in one district people with poor iron ores no longer smelted iron, but boosted the output of textiles or tobacco for which their lands were well-suited, while in another district, blessed with excellent ores, the inhabitants concentrated on producing iron and bought their textiles or tobacco. As a result both of these districts became more efficient producers.

The overall economic output in the whole huge area rose at the same time that its local economies became more integrated. The adoption of new crops from America such as maize, manioc, beans, groundnuts and tobacco were part of this process. Manioc and beans reached higher yields than the crops they were replacing, so that surplus was available for sale to the traders who needed to feed themselves and their slaves. Predictably, the cultivation of these crops spread rapidly along the main arteries of trade. In less forested but moist environments maize fulfilled a role similar to manioc.

But the increase in economic output came at a high price – a significant loss of population. During the eighteenth century about one million slaves were exported from the region while an unknown number, perhaps half a million, died before they reached the coast or during slave raids on the frontier. Although such losses were high enough to stem significant increases in the population they did not lead to an absolute decline in population, (except perhaps during the 1760s to 1780) because fertile women constituted only a third of these exports. The moral cost of slave trading was equally high, because it became "normal" to treat some people like goats with a chilling callousness that bred inhumanity.

The social and political effects of the slave trade were major but they did not lead to a radical break with the past. Thus while social inequality increased, this by itself was not new. Extreme social inequality had always been a feature of the Houses in this area, but now it became even more pronounced. There had been slaves in the sense of servants who had no kinship group of their own and hence were absorbed into their master's household. Such people could not normally be bought or sold. Now a lower class was added to them; slaves often described as "persons for sale" who were treated like chattels. Moreover, near-servile women were added to the household by turning a certain type of bridewealth into a purchase price.

The trade fostered the emergence of a new commercial elite, whose power directly derived from trade. These competed for power with the older leaders and succeeded. The collapse of the Kongo state was succeeded by the domination of this commercial elite, while in Loango and smaller kingdoms north of the Zaire coalitions of business leaders succeeded after 1700 in taking over the reins of government, even while they ritualized their kings into political impotence, just as had happened to Kongo.

Meanwhile, at the hubs of the trading network, two fundamental elements of society namely the House and the village had been adapted to the slave trade as well. The House turned into a business firm. It became much larger and internally more structured into specialized groups such as porters, and carriers or paddlers, household servants assigned to specific duties, or farm hands. The number of dependents of all sorts, including married women, in relation to the free members of the House sharply rose. Yet despite such innovations the House, its leaders and their significance did not change in the minds of people. For them the innovation merely consisted in putting the old organizations to new uses.

Such firms appeared at harbors all the way from Duala to the mouth of the river Zaire and also along the major hubs along the Zaire river. In these places various Houses flocked to exceptionally favorable sites for commerce. As a result market towns arose, serviced by the countryside around them. Once again people did not see towns as innovations, merely as enlarged villages, even though by 1800 some of these counted between 10,000 and 20,000 inhabitants.

Other strikingly novel structures were also perceived as merely new uses of older institutions. The use for instance of the healing association of *lemba* north of the lower Zaire river to regulate peace on the marketplaces along a segment of the caravan road between Loango and the Pool is startlingly new. Yet the association itself was old and was the royal cult in the kingdom of Loango before it was adapted to this new use.

Finally, the trade spawned new ethnic groups. River traders such as the Bobangi, caravaneers such as the Vili of Loango, or groups controlling harbors such as the Mpongwe of the Gaboon estuary or the Duala in Cameroon led such a specialized way of life that they soon began to think of themselves as a different ethnic group, and all their neighbors concurred. At the same time slave traders began to use a set of ethnic labels to differentiate between slaves of different origins. Their catalogue of ethnic categories created a set of ethnic groups which the colonial powers inherited. Yet, once again, this was not a totally new phenomenon. Ethnicity had always existed and ethnic sentiment had in some cases been based on differences in the way of earning a livelihood. Thus once again the ethnic groups which arose now were in the minds of people only new applications of an old principle.

Economic transformation: the southern network

In the south the system was linked to the Portuguese and Brazilian trade. Its organization differed significantly from trade further north. The triangular trade was less practiced; rather firms in Lisbon sold goods from Europe to European businesses in Luanda or later Benguela. The businesses there financed caravans into the interior, led by their own Luso-Africans. These bought slaves from African dealers on markets in the far interior such as Cassange. As demand rose, the networks expanded and after about 1750 more and more agents absconded with the caravans entrusted to their care by the firms of Luanda to join older Afro-Portuguese communities, especially on the Benguela highlands. There they created enclaves near the courts of newly developing kingdoms and entered into trading partnerships with the local kings who became both their customers and protectors. The African demand for European imports followed the same dynamics as in the northern network. Here, however, most of the African suppliers were chiefs and many more slaves were procured in raids and in wars than was the case in the rainforests.

Moreover, in Angola severe droughts recurred at irregular intervals and during a drought many more slaves were offered for sale than at other times. That led to gluts on the market. Slaves piled up in the barracoons (slave barracks) of Luanda or Benguela where many died before they could be shipped out.

The slave trade in the southern network also had economic effects that were significantly different from those occurring in the northern network. The routes ran overland, hence transportation costs were much higher, there was less cabotage, and hence less regional economic integration – although some did occur; for instance, by the end of the century manioc plantations, cultivated by slaves, had been set up along the major routes to feed the caravans. In this network warfare was prominent while the fact that agents rather than owners were in charge of caravans led to greater neglect and abuse of the slaves in transit. All this explains why slave mortality and general population loss was much higher here than in the northern network. More people died during slave raids, more slaves died from mistreatment as they traveled overland, more died in the slave barracks, especially during droughts, and more died during the middle passage as well, because they were already in weak condition when they embarked. So while the exports in the eighteenth century lay at a little over one million and hence were comparable to those of the northern network, the loss of life was much higher: well over two million, perhaps even three. The demographic strain was therefore much greater and in my estimation led to significant depopulation in eastern Angola.

The most significant effect of the slave trade, here as in the northern network, was also the rise of new commercial elites, all Luso-African. This development did not yet affect major political units in the area because there elites were not yet competing for power in the centers of the various kingdoms. Matamba, Kasanje, and the colony of Angola continued as before. Only on the Benguela highlands was there significant innovation. Here a new set of kingdoms (collectively called Ovimbundu) arose from mid-century onwards, as the direct result of major Portuguese expeditions. But Portugal could not impose chiefs nor set up new kingdoms. The new kings were local people who achieved power partly in old established ways, and the organization of their realms was that of older polities. But power was also achieved in new ways, that is by Luso-African support. From the outset the Luso-Africans backed the new kings. Each royal court was soon flanked by a major trading settlement. Kings and Luso-African traders together soon developed a common commercial framework on such a scale and so efficiently that by the 1790s Ovimbundu caravans came to overshadow all others in Central Africa. Politics and trade were by then so interwoven that the area was in effect ruled jointly by the "old" and "new" elites.

The shaping of a Lunda commonwealth

Given its spectacular development it is easy to assume that economic growth totally dominated political change in western equatorial Africa during this century. If so, there should be sharp differences between developments within this area and those occurring beyond it, and there should be a break in the continuity of the political institutions and practices of people within the slaving area. But such sharp differences or such a break do not exist. The whole history of the area must not be reduced to a history of the slave trade. The clearest evidence for this, is the emergence of a huge single Lunda commonwealth, south of the rainforests and from the Kwango valley eastwards to the Luapula valley nine hundred miles away.

By the later 1680s the Rund kingdom became the cradle for a renewed explosive expansion. Once again adventurous captains with bands of warriors swarmed west of the heartland to carve out kingdoms for themselves. The biggest was to become the

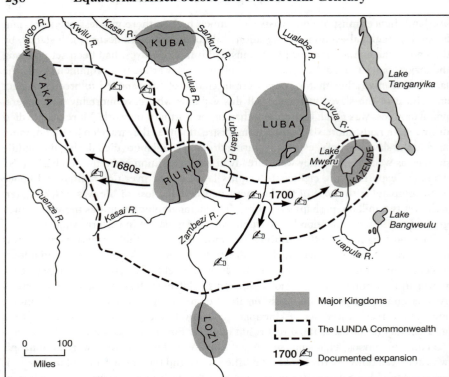

Map 8.6 The Lunda Commonwealth and other major kingdoms *c.*1800 AD
(based on a map by C. Vansina)

main Yaka kingdom. Others expanded south eastwards in Shaba and Zambia. By 1740 one general reached the Luapula river and founded the kingdom of Kazembe there. Why this expansion occurred is still unclear, but the result was the creation of a huge "empire", although an empire only in the imagination of its inhabitants. All its inhabitants recognized the distant emperor as a "king of kings" but that was the only tie common to all in the huge realm. It was therefore more like a commonwealth than an empire and certainly not a single state. Not only was the commonwealth not a state, but none of the constituent kingdoms were states either. The extent of the "emperor's" effective administrative control was barely limited to a territory some sixty to seventy miles around the capital. In 1755 one emperor was even killed by a bunch of stubborn insurgents, who had always rejected the Lunda ideology of government, a mere one hundred and twenty miles away from the court. And in the 1850s, at the height of its power, the Rund court was still struggling to establish administrative control over villages only a hundred miles away from the capital. While it is true that in the later eighteenth century the emperor began to send officials, the *tukwata* or "takers", to collect tribute by force much further away than that, this only occurred *ad hoc*, at irregular intervals. This was not very different from the earlier military expeditions that had originated in the Rund court. The absence of a standing army and the absence of a technology of transportation beyond human portage, go a long way to explain the lack of state formation in these kingdoms. But equally important was the high value the inhabitants placed on their autonomy.

The same factors explain why there never was an imperially planned Lunda expansion. At first glance the settlement of Lunda generals all over southern Shaba in resource rich areas such as the saltpans of the upper Lualaba or the copperbelt, or the rich Luapula valley looks like an expansion planned with economic aims in mind. Yet the rulers who settled there were not able and indeed did not even attempt to control the output of salt or copper. That firmly remained in the hands of the local communities. At best the rulers only derived some income from often irregular tribute payments. Because the commonwealth consisted of a set of kingdoms controlling only small territories around their capitals it is nonsense to imagine that the Rund court controlled the trade routes in Angola's hinterland and in Zambia. The only link with the slave trade consisted in the use by the rulers of the existing trade routes, to increase their wealth and gain followers. By 1800, the Rund "emperor" was sending caravans to trade on his account in partnership with a certain firm in Luanda, while Kazembe was sending his traders to the lower Zambezi. Trade contributed to the greater wealth, prestige and power of the kings, but the kings did not control trade.

Moreover, the absence of a standing army and adequate transport also makes one wary of accepting claims of fast conquests. Kazembe is the only known case of a "quick" Lunda conquest albeit over a limited territory. He did succeed in subduing the people of the central Luapula valley, but it took half a century (from 1740 to 1790). The other celebrated case of conquest was that of the Yaka kingdom in the Kwango valley. Several rival Rund generals settled in the area by the 1680s and they enjoyed overwhelming military superiority. Yet it took them the whole eighteenth century to settle their quarrels, to subdue local leaders, and to set up a central court. Here a conquest occurred but it took a whole century (three generations) to mature and it resulted not in one but in four "Yaka" and one autochthonous kingdom. Among these only one Yaka kingdom was of any size. No other Lunda kingdom was established by conquest and all of them, including the Yaka ones, remained extremely decentralized.

An examination of the renewed expansion of the central Luba kingdom, which also began in the late seventeenth century, leads to the same conclusion. In many cases independent chiefs traveled to the Luba court and *begged* to become subordinates in order to receive the emblems which symbolized this status. These emblems linked them to the prestige of the main Luba court and therefore enhanced their authority at home, both among their own people and against rival claimants. In other cases Luba leaders with prestigious emblems and a small retinue settled in foreign lands. Over a generation or two they gradually gained the allegiance of the local leaders and their followers by sharing prestigious symbols and titles with them. Once again, where prestige was lacking, force could not prevail. The continuing political independence of the Luba people in the Lualaba depression verifies to that.

Such features make it clear that the development of kingdoms in equatorial Africa was not radically different from the development of its many other systems of government, and like these systems it was a continuation of older processes. The rise of the

Lunda commonwealth, the renewed expansion of the central Luba kingdom and the appearance of the other kingdoms in the savannas would have occurred even in the absence of the Atlantic slave trade.

Suggestions for further reading

Birmingham, D. and Martin, P., *History of Central Africa*, Vol. 1, London: Longman, 1983.

de Maret, P., *Fouilles archéologiques dans la vallée du Haut-Lualaba, Zaire*, Tervuren: Musée royal de l'Afrique Centrale 1985.

Harms, R., *River of Wealth, River of Sorrow*, Yale: Yale University Press, 1981.

Hilton, A., *The Kingdom of Kongo*, Oxford: Clarendon Press, 1985.

Janzen, John, *Lemba 1650–1930: A Drum of Affliction in Africa and in the New World*, New York, 1982.

Lanfranchi, R., Clist, B., *Aux origines de l'Afrique centrale*, Libreville: Centre international des civilizations bantu, 1991.

Miller, J.C., *Way of Death: Merchant Capitalism and the Angolan Slave Trade: 1730–1830*, Madison: University of Wisconsin Press, 1988.

Reefe, T., *The Rainbow and the Kings*, Berkeley: University of California Press, 1981.

Roberts, A., *A History of Zambia*, London: Heinemann, 1976.

Thornton, J.K., *The kingdom of Kongo*, Madison: University of Wisconsin Press, 1983.

Vansina, J., *Kingdoms of the Savanna*, Madison: University of Wisconsin Press, 1966.

Vansina, J., *The Children of Woot*, Madison: University of Wisconsin Press, 1978.

Vansina, J., *Paths in the Rainforests*, Madison: University of Wisconsin Press, 1990.

Yoder, J.C., *The Kanyok of Zaire: An Institutional and Ideological History to 1895*, Cambridge: Cambridge University Press, 1992.

9

SOUTHERN AFRICA TO 1795

The southern part of Africa – the region bordered on the northwest by the tropical grasslands and on the northeast by the Zambezi River – has had a different history from that of the tropical middle belt across the continent to the north. The western half of the region is similar to the northern-most parts of Africa. The climate of the area around Cape Town is classified as "Mediterranean" and is not unlike the climate in northern Morocco. Further north in the western half of the region, it becomes more arid, just as the climate of North Africa becomes more arid as one moves into the Sahara, and along the Atlantic coast the Namib Desert has less than five inches of rain a year. As one travels eastward the rainfall gradually increases; but it is less than twenty inches a year, and the natural vegetation is merely sparse scrub, until one is beyond the modern towns of Mafeking, Bloemfontein, and Queenstown. There, on the high veld – the plateau in the eastern half of the region – are temperate grasslands in the Orange Free State and the Transvaal. The Limpopo valley is arid, but there are more temperate grasslands in the Zimbabwe plateau. In the southeast, between the mountain escarpment and the Indian Ocean, most of the coastal lowlands have good summer rains. Almost everywhere throughout the region, however, there are great climatic variations from year to year, with periods of severe drought, so that people can never be sure whether there will be enough rain for a good pasture or a good harvest. No wonder the traditional Sotho greeting is "Pula!" (Let there be rain!) and the basic currency unit in Botswana is the pula.

Southern Africa's location at the southern extremity of the Afro-Eurasian land mass made for a history different from that of North Africa as well as from that of the tropical belt. Whereas the lower Nile valley became the scene of a major ancient civilization, because of its proximity to the fertile crescent of western Asia as well as to tropical Africa, and the Mediterranean shores were vitally affected by the civilizations of the Muslim Middle East and western Europe, southern Africa was far removed from contact with the outside world before the maritime revolution of the fifteenth century. It was at the end of the line for the exchange of information and culture with other people, in much the same way that Patagonia in South America and Tasmania in Australasia were at the end of the line at the southern extremities of their continents.

Nevertheless, southern Africa was not as isolated as those other extremities. Several centuries before the modern era, some of the indigenous people in the region received sheep and cattle from their northern neighbors, and from the second century AD onwards, perhaps earlier, Bantu-speaking farmers with knowledge of iron-working began to move into the region from the north, while the inhabitants of the southern ends of the Americas and Australasia still depended on hunting and food gathering and on implements of stone and wood. The Bantu-speaking farmers became the majority of the population of the region. Moreover, they were familiar with many of the diseases that were endemic in Europe and Asia. As a result, when closer sea-borne contact with the outer world was established in the second millennium AD, the Bantu-speaking farmers of southern Africa had some immunities to help protect them from the European diseases that exterminated the indigenous people of Tasmania and decimated those of Patagonia – and also those of North America.

The environments of southern Africa and North Africa were also similar in the sense that Europeans could survive in both these regions more easily than they could in the tropical lands between. Consequently, the southern and northern extremities became the two regions of Africa to receive the densest immigrations by European settlers. They acquired the largest colonies of people of European origin, both in absolute numbers and in proportion to the number of people sharing cultures that had been domiciled on the African continent for millennia. Moreover, southern Africa contained rich mineral deposits, including copper, tin, iron, coal, diamonds, gold, and uranium. The Bantu-speaking farming communities recovered much of the gold, copper, tin, and iron that lay on and near the surface; but the exploitation of the deeper deposits awaited the introduction of specialized industrial technology in the late nineteenth and the twentieth century. Then, its mineral wealth would make it possible for South Africa to become the richest and the most powerful state in sub-Saharan Africa.

Major processes in precolonial Southern Africa

In recent years, archaeologists, linguists, and social anthropologists have made it possible for us to discern the broad outlines of the major processes in Southern Africa before Europeans began to enter the region in the sixteenth century. Even so, the evidence is very patchy and its interpretation has been controversial. Until recently, scholars explained major changes as solely the product of a series of massive migrations. Now, however, archaeologists such as Martin Hall and historians such as David Beach agree that the story is much more complex.

In this chapter, which should be read in conjunction with Chapter 1 of this book, we outline what we believe to be the most credible reconstruction. Before the first millennium BC, the only inhabitants of southern Africa were scattered and mobile bands, probably of between twenty and eighty people, who lived by hunting game and gathering wild foods. Then, starting about 2300 years ago, it seems likely that some of the hunter-gatherers in what is now Zimbabwe or northern Botswana acquired sheep and cattle from mixed farming communities further north, and in the ensuing centuries more and more hunter-gatherers in the western part of southern Africa added the herding of domestic livestock to their mode of life, wherever the water and soil produced adequate pastures. By 1500, pastoralists were moving seasonally with their sheep and cattle from pasture to pasture, with major concentrations in the heavy winter rainfall area in and near the Cape peninsula. Subsequently, Whites called those who continued the hunting and gathering mode of life Bushmen and those who owned sheep and cattle Hottentots, and they loaded those terms with derogatory connotations. We shall follow scholarly precedents and call them by the indigenous names San and Khoikhoi, and refer to them jointly as Khoisan and their languages, which have some similarities, as the Khoisan languages.

Meanwhile, starting in the first or second century AD, a mixed farming and iron-working culture began to take root in the eastern half of the region, where the rainfall was sufficient for arable agriculture as well as stock farming. This was the beginning of a long process that eventually engulfed the entire eastern half of southern Africa. Newcomers were involved in this process: Bantu-speaking Africans with different physical characteristics from those of the hunter-gatherers – darker skins and more robust bodies. For the most part they probably did not move in large groups or in massive leaps. Rather, it was a process of gradual territorial expansion, as families and family groups split off from established villages and founded new settlements, generally in a southerly direction. Initially, the mixed farmers seem to have settled mainly in river valleys; but after about 1000 AD they filled in the gaps between earlier settlements and expanded into higher elevations. As they settled down in each micro-environment they adapted to its specific opportunities and challenges, which included the qualities of the soil and the natural vegetation and wildlife.

Gradually, as a result of long exposure to different macro-environments, three major cultural groupings of mixed farmers predominated in southern Africa. For convenience, we shall use their modern names, Shona, Sotho-Tswana, and Nguni, although these names were not used in this sense until the nineteenth century. Shona occupied the greater part of the territory of modern Zimbabwe plus the area between the Sabi and Pungwe rivers down to the Indian Ocean in modern Mozambique. Sotho-Tswana occupied most of the present Transvaal, Orange Free State, and Swaziland, and also the eastern part of Botswana and the Lesotho lowlands. Nguni occupied the area between the mountain escarpment and the Indian Ocean, from the vicinity of Delagoa Bay to the Fish River.

The major distinction among these three was linguistic. Their languages were all members of the southern Bantu language group; they had a common syntax and much common vocabulary. According to a recent classification of Bantu languages by lexical statistics, an early split separated the Shona language from the other southern Bantu languages; the Nguni and Sotho-Tswana languages separated from each other at a later stage. From the linguistic evidence, it seems likely that the main bodies of Shona, Sotho-Tswana, and Nguni have lived for about a thousand years as separate communities. Other differences overlapped with the linguistic divisions; for example, the Shona and Sotho-Tswana people tended to live in large villages with populations as numerous as several thousand in some of the Tswana settlements at the western edge of the cultivable region, while the Nguni lived in scattered homesteads each containing only a few patrilineal families of two or three generations. But such differences existed within a common basic culture, which we shall discuss in the next section of this chapter. It is important to know that they were not closed societies. On the contrary, they often readily incorporated strangers into their social units.

Besides the three major clusters of Bantu-speakers in southern Africa, there were several smaller ones. Two of them are particularly interesting examples of adaptation to the limitations imposed by the natural environment. The Tsonga occupied the northeastern coastal belt between the Sabi River and St Lucia Bay. Though some of their lineages claim to have been closely related to Nguni, Sotho-Tswana, or Shona lineages, all the Tsonga spoke a single and distinct Bantu language which had split relatively recently from the Nguni language. Unlike the Nguni, the Sotho-Tswana, and Shona, they were watermen and fishermen. They traveled, traded, and fished on the Limpopo and the other rivers in their area. Tsetse flies made it impossible for them to breed cattle in most parts of their territory, but they had fowl and goats and they grew sorghum.

While the Tsonga were Bantu-speaking food-producers who adapted to an environment where cattle could not thrive, the Herero – the only Bantu-speaking people who lived on the arid western side of the subcontinent south of the tropical grasslands in modern Namibia – adapted to an environment where crop cultivation was not possible. Their antecedents are obscure. When European travelers encountered them in the nineteenth century, the Herero were herders with plenty of cattle but no knowledge of iron-working or crop cultivation.

Hunters and herders in southwestern Africa

In the sixteenth century, the western half of southern Africa had not experienced the full effects of the food-producing revolution and the infiltrations of mixed farmers from the north. Some people there were still hunters and gatherers; others were also pastoralists, with cattle and sheep.

The hunter-gatherers continued to live much as their ancestors had done, using tools of stone, wood, and bone. By the sixteenth century, they had retreated before the herders and mixed farmers to mountainous and arid areas that were not coveted by others, mainly in the western half of southern Africa. There they lived off roots, plants, insects, game, and fish. They were organized in small hunting bands of kinsmen, rarely more than a hundred strong. Each band stuck to a defined territory, wandering around in a continuous search for food, perhaps using a cave shelter as headquarters in bad weather.

Bands of hunters who have survived to the present day in Namibia and Botswana have been studied by modern scientists. Generally short in stature, they are physically tough, with exceptional powers of endurance. They are deeply versed in the habits of their prey and skilled in extracting lethal vegetable and insect poisons, which they smear on the bone heads of their arrows. They no longer practice the arts of painting and engraving, but their predecessors did both until the nineteenth century and have left their record for posterity on innumerable caves and rock shelters from Zimbabwe to the Cape of Good Hope – paintings and engravings that show great imaginative power, a wide variety of styles, convincing portrayal of animal and human forms, a

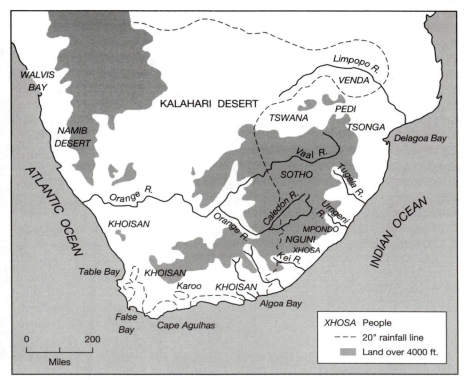

Map 9.1 Southern Africa in the sixteenth century

lively sense of humor, and also a sense of awe. The hunting bands that have been studied by modern research teams represent only one variety of the vast range of the people who formerly inhabited southern Africa. Theirs is the conservative tradition of the bands that avoided confrontation with the forces of change by retreating to areas in Botswana and Namibia that are too arid for even the most extensive pastoral farming.

We know very little about the relationships between farming and hunting peoples north of the Limpopo; by the time European travelers entered that area they found Bantu-speaking farmers occupying nearly all of it. Until the nineteenth century, however, hunting bands continued to hold out in several areas in the eastern half of South Africa and we can reconstruct their relationships with the farming peoples.

The first groups of farmers to occupy an area were usually outnumbered by the local bands of hunters. In these circumstances, the two cultures were able to coexist without much interaction or tension. In the course of time, however, the farming populations became more numerous. Two types of interaction then took place. Farmers took San wives and brought up the children of such unions like any other members of their village communities, and they acquired the farming culture. In this way, the Nguni and the Sotho peoples acquired the genes of the ancient populations of South Africa. Farmers also became patrons of individual hunters. A patron would protect his client and supply him with grain or milk and with pots and ornaments; in return, the hunter would trap or shoot game for his patron as well as for himself.

In some cases, relationships like this became general. This is what happened in Botswana, where the temperate grasslands merge into the Kalahari thornveld. There, to this day, hunting bands are exploited by Tswana chiefdoms, to whom they are bound in systematic symbiotic relationships. Further east, where water is more plentiful, however, the farmers had less need to establish permanent relationships of this sort. In that case, as the farming populations became numerous, the hunters found that they were losing control over the water supplies and that the wild animals were being exterminated. Then, they treated the farmers' sheep and cattle as game. Farmers retaliated, and relations between the two peoples turned to hostility. In the long run, the farmers triumphed because of their greater numbers and more powerful economy. Some hunting bands might retreat for a time, but in the eastern half of South Africa the farmers caught up with them sooner or later and annihilated them.

We have good information about this process in Lesotho. In about the sixteenth century, when the first farmers moved into the Caledon River valley, they were few in number; they lived amicably with the local hunting bands and there was a great deal of intermarriage until the middle of the nineteenth century. Moshoeshoe (pronounced Mushweshwe) (1786–1870), the southern Sotho king, and several of his senior kinsmen took San as well as Sotho wives as a matter of policy to strengthen their authority throughout the area, believing that the first human inhabitants had a special relationship with the land. By the beginning of the nineteenth century, however, pressure on the land increased, and the hunters began to retreat into the Maloti mountains. Later, when the Sotho themselves had lost much of their land to White settlers, they were obliged to establish cattle posts in the mountains. There, they came to blows with the San and eventually exterminated them.

Archaeologists have discovered evidence of the presence of cattle in modern Zimbabwe in the second or third centuries BC, and it seems probable that the expansion of pastoralism throughout the western half of the region began in about the first century AD. By the sixteenth century, pastoralists used the favored areas throughout the western half of southern Africa, wherever the pastures were adequate for their herds and flocks, including the zone of Mediterranean climate at the Cape.

The pastoralists formed larger-scale communities with more complex institutions than hunting bands. Richard Elphick has described their mode of life. They lived in fluid groups whose core members or clans were biologically related to one another. Several clans were often loosely organized in chiefdoms, which claimed control of specific springs and pastures. Pastoral society was unstable and fragile. People quarreled over cattle, fighting with spears and bows and arrows. When, as a result of warfare or drought or personal incompetence, a man lost his livestock, he had two options: he might attach himself as a client to a more successful man in the hope of rebuilding his herds and flocks with gifts from his patron, or he and his family might revert to the life of his ancestors and become wholly dependent on the hunting and gathering mode of life. Moreover, pastoral groups frequently split, when a venturesome man would hive off with his followers onto new pastures. In so doing they generated a series of new political units.

When the Portuguese and the Dutch began to explore the country in the sixteenth and seventeenth centuries, they found Khoikhoi herders occupying the better pasture-lands from the lower Orange River southward to the Cape of Good Hope, and from there eastward to the area between the Gamtoos and Buffalo rivers, where they were in contact with the southern Nguni chiefdoms. A broad belt of country between those rivers formed a frontier zone where Nguni and Khoikhoi made contact. Their relation-ships seem to have been more intimate and more egalitarian than were those between hunting and farming peoples. This was probably because the pastoralists' material culture and social organization had more points of similarity with those of the farmers. A network of reciprocal relations was established. During the sixteenth century, when the pastoralists were perhaps more numerous than the mixed farmers in the contact zone, a Khoikhoi chiefdom split, the new chiefdom entered into symbiotic relations with the Xhosa,the nearest southern Nguni chiefdom, the two chiefs became linked by marriage alliances, and the Xhosa adopted the culture of the Khoikhoi. During the seventeenth century, however, Xhosa numbers increased in the contact zone as a result of population movements from further east. The Khoikhoi then became dependent on the Xhosa chiefdoms and were eventually incorporated into Xhosa society, to form the Gqunukwebe sub-chiefdom.

In short, the interactions among hunting, herding, and farming peoples in southern Africa produced a rich variety of responses. They included a number of eccentric but revealing cases. In Namibia, for example, some of the people who call themselves Damara are physically similar to the Bantu-speaking farmers, but they are hunter-gatherers, they have a subordinate symbiotic relationship with the Nama (a Khoikhoi-speaking herding people), and they themselves speak Khoikhoi and no other language. This shows how various the relationships among physical type, language, and material culture can be.

When we stand back from the details, however, we see that a single trend was manifestly paramount in southern Africa during the millennium and a half that pre-ceded the Dutch settlement at the Cape of Good Hope. Bantu-speaking farmers were expanding slowly but inexorably at the expense of the other inhabitants. The hunting peoples, the herding peoples, and even the Portuguese settlers in the Zambezi valley were being eliminated as autonomous communities, some by assimilation, some by reduction to dependent status, some by outright extermination.

The mixed farming culture

The farmers who occupied the eastern half of southern Africa – its plateau grasslands and coastal belt – had many things in common: their related languages, their pastoral and arable economy, their emphasis on cattle, their use of copper and iron, and their hierarchical, male-dominated social and political relations.

The economy of the mixed farmers was far more complex than that of the people who occupied the western half of southern Africa. Like the hunter-gatherers, they preyed on the game which abounded throughout the region: many species of antelope and also elephants, rhinoceroses, hippopotamuses, buffalo, giraffes, zebras, wilde-beests, and the now extinct quaggas. Like the pastoralists, they herded cattle and goats (and also, in some cases, sheep); indeed, cattle were their most prized possessions. But the mixed farmers also cultivated pumpkins and watermelons, and sorghum and millet which they stored in above-ground or subterranean containers. They practiced a form of swidden agriculture, cultivating a field for several years and then allowing it to lie fallow for a time. They also extracted copper and iron from ores which broke surface in several parts of the plateau. Since metallic ores were concentrated at several locations on the plateau and absent throughout the coastal belt, there was a long-distance trade in copper and iron from places in the plateau where they were available to places where they were not, notably the entire Nguni country below the escarpment. However, this trade was mainly a retail trade, by barter from village to village. There were no market places and no merchant class in southern Africa.

Each village produced most of the goods it consumed – grain, vegetables, and milk (which adults consumed sour); clothes from the hides of cattle and wild animals; pots and other utensils from local woods and clays; and thatching from local reeds. Blacksmiths – the most specialized members of the community – fashioned necklaces, bracelets, and other bodily ornaments from copper, and knives, spears, axe-heads, and hoe-heads from iron.

In the more fertile areas – and this included the Nguni coastal belt – the mixed farmers usually had a rich and balanced diet, based on milk, grains, and vegetables, occasionally enriched by meat. In the 1680s, Dutch survivors of a shipwreck found them to be healthy and robust. In the early nineteenth century, Ludwig Alberti, a perceptive German employed by the Batavian (Dutch) Republic, observed of the Xhosa, who lived near the coast in the western part of the Nguni region, "The abundant health enjoyed by these people must undoubtedly be principally ascribed to the simple food on which they live." But not all seasons were good and not all areas were fertile. Droughts seem to have occurred frequently, every five or eight years; and sometimes in some areas the droughts were serious enough to cause famines.

The people lived in circular huts made of stone or mud and wood, depending on what was available locally, with thatched roofs. While most men married one wife, some prosperous men had two or three, and powerful chiefs acquired many more. The basic social unit was the household, comprising a married man, his wife or wives, his unmarried children, and (maybe) some other dependents. Each married woman occupied a hut; and there were also huts for unmarried boys and unmarried girls.

A village contained a varied number of households. The Nguni lived in small hamlets comprising a single extended family and its dependents. When literate observers first encountered them in the early nineteenth century, they found that Sotho villages contained several households, with between fifty and four hundred people, and that some Tswana settlements, on the verge of the limit of arable farming, were large aggregations of as many as five thousand people, within reach of the rare streams and springs in that area.

The mixed farming culture was thoroughly hierarchical. The married men, who headed the households, were the dominant element – one might almost say a dominant class. Their power and social standing among their peers was measured by the number of cattle they owned and the number of wives and clients they controlled. As historian Jeff Guy has pointed out, cattle and people both represented labor-power. Women were subordinated to men throughout their lives; first, to their fathers, then to their husbands. They did the routine work of sowing, weeding, and harvesting in the fields, as well as fetching the daily supply of water from the nearest stream – an arduous task – and preparing and serving the food. Boys and unmarried men hunted the game, herded the cattle, made the clothes, and, when necessary, defended the homestead from predators. Unsuccessful people, who had no cattle, often became clients of heads of households, who gave them the task of herding some of their cattle, with the right to consume their milk and own a proportion of their progeny.

As far back as we know, the farmers' households and villages in the eastern part of southern Africa south of the Limpopo River formed parts of territorial units under hereditary chiefs. In conjunction with kinsmen and with commoner councilors, chiefs adjudicated disputes and made decisions affecting the chiefdom. Since the power of a chief depended largely on the number of his followers, he was glad to incorporate as clients refugees from other chiefdoms, and often did so. The chief was the richest man in his territory, receiving sheep and cattle for settling disputes; commoners cultivated the fields of his senior wives.

The educational system promoted the political as well as the social order. When the chief had a son who was approaching puberty, he would convene an initiation school for the son and the other boys of his age group. The school would be segregated from the rest of the community and might last as long as six months. There, men would teach the boys the customs and traditions of their chiefdom, including loyalty to the chief, and submit them to a series of tough physical tasks, culminating in circumcision. When he emerged from the school, the graduate was no longer a boy. He had taken a new name and he was a marriageable man. The school also provided the chief's son with a band of followers who were expected to be loyal to him throughout their lives. In most chiefdoms, schools were also convened for girls, where they were prepared for their roles as wives and mothers, but in most southern African chiefdoms, unlike parts of east Africa, girls were rarely subjected to genital mutilation.

The initiation schools transmitted from generation to generation a world view that included spiritual as well as material elements. This was illustrated most clearly in cases of illness or misfortune, when one consulted a doctor (*ngaka)*, who might be a medical specialist or a religious specialist, or both. Some *dingaka* made effective knowledge of the medical properties of local flora and fauna; others specialized in invoking the support of ancestral spirits that had powers over the living generation. Such a ngaka might order the sacrifice of a sheep or an ox to the ancestors; or, as in many other pre-industrial societies, he might decide that a specific person had been responsible for the illness or misfortune, in which case that person might be persecuted as a witch. The system was open to abuse, especially by chiefs, who sometimes used it as a way of eliminating rivals.

Marriage, the next step in the life of a young villager, was an elaborate ceremony, the outcome of a series of complicated negotiations between families. After marriage, the bride lived in her husband's village. The process involved the transfer of cattle from the bridegroom to the family of the bride, marking (in materialist terms) the transfer of female labor from one family to another, since a wife took up residence in her husband's village and became a member of her husband's family.

The political system of the mixed farmers south of the Limpopo was the outcome of the process of fission and expansion which had been going on ever since the second century AD. Chiefdoms varied greatly in size and population, from less than a thousand people to more than 50,000. In larger chiefdoms, there were regional sub-chiefs. Politics was largely a matter of conflict within ruling families: father v. sons, brother v. brothers and cousins.

A chief's authority was limited. He had no standing army and if he tried to act arbitrarily his disaffected followers might set up an independent chiefdom or transfer their allegiance to another chief. Therefore, a successful chief was one who cultivated public opinion. If he needed support for some enterprise, he would convene a public meeting of his male subjects. At such meetings, men might vent their grievances against the administration, but eventually an effective chief would announce his decision and it would be final. Public meetings (*pitsos*) were especially entrenched in the customs of the Sotho-Tswana peoples of the plateau.

South of the Limpopo, those ruling lineages did not create centralized states. When a chief died, the chiefdom often split. There would be a conflict about who was the legitimate heir (and rival claims were easy to make in polygynous families). An ambitious brother or son, who had already established a territorial base with the support of his initiation age-mates, might disregard the authority of the successful claimant. The senior Xhosa chief was to some extent recognized as paramount over all the territory of the southern Nguni, but his authority was ritual rather than political; in particular, he lacked the means to enforce his will over the outlying parts. Among the southern Sotho, on the other hand, each dominant lineage split up into several wholly independent chiefdoms; people knew which chief was genealogically the most senior of his lineage, but the chiefs who were related to him did not allow their followers to appeal to him against their decisions, nor did they perform any of the services due a superior.

African cultural traits endure, in modified form, to the present day. We cannot fully understand contemporary southern Africa without being aware of the persistence of African traditions and belief systems, such as the sense of social hierarchy, the accountability of rulers, and the interaction between spiritual and material explanations of human affairs.

The gold trade and state formation in Zimbabwe

In September 1871, Carl Mauch, a German explorer-prospector based in the Transvaal, came upon the awe-inspiring ruins of Great Zimbabwe, seventeen miles southeast of the modern Zimbabwean town of Masvingo. Great Zimbabwe is the most impressive monument in the African interior south of the Nile valley and the Ethiopian highlands. Covering more than sixty acres of ground, its most conspicuous elements are two complexes of dry-stone buildings, which Europeans have misleadingly called the Acropolis and the Temple. The former is a series of enclosures atop a hill; the latter includes a large number of buildings half a mile away in a valley, many of them encompassed by a massive circular wall (thirty-two feet high and seventeen feet thick at its maximum), which incorporates 900,000 large granite blocks. Recent excavations have revealed that the valley had also contained a large number of small buildings which had been the homes of the majority of the inhabitants. During the 1890s, after settlers had occupied "Mashonaland" under the auspices of Cecil Rhodes's British South Africa Company, prospectors systematically despoiled the ruins of everything that could conceivably yield a profit, including several thousand dollars worth of worked gold. Looting continued into the twentieth century until the government put a stop to it.

In the early published accounts of Great Zimbabwe, Europeans often insisted that it must have had an exotic, non-African origin. Europeans said the same thing about the bronzes of Ife and Benin and about other impressive human achievements in Africa. They could not bring themselves to credit Africans, let alone the ancestors of the modern inhabitants of the area, with the capacity to construct such elaborate buildings. With their reasoning blocked by racial assumptions, they believed that some forgotten "Whites," inspired by Jewish or Arabian models, must have built them. In fact, archaeologists have long since demonstrated that Great Zimbabwe was the head-quarters of an indigenous African state. Now, thanks to recent archaeology, supported by dating derived from the carbon-14 method, by documents written by Portuguese who visited the Zambezi valley (but not Great Zimbabwe itself) in the sixteenth and seventeenth centuries, and by oral traditions obtained from the Shona peoples, some of the history that lies behind the physical monument at Great Zimbabwe has been unraveled.

The basic mode of life of the mixed farmers of the Zambezi–Limpopo area was similar to that which has been described in the previous section of this chapter. There was a similar build-up of the population in the region during the first millennium and a half AD as a result of the introduction and spread of crop cultivation, cattle-keeping, and metallurgy, along with changes in the quality and design of pottery and in the materials and styles of buildings. At all stages, cultural variations within the area were related to differences in the local environments; but these were variations between peoples who were in contact with one another and who ultimately came to speak one of the dialects of the Shona language. Archaeology has also revealed rather abrupt shifts in the material culture at specific sites, and occasional layers of ash indicate destructive episodes. We cannot interpret these shifts and breaks precisely. Informed opinion now lays greater stress than formerly on the dynamics of change within the established population of the area, and there is less insistence on the advent of new types of peoples as a necessary explanation for every fresh cultural trait.

Whereas in Africa south of the Limpopo valley the chiefdoms continued to split and there was no great accumulation of wealth or power by the ruling lineages before the nineteenth century, the archaeological record shows that during the tenth and eleventh centuries AD farmers in the southwestern part of modern Zimbabwe, and at Mapungubwe hill in the Limpopo valley, were starting a process toward state-formation. The process was marked by the concentration of large herds of cattle, the mining of gold, and the opening up of trade with India via Sofala and other Muslim ports on the east coast. It culminated at Great Zimbabwe.

Originally, a great deal of gold ore lay near the surface in a broad belt running from the Mazoe River in the northeast to beyond the Limpopo River in the southwest.

There was also alluvial gold in the Zambezi tributaries. By 1000 AD the inhabitants were not only washing alluvial gold but also recovering and working gold ore. They mined in open stopes sloping downwards, eventually reaching as far as a hundred feet below the surface. They split the rock cover by alternately heating and cooling it; they then cut out the ore with iron picks and took it to the nearest stream, where they crushed and panned it in running water. The Shona continued this method of gold-mining until the nineteenth century. By then, the ores that could be worked by these methods were virtually exhausted, but small quantities of alluvial ore were still being recovered in the twentieth century.

Great Zimbabwe lies some distance southeast of the auriferous belt. People occupied the hill for a period during the first millennium and, after an interval, it was reoccupied during the eleventh century. During the thirteenth and fourteenth centuries, using the local granite which splits easily into regular sheets about six inches thick, they enclosed the hilltop with dry-course stone walls and completed the Great Enclosure, which was probably the royal palace, in the valley below the hill. Because their building methods included features not to be found anywhere north of the Zambezi, theirs was probably an independent invention, free from external aid or influence. But, as in the construction of the pyramids of Egypt, the building of Great Zimbabwe must have involved extremely arduous physical labor and society must have been sharply stratified.

Archaeologists estimate that about 18,000 people lived at Great Zimbabwe in its prime. Most of them lived in small huts packed closely together, while the ruling elite lived well. The site has yielded local pottery of good quality and design; ornaments made of copper, bronze, and gold; remarkable figures of birds carved from soapstone; and also ceramics of Asian origin, including a piece of glazed Persian faience that has been dated to the thirteenth century, and several Chinese celadon dishes of about the fourteenth century.

Great Zimbabwe's wealth was derived in part from its control of the long-distance trade route between the gold-producing reefs to the north and the west, and Sofala, a Muslim trading port subordinate to the city-state of Kilwa, on the Indian Ocean to the east. Gold and elephant ivory were exported in return for cloth and beads.

During the fifteenth century, Great Zimbabwe somewhat abruptly went into decline. Most of the inhabitants left the area, probably because it had been over-exploited and the environment was no longer able to produce enough food and wood for a large population. Some of the people migrated northward and settled in the valley of the Mazoe, a tributary of the Zambezi, where alluvial as well as reef gold was available. From that nucleus, they created another state in the tradition of Great Zimbabwe. Its rulers bore the title Mwene Mutapa, which passed into European documents in the form Monomotapa. Like their predecessors at Great Zimbabwe, the Mutapa dynasty profited from the gold trade, which now became diverted from the route via Great Zimbabwe to Sofala to a route down the Zambezi valley to other ports on the Indian Ocean. The Mutapas controlled the alluvial gold supplies and the northern section of the gold-bearing reef; and they claimed dominion over the valley and escarpment south of the Zambezi from Zumbo eastward to the sea, including the Muslim trading posts on the Zambezi. By the mid-seventeenth century, however, the Mutapa state was in decline, rent by civil wars and the victim of interventions by Portuguese officials and adventurers.

The population of the Mutapa state, like that of Great Zimbabwe, was sharply stratified. The majority of the people were mixed farmers whose style of life was similar to that of the Sotho-Tswana and Nguni of South Africa. But they were also responsible for mining the gold and fighting the military campaigns for the Mwene Mutapa and his aristocracy. The system seems to have worked fairly well under the founder king and his immediate successor, but they were not able to create lasting institutions that would hold the state together after they had died. Instead, they adopted the practice of appointing their male relatives as provincial governors; and by the sixteenth century some of the descendants of these men were acting as independent rulers. When the Portuguese made contact with the northern Shona, they found the Mwene Mutapa living in isolation from his subjects and served by young men of the aristocracy who, on reaching mature age, became invested with various titles that the Portuguese rendered into terms intelligible to themselves, such as captain-general and *majordomo*. But these Portuguese accounts described the Mwene Mutapa monarchy when it was past its prime. It was not necessarily like that in the fifteenth century. In the seventeenth century, several Mwene Mutapas acknowledged Portuguese overrule, but the Portuguese were never able to control them absolutely.

In the 1690s, the Changamire lineage, an offshoot from Mutapa, conquered the Torwa, who had founded a successor state in the vicinity of modern Bulawayo after the fall of Great Zimbabwe. The Changamire rulers exerted power over a large territory and remained free from Portuguese penetration. They wielded a tighter control over gold production and the gold trade in their area than any other rulers in the Zambezi–Limpopo region managed to do. Their capitals at Dhlodhlo and Khami had impressive stone buildings and accumulated vast quantities of finely wrought gold ornaments. They systematically collected tribute from their subjects and they had the final say in the succession to their vassal chieftaincies. Their armies, with 3000 or more warriors, waged campaigns at a great distance from the capital. The Changamire state flourished until it was overthrown by invaders from KwaZulu in the 1830s.

The Portuguese in southeastern Africa

Vasco da Gama opened up the sea route from Europe to Asia via the Cape of Good Hope and the East African coast in 1498–9. During the next decade, the Portuguese harassed the Arab traders in their East African bases and at sea and gained partial control over the commerce of the Indian Ocean. They established their overseas capital at Goa on the west coast of India, built fortresses at Sofala (1505) and on Mozambique Island (1507), and instructed their commanders to locate and exploit the gold of the interior. Reports by travelers to Shona country, such as Antonio Fernandez (1514), whom the Portuguese government sent to investigate the origin of the gold exported from Sofala, showed that "Monomotapa" was no Eldorado. The country of the Shona was difficult to reach and its gold output was modest by Peruvian standards. Nevertheless, throughout the sixteenth and seventeenth centuries, the major Portuguese objective in southeast Africa was to exploit the gold resources of the Shona.

The Portuguese impact on the Shona peoples is a classic example of what could be called "creeping imperialism." The initial Portuguese intentions were exclusively commercial. Trade routes to the gold-producing areas were to be opened up from the coastal establishments at Sofala and Mozambique. The Swahili traders were to be ousted, but the rights of the indigenous Africans were to be respected. By the end of the sixteenth century, the commercial objectives had been partially fulfilled. Using the Zambezi River as their principal route to the interior, the Portuguese founded, fortified, and garrisoned townships on the banks of the river at Sena, about one hundred and sixty miles from the mouth, and at Tete, another one hundred and sixty miles upstream. They also took over the old Swahili trading posts and founded new ones in the goldbearing area southwest of Tete – at Masapa, Luanze, Dambarare, and Ongoe, and even at Maramuca nearly three hundred miles from Tete. These steps enabled them to acquire the lion's share of the gold trade from the Shona country. But they were disappointed in the volume of gold they obtained. Swahili traders siphoned off some of it along trade routes to coastal settlements north of Mozambique, where they usually contrived to evade the Portuguese patrols and ship the gold to Arabia or India.

By the time the Portuguese arrived in East Africa, the Mutapa state was past its prime. Its hold over the eastern Shona was becoming tenuous, as local and collateral lineages claimed their autonomy. Impressed by Portuguese firearms, the sixteenth-century Mwene Mutapa used the Portuguese as allies against their dynastic rivals and insubordinate regional chiefs; but the alliance was not stable. In 1561, overzealous Jesuits obtained a footing at the royal court and even contrived to baptize the Mwene Mutapa and many of his relatives and councilors. When adverse reaction followed, Father Silveira with fifty of his Shona converts were killed. The Portuguese believed Swahili traders had poisoned the minds of influential persons at the Mwene Mutapa's court. Though that may have been a factor, it is more likely conservative forces in Shona society, notably the religious figures, were outraged by the activities of the Jesuits and needed little prodding by foreigners.

In 1569, a new Portuguese king, Sebastião, sent a thousand men under Francisco Barreto with orders to gain control of the gold mines, to see that they were properly exploited, to expel the Swahili traders, and to secure safe access for Portuguese missionaries. The expedition went up the Zambezi to Sena, where most of its members succumbed to málaria. This episode showed that with their sixteenth-century firearms, the Portuguese could occasionally make impressive military demonstrations, at great cost in men, but they were unable to exert permanent control over the Shona.

Another major crisis occurred in 1628, when Kapararidze, a new Mwene Mutapa, tried to reunite his kingdom and to expel the Portuguese. The Portuguese responded by helping Mavura, a rival claimant to the succession, to oust Kapararidze. In return, Mavura acknowledged himself a vassal of the king of Portugal. A further anti-European outburst followed, but a Portuguese military expedition reestablished Mavura as Mwene Mutapa. From then onward, he and his successors depended on Portuguese support. If they tried to act independently, they were overawed. The price of their alliance with the foreigners was a drastic reduction in the size of their territory and in the number of their followers. Finally, in the 1690s, the Changamire conquered most of the northern part of Shona country, ousting the Portuguese from the entire area of the goldfields. They never returned in strength.

One reason the Portuguese had not made better use of their opportunities in southeast Africa was their failure to create an efficient system of local administration. Most local officials, from the captain of the fort at Mozambique downward, like their counterparts elsewhere in Africa and Asia, used their offices for private profit rather

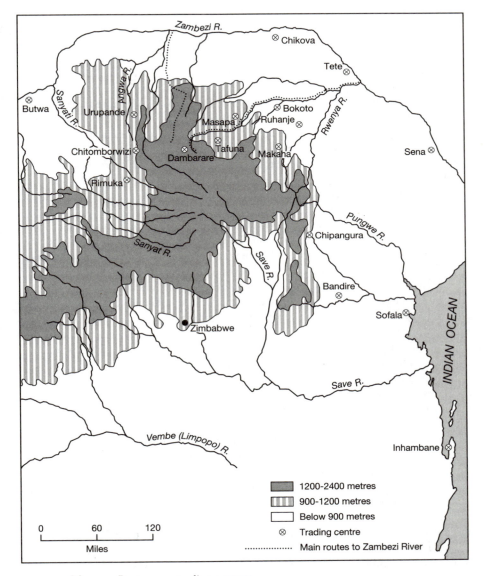

Map 9.2 Portuguese trading centers

than to promote the interests of the Portuguese government. In the interior, except for occasional military expeditions, the Portuguese presence consisted of private individuals pursuing their own interests first and foremost and acting in the interests of Portugal only secondarily, if at all. In the middle of the sixteenth century, a Portuguese adventurer settled at the court of the Mwene Mutapa and gained some influence over him. The viceroy in Goa capitalized on this relationship by giving him the title Captain of the Gates and making him the representative of the Portuguese monarch at the Shona court. This precedent became the norm.

From time to time, Portuguese kings and their advisers conceived the idea of planting a colony of Portuguese settlers in the country of the Shona, to bolster Portuguese power there. In 1677 an expedition of settlers was actually dispatched from Portugal, but little is known of its fate, except that it had no significant results. European settlement in the Zambezi Valley was always curtailed by a heavy mortality rate. The number of settlers reached a peak of perhaps two hundred early in the seventeenth century, but dropped to not more than fifty in 1700. Most of these were absconded soldiers and sailors, along with a smattering of Dominican and Jesuit monks, orphan girls, and prostitutes. Indeed, Indian immigrants from Portuguese Goa became more numerous than Europeans in the Zambezi Valley. Nevertheless, some of the Portuguese and Indian settlers founded families whose achievements were the most enduring and significant by-products of Portuguese power in all of East Africa before the twentieth century.

During the sixteenth century, the Mwene Mutapa granted the Portuguese officials who commanded the forts at Sena and Tete jurisdiction over the lands and the inhabitants of the vicinity. By the end of that century, private Portuguese individuals were acquiring similar titles to land and jurisdiction from the Mwene Mutapa and other African chiefs in return for favors rendered, usually military assistance against African enemies. This process continued during the seventeenth century, especially after the Mwene Mutapa became dependent on Portuguese protection, for that protection was provided by settlers rather than officials. The forces that intervened in the crisis of 1628 were the private armies of Portuguese settlers, who exacted wholesale concessions from the Mwene Mutapas thereafter.

Early in the seventeenth century, the Portuguese government began to acknowledge the rights acquired by these estate-holders. After 1629, when the government obtained pseudo-legal sovereignty over the Mwene Mutapa's realm, it tried to regularize relations along lines that had initially been devised to promote settlement in Brazil. The estates (*prazos*) granted Portuguese individuals (*prazeros*) by African authorities could remain in the hands of the prazero families for three generations, subject to the payment of an annual quitrent. After that, they were to revert to the government. Later in the seventeenth century, the crown decreed that new estates should be created and allotted to Portuguese orphan girls and inherited in the female line for three generations. In the eighteenth century, further decrees limited the size of estates, prohibited absenteeism and pluralism, and obliged heiresses to marry men from Portugal.

These constraints were generally ignored. Some prazos grew in size until they covered a thousand square miles or more. Successive generations of prazeros married spouses who might be Africans, Indians, or members of other estate-owning families.

By the nineteenth century, four or five family groups of mixed descent – we might almost call them clans – owned vast stretches of land on either side of the Zambezi River, from Chicoa to the Indian Ocean. These families wielded virtually unlimited power throughout that area. Neither the neighboring African rulers nor the Portuguese government were able to control them.

Their power derived from their African military followers and their ability to import firearms and ammunition. Two classes of subject peoples lived on a prazo: the descendants of the Africans who had occupied the land at the time it became a prazo, and the slaves whom the prazero had bought, or received as presents from chiefs, or captured in raids. The local people were administered through the heirs of their traditional chiefs and headmen, who were responsible for organizing the payment of tribute in local produce and labor. The slaves provided the prazero with domestic and specialized labor, and the male slaves also served in the prazero's private army.

By the nineteenth century, the distinctions between the two types of dependents were becoming blurred. Indeed, historical studies by Allen F. Isaacman and M.D.D. Newitt have shown that the prazos became more like African chiefdoms as the years went by. The prazeros and their families continued to use Portuguese names and titles and to profess Christianity; but they were barely literate, they spoke local African languages more than Portuguese, they were polygynous, they believed in witchcraft, and they performed the functions of African chiefs, including in some cases the ritual functions. In this way the Portuguese elements were gradually assimilated into the local African culture. They were, however, exceptionally turbulent chiefs. With their armed followers, they were a constant menace to the surrounding African chiefdoms and to one another. Thus the most enduring consequence of Portuguese activity in East Africa during the three centuries following Vasco da Gama's dramatic first voyage was the emergence of a new and independent power structure in the Zambezi Valley.

The Dutch in the Cape colony

A very different type of society emerged as a result of Dutch initiative in the southwestern corner of Africa. French, English, and Dutch ships began to round the Cape of Good Hope toward the end of the sixteenth century. In 1602, the Dutch merchants who had previously been competing with one another pooled their resources and founded the Dutch East India Company, with a charter from the States-General of the Netherlands that gave the company a trade monopoly and administrative powers from the Cape of Good Hope eastward. Whereas the Portuguese had established their Asian headquarters at Goa in India, the Dutch concentrated on the Indonesian spice trade and placed their governor-general in Batavia (Jakarta), Java. During the first half of the seventeenth century, ships of many European nations often put in at the Cape of Good Hope to refresh their crews and to barter sheep and cattle from the local Khoikhoi pastoralists. In 1648, a Dutch ship, the *Haerlem*, was stranded at the Cape, and some of its crew spent a year ashore before they were picked up by the next season's return fleet. On reaching Holland, a member of the party recommended that the company establish a permanent base at the Cape so as to reduce the extremely heavy mortality in ships. In 1652, the directors dispatched an expedition of about ninety men under the command of Jan van Riebeeck, who was instructed to build a fort and a hospital, to grow vegetables and wheat, to breed sheep and cattle, and to set up navigation marks for ships – and thus to provide a safe anchorage and refreshment station approximately halfway between the Netherlands and Batavia. During his ten-year term of office, van Riebeeck accomplished these tasks and founded what became the city of Cape Town.

The directors of the company had no intention of creating a New Holland in South Africa. They never regarded the Cape as performing any useful function beyond that of a refreshment station, and they always treated it as an outlying and subordinate part of their eastern empire. Expeditions from Cape Town showed that no gold, no silver, and no copper were to be had in the vicinity. Consequently, the Cape establishment might have acquired no more significance in African history than the Portuguese forts along the East African coast. In fact, however, a community of European origin developed there as a by-product of the Dutch presence. In the early eighteenth century, some of them were beginning to call themselves Afrikaners. Their descendants would win control of the government of South Africa three centuries after the foundation of the settlement and hold it for forty-six years.

Two factors led to the creation of a settler community at the Cape. One was the calculation of van Riebeeck and the directors that the company would save money if it persuaded some of its employees at the Cape to go off the payroll and instead cultivate land on their own account. The company could then buy their surplus produce and fix the prices, for there would be no other markets available to them. Accordingly, in 1657 nine men were freed from their service contracts and allotted land at Rondebosch, five miles from the fort; others soon followed them. The second factor was ecological. Unlike the Zambezi Valley, the Cape, located at 34° South, was free from anopheles mosquitos, tsetse flies, and other carriers of tropical diseases. Moreover, the indigenous inhabitants of the area – the thinly spread, disunited, semi-nomadic hunters and pastoralists – were not powerful enough to prevent the occupation of the land by men who had firearms and could call on the resources of the company's garrison in an emergency. Consequently, a community of White men, women, and children took root and developed strength and self-reliance in the vicinity of Cape Town in the second half of the seventeenth century.

The so-called free burgher community was recruited mainly from among the company's servants, who were predominantly Dutch and German. Some brought their wives from Europe; a few married orphan girls transported by the company; many of them failed to acquire European wives. A French element was added in 1688–9, when the company provided passage for about one hundred and fifty of the Huguenots who had fled to the Netherlands following the revocation of the Edict of Nantes in France. The company dispersed the Huguenots among the Dutch-speaking farmers and made Dutch the only official language and the Dutch Reformed Church the only church in the colony. Consequently, the children of settlers of French or other foreign origin spoke Dutch and were assimilated by the Dutch colonial majority. As early as 1679, the free burghers (men, women, and children) were more numerous than the company servants at the Cape. In 1699, they numbered 402 men, 224 women, and 521 children. A century later, they were only about 20,000, and because at all stages the majority of the new immigrants were male, men outnumbered women in the free burgher popu-

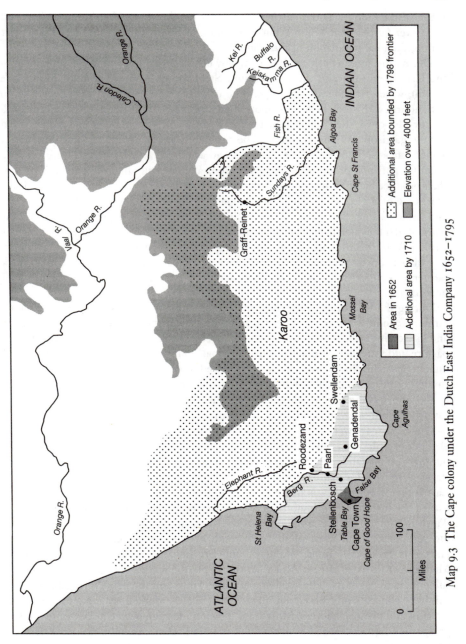

Map 9.3 The Cape colony under the Dutch East India Company 1652–1795

lation of the colony. Today, their descendants number more than three million and form over 60 per cent of the White population of South Africa – but less than 9 per cent of the total population of that country.

During the seventeenth century, company officials tried to confine the settlement to the Cape peninsula and the area around Stellenbosch (thirty-five miles from Cape Town), which was founded in 1679. The colonists were expected to concentrate on agriculture, with stock raising no more than a sideline. By the end of the seventeenth century, however, they were producing more wheat and wine than the company needed for the garrison and passing ships. The problem was accentuated by the conduct of senior officials. The governor and others had acquired large farms and were working them for personal profit, using company labor and ensuring that the company bought their produce before it began to buy the produce of the colonists' farms. The result was that some of the colonists began to move farther afield, and, by specializing in sheep- and cattle-raising, they became more self-sufficient and less dependent on the company. When they needed firearms, ammunition, clothes, or groceries, they could sell or barter sheep or cattle to Cape Town traders or their agents. The company facilitated this dispersion by relaxing its land policies and recognizing the right of each stock farmer to occupy three thousand or more acres of land, provided he paid a small annual license.

During the first three-quarters of the eighteenth century, *trekboers* (nomadic stock farmers) continued to spread outward from the agricultural belt in the Cape peninsula and its vicinity, avoiding the dry Karoo, and occupying land wherever there was enough pasture and water for their stock. Further expansion was then impeded by natural and human obstacles. In the northwest, beyond the Oliphants River, the land was too arid. In the northeast, bands of San hunters carried out raids on their stock from fastnesses in the Sneeuwberg (Snow Mountains) and made White settlement insecure. In the east, the Bantu-speaking southern Nguni farmers formed an impregnable barrier.

The Afrikaners were never self-sufficient. From the start, they were the dominant element of a plural society. When van Riebeeck planned the settlement of the first free burghers on the land, he intended that they should have the services of slaves. Because slaves were used for manual and domestic labor at virtually every outpost of the Dutch East Indian Empire, it was natural for a company official with eastern experience to extend the institution to South Africa. So slaves began to be imported by sea to Cape Town in 1657. This was a momentous decision. Importations continued throughout the seventeenth and most of the eighteenth century. Some came from areas now known as Indonesia, India, Malaysia, and Sri Lanka. Others were Africans from Madagascar or tropical East Africa. At the Cape, the company used some slaves and sold others to colonists. The economy of Cape Town and the neighboring agricultural belt was consequently based on slave labor. Slaves worked as domestic servants, artisans, and manual laborers. Most Cape Town tradesmen owned a slave or two; a few prosperous farmers owned as many as a hundred. Consequently, the stock farmers who moved away from the agricultural belt in the eighteenth century were already accustomed to using unfree workers of another race.

Long before 1652, the Khoikhoi chiefdoms in the vicinity of the Cape peninsula had adjusted their mode of life to the opportunities created by the intermittent visits of

Europeans. When a ship arrived, Khoikhoi brought sheep and cattle and bartered them for tobacco, alcohol, beads, or metal goods, though misunderstandings were common and sometimes led to bloodshed. After 1652, contacts became permanent and more intense, and the pattern of relationships gradually changed. The Khoikhoi, resenting the entrenchment of a White community on their land, pilfered sheep and cattle from the company. Van Riebeeck tried to prevent this by building a series of strongpoints around the settlement and linking them at one time with ditches and at another with a thick almond hedge. The southernmost Khoikhoi chiefdoms then found they were denied the use of some of their pastures. They also lost their monopoly on the role of middlemen when the company sent expeditions to explore the interior and trade directly with other chiefdoms. When fighting occurred in 1659–60 and again from 1672 to 1677, however, the Whites adopted a strategy that would be repeated time after time in their conquest of southern Africa: they took advantage of divisions among the native people and, with local allies, defeated those who resisted. By the end of the century, many Khoikhoi had become detached from their chiefdoms and incorporated in the colonial society. Van Riebeeck employed a Khoikhoi woman whom he called Eva, and she married the company surgeon. Other Khoikhoi became clients of farmers in the Stellenbosch area. Nevertheless, several chiefdoms survived as autonomous polities until after the end of the seventeenth century.

During the eighteenth century, however, the remaining Khoikhoi chiefdoms in the Cape Colony disintegrated. Trekboers occupied the best pastures and gained control of the best water supplies. By barter and pilfer they also obtained Khoikhoi sheep and cattle. Disintegration was accentuated by smallpox epidemics that swept through the Cape Colony in 1713, 1755, and 1767. Smallpox took a heavy toll on the Whites and the slaves, but it had a catastrophic effect on the Khoikhoi who, in their comparative isolation, lacked the proportion of immune persons that previous contact provided for Whites, Southeast Asians, and people from tropical Africa. As they lost their land and their stock, the Khoikhoi chiefdoms broke up into small family groups, most of which became clients of Whites. This suited the trekboers very well; Khoikhoi made satisfactory shepherds and herdsmen and cost very little. Trekboers simply allowed Khoikhoi families to live as their dependents, provided they worked when ordered. These events went largely unrecorded because they took place beyond the purview of company officials; but when Governor van Plettenberg toured the colony in 1778, he did not find a single independent Khoikhoi community.

Not all the surviving Khoikhoi became incorporated in the colonial society. Mixed bands were formed containing Khoikhoi, escaped slaves, freedmen, offspring of White fathers and Khoikhoi mothers, and also an occasional European. Such bands operated on the northern fringes of the area occupied by trekboers, obtaining guns, ammunition, and horses from trekboers or traveling traders. They lived in much the same way as some of the White stock farmers did – by hunting, stock farming, and raiding weaker communities for sheep and cattle, and also for human captives whom they sold to White farmers in the colony. As the trekboers advanced, they pushed these bands further northward, until by the end of the eighteenth century two main groups, who became known as Griqua and Kora (names derived from names of former Khoikhoi chiefdoms), had established themselves on either side of the middle section of the

Orange River, in contact with the colonial society to their south and the Tswana chiefdoms to their north.

Cape colonial society in the eighteenth century

By 1795, the Cape Colony had a population, in addition to the garrison, of about 20,000 free burghers, 26,000 slaves, 1000 African freedmen, and 14,000 Khoikhoi. The colony had four distinct zones. Cape Town itself was the only urban community in the colony – the sole port of entry and the principal commercial and administrative center. Besides the civil and military employees of the company, its population included traders and small businessmen, a few freedmen, and nearly 10,000 slaves. The neighboring agricultural belt, extending to Paarl, Stellenbosch, and Roodezand (Malmesbury), was dominated by White landowners who employed slaves and a few Khoikhoi clients. Beyond that was a vast thinly populated zone dominated by White stock farmers, who owned a few slaves and controlled most of the Khoikhoi who lived inside the colony. Still further away from Cape Town in a northerly direction, Griqua and Kora bands lived by trading and marauding both with the colony to their south and with African mixed farmers to their north. In the east, the trekboer expansion was blocked by African mixed farmers.

The colony was ruled by officials of the Dutch East India Company, subject to instructions from the company directors in the Netherlands, from the governor-general and his council in Batavia, and from senior officers visiting the Cape in transit between Europe and Asia. Their major concerns were to enforce the company's monopoly over the external trade of the colony and to regulate and tax the colonists who conducted the internal trade. The colonists had little say in these matters; but the superior court included a minority of colonists alongside officials, and the executive council (Council of Policy) consulted those court members on matters affecting their community.

Nearly all the salaried officials resided in the Cape peninsula. Beyond that, the company had no interest in spending money to create an effective administrative system. It appointed *landdroste* – general-purpose district officers – to Stellenbosch in 1679, to Swellendam in 1746, and to Graaff-Reinet in 1786. A landdrost was allowed a clerk or two and perhaps a handful of soldiers, but he could do very little without the cooperation of the White colonists in his district. The men who represented the government in each subdistrict and sat with the landdrost on the district court, which had minor jurisdiction in civil cases only, were colonists; they were not paid for their services. This system placed very few curbs on the White community in their dealings with other people. Undoubtedly many crimes went unpunished because of the difficulty of collecting evidence and bringing suspects and witnesses to Cape Town for trial, and many colonists neglected to pay their land taxes.

A similar mixture of monopoly and parsimony was evident in ecclesiastical and educational matters. The company stationed ministers of the Dutch Reformed Church at several places in the colony and paid their salaries. It supervised the work of the church councils and barred other denominations from operating in the colony until 1780, when a Lutheran church was founded in Cape Town. Each minister was meant to conduct a primary school for his congregation, and some did so. But children who were not White were normally excluded from these schools. Moreover, many White children lived too far from the church centers to attend the schools, and any instruction they received in reading and writing was provided by their parents or by traveling teachers. The only secondary school in the colony during the company regime was founded at Cape Town in 1714. It failed within a few years for lack of support. Later in the century a few of the more prosperous colonists sent their male children to Europe for their secondary education, but the vast majority had no such opportunity.

In the Cape peninsula, and there alone, the colonial society was dominated by the Dutch officials. Elsewhere, the embryonic Afrikaner people were dominant. Their power was derived from their control of the basic sources of wealth – land, livestock, capital, and labor; their formal and informal influence over the officials in Cape Town; their virtual control of local administration; their near-monopoly of firearms and ammunition; and their practice of forming commandos, or organized bands of mounted musketeers, to destroy indigenous hunters when they raided their livestock.

The status of the subordinate groups in the colonial society varied. Slaves were regulated in great detail by law. As in other societies based on slavery, the laws were designed primarily to prevent insubordination and insurrection. Besides recognizing the right of slave owners to punish their slaves, the government exercised its authority to maintain their subjection. Slaves were prohibited from owning firearms; they were not allowed to assemble in groups of more than two; they were obliged to carry passes signed by their owners when they were absent from their owners' estates. These laws are of lasting historical interest because they formed the precedent for legislation that was subsequently applied to Bantu-speaking Africans in the nineteenth-century Transvaal and Orange Free State republics and in the twentieth-century Republic of South Africa. On the other hand, the company issued very little legislation that applied to the Khoikhoi clients of Afrikaner patrons. Their status was essentially customary, for it was generally beyond the purview of the officials. In practice they were treated much like slaves and the two groups began to merge.

The lives of slaves and Khoikhoi in the Cape Colony varied with local conditions and the temperament, occupation, and success of their masters. The relationship was characterized by a paternalist ideology that structured and legitimized subordination, exploitation, and the frequent use of violence. The slaves and Khoikhoi, divided into small groups among many different masters, were too atomized to organize concerted rebellions. But, like slaves in the Americas, they resisted their masters' exactions in subtle ways – feigning illness, going slow, destroying property – and they carved out social and psychological space for themselves in their quarters. In desperation, some slaves absconded and survived independently, until, in most cases, they were recaptured and suffered terrible reprisals. Robert Ross has described how bands of escapees lived precariously for several years on the slopes of Table Mountain and Cape Hanglip, on the southeastern side of False Bay. Occasionally, owners manumitted slaves in the Cape Colony, but the freed slaves never numbered more than 8.4 per cent of the free population and that proportion diminished over time.

There were tensions and contradictions within the White colonial community on racial questions. Like other slave-owning communities, they despised menial functions; and like most communities in which slaves had different physical characteristics from slave owners, they tended to equate differences of status with innate racial differences. The civil authorities and the Dutch Reformed ministers rarely opposed these attitudes. To a considerable degree, therefore, the embryonic Afrikaners viewed society in terms of status and racial categories.

On the other hand, the social distance between the races in the Cape Colony was not absolute, for they were bound together in mutual dependency. Subtle and complex processes of acculturation were at work. The slaves had been forcibly detached and deported from their original cultural milieus; the Khoikhoi had witnessed the destruction of their indigenous social system. As dependents of Whites, many of them strove to adopt the manners and the style of living of the dominant class. The acculturative trends were by no means exclusively in one direction. Colonists were influenced by their slaves and Khoikhoi nurses and domestic servants. These processes had durable consequences; slaves and Khoikhoi, as well as colonists, took part in creating a new vernacular language, Afrikaans, which was mainly derived from Dutch but which incorporated loan words from the languages of the Khoikhoi and the slaves, and had a simplified syntax and morphology owing to its use by non-native speakers.

Nor did the three communities remain biologically distinct. Though the government prohibited marriages between colonists and slaves, many colonists had sexual relations with slave women and so did visiting soldiers and sailors. At times, indeed, the company officials allowed the main slave depot in Cape Town to be used as a brothel. Beyond the agricultural belt, trekboer men often cohabited with Khoikhoi women. The children of White men and slaves and Khoikhoi women generally inherited the status of their mothers, but some were incorporated into the free community; consequently, the colonists as well as their subordinates became biologically mixed. It is estimated that about 7 per cent of the genes of the Afrikaner people originated outside Europe.

Mixing continued to occur in later generations, despite the fact that the South African ruling classes increasingly identified themselves as "White" and tried to draw a hard-and-fast line between themselves and people of mixed slave, Khoikhoi, and Afrikaner ancestry, whom they labeled, comprehensively, "Coloured." This distinction began before the Whites expanded eastwards into the area occupied by African mixed farmers. When they did so, Whites identified the farmers as another distinct racial element, whom they called at various times "Kaffirs" or "Natives" or "Africans" or "Blacks." In the late nineteenth century, when Whites imported Indian laborers to Natal, they treated Indians as yet another distinct racial group. Thus, for historical reasons, White South Africans adopted a fourfold racial division.

Later, the Whites tended to divide socially and culturally into two groups: the Afrikaans-speaking descendants of those who arrived before 1795 and the English-speaking descendants of those who came later. But the Afrikaans-speaking community was not limited to Whites; it came to include almost all the Coloureds as well. The racial group, in short, became divided linguistically, while the linguistic group became divided racially. In this complex situation, nomenclature is sensitive. For our purposes in this volume, we use the terms White, Coloured, Indian, and African, recognizing that they are all to some extent misnomers but nevertheless that they became common usage and acquired legal force in the South African context.

Crises in the Cape colony

Toward the end of the eighteenth century, the tensions that had always existed in Cape colonial society were exacerbated by new developments, both local and extraneous. The European Enlightenment, the American Revolution, and the French Revolution made some impact on the minds of the more sophisticated colonists in Cape Town and the neighboring agricultural belt, who always resented the narrow, mercantilist system to which they had been subjected. At the time, however, the company was facing bankruptcy and its directors were more concerned with raising additional revenues from the colony than with relaxing the existing controls. Moreover, the trekboers, who had hitherto coped with their own problems without government assistance, came up against the African farmers in the Fish River area and found that they were numerous and powerful enough to check the expansionist movement on which they had thrived. The result was a series of events that produced a sharpened awareness of identity and common interest among the Afrikaners and alienated them from their European roots. They were also the opening rounds in a conflict that would lead, step by step, to the conquest of all the African farming communities of southern Africa.

In 1779, 404 European colonists who lived in Cape Town and the adjacent agricultural belt had signed a petition deploring the company's mercantilist policy, exposing the selfish and autocratic conduct of its officials, and demanding reforms that included the removal of the restrictions on private trading and the grant of an effective share of political power. In response, the directors made tardy and inadequate concessions. Economic conditions improved during inter-European wars of the early 1780s, when a French garrison occupied the Cape peninsula to assist the Dutch against British attacks. The economic boom collapsed after the construction of defense works ceased in 1785, and it was followed by a depression. By 1795, when a British force attacked and occupied the Cape peninsula, the Afrikaners of Cape Town and the agricultural belt were estranged from both the Dutch East India Company and the Netherlands, and acquiesced in the change of government.

The crisis in the eastern part of the colony was different. Although Whites had made frequent hunting and trading expeditions deep into the country occupied by Xhosa mixed farmers during the earlier part of the eighteenth century, it was not until the 1770s that the build-up of the Afrikaner population in the neighborhood of the Fish River was sufficient to produce a general confrontation between the two societies: White and African. Then, they began to overlap. Several small Xhosa chiefdoms occupied land west of the Fish River, some trekboers east of it. A few White individuals such as Coenraad de Buys detached themselves from their own people and settled at the Great Places of Xhosa chiefs and headmen; several Xhosa became clients of trekboers and worked for them. Previously, the colonial government had tried to prevent this intermingling by ordering its subjects to stay west of a series of frontier lines. In 1778, Governor van Plettenberg toured the frontier area and attempted, equally vainly, to persuade Whites and Africans to recognize the Fish River as a dividing line between the two societies. Quarrels over cattle led to fighting in 1779, when a group of trekboers attacked Xhosa villages, using methods they had devised to deal with indigenous hunters. They soon found that they were not strong enough to impose their will on the more densely settled African farmers. Some of the trekboers then appealed to the government for help.

The government placed a landdrost at Graaff-Reinet in 1786, with orders to try to keep the peace; but it did not provide him with any military force, and he could neither control the irresponsible element among the Whites nor stabilize the frontier. The first landdrost soon fell foul of the trekboers in his district and was recalled. The second, H.C.D. Maynier, was the first company official to become seriously concerned with the harsh way in which some trekboers treated their Khoikhoi clients. He allowed Khoikhoi to come to his office and register complaints. He also tried to curb the trekboers from making further attacks on the African farmers, at least until the bands of indigenous hunters who were still harassing the trekboers in the northern part of the district had been overcome. In 1793, however, a White faction in the south ignored his instructions and launched a rash attack on the Xhosa chiefdoms west of the Fish river, and the Xhosa responded by devastating the homesteads and raiding the stock of the trekboers in the southern part of the district, before Maynier managed to gather a commando strong enough to impose a truce. In 1795 some of the trekboers rebelled against the colonial government, ousted Maynier, and proclaimed the district of Graaff-Reinet to be an independent republic. Similar events occurred in Swellendam.

Thus the regime of the Dutch East India Company in the Cape Colony ended in ignominy: in the west, economic collapse; in the east, an unstable frontier zone and a White rebellion. Its legacy was a weak, interdependent colonial society based on racial slavery and serfdom.

Suggestions for further reading

General Histories

Davenport, T.R.H., *South Africa: A Modern History*. 4th edn. Toronto: University of Toronto Press, 1991.

Thompson, Leonard., *A History of South Africa*. New Haven: Yale University Press, 1991.

Wilson, Monica, and Thompson, Leonard, (eds)., *The Oxford History of South Africa*. 2 vols. New York: Oxford University Press, 1969 and 1971.

Special Studies

Beach, D.N., *The Shona and Zimbabwe 900–1850*, London: Heinemann, 1980.

Beach, D.N., *Zimbabwe before 1900*. Gweru: Mambo Press, 1984.

Bhila, H.H.K., *Trader and Politics in a Shona Kingdom*, London: Longman, 1982.

Elphick, Richard, *Kraal and Castle: Khoi and the Founding of White South Africa*, New Haven and London: Yale University Press, 1977.

Elphick, Richard, and Giliomee, Hermann (eds), *The Shaping of South African Society 1652–1840*. Middletown: Wesleyan University Press, 1989.

Garlake, Peter S., *Great Zimbabwe*. London: Thames and Hudson, 1973.

Hall, Martin et al., (ed.) *Frontiers: South African Archaeology Today*, Cambridge: Cambridge University Press, 1984.

Hall, Martin, *The Changing Past: Farmers, Kings, and Traders in Southern Africa, 200–1860*, Cape Town, 1987.

Inskeep, R.R., *The Peopling of Southern Africa*, Cape Town: David Philip, 1978.

Isaacman, Allen F., *Mozambique: The Africanization of a European Institution: The Zambezi Prazos 1750–1902*, Madison: University of Wisconsin Press, 1972.

Mostert, Noel, *Frontiers: The Epic of South Africa's Creation and the Tragedy of the Xhosa People*. New York: Alfred A. Knopf, 1992.

Newitt, M.D.D., *Portuguese Settlement on the Zambezi*, London: Longman, 1973.

Peires, J.B., *The House of Phalo*, Berkeley: California University Press, 1982.

Peires, J.B., *The Dead will Arise: Nonyqawuse and the Great Xhosa Cattle-Killing Movement of 1856–7*, Johannesburg and London: Rowan Press and James Currey, 1989.

Ross, Robert, *Cape of Torments: Slavery and Resistance in South Africa*, London: Routledge and Kegan Paul, 1983.

Switzer, Les, *Power and Resistance in an African Society. The Ciskei Xhosa and the Making of South Africa*, Madison: Wisconsin University Press, 1993.

Worden, Nigel, *Slavery in Dutch South Africa*, Cambridge: Cambridge University Press, 1985.

10

SOUTHERN AFRICA, 1795–1870

In the late eighteenth century Bantu-speaking African farmers held virtually all the habitable land in the better-watered eastern half of southern Africa. In the Zambezi valley, the inhabitants of the *prazos* still possessed vestiges of Portuguese culture; at Mozambique Island and Delagoa Bay, the Portuguese continued to maintain small bases; and Cape colonists were in contact with southern Nguni chiefdoms in the vicinity of the Fish River. Elsewhere, the African farmers were relatively immune from alien influences. For example, many Sotho (pronounced Sootoo) had never seen a gun or a European.

Between 1795 and 1870, radical changes took place throughout southern Africa. There were two major processes. One was a series of profound disturbances among the African farming communities throughout much of southeastern Africa. The other was an expansion of White and "Coloured" people northward and eastward from the Cape Colony at the expense not only of Khoisan communities, as before, but also of Bantu-speaking Africans. Both processes were punctuated by violence and resulted in the creation of new states.

The *mfecane*

The disturbances among the African farming communities have become known as the *mfecane* in the Nguni languages and the *lifaqane* in Sotho-Tswana. The literal meaning of the word is "crushing." As John Omer-Cooper has pointed out, "It has come to be widely accepted as a name for the process of political change and the accompanying wars and migrations which began in the later part of the eighteenth century and resulted, inter alia, in the emergence of the Swazi and Zulu kingdoms" – and also the founding of new states in present-day Lesotho, Zimbabwe, Mozambique, and Tanzania, and the Transvaal.

The mfecane was a complex process with great regional variations. The events that precipitated the process occurred among the northern Nguni, who lived in a narrow area bounded by Delagoa Bay in the north, the Tugela River in the south, the Indian Ocean in the east, and the Drakensberg mountains in the west. Internal stresses had been developing there since the middle of the eighteenth century. It was becoming increasingly difficult for groups of people to hive off from a chiefdom and find unclaimed land, suitable for their customary farming methods, beyond the established settlements. The customary cattle raids between neighboring villages and chiefdoms were developing into lethal contests for control of water, pasture, arable land, and hunting grounds. These conflicts were exacerbated by deterioration of the environment caused by overstocking, excessive tillage, and severe drought. The social, economic, and political order that had been a natural concomitant of centuries of expansion was incapable of meeting these challenges.

Although the mfecane was primarily an African process, two external factors accentuated its severity. During the late eighteenth century and early nineteenth century, traders at the Portuguese settlement on Delagoa Bay were acquiring large quantities of elephant ivory and also a few slaves from the African communities in the vicinity; maritime traders were exporting the slaves to the Americas. These activities contributed to the tensions and rivalries among the African chiefdoms south of Delagoa Bay. Second, since the early nineteenth century, coloured frontiers-people from the Cape Colony, known as Griquas, using horses and firearms, were a source of instability among the southern Tswana chiefdoms in the highveld north of the Orange River. From time to time they attacked Sotho-Tswana communities and captured women and children and sold them as laborers to colonial farmers.

In the first decade of the nineteenth century, two northern Nguni chiefdoms, the Mthethwa under Dingiswayo and the Ndwandwe under Zwide, using the customary initiation system as a basis for military organization, gained control over most of the other chiefdoms in the area by force or the threat of force and created two rival confederacies, which vied for control and caused considerable disruption.

Dingiswayo's most enterprising warrior was a man called Shaka, a son of the head of the small Zulu chiefdom. In 1816, Dingiswayo assisted his protégé to seize control of the Zulu chiefdom from his senior half-brother. Two years later, Dingiswayo was killed by the Ndwandwe and the Mthethwa confederacy crumbled. Shaka then succeeded to the leadership of what was left of it, defeated Zwide, and began to conquer and incorporate most of the Nguni people between the Tugela and Delagoa Bay.

There, Shaka created a new phenomenon in southern African history: a powerful, centralized, militaristic kingdom. The men were conscripted for service in a standing army that is said to have numbered about 40,000 warriors, organized in age regiments. Each regiment lived in a stockaded village, segregated from the rest of society. The women, the children, and the old men remained in the villages to do the routine work of stock raising and crop production. The army was sent on annual expeditions, farther and farther from the Zulu heartland, primarily to capture cattle. The shattering victor-victories of the Zulu warriors were due to exceptionally rigorous training and discipline as well as to the fact that Shaka armed them with short stabbing spears in addition to the customary assagais (long spears). They used these short spears to close in on an enemy for hand-to-hand combat by disciplined units similar to a Roman legion. Such tactics were previously unknown in local warfare. By 1828, besides consolidating his power between the Tugela and the Pongola, Shaka's regiments had swept through the country south of the Tugela as well as the southern highveld across the Drakensberg mountains, seizing cattle and driving many of the inhabitants away.

Shaka's regime provided many benefits to his subjects. The men were elated by their victories; the kingdom was enriched by the booty in cattle; and national festivals, such as the annual first fruits ceremony, promoted national cohesion. But his rule created many tensions, including tensions within the ruling family. In 1828 he sent his army on an arduous campaign to the south and then, with scarcely any respite, he ordered it far to the north, while he remained at home. There, on 24 September 1828, he was assassinated by two of his half-brothers. One of those assassins, Dingane, managed to hold the kingdom together until it was confronted by Europeans with firearms in 1838.

Modern views of Shaka vary greatly. While all informed historians acknowledge that he possessed exceptional military and organizational talents, some regard him as having played an essentially destructive role. Oral evidence, some of it gathered by White traders from his African enemies during his lifetime and soon after his death, and embellished for their own purposes, suggests that Shaka suffered from serious psychological disorders derived from insecurity in his childhood, that he was a blood-thirsty autocrat who killed his subjects on the flimsiest of pretexts, and that his system of permanent mobilization depended on annual campaigns against other Africans, which could only produce diminishing returns. Others deny that he was exceptionally autocratic or that he was responsible for most of the violence that shattered the traditional order. To some, he is a heroic figure, a symbol of "Black power" in a region that became dominated by "Whites"; and this interpretation has been given wide publicity through an imaginative, fictional biography by the Sotho author Thomas Mofolo. Although verdicts differ on the extent of his responsibility for violence, there can be no doubt that Shaka was a military innovator, and that he, more than anyone, was responsible for the creation of a new political system in southeastern Africa after the old system of small, fissiparous units had broken down.

By the time Shaka died, many northern Nguni had fled. The migrations, which started during the Mthethwa–Ndwandwe conflicts, continued during Shaka's reign. Some people traveled as more or less disorganized fragments. Those who moved in among the southern Nguni became known as *mfengu* (beggars) and those who flooded into the Cape Colony from the north were called *mantatees*. Others migrated as organized bands of men, women, and children, under strong leadership, searching for security in new milieus. The most successful of these bands incorporated local people and set up conquest states modeled to a greater or lesser degree on the Zulu prototype.

Before the rise of Shaka, Sobhuza, one of the northernmost Nguni chiefs, was driven with his followers into the mountains north of the upper Pongola River. There he and his successor adopted the short stabbing spear and a variant of the Zulu regimental system. They managed to preserve their independence and to incorporate numerous Sotho as well as Nguni groups. In so doing they created a multi-ethnic kingdom whose people were knit together by cross-cutting loyalties to their clans, their patrons, their territorial chiefs, their age regiments, and the King and Queen Mother. This was the origin of the state still known as Swaziland, named for Mswati, who ruled from 1840 to 1875.

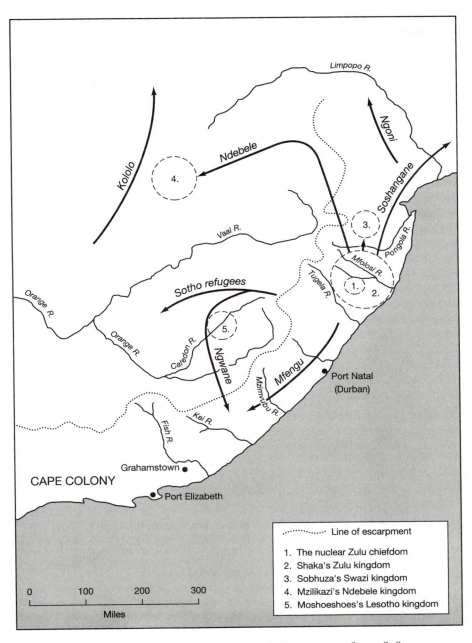

Map 10.1 Shaka's Zulu kingdom and the Mfecane wars 1817–1828

As a result of Shaka's victories over Zwide in 1818, several of Zwide's officers fled northward with their regiments. One was Soshangane, who, incorporating later waves of refugees from the Zulu kingdom and maintaining a tight regimental system, succeeded in dominating Mozambique as far north as the Zambezi River. He exacted tribute from the Portuguese settlements at Delagoa Bay and Sofala and from the Portuguese forts and the prazos on the Zambezi. But Soshangane was less successful than the Swazi rulers in assimilating conquered peoples and developing durable political institutions. Beyond the core of his kingdom on the Sabi River, his power depended on the presence of his regiments, which could not be everywhere at once.

Another dependent of Zwide who fled northward with followers was Zwangendaba, who began to carve out a similar military kingdom in southern Mozambique until 1831, when he was defeated by Soshangane. Zwangendaba then moved further north in successive stages until, in the 1840s, he settled in the western part of modern Tanzania, 1200 miles from his starting point. During this migration, his people annihilated the Rozwi dynasty between the Limpopo and Zambezi rivers, and caused havoc among the inhabitants of modern Malawi and eastern Zambia. They, too, absorbed many of the people they conquered; and they, too, incorporated their male subjects in age regiments, which were mobilized only when needed, rather than on a permanent basis as in Shaka's Zulu kingdom. Zwangendaba's people became known as the Ngoni.

In 1822 Mzilikazi with a small following of about two hundred people fled from the Zulu area to the Transvaal. There they absorbed more northern Nguni refugees and incorporated many conquered Sotho into the growing Ndebele kingdom. The Ndebele regiments made frequent forays against their neighbors in all directions – the Shona across the Limpopo, the Tswana to the west, the Pedi to the east, and the southern Sotho beyond the Vaal – capturing women, children, and cattle. By the mid-1830s, Mzilikazi could muster four to five thousand warriors who dominated an area of about thirty thousand square miles from his headquarters at Mosega near present-day Zeerust. The Nguni elements formed the upper class in the Ndebele kingdom, but many Nguni men married Sotho women and their children were regarded as Nguni.

Not all the Bantu-speaking people of southeastern Africa were incorporated in the states created by northern Nguni warrior leaders. The southernmost Nguni chiefdoms – the Xhosa cluster – were spared attacks from the north. As will be described below, they suffered defeats in a series of wars with their neighbor, the Cape Colony.

Several Sotho chiefdoms, such as the Pedi, survived intact in their mountain strongholds in the eastern Transvaal, and so too did most of the Tswana chiefdoms on the fringes of the Kalahari desert and some of the Shona in eastern Zimbabwe. But several Sotho leaders also founded larger political units than had previously existed among them. Some became migrant warriors themselves, such as Sebetwane, who fought his way northward and created a conquest state in western Zambia. Others occupied defensive positions that became rallying points for survivors of the wars. This process was most effective among the southern Sotho in the valley of the Caledon River. During the early 1820s, bands of northern Nguni refugees and Sotho groups whom they had driven from their homes swept through the Caledon basin. Families, village communities, and chiefdoms were completely broken up; hundreds of people were slaughtered, thousands starved to death, and most of the survivors lost all their sheep and cattle as well as their grain; some even resorted to cannibalism.

By the time of Shaka's death, the Nguni invaders had lost control of the Caledon region, and the surviving inhabitants, Nguni as well as Sotho, were attaching themselves to one or another of two Sotho leaders: Sekonyela, heir to a relatively large chiefdom, and Moshoeshoe, who had started life as the senior son of the head of a small autonomous village community. Both managed to preserve some cattle and to increase their herds by raiding the southern Nguni across the mountains to the south, and both occupied mesalike mountains that formed natural strongholds: Sekonyela on the north bank of the Caledon near modern Ficksburg, and Moshoeshoe forty miles further south at Thaba Bosiu (pronounced Taba Bosiu). Both gradually built up their military capability by procuring guns and horses from Whites. Sekonyela and Moshoeshoe repulsed several attacks by Nguni invaders and became rivals for control of the Caledon basin. Moshoeshoe was the abler of the two and eventually he prevailed, although it was not until 1853 that he finally captured Sekonyela's stronghold.

As a result of these tumultuous events, society throughout the eastern part of southern Africa was transformed by the 1830s. There were dramatic increases in the export of slaves from Delagoa Bay and in the influx of Africans seeking work in the Cape Colony, fed by refugees from the wars. Large areas were partially depopulated and new and larger political communities were created. The rulers of the new states imposed their authority over the surviving members of numerous small chiefdoms; people speaking different Bantu languages and dialects were intermingled to a much greater extent than previously. There was also an accentuation of social inequality. Men who had lost their cattle became clients of men of property; the status of women declined; and in most cases conquering warriors formed a dominant class. The authority of the rulers was most effective in relatively small core regions; beyond that, territories occupied by subordinate chiefs shaded off into territories whose chiefs were semi-independent allies. The structure and style of the states differed immensely. The traditional order was most radically changed in the Zulu kingdom, where the men of fighting age continued to be conscripted into age-regiments and segregated from the rest of society until they reached the age of about forty, and where the traditional liberties of the people were sacrificed to the interests of the state as determined by the king and his military officers. In Lesotho, at the other extreme, traditional family and village life revived, the men were mustered for warfare only when necessary and fought under their territorial chiefs rather than in nationwide regiments, and the state was a fragile association of chiefs and their followers, held together by the personality and skill of Moshoeshoe.

White power in the Cape colony

While these dramatic events were taking place in the east, White power was increasing in the southwestern part of southern Africa. The Cape Colony changed rulers several times during the French Revolutionary and Napoleonic wars. The British conquered it in 1795, returned it to the Dutch (the Batavian Republic) in 1803, and reconquered it in 1806; and British rule was confirmed by the European peace settlement of 1815.

Until 1870, British interest in southern Africa was primarily strategic. Like the Dutch before them, the British used the harbors of the Cape peninsula as bases for controlling the sea route between Europe and Asia. British investment in southern Africa, British imports of southern African produce, and British exports to southern Africa amounted to a small fraction of British investments in and trade with Europe, North or South America, or Asia. Nevertheless, there was a steady increase in commodity production for export, mainly to Britain. Cape wine producers prospered until they lost their preferential tariff in Britain in 1831. After that, wool became the main export and sheep farming the most profitable enterprise. By 1870, wholesale houses, chambers of commerce, banks, and insurance companies had laid some of the foundations of a modern business economy, but there were still fewer than seventy miles of railroad track and most of the banks had collapsed during a severe depression in the 1860s.

The increase in the White population was not spectacular. Only a small proportion of the many thousands of people emigrating from Britain chose the Cape Colony as their new home. The largest such group consisted of about 5000 men, women, and children who settled in the eastern part of the colony in 1820 with assistance from the British government, which intended them to practice intensive agriculture and form a compact barrier against the southern Nguni chiefdoms. The planned agricultural settlement was not a success, but, after early setbacks, some of the British immigrants prospered as wool farmers and merchants while others became traders, professionals, and artisans in the colonial towns and villages.

The White population numbered only about 180,000 in 1865. The majority were the embryonic Afrikaners, descendants of the settlers who had left Europe in the Dutch period. Despite great regional and class differences among them, nearly all of them derived their livelihood from the land and spoke some variant of Afrikaans, which was emerging from the interaction among the diverse inhabitants of the colony and included elements derived from the languages of the Asian slaves and the Khoikhoi as well as a core vocabulary and syntax from Dutch. In varying degrees they were conscious of forming a separate community under alien rule, like the French in Canada. The British settlers, a cross-section of early industrial British society, regarded themselves as forming an overseas extension of that society. That ethnic dichotomy, sustained by linguistic and cultural differences, persisted in the twentieth century as a major cleavage among White South Africans.

After a cautious start, during the 1820s the British regime imposed a series of reforms which weakened the power of the colonial oligarchy. They appointed British magistrates to replace the Dutch district courts which had been controlled by colonists. They brought the law closer to the farming areas by making judges travel regularly on circuit to the district headquarters. They introduced English trial procedures, including the jury system. They founded government schools in the towns and villages, using English as the medium of instruction and syllabi that emphasized British history and culture. They imported Scottish ministers to serve the Dutch Reformed congregations. And they abolished many of the Dutch concessions and monopolies and registered private property in land.

The British regime also gradually came to grips with the racial problem. Initially, it entrenched the dominance of the White population. Not only did it uphold the institution of slavery, but in 1809 it also subjected the Khoikhoi to a form of legal serfdom by obliging them to have a "fixed place of abode," which meant, in effect, working for a White farmer, or living on a mission station, or serving in the colonial regiment (the Cape Corps). In 1812 it even empowered White landowners to apprentice children whom they had raised on their farms for another ten years from the age of eight – a ruling that immobilized their parents also. During the 1820s, however, the humanitarian lobby became influential in Britain and John Philip, the Cape colonial superintendent of the London Missionary Society, shocked by what he found in the Cape Colony, went to England armed with massive evidence on the abuse of power by White farmers and the collusion of local officials. There, he persuaded the parliamentary abolitionists to take up the cause of the Khoikhoi as part of their campaign against slavery. In 1828, the colonial governor, seeing the writing on the wall, issued Ordinance 50 which abolished all racially discriminatory legislation and placed all the inhabitants of the colony on the same legal footing.

Soon afterward, the British Parliament put an end to slavery throughout the British Empire. After first making the slave trade unlawful for British subjects in 1807, the British government had then tried to ameliorate the condition of slaves, but in the Cape, as well as the Caribbean colonies, the slave owners had succeeded in making these reforms ineffective. The British anti-slavery movement then shifted its objective from reform to outright emancipation and in 1833 Parliament passed an Emancipation Act, which included a transitional period of apprenticeship and partial compensation for slave owners. When apprenticeship ended in 1838, the Cape slaves stepped into the legal status already acquired by "Hottentots and other free persons of colour." As J.B. Peires has written, "The Cape was thrust, greatly hesitating and dragging its feet, towards participation in the great Victorian empire of free trade and private enterprise."

For a while, some Khoikhoi managed to make good use of their freedom. By 1831, more than 3000 Khoikhoi had built up a flourishing arable and pastoral settlement on land allotted to them by the colonial government in the fertile Kat River valley in the eastern frontier zone (land which the government had recently conquered from Africans). Nevertheless, as American experience after Abraham Lincoln's 1863 proclamation would also show, emancipation does not necessarily lead to economic or social equality. In the Cape Colony, White colonists retained effective control over the economic resources, including most of the land; and the "Coloured people," descended in varying degrees from Khoikhoi, slaves, and Whites, became a rural and urban proletariat dependent on working for wages in cash or in kind.

By 1851, colonists had destroyed the Kat River Settlement and dispersed its inhabitants; and soon afterwards they entrenched their economic dominance by gaining control of the political system. Initially, the British governor exercised autocratic powers in the Cape Colony, subject only to his superiors in Britain. After significant numbers of British settlers had arrived, however, some of them took the lead in demanding reforms. Following a struggle with the governor, freedom of the press was conceded in 1827, followed by freedom of assembly, so that political issues could then be debated in the newspapers and at public meetings. By 1853, Lord Durham and

Lord Elgin, in coping with a constitutional crisis in Canada, had broken the ideological impasse that had led to the American Revolution, and the Canadian example became a precedent for legal development in other British settlement colonies, in two stages: first, "representative government," in which power was divided between an executive branch subordinate to the British government and a legislative branch elected locally; and second, "responsible government," with an executive cabinet drawn from, and responsible to, the local legislature (but with Britain keeping control over the colonies' external relations until well into the twentieth century). Was the Cape Colony to be treated as a colony of settlement and subject to this evolutionary development? Or was it, rather, a dependency like India, with a preponderance of alien inhabitants to be ruled autocratically for the foreseeable future?

By mid-century the influence of the humanitarian lobby had declined in Britain and, after some hesitation, Parliament opted for the settler prescription. In 1853 the colony was granted representative government – a legislature with two houses, both consisting entirely of elected members; and in 1872 it acquired responsible government, with a cabinet responsible to the legislature. The franchise for both houses of the Cape parliament was open, regardless of race, to any man who occupied property worth £25 or who earned £50 a year. In politics as in social and economic affairs, however, the forms might be color-blind, but the substance was very different. The net effect of the constitutional changes was to transfer power from the British officials to the White section of the colonial population. No Coloured man ever became a member of the Cape Cabinet or Parliament; colonial juries and local officials were almost entirely White. Only a small fraction of the Coloured men registered as voters, and those who did never formed an effective pressure group. The new colonial parliament quickly demonstrated this reality: in 1856 it passed a Masters and Servants Act that went a long way to restoring White control over Black labor, tying workers to five-year contracts and imposing severe penalties for desertion, "laziness," and "disobedience."

The conquest of the Xhosa

Meanwhile, the Cape Colony was confronted with the nearest Bantu-speaking African farming communities – the Xhosa chiefdoms beyond Algoa Bay, some four hundred miles east of Cape Town. The result was a long, drawn-out struggle, that culminated in the conquest of the Xhosa and foreshadowed the fate of African farmers throughout the entire southern African region.

Until 1811, Bantu-speaking Africans and Cape colonists were evenly matched in a frontier zone on either side of the Fish River, where the two societies began to overlap during the eighteenth century. The subjects of the Xhosa cluster of chiefdoms in the vicinity of the frontier zone were far more numerous than the colonists in the eastern districts of the Cape Colony, and they drove the colonists out of the area for the second time in 1802. But the colonists had more horses and guns than the Xhosa, and they regained lost ground with the assistance of Dutch troops during the short-lived regime of the Batavian Republic.

Power tilted decisively toward the Whites in 1811–12, when British troops drove the Africans out of the area west of the Fish River and then built forts alongside the river. In

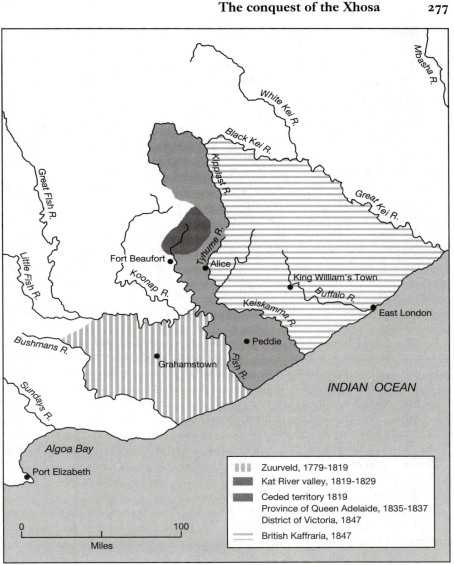

Map 10.2 Xhosa land losses 1795–1850

1820, the strength of the resident Whites increased with the settlement of 5000 British immigrants in the recently conquered territory. That was the beginning of the conquest of the southern Nguni – a process punctuated by wars, advances of the colonial boundary, and forced removals of Africans from the land they had occupied. Most of the wars started with a Xhosa invasion of the colony aimed at regaining lost territory; most ended with a counter-attack staged by British troops, White and Coloured colonial levies, and African allies, destroying crops and villages and capturing vast herds of cattle. The colonial forces won each of these wars, after an initial setback, because they were drawing on the resources of a powerful industrial state, whereas the Xhosa had no such backing and were always impeded by their own disunity. The Xhosa paramountcy had symbolic rather than material authority and no leader succeeded in imposing his authority, as Shaka had done over the northern Nguni or Moshoeshoe over the southern Sotho. The endemic rivalries among chiefdoms and among opposed segments of chiefdoms were compounded in 1835, when the colonial government made allies of 17,000 Mfengu who had arrived in the area as refugees from the Zulu; the Cape government settled them on land conquered from the Xhosa. Many of the British soldiers and settlers, assuming that the Xhosa were not fully human, were extremely brutal. Nevertheless the Xhosa put up a prolonged and often heroic resistance, fighting desperately in 1819, 1834–5, 1846, 1850–3, and 1877–8, by which time they were a conquered people.

As the conquest proceeded, the boundary of British territory shifted further and further eastward and incorporated more and more Xhosa territory. At the beginning of the century, it was fixed at the Fish River; in 1819, it advanced to the Keiskamma; in 1847, to the Kei; in 1858, to the Mbasha; and in 1878, to the Mthatha. When the Mpondo country was annexed in 1894, the Cape boundary met the boundary of Natal along the Mtamvuna River, which thus brought all the southern Nguni under White administration.

Between the Fish and the Kei, the colonial government divided up most of the conquered land into farms for White settlers, interspersed with reserves that would form the "Ciskei" homeland under apartheid in the second half of the twentieth century. Even there, however, Bantu-speaking Africans still made up the vast majority of the population, not only on their reserves but also in the towns and as workers on the White farms. The Xhosa on the frontier were not so much rolled back as overwhelmed and subjugated by the political power of the Cape government and the economic power of the White settlers who had appropriated much of their former land. In the "Transkei," east of the Kei, however, the Africans held on to the land, except in a small region around Kokstad, which passed first into the hands of people of mixed descent and then into the hands of White settlers.

In the Ciskei reserves and the Transkei alike, the Xhosa were exposed to three types of aliens: officials, traders, and missionaries. Magistrates appointed to district headquarters in the conquered territories gradually undermined the authority of the chiefs, transforming them into subordinate officials with limited powers. Traders, selling commodities such as sugar, tea, blankets, and iron pots that Africans rapidly came to regard as necessities, created a chain of shops throughout the territories. Missionaries of several Protestant denominations – Congregational, Methodist, and Presbyterian – created another chain of stations in which they taught Christian theology in combination with nineteenth-century British cultural values and denounced local customs such as initiation, polygyny, and the transfer of cattle on marriage (*lobola*) that were fundamental to African social solidarity. They also founded schools in which Africans acquired a Western education in conjunction with religious instruction.

Each magistracy, each trading station, and each mission became the nucleus of a new social grouping of Africans, who weakened their links with traditional society and adapted to the presence of their conquerors. Economic imperatives accentuated the process. People who could not provide for their needs on the lands that remained to them went out from the reserves to work for White farmers, and although some returned to their homes after a year or two, others remained away.

The results for Africans were uneven. Many of the Mfengu, whose social system had been disrupted by Shaka and who had fled southward and received a privileged status from the colonial authorities, adapted most eagerly to the new order. So did individuals and segments from the Xhosa chiefdoms. But other individuals and groups continued to resist the new order psychologically, even when they had been physically overcome. In the war of 1819 and again in the 1840s, Xhosa prophets invoked religious beliefs to oppose conquest. Noel Mostert explains that by 1856, following "the longest, cruelest, and most penalizing of all the frontier wars, the frontier Xhosa were in a severe state of spiritual, political, and economic crisis after a century of progressive land loss, strenuous assault upon their traditions and customs, and military defeat." Then a young Xhosa girl named Nongqawuse reported that she had had a vision: the people should destroy all their cattle and their grain; when this was done, the ancestral heroes would be reborn, choice cattle and grain and also guns and ammunition would appear, and a great wind would drive all the Europeans into the sea. This report was taken seriously by many of the Xhosa and by early 1857 they had destroyed over 150,000 cattle. But instead of the millennium, there was mass starvation. According to one estimate, nearly two-thirds of the Xhosa people who had lived between the Kei and the Keiskamma rivers died or fled into the colony, where Africans had been admitted since 1828, provided that they worked for Whites.

As people reacted in different ways to their changing circumstances, new cleavages opened up in Nguni society. Rivalries among chiefdoms and ethnic groups were accentuated by the differential treatment they received from their conquerors, notably the division between the Mfengu and the rest. There was also a division between those who persisted in trying to reject alien goods and customs and those who attempted to make use of their new opportunities, such as they were, by mastering the conqueror's knowledge and adopting his customs. These people accumulated imported goods, used plows as well as hoes, wore Western clothes, attended mission schools and hospitals, ceased to observe established rituals, and were baptized. Chiefdoms and families split along these lines. But the division was never absolute: every individual experienced the contrary tugs of custom and Westernization.

The Westernization process would have been more successful in pointing the way toward a harmonious society if those Africans who conformed most closely to their missionaries' prescriptions had received the benefits that were implicit in the Cape colonial legal system. When the colonial reforms were enacted in the 1820s and 1830s, and even when the terms of the franchise were set for the Cape Parliament in 1853, few Africans lived inside the Cape Colony; the land between the Keiskamma and the Kei was then administered as a separate colony. Later, after the Keiskamma-Kei territory was incorporated in the Cape Colony in 1865, followed by other large blocks of territory with African inhabitants, additional parliamentary constituencies were created there, but steps were taken to ensure that few Africans became registered as voters.

By 1872, when the Cape Colony received responsible government, the primary division in colonial society was a correlation of racial and class criteria. The White colonists controlled the economy and the politics and most of them – British settlers as well as Afrikaners – were steeped in a racist ideology. They depended on the labor of the African and Coloured inhabitants; but they would not accept them as equals, however "civilized" they might be.

The Afrikaner Great Trek

Meanwhile, between 1834 and 1841, numerous Afrikaner men, women, and children trekked northeastward out of the Cape Colony. The precise number is disputed, but is probably rather more than 8000. Later, this emigration became known as the Great Trek, and the emigrants as *voortrekkers* (pioneers). They traveled in organized groups of kinfolk and neighbors, with their servants and their ox wagons, cattle, sheep, and other movable property, determined to establish new homes for themselves beyond the limits of British control, either in Natal or on the high veld on either side of the Vaal River.

Most of the voortrekkers came from the eastern districts. They emigrated out of deep dissatisfaction with conditions in the colony, for the world they had known seemed to be dissolving around them since the mid-1820s. They had lost control over the local administration. They were short of labor since Ordinance 50 of 1828 had deprived them of legal authority over the Khoikhoi, many of whom had left the farms for the mission stations and the towns, while others had become self-sufficient land-holders in the Kat River Settlement. And they could no longer obtain possession of large landholdings under the customary loan farm arrangement. The British adminis-tration had introduced a more costly system of quitrent tenure; moreover, by the 1830s there was no fresh land available for Afrikaners within the colonial boundaries and the Xhosa chiefdoms blocked their expansion eastward. Consequently, it was not possible for the new generation to acquire what they considered to be their birthright – several thousand acres of land per family.

The emigration was well under way before December 1834, when the slaves were formally emancipated and masses of Xhosa invaded the colony to start another frontier war; but those events enhanced the scale of the emigration. Colonists who had owned slaves – who included many voortrekkers – discovered that their compensation could only be claimed in London, which placed them in the hands of British agents who charged high commissions. Also, in 1835, after the Xhosa had destroyed many farm buildings and captured thousands of livestock, the victims were appalled to hear that the British Colonial Secretary was blaming them rather than the Xhosa for starting the war, and that he was instituting a policy of treaties with the Xhosa chiefs – a policy that, in their opinion, could only lead to further troubles. In short, the voortrekkers emi-grated because they wished to continue the autonomous, expansive, patriarchal way of life of their parents and grandparents, independent of a government that seemed to have become hostile to them.

Nevertheless, only a fraction of the Afrikaner people left the Cape Colony. Many others probably felt much the same way about the changes made by the British regime;

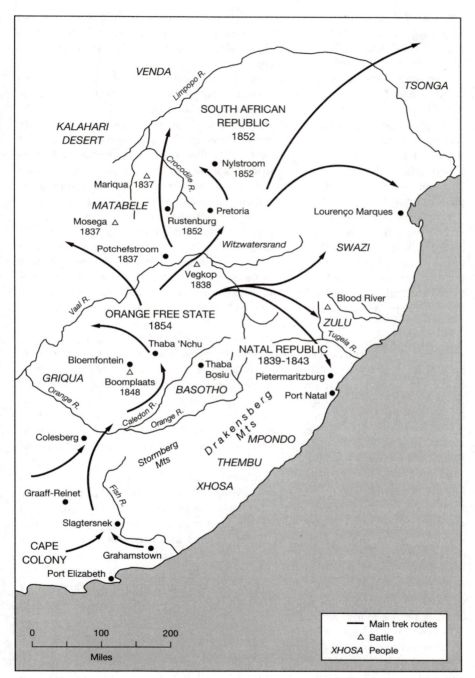

Map 10.3 The Afrikaner Great Trek 1836–1854

but most of them accommodated more or less successfully to the British reforms, and after 1853 they gradually learned to take advantage of the parliamentary institutions. In particular, led by the British settlers, they soon found new ways of maintaining control of the Coloured and African inhabitants.

During 1834 and 1835, small parties of Afrikaners made reconnaissance expeditions to Natal and the high veld. They returned to report that both regions had spacious territories that were only thinly populated – the lush subtropical lands below the mountain escarpment and the fertile grasslands on either side of the Vaal River. These reports were fairly accurate as far as they went (though they overestimated the extent of depopulation); but their authors did not realize that both regions had recently contained quite dense populations of African farmers and that the Zulu and Ndebele kingdoms were keeping them thinly populated by military raids. The voortrekkers' plans to settle there inevitably brought them into conflict with those kingdoms.

Ever since Mzilikazi had settled north of the Vaal River, he had been attacked several times from the south – not only by Zulu armies sent by Dingane, who still regarded him as a rebellious subject, but also by Griqua horsemen armed with muskets. By the 1830s, the Griquas were harassing the other inhabitants – African hunters, pastoralists and farmers – to the north of the central Orange River. They traded guns and ammunition from the colony in return for human captives and, with the support of White missionaries, they had founded two fragile polities, known as Griqualand West and Griqualand East.

When Mzilikazi's scouts reported that considerable numbers of White people with vast herds of cattle and flocks of sheep were occupying land on either side of the Vaal, he sent his regiments to attack them. By 1837, however, there were enough voortrekkers in the high veld to mount an offensive. With African and Griqua allies, they drove Mzilikazi northward from Mosega early in 1837 and later that year sent him fleeing with his followers into the country of the Shona across the Limpopo, where they carved out a new Ndebele kingdom. Having conquered the conquerors of the African inhabitants of the high veld, some of the voortrekkers then proceeded to found settlements on either side of the Vaal River.

By 1838, however, the majority of the voortrekkers had decided to settle in Natal, because its coastline provided an opportunity for trade with continental Europe and the United States, in preference to the landlocked high veld, where they could only replenish their supplies of arms, ammunition, and groceries through the Cape colonial network. One of their leaders, Piet Retief, entered into negotiations with Shaka's successor Dingane for a grant of land south of the Tugela. But Dingane had already been made suspicious of Whites by the erratic behavior of a small group of British traders at Port Natal (Durban), who were harboring refugees from his kingdom, and he was well-informed about the fate of Mzilikazi. He regarded a voortrekker settlement in Natal as a threat to his kingdom and he was determined to prevent it.

In February 1838, after Dingane may have put his mark to a document purporting to cede the territory of Natal (the authenticity of the document is contested), his warriors massacred Retief and his party and attacked the voortrekker encampments below the Drakensberg. In all, they killed over three hundred and fifty Afrikaners and over two hundred and thirty of their servants, and they temporarily extinguished White power in

Natal. In December, however, a voortrekker force, revitalized by fresh leadership, repulsed a massive Zulu attack by forming a circle with their wagons. About 3000 Zulus perished in that engagement, which Whites called the Battle of Blood River. The Zulu nation then split. Mpande seceded from his half-brother Dingane with a large following and allied himself with the voortrekkers. In 1840 Mpande's regiments crushed Dingane's army and sent the king fleeing northward to his death. Mpande then assumed control over a weakened Zulu kingdom, while the main body of voortrekkers carved farms out of the lands south of the Tugela and applied to the British authorities to be recognized as an independent state.

They nearly succeeded. During the middle years of the nineteenth century the British government did not favor the annexation of an overseas territory unless there were strong commercial or strategic reasons. The Cape Colony itself, with its incessant and costly frontier wars, was regarded as a burden necessarily borne for the sake of the harbors on the Cape peninsula. Natal had much less to offer. The trade conducted there by a few British subjects since 1824 was negligible, and a sand-bar made the entrance to the harbor of Port Natal (Durban) inaccessible to all but the smallest ships. Before the voortrekkers arrived, the government had had no hesitation in rejecting requests by the traders and their Cape colonial backers for the annexation of Natal.

In 1842, however, the British government changed its mind. A voortrekker commando had raided southward against a chief whose neighbor, the chief of the Mpondo, had appealed through his missionary for British protection, and the voortrekker *volksraad* (legislature) had passed a resolution for the forced removal to the south of numerous Africans who had returned to their original homelands in Natal after the defeat of Dingane, and who were deemed to be "surplus" to the labor requirements of the Afrikaners. The British government concluded that these pressures would have disturbing effects throughout southern Nguni country right down to the Cape colonial frontier. It was also influenced by the humanitarian lobby, which was denouncing the voortrekkers' dealings with Africans. Accordingly, a British military detachment was sent to Natal where, after some sharp fighting, the voortrekker authorities submitted to British rule in 1842. During the next few years, the majority of the voortrekkers who had settled in Natal harnessed their oxen again, recrossed the Drakensberg, and made their homes on the high veld.

By the late 1840s, numerous White settlements were scattered across the high veld, from near the Orange River in the southwest to the foothills of the Soutpansberg mountains near the Limpopo River in the north. Each settlement comprised a small village surrounded by large pastoral landholdings and formed a distinct community, usually with a nuclear group of families who had left the Cape Colony together. The relations between the settlements were often far from cordial. Differences of opinion on matters such as whether a British missionary or an unordained Afrikaner should conduct religious services and how they should organize themselves politically, compounded by personality conflicts, gave rise to fierce quarrels. Near the Cape colonial border in the southwest there were further complications caused by the presence of the Griqua communities and also a considerable number of Afrikaners who still regarded themselves as colonial subjects and were not imbued with the independent spirit of the voortrekkers.

For a while, the British were sucked into the territory between the Orange and the Vaal. In 1843, consistent with the policy they were then pursuing on the eastern frontier of the Cape Colony, they made treaties with the East Griqua chief, Adam Kok, and the southern Sotho chief, Moshoeshoe; and in 1848 an impetuous governor, Sir Harry Smith, annexed the entire territory between the Orange and the Vaal, including East Griqualand and Lesotho. But he had overreached himself. Smith's annexation went against the grain of contemporary British policy and although the government in London grudgingly accepted it as a *fait accompli*, it refrained from providing sufficient funds for effective administration of the territory. Moreover, the man Smith appointed as local administrator ineptly became involved in local communal conflicts, eventually forming a military alliance with the Whites and the smaller African communities against Moshoeshoe, who defeated him. The British government then sent out commissioners to examine the situation on the spot. In 1852, they signed a Convention at the Sand River with representatives of the Transvaal voortrekkers, recognizing their independence. Two years later, another British commissioner made a similar agreement at the growing town of Bloemfontein with representatives of the White population of the area that was to become the Orange Free State.

The Great Trek was a remarkable feat. Previously, White settlers had been confined to the southwestern segment of southern Africa, where they had flourished at the expense of the relatively weak and thinly spread Khoisan hunters and herders. The voortrekkers broke through into the better-watered eastern half of the continent, where, taking advantage of the fact that the African inhabitants had recently been scattered and disrupted by the mfecane wars, they were able to occupy vast areas. They defeated the Zulu and Ndebele kingdoms that had dominated the region and, although Britain annexed Natal, they gained British recognition of their independence in the interior. More than that: in the Conventions, the British permitted Whites to purchase arms and ammunition in the colonies, prohibited such trade with "native tribes," and revoked their treaty with Moshoeshoe.

To later Afrikaners, the voortrekkers were heroic figures who had brought "White Christian civilization" to darkest southeastern Africa. In the 1930s, the celebration of the centenary of the Great Trek was exploited by politicians to intensify Afrikaner nationalism, and a massive voortrekker monument was erected outside the city of Pretoria. To Africans, on the other hand, the voortrekkers were ruthless conquerors who set the stage for their systematic exploitation. There are ironies in both views. Shaka, the symbol of African power, was partly responsible for the disruption of the African peoples that paved the way for voortrekker settlement. And, while the trek was taking place, most Afrikaners remained in the Cape Colony and were skeptical of the voortrekkers' achievements.

The Afrikaner Republics

The White population of the territories the voortrekkers occupied in the interior grew slowly by natural increase and immigration from the Cape Colony and Natal to number about 45,000 in 1870 (at a time when the Cape Colony had nearly 200,000 White inhabitants). Most of them were still semi-nomadic pastoral farmers; a few leaders owned many livestock and were patrons of the least successful. They claimed vast expanses of land without cultivating it, lived off their herds and flocks, and produced little else for exchange. People of British and continental European origins sold them colonial and imported goods obtained from merchants in the Cape Colony. A few other White foreigners were employed by the voortrekker governments as clergy, teachers, and officials.

The voortrekker communities remained fragmented. The extended family evoked more loyalty than the regional group, the regional group more than any larger community. African chiefs as well as British officials often manipulated these divisions, while Whites in turn exploited the cleavages among Africans.

Two states gradually took shape in the interior: the Orange Free State between the Orange and the Vaal, and the South African Republic (generally known as the Transvaal) between the Vaal and the Limpopo. External influences were somewhat stronger in the Orange Free State, which formed a cultural as well as a geographical bridge between the British colonies and the Transvaal. Both republics adopted constitutions that confined citizenship to White men; the Transvaal document bluntly declared that "The people are not prepared to allow any equality of the non-White with the White inhabitants, either in Church or State." The constitutions also provided for the election of presidents and unicameral legislatures. Although there were a few salaried officials in each little capital town, Bloemfontein and Pretoria, and one or more in each district headquarters, neither state had the means to create an efficient bureaucracy, and local administration was mainly in the hands of unpaid, part-time, military officers, elected by the local citizens from among themselves. After a shaky start (the first president was removed from office by force), the Orange Free State eventually achieved stability under President J.H. Brand (1864–1888). The Transvaal remained chronically unstable; the White factions were not formally united until 1860, and even then they fought among themselves intermittently for another four years.

The voortrekkers never contemplated living without control of dark-skinned people as domestic servants and herdsmen. Needing many more dependents than the servants they had brought with them from the Cape Colony, they turned to the local African farming communities. Commandos often made a point of capturing African children as well as cattle for distribution when a campaign was over, as colonial commandos had formerly captured San children. Voortrekkers also obtained African children by barter from adults who had no food. Captured and bartered African children were called apprentices and, as with Khoisan children during the early years of British rule in the Cape Colony, they were meant to become free at the age of twenty-five (twenty-one in the case of girls), but often did not do so. In addition, many African adults as well as children simply stayed where they were as labor tenants when Europeans assumed possession of their land. By methods such as these, the voortrekkers secured an ample supply of African labor.

Wherever they settled, in Natal and on the highveld, the voortrekkers soon found themselves confronted with a security problem. Many northern Nguni who had lived south of the Tugela before the time of Shaka drifted back to their home areas after the fall of Dingane; similarly, numerous Sotho-Tswana returned to their home areas on the high veld after Mzilikazi was driven northward across the Limpopo. The voortrekkers tried to deal with the influx by passing laws limiting the number of Africans to four or five families on each farm; prohibiting Africans and Coloured people from owning firearms or horses, or being at large in White areas without a pass signed by a White employer; and placing all "surplus" Africans in reserves under headmen who were made responsible for their good behavior and for providing additional labor on demand.

The Republic of Natal began to formulate such a policy, but in attempting to cope with the "surplus," it set in motion the chain of events that led to British intervention. In the Transvaal, too, the government lacked the means to enforce its laws systematically. The reserves were not delimited and relations between Whites and Africans varied considerably from region to region and over time. Generally, Africans who lived in the reserves had security of life and limb and the opportunity to produce their own food in return for the obligation to provide intermittent compulsory labor for White farmers; but where the Whites were particularly capricious there was anarchy. This was always the case in the northern Transvaal, where the White community lacked internal discipline and the officials were themselves guilty of the most flagrant abuses.

Areas where Africans were effectively subjected to White control shaded off into areas where they remained autonomous. Initially, voortrekker leaders tried to acquire titles to land by negotiation with chiefs, and they continued to make treaties when it seemed expedient; but after they defeated Mzilikazi's Ndebele they saw themselves as having won by conquest his entire Transvaal empire, which they construed in the largest terms as embracing everything between the Vaal and the Limpopo and between the Kalahari desert and the mountain escarpment. They claimed to have liberated all the African inhabitants from Ndebele oppression and to be justified in treating them as vassals.

The Africans saw things differently. Many had never been ruled by Mzilikazi, others had been only partially subjugated, and in either case they strove to achieve and maintain their independence after the Ndebele had been driven out. Several British traders and missionaries, including David Livingstone (who was later to be famous as an explorer) encouraged them to adopt this attitude, and increased their capacity to resist Afrikaner demands by selling them arms and ammunition. But, located as the Africans were around the periphery of the trekker settlements and divided as they were by traditional feuds and personal rivalries, they had to depend very largely on their own resources, and the Afrikaner authorities were generally able to deal with them piecemeal. The Transvaal also exploited the fissiparous nature of African chiefdoms by giving sanctuary to the rivals of incumbent chiefs, thus splitting several chiefdoms into two parts – one autonomous, the other under Afrikaner control.

Three clusters of chiefdoms managed to preserve their independence from the Transvaal government until 1870 and later. On the borders of the Kalahari in the west, the government failed to conquer several of the Tswana chiefdoms, which became combined into a British protectorate in 1885 and formed the independent state of Botswana in 1966. In mountainous country in the east, the Pedi rallied the survivors of many northern Sotho chiefdoms that had been disrupted by Mzilikazi and Soshangane, and they repulsed White attacks until 1879, when they were defeated and incorporated in the Transvaal. In the Soutpansberg mountains in the north, the Venda actually reversed the White advance in 1867, when they defeated a commando led by Paul Kruger and made the Afrikaners abandon almost the entire Soutpansberg district. It was not until 1898, when Kruger was president of a much more powerful Transvaal, enriched by gold discoveries, that a republican force of nearly four thousand, with Swazi and Tsonga allies, finally conquered the Venda.

The British colony of Natal

In Natal, which Britain annexed in 1843, Africans vastly outnumbered Whites. The African population continued to rise steeply after the collapse of the voortrekker republic. Many Africans returned to the neighborhoods they had abandoned during the time of Shaka; others fled from the Zulu kingdom, where internal tensions reached a peak in 1856, when rival factions led by two sons of Mpande fought a tremendous battle near the Tugela. British immigrants began to arrive in substantial numbers in 1849, soon outnumbering the few voortrekkers who remained in Natal after the annexation. Even so, it is estimated that in 1872 nearly 93 per cent of the total Natal population of about 320,000 were Africans and less than 6 per cent were Whites (proportions similar to those in Rhodesia – now Zimbabwe – in the 1970s). By 1872 there were also a few Indians, imported by the Natal government to work for European planters on the sugar estates along the coastal belt.

The British annexation proclamation of 1843 included a high-sounding commitment to prohibit racial discrimination: "That there shall not be in the eye of the law any distinction of colour, origin, race, or creed; but that the protection of the law, in letter and in substance, shall be extended impartially to all alike." The early history of the colony is largely an account of how the tiny White community subverted that commitment and obtained substantial control over the entire territory.

The division of the land was a crucial issue. One of the first acts of the British administration was to appoint a commission to deal with this problem, with the result that only about two million acres out of a total of nearly twelve and a half million in the colony were eventually defined as African reserves ("locations"). The rest became the private property of individual Whites or White companies, or remained in the public domain ("crown lands"). Most of the African inhabitants lived in the reserves; some squatted in the public domain; others became tenants of White landowners, including absentee landlords who merely collected rent, a practice known as "Kaffir farming."

From 1845 to 1875, the African inhabitants of Natal were administered by Theophilus Shepstone, son of a Cape colonial Wesleyan missionary. He controlled them through chiefs and headmen, some of whom had prescriptive claims to their offices while others were new men. These African office-holders were responsible for law and order in their reserves, subject in theory to the governor of Natal, who was proclaimed "Supreme Chief," and in practice to Shepstone, the Secretary for Native Affairs. He allowed them to apply customary law in civil disputes among Africans, but magistrates tried criminal cases and disputes with Whites in accordance with Roman-Dutch law adopted from the Cape Colony. The Africans paid an annual hut tax as well as customs duties on imported commodities they bought from traders – payments that amounted to more than the government spent on their administration. This method of controlling Africans contained many of the features of Indirect Rule, which was to become the orthodox practice of British administrators in tropical African colonies in the twentieth century; it also contained the germs of the apartheid system that was introduced in the Republic of South Africa in 1948. Missionaries founded a few schools and hospitals in the reserves but their resources were too meager to have a significant impact and the Natal Africans had scarcely any opportunities for economic growth under colonial rule.

Whites who lived inland were mixed farmers, who employed African labor in return for low wages or tenant rights. Along the coastal belt, experiments were made with tropical crops and by 1870 sugar was being produced on a commercial scale for export. Because Shepstone balked at forcing Africans to become plantation laborers – a very different type of activity from the cattle-herding and grain production to which they were accustomed – the planters used their political influence to persuade the government to make arrangements for the importation of laborers from India and to allot public funds for this purpose. Recruiters employed by the Natal government persuaded Indians to sign contracts ("indentures"), by which they undertook to serve Natal employers for five years, after which they had the option of entering into new contracts or making their own way as private persons. Ten years after arrival, they became entitled to free passages back to India, but they were not obliged to return. The first batch of Indians, who completed their ten years in 1870, set an example that was to be followed by their successors until the indentured system was abolished in 1911: only a small minority returned to India. The rest remained in Natal, where they became market gardeners, shopkeepers, and service workers in and near the two main towns, Durban and Pietermaritzburg – activities which effectively excluded Africans from those occupations and paved the way for African hostility toward Indians.

As in the Cape Colony, the Whites used their political power to buttress their economic advantages. In 1856, three years after the British government had granted representative institutions to the Cape, it created a Natal legislature with a majority of its members elected by the White settlers. Although the salaries of the senior officials could not be reduced by the legislature, and although those officials remained responsible to London until 1893, this was a decisive step toward full settler control of the colony. The use the colonists would make of their political power had been foreshadowed by a commission of settlers who reported on "native policy" in 1854. The commissioners categorized Africans as "savages" – "superstitious," "crafty," "indolent," "bloodthirsty and cruel," "debased and sensual." They also described the Africans as "foreigners" with no right to occupy land in Natal; and they declared that since "Natal is a White settlement," the prohibition of racial discrimination in the annexation proclamation had become "utterly inapplicable."

Moshoeshoe's Lesotho

We can illustrate African responses to White expansion in this period by turning to the history of the southern Sotho and their remarkable king, Moshoeshoe, who was born in about 1786 and died in 1870. Lesotho occupies a central position in southern Africa, and we probably know more about Moshoeshoe than we do about any of his African contemporaries in the region, because missionaries got to know him unusually well and wrote quite perceptively about him, and he himself dictated numerous letters. These sources have to be interpreted judiciously, however; the writings of the missionaries were affected by their cultural assumptions and evangelical goals, and we cannot be sure how accurately the letters attributed to Moshoeshoe reflect his meaning, for he spoke in southern Sotho, whereas his scribes, who were missionaries or mission-educated Africans, wrote out his dictations in English or French. We can remedy these deficiencies by drawing on the traditions still current in Lesotho and on several studies that modern anthropologists have made of aspects of Sotho society.

The senior son of a semi-autonomous village headman, Moshoeshoe first became prominent during the 1820s when, starting with a small band of followers, he repulsed several African attacks on his mountain stronghold, Thaba Bosiu, south of the Caledon river, and incorporated numerous Nguni as well as Sotho survivors of the mfecane wars into a loosely structured kingdom. He attracted followers not only because he was a master of defensive warfare, but also because he restored the morale of people whose lives had been disastrously disrupted. He put an end to cannibalism and encouraged people to settle down again in villages and resume their customary mode of life as mixed farmers. But whereas before the wars they had been divided among numerous separate chiefdoms, they now looked up to him as their great chief. He and his councilors heard appeals from the decisions of their local courts and from time to time he summoned all the initiated men to Thaba Bosiu, where he discussed public affairs with them and announced his decisions.

The first Europeans to settle in Lesotho were two French Protestant missionaries and a lay assistant, who arrived in 1833. Moshoeshoe himself had sent messages inviting them. Bands of Griquas from their chiefdoms west of Lesotho, equipped with horses and firearms obtained from the Cape Colony, were raiding his outlying villages and he had heard that missionaries were men of peace who possessed magical powers. The missionaries had an interest in helping Moshoeshoe to stabilize and extend his kingdom. His favorite, Eugene Casalis, founded a station immediately below Thaba Bosiu. Moshoeshoe consulted him frequently and used him as his secretary and interpreter. He placed other missionaries alongside his subordinate chiefs at strategic points, where their presence deterred potential enemies from attacking them. He also encouraged his people to attend the mission services and schools. By the end of 1847, there were nine French mission stations in and near the Caledon valley, and the missionaries had baptized several of Moshoeshoe's councilors and close relatives — sons, half-brothers, and wives.

Moshoeshoe also made several far-reaching concessions to his missionaries: he adopted Christian burial customs, he ceased to hold initiation schools, and he granted divorces to some of his wives who had been converted. However, he refused to yield to his missionaries' denunciations of the traditional system of polygyny, for he himself had many wives and in the absence of a money economy he needed them to cultivate his fields and to prepare food for himself and his numerous guests. Moreover, although he frequently attended services in the mission churches and became very well-informed about the Bible and sympathetic to the moral code of the New Testament, he declined to be baptized. He realized that if he did so he would alienate his more conservative followers (including his aged and respected parents), as well as the Sotho doctors and prophets who had vested interests in their beliefs and rituals.

Traders from the Cape Colony, bringing wagonloads of merchandise, followed the missionaries to Lesotho during the 1830s and 1840s. In the 1850s, they began to build shops at the principal mission stations, buying grain and cattle and selling manufactured clothing and metalware. The Sotho responded by producing a considerable surplus of grain for the market. Moshoeshoe himself set an example by using imported plows in his own fields and by planting wheat as well as sorghum and corn. He and his people were also quick to appreciate the significance of horses and firearms. By the 1850s, many young men owned some and Moshoeshoe had a large ammunition store on Thaba Bosiu. Although the trade in guns and ammunition was frowned upon by White opinion and prohibited by the Bloemfontein Convention (1854), there were always farmers and traders who were prepared to take advantage of the Sotho demand. Horses flourished in Lesotho; but the firearms were mostly inferior muskets manufactured in Birmingham specially for the African market. While Moshoeshoe encouraged trade, he also took steps to control the traders. He himself, like his father, never drank even the mildest Sotho beer, declaring that a chief should keep a clear head. He agreed with his missionaries in deploring the demoralizing effects of the colonial brandy that traders were selling his people, and in 1854 he issued a proclamation prohibiting the sale of trade alcohol. Five years later, he issued another proclamation asserting his unqualified jurisdiction over traders and prohibiting them from owning any land in Lesotho.

Moshoeshoe was able to control the French missionaries and colonial traders because their interests very largely coincided with his own; but the interests of the voortrekkers with their insatiable appetite for land were almost entirely antithetical. By the early 1840s, Afrikaners and Africans were becoming intermingled in the triangle between the lower Caledon and the Orange rivers as well as further north, and the situation was further complicated by the presence on the north side of the Caledon of several Griqua and African communities, including Sekonyela's Tlokoa chiefdom, who did not recognize Moshoeshoe as their king. After the voortrekkers defeated Mzilikazi and Dingane, they occupied more and more land on the high veld to his north and west, and Moshoeshoe realized that they constituted a serious threat to his state, whereas the British seemed to have no intention of depriving him of his territory. Accordingly, he sought a British alliance. In a treaty concluded in 1843, the governor of the Cape Colony recognized Moshoeshoe as the ruler of all the land between the Orange and the Caledon and also of a strip twenty miles wide on the north bank of the Caledon (except for Sekonyela's territory at the northeastern end).

But Moshoeshoe's relations with the British authorities soon deteriorated. A later governor persuaded him to allow Whites to settle in the triangle between the lower Caledon and the Orange. When, in 1848, governor Harry Smith annexed the territory between the Orange and the Vaal, which included Lesotho, he personally assured Moshoeshoe that the British regime would not interfere in his internal affairs or with his territorial rights; but the officer whom Smith appointed to administer the territory succumbed to pressures from Whites, Griquas, and Africans who lived on the northern side of the Caledon and claimed to be independent of Moshoeshoe. First, he proclaimed a series of boundary lines that separated the territories of those chiefs from Lesotho. Then, when skirmishes broke out among the affected groups, he organized a coalition against Moshoeshoe and his allies. The Sotho warriors defeated this force, repulsed an attack by British regular troops, and conquered and incorporated the Tlokoa. In 1854, this prompted the British to disannex the entire Orange-Vaal territory, leaving Lesotho face to face with the infant Orange Free State, without an agreed boundary between them.

The inevitable result was friction. Whites and Africans raided each others' cattle and vied for control over disputed territory. In a war that broke out in 1858, the Orange Free State commandos invaded Lesotho but broke and fled rather than attempt an assault on Thaba Bosiu. By the time fighting was resumed in 1865, however, Moshoeshoe was aging and losing control over his subordinates, and the Orange Free State had a young and vigorous president in J.H. Brand and a White population that had grown considerably. The Afrikaner commandos gradually got the upper hand by systematically destroying Sotho villages and crops, storming Sotho strongpoints, and persuading several chiefs to agree to treaties that deprived the Sotho of nearly all their arable land. But the commandos never managed to capture Thaba Bosiu, nor were they able to follow up their victories by effective occupation of the land they claimed to have conquered. Bands of Sotho maintained a spirited guerrilla resistance even after their chiefs had come to terms with the invaders. Moshoeshoe, meanwhile, had repeatedly applied to the British authorities for protection, and this was granted in 1868 when Sir Philip Wodehouse, High Commissioner for South Africa and Governor of the Cape Colony, annexed "Basutoland." Moshoeshoe died two years later. By that time, without consulting Moshoeshoe, British and Orange Free State representatives had agreed on a boundary line that survives to the present day: a line that gave the Orange Free State everything north of the Caledon and a considerable area between the lower Caledon and the Orange, leaving a truncated territory which the British called Basutoland, consisting mainly of mountains, with only a narrow strip of arable land on the southern side of the Caledon. Although Basutoland would regain its political independence and the name Lesotho in 1966, it was doomed to be economically dependent on the Republic of South Africa.

The case of Moshoeshoe and the southern Sotho illustrates the importance of three variables in the early contact situation: the style of African political leadership, the condition of the African society at the moment of the first substantial contact, and the class of Europeans who provided that contact. Moshoeshoe was a remarkably humane and intelligent man, the southern Sotho were just recovering from the mfecane wars, and the first Europeans who settled in Lesotho were exceptionally sympathetic missionaries. Consequently, Moshoeshoe eagerly grasped the missionaries' evangelical teachings as well as their material culture. But Sotho conservatives challenged the honeymoon relationship from the first because they resented missionary interference in their customs, and a reaction swept through the society when it became apparent that Afrikaner settlers were infiltrating their territory with the connivance of British officials, and that the missionaries were not capable of stopping them. By the end of the 1840s nearly all Moshoeshoe's councilors and kinsfolk who had been baptized had left the church and resumed the customs the missionaries had banned. During his later

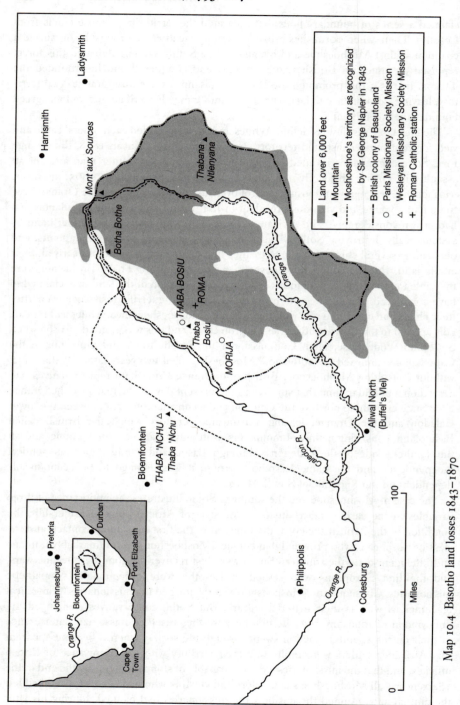

Map 10.4 Basotho land losses 1843–1870

years Moshoeshoe himself revived the initiation schools and seems to have placed greater reliance on Sotho remedies than on Christian precepts; and though both Catholic and Protestant missionaries implored him to accept baptism as he lay on his deathbed at Thaba Bosiu, Moshoeshoe himself died unbaptized.

Conclusion

By 1870, there was a crucial difference between the fate of the indigenous inhabitants of the Americas and that of the Bantu-speaking peoples of southern Africa. Indigenous societies throughout the Americas had collapsed under the impact of European colonization, not so much as a result of brutality in the conquest process (though there was much of that), but essentially because after millennia of isolation from the rest of the world they had no defenses against measles, smallpox, and other diseases introduced by Europeans. Bantu-speaking Africans, on the other hand, shared a common disease environment with Europe and Asia and were able to survive, despite the slaughter and famine of the mfecane, the catastrophe of the Xhosa cattle-killing, and White colonization.

In 1870, southern Africa was a region of great human variety, ranging from prosperous merchants operating in Cape Town, the vibrant, outward-looking, cosmopolitan capital of a White-dominated British colony, to African subsistence farmers in autonomous kingdoms and chiefdoms, such as Mzilikazi's Ndebele kingdom in modern Zimbabwe.

Whites were the most powerful people in the region, but they were by no means hegemonic. They numbered little more than a quarter of a million – a minute figure compared with North America and only slightly larger than that of Algeria. About 190,000 Whites lived in the Cape Colony, 18,000 in Natal, and perhaps 13,000 in the Orange Free State and 30,000 in the South African Republic (the Transvaal). Everywhere they were outnumbered: in the Cape Colony, from the west coast eastward to the Fish River by coloured people – descendants of the Khoisan indigenous inhabitants, of imported slaves, and of Whites; elsewhere by Bantu-speaking Africans. In the region as a whole, Bantu-speaking Africans outnumbered Whites by at least twelve to one.

In 1870, moreover, southern Africa was still peripheral to the capitalist economy of Europe and North America. The Cape Colony, as Hobart Houghton has said, was still "a sparsely populated country largely engaged in pastoral farming and self-subsistence agriculture, too poor to advance rapidly in domestic capital formation, and lacking any exploitable resources to attract foreign capital." Cape Town, with about 30,000, was the only town with more than 10,000 inhabitants. Internal communications by horse or by ox-wagon were over rough roads, impassable after heavy rains. Manufacturing industries were few and small. Exports consisted exclusively of unprocessed primary produce, notably wool and ivory; their value amounted to only about £2.5 million a year, and over 80 per cent of the external trade was carried by British ships to British ports. Conditions were similar in Natal. The Afrikaner republics had even weaker infrastructures and were even more tenuously connected with the European or

American economy; but they, too, were dependent on British trade channels for manufactured goods, since they had not been able to develop a trade route through the tsetse-infested country to Delagoa Bay.

Most White southern Africans, like those in Europe and the United States at that time, believed that they were superior to darker skinned peoples (and "scientific" racism was growing in virulence during the final third of the nineteenth century). But the Whites themselves were divided by an ethnic cleavage. Most British settlers continued to look to Britain, in the last resort, for cultural, economic, and military support. Most Afrikaners, except for a few in the vicinity of Cape Town, had long since severed their European roots and were suspicious of Great Britain and the colonial bureaucracies. There were also great class differences among the South African Whites, who included wealthy merchants, prosperous wool farmers, patriarchal landowners, their poor rural clients, and a small but growing number of urban workers.

All the independent African chiefdoms were experiencing White influences. They were frequently visited by hunters and traders, and most of them had resident missionaries. Although the chiefs employed messengers to keep themselves informed about what was going on elsewhere, they never managed to join forces in resistance to the intruders. In every phase of expansion, Whites exploited the divisions within and among chiefdoms. In 1835, voortrekkers were assisted by a Tswana chief when they drove Mzilikazi north of the Limpopo; in 1840, Mpande's followers fought the decisive battle that overthrew Dingane; Mfengu played major roles in the conquest of the southern Nguni; and the Orange Free State used African allies in its wars against the southern Sotho.

By 1870, many African farmers were taking advantage of their new economic opportunities. As Colin Bundy has shown, besides continuing to produce most of the food they consumed, many Mfengu and Xhosa also grew a surplus of grain, which they traded for imported goods. This development often began on mission stations where, freed from control by conservative traditional authorities, they experimented with new implements such as plows, new crops such as wheat, and new agricultural methods such as irrigation. The Mfengu were particularly eager innovators because their social system had been thoroughly disrupted by the mfecane wars. Similarly, as we have seen, the southern Sotho were producing a large surplus of grain by 1870. Indeed, African cultivators were the main suppliers of grain to the Afrikaners in both republics.

But the capacity of Africans to become stable communities of self-sufficient peasants, producing grain for the market, was offset by their land losses and by White exactions of African labor. Wherever they settled in southern Africa, British immigrants as well as Afrikaners were dependent on laborers drawn from communities outside their own, and they often used violent methods to obtain and control them. In the western districts of the Cape Colony, the laborers were Coloured people; elsewhere, they were Bantu-speaking Africans, except in coastal Natal where the sugar-planters employed Indians. Labor relations in the Cape Colony were regulated by laws which did not overtly discriminate against people on racial grounds but which nevertheless assisted employers by making breach of contract a criminal offense. There, African farm laborers received rations and a small payment in cash or the equivalent in kind, such as a cow for a year's service. In the Transvaal, at the other extreme, local officials who were themselves White farmers were entitled to compel Africans to work for Whites, and wages, if paid at all, were almost invariably in kind.

The Africans' responses to Christianity varied with the efficacy of their norms and institutions. As long as they were independent, most Africans found no greater use for missionaries than as informants about the wider world, as scribes for communicating with White authorities, and (if possible) as suppliers of firearms and ammunition. This was still the case with the Zulu under Mpande. Mzilikazi, too, admitted a few missionaries to his kingdom north of the Limpopo, but he kept them isolated and did not allow his subjects to be baptized. But when an African community's confidence in its traditional institutions and beliefs had been shaken by conquest, its members became interested in the missionaries for additional reasons – as sources of new spiritual insights, magical powers, and social and political ideas that might help them accommodate to their new circumstances.

Moshoeshoe responded positively to the missionaries when the confidence of his people had been shattered by the mfecane; but when it became apparent that his missionaries were not preventing other Whites from encroaching on his territory, he confined them to subordinate roles and relied primarily on traditional Sotho sources of power. Later in the nineteenth century, however, after the southern Sotho had been brought under alien administration, they converted to Christianity in massive numbers; and so did the other African communities.

Few Xhosa converted so long as they felt capable of resisting conquest. In the 1850s, after military resistance had failed repeatedly, some resorted to the drastic remedy of cattle killing – in obedience to the orders of their ancestors as revealed in a prophetic vision. The failure of that remedy made it clear that their customary physical and spiritual resources no longer sufficed, and during the 1860s, for the first time, large numbers of Xhosa adopted Christianity as a means of accommodating to the wider world.

By 1870 southern Africa was on the brink of a radical transformation. Three years earlier, a diamond had been found near the confluence of the Harts and the Orange rivers, in arid country west of Bloemfontein. Within twenty-five years, southern Africa would have a very special niche in the capitalist world economy as the producer of the lion's share of the world's annual output of gold as well as gem diamonds. With its immense appetite for labor, the mining industry became the hub of an integrated regional economy. But there were continuities in the structure of South African society. Embedded in the pre-industrial racial order, the industry split its labor force between well-paid, stable, White workers and poorly paid, migrant, African workers; which paved the way in turn for the twentieth-century policies of segregation and apartheid.

Suggestions for further reading

Bundy, Colin, *The Rise and Fall of the South African Peasantry*, 2nd edn, Cape Town: David Philip, 1986.

Crais, Clifton C., *White Supremacy and Black Resistance in PreIndustrial South Africa: The Making of the Colonial Order in the Eastern Cape, 1770–1865*, Cambridge: Cambridge University Press, 1992.

Delius, Peter, *The Land Belongs To Us: The Pedi Polity, the Boers and the British in the Nineteenth Century Transvaal*, Berkeley and Los Angeles: University of California Press, 1984.

Elizabeth A. Eldredge, *A South African Kingdom: The Pursuit of Security in Nineteenth-Century Lesotho*, Cambridge: Cambridge University Press, 1993.

Fredrickson, George M., *White Supremacy: A Comparative Study of American and South African History*, New York: Oxford University Press, 1981.

Galbraith, John S., *Reluctant Empire: British Policy on the South African Frontier 1834–1854*, Berkeley and Los Angeles: University of California Press, 1963.

Macmillan, W.M., *Bantu, Boer and Briton. The Making of the South African Native Problem*, rev. edn, Oxford: Oxford University Press, 1963.

Marais, Johannes S., *The Cape Coloured People 1652–1937*. Reprinted from the 1939 edn. Johannesburg: Witwatersrand University Press, 1957.

Marks, Shula and Anthony Atmore (eds), *Economy and Society in Pre-Industrial South Africa*, London: Longman, 1980.

Maylam, Paul, *A History of the African People of South Africa*, New York: St Martin's Press, 1986.

Mostert, Noel, *Frontiers: The Epic of South Africa's Creation and the Tragedy of the Xhosa People*, New York: Knopf, 1992.

Omer-Cooper J.D., *The Zulu Aftermath. A Nineteenth Century Revolution in Bantu Africa*, Evanston, Ill.: Northwestern University Press, 1966.

Peires, J.B., *The Dead Will Arise: Nongqawuse and the Great Xhosa Cattle-Killing Movement of 1856–7*, Johannesburg: Ravan Press, 1989.

Ross, A., *John Philip, 1775–1851: Missions, Race and Politics in South Africa*, Aberdeen, 1986.

Ross, Robert, *Adam Kok's Griqua: A Study in the Development of Stratification in South Africa*, Cambridge: Cambridge University Press, 1976.

Thompson, Leonard, *Survival in Two Worlds: Moshoeshoe of Lesotho, 1786–1870*, Oxford: Clarendon Press, 1975.

Thompson, Leonard, *The Political Mythology of Apartheid*, New Haven: Yale University Press, 1985.

Van Jaarsveld, F.A., *The Afrikaner's Interpretation of South African History*, Cape Town: Oxford University Press, 1964.

Walker, Eric A., *The Great Trek*, 5th edn, London: Black, 1965.

(See also the bibliography for Chapter 9, especially Elphick and Giliomee, (eds), *The Shaping of South African Society 1652–1840*.)

11

NORTH AFRICA IN THE SHADOW OF EUROPE (c. 1780–1880)

North Africa, like southern Africa, met the European threat several decades before it reached the equatorial belt between the Sahara and the Limpopo. The threat, however, took different forms in the far north and the far south. The southern tip of Africa had been comparatively isolated from the intercommunicating zone until the maritime revolution of the fifteenth century, whereas North Africa had made contact with a wider world at an early date. The seventeenth-century establishment of a European community at the Cape was a new thing in African history, but the Napoleonic invasion of Egypt in 1789 simply brought one more Frankish army to the Levant, where Frankish armies had marched from time to time since the eleventh century – just as North African armies had marched in Spain and Sicily and North African navies had often dominated the Mediterranean sea lanes. But the reappearance of European power at the end of the eighteenth century was something more than another swing of the pendulum. Europe was then beginning to enter the industrial age, which was to give the Europeans a new advantage in military power. By the 1780s or so, Europe's technological advantage was great enough to be apparent to all but the most backward-looking, but Europe's potential power was not yet effective power. For North Africa, it became effective during the century that followed, first and most intensively for Egypt, last and most weakly for Morocco.

Ottoman reform

These developments must be seen in a broader perspective than that of Africa alone, even of North Africa. In theory, at least, the whole of North Africa east of Morocco was simply a set of Ottoman provinces ruled from Istanbul. In spite of its weakening control during the eighteenth century, the Ottoman Empire remained the pivotal political and military defense against the Christian menace – not only for North Africa but for the Muslim world as a whole. The Ottoman state was a religious state, in a way that no Western state was. The sultan was not only a temporal ruler; he was also the recognized *khalifa*, the successor on earth of Muhammad himself. He ruled in his two different capacities – as administrative head and as a religious leader – through two separate sets of officials. One was the ordinary bureaucratic structure of government administration over provinces and their subdivisions, which was theoretically exercised through slave-administrators but in practice was exercised by local men whose *de facto* authority Istanbul had been forced to accept. The other was the religious and judicial hierarchy, drawn from the class of *'ulamā*, or Muslim clerics. These men supplied the *qadi*, or judges in Muslim law, both temporal and spiritual. Their hierarchy reached its own peak with the office of chief mufti, or *seyh-ül-Islam*, who could depose the sultan himself for a breach of Muslim law. The significant point is that the *'ulamā* were a social and political body with power independent of the sultan.

After the mid-eighteenth century, central control tended to weaken throughout the empire, even as it did in the Maghrib and Egypt. Provincial magnates known as *āyan* increased the powers they had acquired through their wealth, land, or government positions as tax farmers. Some were provincial officials who, like the Karamanli family in Tripoli, made themselves virtually independent. But as the power of the royal slave-administrators declined, that of the slave-soldiers, or Janissaries, increased. Recruited as children from beyond the frontiers in much the same way as the Egyptian Mamluks or the sub-Saharan *'abid* forces in Morocco, the Janissaries constituted the core of the standing army. It was all too easy for any of these military groups to translate its physical power into political power that eventually came to be recognized and imbedded in the informal constitution of the state.

The external threat to the empire came first of all on the land frontiers with Austria and Russia. The first important territorial losses in Europe went back to 1699, and further cessions were made to Austria in 1718. In 1774, the Ottoman Empire experienced its first significant loss of Muslim-populated territory when the Crimea fell to Russia. In 1787–92, the Ottomans recovered militarily in the war against Russia and Austria, but it was already clear that the Ottoman state would have to be thoroughly reformed if it were to survive over the long run.

For nineteenth-century commentators, "reform" meant much the same thing as "modernization" means today; it implied some adaptation of Western technology, at least military technology. The goal was to make the Ottoman Empire defensible against a major Western attack, and that required Western weapons. The first really serious reform effort was made in 1792–93, when Sultan Selim III issued a comprehensive set of administrative and military regulations known collectively as the *Nizam-i Cedid*, the New Order. The immediate objective was to create a corps of regular infantry, trained and equipped along the same lines as European infantry of the period. This force needed officers trained in a new way, which called for new military and naval schools, staffed initially by French officers. It also cost money, because it was intended to supplement rather than replace the Janissaries, and that in turn called for administrative and fiscal reform.

This effort produced two consequences that were to crop up again and again whenever the Ottoman government – or a North African government – tried to put through military reforms. First, it created a new class of people with power: the military officers with specialized Western training, many of them trained in western Europe. Second, it produced a desire for modernization; along with their technical training, these officers inevitably came into broader contact with Western culture, and they

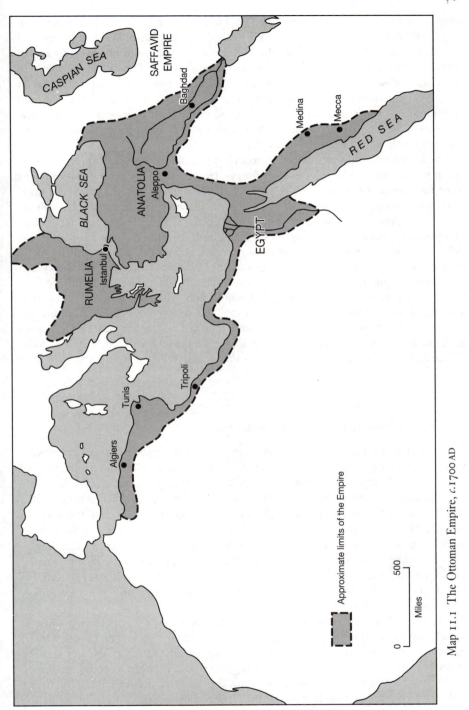

Map 11.1 The Ottoman Empire, *c.*1700 AD

often came to admire some aspects of it. They might not end as avid Westernizers, but they were impressed by Ottoman military weakness in the face of Western power; and they were especially impressed, as the nineteenth century wore on, by the material wealth of industrial societies. In present-day terms, they would be called *modernizers* in the special sense of that term which regards the goal of modernization as the creation of one of the several kinds of societies capable of high levels of production and consumption – levels equivalent to those found in the most developed, technological societies of the time. Modernization in this sense could be many things to many people, not necessarily slavish imitation of the West.

The New Order thus introduced a modernizing military elite into Ottoman society, and it threatened the old order in several ways. By increasing the central government's need for money, it tightened the relaxed fiscal relations between the provincial magnates and the central government. Fiscal reform alienated important people. Military reform threatened the Janissaries even more directly. Others saw the new technology as a possible source of contamination for Islam itself, because the new knowledge was infidel knowledge, and this fear was most prevalent among the 'ulamā. Military modernization, in short, might be essential to save the Ottoman state, but it also threatened to redistribute political and economic rewards within the state. The sultan and the New Order (as the new units were soon called) would gain, while the āyan, the Janissaries, and the 'ulamā would lose a little. In 1807, the conservatives rallied against the reforms, drove Selim from the throne, and returned to the old order. Thus, with modernization silenced for a generation in the Ottoman homeland, Egypt and the Maghrib were left to deal with Muslim weakness and Western strength in their own ways.

Egyptian modernization: the first steps

The province of Egypt, not the Turkish homeland, took the first lasting steps toward modernization. Egypt was also the first major African state to be subdued militarily and occupied by a European power, and the two "firsts" were connected in ways that made the Egyptian experience a precedent for some and a warning for others, though it had special features that were uniquely Egyptian. The new kind of European threat began with the French occupation of 1798 to 1801, an event more directly tied to the strategy of the Napoleonic wars than it was to French intentions in Egypt itself. The Anglo-French wars of the eighteenth century were part of a worldwide competition for empire stretching from India to North America. The French move on Egypt was connected to the Indian strategy, and it was ended by British naval pressure on the French supply lines – not by an Ottoman counter-attack.

The French occupation took place at a time when Egypt was peculiarly open to outside influence. Mamluk rule had reached a nadir in the 1790s. The Egyptian social structure found itself divided between the Mamluk aristocracy at the top and the ordinary peasants, or *fellahin*, at the bottom, with few in between to act as mediators. Some merchants had wealth, but their political power was insignificant. The 'ulamā had more power, but mainly through their religious prestige and command of the educational structure, at the apex of which was the mosque and school of al-Azhar. In these circumstances, the French presence was at once an example of Western power, visible to all, and of Western technological progress, visible only to some. It also disrupted whatever might have been left of the Mamluk political order.

After the French withdrawal, Istanbul once more sent in an effective military force. This balanced the remaining power of the Mamluks and opened the way for an enterprising individual to become the autonomous ruler of the Egyptian province. Muhammad ʿAli began as commander of the Albanian battalion of the Ottoman expeditionary force, a part of the New Order. Through astute maneuvering, he worked with the local ʾulamā to mobilize the middle ground of Egyptian opinion, taking advantage of factional divisions among the Mamluk aristocrats and representing himself as the champion of Egyptian interests against the alien authority of Ottomans and Mamluks alike. Istanbul acquiesced, as it had done so often in the past when confronted by local magnates, and appointed him *wali* of Egypt in 1805. His real power, however, began in 1807 after he had weathered a British naval landing at Alexandria. Selim III's deposition the same year left him free to run Egypt in his own way until his death in 1848.

Muhammad ʿAli's program in Egypt was a direct outgrowth of Selim III's New Order. The changes Muhammad ʿAli made were clearly designed to modernize and strengthen the military force, but military power was not necessarily an end in itself. It is less clear what Muhammad ʿAli had as his ultimate goal. It was certainly not Egyptian greatness or national independence, nor even an early form of Arab nationalism against the Turks. Muhammad ʿAli and his group ruled whatever Arab provinces they could control, but they recognized ultimate Ottoman suzerainty, and the language of administration continued to be Turkish, not the Arabic speech of the country. It could of course be argued that strengthening Egypt was a step toward strengthening Islam against the infidel Europeans, but Muhammad ʿAli was willing to work with Europeans when it suited his purposes, and to work against Ottoman power most of the time. His actions suggest that he was mainly interested in establishing his own power and that of his friends over as large a section of the Ottoman Empire as they could comfortably control.

The intermediate goal of military modernization itself called for sweeping changes in Egyptian society. Some of the most crucial were in education. The existing educational system was based on the village Koranic schools. Higher levels of study led on to the training given the ʾulamā to fit them for leadership in religious and judicial affairs. None of this met the need for military officers and bureaucrats conversant with Western technology. Muhammad ʿAli simply by-passed the existing system without seeking to reform it, creating instead a system of secular state schools modeled on those of Italy and France. Initially, they were staffed by Western teachers, then by Egyptians trained in Europe, and finally, after the mid-century, by Egyptians trained in the system itself.

The government created ancillary services to supplement the new educational establishment. A state printing press brought out books in Arabic – with the help of a translation bureau to make Western knowledge more readily available – military technology at first, then the sciences, and finally even literature. The program also included specialized higher education, with a medical school to begin with, followed by an engineering school modeled on the French Polytechnique. By 1849, its director was a Western-trained Egyptian engineer.

A secular, modernizing program of this kind might have appeared as a threat to the 'ulamā, especially to those attached to al-Azhar mosque. Similar programs were seen as a threat in other Muslim countries and would be, later in the century, in Egypt, but, in the first instance, important Azharites looked on Western learning as a way of reforming al-Azhar itself. Egyptian literature and scholarship had a deeply pessimistic tone in the last decades of the eighteenth century. People were alarmed for the safety of Islamic society; but they were not alarmed enough to lose their belief in the ultimate value of the Arabic language and Islamic culture; and Western knowledge, it was thought, could help rejuvenate older traditions. The translation program, for example, called for new attention to Arabic language studies. It began at the technical level with a search for the Arabic equivalent of Western scientific concepts, but it moved on into a much broader renewal of Arabic literary studies, with attention to classical Arabic as well as the language of ordinary speech, which began to take on literary form through the rise of a newspaper press.

Military modernization demanded economic development. Muhammad 'Ali began with the aim of wide industrialization, with government-operated factories turning out products as diverse as textiles, sugar, paper, glass, arms, and chemicals. Later, emphasis shifted to the more lopsided development of long-staple cotton for export in return for European manufactures. This required capital investment in irrigation works instead of factories, because irrigation water was necessary for summer cultivation in the season of the low Nile. Animal power and some water-powered devices had been used for centuries to raise water to the fields when the Nile was low, but extensive cultivation called for mechanical pumps, or for canals to carry the water from dams far upstream. Egyptian conversion to year-round cultivation was only begun in Muhammad 'Ali's time. The most important steps were to come later, during the British occupation toward the end of the nineteenth century, and again, after independence was regained, with the building of the Aswan high dam in the 1960s. The decision to concentrate Egypt's resources on production for export rather than on diversified industry may well have been correct in terms of short-run gain for the Egyptian state. In the long run, however, it slanted the economy toward a dangerous and fragile dependence on one crop, with minimal protection against shifts in the world market.

The government also needed to redistribute the national income so that more would go to the state to pay for all these programs, and less to private citizens. The first and easiest step was to expropriate the wealth of the Mamluks and other tax farmers left from the old regime. To that end, Muhammad 'Ali revolutionized Egyptian land tenure. Where tax farmers had once been virtual landlords drawing unearned income from the work of the peasantry, a new land survey made it possible to tax the peasants directly. This increased state revenue, though it may have decreased the real living standards of ordinary farmers. Muhammad 'Ali also saw that some of the land was given to his family and other supporters, who held it tax-free. State monopolies were another source of government revenue. The government controlled all exports, buying agricultural products at a fixed and low price and selling them on the world market at a higher price.

Though Muhammad 'Ali is usually called a modernizer, he was one only in a restricted sense of the term. The end product was a modern army in the European fashion, but, at mid-century, the Egyptian economy and society were less, not more, able to move on toward the autonomous development of a balanced economy capable of high productivity and high consumption. Raising agricultural production through state action set the stage for a later weakening of the class of small tradesmen, of the merchant class, and of the 'ulamā, while it simultaneously strengthened the power of the bureaucracy, the army, and foreign commercial interests. That result, however, was hardly apparent until the final third of the century.

Meanwhile, Muhammad 'Ali's payoff was a military establishment strong enough to make him virtually independent of the Ottoman Empire, and to expand his control beyond Egypt. In the 1810s, he sent military expeditions into Arabia against the Wahabi movement; this gave Egypt control of the holy cities of Mecca and Medina. Later, in the 1830s, Egypt occupied Syria and Palestine and threatened a successful attack on Istanbul itself. The prospect of Muhammad 'Ali as a new Ottoman sultan, however, brought in the balancing mechanisms of the European state system. It was already British policy to support Istanbul against other powers, especially Austria or Russia, while France had patronized Muhammad 'Ali. France and Britain now joined together to stop his drive to the north, by a private agreement that he should not take Istanbul. In return, they recognized him as hereditary ruler of Egypt, with the title of Khedive, though he still acknowledged the ultimate, if theoretical, sovereignty of the Sultan.

Secondary empire in the Nilotic Sudan

Meanwhile, from the 1820s, Muhammad 'Ali's forces had been active south of the Sahara, and the push up the Nile into the Sudan had a different character from the struggles over Ottoman provinces. The new conquests lay beyond any previous Ottoman territory, and they fitted a pattern of the greatest importance to tropical Africa in the nineteenth century – the pattern of "secondary empire." This type of empire-building was secondary in the sense that African states exploited a military technology whose source was Europe. Yet the empire builders, whether Africans or overseas Europeans, were free from direct European control.

Viewed schematically, the process was simple, though capable of infinite variation. Repeatedly through history, people who suddenly gained command of a military innovation could lord it over those who remained ignorant of it. This had happened with the use of chariots, again with the first cavalry, still later with armored heavy cavalry. It happened repeatedly during the nineteenth century as rapid-fire weapons were carried beyond their source in Europe. It was not, perhaps, inevitable that those who first gained control of the new weapons should use them to create large territorial units – that they should become empire builders – but the temptation was always present.

The empire builders on the periphery had a different position from those at the center – in this case, from the Europeans whose technology created the new differen-

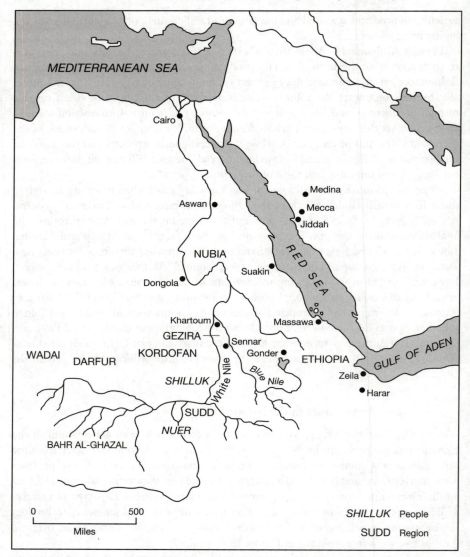

Map 11.2 The Nilotic Sudan in the nineteenth century

tials in military power. Because the Europeans had the knowledge and the industrial plant to create new devices and thus to preserve their lead, they had an advantage that was to last for decades and even centuries. On the periphery, by contrast, whoever first came to control European weapons had only an ephemeral advantage, to last until his neighbors had done the same. In the Ottoman Empire, for example, the first to master the use of modernized forces gained an advantage, as Muhammad ʿAli did for Egypt, but others could and did follow the same path within a few decades. (Muhammad ʿAli's power in Ottoman affairs was also always limited to what states at the center of industrialization, like Britain and France, were willing to put up with.) On the periphery, in the Nilotic Sudan, guns and European tactics were still unfamiliar. The Egyptian advantage was that much greater there, even though it was still temporary. This transitional quality may help to explain why people with a windfall advantage were tempted to use it before it disappeared, and why new military techniques spread so rapidly beyond the original center of diffusion.

This phenomenon was not confined to the offshoots of industrialization. The Zulu technique of fighting as disciplined infantry in *impi* formations owed nothing to Europe, yet it spread throughout southern Africa from the first decade of the nineteenth century in the great outburst from Zululand, laying a train of secondary empire-building stretching from Natal northwest to western Zambia and north more than a thousand miles into what was to be central Tanzania. In southern Africa, nearly simultaneously, European settlers developed an effective tactic of fighting partly on foot, partly on horseback for mobility. They could beat the Zulu impi, as it turned out, but their tactic was less revolutionary against the Xhosa beyond the Fish River frontier, because the Xhosa themselves had adopted the same one. In this case, the periphery of diffusion had passed beyond the periphery of settler expansion before the Afrikaners could capitalize on their advantage. With the Great Trek, however, the Afrikaners could catch up and out-distance the periphery of diffusion by moving onto the high veld and down into central Natal. There, they could enjoy the same kind of advantage the Zulu had enjoyed against less-disciplined infantry a generation earlier. One possible interpretation is to see both the offshoots of the mfecane and the offshoots of the Great Trek as secondary empires, one with its roots in Zululand, the other based partly on the distant technology of Europe and partly on innovations made by European settlers in the Cape Colony and its fringes.

The Egyptian conquest of the Nilotic Sudan was more distinctly based on European models, and it foreshadowed more clearly the kinds of secondary empire-building that were to follow in tropical Africa during the nineteenth century. This time, the military innovation also involved firearms, as it did with the Boer mounted infantry, but the problem of slow reloading time for muzzle-loaded muskets was met in a different way. Egyptian musketeers received intensive training in disciplined loading and firing by ranks, combined with the use of mobile field artillery.

These tactics, already used in Europe during the eighteenth century, were to change in the nineteenth with the invention of newer, more accurate, and faster firing guns. In effect, Europe was on the eve of a permanent revolution in military technology that would give secondary empires a longer lease on life. Those with access to the latest European weapons after about 1860 or so could count on meeting enemies with the last generation's weapons in their hands. In the immediate situation of the 1820s, however, Muhammad 'Ali's modernized armies fought with the weapons and tactics used in Europe during the Napoleonic wars, though at this point nothing quite so elaborate and overpowering was required against the peoples of the Nilotic Sudan.

The rain-watered land south of the desert and the desert fringes was then a patchwork of different political organizations – some sedentary along the Nile valley, including the desert Nile through Nubia, others nomadic in different ways. Arab infiltration had produced a change in language and culture over recent centuries. Although the net Arabian contribution to the gene pool of the present-day northern Sudan is estimated at only about 5 to 10 per cent, most of the nomadic peoples and some of the sedentaries were already Arabic-speaking by the nineteenth century. The result was similar, in fact, to the Arabic impact on the Maghrib and western Sahara, where about the same addition to the population had also brought a widespread change in language. As in the Maghrib, where Berber persisted in the mountains and some of the desert fringes, islands of Nubian speech persisted at a few points on the Nile and in some highland regions. The Beja nomads of the Red Sea hills also kept their original language and much of their older culture, though they too had long since become Muslim. Other nomadic cultures were more strongly Arabian, especially that of the camel nomads who occupied the desert fringes from the latitude of Sennar to the great southward bend of the desert Nile. The *baqqara*, or cattle-keeping nomads, occupied another ecological niche in better-watered lands further south, equivalent to that of the Fulbe of West Africa. They too took on a good deal of Arabic culture along with the Arabic language.

The Arabian cultural penetration was much weaker among sedentary people, and it stopped somewhat short of the point where the sudd blocked the Nile as a viable transportation route. The people here and further south were mainly Nilotes, related to the Luo who had moved off into East Africa (see Chapter 4). The Shilluk lived along the White Nile, principally on its west bank, and were densely settled in a society estimated at about a million people in the early nineteenth century. Although the effective political unit was the village, the Shilluk also had an elaborately stratified society with a complex political ideology and institutions of a kingdom in which the god-king was intimately related to the fertility of the earth. If he became ill or old, he was killed and a more fitting man set in his place.

To the south of the sudd and the west of the main Nile lived other Nilotes in stateless societies like those of the Dinka and Nuer, with a complex adaptation to their difficult environment with its seasonal alternations between drought and flood. These and similar peoples had long been subject to sporadic slave raids from the northern Sudan, which fed the trickle of slaves exported north to Egypt or across the Red Sea to Arabia.

The main agents of the slave trade – and the main agents of Muslim cultural penetration to the south – were merchants, usually called *jallaba*, the Sudanese Arabic word for petty trader. Many were Ja'ali, Arabized Nubians from the desert reaches of the Nile. They claimed aristocratic ancestry in Arabia, but their physical appearance and most of their culture were more Nubian than Arabian. A few still spoke Nubian, but most had shifted to Arabic as their home language. Political troubles in their Nubian homeland in the eighteenth century had driven many of the Ja'ali to the south and west, some as far as Darfur and others up the White Nile, where they were to play an increasingly active political and economic role in the nineteenth century.

In 1820–21, when Muhammad 'Ali began his attack up the Nile, the region's political structures were even weaker than they had usually been in the past. The Funj state of Sennar was limited to the *gezira* itself, the area between the Blue and White Niles. Kordofan to the west was under the vague hegemony of the Sultanate of Darfur.

The Nubian Nile was politically divided, with some sections under nomadic Arab domination, while the region around Dongola had fallen to refugee Mamluks from Egypt. Muhammad ʿAli's first objective was this remaining center of Mamluk power, because Mamluk power in the south could be a danger at some later moment of crisis. Once he controlled the Nubian Nile, he could tap the source of slaves among the Nilotes, and slaves were important as military manpower to an Egyptian state that preferred not to draft the native fellahin.

Muhammad ʿAli's initial expeditionary force was only 4000 men, roughly the size of the army Morocco had sent against Songhai in the sixteenth century. It had to fight the Mamluks for control of Nubia, but the mere threat of force made the Funj sultanate surrender. The Egyptians then detached Kordofan from Darfur and added it to their new empire. By the mid-1820s, they had recruited an army by purchase in the far south and trained it to serve as the occupying force. Khartoum, where the Blue and White Niles join, became the capital of the Egyptian Sudan, but the new government made no serious effort to change either the society or the economy. It confiscated many slaves belonging to the former Sudanese aristocracy, and reopened trade up and down the Nile Valley, but the frontiers first established were left unchanged until the 1860s.

Government and society in the Maghrib: the Ottoman regencies

The external threat to the Maghrib was from Europe, just as it was to Egypt and the Ottoman Empire, and it posed the same problems. The crucial problem was military weakness, but military reforms cost money. New revenue would require administrative and political change, raising once more the basic question: who should control the power of the state? This last question was even more complex in the Maghrib than it was in Egypt, because here the distribution of political power was more diverse.

In Tripoli, the Karamanli family continued as hereditary pashas, but they remained in power only by balancing off the quasi-independent powers of important groups such as the commerce-raiders' guilds and other merchants in the port against the influence of the nomads and semi-nomadic leaders from the hinterland. During the long reign of Yusuf Karamanli (1795–1835), European naval powers began to take a stronger stand against commerce raiding. Even the distant United States mounted counter-raids against Tripoli during the Napoleonic wars. After Waterloo, the British and French consuls became more active in Tripolitanian affairs. When the Karamanli did nothing to modernize the military establishment, they became potential prey to any power that did. The Anglo-French rivalry kept either one from acting on its own, but the revived Ottoman power, the Bey of Tunis to the north, or even Muhammad ʿAli of Egypt were potential and increasing threats to the Karamanli after the 1820s.

The crisis came in the early 1830s, with the nomads of the steppe, the Tunisians, and the threat of British or French intervention all playing a role. The victory, however, went to an expeditionary force from Istanbul, which deposed the Karamanli dynasty and reimposed direct Ottoman rule – to last until the Italian invasion of 1911–12.

In the second half of the eighteenth century, Tunisia too had settled down under its own dynasty, though here the beys, unlike the Karamanli, still recognized Ottoman authority in theory. By 1800, however, Turkish influence in military and court circles

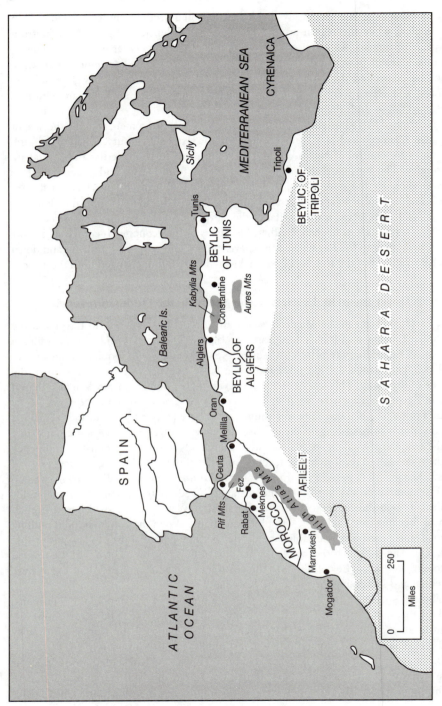

Map 11.3 The Maghrib in the late eighteenth century

was weaker that it was in either Algiers or Tripoli. The ports were better articulated with the life of the hinterland and less dependent on commerce raiding. Yet the European threat was more serious here than it was elsewhere. In spite of Anglo-French rivalries, the British and French consuls forced the beys to make trade concessions and to change some policies, including the abolition of slavery in 1819. Partly to counter this pressure, Tunis moved faster than either of the other regencies to modernize its army and to abolish the remaining Janissaries, though these reforms came still later than they did in either Istanbul or Cairo.

The prosperity of the Deylic of Algiers, built on commerce raiding, had declined sharply after 1700 or so, as the Christian powers were better able to protect their commerce and less willing to pay protection money. Spain still controlled a series of port towns, or presidio, scattered along the Moroccan-Algerian coast from Ceuta east to Oran, but Spain relinquished Oran in 1791, and Algiers was less disturbed by consular pressure on government affairs than Tunis and Tripoli were.

But Algiers had special problems in its hinterland. By 1800, the dey himself had become the political tool of the Turkish garrison and certain factions of the local port oligarchy, and his direct authority was recognized only in the province of Algiers. Further afield, the country had fallen under the control of three beys, each exercising within his own beylic the same kind of authority the dey exercised over his own province. But the dey and the beys together controlled only about a sixth of the present republic. Arab and Berber nomads controlled the desert fringes to the south. The Kabylia, a densely populated mountain area, was an independent Berber-speaking enclave stretching east from the vicinity of Algiers nearly to Constantine. Similar Berber mountaineers in the Aurès mountains were independent most of the time, often in theory as well as in practice. Still other regions were autonomous under the leadership of important Muslim brotherhoods, and many important family heads could assert an independent power against the authority of a bey or the dey himself. It was not merely that the power of Algiers gradually dwindled with distance from the port; the whole territory was pockmarked with different kinds of local government, each related differently to the authorities in Algiers – if not completely independent.

The Sherifian empire of Morocco

Morocco was similar, but the crucial difference was that here a local dynasty stood at the head of the government, whereas the authority of the deys and beys derived from the Ottomans. The sultans of the Sherifian Empire of Morocco had still another source of support. As descendants of the Prophet, their religious authority gave them a shadowy national leadership. The idea of nationality is so suggestive of nineteenth-century Europe that it can be misleading to use the term "nation" of any African state. Yet nineteenth-century Morocco had some of the attributes of nationhood; people over a vast stretch of territory recognized their ultimate allegiance to the sultan and identified themselves with the Sherifian Empire – not only in present-day Morocco but south and east into what was later to be the Spanish Sahara, Mauritania, and large parts of southern Algeria and northern Mali. But the territory of allegiance and the territory of effective government were quite distinct, and they were so recognized at the time. In either Asante or Buganda, the king's authority reached more uniformly to the frontiers than it did in Morocco, where the zone of close control was known as the *bled el makhzen* (literally "government country"), and the wider regions of more tenuous allegiance as the *bled es siba*, usually translated as "country in dissidence," though the translation obscures the main point. People in these regions might not always obey the sultan or pay taxes, but they did recognize his authority.

Makhzen, as a collective term, was not simply the government of the day. It was a social and political group centered on the sultan but including in the first circle of power his ministers, a council of notables, the *ca'id* (provincial governors), and the *qadi* (judges in Islamic law). It was also overwhelmingly Arabic or Arabized Berber in speech and culture. Because the makhzen was such a broad group, the sultan could not fully enforce his personal will, even within the bled el makhzen. Some members of the inner circle had their own independent sources of authority. They were therefore hard to control and even harder to remove from office. It was taken for granted that they and most other officeholders would try to enrich themselves, but they were also representatives of broader circles of interest in which the sultan's immediate lineage constituted only one element. This broader circle included the 'ulamā, who formed a pool of trained manpower for the post of qadi. It included the urban commercial people, who also occupied some government posts, especially in finance. And it included four specific extended lineages of nomadic Arabs, descended from those who had come to the Maghrib with the Hilalians in the eleventh century and later. These "tribes" were known collectively as the *gish* (literally "army"). They had a special obligation to support the sultan in case of need. Earlier, in the eighteenth century, the officers of the corps of slave-soldiers recruited in sub-Saharan Africa would also have counted as an important element in the makhzen, but they were no longer important in the nineteenth.

The makhzen, then, governed the bled el makhzen in much the same way the Dey of Algiers and his following governed the province of Algiers. This bled el makhzen changed size and shape from time to time, but it normally included two great areas of comparatively flat and fertile land: the triangle Fez–Meknès–Rabat and north along the coast to Tangier, and a second triangle from Rabat southward to Marrakesh and west to the Atlantic at Essaouira (formerly Mogador). Fez was the nineteenth-century capital, but Meknès, Rabat, and Marrakesh were also imperial cities that had once served in that role. The four together formed the urban core of the bled el makhzen, along with Tanger, where the European consuls kept their residences and where most foreign relations were conducted.

The bled es siba lay beyond, governed by other authorities in other ways. Some of the siba territory was just as tightly controlled as the bled el makhzen, but it was governed differently. The sedentary Berbers of the Atlas and Rif mountains went their own way, just as similar people did in the Algerian Kabylia and Aurès. Much of the rest of the siba was nomadic or semi-nomadic. In either case, the underlying political system was based on patrilineages of varying depth. Among the nomadic and semi-nomadic peoples, the ultimate patrilineage could be very large, including thousands if not tens of thousands of people, usually calling themselves by the name of their earliest common ancestor, such as the Banu Hillal in Arabic or the Aït Atta in Berber, meaning in either case "the children of Hillal" or the "children of Atta."

The very largest lineages, however, were usually too big to be effective political units. People still recognized their allegiance to the larger kinship units – sometimes called "tribes" or "confederations" (the terminology is not standardized) – but effective governance came through more manageable subsections. Nomads generally had larger effective kinship units than sedentary peoples did. Among sedentary Berbers, the most effective large unit was usually a patrilocal village, ruled by a council made up of the heads of lineage subsections, although more intimate aspects of social and economic life were governed by the extended family that could actually live and work together. Villages, in turn, could be grouped together in units of three or four, managed collectively by a similar council. Even so, the unit rarely exceeded eight hundred or so extended families, and larger units tended to break down if they grew much beyond that.

At the local level, the sedentary Berber political system operated very much like the segmentary political systems south of the Sahara, like those of the Tiv or the Ibo of Nigeria. The point of departure was the fact that only one line of descent, the male line, was taken into account. Each person therefore belonged unambiguously to a single lineage, but that single lineage could be defined by breaking off at one of several possible points up the line toward more and more remote ancestors. It could include merely the children of the same father, or the same grandfather; but, the further back the ancestor, the larger the politically effective lineage.

Lineage units of this kind could play many different roles in many different kinds of society, and they could also take the place of regular government. People naturally join together when threatened by outsiders. When insiders and outsiders were defined by kinship, a threat to one individual became a threat to that person's kinfolk as well, and in a segmentary system, people tended to respond according to their place on the ladder of kinship. If, for example, one of a set of brothers was attacked by his cousin in the male line (father's brother's son), the brothers, along with any junior kinsmen, would be expected to come to his defense. But the father, and men of the father's generation, would be expected to patch up the quarrel if possible. If a similar conflict developed between men from different villages, each could count on the support of his fellow villagers. In this way, opposition between individuals tended to become opposition between nearly equal groups – including many who would be more anxious to find an honorable solution than to fight to the finish. The result was a tendency to arbitrate when possible.

This form of social system, with its implicit possibility of conflict resolution, was extremely common throughout Berber society in the Maghrib, but it was not the system of government in all circumstances. The makhzen in Morocco or a foreign ruler like the Dey of Algiers were higher authorities who overrode the segmentary system at some times and in some places, but if higher authority was removed, segmentary conflict resolution came back into operation. Nor did it usually operate in a pure form, unmodified by other institutions. With the sedentary Berbers of the Kabylia, for example, permanent officers existed within the segmentary system. Each village normally had a council chosen by the lineage heads, with an executive officer to see that its decisions were carried out. This made each village a kind of microstate within a society that was stateless at higher levels. Inter-village conflicts were resolved within a framework of large-scale alliances called *saff*, which were distinct from the kinship system but nevertheless functioned much as kinship units functioned in a segmentary society. For the sake of schematic simplicity, the alliances are sometimes described as made up of alternating villages like the red and black squares on a checkerboard. Neighboring villages, therefore, tended to belong to opposing alliances. A quarrel would bring in other members of the alliance, so that it could be diffused into a spreading network of support – which was incidentally also a network of diplomacy to settle it.

In some parts of the Moroccan Atlas, on the other hand, the alliance system was much weaker, but a form of professional arbitration was provided by lineages of hereditary Muslim saints, called *Igurramen*. They were set apart from the rest of the community by descent from the Prophet and by their reputation for special piety or holiness, the quality called *baraka*. They also practiced a very strict form of pacifism that set them above the ordinary run of lineage quarrels, and incidentally kept them from being a threat to the actual or potential power of any of the other lineages. This combination of pacifism and renunciation of political office was common among Muslims on both sides of the Sahara. We have already seen it combined with commerce in the western Sudan (see Chapter 6), and it was one element in the West African opposition between secular-political and religious-commercial callings. Wherever it appeared, it opened a role for clerics to mediate disputes between other groups and generally to ease the operations of a stateless society that bordered on anarchy.

The fact that their sanctions were merely spiritual kept Igurramen neutral, but they nevertheless exercised real, if disinterested, power, and they could sometimes make a bid for direct secular power – as, indeed, had happened with the Alawite dynasty, still ruling in the nineteenth century.

The kind of power exercised by these communities of saints shaded off into another kind of religious power exercised by the heads of the sufi brotherhoods. The headship of a brotherhood was not necessarily passed by inheritance from father to son as sainthood was, and spiritual and political leadership was held by only one man, not by the whole community; but, whenever central governments weakened, these orders tended to make themselves into governments or quasi-governments. Even within the bled el makhzen, the important marabouts, as the French were to call them, were men to be consulted by a wise ruler.

Alongside regions of segmentary society and those with strong clerical influence, a more secular and autocratic kind of chiefdom was also found in the Moroccan bled es siba. Off to the south, a number of large nomadic Arab lineages dominated the region toward the Atlantic and on down to the Senegal valley, where the Maqʿil leaders of the Trarza, Brakna, or the Mbarek occupied the steppe and barely recognized the distant sultan. In the equivalent steppe position to the north of the desert, the Aït Atta, a very powerful Berber confederacy, dominated both the steppe and the important oases based on the flow of mountain rainfall toward the Sahara. In the Berber-speaking Atlas itself, powerful chiefdoms existed alongside stateless areas. These came into existence when a particular lineage played on the politics of segmentary opposition so successfully that it became dominant within its region. In the late nineteenth century, a leader of this kind dominated the eastern Rif mountains from Tetouan to Tanger, while the western Rif was stateless. In the high Atlas, four great Berber rulers of similar origins shared control over the mountains with pockets of segmentary society.

Relations between the makhzen and any of these principalities or stateless areas were highly variable. The great lords of the Atlas were sometimes at war with the sultan or in open rebellion. At other times, the sultan would give one of them an official appointment as ca'id over the territory he controlled in any case on his own authority. The sultan's main authority over the siba country was religious, inherited by descent from the Prophet, accepted and respected by the urban 'ulamā. As a result, his actual influence was largely diplomatic rather than political, but indirect influence could be supplemented by an occasional show of force. Periodically, he could call out part of the army for a *harka*, or military procession through some part of the bled es siba. The operation was partly a way of collecting taxes, partly a show of the sultan's power and prestige, but mainly a way of putting him in touch with important people who were normally beyond his control.

Some sultans were more successful than others, and the size of the makhzen as well as the sultan's influence within it, rose and fell. The nineteenth century was generally a period of strong makhzen. Mawlay Hassan (1873–94) was among the most successful of all. At a time when so much of the rest of Africa was falling under foreign control, he brought in military and administrative reforms to strengthen the regime within its own territory, and he carried out an active military and diplomatic program on the periphery. By that time, however, France was not simply a distant power overseas; it had become an established neighbor on the Moroccan-Algerian frontier.

The French in Algeria

The French attack on Algiers in 1830 seems out of its proper time. The main conquest of Africa took place only after 1880. Even in the far south, the Great Trek had not yet begun. European concern with North African affairs in the early nineteenth century centered further east on Cairo, Istanbul, or even Tunis. The Ottoman Empire was a part of the European state system, and it lay at the core of the "Eastern question." In European eyes, Algiers, Tanger, and Tripoli were merely weak nests of commerce raiders, and the French attack on Algiers began in the same style as the American raid on Tripoli – as an application of European muscle to force weak states to toe the line, without territorial acquisition as a conscious goal. On this occasion, it started with an unsettled debt. The Dey of Algiers then insulted the French consul. France demanded redress and sent a naval force. Its commanders allowed the show of power to escalate into a military attack on Algiers and two other ports, at which point the dey surrendered, ceding all his powers to the French government. Having acquired something that looked valuable, French officials were tempted to keep it; and the circumstances of French politics made it possible for them to do so.

In fact, France acquired only what the dey had, which was a great deal less than control over Algeria. For that matter, a good deal of the dey's diplomatic influence in the hinterland disappeared when he vanished to a well-heeled exile in Italy. The

French conquest of Algeria therefore began only after the seizure of Algiers itself, and it lasted at least until 1872 with the final military operations against the Kabylia. During these four decades, the French military leaders not only carried out extensive military operations; they also began to create piecemeal a series of policies that were to form an important precedent for French colonial rule in other parts of Africa.

The Algerians, for their part, sometimes collaborated with the new regime, even as they had collaborated in part with the Turks in Algiers. Sometimes they resisted French aggression, and again their resistance was of the same order as the Moroccan siba country's resistance to the makhzen. It was, of course, heightened by the fact that the French were infidels, but the religious difference was not always crucial. Few Algerians thought that a united and powerful Algerian state was desirable. For most, the political unity of a large territory was a deplorable emergency measure, to be ended as soon as possible, once the emergency was over.

Resistance to the French was endemic from the beginning; sometimes it involved armed resistance by the existing political authorities, sometimes wider movements organized under religious leadership. These were important in the early 1830s, but they were superseded in the late 1830s and on to 1847 by a new and larger movement centered in western Algeria. It was both anti-French and pro-Muslim, and it was also revolutionary in its attempt to create a new state with a modern administration and army.

The leader of this movement was ʿAbd al-Qādir, son of the local head of the Qadiriya, the most important of Muslim brotherhoods. He began with a center of power south of Oran, a little beyond the immediate reach of the French armies. His first effort was not so much to drive the French into the sea as to contain them in the ports they already controlled. But he realized that this would require a new kind of state with a more effective administration than any that existed in that part of Africa. In the longer run, it would have ended the complex lineage institutions of the old political order, and it called for a new-style military organization to enforce unification as well as to resist the French. It called, in short, for the kind of military modernization that Muhammad ʿAli had undertaken in Egypt.

Meanwhile, ʿAbd al-Qādir had to use the symbols of power that already existed. At first, he did not even claim political independence but put himself under the temporal and spiritual protection of his neighbor, the Sherifian Sultan of Morocco. He also took the title of *amīr al-muʾminīn*, commander of the faithful, the same title used by contemporaneous religious revolutionaries south of the Sahara. He set out to create a regular government administration that would combine some aspects of a bureaucratic hierarchy with recognition of the power that was. For each district he appointed a deputy or *khalifa*. They in turn recognized and worked through the existing authority of lineage chiefs and others who would join the cause. These men were appointed to the title of *agha*, so that they could act in the name of the central government, and they were also controlled to a degree by agents ʿAbd al-Qādir assigned each of them to supervise fiscal and military affairs.

Up to 1841, the French did not engage him in all-out war, and he used the respite to organize and establish his authority. In the process he had to force some tribal groupings into submission, and he had to fight the shaykh of the important and rival sufi order, the Tijānīya. The core of his military power was a small standing army of about 10,000 men, trained by European advisers and fighting with recent-model weapons. But his chief tactic against the French was to avoid open combat in so far as possible and instead to depend on hit-and-run raids against French strong points. This gave a certain fluidity to the battle lines, but, at the height of his power, ʿAbd al-Qādir was the recognized ruler of about two-thirds of Algeria north of the desert.

After 1841, the official French policy of limited occupation turned to one of outright conquest, including a direct confrontation with ʿAbd al-Qādir's new order. It turned out to be a harder task than anyone in France expected. By 1844, the French were forced to attack Morocco as well in order to cut off outside support. By 1846, they had put some 110,000 troops into the field, or a third of the entire French army. In 1847, they finally defeated ʿAbd al-Qādir, who was betrayed to the French and carried off as a prisoner. But the end of ʿAbd al-Qādir was not yet the beginning of full French rule. Even where the French did rule, they often did so by recognizing a local authority as *bashaga*, just as ʿAbd al-Qādir had done in his own zone. This meant that their ability to enforce their orders varied a good deal according to the time and place. Religious leaders continued to organize sporadic revolts. The French garrison had to face a "rebellion" somewhere almost every year from the late 1840s through the 1850s.

The most serious of these came in 1871, in circumstances that were more nearly those of initial conquest over a region forced to submit to French rule for the first time. It began with a comparatively minor incident, with one of the local bashagas launching a limited campaign that was partly anti-French and partly an attack on a rival saff, or alliance grouping. That outbreak, however, triggered a rising of the whole Kabylia under the shaykh of the Rahmanīyya, who managed to rally a number of other religious fraternities to his cause. Within a short time, the rebels had captured the whole mountain region from the outskirts of Algiers some 200 miles east along the coast, and south to the edge of the desert. These people, however, lacked the arms and training ʿAbd al-Qādir had tried to organize thirty years earlier. The French army moved in with a swift and punitive repression, though it cost them nearly 3000 men to crush the rebels.

The two decades on either side of 1870 were the period when French Algeria crystallized into the political and social order that was to persist through the colonial period. One early question was: who was to run the government, and in whose interest? In the early phase of conquest, military officers were the effective government, and they continued as such in the outlying districts. They were also the main rulers of the Muslim population. Special agencies called *bureaux arabes*, or Arabic Offices, were staffed by men with special language training. Although military rule could be oppressive, many officers in the bureaux arabes came to understand something of the local population and tried to rule in its interest. They were far from suggesting that Algerians should be treated as equals, but they came to believe that France had an obligation to rule Algeria well, and fundamentally in the interests of the Algerians themselves. For a time in the 1860s, they almost brought the French government in Paris around to their point of view.

Their principal opponents and principal rivals for control over French Algeria were the European settlers who had begun to immigrate from the 1830s onward in the wake of the French armies. At first, the movement was separate from official policy. It began simply because the French administration could make land available to individual Europeans. Other Europeans came because they found economic opportunities in the towns, often in connection with the administration or the army. About half these foreigners were from France, the rest came from Malta, the Balearic Islands, or the Spanish mainland. Over time, they adopted the French language and culture and came to think of themselves as French, but as French whose permanent home was Algeria. Unlike the soldiers or administrators, who came for a few years and looked forward to ultimate retirement in France, the settlers expected to live and die in Algeria. By the end of the nineteenth century, more than half were Algerian-born.

By the 1850s, Algeria had 130,000 resident Europeans. The settler community grew slowly through the 1850s and 1870s, with another burst of new arrivals in the 1880s that carried the European population beyond the half-million mark before the end of the century – about 13 per cent of the population in 1900, a proportion that changed little up to independence in 1962.

Unlike sub-Saharan Africa, where colonized and colonizers were instantly distinguishable by physical type and skin color, European settlers in Algeria were set apart by their culture, especially their religion. The French administration recognized Christians of all origins as a separate and legal group of French citizens. Non-Christian Algerians were French subjects, not citizens. French citizens came under French law and enjoyed many of the legal and constitutional rights they would have had in France. French subjects, by contrast, came under Muslim law. Their personal and property rights depended on a different set of rules; and they were subject to special and discriminatory laws and regulations created especially for them by the colonial government. For a time, Algerian Jews were in a third religious category, but in 1870 they were promoted from subjects to citizens. Inequality before the law came to include inequality in education, in civil rights, and in economic opportunity. The French citizens resident in Algeria jealously guarded their privileges. They became cultural chauvinists of the most extreme kind, tending to see the differences between their culture and that of the Muslim Algerians as an innate "racial" inheritance.

Up to the 1860s, the army kept the upper hand, with the settlers increasingly resentful. In 1870, however, the foundation of the Third Republic in France brought a settler victory. In the name of democracy and republicanism, the French citizens of Algeria received the right to elect deputies to the National Assembly in Paris. Algeria was formally annexed to France. The officers of the bureaux arabes were subordinated to the civilian government in each district, and the voice of the settlers became more and more important in deciding French policy. But, as in South Africa, "victory for democracy" in this case meant victory for a democracy confined to a small minority, and the turning point can be located in the 1870s and 1880s.

Although most of the settlers lived in towns, their main impact on the Algerian economy was through their control of the land – even though Algerians still did most of the agricultural work. Up to 1851, the colonial government had redistributed some 1400 square miles, an area half again the size of Rhode Island. Nearly half of this land had belonged to the Regency government, but nearly a fifth had been grazing land held by nomadic or semi-nomadic lineages, who were now forced to settle down as sedentary farmers. Another 15 per cent was confiscated from government opponents like 'Abd al-Qādir's followers. In this first phase, many of the settlers were given small plots and worked the land themselves, while some 36,000 Algerian families lost their land and had either to move away or to take work as landless farm workers.

After mid-century, still more land changed hands. The French confiscated another section about the size of Rhode Island in the wake of the great rebellion of 1871, and made it available to Europeans. Europeans also began to buy land, and began to move into large-scale agriculture, using dry-farming techniques for grain production in the more arid, yet tillable, regions, or cultivating large vineyards where rainfall was adequate. By the end of the century, a pattern of efficient, highly capitalized agriculture under European control was beginning to emerge, alongside the less efficient, under-capitalized agriculture still carried out on the fragmented land holdings of Algerian farmers.

Egypt's loss of independence

In the second half of the nineteenth century, while France secured its formal empire over Algeria, Egypt gradually fell into the informal empire of the Europeans. "Informal empire" is a useful term for that shadowy area in international relations where two states of vastly unequal power were theoretically sovereign and equal, but where the stronger of the two nevertheless exercised more authority over the weaker than was common within the European state system.

Especially in the nineteenth century, European states often preferred informal control overseas to the responsibility and cost of running a formal colony. The extent of that control could vary greatly. It might be no more than pressure on the weaker state to pass a particular piece of legislation or to set tariffs at a rate favorable to the stronger. In more extreme cases, Europeans sometimes took over part of the judicial system – often insisting on the right to try cases involving their own nationals. Or they might manage whole government departments, such as the treasury or foreign affairs, leaving the rest of the internal government in local hands.

The term "informal empire" can cover a wide variety of circumstances. Egypt in the nineteenth century passed through several phases. During the first half of the century, it managed to enjoy some of the fruits of modernization, like a strong army, without paying a very high price in the form of European influence. Egypt enjoyed French patronage in that period, but the French consul had nothing like the kind of influence French and British consuls exercised in Tripoli. The slide toward informal empire came only after the 1860s, though some of it can be traced back to Muhammad 'Ali's failure to create a strong and balanced economy. The new khedives, Sa'id (1854–63) and then Isma'il (1863–79), were more active modernizers than Muhammad 'Ali had been. Sa'id's government built the railroads from Alexandria to Cairo and from Cairo to Port Said on the Red Sea. It began a new and more active drive for irrigation works and perennial agriculture. It commissioned a French engineering firm to begin work on the Suez Canal, which was completed in 1869. Isma'il was even warmer and less critical in his admiration of Europe, where he had traveled and lived for a time in his youth. He pushed ahead on these same fronts, only more rapidly.

This activity raised several serious problems. The Suez Canal changed the strategic situation in the eastern Mediterranean, opening a water passage to the Indian Ocean just when steamships made the Red Sea more useful to navigation than ever before. Britain began to be more concerned about Egypt as a strategic route to its Indian empire. To make matters worse, these improvements were made with borrowed money – not only borrowed, but sometimes borrowed at excessive rates of interest and invested in ways that brought no return, such as in monumental architecture intended to beautify Cairo on the model of Napoleonic Paris. Total Egyptian indebtedness rose from about £7 million sterling in 1860 to more than £100 million in 1876. By that time, the annual interest payments flowing out of the country came to £5 million a year, or more than a third of the value of the annual exports. It was impossible either to pay off the debt or to pay interest on it without demanding a great sacrifice from the Egyptian people, and the need to export in order to pay the interest gave Egyptian economic planning still another bias toward production for export.

The speed of economic growth in the export sector also opened opportunities for foreigners. It was not simply that Muhammad 'Ali's modern educational system could not meet the demand for skilled people, though that was true too. The legal position of foreigners actually gave them an advantage over Egyptians in all kinds of commerce and in some other fields as well. The foreigners' privileges dated back to the so-called "capitulations" agreed to by the Ottoman Empire. These gave European consuls jurisdiction over disputes between Westerners, and they provided special privileges for Westerners tried on criminal charges before Ottoman courts. In the beginning, these privileges were voluntary concessions based on the Ottoman practice of letting each religious or ethnic community look after its own internal affairs.

In the course of the nineteenth century, however, new extensions crept in. Marginal cases tended to be brought to the consular courts rather than to Egyptian courts. After 1873, Europeans won the right to have even criminal cases tried by the appropriate consul, and mixed Egyptian consular courts were set up to hear civil cases in which one litigant was Egyptian and the other foreign. By the 1870s, the number of foreign residents had increased to about 2 per cent of the total population, though most were not from western Europe. Economic opportunities attracted many Greek and Levantine people of working-class background.

By the 1870s, a second kind of pressure for informal empire was apparent. European creditors, mostly bankers, appealed to their respective governments for help in recovering their loans to an Egyptian government now badly overextended. In 1876, the khedive was forced to appoint four prominent Europeans to posts in his own government as "Commissioners of the Debt." With that, Egypt was clearly within the informal empire of France and Britain, with France the senior partner.

The Egyptian debt then entered the broader network of European international relations that centered on the problem of Ottoman weakness. By the 1870s, the powers anticipated an Ottoman collapse, but they were concerned with the division of the spoils, not the fortune of the sultan. Russia and Austria in particular were rivals for the Ottoman provinces in the Balkans. Russia also hoped for an open and uncontested right of passage through the straits from the Black Sea into the Mediterranean. Germany, France, and Britain were all worried that Russia might upset the balance of power by swallowing the whole Ottoman Empire, though France and Britain were also rivals for influence in Egypt and in the eastern Mediterranean generally. In 1876, a successful Russian war on Turkey touched off a new crisis. Britain threatened naval intervention to stave off a complete Turkish collapse. That led, in turn, to a general European diplomatic meeting, the Congress of Berlin in 1878.

At that meeting, the powers managed to avoid a general European war by dividing the spoils so that each of them got something. Russia made territorial gains. Romania and Serbia were detached from the Ottoman Empire as independent states. Britain promised to defend Turkey from further Russian aggression and received Cyprus as compensation for Russian gains. France received permission to occupy Tunisia, though the actual occupation was put off until 1881.

Egypt came into the picture as an Ottoman province, however autonomous. If the powers felt free to dictate to Istanbul, they felt free to do the same to Cairo. In 1878, they forced Isma'il to appoint one French and one British member to his cabinet, and the web of informal control closed a little tighter. Even this disguised rule from overseas was unpopular with many Egyptians. Heavy schedules of interest and capital repayments proved even more so, and Isma'il reacted by dismissing the foreign cabinet ministers. The powers reacted in turn by ordering the Ottoman sultan to dismiss Isma'il himself, and the crisis deepened. Late in 1881, Egyptian troops led by 'Urabi Pasha seized power in Cairo as part of an anti-foreign movement. That left the Anglo-French coalition with a choice between armed intervention or loss of their informal control – with all that implied for their strategic position at the Suez Canal.

On the initiative of the French government, they chose intervention, but then the French National Assembly withdrew its support for the military action. That left the British to act alone. In 1882, Britain sent a military expedition, fought and won a decisive battle, and found itself in control of Egypt. This control was largely unintended, and it was far from happy. To withdraw would endanger the Suez route to India and annoy Egypt's creditors in Britain, but to stay left Britain rather than the khedive face to face with those same creditors in Europe. The result was an informal British protectorate that lasted until 1914 under a variety of legal fictions, a protectorate that amounted in time to British control of Egypt, but with international pressure from other European powers severely limiting Britain's freedom of action.

The collapse of secondary empire in the Nilotic Sudan

From the 1850s through the 1870s, Egypt greatly expanded the range and degree of control it exercised in the Sudan. This was another part of Sa'id's and Isma'il's modernization program. Like the rest of the program, it stretched the country's resources beyond the breaking point, but it scored what looked like successes along the way. In fact, two kinds of expansion took place simultaneously, one official and the other private. The official moves followed the line of the Red Sea and the strategic logic dictated by the Suez Canal already under construction. Egyptian moves along the Red Sea coast, the Gulf of Aden, and into the Ethiopian highlands began in 1865 with the acquisition of the previously Ottoman-owned posts at Suakin in Sudan and Massawa in Ethiopia. In the 1870s, the drive continued with an Egyptian occupation of Zeila (now in

Somalia) and Harar (now in the eastern highlands of Ethiopia) and two frontal assaults on Ethiopia itself – with a disastrous defeat for Egyptian forces each time.

The second and private aggression followed the line of the White Nile and westward up its tributaries. It was carried out by private armies generally under the control of the *jallaba*, or petty traders, creating a secondary empire within a secondary empire. The jallaba had been moving toward the south with their trading posts for some decades, but they received a strong assist from 1839 to 1842 when it was discovered that steamboats could sail up the Nile past the sudd and past the relatively well-organized Shilluk. During the next three decades, jallaba, principally from Nubia, became more active than ever as slave traders and slave raiders among the stateless peoples like the Dinka and Nuer. They set up fortified camps, or *zariba*, manned by slave-soldiers armed with modern weapons. They were not interested in administering the societies that surrounded them, only in trading and securing the passage of goods along the trade routes. It was, in short, an armed trade diaspora like that of the French in seventeenth-century Canada or the Russians in seventeenth-century Siberia, or the contemporaneous Zanzibari in the East African interior. In time, their furthest posts reached as far south as the present frontier between Uganda and Zaire, and west into the Bahr al-Ghazal region to the south of Darfur. Most of the jallaba were Egyptian subjects, and Egypt sometimes recognized their authority in the south, but their real power derived from the fact that modern arms conferred power indiscriminately on whoever first had an opportunity to use them against those who had none.

From the 1860s onward, Cairo tried to deal with the problem of frontier anarchy. It opened a new district capital at Fashoda among the Shilluk, tried to establish an official connection with the prominent jallaba leaders by appointing them as government officials, and sent in prominent English mercenaries to take command of the southern armies. Egypt's final push for control was simultaneous with the financial crisis in Cairo. In 1877, Isma'il appointed Charles Gordon Pasha as governor-general of the Sudan and simultaneously signed an anti-slave-trade convention with Great Britain. Gordon was supposed to suppress the slave trade, but instead he lost control of the jallaba altogether, as the southwest and other fringe provinces lapsed into chronic revolt.

The final collapse, however, came at the core of the Egyptian Sudan, in the gezira between the Blue and White Niles. In 1881, a certain Muhammad Ahmad organized a revolt, declaring that he was the expected Islamic savior, or Mahdi. His forces captured Khartoum and killed Gordon Pasha in 1885. He and his successor then founded a new state that was to rule over the Nilotic Sudan until the British conquest in 1898.

By the 1880s, the movement for Islamic purification and reform had been flourishing for more than a century, and the expectation of a savior was common in the Islamic world. The Mahdi's revolt was one of a series of revolts in Africa and elsewhere that sought to overturn governments judged to be incompletely Muslim. Examples go back in time to Nasīr al-Dīn's effort to build a new Muslim state in southern Mauritania and northern Senegal in the seventeenth century, or to the Wahabi movement in eighteenth-century Arabia. The Mahdi's regime in the Sudan also had overtones suggesting 'Abd al-Qādir's effort to build a new state in western Algeria as a make-weight against European pressure.

Muhammad Ahmad came originally from the desert Nile in Nubia, but he had long since moved south to the gezira as a Muslim cleric of the Samanīya order, one of the reforming brotherhoods founded in Arabia during the eighteenth century. By 1880, he had become the local head of the order with a broad following throughout the gezira and westward into Kordofan. In 1881, he had a series of visions telling him he was to be the Mahdi, not merely for the Sudan but for the entire Islamic world, and he called for a holy war to accomplish this end. The first enemy was the Egyptian regime, locally identified as "Turks," though in fact by this time most officials were Egyptian Muslims, with a sprinkling of Coptic Christians and Europeans like Gordon Pasha. The regime was, in any event, alien enough to arouse the fears of those who felt that Islam was in danger, and the Mahdi's original, pre-revolt following were people of unusual religious zeal marked by a streak of puritanism.

The first successes in Kordofan brought new followers with other reasons for opposition to the Egyptian regime. Some of the old Sudanese ruling class who had once accepted the "Turks" began to have second thoughts. Khedive Isma'il's financial problems and his gradual slide into informal empire were known in Khartoum, as they were in Cairo. The khedive's effort to establish genuine control over the Sudanese periphery also threatened local interests, especially those of the southern jallaba, and they in turn had friends and relatives in the core area as well. The appointment of an infidel governor-general made it easier still to associate the cause of Islam with specific interests, and the British seizure of Cairo in 1882 meant that the later stages of the war, from 1883 to victory in 1885, were fought against British and Egyptian troops under British command. By that time, the movement stood out more clearly than ever as one of Muslim resistance to Western encroachment.

The Mahdi himself died in 1885. His successor, the khalifa 'Abdullah, carried on, though he gradually changed the nature of the regime. The main support within the country still came from the religious enthusiasts, from the commercial classes, and from many of the baqarra, or cattle nomads, of Kordofan and the west. But success whittled down their influence. The ideal of building a universal Islamic state was quietly allowed to drop. Disciplined slave-soldiers replaced the irregular and largely nomadic forces that had won the first battles, and the khalifa retained many of the administrators who had run the Egyptian government. He also became more tolerant of religious differences within Islam, cooperating when it seemed politic with other brotherhoods less puritanical and orthodox than his own. Toward the end, it was clear that he intended his own son to take over after he died. What began as a religious reform movement, in short, increasingly became just another Muslim state, no more religious than the rest, based on the sedentary societies of the sub-Saharan Nile valley and Kordofan.

But the tendency in that direction was cut short once more in 1896 by events in Ethiopia and competitive annexation elsewhere in Africa. Early in 1896, Italy launched an invasion of Ethiopia from its existing colony of Eritrea, but Ethiopian forces armed with modern weapons won decisively at the battle of Adowa. British officials in Cairo had been willing to let the Sudan go its own way, but they now feared that the khalifa would invade Eritrea to take advantage of Italy's defeat. They therefore launched an advance up the Nubian Nile to occupy the Mahdist armies and relieve the pressure on

Italy. Once started, the advance up the Nile built up a momentum of its own, with a popular demand to avenge the death of Gordon.

By 1898, a new factor entered the picture. France had launched a small expedition intending to cross Africa from the lower Congo to Ethiopia. By the time the British reached Khartoum, it had reached Fashoda, the former Egyptian post on the White Nile. The British therefore pushed on to Fashoda, in order to protect the Nile Valley for Egypt. That lead to a diplomatic crisis and nearly to a war between France and Britain. They avoided armed conflict, but Britain concluded that Egypt would have to reannex the Nilotic Sudan in order to protect its strategic interest in the source of Nile water. The result for the Sudan was a second period of government from Cairo, this time by an Anglo-Egyptian condominium that was to last until 1955, though ultimate power always lay with the British side of the partnership.

The fall of Tunisia and Morocco

Tunisia's position became increasingly difficult after the 1830s, what with a renewed Turkish regime in Tripoli and the French in Algeria. Either neighbor could threaten the bey's continued quasi-independence. The bey therefore sought to modernize the army, but at the usual risk of falling into the trap of informal empire in the process. The Tunisian government not only borrowed more in Europe than it could easily repay, it borrowed at such exorbitant rates of interest that any effort to repay – or even to keep up the interest charges – forced it to raise taxes at home. The heavy borrowing added European bondholders and Tunisian taxpayers to the existing pressures. To complicate matters, substantial numbers of French, Italian, and Maltese settlers moved into Tunisia during the second half of the nineteenth century, much as similar foreign immigrants moved into Egypt at the same period. As in Egypt, their presence brought still more pressure from the French, Italian, and British consuls (since the Maltese were British subjects).

By the 1850s, Tunisia could be counted as part of the French informal empire, and the French in fact planned a limited occupation in the late 1860s in order to assure their control. British and Italian protests, however, forced France to agree to turn Tunisian finances over to an international commission. Partly as a result, the Tunisian economy recovered somewhat during the 1870s and the formal French protectorate was put off until a suitable configuration of international relations at the Congress of Berlin removed the opposition and allowed the French to invade in 1881. Tunisia's confrontation with Europe, in short, was very much like Egypt's and the result was much the same – except for the fact that the French protectorate was overt, while the French control of Egypt remained a legal fiction.

Morocco, meanwhile, seized the other horn of the dilemma of modernization. Given a choice between military modernization at the price of a large foreign debt, or military weakness with an old-fashioned army, Morocco stood by the old ways. The policy worked reasonably well, in spite of military defeat at the hands of France in the 1840s and again at the hands of Spain in the 1860s. International rivalries among the Europeans limited the demands any one of them could make on the sultan. Morocco was open to European economic penetration in the second half of the century, but that penetration was comparatively slow. About 1870, when Egypt already had 100,000 resident foreigners and Tunisia had nearly 10,000, Morocco had only 1500. Sultan Mawlay Hassan (1873–95) was especially skilful in preserving the balance of the old political system. He had a small force of European-trained soldiers, but the mainstay of his army remained the old combination of slave-soldiers and military levies from privileged tribes. With a more powerful force, he might have been tempted to extend the makhzen's power over siba country; but lack of power reduced the temptation, and Mawlay Hassan's revenue matched his expenses to the end of his reign.

This comparatively happy situation may have come from luck as well as wisdom; Great Britain had the largest stake in Moroccan trade and acted as an informal protector of Moroccan interests against the Spanish and French on the frontiers. After 1900, however, the old balance began to break down. A new sultan moved toward modernization, which brought on a conservative revolt in the region east of Fez. That, in turn, brought firmer action from France, which sidestepped British objections by promising Britain a free hand in Egypt. Spain was bought off with the promise of a zone of Spanish influence in northern Morocco. By 1904, France had lent Morocco large sums of money and had already taken over the customs and postal services. The slide into informal empire had already begun, but Germany had to be bought off as well before France could formalize the protectorate. Even earlier, the puppet sultan began to lose power internally and France had to bail him out with military support or see him deposed by his enemies. Finally, in 1912, France and Spain divided Morocco into two zones of formal control, though the sultan continued as theoretical ruler under European protection.

This final failure stands in contrast to Morocco's comparative success in keeping out the Europeans, but the Moroccan makhzen nevertheless held out longer than any other government in North Africa. Parts of the bled es siba remained independent of real French control until 1934, nearly the last sections of Africa to be conquered by the Europeans, and the Sherifian sultans continued as heads of state into the 1990s. In spite of European pressures in the nineteenth and twentieth centuries, the old institutions and loyalties were remarkably resilient.

Suggestions for further reading

Abir, Mordechai, *Ethiopia in the Era of the Princes*, London: Longman, 1968.

Abu-Lughod, Janet L., *Cairo: 1001 Years of the City Victorious*, Princeton: Princeton University Press, 1971.

Dunn, Ross E., *Resistance in the Desert*, Madison, University of Wisconsin Press, 1977.

Ewald, Janet J., *Soldiers, Traders, and Slaves: State Formation in the Greater Nile Valley, 1700–1885*, Madison: University of Wisconsin Press, 1990.

Gallagher, Nancy Elizabeth, *Medicine and Power in Tunisia, 1780–1900*, Cambridge, Cambridge University Press, 1983.

Gellner, Ernest, *Saints of the Atlas*, London: Weidenfeld and Nicolson, 1969.

Holt, P.M. and M.W. Daly, *A History of the Sudan: From the Coming of Islam to the Present Day*, 4th edn, London: Longman, 1988.

Marsot, Afaf Lutfi al-Sayyid, *Egypt in the Reign of Muhammad Ali*, Cambridge: Cambridge University Press, 1984.

Montagne, Robert, *The Berbers: Their Social and Political Organization*, London: Cass, 1973.

Prochaska, David, *Making Algeria French: Colonialism in Bône, 1870–1920*, New York: Cambridge University Press, 1990.

Schroeter, Daniel, *Merchants of Essaouira: Urban Society and Imperialism in Southwestern Morocco*, New York: Cambridge University Press, 1988.

Valensi, Lucette, *Tunisian Peasants in the Eighteenth and Nineteenth Centuries*, Cambridge: Cambridge University Press, 1985.

Vatikiotis, Panayiotis J., *The Modern History of Egypt*, new edition, Baltimore: The Johns Hopkins University Press, 1991.

12

THE COMMERCIAL AND RELIGIOUS REVOLUTIONS IN WEST AFRICA

Throughout Africa, the pre-colonial century was a period of revolutionary change in external trade. For tropical Africa, the impact of this new trade was so pervasive as to give the false impression that trade and its consequences would explain everything else that took place. But other trends can also be distinguished, and they had other origins.

Internal trade was still far more important than trade with the world overseas – as it had been in the period of the slave trade. Regional economies in many parts of Africa began to grow in scale and in the intensity of exchange. Throughout tropical Africa, increasing trade led to increased tension between the well-sheltered local and regional communities and the broader institutions that joined them to their neighbors.

A second general tendency was the accelerated pace of culture change. Cultural features from hairdos to new crops and new cults diffused at a faster pace than ever before, and this rapid diffusion tended to make for new regions of common culture that were also expanding in scale. Both trends had been present in earlier African history, but they were now reinforced by world events – specifically, by the industrial revolution in Europe and by African responses to it. And the African initiatives were important; if Africans had not wanted European goods, the story would have been different.

West Africa's experience in the pre-colonial century was similar to that of other African regions in the shadow of industrialized Europe, but here the common trends were mixed together in ways that created a number of special patterns. Coastal West and Central Africa had a longer and more intense experience of maritime trade than any other part of sub-Saharan Africa. Their leaders were familiar with Europeans and with European arms. They had imported tens of thousands of muskets and incorporated them into their military systems. After the 1780s, many more Europeans were resident on the coasts, so strategic surprise could not play the same role it played on the upper Nile or in the East African lake region. West Africans had been using European muskets for more than a century. Having been inoculated with the virus of European weapons, they already had a partial immunity to the dangers of secondary empire-building. European military encroachment was also less serious in these decades than it was in either northern or southern Africa. Western cultural penetration took place, but its agents were more often Western-educated Africans than European settlers.

Other trends common to Africa as a whole were especially strong in West Africa. One such was the movement for Islamic reform and rejuvenation. Revolutionaries who claimed a religious motive had been important since the seventeenth century from the middle Senegal to the highlands of Fuuta Jaalo. Some of these movements actually antedated the Middle Eastern reform movements that began to be important in the eighteenth century, but the new religious currents from the Middle East combined with local factors. From the 1770s onward, they changed the entire political map of the western Sudan, and the locus of political power in those societies shifted beyond recognition.

Revolutionary change in commerce also swept West Africa. All of Africa experienced enormous increases in overseas trade, but for West and Equatorial Africa the change in scale was simultaneous with a change in the principal exports. With the winding down of the trade in slaves, the new "legitimate" trade (as the Europeans at the time liked to call it) was not merely a substitution for the old; it shifted the centers of wealth and power. Those who had profited from the slave trade lost out, and new wealth flowed to those who could supply gum-Senegal, palm oil, or peanuts.

Religious revolutions: the Qadiri phase

Whereas the center of religious revolution in the seventeenth and early eighteenth centuries had been Senegambia and its Fulbe offshoots south and east to Fuuta Jaalo, a new center of reformist preaching and influence appeared in the mid-eighteenth century on the desert fringe just north of Timbuktu. The organizing force behind this movement was the same reforming Qadiriya order that was to supply the organizational base for 'Abd al-Qādir in Algeria. The Qadiriya was a *sufi* order, but it differed from many in being far more orthodox. In the nineteenth century, it was near the heart of the Muslim call for a return to the purity of primitive Islam. The West African head of the order was Sidi al-Mukhtar al-Kunti, whose preaching was effective from the late 1750s to his death in 1811. He made no bid for territorial authority, though his influence was enormously important throughout the southern Sahara and the western Sudan; and the reform message spread along the trade routes from Timbuktu up the Niger through Maasina to the heartland of Mande culture, and downstream toward Hausaland in present-day Nigeria and beyond, into the Oyo empire in northern Yorubaland. Along the desert fringe, it stretched into what is now southern Mauritania in the west, down into Senegambia, and eastward to the Tuareg of Aïr.

Islam had been gaining gradually throughout the western Sudan in recent centuries, but its gains had come as pockets of adherents, not a broad expansion across the countryside. The peasants – the vast majority – clung to their old religion, to the gods attached to lineages, places, or protective functions under a powerful but aloof High God. Islam attracted those whose lives were directed outward from the home village, along the trade routes, and into the courts of the rulers. Many rulers were at least formally Muslim, but they ruled over a population that was not; and few of them tried to convert the general public or even to enforce Muslim law throughout their territory.

New tendencies within Islam in the eighteenth century meant far more in clerical and commercial circles, and these were the source of new Islamic preaching in rural

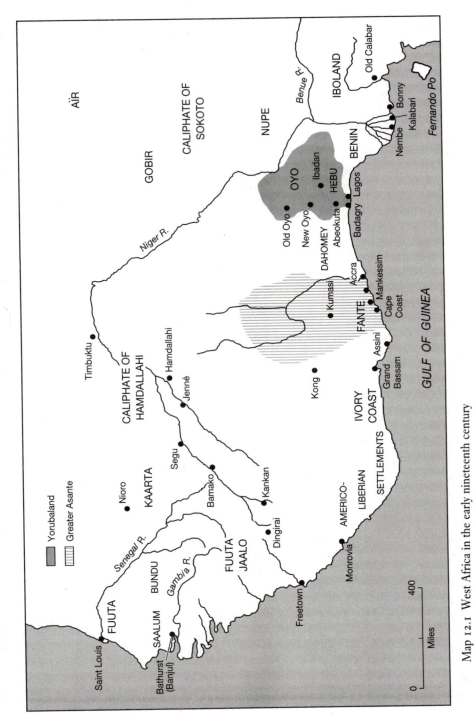

Map 12.1 West Africa in the early nineteenth century

areas. In places like northern Nigeria, the reform movement encouraged popular preaching, but reformist scholars also sought to separate themselves from the cities, which they regarded as centers of non-reformed Islam. Small groups of scholars settled in the countryside, some for mutual enlightenment, but others set out to spread the word to their largely non-Muslim neighbors. The eighteenth-century increase in commerce across the western Sudan also played a role. Islam was the religion of commerce, and it was strong in ethnic groups with a commercial calling, like the Soninke and their offshoots (the Juula, Marka, and Jahaanke among others), who were scattered from the Niger bend south to the forest and west nearly to the Atlantic. The Muslim Fulbe (sg. Pulo), most of whom were cattle keepers from the Atlantic to Lake Chad, were also sprinkled throughout the region as itinerant clerics in courts, towns, and cattle camps. Elsewhere in the Sudan, however, non-Muslim religions were virtually untouched, especially in the southern, or pre-forest, savannas, but also in such large blocs of "pagan" population as the two Bambara kingdoms or the Mossi and their neighbors in present-day Burkina Faso within the great bend of the Niger.

Nor had the first almaamates, spawned by the *jihads* (holy struggles) of the seventeenth and early eighteenth centuries, turned into centers of Muslim power. The rulers of Bundu, founded in the 1690s as a clerical state, kept the title of almaami, but they were no longer trained as Muslim clerics. Bundunke clerical offices and judgeships were reserved for Jahaanke clerical lineages who had their own autonomous villages. In Fuuta Tooro, where the first jihad had failed in the 1680s, a second began in the 1770s. In the 1780s, Abdul Kader ('Abd al-Qādir in Arabic) emerged as almaami, but his armies failed to spread the movement to neighboring states. In 1806, he and the original aims of the revolution died together, defeated in war by the combined forces of Bundu, the pagan state of Kaarta, and a powerful faction within Fuuta itself. The victors preserved the office of almaami and the fiction of Islamic reform, but the Futaanke clique that betrayed the revolution set itself up as a kind of electoral council that appointed and removed the almaami at will.

The almaamate in Fuuta Jaalo had a similar history. After the first victories in the 1720s, the clerical party became a secular-minded oligarchy whose principal interest was to command the flow of trade from the upper Niger to the coast (in what are now Guinea-Conakry and Sierra Leone). The rulers were Muslim, but they did little more than convert their slaves, and they turned more and more to chronic civil war between quarreling factions. After about 1800, they alternated the office of almaami between two dominant lineages descended from the first leaders of the jihad.

By the early nineteenth century, however, the demand for religious reform was more widespread than ever. Preachers and moral leaders called for the reform of the state and the enforcement of *shar'īa* law. During the century from 1780 to 1880, they often called for jihad against Muslim rulers less rigorous in their religion than the reformers thought they should be. More than a dozen leaders with this program succeeded in displacing the old rulers or in founding new states in the western Sudan. For each successful move, however, another dozen or more failed in palace coups now passed over by history. Many leaders, successful or unsuccessful, were no doubt moved by motives that could be qualified as essentially religious, but the call for jihad also became a least-common-denominator appeal for assistance in overthrowing whatever government might be in power, or for seeking to found new states with wider frontiers. A broad pattern of mixed motives can be discerned, but the end result was the substitution of new rulers for old, and new large states for the former small states, and a substantial spread of Islam as a religion.

The new phase of successful nineteenth-century jihads began in Nigeria even before Abdul Kader had died on the Senegal. This call for reform was also associated with the Qadiriya and, specifically, with al-Kunti, but the message was heard in the specific setting of the Hausa city-states, which had been at least formally Muslim for several centuries. In the towns were the merchants and craft workers, the court, and the greatest concentration of Muslim clerics. The surrounding countryside was occupied partly by sedentary Hausa peasants and partly by transhumant Fulbe pastoralists, while Tuareg nomads occupied the desert fringe to the north and could be an effective force in some circumstances. Within this local society, competitive interests separated the nomads and semi-nomads from farmers, rural people from townspeople, Muslims from non-Muslims or less-Muslim, merchants from princes, and ethnic communities from one another.

Usuman dan Fodio, who was to mobilize segments of this society for a successful jihad, began preaching in the city-state of Gobir about 1775. He demanded a stronger religious leadership within the state and complained against specific grievances of the pastoralists. In time, he became the local head of the Qadiriya, and, by the 1790s, his movement had become a potential military threat to the state. The king of Gobir planned a pre-emptive military strike against the religious community, but Usuman ordered a retreat, imitating Muhammad's flight from Mecca to Medina. In 1804, he declared a holy war against Gobir, returned with an armed following, and, by 1808, had captured the city, killed its ruler, and begun building a new capital at Sokoto.

Other revolts followed in other Hausa states. Their usual base was a similar reform program and a similar core of followers consisting of Muslim clerics, Fulbe, and sometimes Tuareg from the north. At times, Usuman dan Fodio could use the prestige of his early victory to influence the choice of leaders elsewhere; he often favored a scholarly Muslim cleric as flag-bearer, usually a Pulo like himself. Other leaders emerged on their own and applied to Usuman for recognition The movement never identified itself openly as a Fulbe drive to dominate the Hausa majority, though the rebels attracted more support from serious Muslims, merchants, and herdsmen than from other groups. It identified the enemy as the old Hausa-speaking ruling class, now condemned as pagan. The mass of the peasantry apparently remained neutral; the bulk of the actual military operations involved two minorities – the rebels and the aristocrats they were trying to expel from power. Nor was this phase of empire building in any sense a secondary empire. Most of the fighting involved sieges of fortified towns, and the dominant force was cavalry supported by archers. Guns, long used nearer the coastal sources of supply, were not important at first. The fighting developed into a state of near-anarchy through much of what was to be northern Nigeria – only to settle down gradually as Usuman dan Fodio was recognized as *shaykh* (or *shehu* in Hausa) and a general government took form.

The new political order that emerged in the late 1810s and early 1820s was mainly the creation of Usuman's brother Abdullahi, and his son Bello. The head of state was considered to be the *khalifa* or successor of Muhammad on earth. The new state's principal capital was at Sokoto under Bello, while a subordinate and semi-autonomous western region had its own capital at Gwandu under Abdullahi. They recognized individual flag-bearers as emir over the territory each had conquered. In practice, this meant that the central government could not easily remove the emirs from office, much less control in detail the internal workings of their governments. Thus, although Usuman dan Fodio had begun with a detailed blueprint of the kind of society he wanted to create and how he wanted to manage it, his successors lacked the power to follow through. The central government could give advice, or use diplomacy, but it could only occasionally use force to correct a difficult situation. Even within the area under close control from Sokoto, old social structures revived under new names. The aggrieved herdsmen drifted back into seasonal transhumance, while a Fulbe and Muslim aristocracy replaced the old Hausa governments in the towns. The tight social stratification of the old regime reappeared with new men at the top.

Similar politico-religious movements appeared nearly simultaneously, but several were independent of and even hostile to Sokoto. In the kingdom of Borno near Lake Chad, the ancient Sefawa dynasty was still in power at the beginning of the nineteenth century, though much reduced from its apogee at the end of the sixteenth century. Its core area lay west of the lake, with a variety of tribute-paying subordinate states north into the steppe and eastward to the Sultanate of Wadai, the next truly independent neighbor. With an impetus from the Fulbe jihads in Hausa country, the Fulbe also rose in Borno. By 1808, they had captured the capital and appeared likely to overthrow the Sefawa. But a local cleric, Laminu al-Kanemi, mounted his own reform movement, opposed to Sokoto and independently of the Sefawa. He first reconquered the capital and the western lands lost to the Fulbe. He then became a kind of clerical warlord and political arbiter with a following of Shuwa Arabs, Kanembu from the east of Lake Chad, and other semi-nomadic peoples. He could appoint and dismiss the *mai*, or king representing the Sefawa dynasty. From the early 1820s, he had his own private army under slave-commanders loyal to him alone. He and his successors ruled through puppet kings until 1846, when a mai made a bid for real power with support from the Sultan of Wadai. Laminu's son then had the last Sefawa ruler killed and established his own family as the new dynasty in theory as well as in fact.

Still another religious revolt occurred in Maasina, in the Niger Valley above Timbuktu, where the river breaks into a thousand branches that form an internal delta over a distance of nearly three hundred miles, from a little south of Timbuktu upstream as far as Jenné. Each wet season, the river rises and spills over its banks to create a shallow lake up to fifty miles wide, though it leaves many small hills that become islands, to which people retreat with their cattle until the flood recedes. Then the moisture and silt left by the river create rich pastures across the plain, as well as the possibility of planting a dry-season grain crop. Like the similar environment of the Dinka and Nuer on the Nile thousands of miles to the east, it was well suited to pastoral occupation, mainly by Fulbe in Maasina proper or by Tuareg just inside the Niger bend. Somono rivermen also fished the Niger waters and carried the important trade that flowed south from the desert edge to Jenné and other trans-shipment points for the overland trip toward the forest. Riverside commercial towns like Sinsani

(Sansanding), Jenné, or Mopti attracted a variety of people from all over the western Sudan – among them Marka, traders and planters who traced their ancestry back to Soninke origins, like the Juula and Jahaanke elsewhere in the western Sudan. The agricultural region just above the delta, however, was mainly Bambara in culture, non-Muslim in religion, and attached to the kingdom of Segu.

At the beginning of the nineteenth century, Islam was strong among the townspeople and river boatmen. Many Fulbe clerics in the towns had connections among the pastoral Fulbe as well. Political control in the delta, however, belonged to the Fulbe Dikko lineage, which was theoretically Muslim but acted more like a predatory war band with a weak allegiance to the rulers of Segu. The court at Segu, like other western Sudanese courts, was also touched by Muslim influence, though the Bambara countryside was not. In spite of this checkerboard of conversion to Islam, Muslims here had been greatly influenced by the reformist teaching of the Qadiriya center of the Kunta leaders of that order near Timbuktu.

News of Usuman dan Fodio's successes in northern Nigeria inspired a more active reformist movement under the leadership of a Fulbe cleric, Ahmadu Lobbo. He followed Shehu Usuman's teachings in some respects, but he was even stricter in his opposition to deviation from a puritanical standard of Islamic virtue, and identified still more strongly with the Fulbe as an ethnic group. About 1816, Ahmadu began to prepare a jihad that was to be partly a civil war against the Dikko rulers of the Fulbe, partly a war seeking the liberation of all Fulbe from the Bambara of Segu, and partly an effort to create a rightly guided Muslim state. He succeeded against the Dikko in 1818, then against Segu, and in 1821 set up a state with a new capital at Hamdallahi.

The Caliphate of Hamdallahi differed from its neighbor in Sokoto. It was much smaller, without subordinate emirates, and with far more of its administrative apparatus in the hands of Muslim clerics. It was also limited to a single geographical region with an ethnically homogeneous population. Though Ahmadu Lobbo and his successors sometimes fought their neighbors – they captured Timbuktu itself in 1826 – their policy was generally non-expansive. As a result, the caliphate lasted fairly peacefully into the early 1860s as the jihad state most faithful to the original Islamic reform program, though its puritanical fundamentalism was also somewhat suspect to the bulk of the West African 'ulamā.

The commercial revolution

The idea of a commercial revolution in nineteenth-century West Africa has often been associated with the winding down of the slave trade and the substitution of other exports. It was that, of course, and the slave trade ended in that century. Other exports also increased rapidly, often in response to economic demand from the growing economies of industrializing Europe.

But an emphasis on external demand can be misleading. For most of sub-Saharan Africa, overseas trade was only a small fraction of the total trade. The evidence for West and Equatorial Africa from the late eighteenth century onward to the colonial period suggests that total long-distance trade within Africa increased more rapidly than overseas trade, that the internal economy was changing rapidly for reasons independent of the European stimulus.

External stimulus was undoubtedly present as well. From the last third of the seventeenth century to the middle of the nineteenth, the prices offered by Europe for African exports increased steeply – including the price for slaves, which began to rise first. Rising slave prices were simply a reflex of the increasing profitability of slave-grown tropical agriculture in the New World, which in turn reflected the willingness of Europeans to buy more coffee and sugar at higher prices. The greater European wealth, created essentially by the industrial revolution, led therefore to a continually increasing demand for slaves, especially for slaves to staff new plantations in Cuba and Brazil. In time, the search for labor was to bring tens of thousands of East Indian contract workers to the Caribbean in a partial substitution for the African slave trade.

Opposition to the slave trade began to be serious from the 1780s. Humanitarian sentiment increased in Europe in the late eighteenth century. The democratic revolutions in France and the United States and the broadening franchise in Great Britain brought political power to middle-class voters who were moved by the inhumanity of the trade. Some of the northern states in America abolished slavery in the wake of the American Revolution. France abolished both slavery and the slave trade for a time during the 1790s, though later governments restored both. The Dutch slave trade in effect came to an end about 1795, while the Danes abolished theirs, with small exceptions, in 1803, followed by Britain and the United States in 1808. The rest of Europe followed after 1815. In 1830, Brazil abolished the last legal slave trade in the Atlantic basin.

The legality of the trade, however, was not always important. Shippers from many countries found it profitable to trade in slaves, whatever the law might say, and countries like Brazil and Cuba were slow to enforce laws international diplomatic pressure had forced them to pass. After 1815, however, Great Britain began using its navy in a large-scale attempt to suppress the trade at sea. In time, France and the United States joined in with small squadrons of their own. These efforts were not enough to stop the slave trade, but they did succeed in capturing some 160,000 slaves at sea, amounting to about 8 per cent of those shipped from Africa between 1810 and 1870. That alone raised the cost of slaves in the Americas and reduced the size the trade might otherwise have reached. The effective end of the Atlantic slave trade came only when American countries began to enforce their own anti-slave-trade laws, as Brazil did after 1850, and as Cuba did after the late 1860s. The American Civil War ended the trickle of illegal imports that continued to add slaves to some southern states through the early nineteenth century.

Meanwhile, "legitimate trade" had already begun to replace the trade in slaves. For that matter, slaves had never been the sole source of West Africa's trade; in the seventeenth century, gold from the Gold Coast and hides from Senegambia had been more important exports. Even during the eighteenth century boom in slave exports, West Africa sold abroad substantial quantities of timber, gum, palm oil, beeswax, gold, hides, and even manufactured products like beads or cotton textiles. Production and commercial facilities therefore existed to be stimulated by rising prices, even before the slave trade declined. Gum from the desert fringe was used in Europe for confectionery and in the textile industry. The price per ton doubled between the 1730s and 1780s, then doubled again by the 1830s. Prices offered for hides and ivory increased tenfold between the 1780s and 1830s, and the price of beeswax increased threefold. Palm oil prices fluctuated widely in short-run swings, but the general level began to rise after 1815, approximately doubling between the 1820s and 1850s. These changes prompted even sharper changes in the volume of exports. Palm oil from West Africa to England alone rose from about 1000 tons a year in 1820 to 30,000 tons a year in the 1850s. Peanut production from Senegambia rose from negligible quantities before 1840 to around 40,000 tons a year by the late 1880s.

While the prices and quantities of particular African exports were rising very rapidly, the prices of European goods sold in Africa rose only slowly or, in the case of cotton textiles, even declined somewhat as machine production drove down costs. This meant that the terms of trade generally shifted in favor of West Africa from the late eighteenth century to about 1860; West Africans received more goods for a given quantity of exports than they had done in the past. But the rise of legitimate trade had some peculiar economic consequences. The total value of West African exports in the 1790s – mostly slaves – was about £4 million sterling. By the 1850s, non-slave exports reached about the same value. On the surface, then, legitimate trade had replaced the slave trade in importance. But the new exports came from particular regions: gum from northern Senegal and southern Mauritania, timber from the riverbanks of Sierra Leone, palm oil from the tropical forests of southern Nigeria. These were not the same regions that had profited from the slave trade. Even the illicit slave trade moved to new places as old suppliers like the Gold Coast or Senegambia dropped out altogether. After the 1820s, new sources like Yorubaland became major slave exporters for the first time in their history.

The economic and social consequences of legitimate trade were also different from those of the slave trade. The society whose people became enslaved was, of course, a net loser, but even the captors received a comparatively small percentage of the total price paid on export. Most of it went to the merchants who moved the slaves to the coast and held them until a European ship appeared. These merchants could some-times change to new commodities, but only if they happened to live near one of the zones of new production for export. Otherwise they had to find a new occupation or change to the non-export trade.

The payoff for the new, non-slave trade went in part to merchants, but producers also took a share. They might be members of an old ruling class, like the Mauritanian lineage heads who controlled semi-desert woodlands where their slaves collected gum. Sometimes peasant producers found new sources of income. The Senegambian peasants who grew peanuts profited directly, and so did large numbers of free migrant workers who began to come annually to work at peanut growing near the Senegal coast or the Gambia River. In the palm oil regions it was again slaves who did much of the work while their owners, the merchants, and the political authorities took most of the new income. But most economic activity was not for export, nor were all new currents of trade bound for Europe. It is probable, for example, that the nineteenth-century kola nut trade from Asante to the savanna country increased even more in value than did the palm oil exports from the Gold Coast.

The European presence

The influence of European culture along the West African coast grew even more rapidly than the growth of overseas trade might indicate. Legitimate trade required more European residents than the slave trade had done. Culture contact on the African coast in the era of the slave trade was unusually low, partly because the slave-trade posts were only lightly manned and partly because the European death rates were so high. Most European posts of the eighteenth century, were more Euro-African than European. Where the typical European strength might vary from a dozen to a few hundred, the associated African population was always much larger including many descendants of European fathers and African mothers. These Afro-Europeans and others of purely African descent occasionally went to Europe for an education, like Philip Quaque, the Anglican chaplain to the main English fort on the Gold Coast. He and others like him helped to found schools teaching a smattering of European languages and commercial arithmetic. These schools were often ephemeral, but, by the turn of the eighteenth century, a scattered, partly European population of permanent residents could be found along the coast from Saint Louis in Senegal to Benguela in southern Angola. Saint Louis in 1810 was representative, with only about ten Europeans but five hundred Afro-Europeans, another five hundred partly Europeanized free Africans, and around 2200 slaves as a culturally African working class.

By the nineteenth century, these Afro-Europeans were among the most important members of local "European" society, partly because the Afro-Europeans stayed on, while Europeans typically came for a few years only. Thomas Joiner of the Gambia had been a slave in Virginia, but he returned to Banjul after the Napoleonic wars and became the largest shipowner and one of the most prosperous merchants in the Gambia. On the Gold Coast, the Brew family, descended from an Irish trader of the mid-eighteenth century, founded a dynasty of Anglo-African merchants and officials who flourished for more than a century. The last three decades of the pre-colonial century were the pinnacle of economic success and power for Afro-Europeans all along the coast. Only in the 1880s and later were they pushed aside by Europeans fresh from Europe. By that time, colonial regimes with exclusive, racist policies had replaced the more informal life of the trading enclaves.

A new and greater intensity of European activity along the coasts was already evident a century earlier. In the 1780s, Europeans planned a dozen or so new settlements for the African coasts, often with an agricultural component alongside old-style fortified trading posts. Most of these plans came to nothing, or, if tried, failed and disappeared. But the British settlement at Sierra Leone had a disproportionate influence all along the coast.

It began in 1787 as a philanthropic project to provide a home for the "Black poor" of London, but the plan soon broadened into a projected agricultural colony and a base for "legitimate trade." Through several changes in emphasis and management, it was used successively as a place of settlement for black American loyalist refugees from the American revolution and Jamaican rebels – both groups of returnees from the New World being Western in culture. Then, from the first decade of the nineteenth century, it became a place for the reception and settlement of slaves recaptured at sea by the

British navy. Sierra Leone then became the focus of a broad, humanitarian effort to promote Christianity and Western culture in Africa through the agency of Westernized recaptives. Missionaries came in larger numbers than ever before. A government-sponsored educational system was soon training a higher proportion of school-age children than were trained in England itself at that time. In 1827, Fourah Bay College opened its doors for the education of an African clergy. The result was a new Anglo-African society, small at first, but increasingly capable of assimilating thousands of new arrivals when the stream of recaptives reached a peak in the 1840s.

A second settlement of returnees had meanwhile been established nearby. In 1822, the American Colonization Society founded a small colony of Afro-Americans at Cape Mesurado. The settlement grew into the city of Monrovia and the colonization effort eventually became the Republic of Liberia. It was unofficially supported by the United States government, but the major effort came from private citizens. Some acted from genuinely philanthropic motives but others simply wanted to rid the United States of its free Afro-American population, which they regarded as racially undesirable. Other private colonization societies sponsored settlements along the coast south and east of Monrovia until some 5000 settlers had arrived before 1850. They were later joined by recaptive slaves landed by the United States Navy, and these settlements became a flourishing set of Afro-American communities. In 1847, the Monrovia settlement sought to clarify its relationship with the United States by declaring its independence. By 1856, the other settlements joined to form an independent Liberia, and most of the European powers recognized the former colony's new status in international law, though informal American influence usually made the new country less independent in fact than it was in theory.

The old trading posts also began to change after 1815. The British returned to the mouth of the Gambia in 1817 after several decades of absence and founded a settlement at Banjul (known as Bathurst during the colonial period), while the French made elaborate plans for the Senegal valley, including a new fortified post at Bakel in 1819, four hundred miles inland, and the first use of steamboats on African rivers. They tried in the 1820s to encourage plantation agriculture in the neighboring state of Waalo; but the scheme was undercapitalized, the European managers died, and the Africans were unwilling to work for the wages Europeans wanted to pay.

In the 1840s, the British tried an even more elaborate scheme on the Niger, one with similar components. They brought steamboats for the river trade and planned a plantation colony at the junction of the Benue and Niger rivers in open savanna country, about two hundred and fifty miles from the sea. They hoped to encourage large-scale cotton production under the direction of an Afro-American specialist hired for that purpose. It was an early scheme for economic development, partly in European-controlled territory, but including an effort to persuade African authorities to set up their own plantations along European lines. The economic aspect was coupled with a missionary effort aimed at "Christianity and civilization" on the model of Sierra Leone.

This project failed dramatically because of high mortality among the European personnel. It nevertheless illustrates the kind of political, economic, and cultural influence Europeans wanted to exert in Africa at that time. They were emphatically not interested in the kind of direct annexation that was to take place after the 1880s. Instead, the goal was informal empire of a limited kind. After the failure of the Niger expedition, for example, the British kept the hope that they might find a strong African power – perhaps the Caliphate of Sokoto – that would accept subsidies and advice and provide in return a protective shield over British commerce as it spread into the interior.

France, the only other European country active in West Africa at mid-century, had similar goals with similar limitations on conquest or annexation. In the 1840s, France too began to set up new trading posts to foster legitimate commerce, such as Grand Bassam and Assini on the Ivory Coast and Libreville in Gabon. Some of the French hoped to establish plantations, especially in Gabon, where they landed the recaptives their navy had taken from slavers at sea, but they had no more agricultural success than the British had in Sierra Leone or on the Niger. Especially in the 1850s and 1860s, they too used armed steamboats on the Senegal as a road to the interior and as a means of putting force behind their goal of informal empire over the riverine states. They too hoped for a special relationship with some large interior state, as an umbrella to cover the advance of French influence. At first they had in mind the Bambara kingdoms of Segu and Kaarta – later the new states established on the same ground by the continuing religious revolutions.

Meanwhile, Liberia and especially Sierra Leone became centers for the less formal penetration of Western culture. Though neither developed the hoped-for agriculture, the settlers in both created trade networks that reached far into the interior. Both developed an important seaborne trade along the coast, sometimes buying condemned slave ships for the purpose. This trade opened a way for many of the recaptives to return to their homelands, especially to Yorubaland in western Nigeria. By the 1840s, many returnees with years or decades of education and experience in Sierra Leone carried home their knowledge of Western ways. By the 1850s, the stream reached more than a thousand people in peak years.

Many returnees found it impossible or impractical to resettle in the home village, even if it had survived the wars. Most were involved in trade or missionary work and settled first at coastal points like Badagry or Lagos, which became a British government post in 1861. Others made their way inland, many going to Abeokuta, which was already a rallying point for the Egba, a Yoruba subgroup whose cities and towns had been largely destroyed by the wars. Concentrated groups of returnees like those in Abeokuta were soon able to play an important role in local affairs, while those who originally settled on the coast often circulated widely through Yorubaland as commercial travelers, catechists, or Christian missionaries.

By the mid-nineteenth century, other returnees also began to drift back from the New World to Yorubaland, especially from Brazil and Cuba. These "Brazilians," called *amaro* as distinct from the *saro*, or "Sierra Leoneans," also turned to commerce and settled for the most part in coastal towns from Lagos west through the present republics of Benin and Togo. There, they merged with an existing community of Afro-Portuguese who had preserved the Portuguese language and Catholic religion. By the 1890s, more than half the merchants in Dahomey were "Brazilians."

Some of the returnees were illiterate or barely literate, relatively untouched by the

West. The ordinary home language in Sierra Leone was not English but Krio, a new language with an African grammatical base and vocabulary from many sources, though heavily influenced by English. Most ordinary returnees had picked up a new African culture abroad, with a few associated aspects of Western culture. Others were fully educated in the Western manner, including education in Europe. Dr J. Africanus B. Horton, the son of an Ibo recaptive, became a British-trained physician who served from the 1850s to his retirement in 1880 as a regular member of the British Army Medical Service. He contributed research reports on tropical medicine to British medical journals, and he published even more widely on African affairs. Samuel Crowther began life as a Yoruba boy, was captured, enslaved, then recaptured by a British cruiser and landed in Sierra Leone. He went on to become one of the first students at Fourah Bay College and later the first African bishop of the Anglican Church, founder of an all-African missionary effort along the Niger River, author of a number of books about Africa, including geographical explorations and a study of the Yoruba language.

None of the returnees from Brazil achieved such intellectual distinction, but several of the Afro-French community on the Senegalese coast published books in French. Abbé Boilat, who went to school in France, published a book-length study of Senegalese society in the 1850s. Other Afro-French rose in the government service, including General Dodds, the French military commander at the conquest of Dahomey in the 1890s.

Africans who reached this level identified with Europe and accepted European culture on its own terms. They admired the technological superiority of the West and often ended by accepting Western cultural chauvinism as well. They saw the appropriate future for Africa in the direction labeled "Christianity and civilization," and they were generally proud to have a part in leading Africa to that salvation. Few suspected at mid-century that a colonial period lay ahead. They assumed that more and more authority would pass into the hands of Western-educated Africans like themselves. By the 1870s, however, a certain disillusionment began to set in. Men like J.A.B. Horton began to worry about the political future, and the rise of pseudo-scientific racism in Europe was cause for alarm. Their disillusionment was muted at first, but it deepened in the 1890s. By that time, it was abundantly clear that "Christianity and civilization" meant rule by Europeans from Europe – with diminished roles for people like themselves.

Political modernization and informal empire: the Gold Coast and Abeokuta

Men like Horton and Bishop Crowther were far more clearly "modernizers" than Muhammad ʿAli had been in Egypt; they understood the West far better than he had done, but they were not in command of independent African governments. Those Africans who did hold power were rarely able to plan ahead over a number of decades. Most lacked a clear understanding of the European threat. European warships were present along the coasts; consuls conducted diplomacy with naval power in the background; but European pressure was intermittent. Even the push for informal empire on the Niger or Senegal was sporadic. Elsewhere, the Europeans encroached only gradually with a new trading post here and there.

Some African governments, however, learned how to meet the West more nearly on its own terms, and they learned mainly from the pressure for informal empire and the local response this inspired. Local European commanders in the early nineteenth century tended to mix more actively in African politics than their predecessors had done. On the Gold Coast, for example, the British governor sent diplomatic missions to Asante in the interior. From 1824 to 1826, he abandoned a time-honored neutrality and entered a war against Asante on the side of the Ga and Fante coastal states. This was the beginning of an informal alliance which ultimately made the coastal rulers dependent on British support. In the 1830s, however, the London government decided to reduce its commitment to African trade. It turned the Gold Coast forts over to a committee of merchants, but the committee's main official on the coast, George Maclean, soon began to arbitrate quarrels among the rulers of the micro-states in the hinterland. This arbitration gradually grew into a kind of legal jurisdiction, in which a British official, with African consent, acted as judge between African litigants, enforcing African law with a few changes to bring it into line with "civilized" practice. When the British government resumed control of the forts in 1843, it found an informal judicial protectorate functioning as a constitutional device to increase the scale of political life. It was, in short, a step toward political "modernization," though designed to meet a potential threat from Asante rather than from Europe. In 1844, the British formalized this informal arrangement by asking each participating state to sign a "bond" authorizing the British governor to act for it in certain judicial matters. The Asante danger forced their compliance, but it was a clear step toward informal empire, even toward colonial rule, because later British officials acted as though the alliance was actually a protectorate.

Afro-Europeans and Western-educated Africans also worked with African governments behind the Gold Coast forts. Several times in the 1850s, they advised the traditional authorities in ways that helped them to resist informal empire, and they worked to create modernizing institutions independent of British control, such as a commercial court projected for Cape Coast.

A new phase began in the late 1860s, when King Aggrey of Cape Coast resisted British jurisdiction on the advice of the Western-educated community. The British deposed and exiled him in 1866, but this act showed many people the need for a larger and more powerful political organization, partly to resist British encroachment but also for protection against Asante if, as was widely expected, the British were to withdraw from the Gold Coast altogether. J.A.B. Horton was one of the leaders of this movement; others were African clergymen and schoolteachers associated with the Methodist Church. Between 1868 and 1873, they mobilized local opinion to support the project of creating a new state that would join all the Fante and other coastal peoples in the central and western Gold Coast. The projected constitution assigned a formal role to the traditional rulers of the existing micro-states, but it balanced their power against that of the new, Western-educated elite. The new state, sometimes called the Mankessim Confederation from its principal meeting place, recruited a military force and set up a rudimentary administration, but the British, neutral at first, decided to annex the coastal states, creating the Gold Coast colony in 1874.

The Fante Confederation achieved little, but it was an important straw in the wind showing where African opinion was tending. Nor was it alone. A similar Ga-speaking Republic of Accra was also suppressed in 1873 by the British occupation. Nearly simultaneously, the Egba United Board of Management, founded by J.W. Johnson, a Sierra Leonean returnee to Abeokuta, made a similar effort at political modernization, balancing a continuing role for the old elite with a secure place for the Western-educated. It held real power in Abeokuta from 1865 to 1872, almost the same period as the Mankessim Confederation, but it failed in the longer run. It was not able to muster the unified support of the Egba people, and it lacked the military power to withstand British pressure from Lagos.

None of these constitutional innovations was as important as the routine day-to-day participation of educated Africans in the affairs of the European posts. The distant roots of the movement for African independence, indeed, can be traced back to the political efforts of Western-educated Africans within the European sphere, often working for the colonial governments – even before the colonial period had begun for most of Africa.

Commerce and political change: Oyo

Countries undisturbed by the religious revolutions or by the direct influence of Europeans along the coast nevertheless felt the impact of the commercial revolution. Broadly speaking, people with commercial interests rose in wealth and power by comparison with the old political and military elites, but generalization at this level can mask a great variety of actual change. Three West African societies – Oyo, Asante, and the trading states of the Niger delta – can be used to illustrate the range of social and political responses to the new flow of commerce.

In Yorubaland, the overriding political event of the pre-colonial century was the collapse of the old empire of Oyo and the growth of a new Yoruba state system to replace it. Commerce was especially important in the later stages of this process, but the fragility of Oyo's political constitution was more crucial to its initial collapse. Eighteenth-century military expansion had left a structure that was both diverse and disunited. At the core was the original kingdom of Oyo, from which the expansion had begun. It was culturally Yoruba and homogeneous. Beyond were other Yoruba states under Oyo's control, but not under its day-to-day administration. Each had its own *oba*, or king, and went its own way. Each was ruled through a system of councils representing important lineages in much the same way that lineage power was checked and balanced in the core kingdom. Still further afield were a number of diverse non-Yoruba tributary states – Borgu and parts of Nupe to the north, Dahomey and other Aja-speaking states to the west as far as the borders of Asante. These were still harder to supervise, and they tended to break away in times of crisis at the center.

In the central government, an oba bearing the title of *Alafin* was balanced against a principal council called the *Oyo Mesi*. The president of the council was the *bashorun*, or military commander, and its members represented the principal non-royal lineages of the capital. The Alafin and the Oyo Mesi had been in chronic conflict throughout the eighteenth century. Much of the Alafin's power came from his constitutional role as ruler over the provinces and subject kingdoms. The council meanwhile drew its power mainly from Oyo itself. Over the eighteenth century, the expansion of the empire brought increasing power to the Alafin at the expense of the Oyo Mesi. Wealth from trade and empire brought wealth to the central government, which made it possible for the Alafin to build up the royal administrative staff, largely royal slaves.

The victory of the monarch, however, was incomplete, because the Oyo Mesi still controlled the armed forces. The final crisis came in the 1820s, precipitated by a military revolt under a certain Afonja, who had built up a private military force of local Muslims, aided from time to time by offshoots of the Fulbe Caliphate of Sokoto. Afonja first made himself independent of the central government, then detached a substantial part of northern Oyo to create the emirate of Ilorin, dependent on Sokoto. Afonja's success then prompted other provincial leaders on other fringes to revolt and to go their own ways.

The running conflict between the Oyo Mesi and the Alafin kept the center from taking effective action until it was too late to pull the pieces together again. The outer provinces all fell away into independence during a period of confused anarchy and fighting that lasted well into the 1830s. Many of the savanna-dwelling people of the metropolitan province around the city of Old Oyo moved south into the forest belt for greater security from roaming cavalry. In savanna and forest alike, walled towns became centers of refuge and power, and they began to fight one another for domination over particular regions. Victory meant the destruction of the enemy towns and the enslavement of their inhabitants, which in turn fed the illicit slave trade to Brazil and Cuba.

In the 1840s and 1850s, the worst of the anarchy was contained and a new constitution began to take shape for Yorubaland. The monarchy was restored in Oyo, but the new Alafin found the old capital untenable. He therefore retreated to the south and established New Oyo at the edge of the forest. Most of northern Yorubaland recognized New Oyo as suzerain, though real power still belonged to a series of towns controlling their own regions. These new towns were larger than Yoruba towns had been in the past, having populations of 20,000 to 60,000 people for greater security, often consolidating several older towns into one. Abeokuta, for example, brought together the remnants and refugees from more than a hundred Egba towns and worked out a new combined constitution. In the 1850s, an alliance of African Christian missionaries, returning saro, and some traditional chiefs founded the Egba United Board of Management. Other towns were also new or refounded, like Ibadan, which began as a war camp but stabilized into a city, and Ibadan's constitution reflected its military origin. From the 1850s to the 1870s, Ibadan seemed close to gaining dominance over all Yorubaland, but the threat inspired other towns to unite for fear of being swallowed up. The result was a new period of chronic warfare lasting from 1877 to 1892 and centering on Ibadan's drive for power.

Meanwhile, the slave trade ended in the 1850s, and legitimate commerce began to be important. The new flow of trade shifted income from those who captured slaves to those who had palm oil for sale. It also shifted income to communities in a position to profit as middlemen – first to ports directly on the sea like Badagry and Lagos, then to Yoruba states further inland, like Ijebu on the land side of the coastal lagoon or Abeokuta still further inland. While new trade brought new wealth, it also brought new dependence on the ports and a web of informal influence from Lagos, though it became attenuated as it stretched inland. When the British finally decided in 1892 to turn this influence into formal empire, it required only a quick demonstration of power against Ijebu. After that, treaties were imposed on most of the remaining Yoruba states. Though these were not yet treaties of outright annexation, they nevertheless gave the Lagos government so much informal control that annexation could follow whenever Lagos decided the time was ripe.

Asante

The Asante experience was somewhat different. The impact of the new commerce was stronger and came earlier in the century. Asante was also smaller than Oyo, more homogeneous in culture, with a more efficient bureaucracy and a less cumbersome constitutional balance between king and council. In most circumstances, the ruler or *Asantehene* had more individual power than the Alafin had. Asante was nevertheless a lineage-based state, just as Oyo had been. People's fundamental connection to society was through membership in their matrilineage. Matrilineages were internally self-governing within a village, and villages were nearly self-governing within the broader state. The state was regarded as having only limited functions – to maintain law and order internally and to protect the populace from foreign attack. In fact, the state in the eighteenth century had done a good deal more than that. Its expansion northward out of the forest had brought gains from tribute and slaves for sale to the coast, in a setting where both trade and warfare were monopolized by the central government.

Government circles of the early nineteenth century contained two discernible parties: an imperialist party that wanted the state to enrich its citizens through military aggression, and a peace party that wanted the same goal through state trade. A different group of citizens was likely to profit from either alternative. Military leadership stood to be rewarded by imperial advance, whereas state traders would profit from a peace policy. Though the Asantehene had a theoretical monopoly of all foreign trade, trade was actually controlled by a Company of State Traders under the head of the treasury, with trade chiefs directing the actual movement of goods. Individual merchants, however, carried on their own operations on their own account. The Asantehene supplied each important trader with a regular advance of capital in the form of gold dust, which the recipient could invest himself or pass on to subordinate agents. He was expected, of course, to make an accounting, and much of the profit went back to the treasury; but everyone who was engaged in trade, down to the lowliest caravan porters, expected to make a private profit as well, and the Asantehene sometimes left a segment of the trade open to private enterprise.

The end of the export trade in slaves after 1810 shifted income from the war party to the peace party, and the growth of legitimate trade favored it even more. From the 1840s, the Asantehene began allowing wealthy traders to invest their own capital alongside the state investment, thus shifting somewhat from state capitalism to a mixed system with room for private capital as well. Even before these changes, a few men had been able to amass great fortunes from their connections to the state trade apparatus. They were much respected and honored by the state, and they came to own many slaves, because slaves and gold dust were the main forms of transferable property. But they were less secure than they would have liked to be, because the Asantehene had the right to inherit any property held in gold dust.

After mid-century, the commercial group became richer and stronger and began to demand the end of the inheritance tax, and of government regulation it thought was crippling trade. The merchants also picked up chance allies among the underprivileged, both slaves and free, who were strongly opposed to the existing system of military conscription, hence to the military group as a whole. The commercial group and its allies were especially strong in the 1870s, and they began to look south to the newly created Gold Coast colony as a model of a better society. In 1883, they staged a coup that brought down the government of Asantehene Mensa Bonsu, but the alliance of rich and poor turned out to be fragile. Their coup was followed by a series of counter coups, while no unifying leadership emerged among the rebels.

This situation left an opening for the Gold Coast government to intervene actively in Asante politics. Political refugees from Asante gathered in the coastal towns where they were allowed to behave like a government-in-exile. By the early 1890s, Asante was well within a British informal empire. In 1896, Britain made the annexation official, being alarmed about the inland advance of the Germans in Togo to the east and that of the French in the Ivory Coast to the west. Annexation by some European power was probably inevitable. The Asante political system had already failed to respond effectively to the social and economic forces released by the commercial revolution.

The Niger Delta

The Ijo of the Niger Delta were closer still to the impact of the new commerce, and their trading states like Nembe, Bonny, and Kalabari had already adjusted their political and social structure to meet the new conditions of seaborne trade. In place of the usual African system of lineages, the new social unit here was the "canoe house," the basic trading organization. In each of these states, the kings were stronger than their eighteenth-century predecessors had been, but they still ruled with the sanction of a council made up of the heads of the individual houses. Each state controlled its own trade zone and the water routes to the interior, with a more informal influence stretching into the hinterland that furnished the slaves for export. As it turned out, this hinterland was also a place where oil palms grew naturally in the forest, so the first adjustment was simply that of adding a new product to the continued movement of slaves toward the sea.

The end of the slave trade and the growth of the palm oil trade brought changes too. British anti-slave-trade patrols based on the island of Bioko (then called Fernando Po) could intervene forcefully anywhere within reach of their ships' guns. Europeans also came to live on the rivers, to buy palm oil and prepare it for shipment, and their hulks moored offshore became a center of European influence. That influence increased as African suppliers became entangled in a web of credit. The Europeans extended goods on trust, to be repaid in palm oil at a later time. Africans had furnished their own capital for the slave trade, but they began to borrow more from the Europeans to trade in oil. Credit led to conflict, which in turn led to the creation of Afro-European "Courts of Equity" to help settle disputes. These courts, made up of African and European merchants, settled commercial disagreements. Their decisions could be enforced by commercial sanctions, but they were also validated in British law by the authority of the British consul assigned to the Bights of Benin and Biafra. Here, as in Egypt or the Gold Coast, informal empire began with European judicial institutions that gave no special advantage to either side in the beginning, but shifted over time to favor the Europeans.

At mid-century, however, the delta states were still clear of informal empire. They had switched successfully from the slave trade to the oil trade, which brought a similar level of profits to the same people trading in much the same way. Trouble began in the 1850s, when steamboats became a regular feature on the lower Niger, trading up to the junction with the Benue and on up both rivers. This carried the riverside trade well into the savanna belt, but it also opened new points of trade on the lower river, in effect giving steamers access to the palm-producing regions previously served by the Ijo canoe routes. The delta states thus found their trade reduced and their future expansion limited. To make matters worse, substitutes for palm oil began to come on the European market at lower prices – peanut oil for some purposes, petroleum for others. The price of palm oil had risen steadily until the late 1850s, but in 1862 it began to decline, and it declined so rapidly that the delta states could not sustain the total value of their exports, even by shipping larger quantities.

Social unrest also spread, as ex-slaves who had begun as canoe paddlers worked their way into the ranks of the merchants. They were unhappy at being denied power and prestige to match their wealth. Revolts broke out in all the delta states from the 1850s onward, with the British navy called in from time to time to help shore up the old regime. In 1869, part of the population of Bonny emigrated to found a new state, Opobo, under an ex-slave named Ja-Ja, who soon established his control over most of the markets Bonny had once dominated.

Through all of this, the British consuls continued to increase their influence over Ijo affairs. By the mid-1870s, the delta could be counted as part of the informal British empire. By the end of the decade, informal British control stretched up the Niger as well, where the National African Company had scores of trading posts along the rivers. In 1884–5, the British became concerned about French and German annexations elsewhere in Africa. They therefore formalized their hold on the Niger by asking the rulers of the Niger coast and riverside to sign "voluntary" treaties placing themselves under British protection – the first major step toward creating the territorial unit that was to be Nigeria.

Shaykh Umar Tal and the Futaanke empire

By the 1830s, religious revolutions in the western Sudan were markedly less revolutionary. Abdul Kader's reform movement in Fuuta Tooro had been secularized and stabilized since the early century. In the Caliphate of Sokoto and in Borno, the new

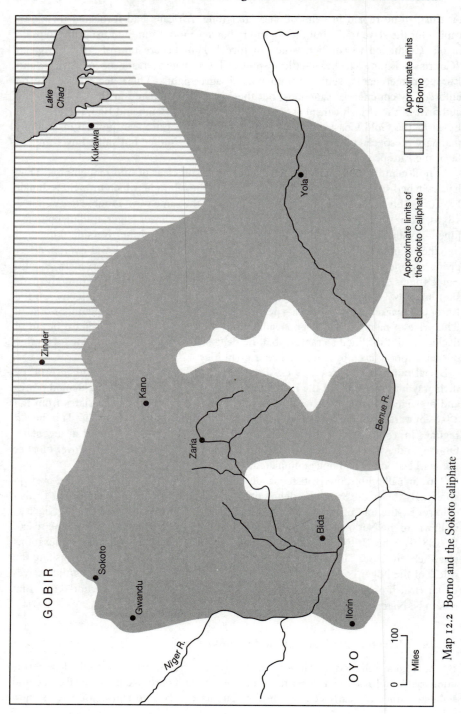

Map 12.2 Borno and the Sokoto caliphate

political structures were in place, and the demand for further change was muted, if not silent. On the Niger bend and in Maasina, the descendants of earlier reformers were fighting one another, as the Kunta shaykhs set themselves up as leaders of dissident Fulbe and Tuareg trying to separate Timbuktu and the Niger bend from the Caliphate of Hamdallahi. Within that caliphate, reform had also lost some of its appeal. In the 1840s, a new group of military men came to power, men who had been too young for the earlier revolution and depended on power politics, not religious fervor, to secure the place of the caliphate in the Niger valley.

At the same time, the earlier reformers had been able to stir men with their demands for a just and godly society, and that demand was clearly not satisfied. As before, people resented the way society treated them, for many different reasons, and the idiom of religion could still appeal to people and unite them behind a leader. Flurries of reform preaching and organization were continuous all through the first half of the century. Several broke into open rebellion, but the existing governments were able to suppress them with apparent ease. It was only with the 1850s that a new and somewhat different kind of movement arose under Shaykh Umar Tal, a cleric from western Fuuta Tooro. He built an empire that was larger and more centralized than Hamdallahi or Sokoto had been, and he carved it out of territory that was mainly non-Muslim.

Umar also preached a new religious doctrine, different from the Qadiriya that had served other reformers. His message was that of the Tijaniyya, a comparatively new religious brotherhood founded in Fez in the 1780s by Ahmad al-Tijāni. The Tijāni doctrine was more exclusive and rigid than was common to sufi orders. Compared to the Qadiriya, it was also more mystical and concerned with the correct ritual practices to bring a sense of direct contact with God. At the same time, it had a weaker tradition of asceticism than did other sufi orders (or such anti-sufi reform movements as the Wahabi of eighteenth-century Arabia). Ahmad al-Tijāni's claim to be the "seal" of the saints was also exceptional; it asserted that he was the final Muslim saint in the same sense that Muhammad was the seal of the prophets. This implied that the Tijaniyya, was different from the other sufi orders in offering not merely *a* way to God, but the only correct way. Some later Tijāni clerics have pushed the claim of exclusivity to the point of making the order appear more a separate sect than a *tariqa*.

By the 1830s, the Tijaniyya was widely followed in the Maghrib and out into the desert, but the main line of transmission to the western Sudan was to come by way of Umar Taal's pilgrimage to Mecca in about 1830. The order's khalifa for the Holy Cities of Arabia appointed Umar head of the order in the western Sudan. With that authority, he made a slow return toward Senegambia with prolonged stops in Borno, Sokoto, Timbuktu, and Hamdallahi before settling down to preach and build up his own following. The base he chose was not his home country but Dingirai, on the frontiers of the Almaamate of Fuuta Jaalo far to the south.

Umar's early appeal was peaceful and widespread. In 1846–7, for example, he traveled with a group of followers from Fuuta Jaalo down the Gambia valley to the Atlantic, then north through the Serer and Wolof kingdoms, and finally up the Senegal valley through Fuuta Tooro, then back to his base at Dingirai. During the next two years, he began military operations that slowly turned his capital into the center of a small state incorporating several of the smaller kingdoms in the upper Niger valley. Toward the end of 1852–3, he declared a holy war and began still more extensive conquests from Dingirai north toward the upper Senegal through a region mainly Mande-speaking and non-Muslim.

Umar's jihad was different from those of earlier reformers in that he tried mainly to conquer new territory for Islam, rather than purifying the practices of Muslim governments. He called for no jihad against the existing almaamates of Fuuta Tooro, Fuuta Jaalo, or Bundu, and he was less doctrinaire than most earlier reformers. He played lightly on the differences between his own Tijāni way and that of the Qadiriya. His main interest in the Muslim territories of Senegambia was their support against "pagans" further east. He called for a great *fergo*, or voluntary withdrawal with wives and cattle, from Fulbe Fuuta Tooro and Bundu to follow him eastward. In Bundu, he played dynastic politics so as to establish an Almaami favorable to his interests, but neither there nor in Fuuta Tooro did he try to establish his direct rule. But, over the next few years, he drew off as much as 25 per cent of the Futaanke population, and half that of Bundu. By 1854, he controlled parts of Kaarta from a new capital at Nioro, in the sahel between the Niger and the Senegal, as the base for a Futaanke empire, sometimes called the Tukolor empire from the name of the sedentary farming class in Fuuta Tooro.

During the rest of the 1850s, his main concern was to continue the fergo from Fuuta in order to build up the new base at Nioro. This inevitably involved a confrontation with the French, who were simultaneously trying to establish their absolute control over Senegal River trade and their informal empire over riverside kingdoms. The Franco-Umarian military confrontation came in 1857, when Umar tried to capture Médine, the French post near the head of Senegal navigation. But the post held out under an Afro-French commander long enough to be relieved by a new force sent upriver by steamboat. The result was not so much a French victory as a standoff, leaving the French the unquestioned masters of Senegal navigation, while Umar kept his conquests between Dingirai and the Senegal and eastward along the desert edge. He still visited Fuuta to recruit followers and soldiers, though he never claimed authority there.

Shaykh Umar's next objectives were still further east. In 1860, he began a new series of campaigns for control of the Niger Valley from the kingdom of Segu northeast to Timbuktu. Segu had a Muslim minority, but it was culturally and linguistically Mande or Bambara and safely "pagan" in religion. Further downstream, however, both Timbuktu and the Caliphate of Hamdallahi were already reformed Muslim, though Qadiri, not Tijāni. Umar first captured Segu, then moved on in 1863 to take Hamdallahi and Timbuktu – his first major capture of already-Muslim territory.

The military operation was successful at first, but it brought on a counter-movement led by the Kunta from the desert north of Timbuktu and others disaffected with Umar's regime. The rebels defeated and killed Umar in 1864. Although Umar's nephew later managed to reconquer large parts of what had been Maasina, he ruled it without recognizing allegiance to what was left of the Umarian empire. The Umarian empire broke apart. Even before Umar's death it had been too big for continuous central control, and the shaykh had already allocated large provinces to one or another of his family or followers – though these provinces were larger and fewer than the emirates under Sokoto. The main sub-capitals were Dingirai for the southwest, Nioro for the sahel, Segu for the Niger Valley, and Koniakari just east of the upper Senegal. Umar's son, Ahmadu Seku, took over the central power and the title *Lamido Juulbe* (commander of the faithful).

Such a large empire tempted French strategists to plan informal penetration under the Lamido Juulbe's shield, but the local French military commanders preferred to try for outright conquest, which they carried through in a series of campaigns beginning in the late 1880s and ending in 1893.

New rulers for Senegambia

Senegambia's experience with religious reform went back at least as far as Nasīr al-Dīn's jihad in the 1670s, but the Wolof, Serer, and Madinka states near the Atlantic coast and along the Gambia remained unreformed until the 1860s. Then, in a short space of only three decades, the old secular dynasties were overthrown by new clerical leaders preaching a purified Islamic state. Finally, in an even shorter space of time, French and British arms prevailed and established another and still newer set of rulers – this time from Europe.

Most of the old guard of secular-minded, though normally Muslim rulers worked within a political framework consisting of one or more royal lineages that supplied rulers in turn, with a council that represented the other important free lineages in that society – balancing, in effect, the royal lineages and one another. Because the lineages themselves were to some extent autonomous units, it was easy for this kind of state to grant autonomy to other groups that might demand it. Over recent centuries, clerics, often with a mercantile background, had asked for and obtained permission to form small autonomous enclaves – often no more than a village and its surrounding agricultural land. There, the clerics and their followers could practice Islam as they wished, free from secular interference. By the early nineteenth century, the kings had created scores of such enclaves, and they were already a source of potential opposition and even an alternate source of authority, should the secular state weaken.

The secular states of the nineteenth century *had* become weak. The constitutional checks and balances worked so strongly against the monarch that few could maintain effective control, either against important lineage heads or even against their own standing armies of slave-soldiers. These slave-soldiers, or *ceddo* (*thiedo* in French), were a serious source of disorder in the countryside, raiding the peasants in their own territory or across nearby frontiers. Beginning in the 1840s, peanut cultivation began to extend inland from the Gambia River and from the coast. The end of the slave trade may have deprived the rulers and ceddo of some income. It certainly diverted income to the peasants who grew peanuts for export, and to the merchants who bulked and transported the peanuts to navigable water. Disorder, in short, gave the peasantry a grievance against authority, while the clerical-mercantile group could provide leadership for a series of revolts that struck almost everywhere in Senegambia, but with great local variation and complexity.

The central role in this series of revolts belonged to Mamadu Ba, commonly called

Ma Ba. He was originally from Fuuta, like Shaykh Umar, but he lived in the tiny riverside state of Baddibu, or Rip, on the north bank of the Gambia. In 1862, he won control of Baddibu and moved on to conquer Saalum as well, occasionally intervening eastward up the Gambia or across to the south bank. But Ma Ba was essentially a religious leader, not a military man; his wider influence came indirectly through his followers. Among these were Lat Joor (Dior), who seized power in Kajoor, and Alburi Njai (N'Diayi), the ruler of Jolof. Another important figure, Momar Anta Mbake, was Ma Ba's friend, the tutor of his son, and the father of Amadu Bamba, who in turn founded the Mourid brotherhood and went on to become one of the most important religious leaders in twentieth-century Senegal. Other revolts continued to the eve of the European conquest.

The British and French in the trade enclaves generally tried to support the old rulers in this series of wars, but the secular side gradually lost power in spite of foreign support. The last act was played out in the late 1880s. It began when Mamadu Lamin Drame led a final religious revolt against the secular rulers of Gajaaga and Bundu on the upper Senegal. That region was already in the sphere of French informal control. France entered and pursued Mamadu Lamin to his death on the middle Gambia. French forces had already defeated and killed Lat Joor of Kajoor in 1886. They drove out Alburi Njai of Jolof in 1890, and they completed their conquest of Fuuta Tooro in 1891, thereby introducing the colonial period to most of Senegambia.

Samori Ture and the Juula revolution

Almost all the religious revolutions sketched so far took place in the northern half of the savanna belt. In the southern half of the savanna (the "middle belt" as Nigerians call it, sometimes called the pre-forest zone further west), the socio-religious setting was different. There, Muslims were only a small minority, and Muslim penetration had only recently been carried by the juula, or merchants. Islam was therefore identified with the merchant community even more closely than it was further north. Almost all juula were Muslim, though not all Muslims were juula. Before the eighteenth century, the juula communities scattered along the trade routes had a tacit understanding with the local rulers: if the juula stayed out of politics, the rulers would stay out of commerce.

This understanding was broken by such events as the Fulbe jihad of the 1720s in Fuuta Jaalo, which opened access to the coast through a single Muslim state. A merchant-led revolution further east created another Muslim commercial state at Kankan. Then, from the coastal side, the krio-speaking Sierra Leoneans began to penetrate as merchants by many different routes through and around Fuuta Jaalo. People in Kankan still remember the middle decades of the nineteenth century as a time of special prosperity for their trade.

The religious reform movement in the northern savannas had repercussions in the south as well, if only by encouraging rebels to follow the fashion of stating their objectives in religious terms. The Tijaniyya made steady gains after the arrival of Shaykh Umar in the 1840s. Within a decade or so, most of Fuuta Jaalo had joined the new tarīqa. But here the more serious call for religious reform came from a Qadiri leader, Modi Mamadu Jue, who organized a rebellion in the late 1840s. His followers were called Hubbu from a term meaning "those who love God." The movement stood for the reforms promised and then set aside by the original jihad more than a century earlier. It failed to overturn the almaamate, but it remained an effective rebel military force into the 1880s.

In the middle decades of the century, another group of rebellions with religious overtones occurred in the region south and east of Kankan. These were in effect, a new installment of the earlier juula revolution. Some juula leaders founded new states, but none survived very long until, in the 1870s, Samori Ture emerged as a juula leader with remarkable military talents. With his conquest of Kankan in 1875, he became the most important force in the region. By the early 1880s, his control stretched from the forest edge northward to include the Buré goldfields and the upper Niger as far downstream as Bamako. But Samori's empire was clearly less Islamic than those created by the early jihads. He was Muslim, but he had joined some of the earlier fighting on the secular side. For a short while he adopted a strongly pro-Islamic policy, taking the title of Almaami in 1886 and using state power to force conversion. But he later dropped the religious emphasis, and it appears in retrospect that Samori was moved mainly by the hope that Islam could help to unify the diverse people he happened to control.

Until the 1880s, Samori built his empire without concern for a European threat. The British and Krio in Sierra Leone served as a convenient outlet for gold and other exports. The French on the Senegal were far away until they began their military advance to the east in 1879. That move was so nearly simultaneous with Samori's own drive down the Niger Valley that both arrived before Bamako in 1883. After some initial brushes with French forces, Samori was able to arrange a truce in 1886–7. That left him free to pursue territorial expansion eastward into the present-day Côte d'Ivoire. The French meanwhile were tied up with their wars against the Futaanke empire to the north.

It seems likely that, about the mid-1880s, Samori had reached something like the limits of territory he could conquer with his original resources and support. It was an empire of diverse ethnic groups, with no earlier experience of political unification, and without even the self-interest of its citizens to justify the material cost of still more territorial expansion. In 1888–9, a major revolt broke out throughout the western part of the empire, which the Almaami suppressed only with great difficulty.

Then, in the early 1890s, the entire scene changed. The French had finished with the Lamido Juulbe in 1891, and this freed them to concentrate on Samori. Samori, in turn, had begun to acquire repeating rifles through his trade with Sierra Leone. He might have used them in a last-ditch stand against the French, but instead he chose to conquer a new secondary empire to the east of his original holdings, meanwhile fighting a series of rearguard actions against the French. Between 1891 and the beginning of 1894, the French conquered the whole of Samori's original empire, though at great cost in the face of a scorched-earth policy that left them little of value. In those same years, Samori's forces conquered a new empire. At its peak in mid-1896, it took in approximately the northern half of the present-day Côte d'Ivoire and extended eastward halfway across northern Ghana.

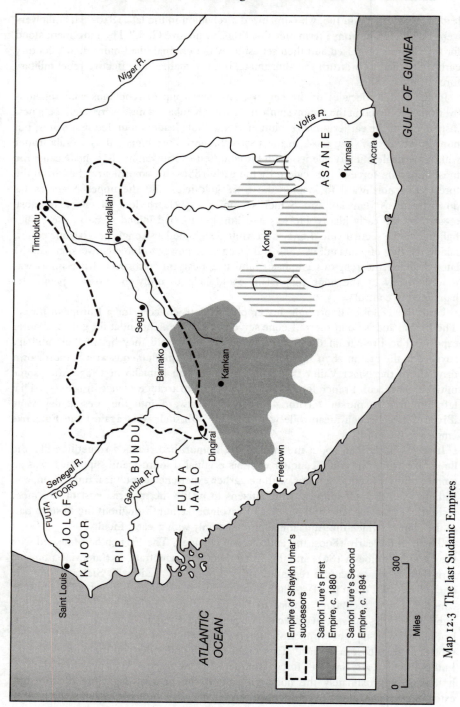

Map 12.3 The last Sudanic Empires

In abandoning his original empire, in short, Samori abandoned the objectives of the juula revolution, abandoned the goal of creating a Muslim state and turned his army into a weapon with which to exact tribute from the conquered people of a secondary empire. It was the most extreme case of secondary empire in West Africa, with many resemblances to Rabih's path of conquest across the central Sudan to Borno in that same decade: his end was the same. It was impossible to hold out against Europeans who had more and better weapons. Samori's second empire fell in two years. A French column seized him in 1898 and exiled him to Gabon, where he died two years later.

Suggestions for further reading

Adeleye, R.A., *Power and Diplomacy in Northern Nigeria. 1804–1906*, London: Longman, 1971.

Ajayi, J.F.A., and Michael Crowder, *History of West Africa*, Vol. 2, 2nd edn, London: Longman, 1987.

Akintoye, S.A., *Revolution and Power Politics in Yorubaland 1840–1893*. London: Longman, 1971.

Brenner, Louis, *The Shehus of Kukawa: A History of the Al-Kenemi Dynasty of Bornu*, London: Oxford University Press, 1973.

Curtin, Philip D., *The Image of Africa*, Madison: University of Wisconsin Press, 1961.

Dike, K.O., *Trade and Politics in the Niger Delta*, London: Oxford University Press, 1954.

Eltis, David, *Economic Growth and the Ending of the Transatlantic Slave Trade*, New York: Oxford University Press, 1987.

Hiskett, Mervyn, *The Development of Islam in West Africa*, London: Longman, 1984.

July, Robert W., *The Origins of Modern African Thought*, London: Faber, 1967.

Last, D. Murray, *The Sokoto Caliphate*, London: Longman, 1967.

Law, Robin, *The Oyo Empire c.1600–c.1836: A West African Imperialism in the Era of the Slave Trade*, Oxford: Clarendon Press, 1977.

Munro, J. Forbes, *Africa and the International Economy 1800–1960*, London: J.M. Dent, 1976.

Person, Yves, "Samori and Resistance to the French," in R.I. Rotberg and A. Mazrui (eds), *Protest and Power in Black Africa*, New York: Oxford University Press, 1970.

Reynolds, Edward, *Trade and Economic Change on the Gold Coast 1807–1874*, London: Longman, 1974.

Roberts, Richard L., *Warriors, Merchants, and Slaves: The State and Economy in the Middle Niger Valley, 1700–1914*, Stanford: Stanford University Press, 1987.

Robinson, David, *The Holy War of Umar Tal: the Western Sudan in the mid-Nineteenth Century*, Oxford: Clarendon Press, 1985.

Smith, Robert S., *Warfare and Diplomacy in Pre-Colonial West Africa*, 2nd edn, London: James Currey, 1989.

Wilks, Ivor, *Asante in the Nineteenth Century*, Cambridge: Cambridge University Press, 1975.

13

A CENTURY OF IRONIES IN EAST AFRICA
(c.1780-1890)

The successive social and economic revolutions that accompanied Africa's increasing involvement in international trade were compressed, in East Africa, into a much briefer time period than on the western side of the continent. The slave trade on the Atlantic coast had grown from minute beginnings in the fifteenth century to a peak in the eighteenth, then changed again in the early nineteenth with the further growth of the Angolan slave trade and the shift along the Guinea coast to ever larger trade in the products of African soil and labor. In eastern Africa, however, especially in the areas that are now Kenya, Uganda, and Tanzania, the slave trade had been insignificant before the late eighteenth century. The rise of a major slave trade, the attempts to abolish it, and the increasing trade in commodities produced within Africa therefore came simultaneously in this region, with drastic consequences for its history.

In one sense, the lateness of these developments made the East African historian's task easy. Here, the tellers of oral traditions are not forced to reach far back into the memories of their ancestors in order to describe the transformation. In most places, it is still possible to reconstruct from oral sources a picture of society as it was before the start of the slave and ivory trades, and then to see what happened after the trade began. This experiment in historical perception is especially valuable whenever the full impact of the slave trade was delayed until the second half of the nineteenth century. The grandfathers of today's old men were then active, and living memories can be taken as a picture of what probably happened earlier in other places, because the changes that were well under way in northern Mozambique by the early eighteenth century, for example, affected some isolated societies only in the 1880s, and, in still other places, had not yet occurred at the time of the colonial conquest.

Slave trading was stimulated in East Africa by two major economic developments. First, the slave-plantation complex, involving imported capital and managers, tropical land, and African slave labor, expanded to the Indian Ocean. In the eighteenth century, the French brought this system to the Mascarene Islands, including Mauritius and Reunion, 800 miles east of Madagascar. They experimented with a number of crops, but, by century's end, sugar had become the basis of the economy. By the final quarter of the eighteenth century, the French demand for slaves had a substantial effect on the East African coast. Whereas the economy of the Mascarenes was simply the Caribbean sugar economy transplanted to the other side of the world, on Zanzibar the plantation idea was applied to a totally different crop – cloves – and involved a different set of entrepreneurs – Omani Arabs from the Persian Gulf. They too wanted slaves from the mainland. The Omanis who remained at the Persian Gulf used slaves as domestics, on date plantations, and as sailors.

The second major stimulus to the slave trade in East Africa was, paradoxically, the British abolitionist campaign. Between 1815 and 1831, the Anglo-Portuguese anti-slave-trade treaties outlawed the Portuguese slave trade north of the equator, thus increasing procurement in the south, in both Angola on the west side of the continent and Mozambique on the east. At the same time, the British negotiated the first of a series of abolition treaties with the authorities in control of the East African trading island of Zanzibar. Again the consequences were paradoxical, for the treaties reduced the price asked for slaves, thereby encouraging people to find new local uses for slave labor, so that in the end, the total number of slaves captured each year within East Africa actually increased.

It was thus one of the great ironies of nineteenth-century East African history that the legal abolition of the slave trade in the region led in fact to its extension into new areas. This was true not only of the revived Mozambique trade to Brazil early in the century, but also further up the coast, where the most rapid growth of slave imports to Zanzibar, in the late 1840s, came at a time when increasing restrictions were being placed on the trade. The end of the slave trade by sea from the southern port of Kilwa in 1873 set off a whole new round of trade on the mainland nearer to Zanzibar. Much the same thing happened in Ethiopia, where the slave trade to the Persian Gulf by way of southern Arabia became economic once the British patrols cut off the direct sea route from East Africa.

The extension of the slave trade as a result of abolition is an irony in two senses: as the Oxford English Dictionary defines it, *irony* is "a contradictory outcome of events as if in mockery of the promise and fitness of things"; it is also a drama whose inner meaning – for those who look back on the events – is quite different from the outer meaning it had for those who were immediately concerned. We have not yet reached the bottom of the irony, in either sense of the term, because the "legitimate trade" that abolitionists wanted to substitute for the slave trade was usually a commerce in the products of slave labor. For instance, cloves were considered "legitimate" even though grown and picked by slaves. Rubber and copal (for varnish) collected by slaves on the mainland were also "legitimate," as was grain grown by slaves on the East African coast. Many prominent abolitionists were quite conscious that they were asking for the local use of slaves who had previously been exported.

On the Indian Ocean sugar islands themselves, abolition led to a labor importation system that shared many characteristics of slavery. The British took the island of Mauritius in 1810, during the Napoleonic Wars. They later abolished slavery, but continued sugar production using indentured laborers, whose contracts were enforced by penal sanctions. They were taken from India either by force or in conditions of extreme distress, and given little real chance of returning to India. Conditions for the new laborers on the sugar plantations were nearly identical to the earlier conditions of slave labor.

Along with the new demand for plantation products came an enormous increase in Europe's demand for ivory. Here was another irony of East African history, that the unequal development of the African and European economies should have gone so far that a trivial demand for combs and billiard balls could revolutionize the economy of the entire region. Ivory had been exported to India for at least a thousand years, and this age-old trade continued in the nineteenth century. But in addition, Europe and America began to find new uses for the soft ivory of East Africa. Hard ivory from West Africa had been used for knife handles. Now the softer varieties from the east were used for combs, piano keys, and billiard balls. Others sources of soft ivory were southern Africa and the Nilotic Sudan, but in East Africa demand outstripped supply throughout the nineteenth century, and the price rose continuously.

It rose even more steeply in real terms than it did in monetary value, for the prices of European and American goods were declining at the same time the price for ivory was rising. This was, of course, a consequence of the industrialization of cloth production in the West. Here is another irony, for the terms of trade with the Euro-American world were clearly shifting in East Africa's favor throughout the nineteenth century: Africans had to exchange less and less ivory to acquire more and more cloth. Yet by the end of a century of "improvement," the East African economy was a shambles. The point here is simple. When Africans hunted elephants, they were not building an industry that could lead to further economic growth; they were simply depleting a limited resource. In return, they received cloth, but they also received guns and powder with which to kill more animals, make war, and enslave one another. Some of these activities were uneconomic in themselves, at least in the social cost to East African society. But dependence on a single major export leads to a fragile economy in any case, and heavy dependence on the export of a non-renewable resource was especially serious in distorting the economy toward activities that would inevitably end after a fairly short period.

Mozambique and Kilwa

In the eighteenth century, Portuguese and Indian traders in Mozambique supplied India with ivory, but then, in the early nineteenth century, the ivory trade shifted north beyond the zone of Portuguese control, and Mozambique turned increasingly to the slave trade. It had not been especially large or profitable in the eighteenth century until the French from the Mascarene Islands shifted to Mozambique as a source of supply. They had begun buying slaves mainly in Madagascar in the late 1730s, but when these slaves acquired a fortunate reputation for "insolence," the French switched gradually to Mozambique. ·

After the turn of the century, New World demand became more important, with Mozambique figuring as a major source of slaves for Brazil. Through the 1820s and 1830s, according to recent careful estimates, more than 15,000 slaves were exported each year from the single port at Mozambique Island. The Portuguese also opened many subsidiary ports up and down the coast for direct trade with the Brazilians. Trade to the French islands continued, carried in Arab boats as far as the Comoro Islands north of Madagascar, then onward by the French. Spanish vessels also called for slaves to Cuba, and even a few United States vessels took on slave cargoes for the Americas.

In the last quarter of the eighteenth century, the coastal trade north of the Portuguese sphere also began to grow, first in slaves, then in ivory. This process began in Kilwa though it ended in Zanzibar. In the late eighteenth century, Kilwa was the center of a rivalry among three major outside powers. For the Portuguese, the island port was

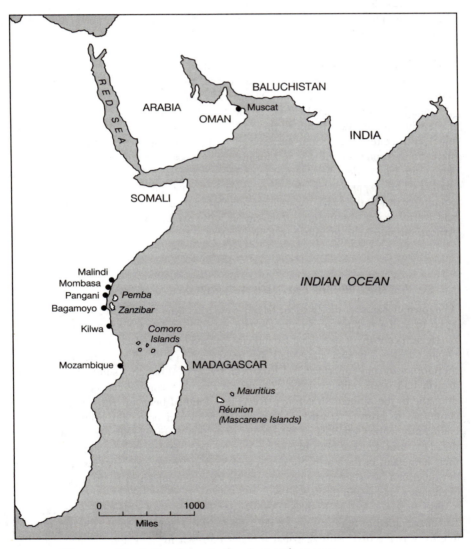

Map 13.1 The Indian Ocean in the nineteenth century

a difficult competitor, just beyond the range of their control and able to draw on the same hinterland. The Yao traders who supplied Mozambique with ivory could also choose to deal with its competitors at Kilwa. A second power, the Omani Arabs, had been pushing south since the seventeenth century, when Portuguese strength in the northern Indian Ocean began to break up. They drove Portugal out of the Persian Gulf by 1650, then from Mombasa by the end of the seventeenth century. The island of Zanzibar, across a narrow channel from the coast, then became the center of Omani influence on the coast and a major trade link between East Africa and the Persian Gulf. The Omanis also had intermittent control over Kilwa's ivory trade. The French from the Mascarenes were the third power drawn to Kilwa; they were not getting all the slaves they wanted from the Portuguese zone, and they too had the hope of reaching the southern hinterland through Kilwa.

Kilwa's trade had two special bursts of activity in the late eighteenth and early nineteenth centuries. First, in the late 1770s, the French began to export great numbers of slaves from Kilwa to the Mascarenes, but this phase was brief, first because of Omani opposition, then because of the Napoleonic wars. The second great jump came with the northward shift of the Yao ivory traders to Kilwa after the turn of the nineteenth century; it became increasingly dangerous for them to pass through the slave-trading zones on the way to Mozambique's coast, and the Portuguese raised the duties on Yao trade when demand for ivory was rising dramatically on the world market. This expansion in the ivory trade not only led to the growth of Kilwa's commerce; it was the basis of Zanzibar's commercial empire in the nineteenth century, and ivory became the major commodity in an expanding trade throughout the East African interior far to the north of Kilwa.

Zanzibar and the East African economy

The town of Zanzibar on Zanzibar Island grew from little more than a fishing village in 1710 to a fine trading center dotted with merchants' stone houses in 1800; in the nineteenth century, it became a capital city, graced by the palace of the sultans of the Omani dynasty. It also controlled the great trade of the East African coast, and therefore attracted American and European traders. Although a solid base for future growth had been built by 1800, Zanzibar's rise as a commercial center was most dramatic in the nineteenth century. Revenues doubled between 1804 and 1819, and continued to grow afterward. Indian traders who had come for brief visits in the eighteenth century established themselves permanently in ever-increasing numbers at the same time Omani Arab plantation owners and caravan traders came down from their homeland in the north. Sultan Seyyid Said of Oman paid his first visit in 1828, but he ended by establishing his dynasty on Zanzibar, which to his predecessors had been only a minor and distant colony.

The Indians, Arabs, English, Americans, French, and Germans who came to Zanzibar traded in one or more of the island's three major exports. The ivory of the interior was the first, with Zanzibar a major entrepôt for its shipment overseas. The second major export product was slaves, also drawn from the mainland, shipped early in the century to the French islands, but throughout the century to the Persian Gulf and beyond. Zanzibar was also a major destination of slaves for the clove plantations, the third pillar of its economy.

Early in the nineteenth century, a rough division of the export trade developed, with Arabs shipping slaves while the Indians exported ivory. The Indian traders had a competitive advantage because they had information about the Bombay ivory market, where most East African tusks were taken. Some Omani Arabs exported ivory, but they were increasingly marginal traders. In 1800, most Indians on Zanzibar had come for brief visits; a decade later, several were in permanent residence, and their numbers grew along with the value of the island's commerce. Many Omanis also came to settle and enjoyed their own competitive advantage in the slave trade, since many slaves were sold for domestic use on the date plantations in the Persian Gulf.

Of these three products, only ivory rose continuously in profitability throughout the century, to become the main engine of the island's economic expansion. As we have seen, the first boost came from the rise in Portuguese duties at Mozambique, previously India's main supplier. Prices in the rest of East Africa immediately jumped, bringing rapid growth in ivory exports between 1800 and 1820. By this time, when the demands of the Indian market had been met, European and American demand began to grow. Traders from Salem, Massachusetts, played a considerable role in direct trade with East Africa, but most ivory went to Bombay, where part of it was reexported to England. The price of ivory rose continuously from $22 a *frasila* (35 lb) in 1823 to $89 a frasila in 1873. Before the American Civil War, when the United States was still Zanzibar's main non-Asian trading partner, ivory produced in the slave-trading economy of Zanzibar was exchanged for textiles made with cotton grown on the slave plantations in the American South. These same Salem traders carried cured beef from Madagascar for the consumption of Cuba's slaves. Whether the ivory was carried to India, to Britain, or to the United States, it was the one product of East Africa that gave sure profits throughout the century, providing capital for other sorts of ventures and leaving a cushion when those ventures faltered.

In the areas that are now Tanzania and Kenya, ivory had long been passed from hand to hand from the interior to the coast, or brought by hunting bands who ranged up to a couple of hundred miles into the interior. The ivory trade of the nineteenth century, however, provided incentives for the development of caravans that traveled a thousand miles or more, some beginning in the interior and making their way to the coast, others marching up-country from the ocean. The dates of the first caravans are uncertain, but it is clear that caravans were making their way from the coast into the interior of central Tanzania by 1811, and by the 1820s the Arabs appear to have gone beyond Lake Tanganyika into what is now Zaire. Caravans organized by Nyamwezi from western Tanzania must have begun even earlier. Whether the caravans were led by Nyamwezi, or Arabs, or coastal Swahili-speakers, they all tended by the 1850s to make their way to the land of the Nyamwezi as the main trade center, then to branch northwest around Lake Victoria into Uganda, southwest around the southern end of Lake Tanganyika, or directly west to Ujiji on the lake shore.

The caravans varied enormously in size, ranging from a mere handful of porters to a line of thousands snaking its way across the landscape. At dangerous spots the traders would wait until several caravans had gathered so as to mobilize greater strength in defense. Larger caravans were better able to bargain with powerful local chiefs about the exact amount to be paid in tolls. Such caravans developed very early their own sets of specialists: the *kiongozi* led the way wearing a long bright red gown and other adornments – often the black and white skin of a colobus monkey and a headdress made from the feathers of a crested crane; a medicine man went along to read omens and to make magical charms for the caravan's protection; tent men, cooks, armed guards, and, of course, porters all went along. In the caravans described by the explorer Richard Burton after his 1857 trip, the kiongozi was followed by the bearers of ivory, with cowbells attached to the points of especially large tusks sounding as the caravan made its way. After the ivory came beads and cloth wrapped in large bolsters. Then came the men carrying rhino teeth, hides, salt cones, tobacco, brass wire, iron hoes, supplies and stores, beds and tents.

The trips were long and difficult, beset by the dangers of thieves and at the mercy of powerful authorities along the way. The many caravans that passed through the same few supply stations were perfectly suited to transmitting infectious diseases. The diaries of the nineteenth-century European travelers who followed the caravan routes are filled with frequent casual references to smallpox, "seasoning fever," and numerous other diseases that gave caravan porters a high rate of mortality. The difficulties of the trip, and the unusually labor-intensive means of transport, with one man carrying seventy pounds at the very most, made caravans an enormously expensive way of moving goods. It paid to carry ivory, which had a very high value per pound, and cloth or beads with which to purchase ivory, but many of the potential export products and consumer needs of the interior were simply not worth the high cost of carrying. Slaves, of course, had the advantage of being able to walk, though the mortality and morbidity rates for slaves moving into unfamiliar disease environments were high, as they were also for porters. The merchants could sustain a moderate loss of life among their human chattel if the price paid for slaves was high enough, but for the slave, death was final.

Ivory was the kind of product that led to a moving traders' frontier. The richest area for great herds of elephants and for their valuable large tusks was always further into the interior, beyond the region where the hunters had already taken their first harvest. By the second half of the nineteenth century, many of the most enterprising traders were pushing into eastern parts of present-day Zaire. Warfare and slave raiding tended to move with the traders' frontier not only because the caravans traded in slaves as well as in ivory, but also because the skills needed for elephant hunting were the same as those for making war and capturing people. In the days of the spear, elephant hunters were highly skilled indeed, although the rapid improvement of imported firearms in the 1870s and 1880s made it possible for even the relatively unskilled to hunt elephants.

The onward passage of the frontier often left economic collapse in its wake. On top of the ravages of warfare and slave raiding, the best of the elephant herds were gone. The only good possibility was to exploit the caravans going further into the interior, and some chiefs were able to collect tolls if they controlled an important river crossing or source of water in an arid region. A few people were able to continue elephant hunting on a smaller scale, as the Gogo did just to the east of the Nyamwezi, and a few points grew into important way stations as the frontier moved westward and it became difficult for coastal traders to make the entire trip without an intermediary supply base.

By the 1850s, the Arabs had founded the town of Unyanyembe in Nyamwezi country. Individual traders maintained storehouses; a general agent was able to dispose of excess cloth, to find porters for caravans, and to supply trading parties with goods.

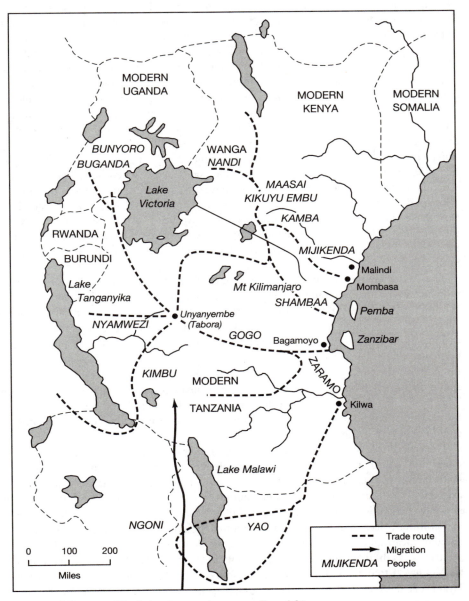

Map 13.2 Trade in nineteenth-century East Africa

Slaves at Unyanyembe produced food to provision the trading parties, and the town had gunsmiths, carpenters, masons, and other artisans. Many Arabs based themselves at Unyanyembe for years, sending agents or going themselves on trading parties along one of several routes further to the west. Local populations in very fertile areas, both near Unyanyembe and elsewhere along trade routes, went into the provisioning business, founding major rest stops for caravans in order to sell their surplus crops. Other farmers sometimes moved their homesteads to isolated wet spots in the middle of very barren areas, where they could then charge very high prices for provisioning caravans.

One puzzling question about the caravan system is why the Arabs participated in it at all. They were not the originators of the caravans, nor were they the first businessmen to respond to the expanded demand. Although the evidence is shadowy, all the major caravan routes into the interior appear to have been pioneered by the interior peoples themselves. In the Kilwa hinterland, the Yao were carrying on trade before the first coastal traders pushed on into the interior. In southern Kenya, Kamba traders, from the area southeast of Mount Kenya, traded successfully in ivory before the mid-nineteenth-century period when coastal merchants deprived them of the route they had pioneered. On the Nyamwezi route, trade goods had reached both Uganda and Rwanda in the eighteenth century, and Nyamwezi traders were at the coast by about 1800, perhaps earlier. Nyamwezi caravans also appear to have traveled more austerely than those of the Arabs, and as a result had lower overhead costs. The Nyamwezi had the necessary political ties in the interior and even developed trade-raiding outposts far into Zaire. Their caravans were reportedly much more numerous than Arab caravans in the 1850s.

The Arabs' competitive position depended on force of arms, access to credit, and influence over Zanzibari trade policies. Of these, force of arms was the least important. While the Zanzibari Arabs had access to superior firearms, they found it difficult to control the arms trade to Nyamwezi chiefs, who quickly caught up in spite of occasional short-lived Zanzibari attempts to place embargoes on the sale of powder to particular chiefs. Up and down the coast, as well as in the centers of Arab presence in the interior, the Sultan of Zanzibar was capable of bringing a considerable force into action on any given occasion, but he was not capable of sustained application of force. This meant that Arab traders could fight back when they were faced with arbitrary or hostile limitations on their trade; although they could improve trading conditions, they could not govern by force of arms.

The crucial role of Zanzibar as an entrepôt offering important trade facilities was far more important than force in making it possible for the island to dominate the hinterland. Credit was an obvious advantage, and capital for the inland trade was readily available from local financiers, most of whom were of Indian origin. These merchants not only charged interest; they also insisted that caravan leaders sell ivory only to them and at lower prices than those prevailing on the open market. Zanzibar also discriminated by means of its tariff structure. In 1864, the duty on ivory from Nyamwezi was $9 per frasila (35 lb) if the tusks had been brought by Arabs, $15 if they had been brought by Nyamwezi traders, and $12 for ivory purchased by Arabs on the coast. That the Nyamwezi traded at all under these circumstances was a clear indication of their competitive superiority.

Zanzibar's advantage also grew from the island's dominant position in oceanic trade. American and European traders preferred the island because there they could purchase full cargoes without having to sail along the coast collecting cargo at every small port. Zanzibar's trade atmosphere was congenial because the duties on imports from Europe were both low and predictable. Local traders also gained some advantage from price competition among the large number of European and American traders on the island. By establishing and using its control over mainland ports, Zanzibar strengthened its position. Muslims had resided for generations in a number of these towns, and many were independent city-states before the Omani encroachment of the early nineteenth century. The local merchant class had not been active in the caravan trade, but had worked instead through inland traders and powers in the hinterland. The Omani took over the towns, established garrisons in some, began collecting duties, and tried to open the trade routes to the interior as much as possible. Bagamoyo, for example, was the coastal terminus of the Nyamwezi route, and the local Muslims (called Shomvi) had traditionally paid their Zaramo neighbors in the interior for the right to trade through their country. In the 1840s, however, the Zanzibari garrison used force to reduce the tolls, and later the payments to the Zaramo ended altogether.

Although Omani control of the coast was limited, it was adequate at most places for regulating trade. At Kilwa, for example, direct foreign trade in ivory and copal was barred by the second decade of the nineteenth century. The island town of Kilwa with its ocean port declined even as trade prospered. The neighboring small towns on the mainland had adequate harbors for the coastal dhows that carried goods to Zanzibar for trans-shipment. The greater part of the Tanganyika coast, both north and south of Bagamoyo, was off limits to foreign traders, who were required by treaty to pick up African goods in Zanzibar, and Zanzibar in any case was a natural entrepôt for the trade south of Bagamoyo, because Indian Ocean sailing ships going further down the coast risked being stranded by the seasonal change of wind. Not surprisingly, Zanzibar collected higher duties on the Tanganyika coast, where its control was tightest, than it did in present-day Kenya. There, Mombasa continued to have a little direct foreign trade, even though it was conquered by the sultan's forces in 1837.

Plantations and their slaves

Zanzibar's position at the division point between trade networks also helped the growth of the slave-worked clove plantations on Zanzibar itself and on the neighboring island of Pemba. The Arab planters were to take advantage of periods when slave prices were low to try out new crops and to staff their own plantations. The caravan trade in ivory provided the poorer Arabs with a chance to accumulate enough wealth to buy a plantation, and some ivory caravans also brought down slaves on the march to the coast.

Cloves originated in the Moluccas of eastern Indonesia and for centuries grew nowhere else. Seeds were carried to the Mascarene Islands by about 1770. In the opening decades of the nineteenth century they came to Zanzibar, probably brought by a French-speaking Arab. The first great expansion of clove production on Zanzibar took place after the treaty of 1822 had abolished the slave-trade to all Christian countries, including the French plantation islands. Cloves would probably have caught on in any event, but were helped by the treaty, which reduced the demand for slaves. The drop in the price of slaves from about $40 in the 1780s to $25 in the 1810s and finally to $20 in the 1820s certainly made the clove plantations far more attractive.

Once the plantation economy was introduced into East Africa, it took on a dynamic of its own. Arabs and other plantation owners expanded production of cloves in profitable times, experimented with other crops and also with opening up land on the mainland coast, and grasped the opportunities offered by the cheap slave prices in the years that followed abolition treaties. The boom prices for cloves and the enormous expansion of production came between 1835 and 1845, after which prices declined through the century, except for one brief period. Because it takes six years for clove trees to bear the aromatic flower buds, and longer still to reach full production, the greatest need for slaves to pick cloves came in the 1850s, when clove prices began to drop. Fortunately for the Zanzibari Arabs, the sultan had signed another slave-trade treaty in 1847, this time prohibiting overseas export of slaves. Slave prices dropped 25 per cent immediately after the signing and the Zanzibaris filled their plantations with slaves, and some of them moved to the mainland coast to undertake grain production.

In 1873, all slave shipments by sea were legally ended, and Zanzibar's slave market closed; in 1876, Zanzibar prohibited slave caravans on land as well. These well-meaning actions led to the final steps naturalizing slavery in East Africa. Grain production on the Kenyan coast grew enormously. By a conservative estimate, the plantations around the town of Malindi alone absorbed a thousand slaves in 1874. Many of Zanzibar's clove trees had been destroyed in the hurricane of 1872, which led to a shortage of cloves and a spectacular rise in prices back to the levels of the 1830s. Slaves were smuggled to Pemba by the thousands from the nearby Pangani valley, on the mainland, which had never before been a major slave-producing area.

The difficulties of the slave trade in the years of abolition led many East African peoples to find local uses for slave labor. In the big grain-producing areas of the Kenya coast, the Mijikenda, the original inhabitants of the coastal hinterland, extended their farms, purchased slaves, and competed with Arab planters in the export business. Further into the interior, the Nyamwezi increasingly used slaves for farm labor, while the free men went off to trade ivory. The Gogo and some Kimbu sold ivory for slaves. The Makonde of the Kilwa hinterland used slaves to farm so that free people could collect wild rubber. None of these were "traditional" uses for low-status labor in East Africa, but in the economic conditions of the 1880s some Africans behaved in much the same way as the alien plantation owners. The lesson was that once East Africa's societies underwent the period of upheaval and transformation that led them to sell slaves, they could not easily return to the relative harmony of earlier times. Abolition did not end the capture of slaves; it merely reduced part of the demand, lowering prices so that locals as well as outsiders could find new uses for slave labor.

Slave-statuses were enormously varied at the coast, depending on whether the slave was newly arrived or had been born on the coast, whether entirely attached to a home religion or partly Islamized, and whether a woman or a man. The slave's status depended also, in part, on his or her skills. The slaves who came to the coast and islands were about equally divided between men and women, but women (unless they were concubines) were likely to hold the lowest-status jobs. Newly arrived women, and some men, did agricultural work under the supervision of overseers, on export-crop farms run for the profit of the slave-owners. Even the export-crop slaves had farms of their own on which they were allowed to work two or more days a week to feed themselves, and lived together with other slaves in villages separate from their masters. Nevertheless, conditions must have been difficult. Despite the presence of significant numbers of women among the slaves, they rarely succeeded in bearing and raising children and in reproducing the slave population. On Zanzibar in 1900–1, after the end of slave importation, two-thirds of the slaves were mainland born; only a third had been born in slavery.

Many slaves had more autonomy than the women who worked on export farms. Some were left free to cultivate on their own, subject only to the requirement that they give the master part of their harvest. Others, mainly male slaves who lived in town, worked at jobs for a daily wage, perhaps as stevedores at the docks, or as porters who carried loads. They then shared their wages with their masters. Still others rose to positions of leadership; these were almost always *wazalia* – slaves born at the coast. They included artisans, fishermen, even sea captains or senior caravan traders. They were expected to give part of their profits to their masters. The many gradations of servile status show that the division between slave and free was not entirely clear. Slaves who wished to rise exploited the ambiguities: sometimes a man who had not yet won the right to take up caravan trading would join an expedition without his master's approval; at other times slave craftsmen would earn money, but withhold the payments their masters expected. The most senior wazalia aspired to coastal citizenship.

The 1870s and 1880s were challenging times for both slaves and masters, and their differing responses led to rising levels of conflict. By the early 1880s the profits on Zanzibar's clove plantations were being squeezed as prices declined. The owners' solution was to find a way to get more work from the existing number of slaves. One slave could pick the cloves of anywhere from ten to twenty trees, and the number undoubtedly increased as losses and mortgages mounted. On the mainland, the expansion of grain plantations in Kenya and sugar plantations in Tanzania led to growing demands for labor. Some owners tried to get more labor out of their slaves by demoting share-cropping, or wage-working, or even artisan slaves to field-slave status. The slaves, meanwhile, were struggling in the opposite direction, trying to rise through the hierarchy.

On the mainland coast, the conflicting expectations of slaves and owners led thousands of slaves to withdraw from the farms and houses of their masters and become *watoro* – fugitives or maroons. The watoro coalesced around their own leaders, and built fortified settlements at a number of places. They acquired arms and carved out a place for themselves in the region's politics, often by forming alliances with renegade Arabs who opposed the sultan's authority. The slave system which, in one sense, reached its height just before conquest, had torn many Africans loose from their home surroundings, but it did not have the power or the authority to keep them in their servile places; the men and women who had been torn from their homes were determined to remake the coastal world on their own terms.

Opportunity and insecurity in the slave trade

The new trade opportunities, and the new dangers, had profound effects on the lives of ordinary people all across East Africa. In some places, young men were able to rise rapidly to positions of control; in others, the need for security made individuals more dependent on their clans and lineages than they had been before. Insecurity led the residents of some areas to cluster in fortified villages larger than the previous norm, while in others nucleated villages broke up as commercial farmers expanded the area under cultivation. Opportunistic men built themselves new chiefdoms at the same time that old political units were being torn apart by the slave trade, by Arabs, or by powerful local rebels. Some chiefs traded their own subjects into slavery, while others built defensive armies and refused to deal with outside traders. The local initiatives were as diverse as East Africa's societies – or as the personalities of their leaders.

Any understanding of the choices that faced East Africans must begin with the opportunities offered by the new kinds of trade, and with a recognition that one person's opportunity might be another's tragedy. There had always been inequalities within East Africa's societies, but there had also been a social contract based on interests shared by the weak who needed protection and the strong who needed followers. The balance between strong and weak had long been shaped by the region's abundant land, and the shortage of people to till or defend it. People on their own, whose kinsfolk had died or left, were able to strengthen the followings of the wealthiest men. The kinless might be pitied, perhaps given chores and sent on errands, but they were welcomed and given security because they strengthened the numbers of a chiefdom or a lineage. Wherever the trade in slaves emerged uncontrolled, the balance between strong and weak shifted, because the strong now had a second option: they could sell the kinless as slaves, or they could provide protection as before.

The opening up of this new possibility led the kinless to lose power, to become more helpless in their dealings with potential protectors. We know this from the life histories of women who found refuge at mission stations shortly after colonial conquest. There was the case, for example, of a woman named Narwimba, who lived in the region between Lake Tanganyika and Lake Malawi at a time when slave trading was at its height. Narwimba had been married, but then entered a period of insecurity when her husband died, in about 1880. She described how she had begged a relative of her husband's to take her in: "And I, on my part, begged him to take me to wife, so that we might be protected." The threat that a woman without protection might be sold in the slave trade gave her "protector" very much more power over her than he might have had in earlier periods.

Not all women were weak and vulnerable in this new situation. There were women chiefs in the interior, and women among the large-scale slave-owners of the coast. In the Shambaa kingdom, each senior wife of the king was given a chiefdom to manage with her sons, and each junior wife received a food plantation near the royal capital, along with the slaves to staff it. Among ordinary women, autonomy often depended on claims to male support. Women had considerable authority as mothers of adult men, and younger women were able to negotiate strong positions for themselves if they could call on the support of fathers and brothers to balance a husband's authority.

For young men within a lineage the new trade conditions operated in two contradictory ways. For a very few of them the possibilities of acquiring wealth on their own through the trade made them independent of their elders, but this happened only to the most fearless and ambitious. The insecurities of the slave-trading era made the lineage indispensable as a guardian of the individual's welfare, for lineage wealth could buy back a member captured by kidnappers or pay the indemnity for a person who otherwise would have been sold into slavery after committing a crime. In some places, a young man or woman who showed no respect or who had a difficult personality might even be sold into slavery by close relatives – in an African recapitulation of the Biblical story of Joseph.

Young men were thus offered opportunities for independence while independence was becoming more dangerous by virtue of the slave trade. Individuals responded differently to the opportunities and dangers, and widely different social patterns emerged from region to region within East Africa. One possibility was to minimize the dangers (and the individual opportunities) by using wealth from trade to support the preexisting pattern of authority. This is illustrated in the oral traditions of the Embu, of the southeastern slopes of Mount Kenya. Elephant hunters would take their relatives along to bargain with the coastal ivory traders. In the final stages of bargaining, each relative would sit on the ivory in sorrow at its loss. The trader could take the ivory only after paying each one to agree to the trade. The hunter's important relatives were paid more, minor ones less. This practice reinforced the relationships and gave them special recognition.

For traders who wanted to rise, the combination of opportunity and insecurity served as a kind of threshold mechanism. An individual could only afford the insecurity that went with personal independence, leadership, and display if his wealth was very substantial indeed. The result was a combination of strong lineages and dependent, insecure individuals on the one hand, but, alongside emerging Big Men, or notables – men who were not chiefs, but who exerted local influence because of their success as traders. A fine line separated the trade notables from the chiefs: for the most part, chiefs could impose their judgments on subject lineages, while big men used the power of persuasion; chiefs could require payment of tribute, while big men gave and received gifts or struck bargains; a chief could pass on his office to his heir, while a notable's goods were divided among his heirs, and his influence was dissipated after his death.

Kamba traditions in Kenya have given a picture of the notables who emerged during the first half of the nineteenth century, the period of the Kamba-dominated ivory trade. Some important Kamba traders used their wealth to achieve prestige and influence by enlarging their lineages through marriage and by adopting dependents whose lineages could not support them in time of famine. These notables distributed their trade goods to local men of influence who could help in recruiting caravan porters. In other societies, chiefs required hunters to bring the tusks to the ruler's court, but the Kamba notables had no such authority. Instead, they took wives from elephant hunters' lineages to ensure the flow of ivory from their in-laws. Nor was wealth alone enough to make one an important notable; personal flair and style were also essential. The great Kamba ivory trader Kivui is remembered for his oratory, his

puns and use of onomatopoeia, his great storytelling. Ndumbu, another trader, commissioned spectacular lattice copper necklaces for himself and his hunters. Other
notables gave feasts.

The spread of slavery together with the periodic abundance of slaves were used by
big men to build their followings. Some Giriama notables in the hinterland of the
Kenya coast created extensive grain farms for the oceanborne export trade, building
their enterprises by adopting dependents who needed food in time of famine, by
marrying many wives, by buying slaves for wives when slave prices were low, and by
purchasing some male slaves. In matrilineal settings, slave wives offered men a unique
opportunity to build lineages. A man could not build a following through normal
marriage, as he might do in a patrilineal setting, because his children would ultimately
belong to their mother's lineage. A slave wife had no lineage, however, so that a man
who married slaves could claim the children as his own in order to build a band of
personal supporters.

For a person whose lineage was too weak to provide security, or who wanted to
escape lineage restrictions, the household of a notable or the court of a chief were
places of refuge. A young man could serve as a soldier, hunter, or porter, a young
woman as a wife or the wife of a refugee-soldier, in return for which they enjoyed the
protection of their patron. They enjoyed their security, however, at their protector's
whim.

The need for security and the frequent armed conflict associated with the nineteenth century made it a century of personal armies and standing armies. The fighting
forces of most eighteenth-century chiefs and kings had been "countrymen's armies" –
fighting forces of ordinary farmers who could be called up at a time of crisis. Nineteenth-century conditions, however, favored standing armies, partly because firearms
made it possible for a small force of well-armed men to achieve greater striking power
than a large force of poorly armed peasants. The fighters could also be paid in trade
wealth or booty; a paid army of strangers had fewer compunctions about slave raiding
than a countrymen's army had. Standing and hired armies were spread all across the
region. Arab trading caravans were essentially private armies on the move. Through
the whole of western Tanzania, standing armies carried on raids and fought one
another. In Uganda, the king of Bunyoro created a standing army of northerners, from
beyond the borders of his kingdom. Even among the chiefless Kikuyu of Kenya,
brigand bands called *thabari* (from the Swahili word *safari*, for a caravan or a journey)
marauded, stole livestock, and burned houses. The Sultan of Zanzibar used a mercenary army drawn from far-away Baluchistan, on the border between present-day
Pakistan and Iran.

Centralized authority and slavery in nineteenth-century trade

The arms trade, the demand for slaves and ivory, the presence of caravans and Baluchi
soldiers, the development of notables and standing armies, all had an enormous impact
on the political fortunes of East Africa's chiefs and kings, but the effect on centralized
authority was not uniform. In some places, powerful chiefs fell; in others, centralized
rule emerged stronger than ever before. In the Shambaa kingdom, about halfway

between Mount Kilimanjaro and the Indian Ocean, the royal capital and most of the populated areas were located in a mountain area that was difficult for caravans. Trade routes passed through the plains below, shifting the entire balance of power away from the king in favor of a minor territorial governor named Semboja, who took control of an essential stopping place for caravans and assembled his own corps of elephant hunters. In the 1860s, Semboja made war on the king with arms acquired through trade and the assistance of his trading allies. First, the king's power to maintain order was destroyed; then the 1870s saw a rapid increase in the demand for slaves to work on the clove plantations of Pemba. By the mid-1870s, it had become profitable for local governors both to prey on their own subjects and to make war against their neighbors for the capture of slaves.

What had been an orderly, prosperous, and peaceful kingdom during the first half of the century thus broke up into a great many embattled chiefdoms, each seeking its own ties with traders, and each selling slaves. Some elements in the Shambaa disaster were unique: its mountain location and the sudden growth of the Pemba slave trade at an already difficult moment, for example, were not reproduced in exactly the same form in other societies. Three other elements, however, recurred across East and Central Africa. First, Semboja used mercenary armies. Second, the change followed a shift in the sources of a chief's or king's wealth. Before the expansion of trade, a chief depended on tribute from his subjects with which to reward his followers; the chief or king who had the most subjects was also the most powerful. After the change, a clever trading chief, or one with access to ivory, relied less on his own subjects, and high slave prices sometimes made the sale of subjects profitable. This would have been unthinkable in a period when the chief's main support derived from the farm work of his people. Third, outside trade and raiding allies became involved in internal disputes all across East Africa, although the outsiders in some cases were other trading chiefs of the interior, coastal traders, or a combination of the two.

The characteristic form of Arab or Swahili interference in local affairs was not a frontal assault on an established ruler. The traders were not powerful enough for that. Instead, individual traders or groups of traders made alliances with particular local leaders. Sometimes two Arab traders competing with one another would make alliances with competing local chiefs, thus raising the overall level of violence, possibly by encouraging a weak local contender to carry on the fight when he would have quit in the absence of outside help. In the chiefdom of Unyanyembe, where the most important Arab trading town of Nyamwezi country was located, three chiefly factions competed for control. The Arab traders were deeply involved in the area's politics; one married a daughter of Fundikira, the chief in the 1840s and early 1850s, and renewed the alliance when his wife died by marrying her sister. After Fundikira died in 1858, the Arabs took sides in the succession wars until they got a chief friendly to their interests.

The great variety of paths to increased centralization in the nineteenth century are illustrated by two neighboring societies in western Kenya: the Nandi and the kingdom of Wanga. The Nandi, who combined herding and agriculture, occupied a plateau area immediately adjacent to the westernmost groups of cattle-keeping Maasai. The dangers of Maasai cattle raiding limited the border Nandi to easily defended forest areas. Then, at some point before 1850, the Maasai were weakened by fighting among their subgroups, and the Nandi, at the same time, gave refuge to a Maasai ritual leader who became the first Nandi *orkoiyot*. It was the orkoiyot's job to predict coming events, to understand the omens favorable or unfavorable to action, and therefore to advise about war and peace. The combination of Maasai decline and increased coordination through the orkoiyot's leadership enabled the Nandi to expand beyond the forest edge at the expense of the Maasai. When, a brief time later, the first trading expeditions appeared, the Nandi were confident that they could control threats from the outside – had they not defeated the former masters of the grasslands? The first Arabs and Swahili (who probably came in the 1850s) were therefore allowed to establish fortified outposts, but then they began to mistreat the Nandi. Local people remember an incident in which young men were imprisoned by the coastal traders, another in which young Nandi women were treated disrespectfully, still another in which the outsiders dumped a bowl of hot porridge over the head of a local young man. When the Nandi objected, the traders responded with a demonstration quite common in these situations. They placed a shield against a tree, invited the Nandi to shoot arrows, which did not penetrate, and then fired through their shields with muzzle loaders. The Nandi went away, but they returned in an attack that drove the traders from the country; and caravans avoided Nandi country from then on. The Nandi succeeded in avoiding the slave-ivory trade almost completely. They were uninterested in arms, having discovered that they could defeat a force armed with muzzle loaders by charging openly, falling down for the brief period of shooting, and then attacking before the enemy could reload.

Earlier in the century, the small kingdom of Wanga, just to the west of Nandi country, had also been visited by Maasai refugees, who served as mercenaries in disputes among local political leaders. When the coastal traders arrived, they too were drawn into local politics. The king of Wanga made his capital a major stopping place for caravans and gained the traders' assistance in defeating his enemies. His power grew throughout the period. One fascinating continuity emerges in the history of both Wanga and the Nandi. When the British appeared late in the century and began to carry out their conquest, the king of Wanga, who had depended for his power on outside allies, ingratiated himself with the British and began to conquer large sections of the region for them. The Nandi, who had reorganized internally to deal with the external threats of Maasai and traders, fought a series of British expeditions over a period of ten years before finally submitting.

The slave trade also altered the nature of slavery itself. The word *slavery* is dangerous to use, because it means such different things at different times and places. Some sort of servile status existed almost everywhere in Africa before the growth of the slave trade, but its East African form changed dramatically during the nineteenth century. We have already seen that wealth was necessary for increasing the strength of a lineage and its ability to reproduce, whether the wealth was used to pay for wives in the form of bridewealth, or for famine food, or for medicines when someone was ill. When a member of one lineage harmed an individual from another, the balance was redressed by the payment of an indemnity. The indemnity was a transfer of wealth that could be regarded as reproductive capacity. The problem with this system was that, if it went no further, a poor lineage would be able to act irresponsibly, accumulating debts and harming others, yet unable to pay. The solution was to transfer one or more individuals, which thus shifted reproductive capacity directly through people rather than through wealth. Nineteenth-century slavery grew out of this institution, as well as from several other related ways of dealing with individuals who had no lineages – war captives, for example, or people who had been driven out of their lineages for incurring too many indemnities.

The growing demand for slaves in the nineteenth century led to the transformation, in many places, of this institution, although slave procurement was by no means uniform across East Africa. In some areas, predatory groups, like the Chikunda elephant hunters of Malawi and Zambia, simply raided their neighbors. In other areas, small-scale kidnapping by aspiring notables was common. Both slave raiding and kidnapping seem to have occurred in places bypassed by the ivory trade, or where the ivory trade stimulated demand for imported goods but then declined. Among the Kamba of Kenya, for example, the period of slave trading came after the decline of the Kamba ivory trade. Some of the southern neighbors of the Nyamwezi, who had dominated the ivory trade before it shifted to Nyamwezi territory, engaged in slave raiding. In other areas, normal judicial processes were subverted in order to produce slaves. Chiefs would impose huge fines for small crimes knowing the fines could not be paid and slaves would be offered instead.

The uses to which slaves were put also changed. Among the Yao, at least some of the slaves were still assimilated to the new master's lineage as adopted kin. In other places, they were incorporated in the standing armies of chiefs. But some also became a separate agricultural labor force, and this appears to have been new in the nineteenth century, not only for the Arabs on grain or clove plantations, but also for Africans who had never before used slave labor. They produced export crops for the Zaramo in the hinterland of the Tanzania coast and food crops for the Nyamwezi. Among some trading, rubber-gathering, or ivory-hunting populations, they began to work the farms at home while their masters occupied themselves with more lucrative activities further afield.

Where East Africa experienced one form of secondary empire in myriad variants following the introduction of firearms, it also felt the impact of the great scattering of peoples from South Africa known as the mfecane, and of the associated military innovations based on age-regiments. Although the empire builders from the south were not all Nguni from the coastal plains of Natal, they usually figure in East African history as Angoni or Ngoni. The largest group crossed the Zambezi in 1835 under the leadership of a single chief named Zwangendaba, and they were known as Zwangendaba's Ngoni until their leader died in the late 1840s, when they split up into a number of smaller states. When they had first started their 2000-mile migration, Zwangendaba's Ngoni totaled only a few hundred people. But their mastery of Zulu military tactics enabled them to conquer along their way. They took many war prisoners, incorporating male captives in servile positions at first, so that each had to obey his Ngoni "father." A captive could become a full member of Ngoni society, however, by founding his own lineage through the capture of wealth or women in warfare. Any age-regiment therefore included not only original Ngoni, but also captives who were in the process of becoming Ngoni in what has been described as a snowball state. From the 1840s on, separate groups of Ngoni stopped migrating and settled down in Malawi, eastern Zambia, and southern Tanzania, where they created new social forms combining local and Ngoni elements.

Southwestern Tanzania, which was already undergoing transformation as the result of the coastal trade, also had to deal with the Ngoni threat. In the process, a number of local armies adopted Ngoni military tactics, and some Nyamwezi chiefs hired roving bands of Ngoni mercenaries. Mirambo, the greatest of the Nyamwezi chiefs, spoke the Ngoni language and (like others among his neighbors) assembled a wild and rootless band of armed followers called *ruga-ruga*, who were modeled at least in part on Ngoni age-regiments. Among the ruga-ruga were war captives, escaped slaves, deserters, runaways, and all sorts of desperate characters who had been cut loose from their lineage ties. Their tactics were to strike terror among their enemies: they would wear red cloths, to which they would point at the start of a battle, saying, "This is your blood." They wanted to shock the opposing army into submission. Mirambo and other chiefs rewarded them with slaves and land, so they could start their own lineages. The age-regiment pattern thus had an origin independent of the coastal trade, yet it fitted in perfectly with politics and warfare in the age of slave and mercenary armies. In one sense, the two varieties of secondary empire met and combined here in central Tanzania.

Alongside the insecurity, disorder, and ruga-rugas, some benefits grew out of the nineteenth-century economic changes, one of them being the expansion of regional trade. Neighbors who traded ivory with one another often expanded their mutual trade in commodities for local consumption rather than export, along routes which ran in every direction, as opposed to the overseas routes which simply ran from the interior to the ocean. Lake Victoria, for example, was criss-crossed by a network of trade ties among lakeshore populations. The islands of the southeastern corner provided dried fish, grain in times of drought, and timber for boat building; the northeast provided salt, while Buganda in the northwest supplied barkcloth; other lake regions sold tobacco and coffee beans. Similar local trade networks developed all across East Africa.

Insulation, religious innovation, and centralization

Contact between Africans and Europeans in the nineteenth century led to scattered instances of intellectual, religious, economic, and military change. On some parts of the Guinea coast, we have seen that intellectual and political leaders literate in European languages emerged at just the time the political independence of their homelands was being eroded. Other leaders sought firearms or other aspects of alien technology, but those who succeeded best in preserving their political autonomy, before the full European invasions of the 1800s and after, were those who best insulated themselves against disruptive foreigners bearing guns. Success came from the care with which they controlled outside influences, often combined with an advantageous location far from seaports and other centers of foreign presence.

This pattern is strikingly illustrated by highland Ethiopia, which began the nineteenth century as a region of numerous princes, most of them adhering to the country's ancient Christianity, each ruling a small territory and squabbling for control over a larger one. Many of the Christian highland princes were dependent on mobile armies of neighboring lowland Muslims. Those nearest the coast had the best opportunity to obtain arms from Europe, but the highlands were to be unified most effectively by Menilek of Shoa, whose kingdom, centered on the present city of Addis Ababa, was in the far south of the Christian zone.

The process of centralization did not begin with Menilek; it unfolded through the second half of the nineteenth century. Over a fifty-year period the kingdom's territory tripled and added millions of people. The first of the centralizers was a king who took the throne in 1855. He took the name Tewodros II, which had powerful symbolic connotations in Ethiopian traditions, for it was said that a king named Tewodros would come some day, would restore order, and would rule the kingdom justly and peacefully for forty years. Clearly Tewodros had hopes of ending the unhappy era of the warring princes. He tried to impose centralized discipline on an army that was accustomed to feeding itself by plundering its own peasantry. For a period, Tewodros succeeded in disciplining the army, in winning the support of the peasantry, and in beginning to expand his kingdom. He could not see the ultimate success of his vision because his small base in the northern highlands would not support the large army needed to centralize the kingdom. He tried to solve this problem by welcoming Europeans, in the hope that they would help him to import or manufacture weapons, making his small army more powerful. He also tried to expand his resource base by confiscating lands owned by the church, but this provoked the enmity of the clergy. Tewodros's successes lasted only a few years, and by the mid-1860s there were uprisings against him led by many of the regional chiefs. The army returned to plunder, and peasants rose in rebellion. Tewodros's reign ended as a result of a dispute with the Europeans he had welcomed to his kingdom. In 1867 the British sent a punitive force against him, and the Ethiopian people along their route eagerly joined forces to help overthrow him. In 1868, as the British drew near, the king committed suicide.

Tewodros was succeeded by Yohannes IV, whose position seemed enviable at first glance because he had European weapons, military power, and the ancient title of king of kings. But he too suffered the weaknesses of a northern base, near borders with powerful outsiders: he was threatened from two fronts – the Sudan, where the Egyptians were a threat at first, and the Mahdi a later one, and the Red Sea coast, where the Egyptians were again the early threat, but here were supplanted by the Italians. Menilek was active from Shoa by this time, as the king's main competitor. Despite the fact that Emperor Yohannes defeated Shoa in 1875, he accepted a weak truce because of the Egyptian presence in the north. The emperor died in 1889, in battle against the Mahdist forces from the Sudan.

In his early competition with Yohannes, Menilek had the enormous advantage of a southern base. He was insulated from the outside threats in the north, and he was able to expand southwards into the slave-source areas beyond the limits of the Christian and Muslim zones. By expanding in this direction and exploiting the slave trade, Menilek was able to escape from the economic limitations of the kingdom's highland base.

The time of Menilek's rise to power was one of increasing demand for slaves from the Ethiopian region. That demand first increased early in the century, when Russia conquered the Caucasus, cutting off that source of slaves for the Ottoman Empire. Then, after 1847, when the British treaty with Zanzibar prohibited the export of slaves from the Zanzibari sphere, Ethiopia became an alternate source. Slaves could be carried across the Red Sea to Arabia and on to the Persian Gulf and Iraq, in spite of British attempts to halt the trade by naval action on the Red Sea. Menilek and other Ethiopian leaders relied on tolls from trade, and especially the slave trade, to buy arms for their empire-building wars. Menilek's kingdom of Shoa had the best of both worlds; its subjects were neither slave traders nor enslaved. They merely charged tolls, taking care to expand through the 1870s and 1880s in directions that enabled them to control increasing quantities of trade.

After Yohannes's death in 1889, and his emergence as king of kings, Menilek succeeded in uniting both the north and the south. The part of Ethiopia that escaped his control was the mainly Tigrinya-speaking highland area in the hinterland of the Red Sea coast, that had already been taken over by Italy and incorporated in the colony of Eritrea. By Menilek's time, it was essential to have a large supply of modern arms, and he was fortunate in being able to secure them in time to defeat an Italian invasion in 1896. He also used them to build the secondary empire that was to survive as the independent state of Ethiopia.

On the great island of Madagascar, as well as in the large and prosperous kingdom of Buganda in the southern part of present-day Uganda, efforts to keep foreigners under control were combined with spectacular movements toward literacy and the adoption of European religion. In both cases, Africans borrowed elements of European culture and used them to further projects that had deep roots in their own societies. The borrowings then became integrated into Malagasy and Ganda history, following a course very different from one Europeans would have imagined. In the eighteenth century, Madagascar had been divided among a number of separate and competing political units of varying composition: kingless kinship groups governed by elders; small chiefships which spread by multiplying, as new leaders in each generation moved out across the landscape; and independent kingdoms. The central developments of the nineteenth century were to take place in the kingdom of the central highlands, in the region called Imerina, which began by uniting four earlier Merina kingdoms, and then expanded to conquer many of the island's polities and to dominate others.

Centralization already held some appeal for the ordinary people of Imerina whose agriculture, based on the intensive cultivation of rice, required large-scale organization. People in any one locality were organized in kinship groups within which people intermarried, each one occupying a territory that held the tombs of its ancestors. These groups were not large enough to build and maintain the irrigation works necessary for rice cultivation. For this, they relied on political leaders. The king's contribution to a bountiful rice harvest came not only from his organization of public works; it came from his role as a ritual leader. The most important royals and nobles in each of the four kingdoms controlled the ritual objects – the *sampy* – which had the power to bring fertility to the land, increase the rice harvest, prevent epidemics, and establish good relations between kings and subjects.

In the late eighteenth century one of the four Merina kings, Nampoina (short for Andrianampoinimerina), began to dominate the others, and by 1806 he had created a unified kingdom. He was able to do so by taking advantage of the slave trade to Mauritius and Reunion, the French plantation islands east of Madagascar. Slave labor became fully indigenized within Imerina after Nampoina's successor signed a treaty, in 1817, outlawing the slave trade. From that point, slaves captured in the island's wars could be put to work within the kingdom. A system of stratification emerged, over the course of the nineteenth century, in which both slaves and free farmers carried a heavy burden of labor, and the political elite (especially the most powerful generals) were able to enrich themselves. Free peasants were subject to conscription into the army to fight the kingdom's wars, and then also to staff the garrisons that controlled the outlying non-Merina areas. The peasants were subject also to compulsory labor on public works. The burden of forced labor varied from one time and place to another, but it was heaviest where substantial numbers of privileged people enjoyed labor exemptions, leaving few farmers to carry the burden. Because slaves were exempted from labor dues, the labor system saw a shift of peasant farmers into public service, and of slaves into rice-growing.

The conversion of substantial numbers of Merina to Christianity established one of the central tensions in the politics of the nineteenth-century kingdom. Christianity, which was first introduced by British missionaries under royal patronage in the 1820s, served the purposes of kings and queens who were trying to achieve political centralization by freeing themselves from the ritual authority of the pre-unification nobles. The power of the old rituals survived royal rejection, however, and could not easily be ignored. The result was that royal policy swung sharply back and forth, for and against Christianity, for and against the sampy – the ritual objects of the old nobles. The struggle over how to deal with the sampy had begun even before the introduction of Christianity. Nampoina, the founding king who had died in 1810, relied on soldiers who were not of noble birth, and who did not control the ritual objects. He took great care, however, to award marks of high status among his personal supporters to the guardians of the most revered of the sampy, the Kelimalaza. When Christianity was introduced, the soldiers in the standing army, who did not have roots in the old nobility, and who were supplanting it, were among the first drawn to the new religion. In a later period, adherents of the London Missionary Society formed a leading faction in the army.

Nineteenth-century history was characterized by a series of sharp movements, by the kings and queens of Imerina, first to concentrate control of the sampy in royal hands, then towards Christianity and a rejection of the sampy, and then further towards the older rituals and away from Christianity, with each initiative provoking resistance from the losing side. The question was finally resolved under Queen Ranavalona II in 1869 who, when threatened with revolt from followers of Kelimalaza in the southern part of the kingdom, ordered that all sampy be burned, and created a state church. From this point on, Protestant Christianity was the religion of the state. Attendance of church and school became a mark of loyalty to the queen, and the old rituals were to be wiped out. This was to be the final triumph of the army over old leading families. But in the countryside people did not so easily accept the death of the sampy, which were locally revived and revered, invisible to outside observers, even after the originals had been burned.

Powerful leaders close to the royal court had access to great wealth. They held monopolies in many of the goods of Madagascar's external trade, which they were able to control through the military garrisons and customs posts. Those close to royal power were easily able to acquire slaves taken in war, and they were exempt from forced labor. The trade monopoly was broken, however, during the years of Radama II, whose relationship with the army leaders was strained, and who reigned for only two years before he was strangled to death in 1863. Radama opened the island to foreign traders, and agreed that they would remain under the protection of their own consuls. This was the start of Madagascar's economic decline. Then, in 1883–5, the French made war against Madagascar, bombarded the port of Tamatave, and blockaded a number of ports. The threat of further French action was averted when the kingdom agreed to pay France an indemnity of ten million francs. Labor demands became ever more severe, and bands of labor deserters took to banditry around the edges of the kingdom. A period of final decline led to the French invasion of 1895.

The same openness to literacy, new technology, and alien religions characterized Buganda in the second half of the nineteenth century, except that here Islam was introduced first, followed by Protestant and Catholic Christianity. The changes came, as in Madagascar, at a time when Buganda had been expanding and when its *kabaka* (or king) had been gaining power at the expense of his neighbors and of local leaders within the kingdom. Over several decades each successive kabaka had made a greater proportion of the administrative positions appointive, rather than hereditary. Buganda had also gained control of the trade route around the western side of Lake Victoria. Mutesa, who was kabaka from the late 1850s until 1884, was intensely interested early in his reign in the culture, religion, and technology of the Zanzibari traders who came to his court. He was eager for increased numbers of firearms, especially the advanced weapons that were more effective than the usual trade guns, and along with the guns came incidentals such as Zanzibari-style soap, clothing, and bed frames.

Mutesa was also fascinated by theology. In the late 1860s his court adopted the Islamic calendar, fasting, and the reading of the Koran. Those who adopted new religions most easily were the teenage pages who had come from all parts of the kingdom to live at the royal court, in order to seek Mutesa's favor and win advancement as chiefs. They were largely cut off from their local roots, intensely competitive and pragmatic, and impressed by the new technology and culture from the coast. For a while, those who were best at the study of Arabic and Islam were the ones who most easily won the kabaka's favor. A crisis came, however, when the Sultan of Zanzibar proved unable to send help against the threatening Egyptians from the north. New and stricter Muslim teachers began to ridicule the kabaka's practice of Islam, leading to insubordination among the most devout of the royal pages. The kabaka had found that he could not do without the foreigners; now he learned that he could not tolerate having them either. In 1876, the first of Buganda's religious persecutions began with the execution of Muslims.

Mutesa tried to cope with the situation by playing off religious groups against one another. He invited Protestant missionaries to balance against the Muslims, Catholics to balance against the Protestants, and then returned to the local spirit cults, to balance against them all. Mutesa's successor was unable to control all these forces. Out of desperation, he ordered the execution of a set of Christians in 1886, only to lose control altogether. A combined army of Muslims, Protestants, and Catholics defeated him in the field but then reinstated him on their own terms. Up to the 1890s, conversions, literacy, religious enthusiasm were all matters for the court – for pages and chiefs. But with the kabaka's defeat, the arrival of the first British forces, and the triumph of the Protestants in the early 1890s, religious enthusiasm swept Buganda. Thousands attended services; new converts besieged the missionaries, books in hand, seeking to clarify the meaning of obscure passages.

Buganda and the Merina kingdom both began their centralizing years in positions that were relatively insulated from foreign traders and political representatives: Buganda away from the main Nyamwezi trade route, and the Merina kingdom in the interior of the island. In both, however, the central actors in royal politics, who were struggling to overcome the older loyalties associated with local religions, welcomed alien religious ideas at their core. The new religions, however, proved just as capable of creating divisive loyalties as the old ones, and in both places periods of royal enthusiasm for the new religions alternated with periods of persecution.

The religious and cultural transformations of Madagascar and Buganda, like the economic changes emerging from the abolition campaign, foreshadowed patterns of collective behavior characteristic of the twentieth century. In abolition, the European insistence on "legitimate" trade showed the first clear preference for using Africans as exporters of primary products, and consumers of European-made industrial goods, in place of the earlier use of African labor exported in the slave trade. In the cultural realm, the characteristic ambivalence toward European culture, combining great admiration and great distaste, was already emerging in the two kingdoms. Factions formed for and against the foreigners in favor of Islam, Protestantism or Catholicism, or local religions. All of these divisions were to continue in different form during the colonial period. Perhaps the most profound continuity of all came in the division between the administrative elites with leisure to debate these questions, and the slaves of Madagascar in the nineteenth century – or peasant farmers everywhere in the twentieth – who were just as avid in their search for answers but less comfortable.

Suggestions for further reading

Alpers, Edward A., *Ivory and Slaves: Changing Patterns of International Trade in East Central Africa to the Later Nineteenth Century*, Berkeley and Los Angeles: University of California Press, 1975.

Ambler, Charles H., *Kenyan Communities in the Age of Imperialism: The Central Region in the Late Nineteenth Century*, New Haven and London: Yale University Press, 1988.

Cooper, Frederick, *Plantation Slavery on the East Coast of Africa*, New Haven and London: Yale University Press, 1977.

Ellis, Stephen, *The Rising of the Red Shawls: A Revolt in Madagascar, 1895–1899*, Cambridge: Cambridge University Press, 1985.

Feierman, Steven, *The Shambaa Kingdom: A History*, Madison: University of Wisconsin Press, 1974.

Glassman, Jonathon, "The Bondsman's New Clothes: The Contradictory Consciousness of Slave Resistance on the Swahili Coast," *Journal of African History*, 32 (1991), pp. 277–312.

Kimambo, Isaria N., *A Political History of the Pare of Tanzania, c.1500–1900*, Nairobi: East African Publishing House, 1969.

Koponen, Juhani, *People and Production in Late Precolonial Tanzania: History and Structures*, Uppsala: Scandinavian Institute of African Studies, 1988.

Muriuki, Godfrey, *A History of the Kikuyu: 1500–1900*, Nairobi: Oxford University Press, 1974.

Sheriff, Abdul, *Slaves, Spices and Ivory in Zanzibar: Integration of an East African Commercial Empire into the World Economy 1770–1873*, London: James Currey; Athens: Ohio University Press, 1987.

Wright, Marcia, comp. 1984, *Women in Peril: Life Stories of Four Captives*, Lusaka: Neczam.

14

UPSTARTS AND NEWCOMERS IN EQUATORIAL AFRICA (*c*. 1815 – 1875)

It is often believed that the special character of the nineteenth century in equatorial African history consists in the spectacular rise of the level of intercontinental trade with Europe. Even though the trade itself was old by 1815,* the volume of imports and exports rose tenfold and more before 1880, exceeding anything even dreamt of in earlier days, as the industrial revolution poured its cheap manufactures on Africa's shores. Brawn was no longer essential in this machine age and the slave trade, it is said, now gave way to a "legitimate trade", a commerce in raw materials to feed the machines in Europe. In fact the slave trade remained as active as ever, although it is true that the demand for other products profoundly altered the character of all commerce. In addition the increasing volume of commerce inexorably led to an ever-growing expansion of the networks that fed the coastal markets until by 1875 every bit of equatorial Africa was reached by the tentacles of trading networks which ringed the area on every side.

Yet most Africans later did not remember the nineteenth century for its trade. Oral traditions recall it as a time of newcomers and upstarts, for whom might was right, a time of turmoil and brutality. In most of the rainforests these upstarts were pictured as local *nouveaux riches* who used their clout to wrest power from older leaders, while further south most upstarts were foreigners from far away. In some places, the memory of the arrival of whole new populations rather than new leaders holds center stage. It is very rare that people recall only the continuation of older and peaceful patterns of life. Trade, if mentioned at all in such reminiscences, is merely the scenery in a drama about heroes and heroic villains. And yet . . . such memories do not include the fact that the newcomers, the turmoil, the upstarts, and even the flourishing of older societies were usually linked closely to the intercontinental commerce. Hence why not give pride of place to commerce?

The dilemma is that if one privileges intercontinental trade one risks casting the African actors in the role of puppets reacting to foreign strings, while if one ignores this

---

* The date 1780 used as a starting point for the other chapters in this book is not significant in equatorial Africa: 1815 is its equivalent here.

trade the prizes and much of the motivation of the struggle between leaders are ignored. Surely both approaches stand in error. To overstress trade is to forget that all producers and most merchants or raiders in the nineteenth century were Africans, who freely participated in the overseas trade, that African demand for European goods fueled this trade just as much as European demand for African products, that African institutions, from commercial law to currencies and courts, from markets to the provision of protective charms for caravans, made commerce possible. Moreover, African leaders and followers continued to pursue many aspirations and a host of other activities unrelated to commerce. Yet to neglect trade is to forget that the potential for wealth and the power of the gun was tied to this commerce, and thus that commerce was inexorably tied to every aspiration for power. This attitude also ignores that in many parts of the area commerce altered the whole tenor of daily life as the result of the innovative adoption of new goods, practices, ideas, or values, carried from one community to another along the trading routes. Therefore to use the structure imposed on the geographic space of equatorial Africa by the trading networks as a framework for presenting the history of its peoples, also draws attention to the growth of closer interaction between African communities and illuminates innovations that resulted from such dynamics. Such a framework describes the historical experience of equatorial Africans in the nineteenth century well enough, provided that the reader remembers that this is only a device to facilitate the exposition. In the end the leading actors, old and new, are responsible for historical change, not an impersonal force called intercontinental commerce.

The Atlantic trade in the nineteenth century

The Napoleonic wars practically stopped commerce on the coasts north of Ambriz and seriously disrupted the Angolan trade as well. But by 1815 the slave trade on both segments was picking up again even though this trade was by then outlawed north of the Equator. This prohibition explains why commerce in the north first acquired its new features between c.1827 and c.1850. New commercial firms of British, Dutch, French, Brazilian, Spanish (Cuban), and later German and Portuguese firms began to build many new trading establishments all along the coast from Victoria to Ambriz. There they sold increased tonnages of the old staple goods: textiles, guns, liquor, metalware (especially copper and brass objects), beads and sundry goods. They bought ivory as of old, but also new, bulkier and less valuable productions such as palmnuts and kernels in Cameroon, timber in Gabon, dyes, wax and honey in Angola or redwood and even the occasional load of copper ore on the Loango coast. As the century unfolded, especially after steamships became available in the 1850s, they bought not only much greater tonnages of these products but also cotton, coffee, sugarcane and sugar products, and after 1879 rubber. While precise calculations of the growth in volume of the total trade between 1815 and 1880 cannot yet be made an estimate of a fifty-fold increase is reasonable. And yet trade in the late eighteenth century was already voluminous: at that time some 50,000 guns a year for instance were imported on the Loango coast. Figure after figure shows that by 1880 the coasts around the Cameroon estuary and the lands from Loango to Ambriz were fully part of the world economy. For example by 1875–80 the market at Boma on the Lower Congo (as the Congo/Zaire river was then called) was clearing some 100 tons per day of groundnuts, sesame, and palm products, probably produced in the region. Such a tonnage requires approximately 3400 porters to move it every day, and we can only guess at the numbers of people (mostly slaves) required to produce such quantities.

That was the "legitimate" trade, but these firms were far from innocent. Legitimate firms sold much of their cargo of textiles or guns for Mexican gold brought by slave traders they met in African ports, and this was the source for most of their profits. This arrangement enabled the slave traders to buy slaves. The slave trade itself was now carried mostly by Brazilian, Cuban and some Portuguese ships. Between 1820 and 1867 one million slaves were exported from both coastal segments, at rates as high as those of any decade of the eighteenth century, and with similar effects. The abolition of the trade led to the establishment of a British naval base at Clarence on Fernando Po (Bioko) in 1827 and a French one at Libreville in 1839, and forced traders to go clandestine on a large scale. After the abolition of the trade to Cuba (1845) and Brazil (1845) new legal niceties were invented whereby children were exported to the French Caribbean as *engagés* (1857 onwards) or adults to São Tomé as *libertos* (1869 onwards). As late as 1860 a Dutch naval officer could still estimate that 30,000 slaves a year were exported from the Congo estuary alone. Such exports ended only around or even after 1900, while slave trading and raiding in the interior for resale elsewhere in equatorial Africa lasted at least until about 1911.

The trading areas within either the northern or the southern segment of the Atlantic trading system can be divided in coast and inland sectors. The coastal sectors were directly affected by the legitimate trade, the inland sectors only indirectly. The boundaries between coastal and inland sectors were, for the northern segment, the Bamileke plateau and the western edge of the navigable tributaries of the Congo river, and for the southern segment, the valley of the Kwango river. Within the coastal sector itself the trade had different effects on the main harbors, where most of the new wealth was concentrated, on the agricultural lands surrounding them, which produced the crops for the export and imported slave labor from inland to do so, and on a hinterland further away, a region in which the new dispensation often wrought great turmoil.

The Atlantic trading area: the northern segment

Despite the foundation of trading posts at dozens of new points along the coast the main ports of trade remained Douala, the Gabon estuary, Loango, and the Cabinda-Boma complex in the estuary, and all these places were still controlled by African powers. The trading posts were collecting points for these harbors and only had a local impact, except for Kribi founded in 1828 on the Cameroon coast. Before this port was built the hinterland of southern Cameroon had never been affected by the international trade. Now it was suddenly invaded by traders, which caused great upheavals. But despite this structural stability, the increased scale and complexity altered the character of trading and brought the struggle between established authorities and upstarts to a new level.

This is most evident in the Loango coast, which was the heart of the whole northern

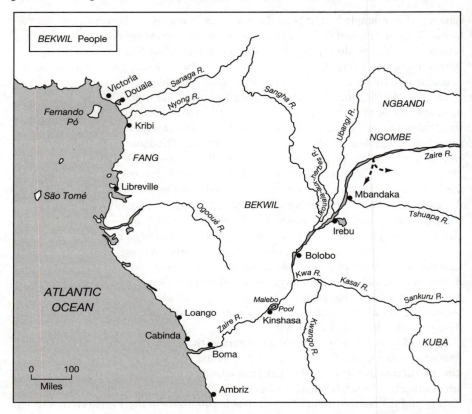

Map 14.1 Northwestern central Africa in the nineteenth century (based on a
map by C. Vansina)

segment in the eighteenth century. Already then in a "junta revolution" of their own,
merchant families had relegated the older rulers to ceremonial roles, and ruled the
main towns. Now in response to the rise of legitimate trade and the suppression of the
slave trade an even more powerful type of merchant arose by 1845 in Cabinda and
Boma. Cabinda was specialized in legitimate trade while Boma became the hub of the
clandestine slave trade conducted in the estuary of the Zaire river. Yet both were but
parts of a single system. By then shipwrights in Cabinda were building seaworthy ships
to convey goods from Cabinda to the estuary by sea, while slaves traveled overland
between the two ports. Among the entrepreneurs in Cabinda who managed the whole
system, none was more famous than Chico Franque whose career spans the period
from 1815 to 1875. Heir to a father who had already made a modest fortune in the
slave trade, he was educated in Brazil (not unusual then). On his return he found trade
still in the hands of three powerful families, each commanding a fighting force of some
seven to eight hundred. But thanks to his contacts with a Brazilian firm and his acumen
he flourished. He started to build ships, organized coastal shipping between Luanda
and Cape Lopez, and in the 1860s even sent a few ships directly to Brazil. He

forwarded merchandise and slaves to Boma, set up farms that produced food and cash crops, and conducted his business as a well-informed equal of slavers, legitimate traders, and North American whalers. He used his growing power to oust one of the other families by force c.1849, and contracted marriage alliances with the two others. Commercial information reached him from as far as Luanda where he had relatives, and Portugal where two of his sons were educated. Between 1840 and 1860 he undoubtedly was "the" merchant prince of Cabinda. Later the firm lost some of this power, but in 1885 the Franques and one other family in Cabinda were still powerful enough to deliver the territory by treaty to Portugal rather than to the Independent Congo State.

None of Boma's entrepreneurs, not even Nemlao, the foremost among them, was as successful as Franque. As in Cabinda public authority was exercised by a coalition of leading Houses, the "Nine kings of Boma" whose dissensions were arbitrated by the priest who kept Boma's most feared charm. Government by coalition of this type was the rule from Loango to Boma. Given the intrinsic fragility of this type of rule, it is remarkable that public order never broke down into chaos even though trade was far more intensive around Cabinda and in the Congo estuary than elsewhere and even though a growing number of Europeans resided in well organized settlements of their own there. But the price paid for order was a regimen of daily violence against the weak. After 1879 Boma became the nursery of the later Congo Independent State and its patterns of violence spread over much of that country.

During the 1830s the three major settlements in the Gabon estuary were controlled by different Houses, led by hereditary *oga* ("kings"). They jockeyed with each other for the best location on the estuary to benefit most from the Atlantic trade while attempting at the same time to monopolize the routes into the interior. Moreover, a few "upstart" entrepreneurs managed to enter the fray as well. The best known among these, Ntoko, succeeded in building up a supply network in ivory and slaves that outperformed the others and to found his own settlement on the estuary as well. He even attracted an American Presbyterian mission to his place. But ultimately his arch-rival "King Denis", an oga, triumphed when he allied himself in 1839 to the French navy and ceded land to them. Thus were the seeds for the future colony of Gabon sown. In 1849 the navy base became Libreville, or "Freetown", when the French settled fifty-two freed slaves brought there from Dakar. Barely a decade later Libreville became the French gateway for forays inland.

In Douala on the Cameroon estuary "King Bell" lost access to the northern routes and their hinterland across the estuary, although he succeeded at first in keeping the upper hand south of the estuary. Later, by the 1840s the Bell family found it very difficult to maintain supremacy even within the town. The slave trade was then effectively being suppressed by interventions of the British consul of Fernando Po, and a Baptist mission had been established in town. Both events weakened the king more than his competitors because the richest lands for the production of palm oil lay to the north of the estuary and their profits went to his adversaries. In town the mission bolstered the power of the Houses of the main rival of the king. By 1856 strife between the competing Houses there became so bad that even the secret association, whose task it was to maintain a negotiated public order, failed and the British consul became the arbiter between the factions. Meanwhile the number of slaves from inland regions who worked on the plantations and in town had grown to such an extent that they began to be seen as a major threat. One of the older associations of free men began to terrorize them by 1858, but the slaves reacted by forming societies of their own and by carrying out boycotts. The new conditions totally overwhelmed the capacity of the local social structures to cope with them. The chaos grew in Douala to the point that "the chiefs of Douala" begged Queen Victoria in 1877 to annex their town. Britain declined the offer, but in 1885 a German consul did annex Douala and thereby laid the foundation for German Kamerun.

As trade grew to unprecedented heights and flooded the caravan trails with unheard of wealth, it also caused extreme turmoil in the form of major migrations in the deep coastal hinterland. The case of the hinterland of Kribi after 1828 shows it best. When people on the central reaches of the Nyong river began to hear about all this new wealth and then saw traders arriving from the coast with precious goods from overseas, they became quite anxious both to gain from the trade and to obtain direct access to this wealth. All the peoples of southern Cameroon began to raid their neighbors for slaves and for stocks of ivory. Some of them migrated towards the coast, while others expanded deeper inland in order to dominate the local population there. The turmoil of raids and migrations eventually affected the whole area. Meanwhile the Fang people in the mountains north of and behind the Gabon estuary felt the same urge. By the 1840s they began to migrate towards the coast, the Gabon estuary and the middle Ogowe river, the major artery of trade, and within thirty years they had displaced or absorbed the original population in this whole area. South of the middle Ogowe large numbers of farmers fled wars and raids to settle in remote backwaters, while smaller numbers did the contrary in the area of the upper Ogowe. They moved towards the trading roads, following the main caravan road to Loango. By the 1890s their advanced parties were setting up camps deep within the forests of Mayombe behind Loango. Along the major and oldest route from Loango to Malebo Pool such major upheavals did not occur although competition between local leaders for access to the benefits of trade increased.

The inland sector of the northern segment of the Atlantic trading network was structured by a mighty coronary artery, the river Congo and covered the lands drained by its tributaries. Its heart was the markets at Malebo Pool still controlled by Tio middlemen, who beat off every attempt by Bobangi carriers to oust them from the four major markets around the Pool. From the Pool to the equator, where modern Mbandaka stands at the mouth of the Tshuapa river, the Bobangi dominated trade on the river, while upstream the Ngala relayed them. In comparison other carriers were minor players. A string of market towns along the Congo river constituted the backbone of these societies. By the end of the period their populations were estimated at between 10,000 and 25,000 inhabitants each. Each town acted as a hub for a large hinterland from which it drew food and necessities for daily life as well as slaves and ivory.

Each town consisted of several major Houses, organized as business firms, containing many hundreds of members, and located next to each other along the river bank. The leaders both competed with each other and collaborated to maintain a minimum of public order. Leadership within each House was open to challenge whenever its fortunes were declining. Succession to its leadership was not predetermined at all. While a son often succeeded, it happened just as often that a talented slave in charge of a good part of the business operations gradually took over from the nominal head or even suddenly took control at the death of the leader. Thus by the late 1870s the most prosperous House in the Malebo Pool – it occupied a whole town of its own at Kintamo (now in Kinshasa) – was dominated by Ngaliema, who had been acquired as a slave not many years before. This was not exceptional as the histories of other towns show. But leaders could also fall from power: some among them are known to have been reduced to slavery overnight. Such extreme social mobility up and down often made daily life in such settlements insecure and often very unpleasant because competitors always tried to extract the maximum amount of labor from those whom they controlled and used extreme violence to achieve their ends.

The great Congo commerce had already led to regional economic specialization in the previous century (see Chapter 8). In this century this trend further intensified. All along the Zaire River from Kinshasa to well into its great bend the lifestyles were becoming more similar. A pidgin language, now called Lingala, was becoming the common trade language over much of the area, while commercial customs had been largely standardized. Leaders began to force social links over great distances. By the 1880s the Tio king, for instance, had married wives from as far away as the lower Ubangi river. Indeed he even had a Zanzibari wife presumably originally from the company that had traveled with Stanley in 1877. Blood brotherhoods which created permanent alliances between leaders were also common and linked people from equally distant places. Scores of cultural features were carried along with trade, from knives of office, originating in the Ubangi bend but treasured as far as Malebo Pool, to standardized house shapes, fishing techniques, new crops such as cassava, citrus fruits, tobacco and maize, intensive agricultural techniques, and even some religious cults and beliefs, for instance the belief in an underwater spirit guardian who traveled with every merchant or boatman and from whom they derived their luck or misfortune. This process went so far that early European visitors thought that one single "tribe", the "Bangala", speaking its own language Lingala, occupied the whole area. The merchants had thus created a single common culture over a huge area of Equatorial Africa. Today these "Bangala" rule modern Zaire.

Further up the tributaries the various local populations in the inner Congo basin were less affected, but even hundreds of miles away from the main river, the exigencies and modalities of the nineteenth-century trade powerfully affected local societies. For instance, by the 1880s among the Bekwil five hundred miles upstream from Kinshasa and two hundred miles away from the Congo, a typical struggle between old and new elites erupted. In the villages nearest the Sangha river, the main route for commerce here, entrepreneurs began to build up membership in their houses and to compete with each other, while disregarding the customary authority of the hitherto powerful village chiefs. To express their aspirations and achievements the new men subverted a well-established masked village dance, by introducing a gorilla mask which they adapted as their own. Each performance now became a display of intimidation whereby gorilla maskers drove out the others, and then one gorilla masker pushed and shoved all the others into submission to him. Everyday brawls between competing Houses became more common and in the end some villages became ungovernable.

Beyond and in between the regular trading routes there were also zones of turmoil which suffered from slave raids. The Mongo inhabitants of Mbandaka conducted slave raids on the remote villages of the Likouala-aux-herbes, while inland Mongo people south of the Tshuapa river and all along its affluents recall the slave raids of pirates, who paddled up the rivers to loot unsuspecting villages so often that many of them were finally forced to flee out of range further upstream. As a result of repeated attacks of this sort all the populations then living in the vicinity of the lower Ubangi fled upstream to the valley of the Lobaye river in the Central African Republic.

Between the Ubangi and the great bend of the Zaire river meanwhile the powerful older dynamics of political competition were still at work. In the eighteenth century, innovation and counter innovation had once again produced greater military efficiency, insecurity and war. The effects reverberated through much of what is now northern Zaire, from the expansion of the Azande (see below) in the east to that of the Ngbandi on the lower Ubangi river in the west. One of the peoples involved were the Ngombe, or "inland warriors", a name given to them by the people living on the northern bank of the western part of the great Zaire bend. Pressed from the north and east by the even better organized Ngbandi the Ngombe first conquered lands north of the great river bend. Then around 1800 they crossed the river and began to wrest the whole area north of Mbandaka away from its original Mongo inhabitants. The wars here were bitterly fought, settlement by settlement and with varying fortunes during most of the century, as is attested by the ruins of scores of once fortified sites, by vivid oral memories and by early written records. Decade after decade these hostilities produced captives, who were sold as slaves to the merchants on the rivers. In these lands the spheres affected by major internal and external processes of change overlapped and tragically amplified the violence and turmoil that accompanied each of these dynamics.

The Atlantic trading area: the southern segment

Until the later 1830s slave trading in the southern segment of the Atlantic continued as before. Metropolitan credit was given to major merchants in Luanda, who sold slaves to Brazilian firms. Both in the towns and inland various Luso-African communities gained more and more influence so that the colonial authorities came to totally rely on them to act on their behalf in the interior. Luanda was still the main harbor and market place although Benguela was growing. Both harbors were closed to all but Portuguese or Brazilian shipping. Structurally the coastal sector of the southern segment consisted of those harbors, the colony of Angola with its potential for plantations behind them and an inland stretch as far as the Kwango and upper Cuanza rivers to the east. So dominant was the slave trade that by 1820 it accounted for 85 per cent of all government revenue and 90 per cent of all exports. Earlier attempts of a few farsighted governors to diversify the economy had little effect.

When Portugal abolished the slave trade in 1836 its decrees were at first ignored. A major decline in the trade occurred only when further measures were taken in the 1840s. These included the creation of a prize court in Luanda, the suppression by the

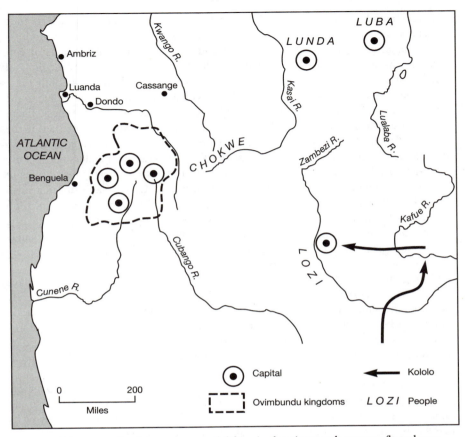

Map 14.2 Southwestern central Africa in the nineteenth century (based on a map by C. Vansina)

British navy of the trade south of the Equator, and the opening up of the harbors to free competitive trade by ships of all nations. Then in 1850 Brazil abolished the slave trade. Then the export trade collapsed. As a result half of the European inhabitants of Luanda left the colony in 1850/51. But a clandestine traffic in slaves still continued side by side with legitimate trades. Indeed as late as the mid-1850s an Angolan governor was still smuggling cargoes of slaves into Brazil. Slave exports finally ceased in the 1860s, to be replaced by the export of *libertos* or bonded labor at the rate of a few thousand people per year. In the far interior, however, the slave trade continued unabated because of a growing internal demand for servile labor in the hinterland of Luanda and further inland. The formal abolition of slavery in 1875 had no effect on the trade which ceased only after the great famine of 1911.

From the 1830s onwards the government stimulated the trade in ivory and wax to replace the export of slaves. In 1834 it abolished its buying monopoly of ivory. As a result the price paid for ivory in Luanda jumped by 300 per cent and the trade grew by leaps and bounds in the 1840s and 1850s when the product became the prime revenue earner for the government. From the 1840s onwards also tiny quantities of products such as palm oil, coffee, sugar, groundnuts and cotton grown on plantations or collected in the wild, began to be traded as well. A decade later many plantations of coffee, cotton, groundnuts, and sugar were set up in the colony itself. Both these plantations and the caravans that carried the bulky legitimate goods of low value to the harbors required more slave labor than had been needed in earlier times. There resulted a shortage of labor and a sharp rise in the value of a slave on the markets in the interior. Planters bought slaves in large numbers, especially during droughts when so many could be obtained at once that the price collapsed. Thus the planters north of the Cuanza took advantage of the dramatic drought of 1855–57 to cheaply buy masses of refugees from south of the river. Then the civil war in the United Sates fueled a small boom in cotton prices, which led to a further expansion of plantations. In 1866 steamships began to ply the route from Luanda to Dondo on the Cuanza regularly, which made it easier and cheaper to export the bulky cash crops. This immediately produced a spectacular increase in exports, yet not enough to offset a contemporary slump in the much more valuable ivory exports.

During the 1840 and 1850s the determination of authorities to stamp out the slave trade in the hinterland of the colony, in and around the lands of Kasanje merely increased the bitter struggles there between those who were clinging to the slave trade and those who were promoting the trade in ivory and wax. Because the government was always forced to rely in part on the military power of local Luso-African allies, its intervention only created more havoc, until its troops were chased out of the region in 1861.

The wrenching shift from slave exports to legitimate exports in the overall economy of this segment of the Atlantic trade between the 1830s and the 1870s had a strong impact on Angolan society. Luanda itself declined dramatically at first as many of its merchants, grown rich in the era of the slave trade, left the country in the 1840s and 1850s. By the mid-1840s already only one hundred and forty Europeans remained in the rural area around Luanda, that is too few to maintain control over commerce in the interior. The city's population then stood at 5600. Then the legitimate trade picked up and so did the city's population. By 1850 it had more than doubled to 12,500 and by 1864 it stood at about 17,000. But the number of European inhabitants halved in 1850 and then remained stagnant at about one thousand. With the passage of time Europeans were thus becoming a smaller and smaller fraction of the whole. Moreover internal dissensions between the major trading houses and the government as well as between Portuguese officials and creoles were growing. The town fell more and more under the economic and political control of the Luso-African settlers. In the nearer hinterland, Luso-Africans, a handful of chiefs, and a number of resident Vili from the Cabinda and Loango coasts, who had earned their wealth earlier in the slave trade, controlled the plantations. Further inland these same groups formed various factions, led by powerful entrepreneurs, and competed with each other for control of the slave, ivory and wax trades in a general atmosphere of lawlessness. The contrasting investment of two famous Luso-African leaders in the interior, Manuel Antonio Pires and Fernandes da Cruz, nicely illustrate the strategies of slave traders and of legitimate traders. By 1860 Pires had forcefully dominated the trade in his town and a large area around it, at the eastern edge of the colony, for thirty years. He disposed of a military force of seven hundred slaves and countless food-producing concubines and was still positioned for trading in slaves only. In contrast, Fernandes da Cruz, who died in 1860, left over one hundred farms and plantations to his heirs along with three hundred slaves to work them, an estate fully adapted to the "modern" plantation economy.

Given the demographic conditions as well as the uncertainty of their revenues, the metropolitan authorities lost most military and administrative control in the colony to various groups of Luso-Africans. Even the city council of Luanda was dominated by the interests of Creoles. The nadir for government power occurred in the mid 1860s when the ivory trade slumped. A devastating epidemic of smallpox in 1864 made the situation worse. It killed off a significant portion of the population and halted trade for a year. Because most government income came from taxes in the export of ivory the public deficit ballooned to the extent that the authorities had to withdraw from nearly all the territories they had gradually incorporated into the colony during the 1850s and 1860s.

By the mid 1870s, however, government's fortunes took a turn for the better. The rubber boom had begun and exports of coffee had tripled in three years, while prices were rising. This attracted a wave of new settlers from Portugal and these immigrants began to whittle away at the plantations of the chiefs and Luso-Africans. At first the latter resisted vigorously and efficiently. But a major famine from 1873 to 1876, followed by a raging epidemic of smallpox which killed a high proportion of the laborers on the plantations, forced many of them to sell out to the newcomers. By 1878, six hundred settlers, mostly new arrivals, were ensconced in the colony inland from Luanda. By 1898 they numbered over 6000. The demographic trend had turned in favor of the metropole. Moreover, the catastrophes of the 1870s had so weakened the older local elites that they no longer had the military force or the wealth needed to prevent ever more brazen dispossessions. By the 1890s the Luso-Africans in and around Luanda were reduced to impotent political agitation. Yet their community ultimately triumphed. For it eventually spawned the "Popular Movement for the Liberation of Angola" (MPLA) which took over control of the government of independent Angola in 1975.

Contrary to what happened nearer the coast the growth of the legitimate commerce in wax and ivory did not at first create great turmoil in the vast inland sector of the trading area. The Ovimbundu kingdoms on the Benguela plateau reacted by diverting their slave trade to Benguela in the south and merely added a trade in ivory and wax. At first they gathered these products in their own lands, but soon wax and ivory from eastern Angola formed the bulk of the exports. The alliances between rulers and Luso-Africans became even closer especially in the three major kingdoms which by mid-century dominated the highlands: Mbailundu, Bie and Huambo. Profits were higher than ever before and the trading networks soon reached as far as the copper belt and even crossed Africa. Ovimbundu caravans also succeeded in breaking the Imbangala monopoly at the Lunda capital in the 1840s and from there expanded northwards as well.

An Ovimbundu caravan was a large and well-armed body of men usually pooling the

resources of several entrepreneurs, although kings and the wealthiest Luso-Africans could afford to finance caravans of their own. The entrepreneurs usually accompanied their caravans, but the kings never did. Because they were supplied from Benguela, where more guns were sold and at a cheaper price than in Luanda, they were also better armed than the competition and had more guns for sale as well. That and their sheer size set them apart from the competition, whether Imbangala or Chokwe.

The introduction of legitimate trade had a spectacular consequence in eastern Angola because it caused the expansion of the Chokwe. By 1840 the Chokwe people occupied a small but densely populated territory near the headwaters of the rivers Kasai and Kwango. Their home was in dense woodlands on poor soils surrounded on most sides by vast tracts of almost deserted forests. They were then known as expert metallurgists, hunters and gatherers of honey. During the drier half of the year small groups of closely related men roamed far and wide in pursuit of game and honey. The most remarkable feature of their social organization was the extreme independence of most men from any control by their chiefs. Formally the Chokwe were organized in four major chiefdoms whose leaders boasted of titles which gave them a position in the overall titulature of the Luanda commonwealth, but in practice this meant something only to the aristocrats themselves.

Until the 1840s the Chokwe's country was a backwater bypassed by the caravans. But the sudden urgent demand for ivory and slaves soon brought in Ovimbundu traders. The Chokwe soon became the major providers of wax and ivory which they sold in return for guns, cloth, beads and other goods. Chokwe parties then sold cloth and sundry commodities further inland to buy female slaves whom they married and thus absorbed in their households. By the early 1850s local overpopulation in their homeland and the lure of richer hunting grounds farther afield took hunters further and further away to the sparsely populated areas in the north and northeast. Tolerated at first by the local inhabitants the Chokwe ended by dominating them because of their rapid population growth resulting from the absorption of foreign women and the military superiority inherent in the ability of their smiths to care for guns and repair them.

The Chokwe expansion began around mid-century. By 1870, the start of the rubber gathering boom accelerated emigration from the homeland as more women and children accompanied the men to gather rubber while their men hunted. During the 1880s bands of Chokwe hunter/warriors overran the core of the Rund kingdom and the Chokwe became dominant over most of northeastern Angola and adjacent lands, wherever the original population densities had not been high. The violent phase of their expansion faltered only in the 1890s when local African leaders allied to the army of the Congo Independent State to thwart them. But even so emigration continued towards the copperbelt in Shaba and the Congo state finally subdued them only around 1920. When the expansion ended the Chokwe were left in control of a very large territory in north central Angola and adjoining parts of Zaire, where they absorbed the original population and imposed their language and culture.

Meanwhile different dynamics obtained in the densely populated areas in what is now the western Kasai province of Zaire. There the Chokwe found no room to settle. They banded together in larger caravans to raid and trade, in competition with

Ovimbundu and Imbangala caravans. But by 1879 there arose a very able leader among the Luba (Kasai) people living in the valley of the central Lulua river. He and his successor unified the country and he was able to deal as an equal trading partner with the Chokwe and to hold them in check. In the 1870s and 1880s these leaders assisted the first European expeditions in the area and were supported by them. This stood in stark contrast to the fate of the other Luba in Kasai living further south and east. By the later 1880s they were heavily raided for slaves by Chokwe and Ovimbundu caravans from the west as well as by slaving parties, from the east, who worked for Tippu Tib, the major Zanzibari slave trader then settled on the Lualaba. Feeling helpless, thousands of Luba fled their homelands to settle near state and mission stations in the 1890s, most of which were located in the country of their successful brethren. Soon the hosts and the newcomers were locked into bitter disputes over land and the ethnic group split in two: the Lulua hosts and the Luba-Kasai settlers. The Lulua leaders clashed with the state authorities, while the Luba-Kasai, as displaced persons, could only make the most of the colonial regime and especially of its educational opportunities. As a result they eventually became a colonial elite in southern Zaire. When the colonial regime began to lose its grip in 1959, the rivalry between Luba Kasai and Lulua broke out in civil war which only ended when most of the Luba-Kasai were forced to return to their ancestral homelands.

Out of the south: the Kololo

Some of the armies fleeing northwards from the *mfecane* or South African drought and Griqua raids in the 1820s reached southern central Africa by the 1830s. Among them only the Kololo had a lasting impact there. The Kololo crossed the Zambezi above the Victoria Falls and first turned eastward, lured by reports about the wealth in cattle of the peoples in southern Zambia. The local populations and their very small political units were no match for the tightly knit, well-armed Kololo regiments. But the latter felt threatened by the more powerful Ndebele who followed on their heels. Even though by 1840 the Kololo had defeated a Ndebele force in southern Zambia, their leader, Sebituane, feared further incursions and thought it prudent to move out of range. He invaded the Lozi kingdom on the upper Zambezi, the richest, most prosperous, and perhaps most populous country in all of Zambia. The country was then in the throes of a civil war over the succession to the throne and Sebituane encountered little resistance. Still he was only secure there by 1850 when he had warded off further attacks by Ndebele and other southern African regiments. In that year he renewed the ties which the previous Lozi king had entertained with Luso-African traders and he even joined some of their parties in raids eastwards towards the middle of the Kafue valley. Then he incorporated the lands between the upper Zambezi and the middle Kafue into his realm. Under his successors a strong Kololo state took shape. Older Lozi institutions were adapted and joined to institutions of government which stemmed from the original homelands of the Kololo. The new state was more centralized than anything known up to that time in the region and the realm was far larger than the Lozi kingdom had been. But the Kololo failed to dislodge the Lozi princes from the swamps where they had taken refuge, and they failed to develop an ideology which won the allegiance of the conquered subjects. In 1864 a Lozi prince succeeded in ousting the Kololo ruler and recaptured the kingdom.

A period of political instability followed until 1885 when a new ruler, Lewanika, finally succeeded in crushing all opposition. Lewanika then skillfully used Barotseland's position at the crossroads of the Atlantic and South African trades to reinforce the internal organization of the state and even to expand to both east and westwards. Eventually he succeeded in preserving his realm as a separate entity within Northern Rhodesia.

Traders from the Indian ocean

In earlier centuries, intercontinental trade based on the Indian Ocean had only affected equatorial Africa in an indirect way. But the network was completely refashioned and refinanced from the late eighteenth century onwards. It was now aimed at the export of slaves and ivory and expanded rapidly after 1800. The traders reached eastern equatorial Africa from c. 1830 onwards. At that time Kazembe on the Luapula was at the zenith of his power. Traders from Tete on the lower Zambezi valley visited his capital regularly and the first traders from the Swahili coast were arriving there as well. Soon the flow of goods intensified and Kazembe's capital became a way station on a route that went on westwards as far as northwestern Zambia where the first Zanzibari trader was active before 1850. The kingdom was secure from foreign enemies which induced people to travel and increased cultural interaction. But the glitter of Kazembe's court life was paid for by heavy taxes which the Lunda lords imposed on the villages. Political stability and security were bought at the price of systematic terror and coercion, which in turn gave rise to generalized but important discontent among its population.

The Kazembe's nemesis was the Sumbwa (western Tanzania) merchant adventurer named Msiri. He first arrived there around 1860 following in the footsteps of his father. He was allowed to settle in Shaba and gradually became involved in local politics. Others from western Tanzania flocked to him, and with the help of their guns he made himself the head of a small territory where he enjoyed the support of the local population because his guns defended them against Luba raids. When he dared to intervene militarily in a quarrel within Kazembe's family, the king was so outraged that he ordered the execution of all Zanzibari and western Tanzanian traders who happened to be at his capital. The Zanzibari counter-attacked and killed the king in 1872. That left Msiri in control on the copperbelt. For a time no Kazembe could keep his throne unless he allied either with the Zanzibari traders or with Msiri's people, now known as the Yeke. Throughout the 1880s the Yeke dominated even the old heartland of the kingdom until a Kazembe recovered part of the Luapula valley in 1892 and turned it into a haven for the many refugees who were then fleeing Zanzibari slave traders.

Msiri's realm was growing even stronger through a centrally controlled trade in copper, salt, and ivory, as well as through political marriages, for example to the daughters of a prominent Luso-African trader, and of an Arab trader from the east coast respectively. In 1880 his father died in Sumbwa country and Msiri took the title

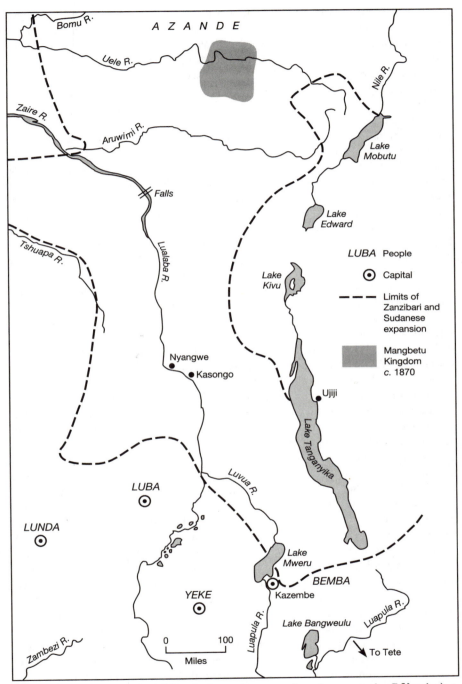

Map 14.3 Eastern central Africa in the 19th century (based on a map by C. Vansina)

of *mwami* or king. During the next decade his realm became a secondary empire. Msiri's power ultimately rested on military technology derived from industrial Europe and on intercontinental trade. He used it to create a tightly controlled state where coercion was far more efficient that it had been at the time of the Kazembes. Coercion was accompanied by an increased pace of imposed technological, social, and cultural change, ranging from new mining techniques, to a flood of laws designed to reconcile Sumbwa customs with those of the local people. Although the Yeke adopted some local cultural features, including the local language, they wanted nevertheless to refashion local society in the image of their own practices. The scope of the new regulations was far more extensive than had ever been the case in the Lunda past. They covered the whole gamut of social relations from bridewealth to the proper composition of local groups. A Sumbwa ideology of kingship, its symbols of office, and some related religious beliefs were also imposed. Moreover, and this had been unheard of before, all these detailed laws claimed to be applicable to every single village and every household in the land, and Msiri attempted to enforce all of them. The difference between Kazembe's and Msiri's rule is vividly remembered in the memories of the local populations. It was the difference between a decentralized kingdom, such as had been common in Central Africa and a new system, the centralized state.

Meanwhile Msiri's caravans of ivory and copper reached both Benguela and the coast opposite Zanzibar. He raided deep into central and western Zambia, threatened to subdue the central Luba kingdom and dominated the wreck of Kazembe's kingdom. His capital, Bunkeya, became possibly the largest city in Central Africa. Not surprisingly, however, his subjects soon became even more alienated than they had been under Kazembe. The very people who had helped him to rise from trader to king rebelled in 1886 and the rebellion turned into chronic guerrilla warfare. By then Europeans had appeared in the areas. Missionaries settled at Msiri's court, then both the Congo Independent State and the British South Africa Company offered him protectorate status which he refused. In 1891 an official of the Congo state killed him during a quarrel. Thereupon the Yeke state disintegrated as the local rebellion now engulfed the realm. Msiri's son had to become an ally of the Congo state against his own subjects to survive. Even with the alliance the war ended only in 1900, barely a decade before the first industrial copper smelter began to operate on the copperbelt.

The coming of powerful merchant caravans to southeastern equatorial Africa did not overwhelm all the local political dynamics as the case of the Bemba chiefdoms shows. By 1800 there were several rival chiefdoms in northeast Zambia all ruled by Bemba chiefs belonging to the same clan and claiming to be relatives. By 1835 one of them became superior in power and prestige to the others and brought nearly all of them in the orbit of a single still loosely organized kingdom. Internal unification accelerated in the 1860s in the face of a Ngoni threat, which vanished after the Bemba king defeated them utterly c.1870. By then the Bemba had found a niche for themselves in the trading economy as providers of slaves. The chiefdoms no longer attacked each other. Instead they raided their neighbors for slaves and ivory which they sold to the Zanzibari merchants at the margins of their lands. Their reputation as invincible warriors grew even stronger than the Ngoni and their role as providers of slaves left them secure from Zanzibari raids. Over time, however, they came to depend more and more on the guns and ammunition imported from the east coast. When in 1898 the British cut off their military supplies, Bemba power quickly collapsed.

Internal political dynamics also remained the major force in the central Luba kingdom until the later 1850s. During the reigns of two very able rulers the kingdom continued to expand from the beginning of the century through the 1860s both by military means and by the rallying of hitherto independent chiefs. When Zanzibari traders first crossed Lake Tanganyika from Ujiji in the 1830s they discovered that they could raid for ivory and slaves with impunity in the uncentralized lands west of the lake, but not in the Luba kingdom. There a few among them settled peacefully near the capital. But then c. 1860 very large and well-armed Ovimbundu caravans began to enter the country from the west. The king at first encouraged them to plunder the lands of his enemies on the western frontier, but later even allowed them to ravage villages in his own realm, which alienated large numbers of his subjects and this discontent erupted into insurrection after his death c. 1870. Civil war between contenders for the throne and popular rebel leaders then engulfed the country. Calm returned only in 1917 when the colonial authorities finally achieved full control of the area.

By 1869 several leading Zanzibari merchants had reached the Lualaba just north of the furthest reaches of the Luba kingdom where they jointly founded a settlement at Nyangwe. A major market sprang up there. Five years later this coalition of traders was forced to accept the primacy of a trader who was more powerful than them. He was Tippo Tib, a merchant from Tabora in Tanzania. Hitherto Tippo Tib had raided and traded from Kazembe to the eastern fringes of the central Luba kingdom and north of it. There, on the fringes of the rainforests, he was able to establish a credible claim to be the legitimate successor of a small ruler he found there and began to lay the basis for a territory of his own. Once recognized as undisputed *primus inter pares* at Nyangwe in 1874 he founded a capital, Kasongo, nearby and organized a substantial realm. He built roads, laid out plantations, imposed a monopoly on the sale of ivory, recognized local leaders as chiefs, appointed his own officials to supervise them, to collect tribute, to "speak justice", and to recruit soldiers. In 1876 he welcomed Stanley and accompanied him downriver deep into the rainforests, an environment which hitherto had defeated the other Zanzibari merchants. But Tippo Tib's local soldiers knew these environments well and with their aid Zanzibar raiding parties expanded their range downstream from that time onwards. In 1887 they reached the Uele and Ituri far to the north, had entered the central Congo basin from the east, and were operating in the lowlands between the Lualaba and the mountains of the western Rift Valley. They also were imposing a territorial organization over a large part of this area as well. By 1890 Tippo Tib returned to a respected life of ease on the coast at a time when clashes with Congo state troops over stocks of ivory began to occur. These escalated into a major war by 1892. Despite the defeat of the Zanzibari in 1894 the officials of the Congo state found themselves militarily in a weak position. They also realized that the Zanzibari system of exploitation was more efficient than their own. Hence they left most of the junior Zanzibari entrepreneurs and their system of government in place. Indeed they dismissed the last of these people only c. 1920. This administrative continuity explains why the Zanzibari were able to bequeath the Swahili language, many Swahili customs, and to a lesser degree Islam to much of eastern Zaire.

Traders from the Nile

By 1800 *jallaba* parties (nicknamed after their favourite costume) were traveling south of the Bahr al-Ghazal river, in a land that was soon to acquire the tragic name of Dar Fertit or "land of slaves". There they set up fortified camps called *zariba* which they used as bases for raids and safe havens for their booty until it could be shipped northwards. Most of these traders came from Darfur where the Sultan regulated their raiding expeditions by granting permits in return for a substantial fee. But around mid-century the Jallaba were joined by competitors based in Khartoum. These were European slave traders at first, but in the 1860s and 1870s Coptic Christians took over from them. They soon controlled the Nile route while the jallaba went overland across Kordofan to Egypt well to the west of the Nile. The famous al-Zubayr Rāhma Mansūr was a Jallaba leader and so was Rābih Fadlallāh who followed him as major war leader after 1879.

Meanwhile jallaba and Khartoumers were steadily raiding in Dar Fertit until whole populations there were wiped out or fled away, leaving the land deserted. Thus most of the Banda-speaking peoples migrated westwards during the whole century. That movement in turn exerted great pressure on the inhabitants of the western part of the present-day Central African Republic. Hemmed in by the southward pressure from Bagirmi to the north, the eastward pressure from the Fulbe in Adamawa to the west and the northward pressure from people fleeing from the slave trade on the lower Ubangi they seemed doomed. But by the 1880s they were finally desperate enough to achieve political cohesion by electing common war captains and they even managed to chase Rabīh out of their lands. But as soon as danger receded they reverted to their cherished local autonomy. The jallaba and Khartoumers raided further and further southwards without much resistance until they encountered warlike troops belonging to the expanding Azande principalities north of the Bomu valley.

In the seventeenth and eighteenth centuries the populations living near and south of the headwaters of the Ubangi river were still locked into an escalating and merciless competition for power, which had begun half a millennium earlier on the northern bank of the River Zaire. By 1700 the drive for internal cooperation against outside enemies had led to military innovations, coalitions between large lineages and the formation of principalities. Half a century later, Ngura, the leader of a small principality on the eastern side of this cluster of violence discovered that his neighbors to the east were much less well coordinated than this chiefdom and hence militarily quite weak. He embarked on a conquest of their lands both to increase his power and to relieve some of the pressure exerted on his principality by his western neighbors. The invaders absorbed or chased the older settlers away and built up a new set of competing and warlike principalities. During most of the nineteenth century the rivalry between these entities fueled further expansion and conquest east and southwards. The result was the creation of a new and highly militarized type of society, a new culture, and a new ethnicity called the Azande.

The Azande were at first a match for the slave traders. As late as the 1860s one of their princes defeated a 1000 men-strong raiding party and even overran a major *zariba* in the area. The traders reacted by allying themselves to some princes against others and thus were still able to export slaves and ivory. The Azande for their part allied with Khartoumers against Jallaba. But in the 1870s many principalities began to crumble and became temporarily tributary to Zubayr in the west and Khartoumers in the east. Only a block in the center remained independent. When the Mahdi rose however the Azande recovered their independence but only to be conquered from the later 1890s onwards by colonial forces. These ultimately divided the principalities between Sudan, Ubangi-Shari (later the Central African Republic), and the Congo Independent State.

Meanwhile, beyond the Azande lands in the area south of the Middle Uele, a major kingdom, called Mangbetu by its founder Nabiembali, had sprung up in the rainforests around 1830. These were very rich lands which had attracted immigrants for a thousand years. This situation had led to a very complex political history as various groups tried to defend their holdings or to acquire land there. Because these groups were of very different origins, many social and cultural innovations accompanied this process. By the late eighteenth century various very large Houses had become centralized chiefdoms and were still competing. Nabiembali's father created one of the strongest among them and his son succeeded in incorporating all the others in his lands. He also halted the advance of the Azande on the Uele. His kingdom was so new, however, that it never developed a specialized political organization commensurate to the task of governing so many people over such a large area. Nor did Nabiembali create an ideology sufficient to capture the loyalty of its subjects. In 1859 the system began to splinter as Nabiembali's sons began to challenge his authority. Later upstarts unrelated to the royal House overthrew some of the main Mangbetu chiefs, while other scions of the royal House moved away to find new domains. When the North African slave traders first met Mangbetu forces north of the Uele river in 1865 they were soundly defeated by a princess. But later as civil strife worsened they found allies in the region. In 1873 a coalition of forces killed the Mangbetu king whereupon the kingdom broke up. Paradoxically this break up led to a renewed Mangbetu expansion over a much larger area south and eastwards for reasons similar to those which had led to the Azande expansion. For the next seven years the slave traders and their Azande allies became the dominant force in the land. Then followed intrusions by Egyptians (1880) and Zanzibari slave traders (1887) before the area finally fell to the Congo Independent State (1891).

The Azande and Mangbetu expansions united more than fifty distinct populations in the Uele-Bomu region and fused their culture and social mores into a single, rich new way of life. Scholars have contrasted the Azande achievement in the areas of technology, warfare and law (rather like the ancient Romans), to that of the Mangbetu who were praised for the refinement of their arts and thought (rather like the ancient Greeks). This is mistaken. By the end of the century the whole area was sharing in a single way of life, strengthened by intensive interaction. The variabilities in life style were due more to the relative richness of the local districts than to any ethnic nomenclature. People in the southern lands were more at ease, because agricultural production and most resources were abundant, while the northernmost lands were less affluent because the climate and soils posed more risks for farmers and resources were on the whole scarcer.

Conclusions

New men, upstarts, and some leaders in the old style modeled the fate of equatorial Africans in the nineteenth century often by using international trade, industry, and capital to realize their expectations. In doing so they ensured that this trade ultimately affected the whole area. Thus commerce became the dominant dynamic in many places, albeit not everywhere, as is shown by the vigorous continuation of the older internal dynamics, for instance in the Ubangi and Uele area, or in the Kuba kingdom.

Many of these new men founded families which continued to play a role during the colonial period. Thus the 1880s are not an absolute divide between radically different pre-colonial and colonial worlds. Alliances concluded in the early colonial period (1889 to 1920) between such elites and colonial officers ensured a certain continuity and allowed some of these families to take full advantage of the new opportunities offered by colonial rule. Some of them have re-emerged among the elite of post-colonial Africa. For example, the Franques now play a major role in Cabinda and in Luanda, the descendants of Msiri backed a failed bid after independence to create a separate state in Shaba and in Uele colonial and post-independence politics alike still involve the families of the upstart chiefs of the 1860s and 1870s. In contrast very few descendants of the pre-nineteenth century elite families still exert any influence today. Thus the upstarts of the 1880s are often the forebears of the so-called "traditional families" which guide the destiny of Equatorial Africa today.

Suggestions for further reading

In addition to the relevant reading for Chapter 8 see also:

Austen, Ralph, A., "Slavery among Coastal Middlemen: The Duala of Cameroun," S. Miers and I Kopytoff (eds), *Slavery in Africa: Historical and Anthropological Perspectives*, Madison: University of Wisconsin Press, 1977.

Cordell, Dennis, D., *Dar al-Kuti and the Last Years of the Trans-Saharan Slave Trade*, Madison: University of Wisconsin Press 1985: Part 1, pp. 1–51.

Dias, Jill, R., "Changing Patterns of Power in the Luanda Hinterland: The Impact of Trade and Colonization on the Mbundu ca. 1845–1920," *Paideuma*, 32 (1986), pp. 285–318.

Keim, Curtis, A., *Precolonial Mangbetu Rule: Political and Economic factors in nineteenth-century Mangbetu history (Northeast Zaire)*, Ann Arbor: University Microfilms International, 1979.

Laburthe-Tolra, Philippe, *Les seigneurs de la forêt*, Paris: Sorbonne, 1981.

M'Bokolo, Elikia, *Noirs et Blancs en Afrique Equatoriale: Les sociétés côtières et la pénétration française (vers 1820–1874)*, Paris: Mouton, 1981.

Metegue-N'nah, Nicolas, *Economies et sociétés au Gabon dans la première moité du XIX e siècle*, Paris: L'Harmattan, 1979.

Martin, Phyllis, "Family Strategies in Nineteenth-Century Cabinda," *Journal of African History*, 28 (1987), pp. 65–8.

Miller, Joseph, C., "Cokwe Trade and Conquest in the Nineteenth Century," in T. Gray and D. Birmingham (eds), *Pre-colonial African Trade*, London: Oxford University Press, 1970.

Miller, Joseph, C., "The Confrontation on the Kwango: Kasange and the Portuguese, 1836–1858," in *Reuniaõ Internacional História de Africa. Relação Europa-Africa no 30 quartel do Séc. XIX*, Lisbon: fundaĉão Gulbenkian, 1988, pp. 535–72.

Pélissier, René, *Les guerres grises: Résistances et révoltes en Angola 1845–1941*, Orgeval: 1977.

Prins, Gwyn, *The Hidden Hippopotamus*, Cambridge: Cambridge University Press, 1980.

Roberts, Andrew, D., *A History of the Bemba: Political Growth and Change in Northeastern Zambia before 1900*, Madison: University of Wisconsin Press, 1973.

Roberts, Andrew, D., *A History of Zambia*, London: Longman, 1976.

Schildkrout, Enid, Keim, Curtia A., *African Reflections: Art from Northeastern Zaire*, Seattle and New York: University of Washington Press and American Museum of Natural History, 1990.

Tippu, Tib, *Maisha ya Hamed bin Muhammed et Murjebi, yaani Tippu Tib*. Swahili text with trans. W.H. Whiteley. Nairobi: East African Literature Bureau, 1966.

Vansina, Jan, *The Tio Kingdom of the Middle Congo, 1880–1892*, London: Oxford University Press, 1973.

Vellut, Jean-Luc, "L'économie internationale des côtes de Guinée inférieure au XIXe siècle," in *Reuniaõ Internacional História e Africa. Relação Europa-Africa no 30 quartel do Séc. XIX*, Lisbon: fundação Gulbenkian, 1988, pp. 135–206.

Vellut, Jean-Luc, "Notes sur le Lunda et la frontiére luso-africaine (1700–1900)," *Etudes d'histoire africaine*, 3 (1972), pp. 61–166.

Wirz, A., "La rivière du Cameroun Le commerce pré-colonial et controle du pouvoir en société lignagère," *Revue Française d'histoire d'Outre-mer*, 40, 219 (1973), pp. 172–95.

15

THE EUROPEAN CONQUEST

The decade of the 1880s was a major turning point in African history. Until then, the European impact on much of the continent had come through gradual encroachment, economic penetration, or religious missions. It now turned to overt annexation, with half a dozen European powers moving rapidly from one conquest to the next, often without waiting long enough to establish a firm administration over territory first acquired. Europeans, then and later, wrote of these events as the "scramble" for Africa that brought most of the continent rapidly and brutally into the colonial period.

European conquest had already come to much of southern Africa, to Algeria, even here and there in tropical Africa, as with the French military push to the upper Senegal in the 1850s. But the empire-building of the pre-colonial century had been mainly African – Shaykh Umar in the western Sudan, the caliphate of Sokoto in northern Nigeria, the Zulu and other offshoots of the mfecane in southeastern Africa, the secondary empire of the Egyptian Sudan, or, further south, a congeries of secondary empires on the fringes of the Zanzibari sphere in East Africa.

Some of this empire-building had involved European mercenaries; some European weapons in African hands; some degree of informal control from Europe; but the prevailing European mode of dealing with tropical Africa in the first three-quarters of the nineteenth century had been to avoid direct administration of large and populous alien territories. The industrial revolution had already begun to alter Europe's relations with the non-Western world, but its influence was felt first through the new currents of trade, second through the European weapons that created disequilibria of power on the local scene, and only third through the direct use of those weapons under European control.

The European background: technological factors

The new phase that began in the 1880s owed something to the earlier impact of Europe on Africa. The rise of secondary empires and their inherent instability is a case in point. They provided a constant and gnawing temptation to European strategists to intervene in order to assure stable conditions for trade or investment.

The new industrial technology provided further incentives to conquest. Some of these technical and economic changes profoundly altered worldwide distribution of resources. Earlier in the century, the search for grain and meat helped spark European expansion across the temperate plains of North America, Ukraine, or Argentina. The 1880s and 1890s were the prime period for Europe's conquest of the wet tropics – not just Africa, but Southeast Asia and the Amazon basin as well. This happened in part because European industry needed tropical products like vegetable oils and rubber. New medical technology made the wet tropics safer for alien visitors. New weapons made the conquest of any non-Western region cheaper than ever before – so cheap that Europeans were tempted to pick up territory whose potential value was doubtful or unknown.

Until the middle of the nineteenth century, people brought up in Europe died in tropical Africa at appalling rates. In the early nineteenth century and before, that loss of life was part of the cost of any European activity in tropical Africa – commercial, missionary, or military. Before the 1850s, the annual mortality of newly arrived Europeans varied between 250 and 500 per thousand. The first breakthrough toward greater safety came with the 1840s. Even though the true cause of malaria and the germ theory of disease still awaited discovery, European doctors found that the regular doses of quinine, extracted from the bark of the South American cinchona tree, could place an anti-malarial agent in the bloodstream ready to counter the parasites when they entered through an infective mosquito bite. The doctors also abandoned harmful ways of treating fevers with mercury and extensive bleeding, so that those who *did* contract malaria had a better chance to recover.

Over the second half of the nineteenth century, European death rates in Africa dropped from around 250 to a little more than 50 per thousand per annum. That was still more than five times the death rate for young men of the same age in Europe, but it was the decrease that captured public imagination. In 1841–2, a British government-expedition up the Niger River, lost 28 per cent of the European personnel to malaria in less than two months up the river. Only thirty-four years later, in 1874, the British sent a military force of some 2500 European soldiers on a punitive expedition to sack Kumasi, the capital of Asante. That force also stayed in Africa about two months, and its losses by death from disease were less than 2 per cent. The British never again used European troops on that scale for the conquest of tropical Africa, but they did prove to their own satisfaction that the loss from disease could be kept to levels considered tolerable by the standards of the day.

The worst of African health conditions for Europeans applied to tropical Africa only, which may be one reason why the encroachments of the early century came in the north and the far south. The disease environment of the Mediterranean was similar on either side of the sea. A study of British military mortality over the period 1817–36 (before tropical medicine became an effective tool) showed the comparative death rates for British troops serving in different parts of the world. Annual deaths per thousand from disease showed 10 per thousand for the Cape of Good Hope, 13 for Gibraltar or England itself, 75 to 85 for India or the West Indies, but 480 for Sierra Leone. The danger was considerable in any part of the tropical world, but it was worst of all for Africa.

In 1901–2, came a second breakthrough with the discovery that mosquitos were the infective vector for both malaria and yellow fever. Anti-mosquito campaigns joined prophylactic drugs, and, on the Gold Coast, the death rate for European officials dropped by half immediately after 1902, fluctuating between 13 and 28 per thousand per annum until the First World War. After 1922, it dropped to less than 10 per thousand. During the high noon of the colonial period, in short, health conditions in Africa were worse than they were for Europeans who stayed home, but in Africa they were far better for Europeans than they were for Africans.

Iron metallurgy also made revolutionary strides during the second half of the nineteenth century. Iron products available in Europe or Africa before that time could be divided into three categories according to their carbon content. The earliest form of usable iron was wrought iron, with less than 0.1 per cent carbon. It was relatively soft, malleable, easily shaped for a variety of uses, but also relatively expensive to make. More carbon, in the range of 0.1 to 2 per cent, yielded steel that was less malleable but harder and far better at holding an edge. Still higher carbon content, in the range of 2.5 to 4 per cent, yielded cast iron or pig iron. It was cheap to produce in the nineteenth century, but it was brittle and inelastic. Up to the nineteenth century, it was very expensive to convert pig iron into either wrought iron or steel. The breakthrough to cheaper high-quality iron products came in a series of new inventions of the 1860s and 1870s. The Bessemer converter could change pig into wrought iron at a fraction of the former cost. The Siemens-Martin process made it possible to do the same at even lower fuel costs, and the "basic" process of steel making made it possible to use easily available phosphoric ores. As a result, the cost of crude steel dropped by 80 to 90 per cent between the mid-1860s and the mid-1890s. The combined steel production of France, Belgium, Germany, and Britain rose eighty-three-fold between 1861 and 1913, a continuous rate of gain of more than 10 per cent per year. Steel took the place of iron in railways, buildings, ship construction, and a thousand other uses.

Africa felt the impact as a new supply of better and cheaper weapons became available to the Europeans and their African allies. Firearms technology had been comparatively stable during the eighteenth century. The standard infantry weapon of the late seventeenth century was the flintlock musket which was loaded by ramming powder and shot down its smooth, wrought iron barrel, and it lasted nearly to the middle of the nineteenth century. It took up to a minute to reload and was inaccurate at ranges beyond fifty yards. This was the weapon that spread so widely through tropical Africa in the era of the slave trade. Finer and more accurate weapons were known in Europe from the early eighteenth century – rifles, for instance, with spiral grooves inside the barrel to spin the projectile and thus improve its accuracy – but they had only limited military usefulness, mainly because the bullet had to be tapped down the muzzle, turning with the rifling as it went. It took up to four minutes to load and fire, but an early nineteenth-century rifle was more accurate at three hundred yards than the smoothbore musket at fifty.

Two inventions brought rifles into general use. One was a bullet with a hollow base, which expanded against the sides of the barrel when fired so as to catch the rifling. This made a rifle as easy to load as a musket, and the new rifles were first used in South Africa against the Xhosa in 1851. The second invention was the percussion cap, replacing the flintlock, and opening the way to breech-loading rifles, first used on a large scale in the American Civil War. The British first used them in Africa against the Ethiopians in 1868. For Africans who depended on the common muzzle-loading musket, the change was catastrophic; they now had to confront European-style troops with something like ten times their own rate of fire and with equal accuracy at six times the range.

From then onward to the First World War, the Europeans continued developing new guns faster than African states could arm themselves with the latest model but one. It was this pace of continuous innovation rather than the mere introduction of breech-loading rifles that maintained the European advantage. In the 1880s, magazine rifles like the Winchester repeater began to replace the single-shot breechloaders of the 1870s. Early machine guns had meanwhile been in use since the 1860s, and the British used some Gatling guns, though not very effectively, on the march to Kumase in 1874. The real breakthrough was the Maxim gun, which the British first used in Africa against the Egyptians in 1882. It became the standard machine gun with Europeans in Africa from then onward. Light "mountain guns" firing explosive shells and capable of transport on the backs of donkeys made their appearance even earlier, in the 1840s, though artillery was less important in tropical Africa than elsewhere because tsetse flies limited the use of animal power to move heavy guns. Rockets, on the other hand, could be head-loaded by porters and were used against Asante in 1874.

The differential in military power between the Africans and Europeans would never again be so great as it was between about 1880 and 1920. Rifles or, later on, automatic rifles were few indeed under African control. Even fewer machine guns or mountain guns fell into African hands before the First World War. Up to that time, conquest in Africa was not only cheaper than it had ever been in the past; it was also far cheaper in lives and money than operations against non-Western armies would ever be again.

In 1896, Ethiopians armed with modern weapons defeated the Italians at Adowa, an event unique for its time but foreshadowing a shift that was to become general. The final conquests of the interwar period were no longer cheap, as the Spanish and French found from their operations against the Riffian Republic of northern Morocco in the early 1920s, or as the Italians found in their conquest of Libya in the 1920s and of Ethiopia in the 1930s. The Africans were still outgunned, but they now had machine guns and up-to-date rifles. The balance shifted even further after the Second World War. By the 1950s, African rebels could count on European or Asian friends to supply them with arms. New guerrilla tactics made it possible for small numbers of insurgents to tie down much larger numbers of foreign soldiers. Territory that had been comparatively cheap to conquer became infinitely expensive to hold – as the French were to discover in Algeria of the 1950s and the Portuguese in Mozambique and Angola of the 1960s and early 1970s.

Permissive factors: political and intellectual

The technology of government administration was still another factor that made the conquest of Africa possible. We often think of technology in purely material terms, though the techniques for ruling an empire can be just as important as the techniques

for arming its soldiers, and the ability to exercise close control over a subject population is comparatively recent in world history. Great empires of the past always found
it hard to know what their subordinate agents were actually doing, harder still to
control them. It was a rare central government that could appoint and remove officials
at will.

European countries had been strengthening their administrative powers since the
fifteenth century, but even in the most centralized states, like France or England in the
eighteenth century, areas of public power remained in private hands. Men who had not
been chosen for their diligence or loyalty nevertheless acted for the government. Some
were officials who had bought their offices; some were guild or other corporate officials
with the right to govern within their own spheres; still others were rural gentry and
nobility with customary jurisdiction over those who worked the land. Governing at a
distance posed special problems; provinces tended to become autonomous, while
overseas colonies like those in the Americas often became independent states.

It was in the century between the 1780s and the 1880s, that new administrative
techniques began to take hold in Europe itself. Reform began on the Continent with
the French Revolution and its Napoleonic aftermath. In Britain, it followed the
Napoleonic wars and continued through the mid-century, as successive administrative
reformers captured local power from the justices of the peace, made local government
and Parliament alike more responsive to the opinion of middle-class voters, and
created a bureaucratic civil service capable of providing relief to the poor, police
services to the towns, factory inspection, and ultimately municipal services to supply
gas, water, sewage, streetcars, and even education for the mass of the population.
These innovations were more welcome at first than they were to be in the long run. By
the twentieth century, bureaucracy could all too easily become an instrument of
oppression – or, at best, a somewhat impersonal institution primarily concerned with
its own aggrandizement.

In any event, nineteenth-century Europeans were better able to administer their
overseas empires efficiently. The Dutch regime on Java or the British *raj* in India
adapted the new government practices in Europe to their own local conditions. The
professionalization of the European officer corps was felt immediately overseas, where
army officers often served as administrators. In time, imperial administration itself
became a recognized profession with its own special training, a movement that began in
1806, when the British set up the first training school for the future rulers of India. In
1887, France too began a systematic program of training for the professional administrators expected to govern Africa and Indochina.

By the 1880s and 1890s, the sum of a thousand minor changes meant that Europeans could plan and set up colonial governments that could actually govern with fair
efficiency. Planners could then look overseas with confidence – sometimes overconfi-
dence, as it turned out – that they could actually carry out a series of policies decided in
advance. Imperial governments might now contemplate goals that were far beyond the
capability of any government a century or so earlier.

This confidence was one facet of a much broader pattern of European attitudes in
the late nineteenth century. Europeans saw around them the material products of the
industrial age – railways, telegraphs, cheap cotton textiles, and a rising gross national

product. It was only natural to reassess their own position in the world, to increase the value set on their own culture while simultaneously lowering their estimation of others. For centuries, Europeans had a certain xenophobic dislike of others. Amerindians were considered mere savages. Africans were perhaps "lower" still, since they had long since entered the fringes of European society overseas through the slave trade. Asians, from Turkey to Japan, were thought of as barbarous heathen, though here dislike was sometimes mingled with respect for Asian power, or admiration for Asian products such as Chinese porcelain and Indian fabrics. But even that respect tended to diminish in the nineteenth century, as the Europeans saw themselves far ahead and increasing their lead in all things technological.

The Europeans' re-evaluation of themselves was reinforced in the early nineteenth century by new currents in biology. European thought in many fields was strongly influenced by the assumption that the natural order of the universe was a "great chain of being," an assumption whose intellectual roots went back to Plato. It implied that all created things would fit into hierarchies of value – in biology, for example, into phyla ranging from the higher animals to the lower, a classificatory system still used today. As biologists of the late eighteenth century became concerned with the place of human-kind, it seemed natural to classify *Homo sapiens* as the highest animal. It was also natural to expect the varieties of mankind to fit into a similar hierarchy from highest to lowest. Because the classifiers were European, it was equally natural to place the European variety at the top, and to grade others downward from there. Since skin color was the most obvious physical difference the biologists automatically placed the people with pinkish-yellow skins like their own at the top, and found it easy to place the tropical Africans with their dark brown skins near the bottom, and this arrangement had the virtue of conforming to the existing social status of "blacks" and "whites" on the American plantations. It also followed, in the eyes of these biologists, that the superiority of the "higher races" was part of the natural order of things, that it governed their intelligence, their aptitudes and capabilities, hence their "natural" role in history; and the same was true of the "lower races."

These "scientific" doctrines of racial inequality have long since been found to be completely wrong. But, before they were abandoned, the new biology of the nineteenth century enjoyed widespread respect as part of Europe's "scientific" triumph. Many detailed and explicit theories based on pseudo-scientific racism were put forward in the 1840s and 1850s, and they gained prestige by association when Darwinian evolution became popular after the 1860s. By the 1880s, learned circles in Europe took it for granted that physical appearance was indeed a mark of the deepest significance in determining culture and the course of history. From then to the first decade of the new century, racism flourished virtually unopposed. About 1910, a few scientists began to point out that culture was learned, not inherited, but the impact on the scientific community was not widespread until after 1920. Scientific support for popular xeno-phobic racism was important even later – witness its place in the ideology of National Socialist Germany to the end of the Second World War; and it can still be used to reinforce racial prejudice, although its support from the scientific community is negli-gible.

The high tide of pseudo-scientific racism thus came between 1880 and 1920. This was, incidentally, the period of the greatest differential in military power between Africa and Europe, and it was also the period when Europe conquered most of Africa. The fact that conquest took place at the relative peak of European power was not simply fortuitous, though the mere coincidence in time is not enough in itself to establish the power differential as either a necessary or sufficient cause of the conquests. European power also reinforced pseudo-scientific racism, since military power could all too easily be read as a sign of European superiority in other fields as well. Though racism did not cause the European invasions in any obvious way, it nevertheless had a profound influence on the way the colonial regimes were organized, simply because it was the popular philosophy-in-office when they were set up.

The conquest: European aspects

Though these permissive factors did not cause the European conquest, they made it easier to promote or justify – once a specific act of aggression appeared to be desirable. Two conditions in Europe of the late nineteenth century, however, have been put forward as the immediate cause of empire-building in Africa. One was international competition within the European state system. The other was the nature of European capitalism at this particular stage in its development.

During the middle decades of the century, competition between European powers had been relatively loose. The long years of peace following Waterloo had been seriously interrupted only by Russian pressure on Turkey and by the rise of unified monarchies in Italy and Germany. International competition became notably tighter with the outbreak of the Franco-Prussian War in 1870. Germany then demonstrated that it was both united and advancing rapidly on the road to industrialization. The victorious German Empire was a new factor in the balance of power, while the French loss of Alsace and Lorraine helped to fuel French nationalist sentiment and French demands for countervailing gains elsewhere.

If the European balance of power can be imagined as a kind of seesaw, before 1870 the fulcrum was relatively wide. Small realignments to prevent one end or the other overbalancing the whole were no threat to the general equilibrium. From 1871 to the First World War, however, it was as though the fulcrum had been narrowed – not, perhaps, to a knife edge, but enough to require a response to comparatively small changes on the other side. This meant that any apparent change in relative advantage overseas – like the acquisition of territory in Africa – was likely to elicit a counteraction from other powers. This tight balance may not have caused the European scramble for African territory, but it could speed up the process once it had begun.

The second alleged cause of European conquest in Africa was the rise of industrial capitalism as a source of funds for investment. It is argued that the European need to find profitable and safe places to invest these funds drove them to seize less-developed territory overseas. This argument, often associated with the name of A.J. Hobson, had an important following in the first half of the twentieth century. The role of the need to invest excess capital once loomed large among explanations of European imperialism. As far as tropical Africa is concerned, it has fallen by the wayside in recent decades, as it became clear that European capital investment in Africa was insignificant outside

Egypt and South Africa. We have already seen that European investment in Egypt was one of the reasons why Egypt fell first into the Franco-British informal empire and then into real, if disguised, control by Great Britain. In South Africa, the investment was in minerals. In the 1870s, the discovery of the rich diamond deposits at Kimberley in Griqualand West brought in both British capital and British political control through the Cape government. When, in the 1880s, European prospectors discovered the gold-bearing reef of the Witwatersrand, they began the exploitation of the largest source of gold in the world, with very heavy investment of European capital.

In tropical Africa, trade competition was a more important economic incentive than capital investment was, but even here Africa had little to offer as an outlet for European manufactures, and hardly more as a source of strategic raw materials. Great Britain had more trade with Africa than any other European country, yet British exports to Africa in the early 1880s rarely amounted to more than 5 or 6 per cent of all British exports, and British imports from Africa were less than 5 per cent of all imports. Nor were the 1880s an important decade for British African trade. The peak decade of the recent past was 1860–70, and the value of British African trade in the 1880s was less than that of any decade since the 1840s. That economic incentives operated at all was only because British traders to Africa feared that European competitors might annex a section of the African coast and cut off their access to the market, not because the total value of African trade was enough to make it a matter of national concern. Traders to Africa therefore asked their governments to annex African territory, so as to have a protected trade zone of their own. Trade competition was thus like international competition in general – a force to accelerate, but not to initiate competitive annexation.

The combination of permissive factors with others that would accelerate the scramble, once started, was nevertheless an explosive mixture. The only thing missing was the trigger or the lighted fuse to set it off. For the years 1879–82, diplomatic historians have isolated a number of different triggers. One can argue over which was first or most important, but in fact a number of triggers were pulled nearly simultaneously in different parts of the continent. If one or another of these had never existed, the others would have done the job. Behind the diplomatic and military events, psychological factors and the social and political process were more important in inducing Europeans to push for expansion into Africa. Similar conditions allowed that advocacy to prevail over alternate policies.

One part of the pattern was a certain tension between officials on the periphery of European control, who normally wanted to expand the sphere of their control, and other officials at the center of European affairs, who normally opposed expansion. In this instance, we have to do with one of those uniformities in human behavior that occur often enough to be a recognizable pattern, but not often enough to predict the outcome of each similar case.

The man-on-the-spot at the fringes of a European empire had a particular political and psychological position. He was the representative of a European power, technologically and militarily more powerful in most cases than his independent Asian or African neighbors. Especially in late-nineteenth-century Africa, his available military forces were usually far superior to those of the Africans. This disparity in forces, combined with the cultural chauvinism and racism of the period, tended to make the men-on-the-spot less willing than they might have been to compromise in conflicts with their African neighbors.

This tendency was all the more serious in that men-on-the-spot were separated from their own societies and therefore from social controls over conduct. Their local circle of vision was limited to a narrow, cross-cultural situation; and cross-cultural tensions are especially hard to resolve, because different cultures live by different rules for conflict resolution, just as they do in other spheres of human relations. The result for the European man-on-the-spot was likely to be an annoying series of frustrations, experienced along with "the flies and the heat" and other disturbing aspects of an alien setting. Given the power to do so, it was tempting simply to take over the alien society across the frontier, moving from a diplomatic to a colonial situation. Then the European rules could prevail. At the periphery, annexation seemed to be the sovereign solution for diplomatic or military problems.

The central governments, however, had quite a different circle of vision. The realities for central officials were the realities of metropolitan politics – including the politics of personal advancement within the government service. Demands for a forward movement of the frontiers were recurrent from a multitude of men-on-the-spot who could not be satisfied simultaneously. Central officials had to deal with a number of special constraints. Taxpayer resistance, even to cheap conquests overseas, was one. The danger that each confrontation settled by force would lead to another in a continuous escalation was a further constraint. In the background was the possibility of needlessly offending other European powers over inconsequential slices of distant territory, in a situation where the heart of European power politics was still in Europe.

In most circumstances before the 1880s, these tensions were settled in favor of the center, simply because the central governments appointed men-on-the-spot, gave them orders, and removed them from office when necessary. But central officials could be caught napping or manipulated by political circumstances. In that case, a man-on-the-spot, such as Maclean on the Gold Coast of the 1840s, or Harry Smith in South Africa, or Faidherbe on the Senegal in the 1850s, might move forward because central authorities were apathetic or ignorant of what was going on. None of these moves, however, triggered competitive annexation. The level of international tension was still too low, and no other European powers felt threatened enough to act in response to first moves. As a result, for most of tropical Africa before the 1880s, though European authority increased spasmodically around the coastal posts, the general rate of expansion was slow.

From the 1880s onward, new circumstances freed men-on-the spot more often from central constraints. The rise of competitive tensions in Europe relaxed people's vigilance against expansion in Africa. In Africa itself, the rise and spread of secondary empires during the middle decades of the century was a source of instability; and instability beyond the European frontiers was bad for trade and created a possible foothold for European rivals.

The instability of secondary empires came from their source of power. A partial monopoly over European arms was a kind of windfall gain that was easily lost. It could be lost to neighbors who had found their own source of modern arms, or to subordinates who took the arms under their immediate control and hived off on their own course of empire-building. The Zanzibari trading-post domination of East Africa was fundamentally unstable. Nothing prevented the political authorities of the interior – whether Zanzibari or local – from setting up their own spheres of control, as Msiri and Tippu Tib did. After the 1880s, the interior of East Africa as far as the Congo River basin tended to break down into a series of smaller but tighter secondary empires.

The Egyptian secondary empire in the Sudan broke down initially because the Mahdi captured its sub-Saharan center at Omdurman, but the Mahdi was not able to hold onto his own peripheral areas. One section, the Equatorial Province on the upper Nile, held on for nearly ten years as an independent state under Emin Pasha, a European mercenary. Rabeh Zubayr organized another offshoot to the southwest, which raided widely in what was to be the Central African Republic and ended by capturing Borno and establishing a new dynasty.

The Boer republics in South Africa were also secondary empires, which had originally split off from the Cape Colony. As time passed, they tended to send out their own offshoots of independent Afrikaner settlers. Some made their way overland as far as present-day Angola, where their descendants lived until the 1970s. Others formed independent republics like the evanescent Stellaland and Goshen. Even the Boer republics themselves seemed stamped with instability in the eyes of British officials in Natal or the Cape.

The frontiers of territory settled by overseas Europeans domiciled in Africa were, in any case, a special situation, in which the balance between aggressive men-on-the-spot and central constraint was harder to maintain, and peripheral aggression became common even before the 1880s. The combination of settlers, military officers, and local government officials tended to prevail in Algeria and South Africa. Expansion in Algeria had gone on steadily after the capture of Algiers in 1830, whether or not it was intended by the government in Paris. By the time of the great Algerian rebellion of 1871–2, creeping aggression had given France control of the *tell* and the high plateaus. Similar expansion had been continuous in South Africa, by the British colonies and the Boer republics alike, ever since the end run of the Great Trek had turned the flank of the Bantu-speakers' frontier.

In southern Africa, however, the situation bred additional tensions among different groups of local Europeans. Some were recent settlers who regarded themselves as metropolitan Europeans and who felt a primary allegiance to Great Britain, but the majority, even within the British sphere, belonged to the Afrikaner "European" community. Beyond the British frontiers, similar people felt a primary loyalty to the relatively new Boer republics. In time, Britons, republican Afrikaners, and colonial Afrikaners were to compete for the diamond-bearing regions around Kimberley, for Zimbabwe, and for almost all the remaining fringe areas to the east and west of the Boer republics. The only non-British intervention south of Angola and Mozambique was the German push into Namibia (which became German South West Africa).

One episode in these rivalries served as a potential trigger for the scramble throughout tropical Africa. It began with a British effort to bring order to the turbulent transfrontier region surrounding the Boer republics. The republics under settler control were aggressive against their African neighbors, threatening from time to time to provoke a general frontier war. A prelude to the crisis came in 1871, when Britain annexed the diamond fields around Kimberley, a territory also claimed by the Orange Free State and the South African Republic (Transvaal). Then, in 1877, Britain annexed the South African Republic itself with the apparent acquiescence of most of the Transvaal settlers. In 1879, local British officials followed this up with a move against the Zulu state – a typical petty aggression on the initiative of the local commander, and not cleared with London. The Zulu defeated part of the British force, but Britain sent reinforcements, won in the field, and established an unofficial protectorate over Zululand. This action removed the Zulu threat to the Transvaal as well, making it safe for the Transvaal Boers to break once more with Britain and to redeclare their independence. They defeated a British force in 1881. This time, Britain recognized the facts as they were and let the Boer republics remain independent until the Anglo-Boer War at the end of the century.

In this case, however, the failure to escalate and to gain a military victory led Britain to treat the Transvaal as a potential rival, and the Transvaal became increasingly formidable after the discovery of gold there in the 1880s. Up to that point, the British had tried to avoid extensive annexation in southern Africa; now, to shore up their international legal position, they annexed or declared protectorates over whatever African territory remained to the west of Transvaal, and they claimed all of the unannexed coastline between the Portuguese post at Delagoa Bay and the Cape of Good Hope. The men-on-the-spot, in short, had provoked a crisis over Zululand alone, but the associated problems of dealing with a secondary empire, plus the new significance of the goldfields, led to the paper annexation of virtually all the remaining African territory south of the Limpopo River. These annexations in turn alarmed other Europeans and helped push them into the scramble for territory elsewhere on the continent.

In other parts of Africa, at nearly the same time, other special situations freed men-on-the-spot from the earlier constraints. French military officers in West Africa, for example, gained a new freedom from central control following France's defeat by Prussia in 1871. A segment of the French public, especially sensitive to the loss of national honor, welcomed military victories almost anywhere. When, in 1879, the French government projected a railway eastward from the upper Senegal, the French military in Senegal were able to turn the operation into a war of conquest against the Umarian Empire, contrary to the intentions of the Paris government. At times, their political allies in France could apply pressure to the central government; at other times they simply disobeyed or misrepresented the orders they received, secure in the knowledge that victory would bring advancement in rank – and protection from civilian superiors in the court of French opinion.

Once started, this process was to continue for more than twenty years as the French moved from the Umarian Empire to a prolonged series of wars with the equally large secondary empire created by Samori Ture from upper Guinea-Conakry eastward to the northern Gold Coast. In time, the west-to-east progress from Senegal was joined by incursions from coastal posts like the Ivory Coast.

Both the French initiative and the west–east direction of conquest are symbolically portrayed on the present map of West Africa. The British central authorities prevented the British territories in the far west – Gambia and Sierra Leone – from making a quick response. Those colonies therefore lost most of the hinterland area their trade had once served. In time, the French push to the east alarmed British authorities at home. Liberia and British coastal posts to the east therefore had an opportunity to protect themselves with counter-annexations in their own hinterlands. As a result, each non-French enclave in West Africa kept a larger hinterland in proportion to its distance from Senegal. Thus, Sierra Leone is larger than Gambia, Liberia is larger than Sierra Leone, the Ghana is larger still, and Nigeria is largest of all.

Missionaries could also play a role in encouraging European conquest. They had much the same cross-cultural frustrations as their civil and military counterparts, but they were not government officials. They might prefer working under a colonial government to working under African authorities, but they could rarely trigger annexation by themselves. In some circumstances, however, their pressure on the home government could swing the balance. A case in point involved the kingdom of Buganda in the early 1890s. British military men there urged the annexation of Buganda, to the north of Lake Victoria for the usual reasons of forestalling other powers and to protect the sources of the Nile, but the home government was still reluctant. The cost of administering a country five hundred miles from the coast would have been prohibitive without a railroad, and existing traffic could not justify a railroad on economic grounds alone. The British missionary movement saw to it, however, that the choice presented to the public in 1893 and 1894 was either annexation regardless of cost, or else withdrawal that might bring on the martyrdom of an Anglican bishop and hundreds of African converts. In this case, with much reluctance, the British government allowed the annexation of Buganda and surrounding territory that was joined together to create the Uganda Protectorate.

A felt need to protect existing strategic interests could also weaken European constraints. The British government about 1880, for example, was not interested in acquiring new territory in Africa, but it was very much interested in protecting the empire it already ruled in India. One route to India lay around the Cape of Good Hope, while another went through the Suez Canal and the Red Sea. A weak Egypt controlling Suez, or a weak Turkey controlling the Arabian side of the Red Sea was no threat to the imperial lifeline, as it was called, but a strong European power capable of cutting the route through the Mediterranean and the Red Sea would have been seen as a definite threat to vital British interests. Where vital interests of this kind were concerned, it was no longer a matter of restraining men-on-the-spot. In this situation, diplomatic and even military initiatives might come from the central government itself.

This is one reason why Britain acted so forcefully from 1878 to 1882, first in defending Turkey against Russia and then in pressing its own intervention on Egypt. Egypt's debt was a factor as well, since British banks held the largest share, but the most pressing immediate cause of British intervention was a rebellion by Egyptian army officers that seemed to threaten the stability of the Egyptian government. British investments and British trade were important enough to bring British action against the upstart military. Once the rebellion was defeated in a single battle, however, the problem of assuring the future safety of the canal made it difficult for the British government to withdraw. The end result was to leave British officials running an Egyptian government – and hence caught up in a whole new set of circumstances where new men-on-the-ground in northeast Africa had to confront a new set of temptations that would lure them on into the Sudan.

Meanwhile, still another train of events began in the mid-1870s in the Congo basin and led by another route to the scramble for that part of Africa. For more than a decade, King Leopold of the Belgians had been fascinated by the possibility of glory and profit to be derived from the creation of a Belgian overseas empire. From the mid-1870s, his attention centered more and more on the Congo basin; but he was only a constitutional monarch, and the Belgian government and parliament refused to accept his views. Leopold got around this impasse by forming a series of private corporations with ostensible scientific and humanitarian aims and a measure of international support. These companies masked Leopold's personal control and financial interest in the creation of a private empire. It was, in effect, a secondary empire run from Europe, though not by a European government.

Private control made an important practical difference. Leopold's men-on-the-spot were not responsible to a strong central government with other interests in Europe itself. In 1879, even before the full nature of his project became apparent and before Leopold had asked for international recognition of his Congo Independent State, the pressures of competitive annexation elsewhere in Africa reached Central Africa. A traveler on leave from the French navy came down out of the interior to the coast north of the Congo with a series of treaties in which he claimed that African authorities had ceded to France sovereignty over the region westward from Stanley Pool (Pool Malebo) to the Atlantic. In most circumstances, the French government would not have recognized unofficial treaties of this kind, but this time the French Assembly was piqued by recent British acquisitions, including Britain's unilateral seizure of Egypt. It therefore accepted the treaties as official, and they became the pretext for annexing the territory that became the colony of Middle Congo, later the Republic of the Congo.

By the end of 1882, the new annexations in South Africa, Egypt, the western Sudan, and Central Africa had attained the critical mass needed to alert European governments to the danger of being left out. At that point, competitive annexation began in earnest. From 1883 to 1885, Portugal tried to make good its claims to the coast in its old trading zone on either side of the Congo mouth, and it began shoring up its claims to the hinterland of its other coastal holdings. Germany seized coastal enclaves that later formed the basis of its claims to Togo, Cameroon, Tanganyika, and Namibia. Britain hastened to formalize its existing informal relations with African rulers all along the coast, especially near the mouth of the Niger. France took advantage of these British preoccupations to begin an attack on Imerina, the most important state in Madagascar.

By 1884, the rapid pace of competitive annexation threatened the peace of Europe, and that threat led to a Berlin West African Conference in 1884–5. It dealt mainly with the Congo and Niger basins, but separate, often informal, agreements also served to lay down the ground rules for the rest of the European conquest. An intricate diplomatic charade emerged, in which European powers marked off the African map and agreed among themselves which of them should be allowed to claim and then to conquer various parts of Africa. This paper division of Africa was virtually completed by about 1900, with lines on the map that looked very much as they were to look in 1914 – or in

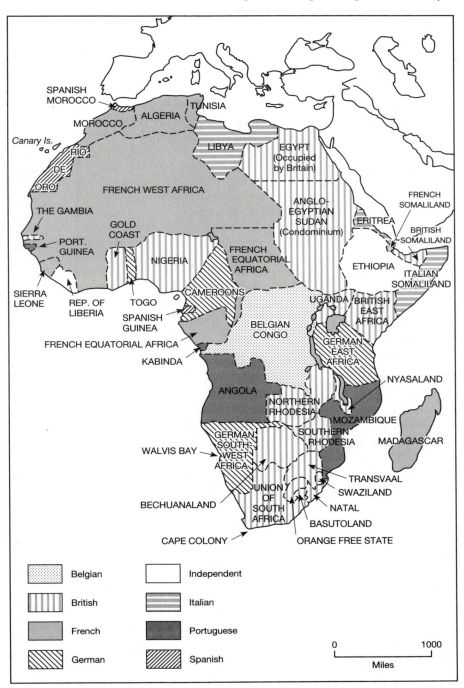

Map 15.1 Africa partitioned 1914

1960 or 1990, with allowance for subsequent independence and the fact that German Africa was redistributed to the victorious allies in 1919. Paper annexation, however, was only the framework for colonial Africa. The reality drew far more heavily on the actual process of conquest taking place in Africa itself.

The conquest: African aspects

Actual conquest followed the treaty making with a delay of up to twenty years. Most of Africa came under some form of European administration by 1920, though a few territories on the fringes of the Sahara had still to be conquered in the 1920s and 1930s. These military operations were different from European wars, in which the destruction of an enemy army and the temporary occupation of its territory were the main objectives. Here, the objective was to put Europeans into permanent command over African societies. The possible ways of doing this were as variable as the African political structures themselves. What was appropriate for a micro-state or a stateless society would not work in a great empire like the Caliphate of Sokoto. What might work in Rwanda, where the population was as dense as that of western Europe, would not work with Saharan nomads.

The Europeans almost always had the physical ability to win each campaign, but military victory alone was no guarantee that they could then govern indefinitely without imposing a continuing drain on the taxpayers at home. African leaders therefore had a far better bargaining position than their military weakness implied. They could not prevent military defeat, but they could help determine the forms and conditions of colonial rule that followed.

One part of their bargaining advantage was the existence of allies in Europe. The same segment of European opinion that initially opposed expansion overseas tended to keep a watching brief on empire in Africa, and it had significant weight, even at the height of the scramble. France, in many ways the most aggressive of the European powers, normally had a large parliamentary bloc opposed to empire, and that bloc brought down several governments even after the fiasco of the Egyptian expedition of 1881–2. In Britain, Liberals were normally anti-expansionist, and official policy only reluctantly supported expansion during most of the years between 1880 and 1914. In Belgium, parliamentary opposition to empire-building overseas had forced Leopold to go it alone. German expansionism in Africa grew out of a special configuration of domestic politics in the mid-1880s, and a colonial reform movement became a political force after about 1900.

The anti-imperialist sentiment in Europe helped African resistance, because colonial administrators and military officers knew they faced opposition at home. An African rebellion would provoke that opposition, and expensive military operations were unpopular with an even wider public. Though European officials had overwhelming force, concessions to avoid rebellion were worthwhile. It was better to accept African surrender on conditional terms than to face the criticism that was bound to follow expensive military operations.

This is not to say that all African leaders enjoyed an equal bargaining position. In many cases, they could do nothing to stave off defeat and annexation on the victors' terms. In others, chance or accident gave African rulers more real power under colonial rule than they had ever enjoyed before. In their confrontation with Europe, Africans had subtle choices to make in deciding how to meet the Western challenge. One choice had to do with their reactions to Western power. They could collaborate and try to seek the favor of the new masters, resist to the end, surrender when defeat was imminent, or attempt to bargain for advantage. The choice was very broad, with many variations.

A second, independent decision had to do with the response to Western culture, including under that head the whole range from firearms and literacy to religion, language and dress. The choice was not usually a simple "for" or "against," as in the South African dichotomy between "school people" and "red." Africans could choose Western weapons and reject Christianity, or the other way round. Nor was the African response to Western power necessarily related to their response to Western culture. They could accept Christianity, yet fight to the end against Western rule just as they could accept Western rule as inevitable and collaborate with the colonial government, yet remain all the more faithful to Islam.

Defensive Westernization had begun in some parts of West Africa even before the colonial conquest. The Fante Confederacy, the Republic of Accra, and the Egba United Board of Management in Abeokuta were all attempts to graft Western methods in politics and government onto the older political forms. All three failed in the short run, largely through British opposition, but the effort continued in Abeokuta. About 1904, for example, the Egba United Government was planning to introduce a written criminal code on the Western model and to carry out other administrative reforms. These efforts were never fully implemented, but the Egba United Government ruled Abeokuta as an independent state down to 1914. Though informally a British protectorate, it was nevertheless the last major state in West Africa to lose its independence. With better luck or a more fortunate geographical position than the one it had astride the railway line to northern Nigeria, it might even have survived without formal colonization, much as Liberia did.

In Buganda by 1900, the Christian chiefs had made themselves into a new oligarchy which had won power for itself against the *kabaka* and other chiefs. The oligarchs were quick to see the advantages of literacy and of European weapons. They also saw the weakness of their military position and did nothing to oppose the British annexation of the country. Many, indeed, served the British as subordinate officials administering other sections of the Uganda Protectorate. Nevertheless, they retained a latent power to make British overrule either cheap and comparatively easy or extremely difficult.

Their great success was to translate their bargaining position into a written agreement, the Uganda Agreement of 1900, by which the British government spelled out the concessions it would make in return for Ganda acquiescence in British overrule. The political effect was to keep the title and office of kabaka intact but to assign real power to the *Lukiiko*, a representative body with some of the characteristics of a parliament and others of an oligarchic council. The agreement also assigned ownership of the best land in fee simple to the individual members of the new Christian oligarchy. As a basis for dividing power between the British and a local aristocracy, the agreement worked with remarkably little friction for half a century. The interests it protected, however, were mainly those of a single social class. By the time of independence, a new generation of nationalist leaders had come to see the kabaka and his government as part of the apparatus they hoped to replace by a new and independent government for the whole of Uganda.

Most African kingdoms were merged into new colonial units, as Buganda had been merged into the Uganda Protectorate, but a few managed to come through the colonial period with their territorial integrity virtually intact – Tunisia, Egypt, and Morocco in North Africa; Zanzibar, Rwanda, and Burundi in East Africa; Lesotho and Swaziland in the south. In each of these cases, not only the kingdom but the kingship survived under some form of European protectorate, though the amount of actual power in the hands of the king varied greatly. Some were mere figureheads, while others enjoyed more real power than European constitutional monarchs of that period.

These pre-colonial polities survived into the colonial period for different reasons. Zanzibar and the Muslim states of North Africa had a special position in European eyes. Most of them had been recognized for centuries as political entities in European international law. Most of the states in tropical Africa were not so recognized at the nineteenth-century peak of cultural chauvinism. Zanzibar and most of the North African states had also fallen deeply into the web of European credit, financial manipulation, and informal control well before the 1880s. When that control was formalized, it eased intra-European diplomatic tensions somewhat to preserve at least the fiction of a "protectorate" status rather than to demand outright annexation.

A protectorate in European international law could be many things, but the protecting power usually took over some, but not all, of the attributes of sovereignty – often control of financial and foreign affairs – leaving other matters to the protected government. In fact, the protectorates that France established over Tunisia in 1881 and Morocco in 1912 were more substantial than that. The French set up a regular European bureaucracy but left the sultan and bey as figureheads. The British protectorate over Egypt from 1882 onward was even more fictitious. The British recognized Turkey as the true but distant suzerain, and Egypt was not even officially a protectorate. Yet British control as real and thorough as French control over Tunisia remained informal until Turkey entered the First World War in 1914. Zanzibar was in the British informal empire even before 1880, so that the protectorate of 1890 merely tidied up the situation by formalizing the reality.

Rwanda and Burundi kept their identity for very different reasons. They were in the heart of Africa, nearly the last region to be occupied by the Germans during the decade before 1914. By then, the Germans had had some experience with the problems of colonial rule. In Rwanda they found a dense population ruled with apparent stability by a king and aristocracy. Class relations between the Tutsi overlords and the Hutu peasantry were congenial to the social attitudes of the administrators from Europe. Hence the decision in favor of the least expensive alternative, that is, to let the Tutsi keep the forms and much of the reality of power, though the Germans meant to shift slowly toward European norms over the coming decades. In Burundi, they found a much weaker state, but they ended by backing the ruling Tutsi there, following their own example in Rwanda.

Lesotho and Swaziland were again different. They kept their identity through skill and luck in manipulating the rivalry between Britain and the Boer republics. Lesotho's experience came first in time and served as a precedent for the other. Moshoeshoe, the aging king, was under strong pressure from the Orange Free State in the 1860s. He repeatedly asked for and eventually received annexation by Great Britain as the lesser of the two evils. Britain in turn passed on Basutoland (as it was then called) to the self-governing Cape Colony. In 1880, however, Cape politicians bungled the job by trying to disarm the Sotho. The attempt provoked a widespread Sotho rebellion that was nearly simultaneous with the Anglo-Zulu and Anglo-Transvaal wars. The rebellion was both annoying and expensive, and it gave force to the Sotho request for direct control from London rather than Cape Town. London agreed, appointing a Resident to advise the Sotho king, and future residents tended to rule through diplomacy and the manipulation of Sotho politics rather than overt force.

The Sotho example was important again after the Anglo-Boer War, when the British wanted to diminish the authority that the Transvaal had gained over the Swazi kingdom on the eve of the war, but without offending the Transvaal Europeans any more than was necessary. Their solution was to separate Swaziland from the Transvaal and to allow the Swazi king a degree of autonomy under British overrule. Here, as in Lesotho and also in the Bechuanaland Protectorate (Botswana), the solution left the African rulers with far more authority than African rulers managed to keep elsewhere in southern Africa.

Some African rulers also managed to hold on to their power by timely surrender and collaboration, even when European rivalries were not in the picture. Northern Nigeria is one example. By the late nineteenth century, the Caliphate of Sokoto had settled down to be an incorporative empire, no longer actively expansive. Ultimate control lay with the Caliph, but most day-to-day command was in the hands of the emirs of a dozen or so provinces. From 1887 onward, officials of the Royal Niger Company began gradually establishing their authority over any African territory within convenient reach of the navigable waters of the Benue and the lower Niger. In the late 1890s, the Company began to impinge on Sokoto's outlying emirates – Ilorin, south of the Niger in Yoruba country, and Nupe, just to the north of the river. In 1897, a small Company force of about five hundred African soldiers made separate attacks on both Ilorin and Nupe. As a result, the Company claimed both emirates and replaced the emir of Nupe with one more favorable to its interests, all without raising a unified resistance from the caliphate as a whole. The caliph in his turn was fearful of the French advance from the west, German feelers sent north from Togoland, and the presence of Rabeh's force from the Nilotic Sudan in Borno to the east. As a result, each emirate had to meet the European-commanded forces on its own.

This combination of strong provincial government with the lack of a military effort from the caliphate as a whole was almost ideal for conquest by very small forces under European leadership. In the years 1902 to 1906, a British force barely exceeding a thousand men advanced in a series of brief campaigns to conquer the emirates one by one. Each emirate in turn surrendered after one or two sharp engagements. Some emirs were confirmed in office. Others resisted briefly and were deposed. Some tried to flee toward the eastern Sudan to find refuge from infidel rule, but many of the most important refugees were caught and killed at the battle of Burmi in 1903.

Whenever an emir fled or was deposed, the British usually had a choice of candidates from other branches of the ruling family. As a result, the governor slipped into the position formerly held by the caliph. He confirmed and removed emirs. He appointed a Resident for each of the major emirates, and the Resident's advice was binding. In theory, British control was complete, but the situation was precarious. The total military force was tiny for the size of the country. The number of civilian administrators was smaller still. The result was not simply indirect rule through African authorities. It included a conscious policy of leaving considerable latitude to the local ruler, and a conscious decision not to press for rapid Westernization. The British not only refrained from all interference with Islam where it was dominant; they even discouraged Christian missions and Western-style education out of deference to local wishes. As a result, change toward Western norms was far less than it was elsewhere in colonial Nigeria; the pre-colonial social and political order was preserved more than it was in most parts of colonial Africa. The old ruling class remained in power as effectively as it did in Rwanda or Burundi – and far more effectively than equivalent groups did in North African protectorates like Morocco or Tunisia.

The Ethiopian experience was a nearly opposite reaction to European power. In contrast to the northern emirs' successful policy of surrender and survival, the Ethiopian central government found it possible to fight and survive. In escaping colonial rule altogether (apart from the brief Italian occupation of 1935–41), Ethiopia was nearly unique on the African continent. (Liberia was the only other exception, and Liberia's rulers were Afro-Americans, who were Western, not African, in their way of life.) Yet the northern Nigerian emirs and the Ethiopian aristocracy had a similar reaction to Western culture. Both sought Westernization for defensive purposes only, and both defended their power and culture with remarkable success until they were overthrown by military coups in the 1960s and 1970s.

In other respects as well, Ethiopia in the twentieth century was not so much an exception to the normal pattern of African history as it was a country where historical trends found elsewhere combined in a particular way. The fact that the Ethiopian monarchy was the only long-standing Christian state in Africa was, of course, a unique element, and one that tended to give Ethiopia a superficially favorable image in Europe. But Ethiopia's success in keeping out the Europeans depended far more on the fact that the small Christian kingdom became the nucleus of a secondary empire. It achieved a stability unusual for secondary empires by drawing on older sources of loyalty, and the emperor's supply of modern rifles and artillery came from a combination of skill, luck, and the configuration of European strategic interests centering on the upper Nile and the mouth of the Red Sea.

The empire Menelik built had the new imperial structure from a Christian core area whose people spoke semitic languages like Tigriñya or Amharic; but it did not include all such populations, and the majority were non-Christian and non-semitic. Menelik's capital at Addis Ababa lay near the southern frontiers of Christian Ethiopia. It then became the geographical center of a much larger secondary empire. Menelik's conquests included a fringe of Nilotic peoples to the west, the Sidamo states to the south, the Muslims of the eastern highlands centering on the city-state of Harar, the vast Somali-speaking semi-desert of Ogaden stretching still further east, and finally the nomadic peoples of the Danakil lowlands, who were not actually brought under effective administration until the very eve of the Italian invasion in 1935.

The fact that Menelik and his successors were able to create an empire larger than most European colonies was important for Ethiopia's future. The scale of political organization was not only small, it was far smaller than optimum size for political or economic development in the technological conditions of post-colonial Africa. Even at the time of the conquest, large states like Ethiopia had options that were simply not open to small states – still less to the thousands of village-sized micro-states or to the peoples of stateless societies. Such small political units had no real chance of successful resistance, either against the Europeans or against larger secondary empires.

Stateless societies, on the other hand, created different problems for the invaders. No one had the authority to make a formal surrender, and no one held an office he could exercise on behalf of a colonial state. In this situation, the kind of cheap conquest and cheap administration the British imposed on the Sokoto caliphate was not possible. The Ibo, or the Tiv of the Benue valley, were far more expensive to conquer, and such conquests took much longer. The Europeans tried to accept the "surrender" of important people, but in fact no one had the power to make more than a personal decision to cooperate with the new rulers. Effective colonial rule could begin only when a large majority had made a similar decision. The conquest of Tiv or Ibo country began with military expeditions marching through to demonstrate British power. Administrative posts were then set up at selected sites, and officials gradually began to collect taxes and enforce a new kind of law. Missionaries with schools and some rudimentary health services also helped to show the advantages of peaceful compliance. In this setting, separate reactions to European power and European culture had to be made by individual men and women, a process that is better illustrated for Ibo country by Chinua Achebe's novel, *Things Fall Apart*, than by any formal works of history.

African as well as European empires had tried in the past to rule over stateless societies. The Moroccan makhzen had problems with the stateless Berber polities of the Atlas and the desert, and the French inherited these problems in turn. Adopting the strategies of the makhzen, the French sometimes made alliances with the great *ca'ids* of the Atlas, whose power had already spread across the previous web of kin relations. Or they tried working, as successive Moroccan governments had done for centuries, with the leaders of the great Muslim brotherhoods. Like their predecessors, the great "marabouts" of the twentieth century were sometimes willing to help preserve order in the countryside in return for government favor. Like the British in northern Nigeria, the French in Morocco found themselves slipping consciously or not, into the former role of the sultan.

Insufficient scale in political organization was also a recurrent problem for leaders of the African resistance to conquest. One response was to create new states as a direct response to the European threat. It was especially common in Muslim North Africa, with precedents going back to the example of 'Abd al-Qādir in western Algeria of the 1840s. Many of these new states were based on the existing institution of the Muslim brotherhoods in the same way that 'Abd al-Qādir had used the Qadiriya in Algeria.

The role of a brotherhood could be especially important among nomads because kinship-based political organization was often ineffective in the face of a foreign threat.

The Sanusiya was one of the most durable and effective brotherhoods in this respect. Its membership stretched from the Nile valley to Lake Chad to the Mediterranean, but its range of effective political authority was much smaller. It nevertheless opposed an attempted Turkish reconquest of Libya up to 1911, and, after the Italians replaced the Turks in control of the ports, it established independent control over Cyrenaica for a time. Italy nevertheless established effective control by 1932; but the Sanusiya took the field again on the Allied side during the Second World War. At the end of the war, the United Nations recognized the head of the order as king of all Libya, and his successors remained in control of the country until the last was removed by a military coup in 1969.

About 1900, Muhammad Abdille Hassan created a similar state among the Somali herdsmen on the borderland where Italian and British Somaliland joined Ethiopia. Again, the organizational base was a tarīqa and Muhammad succeeded in defying the Europeans until 1920. His movement was like the Sanusiya, in that he favored Westernization for defense only but otherwise held to the most conservative forms of Islam.

Similar movements could, however, follow the current of Islamic modernism. One of the most important of these staged a rebellion in the Rif mountains between the Spanish and French zones of Morocco. It began about 1920 under the leadership of Muhammad ʿAbd al-Krim, and this time the nuclear tarīqa was not one of the ancient sufi orders, but the Salafiya, an order recently founded to combat sufism and to reform Islam. ʿAbd al-Krim called his state the Republic of the Rif, and he tried for international recognition from the European powers. He failed in the long run, but resistance to the Spanish occupation continued from 1921 to 1927.

Although these twentieth-century resistance movements were only successful as holding operations, they exemplify the changed military balance. It took a Franco-Spanish force of some 200,000 European troops finally to subdue ʿAbd al-Krim, who had managed to acquire about two hundred machine guns – compared with none at all in African hands during the conquest of tropical Africa three or four decades earlier. In the early 1930s, Italy's campaigns against Libya were on a similar scale and were extremely expensive, given the small number of opponents. Muhammed Abdille Hassan was less significant as a resistance figure, but, for all their disdain, the British gave back-handed credit to his stand when they sent aircraft from the *Ark Royal* to bomb and destroy his last headquarters. The final act was most expensive of all, with nearly half a million Italian troops involved in the conquest of Ethiopia in 1935–6.

State-building resistance movements were also common, if less spectacular in sub-Saharan Africa. Moshoeshoe's foundation of Lesotho in the mid-nineteenth century is a case in point, as is Almaami Samori Turé's success in conquering a new empire to the east even as he lost his original base to French conquest. Elsewhere during those decades, however, the pace of conquest was often too rapid to allow time for political reorganization. One result was a pattern of initial and ineffectual resistance by existing, small political units, followed, up to a decade later, by a second and more effective resistance movement with a wider territorial base. The nature of and connection between the two movements is sometimes obscured by the tendency of European historians to label the second and broader war of resistance mere "rebellion," since by then the Europeans had acquired sovereignty over Africa in European international law.

The conquest of Rhodesia (now Zimbabwe) is a classic case in point. It began in 1890, when the British South Africa Company sent a military force into Shona territory, which it occupied without serious fighting. The Shona had no strong central kingdom in any event, and little previous warning of the European threat. Only the Ndebele kingdom offered serious primary resistance in 1893–4, but the Ndebele, an offshoot of the wars of the mfecane, still used the impi formation of disciplined spearmen. British South Africa Company troops defeated those units without difficulty, and the Ndebele kingdom disappeared. In the years that followed, Shona and Ndebele alike were dissatisfied with British occupation, with the loss of their land and cattle, with forced labor, and with other abuses that followed European domination. The old political structures were gone, but the religious authority of a spirit called Mlimo stepped in, speaking through a human medium to urge a mass uprising by both peoples. The revolt came in 1896–7, first among the Ndebele, then among the Shona – who this time used guerrilla tactics and avoided open, set-piece battles. It was no mere war between soldiers; the initial rising managed to kill about 10 per cent of all the Europeans in the Ndebele kingdom, and the repression was even more bloody in its destruction of African lives.

Another source of resistance could be found in the web of economic interests and informal alliances that were incorporated in the major trade networks. This appeared in a spectacular, if ineffective, manner in the initial resistance of the Tanzanian coastal peoples to the German advance. In 1888, Sultan Khalifa of Zanzibar leased the coast to the German East Africa Company for fifty years. When the Germans first began to set up coastal trading stations, however, they met with armed resistance drawn from a wide area and organized by Bushiri ibn Salim, a coastal Afro-Arab. The German forces turned out to be unbeatable, and the whole affair ended with Bushiri's defeat and death at the end of 1889. But at least 100,000 men had come to the coast to fight and they represented a wide array of different ethnic groups – Shambaa, Zaramo, Zigula, Yao, Ngoni, Ngulu, Kwere, Hehe, Kami, Sagara, Makonde, Mbugu, Arab, and Swahili. It is worth noting in this case that other Africans, whose economic interests were opposed to this grouping – among others, the Nyamwezi and some of the wealthiest of the Arab plantation owners – allied themselves with the Germans.

The Maji-Maji revolt in German East Africa a few years later was similar in scale, though its organizational base was closer to that of the Ndebele and Shona than it was to that of the coastal Arabs. Once Bushiri's revolt had ended, German forces moved into the interior. Southeastern Tanzania was a politically fragmented region, easily penetrated by moving military columns sent to overawe the rulers. Many rulers surrendered, and those who chose to fight did so alone and went down to rapid defeat. By 1905, the country was considered sufficiently "pacified" to be held only lightly from a series of semi-fortified military posts. Then revolt broke out nearly simultaneously throughout all of southeastern German East Africa, a region that was politically and ethnically very diverse. The suppression of this "revolt" was far more expensive to

Germany than the initial conquest had been, and the last of the fighting continued into the latter part of 1907. Here, as in Rhodesia, religion, not pre-colonial political units, made the wider scale possible. The name Maji-Maji came from the Swahili word for water, and the revolt spread as far and as rapidly as it did through water magic associated with the cult of Kolelo.

The Maji-Maji and the Rhodesian rebellions had other points in common. Both were mass movements, not the actions of a few armed dissidents. Both were brutally suppressed, and with similar consequences. On the face of it, suppression left the Africans no residual powers, no bargaining position of the kind some had managed to secure in other circumstances. In that sense, the revolts appear completely futile, but in fact they left a mark on the administrations that followed. Both the Germans and the British South Africa Company were impressed by the seriousness of the revolts and the costs of suppression; both also recognized that their own administrative abuses had been at fault. Both tried to reform their methods, and future administrators were somewhat more sensitive to the fact that their power over African societies was limited. In the much longer run, these early revolts also served as examples of broad-based resistance – examples that were to be followed effectively by the leaders of independence movements some fifty years later.

The Anglo-Boer war and its aftermath

Of all the wars of conquest the Europeans waged in Africa between 1880 and the First World War, the most anomalous of all was the British conquest of the two Boer republics between 1899 and 1902. It was the only war of that period that used large numbers of troops from Europe or that seriously strained the resources of a European power. Its underlying cause was the South African Republic's difficulty in managing the new gold-mining industry without local resources in trained personnel, or the political power to manage the flood of British capital investment. The republican Afrikaners were essentially pastoral farmers with no industrial experience. The mines were therefore developed and operated by foreign (largely British) capital, using imported technicians and skilled workmen, with Africans for unskilled work. By 1899, there were probably more foreigners than Afrikaners in the European male population of the South African Republic.

President Paul Kruger and the *volksraad*, or legislature, tried to cope with the influx by keeping political power in the hands of the original Afrikaner settlers. The *uit-landers*, or foreign newcomers, were denied the vote for fear that they would subvert the state. The problem was intensified by the fact that key British and colonial officials and politicians wanted to re-annex the Transvaal, so that Kruger's fears were well founded. The leader of the local expansionists was a British-born Cape politician, Cecil John Rhodes, one of the most successful mining magnates in Kimberley or the Witwatersrand. In addition to his mining interests, Rhodes became Prime Minister of the Cape in 1890. From Britain, he soon gained the support of Joseph Chamberlain, a Birmingham businessman who was Colonial Secretary in the British cabinet during the crucial years 1895–1902; and Alfred Milner, Chamberlain's choice as British High Commissioner in South Africa from 1897 to 1905.

In 1895 Rhodes concocted an "unofficial" plot to overthrow Kruger's government through a rebellion, combined with an invasion of the South African Republic, but the Jameson Raid – named for the Rhodes lieutenant who led the invasion – failed. The military effort was a small force of troops associated with the British South Africa Company. Rhodes launched it with the expectation that the uitlanders around Johannesburg would rise to its support. The rebellion inside the country never took place. Rhodes was discredited by this fiasco, but Chamberlain and Milner went on to make a series of demands in the name of the British government, mainly aimed at opening up the franchise to the mass of uitlanders.

In 1899, the South African Republic and its ally the Orange Free State declared war on Britain, having first imported large supplies of modern weapons from Europe by way of Delagoa Bay. The two Boer republics were encouraged by the sympathetic attitude of American and Continental governments, and they hoped to repeat their successful resistance of 1881. Foreign governments, however, provided no substantial aid, nor did the British government yield when Boer commandos invaded the Cape Colony and Natal and won several quick victories. Instead, the British built up a vast military machine in South Africa that eventually numbered nearly 450,000 men in uniform, against a Boer army of about 88,000, including volunteers from the Cape Colony. The British forces soon gained control of the vital railroads and occupied the Witwatersrand and the republics' capital cities; and, although the Boers then resorted to guerrilla tactics, the British gradually wore down their resistance, destroying their sources of supply in a series of raids that included the burning of farm buildings and the removal of many civilians to "concentration camps." In May 1902, the last of the Boer commandos laid down its arms, and the republican governments submitted to British rule.

Milner, Chamberlain, and most British Conservatives – especially those with investments in the gold-mining industry – supported the war in the hope that victory would lead to British immigration on a large enough scale to "modernize" and "anglicize" the Afrikaners and reduce them to a minority in the European population of southern Africa. They expected that the entire region would become a wealthy, powerful, and loyal bastion of the British Empire. But, as so often happens, the calculations of the war-makers were not fulfilled. No large-scale British immigration took place; the Afrikaners continued as a secure majority in the European population; and the long war only increased Afrikaner distrust of the British. The Dutch Reformed clergy led the cultural resistance movement and helped to inspire a vigorous outpouring of protest literature in Afrikaans.

In Britain, the length of the war and its cost in men and money created widespread revulsion against the militarists. In the general election of 1906, the Unionist party responsible for the war was overwhelmingly defeated by the Liberal party, which had been far less enthusiastic in supporting it. The policy of the new government, however, differed from the old in its means rather than its ends. The Liberals, too, wanted a loyal and powerful southern Africa; but they thought the way to go about it was through concessions, not coercion. They therefore granted both the former republics a wide measure of self-government in internal affairs, with the vote restricted to men of European extraction, in the hope that this would win the support of the Afrikaner elite and repair the psychological damage done by the war.

Thus, from one point of view, the Afrikaner republics were like other secondary empires that collapsed or fell under the control of a European power during the period of the scramble. From another point of view, however, the British won the war but gave the Afrikaners the reality of victory, including the right to extend their dominance over the African majority. In this sense, the Afrikaner leaders retained more real power after their defeat than any other local authorities did anywhere else in Africa. The main cause of this victory was the strength of pseudo-scientific racism in Britain. The British in London were willing to assume that appropriate concessions would bring the defeated Afrikaners into the family of self-governing settler territories – those that would later become the independent members of the Commonwealth of Nations – if only because these "European" Africans were "White," while the other defeated secondary empires were ruled by "Blacks." But the end result was to sacrifice the interests of the majority of South Africans in order to conciliate this European minority. The position of "non-Whites" within South Africa was to deteriorate during the next eighty years, while that of the local European became more dominant within South Africa, and South Africa became more independent of Britain.

Suggestions for further reading

Ambler, Charles H., *Kenyan Communities in the Age of Imperialism: The Central Region in the Late Nineteenth Century*, New Haven: Yale University Press, 1988.

Boahen, A. Adu, *African Perspectives on Colonialism*, Baltimore: Johns Hopkins University Press, 1987.

Crowder, Michael, *West Africa under Colonial Rule*, London: Hutchinson, 1967.

Gann, L. H., and Peter Duignan, *Colonialism in Africa. 1870–1960*, 5 vols, Cambridge: Cambridge University Press, 1969–75.

Hargreaves, John D., *West Africa Partitioned*, London: Macmillan, 1974.

Iliffe, John, *Tanganyika Under German Rule, 1905–1912*, Cambridge: Cambridge University Press, 1969.

Landes, David, *Bankers and Pashas*, London: Heinemann, 1958.

Low, D. Anthony, and R. Cranford Pratt, *Buganda and British Overrule, 1900–1955*, London: Oxford University Press, 1960.

Marais, J.S., *The Fall of Kruger's Republic*, Oxford: Clarendon Press, 1961.

Pakenham, Thomas, *The Scramble for Africa: The White man's Conquest of the Dark Continent from 1876 to 1912*, New York: Random House, 1991.

Pennell, C.R., *A Country with a Government and a Flag: The Rif War in Morocco, 1921–26*, Wisbech: MENAS Press, 1986.

Ranger, Terence O., *Revolt of Southern Rhodesia, 1896–97*, London: Heinemann, 1967.

Thompson, Leonard, *History of South Africa*, New Haven: Yale University Press, 1990.

Wrigley, C.C., "The Christian Revolution in Buganda," *Comparative Studies in Society and History*, 2 (1959), pp. 33–48.

16

THE IMPACT OF EUROPE

The colonial conquests introduced myriad changes in every aspect of African life. Even in those places where the fundamental matrix of African culture remained intact, a continuous process of adjustment and readjustment from within was still required to absorb the impact of the West. It may not be possible to do justice to such a complex set of circumstances for the whole of a continent, at least within the space available in a general history of Africa; but in the chapters that follow we shall try to do so, first by looking at the European factor as a common denominator, even though it varied from region to region, then, from a more African perspective, by examining one by one the economic, intellectual, and social aspects of change. In a final chapter, we shall deal with the end of colonial rule throughout much of the continent, as well as with the continuance of European domination in the far south. (The complex set of changes of the post-colonial period that began in the early 1960s is another story, and cannot be dealt with here.)

The aims of administration

When the European powers conquered their new African territories they had few specific plans or ideas about what to do with them. Much had been acquired simply to keep other powers out. Specific possibilities suggested themselves – gold mining here, cotton growing there, or building railways to drain particular exports needed in Europe; but long-range plans for economic, social, or political change were very few indeed.

At another level, however, the Europeans shared certain presuppositions and rudimentary qualms, even though these stopped short of systematic planning. For instance, all believed that they had come to Africa to keep the peace. They intended to stop intra-African warfare and to suppress those African customs they regarded as repulsive. For whatever reason, they all meant to set up administrations that could control the African populations, either directly through their appointed officials or indirectly through the existing African authorities. This rudimentary goal was bound to cost money, because it required a level of government separate from and superior to the existing African governments. This meant that revenue had to be found, above and beyond what had previously gone to the African governments. It might have come from Europe, but European taxpayers expected the colonies to pay their own way, at the very least. Colonial governments therefore acquired a second common goal; they needed to promote some form of economic development to produce taxable income.

As a guide to the way these goals might be achieved, Europeans also brought with them a heritage of ideas about overseas empire. This body of ideas took into account such considerations as the best kind of relationship between the colony and the metropolis, and between colonizers and colonized, as well as a wealth of ideas about how to accomplish many specific purposes. It was a kind of dialogue running through Western history from the sixteenth century onward, given new emphasis in the nineteenth century, as Europeans re-examined their place in the world in the light of their new industrial achievements at home and new empires abroad.

Some of these ideas, like pseudo-scientific racism or the new administrative techniques, had, of course, played a role in encouraging Europeans to acquire overseas empires to begin with. They came on the scene again as background for the policies that were followed once the conquest was completed. Racism contributed to the European view of non-Western peoples, and that view had shifted in important ways during the second half of the nineteenth century. Earlier, from about the time of the French Revolution to the 1850s, the dominant view can be labeled "conversionist." Europeans "knew" that they had the one true religion and that their way of life was superior to all others. They took for granted their own duty to spread Christianity throughout the world. They assumed that others would heed the message when they heard it, recognize the superiority of Western culture as a whole, and want it for themselves. They also assumed that culture change would be fairly easy, an assumption that rested in part on the recent success of mass education in Europe. Conversionism carried the unstated assumption that cultures might be unequal at a particular point in time, but it inclined to the view that all people are made in the image of God, with the ability to reason and the capacity to recognize the best. It was, in short, cultural chauvinism of an extreme kind, but it was not racist.

Then, with the rise of pseudo-scientific racism in the second half of the century, conversionism was badly eroded. Racists argued that non-Europeans were inherently and permanently inferior; their culture was part of their inherited racial status and could not be changed. Christians still argued that all men were spiritually equal before God, but many Christians admitted that the capacity for salvation in the next life might not imply a capacity for high achievement in this one. If Africans were racially incapable of Westernization, they rationalized, then it might be better for them to develop "in their own way." As conversionism faded, the doctrine of trusteeship took its place. If Europeans were indeed superior, it was argued, they had special obligations toward Africans – obligations equivalent to those of fathers to minor children, of men to women, of the strong to the weak. These obligations were increasingly seen as the source of Europe's moral right – even moral duty – to establish colonial rule in Africa.

By the end of the nineteenth century, the idea of trusteeship had overwhelmed the conversionist faith, but in several different versions. Much depended on the supposed extent of African incapacity. Those who thought best of African abilities argued that the period of trusteeship would be limited. In time, African colonies would develop enough to emerge as independent states, though still inferior to the West. At the opposite extreme, other Europeans believed that Africans on their own could never achieve anything of consequence. The best they could gain would be acceptance within an overseas European society as a permanent caste of servants. That view was most common among settlers in southern Africa, but it was held by a substantial minority among Europeans in Europe too. With appropriate alterations, it was also applied by the settlers in the Maghrib to Muslim North Africans. But the dominant position lay somewhere between these extremes, with an emphasis on European obligations as well as African duties. There was nevertheless an expectation that the relationship of trustee and ward would be very long, if not permanent, just as the qualities supposedly passed down through racial inheritance were claimed to be permanent.

The means of administration: first stages in tropical Africa

The first stages of colonial rule, to about 1920, were marked by a great variety of administrative expedients. Some were conceived in the spirit of the new racism. Others were mere stop-gap measures that took on a life of their own. Still others were carry-overs from the more egalitarian practices of the earlier nineteenth century.

In the very earliest phase, many African rulers were merely asked to sign a paper and to fly the appropriate European flag. It was only later that the Europeans came back in force, to stay and to give day-to-day orders. But they rarely came in sufficient numbers to see those orders carried down to the level of the ordinary subject. African inter-mediaries had to be called upon. Theorists of administration constructed elaborate frameworks on paper in which they argued the advantages of "direct" or "indirect" rule. Under direct rule, the chain of command ran through echelons of European officials as far as possible. By contrast, the theory of Indirect Rule stressed the desirability of ruling through African authorities like the emirs of northern Nigeria. In fact, all administrative systems gave orders through *some* African intermediaries. The crucial question was the identity of those intermediaries and the degree of formal or informal authority they could exercise.

The range of choice was very wide indeed. In many cases where the African ruler retained some bargaining power, his authority over local affairs was left intact. It could even increase; with political support from the Europeans, he could gain a freer hand against political rivals within his own kingdom. In other places, where the African kingdoms had been swept away, colonial rulers made contact with their African subor-dinates only at the level of the village head. Authorities at that level lacked the prestige and traditional power of kingship; but they were so numerous, and the colonial officials so few, that they could often usurp power informally without fear of being caught.

Sometimes the Europeans tried to recruit their African subordinates without regard to past authority. The Germans in East Africa, for example, began on the coast by simply taking over the Zanzibari administration, which placed a *liwali* in charge of each town, with *akida* serving as his assistants for surrounding rural areas. The Germans then made the akida into tax collectors and greatly increased the numbers. As a result, the akida became the principal intermediaries between the German district officers and the village headmen. These akida were also recruited from among the coastal aristocracy of Afro-Arabs, not from the local ruling class of each district. Later on, many were the first graduates of the German schools set up in the coastal towns. The result was a very important though unintended shift in political power away from one segment of the Tanganyikan population and toward another.

In the Congo Independent State, petty officials might be recruited far more carelessly from the ranks of African soldiers. As the principal agents to enforce the state demands for wild-rubber collections, they became petty tyrants with the right to punish anyone on the spot by whipping. For collective resistance, or simply for failure to meet their demands, they could call down a punitive expedition to destroy a village or punish a whole district.

Whoever may have been chosen to exercise authority for the Europeans, it was rarely possible to impose European government as it was understood in Europe. African subordinates did not fit directly as petty bureaucrats in a Western administrative structure. They became, rather, the clients of European patrons, and this client–patron relationship was common in pre-colonial Africa. It was much looser than the kind of authority implied by a European chain-of-command. Thus, while the colonial state seized all powers of government in theory, it lacked the manpower and the knowledge to exercise the powers it claimed. In effect, its African subordinates were allowed to rule, though with some rough guidelines about the kind of rule they were to provide. The revenue system was often that of a tributary state, where the tributary ruler collected taxes from his subjects and passed some part of them on to the Europeans. So long as the African ruler could maintain this relationship, he was free to order his subordinates in his own way, and this client–patron, or tributary, relationship lasted until the Europeans secured enough control to place all subordinates on salary, with the power subsequently to remove them. The chiefs understood this distinction. As a group of headmen in Uganda argued: "If you pay me to wash my table, it will then become your table." But the client–patron relationship gradually evolved toward more systematic administration.

European governments sometimes ruled indirectly through another kind of tributary by subcontracting colonial government to private companies. From the early stages of European expansion overseas, joint-stock companies had occasionally been endowed with the power to govern, to maintain armies and navies, to fight wars, and generally to do all that the granting government itself might have done. The company usually received commercial monopolies or other privileges designed to yield a profit, which could then be used to pay the cost of fighting wars and ruling the colonies. The system was supposed to be cheap for the home government and profitable to the companies.

Profits rarely matched the costs of colonial rule – being sometimes higher, sometimes lower – though company rule had the further advantage of disguising the government's actual role in matters likely to arouse criticism. Germany began its conquest of East Africa by chartering a German East Africa Company, giving it full control of the Tanganyikan territories it might acquire after 1885, though its charter was revoked in 1889. Britain chartered a Royal Niger Company for the period 1885–1900, an Imperial British East Africa Company for the occupation of Kenya 1888–

1893, and Cecil Rhodes's British South Africa Company over the period from 1889 to 1923 for the conquest and administration of what was to be the Rhodesias (later Zambia and Zimbabwe). All these companies except the British South Africa Company lost their government functions within a few years. In practice, they were either too weak or too strong. The British East Africa Company failed financially, and the German East Africa Company was unable to handle Bushiri's revolt in coastal Tanganyika without calling for imperial troops. The Royal Niger Company had begun as a successful commercial company, but it had to be pushed aside so that African troops under imperial control could oppose French rivals and conquer the Caliphate of Sokoto. On the other hand, although the British South Africa Company was implicated in the Jameson raid, it was allowed to keep its charter and its administrative powers until 1923.

Leopold of Belgium's private Congo Independent State was a form of company government. It was made up of an interlocked nest of capitalist corporations, but its powers to exploit the African population were used more drastically than elsewhere in Africa. After 1892, it claimed a monopoly over the entire rubber production of the colony, paying the gatherers a very low price and using the armed power of the state to force villages and individuals to deliver quotas. It used naked military power to back up a system of forced labor and labor taxation. From all this, the Congo State not only made a magnificent private profit for the king and his friends; it also transferred part of its profits to the Belgian government, the only colony in Africa that paid off directly to a European government.

In addition to these companies that governed whole colonies, other European corporations operated at a more local level – in effect, subcontracting the control and exploitation of a single region or a single product. The government of the Congo Independent State allocated spheres of this kind for mining, railway building, and rubber collection; and some of the subcontractors made fabulous profits – as high as twenty-fold within less than a decade for some rubber companies. High profits, however, were not universal; the French companies chartered for the colony of the Middle Congo and the Portuguese companies chartered for Mozambique were far less successful. Some made a little profit, but on balance they seem to have shown a net loss, even though their methods were no less brutal than those of their Belgian counterparts.

Elsewhere, more liberal practices survived from the conversionist phase in European thought. Before the scramble began in earnest, Britain held only a few coastal enclaves in West Africa, and some, at least, of the British officials believed that these towns should be governed in the best possible way – which, to their view, was the way towns in Britain were governed, with elected town councils and a mayor. Some precedents went back even further. From the mid-eighteenth century, British and French officials of the Senegambian trading enclaves began to recognize a prominent and influential citizen as "mayor." In 1800, the British also appointed a mayor and aldermen for the municipality of Freetown in Sierra Leone. Though the institution died out for a time, it was refounded in the 1890s. In the 1850s, the British set up similar municipal governments for Accra and Cape Coast on the Gold Coast, later for Sekondi as well, and for Lagos and Calabar in Nigeria. But the rise of the ideology of trusteeship cut off this trend toward popular government. No town annexed by Britain after 1900 achieved an elected city government until the 1950s.

The political pattern was similar in French West Africa. The ancient appointed mayoralties for Saint Louis and Gorée changed in 1848 into elected municipal councils, with the additional right to send representatives to the National Assembly in Paris. That was a one-shot affair, since the Second French Empire of the 1850s and 1860s was not very democratic, even in its government of France. With the foundation of the Third French Republic in 1870, however both the elected city governments and the elected deputies to the Paris Assembly were restored. The deputies were usually French or Afro-French at first, but the African inhabitants of the four coastal towns or communes that made up Senegal at that time were entitled to vote on the same basis as the French. As in British West Africa, however, the spread of constitutional liberalism stopped there. None of the territory France gained after 1880 entered this charmed circle of electoral politics until after the Second World War.

That pattern of early political gains, reversed sometime between 1880 and 1900, was the case for South Africa as well. The Cape Colony and Natal achieved representative government in 1853 and 1856 respectively. The right to vote depended on the ownership of property, but the franchise was color-blind, at least in theory. In practice, Natal began to restrict African suffrage as early as 1865, so that only a handful of Africans voted in Natal. They did better in the Cape, however, having a majority in a few constituencies by the 1880s, but then special restrictions began in that colony as well.

For sub-Saharan Africa in general, the decade of the 1910s marked the peak of African electoral achievement before the Second World War. The Reverend Walter Rubusana became the first African member elected to the Cape Provincial Council and Blaise Diagne became the first African Senegalese elected to the French National Assembly. In Senegal, the Africans managed to hang on, and Diagne had a series of elected successors. Not so in South Africa, where Africans, Asians, and Coloured people were excluded from the central parliament of the Union of South Africa from its foundation in 1910, and they were later excluded from the Cape Provincial Council as well. Their right to vote, even in the Cape, was gradually restricted until it was removed altogether in the 1950s, just when colonial constitutions in tropical Africa were again moving toward electoral democracy.

The high noon of colonial rule in tropical Africa

The interwar decades marked a new phase in European colonial administration, when some form of the doctrine of trusteeship was dominant, now reinforced by what were taken to be the "lessons of experience" drawn from the early colonial period. Administration became more efficient and more homogeneous. The most brutal forms of exploitation subsided somewhat, but ordinary Africans gained little say in the way they were governed and even lost some of what they had had in the nineteenth century.

In the first decade of the twentieth century, events in Africa tended to strengthen the anti-imperialist faction in most European countries. In Britain, the Anglo-Boer War of 1899–1902 was an important catalyst, though British anti-imperialists were curiously blind to some important distinctions. They sympathized with the Boer effort to stave off British rule, but they made no serious objection to European racial dominance in southern Africa. British anti-imperialists were also active in exposing colonial scandals in non-British Africa, but they were remarkably quiet about the oppression of Africans in British territories.

German opinion was especially moved by the atrocities committed by their forces during the suppression of the Herero rebellion (1903–7) in South West Africa (now Namibia), and these feelings were reinforced by the impact of the Maji-Maji rebellion in Tanganyika (1905–7). The Belgian public began to hear murmurs of scandal from the Congo as early as the 1890s, especially atrocities growing out of unbridled exactions of forced labor and forced deliveries of wild rubber. In 1908, the Belgian parliament responded by annexing the Congo Independent State and bringing it under Belgian control. Similar atrocities in Angola, Mozambique, and the French colony of Middle Congo raised a similar outcry for more efficient and humane central control and an end to concessionary companies. Reforms were not immediate, nor effective in every case, but the European governments learned something from the public furor and international opprobrium.

The interwar years also revealed the fact that African resources were not the boundless treasure trove some imperialists had claimed during the height of expansionism in the 1890s. Wild rubber had produced great wealth for a few but at great cost to the Africans. By 1910, the rubber boom was gone forever; plantation-grown rubber from Southeast Asia replaced wild rubber in the world market. Other tropical products such as peanuts from West Africa, sisal and coffee from Tanganyika, cloves from Zanzibar, and cotton from Uganda or the Sudan were exported profitably enough, but only in limited circumstances. The perceived lesson about economic development was that private investment in Africa outside the field of commerce could only pay when it concentrated on directly exploitable resources like mineral wealth in copper, gold, or diamonds. Outside of North and South Africa, very little private investment went for anything but commerce or mining.

Still another "lesson of experience" had to do with education. Conversionists in the mid-nineteenth century had trusted to the "civilizing" value of Christian education. The missions and the colonial governments still offered education on the Western model, if only to fill the demand for clerks and catechists. But the result was not a new generation of submissive clerks who "knew their place" in the colonial order of things. The Western-educated Africans were often discontented with the role assigned them, more argumentative and troublesome by European standards than the "unspoiled, bush African." Many officials preferred to deal with the traditional African authorities, rather than to suffer the "insolence" of the journalists, lawyers, and other intellectuals who were beginning to emerge as a new elite around the West African port towns or from South African centers of missionary education like Lovedale in the eastern Cape and Adams College in Natal – or even from the more recently established centers in East Africa or Malawi.

These lessons of experience blended with other tendencies of thought like pseudo-scientific racism, which was still triumphant in the 1920s and into the 1930s. Administrative theory and practice were also affected by European influences having nothing to do with Africa. The First World War was crucial; France, Belgium, and Britain all lost a high proportion of their most able young men of that generation. Even in Europe the result was a kind of historical hiatus, where many trends and developments that seemed imminent before 1914 simply failed to take place until after 1945, and the Great Depression of the 1930s was a further damper on innovation.

Specific theories of administration helped to mediate between these general conditions and the policies that were put into effect. In France, one school of thought called for association between the colonies and the ruling power. Its advocates looked back with horror to nineteenth-century conversionism, which they called the theory of *assimilation*, in the sense that the colonized were expected to assimilate French culture. Associationists held that such assimilation might be desirable; but it was not possible, because non-Western people were racially inferior. It was better, therefore, to aim for mere "association" between the subject peoples and France, so that the colonial subjects could develop within their own, more limited capabilities. The expectation of a permanent relationship between superiors and inferiors was, of course, part of the general idea of trusteeship, of which associationism formed one strand.

The equivalent school of thought in Britain was identified with the idea of "Indirect Rule", usually written with initial capitals to distinguish it from the less specific idea of ruling through the existing African authorities. The adherents of Indirect Rule attached a whole body of justification and additional corollaries. They played down the conversionist role of Christian missions and Western-style education. Instead, they encouraged Africans to develop in an "African" way by using Hausa or Swahili as the language of administration in place of English, by establishing strict social segregation between Africans and Europeans, and sometimes by restricting European immigration to a colony. But the expectation was again a long period of trusteeship, or association between colonizers and colonized, without basic changes in the way of life of either.

These theories were hard to apply, if only because most administrators had contradictory attitudes. They genuinely believed that Africans and African cultures were inferior, and they genuinely believed that their own way of life was the best the world had known. It was therefore very hard to use any other standards of judgment, even when they conceded in theory that Africa had to develop in its own way. They wanted to rule through indigenous authorities, but they tended to push those authorities into the use of Western techniques of government, with typewriters, mimeograph machines, and the rest. This meant a need for typists, secretaries, and clerks who could do double-entry bookkeeping.

Those who worked for European administrators also had to function in French or English or Portuguese. Colonial governments therefore continued to make Western-style education available. They might try to limit the content of that education, as the Belgian Congo did by creating a broad base to the equivalent of high school, then virtually prohibiting education for Africans at the university level. But such limitations rarely worked; it was simply impossible to give people access to education in the language of a technologically advanced society and still expect them to remain "unspoiled, bush Africans." Africans educated in Western schools rarely converted completely to Western culture, but they did begin to learn how Western culture worked, and they could borrow what they felt would help them to achieve their own goals for their own societies.

The conversionist faith had few vocal supporters during the 1920s and 1930s; but several colonial measures suggest that it still had a following of sorts, and it was to emerge strongly after the Second World War. Meanwhile French policy made it possible for an African meeting certain educational and cultural standards to advance from the status of a French subject to that of a French citizen on a footing of full legal equality with Frenchmen from France. Portuguese authorities made a similar concession. Though the numbers of these *assimilados* (in Portuguese Africa) or *évolués* (in French) were a tiny part of the whole, these men and women were a significant factor in social and political life. In less formal ways, British officials in West Africa, more than elsewhere were able to make appropriate allowances for the English-trained lawyers, medical men, and others who could pass as "gentlemen."

Beyond these practical "lessons" and common theory, a great deal was borrowed back and forth among European administrations. All came to share a family resemblance, from Morocco and Egypt down to the Cape of Good Hope. The private companies were phased out. African authorities who had begun with unusual latitude or unusual power over local affairs gradually found their power reduced. Colonies that began without institutions for consulting African opinion developed ways to work with African intermediaries, if only at the lowest level. In the British colonies, the governorship of Frederick Lugard over Northern Nigeria before the First World War became the model of Indirect Rule, widely imitated elsewhere in British tropical Africa. In some cases, where no chiefs or other traditional authorities were visible, as among the stateless Ibo, the British created "warrant chiefs" following the rationale that this was an "African" way of governing and therefore preferable to Western institutions for local government, such as elected councils.

But colonial powers that tried to preserve African institutions sometimes found them breaking down under the demand for efficiency in government or the impact of social and economic change. After 1910, for example, the Belgian administration in the Congo decided to rule through the chiefs. At the first stage, it ordered local administrators to discover and recognize existing chiefdoms. By 1917, they had discovered about 6000, which was far too many for efficient government. In line with the idea of "improving" African institutions rather than borrowing from Europe, they grouped smaller chiefdoms, calling each group a sector. By 1953, they had pared down the 6000 chiefdoms into 460 chiefdoms and 519 sectors as the recognized units of "native local government." Each of these units was supposed to enforce local African law. But local African law was truly local, and many Africans actually lived in towns and mining camps with ethnically mixed populations. By 1931, the administration had to make an exception for these population centers, recognizing them as exempt from customary law (*centres extra-coutumiers*), though a kind of African common law came into being, especially in Kinshasa (the later Shaba province). These centers then grew so rapidly that, by 1960, a quarter of the Congolese population lived in them. Much the same happened elsewhere in Africa, wherever urbanization brought people together. The only choice was to impose some form of common law, and the choice usually went to some modification of a Western legal code.

Above the level of African intermediaries, colonial government was remarkably uniform, regardless of the European power in charge. The key administrative unit was a territory variously called a district, *cercle*, or *territoire*. The head of each district – variously called *commandant de cercle*, Commissioner, or District Officer – was in charge of all aspects of district administration, from judicial appeals to tax collection, road building, and schools, usually with one or two assistants plus specialized personnel for engineering, medicine, agriculture, or education. The general administrative officers were recruited with care, and they had to pass through a period of special training.

They were also amazingly few for the extent of territory they governed. The whole of French Equatorial Africa in the mid-1930s was run by only 206 administrative officers, with 400 specialists and technical officers to assist. The whole of British tropical Africa at the same period (leaving aside Egypt, the Sudan, and southern Africa) was governed by about 1000 general administrative officers, plus another four or five thousand European specialists, while the Belgians ruled the Congo in 1936 with 728 officers in charge of the 104 territories. In Rwanda and Burundi, however, where African kingship had been preserved, they ruled with an administrative staff of less than 50 Europeans. The ratio of subjects to administrators thus varied from the neighborhood of 1500 to one in the heavily administered Belgian Congo, to 70,000 to one in the lightly administered Rwanda and Burundi. These figures cannot be precise for lack of accurate population data, but the range of difference within Belgian Africa alone is about the range of difference in other colonies as well. It is clear, in any event, that most day-to-day governing had to be done by African intermediaries.

Above the level of the district, the larger colonies had an intermediary level of provinces, grouping several districts. Then, at the center, sat the governor assisted by his staff and usually sharing power with some form of administrative or legislative council. These councils might consist only of the heads of government departments, sitting as a kind of advisory cabinet, but they often included important non-official interests such as a few traditional rulers, the chambers of commerce or agriculture, or key trading firms.

The Nigerian constitution that lasted from 1922 to 1946 can serve as an example. The governor had a legislative council of forty-five members, and he was obliged to consult it concerning new legislation or other important matters. Two-thirds were officials from the governor's staff, which meant that he could order them to vote as he saw fit. The other third were partly appointed by the governor to represent banking, trading, shipping, and the interests of African traders, but four members were elected from the coastal towns that had been allowed to keep municipal freedom – three from Lagos and one from Calabar. Similar constitutions with appropriate local variations were in effect elsewhere in British tropical Africa. In East Africa, for example, governors usually appointed a representative of the Indian minority, and sometimes a single European missionary to represent African interests.

African colonial constitutions of the interwar period were peculiarly stable; not because they bred general satisfaction with the colonial order, but because governments were unresponsive to African views. Some protest was heard in council meetings, but most took place outside the political arena, expressed through religious movements, strikes, riots, or the organized refusal of farmers to sell their crops at the prices offered. Toward the end of the 1930s, these protests combined with reformist pressures within Europe itself to produce signs of change, but these projected reforms were overtaken by the impact of the Second World War.

Alien communities in Africa: the problem of plural societies

From the broadest perspective of world history over the past three centuries, the Europeans conquered most of the world; and their impact on the conquered countries fell into one of three highly significant categories, depending on the demographic mixture of Europeans and local people. One category, exemplified by the United States or Australia, was the case where the Europeans were so numerous and the local inhabitants so few that blanket migration brought Western culture to a whole continent, leaving only small enclaves of unassimilated "Indians" or "Aborigines" to preserve their original way of life as they saw fit, or as best they could. By contrast, in British India or the Dutch East Indies – and in most of tropical Africa – the European administrators, businessmen, missionaries, or others acting for European interests were only a few temporary residents. If a self-sustaining European community of permanent residents spanning several generations ever came into existence, it remained a tiny enclave.

Between these extremes lay a third possibility, the cases in which the permanent community of overseas Europeans became a significant factor in colonial society and politics. When this happened, the local society was divided into two or more separate communities, each with its own way of life, yet living side by side and mutually engaged in that society's affairs. Culturally plural societies of this kind came in many variants. Some had a nearly equal balance between two cultures, as in Malaysia where the number of Chinese and Malays was nearly equal during the colonial period, while the dominant European community was very small. Others were numerically unbalanced toward one culture. Some plural societies integrated rapidly, merging to form a common culture, even though individuals might also retain important aspects of their ancestors' way of life. That happened notably in Hawaii, where people of many different Asian cultures, local Polynesians, and Western settlers assimilated a local variant of the European way of life – and in little more time than that of the African colonial period. Elsewhere, as in the Andean countries of Peru and Bolivia, Spanish and American Indian cultures lived side by side in the same society for nearly four hundred years without producing much cultural integration outside the field of religion or beyond the social group of mixed Indian and Spanish descent.

The amount of political or economic power a community could command made a big difference. Where overseas Europeans had the support of the colonial government, a comparatively small number could exercise an enormous influence on the country's affairs. The European minority in Kenya toward the end of the colonial period was only about 1 per cent of the whole Kenya population, but its influence was immense. The East Indian minority at the same time was about 3 per cent. It too had inordinate power because its wealth per capita was greater than that of the African majority, but it had nothing like the weight of Europeans.

The African examples of cultural pluralism in the nineteenth and twentieth centuries fit into a special sector of the whole category. The intrusive aliens were always less than a quarter of the whole population, and less than 10 per cent everywhere except Algeria and South Africa. They came mainly from India to East and southeast Africa and from Europe to northern and southern Africa and scattered areas between – with smaller numbers of Lebanese traders dispersed through West Africa joining the small communities of Afro-Americans in Liberia, Indonesians and Malays at the Cape, and Arabs already settled in the East African port towns well before the colonial period.

The European movement into Africa coincided with the nineteenth- and twentieth-century peak of racism and cultural chauvinism in Europe itself. These attitudes were extremely important to the settlers' feelings of self-confidence and their ability to justify their dominant position, to claim a monopoly over political power or a right to exploit the local people economically. They were also important to the European sense of community and solidarity with others of their kind. Almost everywhere, this led to patterns of residential segregation in urban housing, to social segregation in public facilities, and to overt legal inequality before the law. In less official ways, it led to sharp community resistance to culture change, especially to change that seemed to veer toward the African way of life. "Going native" was seldom illegal, but it brought down on the individual the most severe social and economic and even official government pressure. As a result, culture change in the African plural societies almost always meant assimilation of European culture by Africans, very rarely the assimilation of African culture by Europeans. This in itself was a departure from the kind of Afro-European relations that had once prevailed in coastal trading ports, where many Europeans learned African languages, married African women, and left Afro-European families who became prominent in local society. The whole settler community of the prazeros in the Zambezi valley from the seventeenth to the nineteenth century Africanized their culture. Before 1750 or so the Dutch community at the Cape mixed biologically with the local Khoikhoi far more easily than their descendants were to do with Africans in later centuries. European cultural attitudes, in short, began to harden even before the dawn of the colonial era.

Table 16.1 is a rough measure of the seriousness of the settler problem in colonial Africa. Before 1880, Europeans were a significant problem only in Algeria and South Africa, but they became important in many places before the end of the colonial period, even when they were not very numerous. The various political units fall into four different groups. South Africa is in a class by itself, with the culturally European population constituting 30.1 per cent, even though the racially "pure" Europeans came to only 20.8 per cent (and that itself was a peak figure; by the mid-1970s, they were less than 17 per cent, and the figure has declined ever since, because the African birth rate far exceeds the European). If Indians and others permanently domiciled in South Africa are taken into account, the total population of non-Bantu-speaking African origin as of the late 1950s would have been nearly a third of the whole. Only an insignificant percentage of any racial or national grouping had migrated to South Africa since 1930, and the vast majority were born in South Africa. Their integration into a broader South African society – culturally plural though it was – made South Africa significantly different from any other country. Even Algeria, whose European population was nearly 11 per cent on the eve of independence, represented another

Table 16.1. "Europeans" resident in Africa toward the end of the colonial period

Country (present-day names)	Percentage of total population classified as "European" (1956)
Union of South Africa	30.1*
Algeria	10.9
Rhodesia (Zimbabwe)	7.2
Tunisia	6.7
Former French Morocco	5.4
Zambia	3.0
Malawi	2.7
Angola	2.5
Mozambique	1.0
Kenya	0.9
Zaire	0.8

Source: United Nations, *Economic Survey of Africa since 1950*, New York, 1959, pp. 13, 15.
* Counts the "coloured" population as culturally Western. On a racial basis alone, the "European" percentage would be 20.8. Egypt is omitted for lack of equivalent data.

order of magnitude, and, indeed, the great majority of the *colons* left voluntarily for France as political refugees when Algeria became independent in 1962 – as the Portuguese of Angola and Mozambique would do in 1974 and 1975.

The problem was less severe in the other territories, and the nature of the European settler population was somewhat different in each case. In Tunisia, for example, the settlers arrived in large numbers early in the colonial period. By 1921, they were already thought to be more than 7 per cent of the population – more than they were to be thirty-five years later. In Algeria as in South Africa, the "European" population at the time of independence was predominantly African-born. The movement into Angola, Mozambique, Kenya, and Rhodesia, on the other hand, came largely after the Second World War. The European population of Rhodesia and Kenya, for instance, more than doubled between 1946 and 1955, while the settler population of Angola and Mozambique increased nearly as fast and kept on increasing after the late 1950s, when migration into the rest of southern Africa slowed down. As a result, the "European" populations of these tropical African territories were genuine Europeans from Europe in much higher proportions than was true for either South Africa or the Maghrib, with obvious and serious consequences for the way these people regarded the permanency of their position in Africa.

Another important consideration was the relationship of the European community to the land. In Morocco, settlers came to own about 8 per cent of the land under cultivation; in Tunisia, as much as 40 to 45 per cent in the rich plains south and west of Tunis; and in Algeria, nearly a third of the cultivated land. But most of the best land was managed in large units, and most agricultural work was done by Muslim North Africans. At the end of the colonial period, only about 5 per cent of the European population of Algeria was actually settled on the land.

Settler farm managers were also common in tropical Africa, but in South Africa "European" farmers owned virtually all the productive land outside the African reserves, which amounted to less than one-eighth of the total area. In the western Cape Province around Cape Town, virtually all the rural population were Afrikaans-speaking "Europeans" or people of mixed race, called Coloured in South Africa, while the Bantu-speaking Africans lived in special locations near the principal towns and worked mainly in urban employment.

Land ownership, in turn, was related to the settler community's sense of permanency. In Kenya, for example, most of the European community were not engaged in agriculture; but many important settlers were landowners, and a high proportion regarded themselves as permanent residents who had come to raise their families and ultimately to retire there. On the opposite side of Africa, the city of Dakar in Senegal had about the same proportion of Europeans as the city of Nairobi had in Kenya, but virtually all of the French Dakarois considered themselves temporary residents. Some intended to stay for a period of years, others for the remainder of their working lives, but almost all meant in the end to return to France and to educate their children for careers in France.

The type and extent of political power available to the settler communities varied greatly between northern and tropical Africa – with South Africa and Rhodesia in a class by themselves. In the two French protectorates, Morocco and Tunisia, the settlers' most effective political voice was pressure on the Ministry of Foreign Affairs in Paris. This was especially the case for the large companies and other important interests. In Tunisia, however, the settlers themselves helped to elect a local council with limited powers over the protectorate's budget. Algeria was similar, with local Europeans controlling two-thirds of a representative body called the Financial Delegations, while local Muslims controlled the other third. The settlers, however, were not satisfied. They tended to want Algeria's full integration with France – political assimilation as it was sometimes called – but in a way that would exclude Muslim Algerians from power and from equality before the law. Some French liberals in the mid-1930s and later tried to push the government toward another kind of political assimilation with full civil and political rights for the Muslim majority. They failed in the face of settler opposition, and the political reality in Algiers was that the settlers and the French army exercised even greater power in practice than they did on paper.

Much the same thing happened in other colonies run mainly from the imperial center in Europe. The Portuguese and Belgian colonial governments were theoretically autocratic, but the local Europeans had their say informally. In most of the French and English colonies in West and Central Africa, the settlers had formal representation, either through appointment to bodies like the Nigerian legislative council (following the constitution of 1922) or, in most French territories, through the Europeans' right to elect representatives to colonial councils. These colonial councils, however, also contained the appointed representatives of other interests, including those of important African chiefs, and their powers were mainly limited to the approval of the colonial budget. In British East Africa, especially Kenya, the settlers gained a more effective mini-parliament that functioned as a legislative council, but they failed in their effort to make their interests dominant, as the settlers in South Africa and Rhodesia had already done.

The pattern of politics in southern Africa

The striking difference between the settler problem in South Africa and elsewhere was not merely the size of the "European" community. That community gradually succeeded in making itself dominant over the African majority and independent of control from Europe. This dual victory, largely won in the first third of the twentieth century set a pattern that survived to the end of the 1980s, in spite of the winds of change that brought independence under African control to every other part of the continent.

The victory of the Europeans in the far south began in the aftermath of the Anglo-Boer War. The British were conciliatory to the defeated; the Boers of the Transvaal were allowed local self-government, and their first elected leaders were Louis Botha and Jan Smuts, former Republican generals who nevertheless pursued a moderate policy. They did so partly because they realized it was expedient to conciliate the owners of the mines, but they were impressed by the genuine good the British seemed to offer. In 1910, the British encouraged the formation of a Union of South Africa, bringing together the two British colonies of Natal and Cape Colony, and the former Boer republics of Transvaal and the Orange Free State. This was not a federal state like Canada or the United States, but a unitary state where the central parliament could override the local, provincial governments. It also followed the British model, with executive power vested in a cabinet responsible to the elected parliament. But only "European" men could become members of Parliament, and only European men could vote in any province but the Cape.

Since the parliamentary electorate was overwhelmingly "European" from the start, South African political divisions were based mainly on the historic and cultural cleavage between Afrikaners and those of British descent. Some political parties were led by Afrikaners, and dedicated first and foremost to the promotion of Afrikaner interests. Other parties were led by British South Africans, and were dedicated to the promotion of *their* interests. Still others were middle parties, comprising both Afrikaners and British South Africans, dedicated to the reduction of the historic tensions between the two groups. Because the British South Africans were a minority, even of the European population, no British party has ever won a parliamentary majority. The main struggle therefore was played out between the Afrikaner and middle parties, with the outcome determined primarily by the conduct of Afrikaner voters.

The political history of South Africa since 1910 falls into two periods, each of which started with middle-party government and developed into Afrikaner government. From 1910 to 1924, the dominant party was a middle party led by Botha and Smuts, aimed at the gradual fusion of the two European nationalities and at cooperation with Britain in international affairs. Then, from 1924 to 1933, the dominant party was an Afrikaner party, which promoted economic nationalism as well as detachment from Britain. This cycle ended during the Great Depression, which drew the two main parties together to form a new middle party, the United Party. In 1948, however, a new and more radical Afrikaner party, the National Party, came into power and began moving toward a policy of strict separation between the races, called *apartheid*. In so far as possible, it sought to separate the races geographically, so that the African majority would be forced to live in the reserves, now called "homelands," and the most valuable part of the country would be reserved for Whites – though Africans would still be allowed to enter as temporary workers without political rights of any kind. The National Party held office until 1994, however. In 1990, F.W. De Klerk became President and persuaded the National Party to open negotiations with the African National Congress (ANC) and other non-white factions. The result was South Africa's first non-racist election, in 1994, and an electoral victory for Nelson Mandela of the ANC thus completing Africa's movement towards genuine independence of European control.

Theoretical independence from Britain had long since become a fact. In 1910, the Union of South Africa began as a "self-governing colony," like Canada, New Zealand, or Australia. Over the next decades, all these territories – with British acquiescence – became gradually more and more self-governing, with growing independence even in foreign policy. In 1931, the British Parliament passed the Statute of Westminster which granted legal independence as well. At first, South Africa claimed its right to independence but remained a monarchy, with the king of Great Britain as king of South Africa. Republican sentiment, however, was still strong among Afrikaner nationalists, who were dismayed when middle-party governments participated along-side Britain in both world wars – though the declaration of war against Germany in 1939 passed the South African Parliament by only a small majority. In 1961, South Africa abandoned the monarchy and became the Republic of South Africa, simul-taneously dropping out of the British Commonwealth, whose new Asian and African members were increasingly critical of its racial policies.

By that time, successive South African governments had whittled away the limited franchise rights originally enjoyed by the African and Coloured inhabitants of the Cape Province. In 1936, African voters were removed from the common electoral rolls and given the right to elect three Europeans to represent them in Parliament, and in 1957, after a long constitutional struggle, the Coloured voters were given four such European representatives as well. But even these seats were abolished, in 1960 and 1968 respect-ively. For the next quarter century, only Europeans (including women who were enfranchised in 1930) were allowed to vote for members of the South African Parlia-ment.

Meanwhile, African resistance and African political activity on the fringes of the constitutional, European-dominated forum had long since made their appearance. One of the ironies of modern Africa is the fact that indigenous Africans in the far south were more exposed to Western cultural influences and more involved in modern industrial life than those further north, yet they were to be under European domination longer. As early as 1900, most South Africans had been influenced by Christian missions. By 1960, nearly 60 per cent were Christian. Most had been to some kind of Western-style school, however briefly.

Like subject peoples in other countries and in other periods, modern South Africans developed ways to compensate for their economic and political depravations. Most learned to appear deferential in the presence of "Europeans," but without surrendering their integrity as human beings. Many transformed Christianity to make it fulfil their own social, aesthetic, and psychological needs. And, despite the fact that the migrant labor system broke up vast numbers of families, Africans established strong community ties even in the segregated city locations. Indeed, the growing point in South African culture was a proletarian ebullience, a spirit that was well portrayed by Ezekiel Mphahlele in *Down Second Avenue.*

In South Africa, African political organization – as distinct from resistance to conquest – began toward the end of the nineteenth century. The principal organizations were the African National Congress (founded in 1912), the South African Indian Congress (founded in 1920 as an amalgamation of pre-existing Natal and Transvaal organizations), and the African Political Organization (whose members were in fact Coloured people). To begin with, all three bodies were fairly small, Western-oriented elite groups, lacking mass support. Their purpose was to realize the promise inherent in the Cape colonial system, first by gaining full equality for the well-educated members of their own communities, later by progressively educating and incorporating the masses. The precedent they had in mind was the step-by-step extension of the parliamentary franchise to all classes and both sexes in Britain. By rational argument and peaceful pressure within the framework of the law, they sought to persuade the existing electorate to reverse the segregationist tide.

For many years, the African National Congress remained under the control of lawyers, clergy, and journalists. Their stated objectives were to inform the electorate about "the requirements and aspirations of the Native people," to enlist the support of sympathetic Europeans, to promote unity among the African peoples, and, above all, to redress African grievances "by constitutional means." The ANC protested each installment of segregationist legislation from the Land Act of 1913 through the Parliamentary Representation Act of 1936, usually making its protests inside South Africa but sometimes sending delegations overseas – to England in 1913 and to Versailles in 1919. Though the ANC usually acted alone, its leaders were in close touch with liberal Europeans, and on occasion they sponsored multiracial conferences. By 1948, it was clear that this type of opposition was barren. Instead of being admitted to equality, Africans were subject to new forms of discrimination. All the reformist opposition had achieved in forty years was a succession of rearguard actions, each ending in defeat.

Some Africans also tried before 1948 to create revolutionary movements. In 1919, Clements Kadalie, an African from Nyasaland (later Malawi), founded the Industrial and Commercial Workers Union (ICU), which became the most spectacular mass movement of the interwar years. With the help of a small group of European socialists, he organized an impressive series of industrial strikes. Like its contemporary, the Universal Negro Improvement Association of Marcus Garvey in the United States, the ICU was poorly organized and it disintegrated in the late 1920s, partly from internal weaknesses and partly from official suppression.

The Communist Party of South Africa was founded in 1921 by Europeans. It was the only political organization in South Africa that recruited members from all racial groups and that had a multiracial executive. But it suffered from ill-judged directives from Moscow, like other Communist parties outside the Soviet Union in that period, and from a series of internal schisms. It never gained a wide following, and it was banned in 1950. Nevertheless, it exerted considerable influence on the ICU, and, by 1948, socialist ideas were attracting the younger and more frustrated members of the ANC and the Asian and Coloured organizations.

Meanwhile the South African government had established control over German South West Africa (Namibia) during the First World War and retained it in the peace settlement under a mandate from the League of Nations. After the Second World War, all the other mandatory powers turned their mandated territories over to the United Nations as trust territories scheduled for independence in the near future. South Africa refused. Namibian independence was delayed until 1988, when South Africa was obliged to accede to international pressure and the fear of a guerrilla insurrection.

When the four British colonies united in 1910, politicians in Britain as well as southern Africa generally assumed that sooner or later the Union would incorporate Rhodesia, Basutoland, Bechuanaland, and Swaziland, which remained under British control. In 1922, the British government decided to terminate the administrative powers of the British South Africa Company in Rhodesia, and it gave the local electorate, most of whom were European settlers of British origin, a choice: Rhodesia could either join South Africa or become a separate self-governing colony, in which case Britain would retain ultimate responsibility for the territory. To avoid Afrikaner domination, the voters opted for colonial self-government, but Britain refused them full independence under the Statute of Westminster. Nevertheless, the Rhodesian government's racial policies closely resembled those of South Africa, even though Africans outnumbered the local "Europeans" by twenty to one. Britain also listened to African opinion in the other three territories and kept them under direct rule from London, because their people feared the patterns of racial oppression they had experienced in nearby South Africa, where many had worked as migrant laborers.

European "tutelage" in Egypt

Europe's impact on Egypt during the colonial period was very different from what it was on the great and diverse mass of tropical Africa, or even on the culturally similar Arabic-speaking territories of the Maghrib. The French invasion at the end of the eighteenth century, the modernizing policies of Muhammad ʿAli, and the unrestrained Westernization of Khedive Ismaʾil in the 1870s had brought Egypt into the penumbra of Western-style politics. From 1866 to 1879, the khedive had permitted an elected representative assembly, though the only people it represented were the old aristocracy and the new class of Western-educated officers and officials, plus some of the tiny Egyptian middle class. Effective representation of the whole population was not intended. The assembly was nevertheless a forum in which various shades of opposition to the khedive could be expressed. It was these threads of disaffection that Colonel ʿUrabi Pasha pulled together in 1881–2, along with an effort to escape the European threat.

His rebellion was at first successful against the khedive, but then he lost to the British invasion. The result was a barely disguised British protectorate, though British control over Egypt was different from other protectorates of the period – from those

France established over Tunisia and Morocco, for example. Britain was not interested in lasting control over Egypt. It was interested in the security of the Suez Canal. It therefore chose not to offend other European powers, as it would surely have done if it tried to annex Egypt to the British empire. The result was mixed. The Ottomans were still theoretically sovereign, but a series of local monarchs of Muhammad ʿAli's dynasty reigned until 1962 under the successive titles of khedive, sultan, and finally king. For the British, to preserve the office of khedive seemed a way to conciliate important people in Egypt and weaken opposition to British overrule. On the other hand, the ʿUrabi rebellion expressed an opposition to a discredited khedival regime. By returning the khedive to power, the British reintroduced a corrupt ruler and, through his influence, allowed the return of a political class that was to be equally corruptible in its turn.

Other Europeans continued to exercise certain rights acquired in the days of informal empire. The international body charged with the liquidation of the Egyptian foreign debt still operated, which meant that the British-controlled government had to continue repayment to Egypt's European creditors. The British were also limited by the treaty of rights Egypt had already surrendered to various European powers. By these concessions, resident foreigners not only had the right to be tried by consular courts; they were also exempt from certain taxes imposed on Egyptian subjects. Britain might modify these rights, but only with international agreement. In fact, many special rights for foreigners lasted until 1949.

With these advantages, foreigners continued to stream into the country, attracted by a new spurt of economic growth. They remained at 1 or 2 per cent of the Egyptian population in spite of enormous local population growth. By 1897, there were 100,000 resident subjects of European powers, plus another 40,000 born in some other part of the Ottoman Empire – mainly Syrians, Turks, and Circassians. These "European settlers" were principally city people and they remained city people, concentrated in the skilled trades and commerce. They were also mainly from the eastern Mediterranean, not from Britain or even Western Europe. The British officials in high administrative posts or top positions in British firms were comparatively few. Alexandria was the settlers' city, and it became a "European city" on the African continent in the same way that Nairobi or Dakar were to be European cities, even though most inhabitants were African.

In spite of urban concentrations, foreigners also penetrated far into the agricultural economy. The government sponsored irrigation works to increase production, especially of cotton for the British textile industry. Foreign technicians designed these works, and foreign capital made their construction possible. Large land companies that built subsidiary irrigation works then sold off the land in smaller units to the Egyptians who would actually manage production. Some large farms, however, remained under foreign control and management – some 13 per cent of the arable land in 1900, increasing to 15 per cent by 1913 – while Egyptian agriculture moved toward a dangerous dependence on cotton, rising from 12 per cent of the total value of agricultural production in 1879 to 22 per cent by 1913.

The decision to retain khedival government meant that British officials had to use a form of "indirect rule," and a form in which theory and practice were often quite distinct. The principal official bore the unlikely title of British Agent and Consul-

General. In theory, he was simply an adviser to the khedive; the Anglo-Egyptian agreement provided that his advice had to be taken and acted upon. In effect, the consul-general had the power to order the appointment or dismissal of ministers of the Egyptian government, including the prime minister. He could also see to it that British "advisers" were appointed to help out the heads of various government departments and bureaus, and their advice also had to be taken. They became, in short, the effective department heads. The commander-in-chief, or *sirdar*, of the Egyptian army was a directly appointed British official, who also served as governor-general of the Sudan after its reconquest from the Mahdi.

Britain had, in short, the opportunity to run the government of Egypt in any way it chose, but it chose not to run it quite so intensively as its theoretical power allowed. The consul-general had a kind of veto power over the khedive's acts, but he used it sparingly. The khedive retained enormous power – far more than remained to any king or queen of England at that time. The British also refrained from detailed interference in certain spheres of government, such as the Egyptian court system, local government, and the police. Their intervention was most intense in foreign and military affairs, fiscal administration, and economic development of the agricultural sector.

The political balance that emerged in Cairo was a shifting equilibrium between the consul-general, the khedive, and the representative council that developed over the decades into a kind of Egyptian parliament, though one with a restricted electorate. This body began in 1883 as a thirty-man legislative council, a bare majority being elected, the rest appointed by the khedive. During the decade before the First World War, the elected element increased and political parties began to function. Saad Zaghlul then emerged as a parliamentary spokesman for Egyptian independence. In 1918, he founded the Wafd party, which was to be the dominant nationalist party until 1952. It operated at first under his own leadership and then, after 1927, under Mustapha el-Nahas Pasha. Meanwhile, Britain formally annexed Egypt when Turkey entered the First World War on the German side. It then granted Egyptian independence in 1923 under a constitution that increased the powers of the khedive and the Parliament alike. But Britain also retained effective control over the Suez Canal, over the Sudan, and kept a strong influence in Egyptian affairs generally. Egypt was independent in name only, but the relaxation of British control made it possible for Nahas Pasha and (after 1937) King Farouk to build their personal fortunes and the power of their followers.

After the Second World War, political protest from the mass of the Egyptian population became important for the first time. A Communist party became active. On the right, the Muslim Brotherhood became a significant mass movement. Founded as far back as 1929, it now combined Islamic conservatism with other elements suggesting European fascism. The power of the brotherhood peaked for the first time in the years 1947–9, nearly simultaneously with the Israeli victory in the struggle over Palestine in 1948–9. The lost war discredited both the king and Nahas Pasha, leaving an opening for new leadership of some kind. In July 1952, the army staged a coup d'état that marked the beginning of the Egyptian revolution. Colonel Gamal 'Abd al-Nasser emerged as the most important leader in a movement that simultaneously opposed the monarchy, the old-regime politicians, and the continued British military presence in

Egypt and the Suez Canal zone, and one that promised social and economic justice for the Egyptian people.

The Nilotic Sudan was a further issue in Anglo-Egyptian relations until the mid-1950s. In 1898–9, when the British led the reconquest of Egypt's Sudanese empire from the Mahdi's successor, they had done so in Egypt's name and with many Egyptian troops. At the same time, the British government resisted the idea of recreating a secondary empire under sole Egyptian control. Its solution was to make the Sudan a condominium, theoretically shared between Egypt and Britain. In fact, the British were the dominant partner from the beginning to the end. They governed the Sudan more systematically than they governed Egypt, with a regular system of district administration, similar to that used in other parts of Africa. A special elite corps of administrative officers – the Sudan Service – was recruited for the purpose. They also carried policies of social and legal change further than they bothered to do in Egypt, bringing in English as the language of administration, and as the language of education in the southern Sudan, beyond the region of previous Muslim dominance. They introduced European codes of civil and criminal law as modified by previous experience in British India. After the mid-1920s, they began to introduce indirect rule through existing Sudanese authorities, by-passing some of the Egyptians who had been in charge. As a result, the Sudan and Egypt tended to grow apart rather than closer together. Many Egyptians saw the Sudan as a region for future colonization by excess Egyptian population, but a new generation of Sudanese looked with foreboding on the possible consequence of British withdrawal and Egyptian dominance. As a result, Sudanese independence was thrown into the hat along with other issues to be worked out between Egypt and Britain in the wake of the Egyptian revolution.

Africa in two world wars

By 1914–18, the main phase of colonial conquest in tropical Africa had finished, though the tail end remained to be completed in the 1920s and even the 1930s. African participation in the war was therefore inevitable. Africa was the most important region outside Europe where "German" and "Allied" territory had common frontiers. With command of the seas from the beginning of the war, the Allies had no practical difficulty walking over the Germans occupying Togo, Cameroon, or German South West Africa. Most of the fighting there, as in the original conquest of Africa, was done by African troops serving under European command. In addition, thousands of Africans were recruited in the French colonies to serve in France.

The most contested fighting in Africa was in the east, where the German governor of Tanganyika organized an African military force strong enough to tie down thousands of "European" South Africans, Indians, and East Africans nearly to the end of the war, fighting a long campaign of movement that reached southward into Mozambique and ended with his surrender in northern Zambia. In the process, Kenya alone lost tens of thousands of men forcibly recruited into the carrier corps – most of whom died of disease.

The Second World War was far more significant for Africa, because it served as an important catalyst in the liquidation of colonial rule, though in ways that were far from obvious at the time. The second war may, indeed, be seen as having begun in Africa long before it broke out in Europe – not with the German invasion of Poland in September 1939, but with the Italian invasion of Ethiopia in 1935. From one point of view, this campaign can be regarded as the last in the conquest of Africa, but it was different from the earlier scramble for Africa. It grew out of Italy's – and Mussolini's – position in Europe. Far from being a cheap little war, like the British conquest of northern Nigeria with less than 2000 African troops, the Italians deployed more than 120,000 Italian soldiers at the beginning of the campaign and would use nearly half a million Africans and Italians before it was finished. They also used air cover, poison gas, and other new tactics.

The main phase of the war was finished within a year, in spite of some continuing guerrilla resistance. Emperor Haile Selassie fled to England, to create what amounted to an unofficial government-in-exile until he could secure foreign help to regain his position – an option not available to African rulers at the height of the scramble. Help came in due course. In 1940, when Italy entered the European war on the side of Germany, the Italian forces in Ethiopia, Somalia, and Eritrea were cut off and caught between British, Indian, and African forces in the Sudan and Kenya. The result was a rapid and comparatively easy campaign leading to Haile Selassie's return in 1941, after only five years of Italian occupation.

The war in North Africa was more seriously contested. Italian control of Libya opened the way for a British diversionary attack westward from Egypt beginning late in 1940, just after the fall of France. In the Spring of 1941, however, German and Italian armies drove southeast through the Balkans and simultaneously pushed the British from Libya far back into Egypt. After a seesaw in the western desert, the British barely held at El Alamein in the early summer of 1942, with the Germans only seventy miles from Alexandria. By November, a seaborne Anglo-American force attacked Morocco and Algeria, and the Allies once more drove west from Egypt, meeting in Tunisia in May 1943 to complete their control of North Africa as a springboard for further advances on Sicily, Italy, and finally France.

While these battles in North Africa were essentially a sideshow, the Axis lost nearly a million men killed or captured there. The North African campaigns of 1943 were also the turning point in the European war in the west, but that merely highlights the fact that it *was* a European war, in which the Europeans did the bulk of the fighting over European issues, even though they fought on African soil. African troops participated, like those from British East Africa who helped secure Madagascar for the Free French, as they had earlier fought in Ethiopia. African troops also participated in the defense of India along the Burma frontier – and still later on in such colonial mopping-up operations as in the French reconquest of Indochina after the Japanese surrender.

But the main influence of the war on Africa came in other ways. People of the African colonies were required to make a substantial effort that included real sacrifices in living standards, conscription of young men, and the same range of wartime short-ages experienced elsewhere in those years. Out of this experience came a new sense of frustration with colonial rule. For some it also brought a broadening of horizons. The servicemen returning from distant theaters of war had a new and more intimate sense of what the rest of the world was like.

The seriousness of the wartime pressures brought a more realistic understanding of the power position of the colonial masters, especially in places like Morocco and Algeria where the fighting had actually taken place. The post-war move to independence on the part of Pakistan, India and Sri Lanka was another piece of evidence that the worldwide colonial regimes were neither monolithic nor unbeatable. The Second World War ended the high noon of colonialism in Africa. After that, pressures for independence were to increase and build on their earlier beginnings, while the colonial powers on their own began to move in new directions that were themselves a response to the new conditions of the post-war world. But these post-war conditions were not a result of the war alone. In Africa in particular, they had been formed over decades of fundamental change in the basic conditions of life.

Suggestions for further reading

Beinart, William and Bundy, Colin, *Hidden Struggles in Rural South Africa: Politics and Popular Movements in the Transkei and Eastern Cape 1890–1930*, Berkeley: University of California Press, 1987.

Berque, Jacques, *French North Africa: The Maghrib between Two World Wars*, London: Faber, 1967.

Boahen, A. Adu, *African Perspectives on Colonialism*, Baltimore: Johns Hopkins University Press, 1987.

Bourdieu, Pierre, *The Algerians*, Boston: Beacon Press, 1962.

Coquery-Vidrovitch, Catherine, *Africa: Endurance and Change South of the Sahara*, Berkeley, University of California Press, 1989.

Gann, L.H. and Duignan, Peter, *Colonialism in Africa, 1870–1960*, 5 vols, Cambridge: Cambridge University Press, 1969–72.

Gray, Richard, *The Two Nations*, London: Oxford University Press, 1960.

Harlow, Vincent, Chilver, E.M., and Smith, Alison (eds), *History of East Africa*, Vol. 2, Oxford: Clarendon Press, 1965.

Isaacman, Allen and Barbara, *Mozambique: From Colonialism to Revolution, 1900–62*, Boulder: Westview Press, 1983.

Kennedy, Dane, *Islands of White: Settler Society and Culture in Kenya and Southern Rhodesia, 1890–1939*, Durham: Duke University Press, 1987.

Marks, Shula, *The Ambiguities of Dependence in South Africa: Class, Nationalism, and the State in Twentieth-Century Natal*, Baltimore, Johns Hopkins University Press, 1986.

Marks, Shula and Rathbone, Richard (eds), *Industrialization and Social Change in South Africa*, London: Longman, 1982.

Marsot, Afaf Lutfi al-Sayyid, *A Short History of Modern Egypt*, Cambridge: Cambridge Press, 1985.

Mason, Philip, *The Birth of a Dilemma*, London: Oxford University Press, 1958.

Miers, Suzanne, and Roberts, Richard (eds), *The End of Slavery in Africa*, Madison: University of Wisconsin Press, 1989.

Mokgatle, Naboth, *The Autobiography of an Unknown South African*, London: Hurst, 1971.

Moodie, T. Dunbar, *The Rise of Afrikanerdom: Power Apartheid and the Afrikaner Civil Religion*, Berkeley: University of California Press, 1975.

Mphahlele, Ezekiel, *The African Image*, London: Faber, 1962.

Mphahlele, Ezekiel, *Down Second Avenue: Growing up in a South African Ghetto*, London: Faber, 1971.

Prochaska, David, *Making Algeria French: Colonialism in Bône, 1870–1920*, New York: Cambridge University Press, 1990.

Thompson, Leonard, *The Unification of South Africa 1902–10*, Oxford: Oxford University Press, Clarendon Press, 1960.

Vail, Leroy and White, Landeg, *Capitalism and Colonialism in Mozambique*, Minneapolis: University of Minnesota Press, 1980.

Vail, Leroy, and White, Landeg, *Understanding African Voices: Power, History, and Oral Literature in Southern Africa*, Charlottesville: University of Virginia Press, 1991.

White, Landeg, *Magomero: Portrait of an African Village*, Cambridge: Cambridge University Press, 1987.

17

THE COLONIAL ECONOMY

African economies had been changing long before the European impact. They continued to change during the colonial period, and much of the initiative for this change came from Africans themselves, each responding in his or her own way to the range of options they could invent or discover in the material and technological environment they inhabited. The colonial period also brought new conditions imposed from the outside. These new conditions were of two kinds. One was the direct result of colonial rule – the conditions imposed by the colonial state. The second kind was the consequence of Africa's increasing integration into a worldwide economic order. A world economy had existed even before the pre-colonial century, but the industrial age brought a far more intense web of interconnection for people everywhere. Africa felt that pull long before the colonial period began, and the influence of the world economy was to continue after the colonial period had ended.

Economic policies

Europeans tried to do many different things in Africa, but the range of things tried most frequently was narrow enough to permit generalization. All colonial governments had certain common points of view about economic policy, however much they differed in detail. One of these was the general expectation that African colonies should pay their own way, that they should have a balanced budget. This expectation may seem too obvious to mention, but it became important because most new colonies could *not* pay their own way. The Europeans insisted on imposing a bureaucratic superstructure on top of whatever government existed in pre-colonial times. They needed a modern military establishment to hold the country and to guard against rebellion. All this cost money, and colonial governments had to be concerned about those who would be asked to pay the cost. The European taxpayers could express their displeasure through the central government in Europe. African taxpayers lacked the constitutional outlet, but they could be driven, and sometimes were driven, to rebellion by excessive taxation. The colonial state had the power to suppress rebellions, but only at a cost far exceeding any additional tax yield involved.

The result was the nearly universal goal of economic development, which individual colonial administrators tried to achieve by making the best of local conditions. The kind of development they might plan depended on a number of crucial variables. One was the type of political control they had to work with – light administration and indirect rule as in Rwanda or northern Nigeria, more direct administration as in the Belgian Congo or French West Africa, a company regime as in the early decades in Rhodesia, or a parliamentary system with European overrule as in Egypt. Each kind of colonial administration implied a different decision-making process and a different set of possible outcomes, with different combinations of European and African interests at play.

Resource endowment was still another determinant of economic policy, especially in the light of changing technology. The economic demand that reached Africa changed with the world economy. In the early nineteenth century, new machines needed lubricating oils, and industrial workers needed soap, hence the new demand for fats and oils from the tropical world. Toward the end of the century, that demand led to the development of petroleum, among other substitutes, so that the tropical vegetable oils were no longer so important. But petroleum led to the internal combustion engine, and light engines made automobiles possible; automobiles, in turn, were in the background of a vast new demand for rubber from the 1890s onward. High rubber prices led to the ruthless exploitation of Central Africa through forced gathering, but they also led to more efficient rubber plantations. After 1913 or so, wild rubber virtually disappeared from world markets, which meant that Africa ceased for a time to be a source; and when African rubber revived, it was not until the 1920s and then mainly in Liberia, which in turn developed a deep dependence on that single crop and on the firm that introduced it.

The world market also wanted minerals from Africa, under conditions in which both demand and supply shifted with changing technology. Gold had been exported since the Middle Ages, but the past gold exports were mainly from placer deposits that were easily worked with pre-industrial technology. The vast South African gold deposits, the largest found anywhere at any time, were unknown to the outside world until the 1880s, but the technology for working them was also unknown until the nineteenth century. The quantity of gold in the South African fields was enormous, but it was found in hardrock veins that ran very deep, and the gold content per cubic meter of ore was comparatively low. To mine it at all required crushing and hoisting machinery, and to mine it profitably required a complex technology for underground hardrock mining and another for extracting the gold from the ore on the surface. Other important minerals had been known and worked for centuries – the gold of Zimbabwe or the copper of Shaba and Zambia, for example. African iron ore, on the other hand, was comparatively unimportant outside Algeria and South Africa until the very end of the colonial period. African bauxite deposits had no importance at all until aluminum technology developed between the two world wars.

Technology and resource endowment were intimately, if indirectly, related to a third crucial determinant of economic policy: the size and importance of the settler community in particular territories. European capital was invested where exploitable resources promised the most attractive returns. Settlers tended to follow capital investment in technologically complex enterprises. Egypt, for example, attracted very large investment – more than £11 sterling per capita by 1900 in the public sector alone, with nearly £8 sterling per capita added in the private sector between then and 1914. That was more investment per capita than anywhere else outside South Africa. But most of this investment went into transportation and irrigation works, which could be handled by Egyptians without large-scale immigration of skilled workers, and most foreign immigrants to Egypt went into commerce and services. Agriculture, however, attracted a larger proportion of European settlers to the Maghrib, East Africa, and the eastern Congo. But the tightest connection between European settlers and European capital was in the mineral production of southern Africa from the Witwatersrand north to Shaba and the Zambian copper belt. On the eve of the Second World War, outside per capita investment was estimated at £56 sterling per capita in South Africa, £38 in the two Rhodesias (Zimbabwe and Zambia), and £13 in the Belgian Congo, but not more than £10 anywhere else in tropical Africa. South Africa and Southern Rhodesia also attracted the largest number of settlers and endowed them with the largest measure of political power.

Racial dominance and economic growth in South Africa

South Africa was drawn into the fringes of industrialization faster than any other part of the continent. The economic impetus went back to the diamond discoveries of the 1870s, followed by Witwatersrand gold in the 1880s. Both minerals required very heavy capital investment. This meant an early concentration of ownership and management. By 1899, De Beers Consolidated Mines had amalgamated and concentrated the diamond industry and possessed a virtual world monopoly on diamond sales through a London syndicate. Gold mining came to be organized in a hierarchy of interrelated companies and through an industry-wide Chamber of Mines. Capital and technical personnel flowed in from Britain, continental Europe, and the United States. "European" farm owners in South Africa were drawn in as suppliers of food to the mining camps and cities. The Chamber of Mines organized the recruitment of unskilled African labor from all the colonial territories in southern Africa and Mozambique.

The Anglo-Boer War of 1899–1902 brought a temporary decline of mining, and it destroyed many farms, but recovery was well under way by 1914, and the First World War stimulated local manufacturing to replace distant sources of supply. A decade of relative stagnation followed in the late 1920s, but after 1933 southern Africa entered a period of economic growth that persisted with only minor setbacks to the mid-1970s. Although mining remained important, manufacturing became the sector with the most rapid growth. Manufactures exceeded the value of mineral products by the early 1950s.

After the Second World War, the source of capital investment was more diverse. Where Britain had once been dominant, the rest of the industrial world, including the United States and Japan, now played a larger part. This growth was remarkable, but it was unevenly distributed to a few industrial areas: the Witwatersrand, including Johannesburg and Pretoria; the main ports from Cape Town through Port Elizabeth and East London to Durban; and, more recently, the region of Salisbury in Rhodesia (now Harare in Zimbabwe). Most of the European farm managers were gradually pulled into the growth sector, with massive supports from their governments, but the rural areas of dense African population tended to become poorer, not richer. Whereas they had once been self-sufficient in food, with a peasantry that sold cash crops to the towns, most became deficit areas to which food had to be imported and paid for by the earnings of migrant labor in the mines, industry, or "European" agriculture. The unequal distribution of wealth in South Africa increased until, by the late 1960s, the Republic produced 90 per cent of the region's gross domestic product, Rhodesia produced 8 per cent, Namibia produced 2 per cent, and the three territories with African governments – Botswana, Lesotho, and Swaziland – jointly produced only about 1 per cent.

The product of economic growth was also distributed unevenly among the various racial groups, following a pattern that emerged at the beginning of the diamond and gold mining era. Skilled workers at first had to be attracted from abroad by wages competitive with those offered elsewhere in the industrialized world. Unskilled workers could be recruited in rural Africa to work for a year or so at a time before returning to their homes. They were paid low wages on the assumption that village agriculture provided the main support for their families, and most remained unskilled. The result was a two-tier labor system – one level of skill and remuneration for Europeans and another for Africans. In the course of time, as local "Europeans" acquired the necessary skills, the mining industry became less dependent on operatives from overseas. But the two-tier system persisted, and the pay differences increased rather than diminished. Europeans were allowed to organize unions for collective bargaining under the threat of a strike. Africans were excluded from "European" unions, from strike action, and from the bargaining process. The South African government also applied a so-called Civilized Labor Policy, reserving certain jobs for Europeans regardless of their ability, thus providing sheltered, high-wage employment for the least capable in that category.

Mining and industrial firms might try to reduce the number of highly paid European employees and increase that of Africans, upgrading the level of their skills, but the political power of the European workers always loomed in the background. A series of confrontations occurred, culminating in a serious European miners' strike in 1922 that had enduring consequences. The strike turned violent, and the government called in the army to suppress it, at the cost of two hundred and thirty lives. The suppression of the "Rand Rebellion," as it was called, was a short-term victory for the Chamber of Mines, but the mine owners never again tried to break the two-tier labor system. The power of the European working class was also underlined at the next election, and its privileged position became an accepted reality of South African political life. In 1935, the average cash wages paid each European miner were eleven times the wages paid the average African miner. By 1960, the difference had increased to sixteen times, and the Europeans also received far more in fringe benefits than the African miners did. Even in industry and the building trades, the differential was five to one.

The "European" South Africans, in short, derived immense material benefit from urbanization and industrialization – as industrial and commercial managers, bureaucrats, skilled workers, and capitalist farmers. Indeed, by the 1960s, their standard of living was among the highest in the world. By contrast, poverty prevailed among the

Africans, including those who lived in the three countries under British rule. The lands left to them became overpopulated and remained undeveloped areas, often in the condition of rural slums. Many if not most adults – especially men – were obliged to leave the reserves temporarily or permanently to work for "European" farmers or urban employers on conditions over which they had scarcely any control. Data permitting a full picture are not available, but rough estimates for 1954 put the average family income of Coloured and Indians at about 19 per cent that of Europeans, of urban Africans at 13 per cent, of African farm workers at 7 per cent, and of Africans on the reserves at 6 per cent. "Europeans" generally enjoyed excellent nutrition and medical services; kwashiorkor and other deficiency diseases were widespread among Africans.

African agriculture and colonial planning

Agriculture was the main activity for most of Africa, and economic development meant agricultural development, which implied new crops and new techniques to increase total yields. But total yield meant one thing to African farmers and another to colonial administrators. Africans were likely to look at that part of the total production they were allowed to keep for their own use. Planners were likely to look only at the increased yields that could be channeled into exports, because exports alone built up the foreign trade balances they needed to pay the external costs of running the colony. Foreign balances were also needed to pay for imports, and import duties were the easiest forms of taxation to collect.

By the First World War, planners had already come to think in terms of two alternate models for agricultural change. One was to count on the individual African farmer's response to the price offered on the market for his produce. The second was to take land from the Africans, bring in European managers, and set up plantations using African labor.

Most colonial administrators thought that peasant agriculture was safer but less likely to produce striking increases in yield. Planners saw the peasants as backward, conservative people who were fearful of abandoning the methods of their forefathers. Recent studies in agricultural history, however, tend to show that African farmers were not unthinking traditionalists. Their knowledge of local conditions and suitable techniques was often far better than that of the European "experts" who came to give them advice about what to plant and how to take care of it. They were usually willing to change, even anxious to change, if they could see the possibility of substantial profit at small risk. They were unwilling, however, to divert their efforts when future yields and prices were uncertain. They sometimes lacked the technical knowledge needed for new crops, and they almost always lacked capital for major investment in tractors, fertilizers, irrigation works, or even for a small-scale investment in, say, the planting of tree crops that would not yield for a period of years. Plantations under European control seemed more likely to yield exportable produce, but they involved a greater disruption of African society, creating predictable social and political problems. It was also hard to find capitalists willing to risk investment in a new enterprise.

In any event, planners made decisions for or against peasant production, for or against plantation or settler agriculture, often with less care than was called for.

Sometimes the decision was not even conscious but was simply made by default, but decision-making was consistent enough to create a degree of uniformity across large regions regardless of colonial boundaries. Throughout West Africa other than Liberia, the final outcome favored peasant agriculture in African hands. European government investment was generally limited to infrastructure like roads, railroads, and port works. Private investment was largely by commercial firms dominating the export of the final product and the import of European goods. This West African pattern grew partly from the fact that Europeans had been trading in West Africa for centuries in goods that the Africans produced and delivered to them for export. Africans had shown themselves willing and able to respond to reasonable price incentives, so the precedent held.

West African officials had adopted "Indirect Rule" as a relatively cheap way of governing. Land alienation on a large scale would have compromised the chiefs' power to govern for Britain. The most important direct confrontation came in 1907, when the Lever soap interests began asking for a palm oil plantation concession somewhere in British West Africa. The British government turned down the request, largely from political and social considerations. As a result, Lever applied to Belgium, organized a subsidiary, the Huileries du Congo Belge, and got a concession of 1.9 million acres in 1911. Measured against exportable product, the Belgians may have been right. Between 1909 and 1936, Congolese palm oil production increased tenfold, while Nigerian production merely doubled. But the British decision was not based on the predicted exportable product alone.

In French West Africa, the dominant outcome was peasant production, even though the government leaned toward plantations a good deal of the time. Part of the problem was to make land available to European capitalists without doing great injustice to its African owners. The problem was further complicated by shifting cultivation. Land cropped for a few years would be allowed to grow up as bush to regain its fertility. The land most often belonged to a lineage or a village, which then assigned it to households for temporary use. French officials tried the device of registering all land under individual ownership, so that African farmers might be persuaded to sell their share to a plantation; but the scheme failed.

For a time after 1935, the French West African government turned more actively to a policy favoring plantation agriculture. A few hundred thousand acres in French Guinea, Dahomey, and the Côte d'Ivoire were granted to Europeans in the late 1930s, but most of these concessions were unused and had lapsed by the time of independence. The most acceptable explanation for this outcome seems to be that plantations might have been successful had the government been willing to intervene really decisively against African interests in favor of the European planters. But that intervention would have required forced labor as well as expropriation of the best African-held land, and the colonial government was not willing to go that far. Without that intervention, plantations could not compete with African peasant agriculture.

Plantations did become competitive, however, in large parts of East, Central, and southern Africa, where decisive government intervention favored the European planting class. In Kenya, Rhodesia, and parts of Kivu Province in the Belgian Congo, as well as in South Africa, large tracts of the best land were taken from the Africans and reserved for European management and ownership. In Kenya, the result was the "white highlands" policy, by which some 16,000 square miles were reserved for cultivation by European managers on long leases. It was the government intention that European-managed farms should produce most of the export crops, while smaller and less heavily capitalized African farms would produce food for local consumption. Certain crops, like coffee, were reserved by law to farms under European ownership. As a result, by the early 1950s, "European" production accounted for 95 per cent of Kenya's agricultural exports, though it constituted only about a third of total farm production.

In Rhodesia and South Africa, the territorial division into African and European sectors went even further. The South African Land Act of 1913 was crucial in creating the pattern that persisted thereafter. It divided the whole country between the "Native Reserves," where land could only be owned by Africans, and the rest of the country, where it could only be owned by people classified as "White" (except for a few places where Coloureds or Asians could own land). In theory, Africans could move into the "White" areas only as temporary sojourners, never as permanent residents. This theory was supported by rigorous pass laws, which governed the legal right of non-Whites to move freely about the country. The 1913 Act and its successors set aside nearly 88 per cent of the land in South Africa for only 20 per cent of the people. Some "European" South Africans actually worked their own farms, but most of the work on "European" farms was done by Africans – an increasing proportion as time went on. By 1951, some 30 per cent of the African population actually lived and worked on European farms. By the 1960s, Africans outnumbered the Europeans on "European" farms by a ratio of ten to one. But the fact of ownership reserved by law gave the European farmers an immense advantage. Their per capita annual income was many times that of their African employees. The combination of the best land, the best agricultural education, and the best access to capital meant that European farmers were also the most productive. By the mid-1950s, European farms produced 98 per cent of South Africa's marketed wheat, 92 per cent of the marketed maize, and 96 per cent of the marketed wool.

The agricultural pattern of the Maghrib was similar. Some of the nineteenth-century settlers from Europe had been farmers who worked their own land, but in the interwar years the Europeans tended to manage larger and larger units. In 1914, for example, 6 per cent of the active agricultural population in Algeria were European settlers or their descendants; by 1930, the figure had dropped to 3 per cent, though Europeans were more than 10 per cent of the whole population. By 1934, the 26,000 European landowners held an average of more than two hundred acres each, while more than 400,000 Algerian landowners held an average of only forty-three acres each.

In the Maghrib as in South Africa, the combination of capital, technical knowledge, and the best land produced high yields on European-managed farms, and low yields where the Africans farmed their own land. Tunisian wheat yields in the early 1950s were three times as high on "European" as on African farms. In Algeria on the eve of the war of independence, European farmers produced 66 per cent of all wheat, virtually all wine, and 84 per cent of the olive products. As in South Africa, an inordinate share of the gross territorial product was diverted to the European settlers.

One alternative kind of agricultural planning was to combine high capitalization and technical assistance while leaving African farmers in charge of their own land, not simply as day laborers working for a favored community of foreign origin. To do this required government initiative and capital, but it could be attractive where large irrigation projects called for government capital in any case.

One of the projects regarded as most successful in interwar Africa was the Gezira scheme in the Sudan south of Khartoum, between the Blue and White Niles. It began in 1925 with a dam across the Blue Nile at Sennar. Land lower down could then be irrigated by gravity flow through a series of canals. Rather than simply expropriating the land, the government gave each of the original owners a long-term lease. It then redistributed the land, often to the original owners, in blocs of about forty acres. Each new tenant was instructed in cotton growing and required to plant about a quarter of his holding in cotton. The rest could go into food, fallow, or fodder for animals, as the tenant might choose. During the colonial period, the government allowed a private syndicate to take charge of transportation, ginning, and marketing. When the cotton was exported, the proceeds were divided so that the government got 40 per cent to pay for the land, irrigation works, and supervision, the tenant got 40 per cent, and the syndicate got 20 per cent. The tenant also retained full rights to dispose of the product from the other three-quarters of his holding as he saw fit.

The scheme seemed to be a success from the start. Extensions brought the total irrigated area to a half million acres by 1929 and to more than a million acres after the Second World War. At the time of independence in 1955, it supported a half million people and provided nearly half the total value of Sudanese exports. The Sudan paid a price, however, in undue dependence on a single export commodity, just as Egypt did. Recent critics have suggested that the flow of gross domestic product was unfair, and the high level of planning distorted the economy that might have developed more equitably under a market-based system.

Other irrigation schemes of this type were less successful. The French took the Gezira as a model for a similar project in the French Sudan (now Mali). The original project of 1932 called for dams to irrigate some 400,000 acres, or about the area of the existing Gezira project. Tenants on previously uncultivated land were to grow cotton, and rice as a food crop. The French government set up the Office du Niger, a public enterprise, to build the dams and irrigation canals. By the time of Malian independence in 1962, however, only 18,000 acres were actually irrigated and settled by some 37,000 people. In contrast to the Gezira's comparative success, the Office du Niger could not even repay the cost of the original public investment, and individual settlers were often unhappy with the way in which their lives and work were administered.

Agricultural change on African initiative

Senegambia peanuts, Gold Coast cocoa

In spite of directed development schemes, settler and plantation agriculture, African farmers did most of the work and made most of the decisions about African agriculture and herding, even though they might not dominate the export sector. The most important aspect of agricultural change in the colonial period was therefore the piecemeal adjustments made by individual farmers in response to the opportunities they could discover and use. These changes are often hard to trace, because European observers often paid little attention to what people produced for their own consumption or for local markets. Shifts in local production and consumption could often be of the greatest importance – like the spread of maize and manioc throughout tropical Africa, a shift that was still going on in the colonial period, though it had started in the sixteenth century. The end result was a basic and permanent change in Africa's capacity to support its human population.

Some crops that were later to be exported began as food crops for African consumption, even though they may have originated outside Africa. Peanuts are an important example. The first peanuts came from America to West Africa in the seventeenth century, perhaps even earlier. By the early eighteenth, they were cultivated in the northern belt of the savanna from the Atlantic eastward into present-day Mali. By the nineteenth century or earlier, they reached northern Nigeria as well.

In the nineteenth century, Africans began to export peanuts. We have already seen how this change influenced the religious revolutions in Senegambia. In the 1830s, merchants in the Senegambian trading posts discovered that peanuts could be sold in Europe. Production for export began to spread seriously in the 1840s, with France as the most important market overseas. The first regions to develop were northern Kajoor and Waalo (where camels brought down from Mauritania provided comparatively cheap transportation to the ports), and to the banks of the Gambia and Saalum rivers, where efficient river transportation had existed for centuries. Gambian peanut exports rose to 10,000 metric tons a year in the early 1850s, then more slowly to a range of 15,000 to 20,000 metric tons annually in the final quarter of the nineteenth century.

This new activity called for the reorganization of productive resources. In the Senegambian peanut belt lots of land was available, but labor was not. Many Africans responded by moving to take advantage of the new opportunities. Some men, and sometimes whole families moved as much as three or four hundred miles through a dozen political jurisdictions to take up land near the Gambia. Here the workers hired land from the local lineage heads, sometimes paying in labor. They then planted part of the land in peanuts and part in millet, maize, or some other food crop that would carry them through the coming year. These "strange farmers," as they are called in Gambian English, sold the crop at the end of the season and bought an assortment of imported goods for resale on their return home. Their annual pattern of activity thus began with seasonal work in agriculture, from which they earned capital for investment in a single venture in long-distance trade, over routes that could take as long as a month to travel in either direction. As early as 1848, most of the peanuts exported from the Gambia were grown by strange farmers from the interior, though local people who were not landlords also profited from river shipping and bulking the peanuts for sale to the large French firms that came to dominate final export to Europe.

Peanut production in Senegal rose at first a little more slowly than it did on the Gambia, probably because the Senegal River flowed north of the best peanut land, which meant that camel caravans were needed to move the crop to the river ports or to the coast at Dakar, Rufisque, or Saint Louis. Then, in the 1870s, the government of Senegal built a railroad from Dakar to Saint Louis at the mouth of the river, passing through some of the best peanut-growing territory in the kingdom of Kajoor – even though Kajoor was still independent. The railroad was a financial failure and had to be subsidized by the French government, but peanut production boomed, reaching 140,000 metric tons exported through French-controlled ports.

In the 1890s, Senegalese peanut farming entered a new phase, as African farmers began moving eastward into parts of Kajoor and Jolof, where Fulbe herdsmen had once been the only occupants, and then only seasonally. Some of this movement took place on the individual initiative of pioneer families, but, after 1912, the Murīdiya, a religious brotherhood, entered the picture. This new brotherhood was an offshoot of the Qadiriya. The founder was Amadu Bamba, whose father had been associated with Ma Ba and other jihad leaders of the 1860s and 1870s. The leaders of the new order insisted that each individual submit completely to the authority of his shaykh – that is, to the authority of one of the clerical leaders, who represented in turn the supreme authority of the Amadu Bamba and his successors. One acceptable form of submission was to join a *dara*, or farming group, in effect an economic unit that worked the shaykh's land. These dara became the units of agricultural colonization pushing eastward into new land.

In the early colonial period, the French suspected the Mourids of "religious fanaticism," but they changed their opinion after 1912, and Mourid leaders rose to positions of great political power in colonial and independent Senegal. On the eve of independence, Mourids made up about 20 per cent of the Senegalese population, and the brotherhood controlled about a quarter of Senegal's peanut production. Less fortunately, its agricultural colonization was too intensive for the marginal land it brought under cultivation. Much of it suffered so severely, that it may never recover the fertility it had under wiser use before the 1920s.

Gold Coast cocoa was also notable as an export crop developed largely through African initiative. That crop also came originally from America, but it was suited to the forest zone, not the savanna. In recent years, the West African forests from the Côte d'Ivoire through Ghana and western Nigeria have accounted for about two-thirds of world cocoa production. Cocoa was first introduced as a plantation crop to the offshore island of Bioko (Fernando Po). Seeds may have reached the Gold Coast forest at several different times, but one introduction took place in 1879 by a contract laborer who returned from Fernando Po to the forested Akwapim ridge in the hinterland of Accra. Gold Coast cocoa was first exported in 1891, and the total reached five hundred metric tons by 1900. By 1911, cocoa exports reached 40,000 tons and for the next half-century the Gold Coast was the largest single cocoa producer in the world.

The speed of this development was impressive, and it reflects the organizing activity of African entrepreneurs, at first mainly from the Akwapim ridge. They began with small plots of three to six acres on the ridge itself. Because cocoa trees need shade, cocoa could be underplanted in forest conditions, leaving large trees standing. Suitable land on the ridge soon ran out, and farmers from Akwapim then began to buy or rent land in the lightly inhabited forest country to the west. Most societies on the ridge were accustomed to individual land ownership but most forest societies further west vested control in the lineage head, who could, however, sell land. One problem for the cocoa entrepreneurs was to get together enough money to purchase a tract as a single transaction. They met this problem by forming buying cooperatives, which could make large purchases and then subdivide among the individual members. Before 1914, in the single state of Akim Abuakwa, some eight hundred square miles were sold off to strangers to be turned into cocoa farms.

As the movement continued into the 1920s, others joined in – Fante from the coast, Krobo, Shai, and Ewe from the northeast. Entrepreneurs in southern Ghana used the profits from one farm to recover enough capital to make a second purchase, usually at a distance, as the frontier of cocoa planting moved west and north. In this way, the individual farmer might find himself with three or four plots scattered across the southern Gold Coast. In Asante, chiefs were less willing to sell off their forest land, but Asante farmers went into cocoa planting independently, often using capital from the rubber boom that ended about 1913.

Others came into the cocoa industry as middlemen, buying from the farmers, bulking, and reselling to other traders or directly to the European export firms. Still others used the proceeds from cocoa farming to invest in other sectors of the economy, most significantly in their children's education, so that Akwapim became famous for its many privately supported schools and its contribution of Western-educated people to the government service and the professions.

The intensity of cocoa development soon caused a labor shortage, especially at harvest time during the dry season. Since that was a period of underemployment in the savanna country, young men began to move south for seasonal work – at first from northern Ghana but then from Upper Volta (now Burkina Faso) and other French colonies. By the end of the 1950s, as many as 320,000 non-Ghanaian migrants were crossing the frontier each year. The new agriculture not only moved cocoa farmers out of their relatively isolated ethnic homelands; it also moved immigrants over hundreds of miles into a new socioeconomic setting on a larger scale than that of any pre-colonial society. This increase in scale, in Ghana and elsewhere, could work at least two ways. In some circumstances, it helped to create a sense of solidarity in the new nations that emerged after independence; a person could begin to think of himself or herself as a Ghanaian as well as an Asante. At the same time, as people encountered others who were linguistically and culturally different, new ethnic rivalries emerged in the towns and mining camps, rivalries that had no roots in the distant past.

Ghanaian enterprise in the cocoa industry was unusual in its individual or small-group initiative, free of pressure from the colonial state and the traditional chiefs alike. In the longer run, however, the cocoa farmers were to work with the chiefs for political and economic ends, especially in 1937–8, when they withheld their cocoa from the market and broke an attempt of European firms to fix prices. The early development of the industry had local initiative, new leadership, and voluntary cooperation. The farmers worked together to buy land and to build access trails and bridges – often organized through new agencies like the Christian churches.

Uganda cotton

In other countries, the initiative came from the top down. Cotton growing in Uganda is a useful example. The political background was the Christian revolution in Buganda in the 1880s and 1890s. The victors signed a formal treaty with Britain – the Uganda Agreement of 1900. Its terms covered Buganda only, but it set a precedent for the neighboring provinces of Bunyoro and Busoga as well. The crucial fact was that important chiefs emerged with political authority that allowed them to mediate between the British officials and the individual peasants.

The impact of the world economy reached Uganda suddenly in 1901, when the railroad from Mombasa reached Kisumu on Lake Victoria. Up to that time, head-loading from the coast to Lake Victoria to the coast had cost an estimated £200 sterling per ton; while the railroad charged only £2.40 per ton. Unlike the Gold Coast, where peasants had operated for centuries on the fringes of the world market, the Ganda peasants were not accustomed to the broader market forces. The British government was anxious to generate traffic for its expensive railroad; the colonial government was anxious to have an export crop so as to create taxable income. The British Cotton Growing Association was anxious to promote cotton growing in the British Empire so as to cut dependence on foreign sources. Even the missionaries played a role through The Uganda Company, Ltd, which was partly a commercial firm eager to make a profit from ginning and shipping cotton, though it also had financial connections to the Church Missionary Society, the most active of the Protestant missions.

The government, the association, the company, and the missions all went to work together. The association provided seeds and technical advice and set up central cotton gins to prepare the crop for shipment. The Uganda Company, the government, and the missions enlisted the help of the chiefs (who were the main legal landlords in the province of Buganda). The chiefs distributed seed to their tenants and made sure that it was planted and harvested according to instructions. This more-or-less involuntary first cultivation proved its economic and agricultural feasibility, and other farmers took it up on their own initiative. The Uganda Company, for its part, helped export a crop that rose in value from £43,000 in 1903–4 to £307,000 in 1910–11. By then, it already amounted to more than half of Uganda's total exports; by the early years of the First World War, it reached 70 per cent.

Concentrated cash-crop production drew migrant labor into Buganda province from other parts of the protectorate even before 1914. During the interwar years, the flow increased, with thousands walking across colonial frontiers from Rwanda, Burundi, western Tanganyika, and Kenya. By 1946, the estimated annual flow of migrants had reached 140,000 from Rwanda and Burundi alone. Many of these migrants came for a season only, but others began to settle down for a period of years. They learned Luganda, assimilated Ganda culture – and the second generation were more Ganda than not. The socio-economic consequences of migration also spread back to the source. In positive ways, Rwanda and Burundi were relieved of overcrowding and starvation in time of famine. Migration also had less favorable consequences, leaving families without husbands, to subsist, if they could, on remittances and sub-marginal agriculture.

The social consequences in Uganda were also important, and quite different from those that followed cocoa or peanuts in West Africa. In the Gold Coast for example, African initiative not only sparked the cocoa industry from the beginning; African entrepreneurs also appeared in specialized activities like commercial seed production and commerce – in many branches, from cocoa buying to distribution and retailing of imports from abroad, to trucking migrant workers from the north. In Uganda, the main African initiative came from the chiefly class, but the chiefs were usually administrators and they stayed in administration. The peasantry grew the cotton, but they remained cotton growers; Europeans stepped in as the main operators of ginneries. East Indians in large numbers entered retail trade, buying cotton and other export crops and supplying imported commodities to the countryside.

One result was that Indians came to dominate petty commerce, and ordinary Ugandans developed a deep resentment. This resentment was one root of the expulsion in 1971 of some 80,000 Indians who carried British passports, and the result was an economic disaster because skilled Africans were not available to fill the gap and to maintain the flow of agricultural exports and retail trade. The pattern of agricultural development in Uganda may well have been all too paternalistic. Peasants learned to respond, but only to incentives laid out for them by others. With the move toward independence, able and intelligent Africans were attracted into the government service rather than to trade, so that African paternalism replaced colonial paternalism; and the country missed the healthy play of individual initiative found in West Africa.

Foreign investment and African economic growth

Most economists looking back to the colonial period agree that a principal brake on African economic development was a lack of capital investment. Some capital might have been generated within Africa by appropriate government policy, but the main problem was lack of capital from overseas. Colonial governments did put some money into infrastructure like roads and ports, even a little into agricultural schemes like the Gezira project, but the overall rate of investment was low. Private investment from overseas was especially weak. Up to the Second World War total foreign investment in sub-Saharan Africa has been estimated at about £6 billion at current prices, half of it government and half private. The bulk of private investment was in minerals and mineral-associated industry, heavily concentrated in the south. Private foreign investment in agriculture was also concentrated in the far south and in North Africa.

In the post-war decades, the annual rate of foreign investment increased to several times the pre-war rate, but private investment continued at less than half the total. With the approach of independence and on into the early 1960s, aid from overseas in the form of free gifts or loans at low rates of interest became increasingly important. In the peak year, 1964, it reached more than one billion dollars from western Europe and North America alone, but total aid then declined in the late 1960s and on into the post-colonial decades.

Throughout the colonial period, foreign investors, both private and public, placed their funds overwhelmingly in the export sector. The result was lopsided economic development centered on foreign trade. Part of the cause was government interest in viable export crops or mineral production, but European officials and investors also looked at Africa from a Europe-centered point of view. They knew about European economic demand, but not about the African economy. They therefore placed investment to meet the demand they knew, for wine from Algeria or cotton from Egypt, for example. In theory, capitalist investment should have been placed so as to give the investors the greatest possible return on their money, but they rarely thought of investing in enterprise that served local needs. Thinking instead of European needs, private and public investors alike acted to maximize the security and productivity of the home economy in Europe, rarely to maximize the productivity of the colonial economy, or even to maximize the return on private capital invested overseas. The exception was South Africa, where the inordinate incomes of the European caste helped provide a substantial local market and a local source of capital.

The growth of cotton production in Ubangi-Shari (now the Central African Republic) between the wars is a telling example of uneconomic investment and uneconomic development. Given the colony's great distance from the sea, it might have been economically rational to encourage small-scale industry, drawing on local raw materials and then selling the manufactured product in a local market – like small textile factories using local cotton to make cloth. The French administration decided instead to push cotton as an export crop. Cotton could be grown in Ubangi-Shari, but the crop had to be carried overland to the Ubangi River, down the Ubangi and Congo to Stanley Pool, then by rail to Pointe Noire, and finally by sea to France. Transportation and handling costs were so high that the peasants received only a small fraction of the price paid in France – such a small fraction, in fact, that planting cotton was not worth their while. The colonial government therefore resorted to forced cultivation; each farmer in certain designated regions was required by law to plant a certain area in cotton (about one acre in the 1950s). Forcing the farmers to grow uneconomic crops was expensive for the government, which had to set up whole echelons of sub-administrators whose job it was to enforce the law at the local level. That too was uneconomic. Successive governments appealed to European enterprise to help with ginning, bulking, and transportation to the coast, but they ended by subsidizing cotton-buying companies, subsidizing river and rail transportation, and paying very heavily indeed to suppress a serious rebellion in the late 1920s – a rebellion that was directly traceable to African resentment over forced labor and forced cultivation.

But the plan succeeded after a fashion. By the late 1950s, French Equatorial Africa (including Ubangi-Shari) produced about 10 per cent of the cotton fiber used in France, which was 80 per cent of the cotton reaching France from its overseas empire. By that time, cotton export could pay its own way, but only after having warped the economy toward a form of production that was, for several decades, unprofitable to the peasants, unprofitable to the colonial government, unprofitable to French cotton-buying firms, and probably unprofitable to the French metropolitan government as well.

European investment tended to produce lopsided African economies in another way as well. Wherever European capital was invested, it tended to bring in the latest European technology. This occurred in the new mines of the Witwatersrand of the 1890s, in Katanga in the 1920s, and in the Orange Free State goldfields in the 1950s. It was also the case with agricultural investment in the Maghrib, South Africa, and the settler areas in between. Highly capitalized and technologically advanced enterprises could produce for the world market, but they became one advanced sector in economies that were otherwise far less advanced. As a result, resources and manpower were pulled into the advanced sector, while the less advanced remained technologically backward, starved for capital and government attention.

This tendency was reinforced by the colonial governments' emphasis on production for export. The fact that half the foreign investment in sub-Saharan Africa was government investment was a major factor. Governments are more free of market constraints than private capitalists are. A government could choose to place its investment so as to favor local production for a local market and the long-term goal of maximum gross territorial product. Or, it could go instead for ports, railways, and other facilities to clear the way for exports to the coast and on to Europe.

The continent's general web of transportation and communication facilities was so distorted at the end of the colonial period that a telegram from one colony to its neighbor, only a few hundred miles away, often had to go by way of Europe. Even if private investors had the information to make possible a careful selection of the most profitable forms of investment for local sale, prior government investment had already set the boundaries of what was and was not profitable. By investing in the export-centered infrastructure, governments attracted what little private investment came to Africa into the same sector. Government investment, in short, was often placed with a mind to other goals than maximizing local productivity, and that fact alone could guide the private sector into an emphasis that was not necessarily the most conducive to long-term economic growth. This was especially true of rail lines; those planned and built in early colonial times did a lot to mold the forms and direction of economic development in the decades to come.

Railroads

Africa was a continent badly suited to the early development of a dense railroad network. Population was sparse through most of the savanna country; centers of agricultural production were scattered; and agricultural exports were often seasonal, creating a peak load for a few months but leaving the railroads under-used during the remainder of the year. As a result, most investment in railroads for tropical Africa was unprofitable. Only South Africa developed a linked system comparable to those of Europe or North America, though the French government in the Maghrib built a rudimentary network. The Anglo-Egyptian Sudan and Nigeria also achieved more railroad development than the rest of tropical Africa. In general, however, profitable railroads were those that served the major centers of mineral extraction from Katanga southward. Elsewhere in tropical Africa, railroads were either built with the government's clear understanding that it was subsidizing other forms of development, or were started by private investors who hoped to make a profit but failed. The railroad then ended with some form of government subsidy or outright government ownership.

In East Africa, the unprofitability of railroad construction was recognized in advance, but the Uganda Railway built from Mombasa on the Kenya coast to Lake Victoria between 1895 and 1902 is a classic early example of railroad building for political ends – that nevertheless brought important economic consequences in its wake. (And the neighboring line from Dar-es-Salaam to Lake Tanganyika in German East Africa was built with similar motives and results.) The Uganda Railway grew out

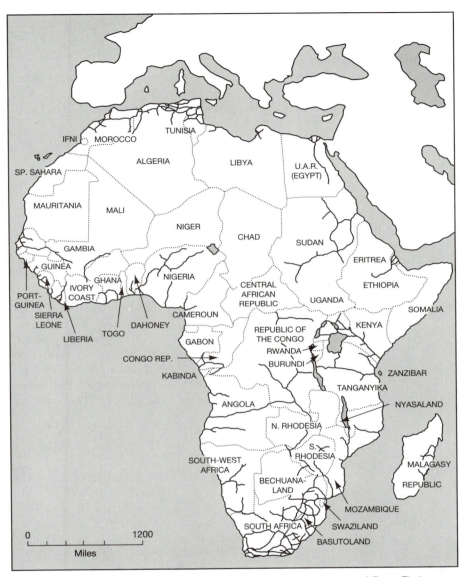

Map 17.1 Railroads of Africa 1960 (based on L.H. Gann and Peter Duignan, *Colonialism in Africa*, Cambridge: Cambridge University Press, 1975)

of the larger strategy of the scramble for Africa. Britain was already in Egypt and concerned about the fate of the Nilotic Sudan. It seemed important to control the outlet of the Nile from Lake Victoria, rather than to let the territory that was to be Uganda fall to Germany or the Congo Independent State. Because no existing traffic could justify the investment, and the colonial governments lacked the resources to build a railroad on their own, construction required a separate act of the British Parliament. This was an open and conscious subsidy paid for by the British taxpayers and justified to them as a way of combating the slave trade and of cutting the costs of administering Uganda so far from the coast.

Once the line was built, however, the colonial governments of Kenya and Uganda were anxious to reduce their operating losses by trying to shape economic development so as to create traffic. Because the railroad passed through the relatively cool and well-watered highlands, it was natural to think of agricultural development, and the "white highlands" policy followed as an indirect result of railroad construction for humanitarian and political ends. Further inland, in Uganda, the railroad was the obvious incentive that sparked government sponsorship of cotton cultivation. Indirectly, then, the rail line was an important factor both in creating a settler problem in Kenya and in setting the stage for the paternalistic character of economic development in Uganda.

Most rail lines had political objectives, and all had political consequences. Many were built to link a particular hinterland to a particular port, usually within the framework of a single colonial territory. The transportation systems thus created a physical reality that gave meaning to the colonial boundaries, however accidental their creation may have been during the scramble. In the French West African territories, feeder lines of this kind brought exportable goods to Dakar from Senegal and the French Sudan, to Conakry from French Guinea, to Abidjan from the Côte d'Ivoire and Upper Volta, to Lomé from Togo, and to Cotonou from Dahomey. But these lines were never joined up to create a French West African rail network. By contrast, Nigeria, the other colonial federation in West Africa, built a rail network that served the northern hinterland through Lagos in the west and Port Harcourt in the east. This rail network helped to tie the north to the two southern regions and to create inter-regional interchange during the crucial decades of the colonial period. This history of intercommunication in Nigeria was one factor that helped to keep Nigeria a single country in spite of the attempted secession of Biafra during the years 1967–72. French West Africa's lack of unified rail infrastructure was a partial background for its breakup at the time of independence.

The French also tried and failed to link up their other federation of Equatorial Africa. It was no easy task. The closest rail link to the savanna country in central Chad was over Nigerian railroads or those of the Anglo-Egyptian Sudan. Exports from Ubangi-Shari could have reached the sea most easily through Cameroon, but Cameroonian railroads reached only a short way inland from the port at Douala. French colonial planners chose instead the river route. The navigable course of the Congo and Ubangi rivers gave a clear run from near Bangui southward to Brazzaville on Stanley Pool. The rapids below the Pool required overland transportation to the Congo estuary, but the Congo Independent State filled that gap during the 1890s with a railway from Matadi to the southern shore of the Pool at Leopoldville (later Kinshasa). At first, that railroad carried goods for the French colonies as well, but in 1914 the French decided to build a separate line from the Pool to the coast through French territory.

The result was the Congo–Océan railroad, only three hundred and seventeen miles long but one of the most notorious errors of the colonial era. It was prompted by

French national pride and strategic considerations, but it was completely unjustifiable on economic grounds. Construction began only in 1921, and the line was not completed until 1934. Meanwhile, the Belgians across the river rebuilt the line from Matadi to Kinshasa, increasing its capacity tenfold by 1930; it could easily have accommodated the traffic of French Equatorial Africa as well as that of the Belgian Congo.

The Congo–Océan also posed construction problems. It ran through a thinly populated region, which meant that workers had to be recruited elsewhere; and they were recruited by force from all parts of French Equatorial Africa. By the time the line was finished, some 127,000 individuals had worked on it for at least a short period – more than 1 per cent of the male population of the whole federation. Many of these men came from the savanna country in Chad and Ubangi-Shari. They were therefore unprepared for the diseases they encountered in the forested Mayombe highlands the railroad had to cross. They were also underfed and ill-housed. As a result, the overall death rate reached 100 per thousand per annum, and as high as 240 per thousand at the peak of mortality – a total of forty-five dead for each mile of narrow-gauge track.

Even after it was finished, the Congo–Océan ran at a loss, and the loss, like the cost of construction, was charged to the colonial governments. It was therefore passed on as a tax burden falling most heavily on the same peasants whose fathers and grandfathers had built the line. Government regulations forced as much traffic as possible to pass down the all-French route by river and rail. Peanuts from Chad and cotton from Ubangi-Shari were sold at the world market price, and the high-cost transportation to the sea meant that peasants in Chad and Ubangi-Shari received less than they might have done if the crop had passed through Nigeria, Sudan, or the Belgian Congo.

The interplay of politics and economics worked somewhat differently in southern Africa. Railroad building there was economically feasible, as it rarely was in tropical Africa, but railroad politics tended to reinforce the rivalries of port towns, with each trying to secure or extend its economic domination over its hinterland. In the 1870s (after the diamond fields had opened at Kimberley) Cape Town, Port Elizabeth, East London, and Durban all began railroads aimed at extending their reach to the new mining area. After gold was discovered on the Witwatersrand, these same lines were extended toward Johannesburg, but the Transvaal was concerned about its own strategic position, if all access to the sea ran through the British colonies. It preferred to work out its own rail link to Lorenço Marques in Mozambique, which was incidentally the shortest route to salt water.

Railroad promoters in Cape Town were already extending the railroad from Kimberley northward, passing west of the Transvaal through Botswana and on into Rhodesia, until it finally reached the Zambian copper belt in 1909 and ultimately tied in to the Belgian system serving Katanga. (It was, incidentally, from a base on this rail line that Cecil Rhodes organized the Jameson raid into Transvaal, and the northern sections were initially financed by Rhodes's British South Africa Company.) But Cape Town in the last analysis was simply too far away to dominate the hinterland north of the Limpopo, much less north of the Zambezi.

Later rail lines reached out from Rhodesia through Mozambique to Beira. Finally, in 1976, the Tanzam railroad from Tanzania reached the copper belt in Zambia, with help from the People's Republic of China. Here again, the main objective was not economic but strategic – to free Zambia from dependence on rail lines passing through either Rhodesia, Angola, or Mozambique, all of which were still under European domination at that time.

Migration

Throughout Africa, economic change meant that people had to concentrate where resource endowment made development possible. They moved from a broad distribution based on agriculture largely for their own consumption into new patterns of concentration at railroad junctions, mines, plantations, administrative centers, or the port cities that grew up along the coasts to handle the export trade. The change of residence usually began with a temporary move, often seasonal and undertaken by young males alone. The migrants then returned again and again, brought their families or married in their new homes, and finally stabilized as new residents. This pattern of seasonal migration as a phase leading to a permanent change of residence was common to all of North and tropical Africa.

In South Africa, however, another form of migration developed that involved a regular and systematic oscillation of workers between nearly self-subsistent farming in the African reserves and wage work for "European" farms, mines, or in the towns. The governments in southern Africa discouraged stabilization of labor in the new centers. This opposition to permanent migration by Africans goes back to the Afrikaners' eruption onto the high veld and into Natal in the wake of the Zulu mfecane. The European migrants at that time had two different and partly contradictory goals for the Africans they had conquered. They wanted land for themselves, and they took the best land available. This implied a need to drive away the original owners. But the European farmers also wanted some Africans around – just enough to meet their demand for labor. Even before 1900, the South African colonies and republics passed laws designed simultaneously to drive off "excess" labor, to control the African labor force, and to make sure that additional labor could be recruited when needed. One set of laws limited the number of Africans who could remain as "squatters" on "European" land. Vagrancy legislation helped give the European farmers legal means to drive off African workers they did not want to employ.

All Africans were meanwhile forced to pay high rates of direct taxation – hut or poll taxes – the intention being to force them into the wage sector, on the theory that African farmers were under-employed on their own land. Taxation of this kind began in Natal in 1849. In time, it spread to nearly the whole of colonial Africa. At first, the payments were set high enough to pinch. Some governments demanded a month's wages each year, in a single payment, occasionally even more. And the rates could be adjusted to meet specific goals. The Transvaal legislation of 1870, for example, provided that Africans working and living on "European" farms should pay only 12.50 pence each year. Those who worked for Europeans but lived elsewhere paid twenty-five pence, while those who lived and worked on their own land had to pay fifty pence.

After gold mining began on the Witwatersrand, labor recruitment became more systematic. The Chamber of Mines set up a central recruiting organization to serve the whole industry, and it soon reached outside the Transvaal and even beyond the British South African colonies. By 1910, non-South African recruits from Mozambique had become the main source of unskilled labor for the South African mines. During the interwar years, South African practice and theory agreed that African labor would be migratory in regular oscillations. The underlying justification was that Africans should be supported by the land in the reserves, unless their labor was needed in "European" South Africa; but then they were to come as temporary sojourners only, never as residents with a right to remain. In fact, the reserves could not support all the people assigned to them; periodic labor in the towns was a necessity, both for the workers and for the industry they served. South African legislation meanwhile tended to limit the period of each visit, and the presence of women and children on the reserves was a pull that made for periodic visits "home." In effect, the low wages paid African labor in the cities and farms were subsidized by the labor of women and children on the reserves.

But oscillating labor was not cheap, even though the wages were low. Short-term migrants were unskilled and inefficient, and it was expensive to train them for the new jobs. Some people in the mining industry came to realize at an early date that the cost per unit of work performed was inordinately high. In the early 1920s, Union Minière, the largest mining company in Katanga, began to stabilize mining labor by encouraging workers to bring their wives and families and settle down as long-term residents of the mining towns. Union Minière's labor turnover dropped from 96 per cent per year in the early 1920s to less than 7 per cent ten years later. In the 1930s, mining companies in northern Rhodesia also shifted to a policy of stabilizing the labor force.

These experiments were known, of course, in South Africa, but there "European" trade unions and European opinion generally feared that stabilized labor would ultimately mean African competition for the skilled jobs reserved for European workers. Still further in the future, it might threaten to integrate the races. South African mines, and to some extent industry as well therefore kept to oscillating labor as a matter of policy, though some stabilization took place as a matter of fact. At any moment in the 1950s, half a million Africans with households in the reserves were absent, at work elsewhere in South Africa. By implication, more than two million men spent their lives shifting back and forth between work in the "White" portions of the Union of South Africa and relatively inefficient agriculture in neighboring countries or the South African "native reserves."

For North Africans, industrial Europe was a similar magnet for labor migration, with a similar tendency toward oscillation. Algerians began going to France as temporary migrants during the interwar period, still more came from all the Maghrib after the Second World War. The total rose from 40,000 in 1946, to nearly a quarter of a million on the eve of the Algerian war for independence in 1954, to nearly a million in 1970. The size of the migration, in short, was about the same in the 1960s as the movement of Africans into "White" South Africa. After the Algerian war of independence, the number of Africans working in France was much greater than the number of Europeans still resident in the Maghrib.

As in South Africa, the North Africans gradually became dependent on wage work in France. As early as 1954, it was estimated that migrants' remittances were equal to the total wages paid by Algerian agriculture, so that work in France directly or indirectly supported about a quarter of the Algerian population. At the same time, the French economy became increasingly dependent on a labor force drawn from North Africa or from parts of Europe that were less developed at that time, such as Spain and southern Italy. As in South Africa, Algerians and other migrant workers were discouraged from settling down as permanent residents; their lack of skills forced them into the worst-paid jobs; and their legal rights were limited; but they were not subject to the full range of overt discrimination Africans had to accept in South Africa.

Migration was equally intense in tropical Africa, but there the population moving to the cities and centers of export agriculture tended to settle permanently after an experimental period of seasonal migration. Along the Guinea coast west of Nigeria, the principal flow was southward from the savanna into the forest belt and the coastal cities. In Senegal, it was westward to the peanut-growing region or ports like Dakar. Seasonal migration continued even after the Second World War, with about four seasonal migrants for each permanent migrant in a typical year, but the permanent migration was more important over the years and brought about a really significant shift in population. West of Nigeria, before 1920, the forest and coastal region had about a third of the total population; by 1970, it had half the total, and this shift implied the permanent displacement of about three million people, who, with their descendants, came to make up about a fifth of the coastal and forest population. Nigeria was a little different, with growth centers in the savanna as well as the forest belt. Some people, especially skilled and clerical workers, moved north from the forest to cities like Kano or Kaduna, while other, less skilled workers were simultaneously moving south to the coastal towns or the cocoa and kola regions in the forest.

Much of the population movement in East Africa was outward from overpopulated territories like Rwanda and Burundi, but otherwise it was mainly within colonial boundaries. The Kenya highlands and cities like Mombasa and Nairobi attracted people from other parts of Kenya. Tanganyikans also moved to the towns, to sisal plantations near the coast, and to the clove plantations of Zanzibar and Pemba offshore; though some were attracted as far away as the gold mines of South Africa.

People also moved for non-economic reasons, to avoid forced labor, for example – especially from French West Africa to the British colonies, where forced labor was far less extensive in the interwar period. Muslims from all over Africa traveled to Mecca as a religious duty, and many took years, working along the way. Some settled down and never returned home. Sudan in particular attracted a large concentration of pilgrim-settlers. The census of 1955 showed that fully a fifth of the whole Sudanese population came from further west, perhaps a third of these from west of Lake Chad.

Migration of political refugees was also common. Some Muslims in the Futaanke empire of the upper Niger valley fled eastward into Nigeria when the French defeated the Lamido Juulbe. Others from Nigeria fled still further east when the British conquered northern Nigeria. These movements only foreshadowed the much more extensive refugee movements that came with and after independence. Tens of thousands of Tutsi fled from Rwanda when the Hutu peasantry rose against their former masters in 1962 and afterward. Even more Hutu fled from the Tutsi government of Burundi in the late 1960s. These ethnic expulsions and refugee movements, however, were to be far more pronounced in the post-colonial period.

In its broadest setting within the sweep of world history, the African migrations of the colonial period and later were part of a much more extensive and worldwide movement from the less industrialized to the more industrialized zones of the world economy. It included the movement of peasants into cities, of Koreans into Japan, of Turks into West Germany, and of Mexicans to California, just as it also included, as part of a broader picture, the South Africans in Soweto and the Algerians in slums outside Paris or in *bidonvilles* on the outskirts of Algiers. In each case, the specific problem has its own particular characteristics – just as South African race relations grew out of the special circumstances of South African history – but they all share other characteristics with the world elsewhere in the second half of the twentieth century.

Migration, in this broader context, appears to be a secondary offshoot of industrialization, which has the economic power to order a redistribution of resources and people toward the centers of growth. For Africa, migration and culture conflict growing out of migration can be traced back to the era of the slave trade. In the pre-colonial century and the colonial period, it was part of the African effort to respond to the industrial demand for its raw materials. Similar adjustments were to continue into the post-colonial period, with increasing numbers of people involved, and with political, economic, social, and ethnic factors creating new situations and problems of increasing complexity.

Suggestions for further reading

Austen, Ralph A., *African Economic History: Internal Development and External Dependency*, London: James Currey, 1987.

Berry, Sara, *Cocoa Custom and Socio-Economic Change in Rural Western Nigeria*, London: Oxford University Press, 1975.

Bundy, Colin, *The Rise and Fall of the South African Peasantry*, Berkeley: University of California Press, 1979.

Cooper, Frederick, *On the African Waterfront: Urban Disorder and the Transformation of Work in Colonial Mombasa*, New Haven: Yale Press, 1987.

Cruise O'Brien, Donal, *The Munrides of Senegal: The Political and Economic Organization of an Islamic Brotherhood*, Oxford: Clarendon Press, 1971.

Denoon, Donald, *Settler Capitalism: The Dynamics of Dependent Development in the Southern Hemisphere*, Oxford: Clarendon Press, 1983.

Fieldhouse, David K., *Black Africa 1945–1980: Economic Decolonization and Arrested Development*, London: Allen and Unwin, 1986.

Hill, Polly, *Migrant Cocoa Farmers in Ghana*, Cambridge: Cambridge University Press, 1963.

Johnson, Douglas H., and David M. Anderson (eds), *The Ecology of Survival: Case Studies from Northeast African History*, Boulder: Westview, 1988.

Manning, Patrick, *Slavery, Colonialism and Economic Growth in Dahomey, 1640–1960*, Cambridge: Cambridge University Press, 1982.

Munro, Forbes, *Africa and the International Economy*, London: Dent, 1976.

Richards, Paul, *Indigenous Agricultural Revolution*, London: Hutchinson, 1985.

Tignor, Robert, *The State, Private Enterprise, and Economic Change in Egypt, 1918–1952*, Princeton: Princeton Press, 1985.

Van Onselen, Charles, *Chibaro: Mine Labour in Southern Rhodesia, 1900–1933*, London: Pluto, 1976.

Van Onselen, Charles, *Studies in the Social and Economic History of the Witwatersrand 1886–1914*, 2 vols. London: Longman, 1982.

Wilson; Francis, *Labour in the South African Gold Mines 1911–1969*, Cambridge: Cambridge University Press, 1972.

18

A CLASH OF CULTURES: AFRICAN MINDS IN THE COLONIAL ERA

Colonial conquest was accompanied by a gigantic clash of cultures, European and African, which unleashed consequences that are still shaping Africa today. To understand why this should be so, one must realize the place of culture in practical life. "Culture" includes what we call religion, ideology, and science, is transmitted through education, and is expressed by language. Culture is crucial because it shapes our very perception of "reality" and thus provides us with the insights about the world which determine our assessment of a given situation and guide our actions. Technically the term refers to an overall cognitive constellation of basic concepts, representations, and interpretations which make the outside world meaningful. Any person shares his or her cultural makeup with many others and the basic axioms of culture are inherited, from forebears many, many centuries ago, just as language is. The term "civilization" refers to such a widely shared cultural legacy which is the product of a millennia-long history of development.

The Europeans who conquered Africa partook in a common civilization, the product of a common history over more than a score of centuries, in which Christianity had been the unifying principle. They distinguished between various types of cognition which were labeled religion, science, or secular ideology, and they had created specialized organizations to dispense religion, further science, and transmit culture through formal education. This civilization was based on and transmitted through writing. Christian religions were founded on the dogmatic interpretation of a set of holy scriptures. The importance of writing in transmitting culture also explains why formal schools existed to initiate the youth.

In northern Africa the Europeans found kindred civilizations (Muslim and in Ethiopia Christian) with whom they shared writing, a related religion, and special institutions to dispense religion and education. The situation there was familiar to them. But in tropical Africa they encountered civilizations based on orality, there was no distinction between religion, science, and ideology, and there were no specialized agencies to dispense culture. Religion, education, science, or ideology were all part and parcel of every type of activity, from farming to healing, from commerce to ruling, even though there often were ritual specialists and often initiation rituals were accompanied by intensive teaching. The situation confused Europeans to such an extent that many concluded that "Africans" were devoid of religion, education, and learning. Hence they were uncivilized and by definition "savages". This suited the conquerors because it dehumanized tropical Africans and thereby denied them any rights. Moreover the conquest could be whitewashed by the claim that aggression was a moral duty, a civilizing mission, which had the noble aim of freeing Africans from savagery and of teaching them "civilization". In practice this program was a declaration of war on all African civilizations. It led to a struggle for the minds of Africans that was to be just as significant for Africa's future as the political and economic conflicts have been.

Thanks to the existence of holy scriptures and specialized agencies such as mosques and Koranic schools, the Europeans did not try very hard to destroy the Islamic and Christian civilizations of northern Africa. But they attacked the civilizations of tropical Africa and succeeded after forty years of coercion (1880–1920 in most cases) to destroy their vitality and coherence. By 1920 they had annihilated all the older social foundations of society and were replacing them by their own administrations, their courts of law, churches, schools and hospitals. They thus succeeded in destroying the social context and hence much of the meaning and relevance of the old civilizations. By introducing their churches, literacy, and schooling they induced a deep cultural alienation in the minds of very large numbers of tropical Africans. But they failed to transplant their own civilization, lock, stock and barrel. Rather they left both considerable cultural confusion and disunity in their wake. Confusion reigned in the minds of most Africans between insights, patterns of thought, and knowledge which stemmed from the older worldviews and others which derived from European worldviews. Cultural disunity stemmed from the contrasts between a heavily Westernized elite and the bulk of the urban and rural populations alike which was much less affected. We follow the various facets of this clash of cultures through the period by addressing successively the impact made by European religion, literacy, education and political ideology.

Revealed religions

Judaism, Christianity and Islam all share the fundamental belief that God revealed His plans for humanity Himself (Christianity) or through prophets, who left a divinely inspired or even divinely dictated (Islam) record of this revelation. Christian and Muslim revelations were addressed to all people in the world and hence it was a holy duty for Christians and Muslims to spread the gospel. The first proselytizers were traveling holy men, but soon both Islam and Christianity also relied on political hegemony to further conversion. Thus was northern and northeastern Africa converted. Later Christianity (but not Islam) often used monasteries to convert pagans as happened in much of Europe, or in Central Ethiopia before 1450. Muslim holy men were often joined by traders and by their efforts Islam was carried to inland West Africa and the East African coast.

Christianity

In the early age of European expansion Catholicism spread wherever Spaniards or Portuguese set foot and mainly used monasteries to gain converts. But overseas the monastery soon turned into something novel: the mission station. In Africa mission activity received a boost from the Catholic Reformation of the mid-sixteenth century and met with a lasting success in the kingdom of Kongo and in Angola during the seventeenth century. In contrast Protestant proselytizing activity remained quiescent until the late eighteenth-century revivals in Germany and England. Protestant mission stations came to Africa in the 1790s. They were modeled on the Christian rural communities of revivalists in Central Europe. Missionary activity south of the Sahara picked up from the 1840s onwards and soon gathered momentum as a Protestant Catholic rivalry heated up. Thus a religious scramble for Africa was in full swing even before the political scramble for Africa broke out. Colonial conquest however facilitated the establishment of mission posts by both rivals and further intensified their activities.

A mission was founded by leasing a plot of land from the local authorities or being granted one by the colonial government. At first funds came from local collections in Europe, but grants from the colonial government for such activities as education and health became more important after 1920. The early missionaries favored two strategies. One was to woo a major African ruler, in the hope that his conversion would lead to that of his subjects and thus "Christian kingdoms" would arise. This occurred often in southern Africa, where the pattern was very successful in Botswana, or Madagascar, less so at Msiri's capital. The other strategy was to attract the downtrodden. Especially in East and Equatorial Africa missionaries bought or liberated slaves and provided refuge for people uprooted by war or disease. These people gradually agreed to be baptized and publicly to be identified as Christians and were settled in mission villages. But this threatened local African leaders ranging from village headmen, and leaders of associations in which the youth were inducted, to diviners and healers, and they offered strong resistance to such conversions. Nevertheless, in the period of active colonial conquest the missionaries prevailed because they enjoyed the backing of the military and African leaders were forced to abandon control over Christian villages to them. Since at that time a colonial administration on the ground scarcely existed some missionary societies took this opportunity to take complete control and to create "Christian kingdoms" of their own. The most extreme cases of this kind occurred in Belgian-controlled Africa where several Catholic orders succeeded in creating virtual states of their own, so that by 1914 the Belgian government was forced into an open struggle with the missionary orders. They only gave in when the Vatican sided with the government.

The very trauma of colonial conquest also favored conversion. People were losing faith in their own religions because these were failing to protect them against war, epidemic, famine and conquest. And meanwhile missionaries were deriding their beliefs and ritual practices as inefficient fancies. In earlier times such emergencies had often led to the appearance of a revelation preached by a diviner or a seer who started a revival movement to cleanse the community of evil-doers and start anew. It is therefore not surprising that in these straits whole communities sometimes suddenly embraced the revelation of Christianity. Moreover, in the initial decades of mission work actual conversion was the work of African assistants who "translated" the Christian message in terms that made sense locally. They were the equivalent of the old seers, and the ones who provoked such movements of group conversion. At the same time they often also were the first articulate, literate, and respected elites in the new colonial order.

By the 1920s and 1930s most missions had shifted their tactics from converting adults to enrolling children in schools where they could be indoctrinated. Moreover especially where Protestant and Catholic missionaries were close rivals, they used health services and even gifts of food or clothing to attract converts. Much of the later growth of Christianity was linked to education, although particular political and economic circumstances still triggered off a few truly massive episodes of adult conversion in this period. Perhaps the best known of these occurred in Rwanda during the later 1930s when many tens of thousands of Hutu seeking European patronage suddenly flocked to the Catholic church.

The decision to join one church or another, or in some areas to become Muslim or Christian, was usually predicated on quite mundane considerations, such as the perception of the official or non-official character of a church, the desire to enroll in the school which best taught the language of the colonial authorities in order to secure skilled employment, the degree of non-interference by various denominations in daily life, for example in matters of polygyny or leisure activities, and the perceived arrogance or empathy of individual missionaries. As a result doctrinal differences between Protestant and Catholic churches, and even between Christianity and Islam were often secondary. In any case conversion soon was no longer an all or nothing affair. Friction was inevitable in the early days when African Christians refused to take part in other public rituals and then often either had to break with their original communities or to become "backsliders" in the eyes of the Christian community. Later, however, when sizeable numbers of Christians made a boycott by others no longer realistic, and in the context of Protestant Catholic competition, standards relaxed and tacit negotiation within the communities themselves decided what practices by converts were acceptable. Often this led to a situation where many converts simply added Sunday worship to existing religious practices. In one instance in Zaire for instance, and as late as 1967, the senior evangelist of the local mission on Sunday was also the senior ritual specialist to maintain fertility on Thursday.

The question of an African clergy became an important source of conflict between the converts and the missionaries. In spite of the message that all people were equal before God, most missionaries until the Second World War at least, thought that people were unequal by culture and perhaps by race. They preached equality of the soul but not of the person. In consequence many among them did not believe in training an African clergy to replace themselves. Yet some African priests, ministers, and even bishops had been ordained in past centuries and institutions like Fourah Bay College were founded to train an African clergy. Nevertheless in the colonial era training developed only very slowly. The first priest trained in a seminary of the Belgian Congo was ordained as early as 1917, but others followed in numbers only in the 1930s and the first Catholic bishops were consecrated only in the 1950s. The Protestant denominations were generally just as slow in their training programs. Such discrimination aroused resentment from the early colonial period onward, especially in coastal West Africa and in southern Africa where missions were well established by 1880. Especially in Protestant churches, particularly in southern Africa, this resentment led to the desertion by whole congregations from the parent missionary church and the foundation of independent churches. When such new African churches dropped institutional links but maintained doctrinal orthodoxy they were called "Ethiopian churches," but when they also innovated in matters of dogma and liturgy they came to be known as "Zionist churches."

By the time of independence, fifty million Africans, roughly one half the population outside Muslim areas, had become Christian and Christian worldviews were strongly influencing the other half. The new religion had now put down deep roots in African consciousness and was being firmly established in its African, rather than western socio-cultural settings. On the fringes of the major churches African independent churches were rapidly multiplying. Meanwhile leadership of all the churches was passing into the hands of an African clergy.

Islam

There were far more Muslims in Africa during the nineteenth century than adherents to any other single religion. Islam was similar to Christianity, but the two religions had always been bitter enemies, and no colonial power after 1911 was Muslim. Yet during the colonial period, when its Christian antagonists ruled, it continued to expand and at a rate higher than had earlier been the case. This constitutes a paradox. One can understand that the strength of Muslim grassroot structures and ancient hatred prevented Christian missions from making any headway in northern Africa. This situation also explains why the colonial governments continued state support in favor of mosques, pious foundations and institutes of higher learning, especially in the protectorates. But why was Islam so successful elsewhere? Its expansion was spectacular in inland West Africa. The process of conversion there drew both on the profoundly African roots of Islam as well as on the heritage of enthusiasm left over from the great nineteenth-century *jihads* (holy struggles), but it was helped by the decision of colonial governments to keep Christian missions out of the area. In East and Central Africa, and even more in South Africa on the other hand, Islam spread less rapidly than Christianity did. It has been argued that West Africans preferred Islam to Christianity as a way to protest about colonial rule, but this impulse did not help them much in East Africa. Yes there were fresh Muslim converts there, but there were far more Christian converts. In southern Sudan Islam actually may have lost some converts while Christian missions made great gains. Further eastwards in the horn of Africa the situation remained static, for all around the fringes of Ethiopia, old religious animosities were so strong that peoples' very identities were expressed in religious terms. Islam gained there only among the Boran and in the Nubia mountains. All in all it is evident that the attitude of colonial authorities was a major but not a decisive factor in these developments. Thus while the French and British discouraged Christian missions in territories they felt were either Muslim or "near-Muslim" they encouraged such missions elsewhere. Meanwhile Portugal and Belgium did all they could to hinder Muslim proselyt-ism.

In North Africa the major debate of the period was the relationship between Islam and modernization. A minority of secularized and Western-educated intellectuals rejected religion altogether. At the other extreme a vocal group of preachers held that everything modern or Western was evil in itself, though their following dwindled from decade to decade. Otherwise many positions between these extremes were possible, and all of them were argued most passionately at al-Azhar university in Egypt. Even before 1882, Jamal al-Dīn al-Afghāni had claimed that all modern progress had been revealed in Islam and could be reconciled with that religion; if only Muslims would unite under a single caliph, they would be more than a match for Christians. This form of Muslim nationalism was an important factor in 'Urabi Pasha's revolt in 1880–2. Later Muhammad 'Abdu, who became *mufti* of Egypt, elaborated this position further. By the interwar period though the most important split in Egypt was no longer between the 'ulamā and the rising modernists. Now a group of "new traditionalists" known as the Muslim Brotherhood arose. They wanted a return to a pristine Islam, adapted to a modern setting. In this they were the forerunners of the modern Islamic fundamental-ist movements. The Brotherhood became as much a political as a religious movement. It organized in secret cells, had a military wing and ran schools and a medical service. In the 1940s and 1950s the Brotherhood became a major force in Egyptian politics when it boasted as many as 200,000 members. In 1956 it was violently suppressed after the military coup of that year had ushered in a socialist Egyptian revolution.

Further west in North Africa, the older tendencies of *sufi* Islam continued stronger than ever as the continued power of the Sanusiya in Cyrenaica and the rise of the Tijaniyya throughout the Maghrib show, even though the Tijaniyya was apolitical or even pro-French. Yet alongside these older tendencies the influence of Islamic mod-ernism, frequently traceable to Muhammad 'Abdu, was also noticeable. The modernist opposition to European rule tended to take the form of participation in Western-style political movements like the Destour and Neo-Destour parties in Tunisia, or the Istiqlal in Morocco. Those grew into the political parties that finally won independence from the French. Of the brotherhoods only the Sanusiya triumphed and took over Libya's government in 1952.

In West Africa modernism was far weaker. The Tijaniyya became the largest order surpassing the Qadiriya, which nevertheless also remained strong. Here too however new religious orders appeared. The Murīdiya in Senegal, an offshoot of the Qadiriya, was perhaps the most important among these, and for reasons other than its crucial role in the production of groundnuts for export. Another new order, the Hamaliya, an offshoot of the Tijaniyya, founded in 1925 near Nioro, also became very influential. Although it had fewer followers than the Murīdiya it was more widespread and a more consistent source of opposition both to the French and the old African elites. It appealed to the downtrodden, admitted both women and slaves, and created close-knit congregations which had something of the character of a secret society, intentionally isolating itself from the rest of the population. Other influences stemmed from Asia, through the Ahmadiya. This was the only order which proselytized on the model of Christian missions, setting up outposts in heathen lands to spread its version of world religion through the agency of paid teachers. One can hardly call the order Muslim if only because its adherents claimed that Muhammad was not the last of the prophets and also because its doctrine incorporated Christian, Jewish, Mazdean and Hindu elements but in the end it helped to spread Islam itself.

On the East African coast Islamic brotherhoods left much less of an imprint on public life. Several of them vied with each other to attract either the downtrodden or the better-off but without becoming significant movements. Still the perpetuation of Islam in the Zanzibari enclaves around Lake Tanganyika and in eastern Zaire owes much to the endeavors, from the 1920s onwards, of 'ulamā sent by one of them to maintain, purify and extend the faith there.

Tropical African religious movements

The older religions in tropical Africa did not die out. Indeed even by the end of the period they still held the allegiance of half the population there. At the onset of the period they were subjected to severe strains because they failed to protect their adherents against the decimation brought by war, epidemic, famine and conquest. In many cases religious leaders reacted by creating new protective charms and rituals. These were believed to turn bullets into water or otherwise nullify European technological superiority and thus to avert conquest, or after conquest had occurred to recover freedom. Examples of such movements include the actions of Dinka and Nuer prophets who opposed the conquests of Egypt during the nineteenth century, or the later war-charm movements in Madagascar and the Congo basin. Maji-Maji which erupted in 1905 to 1907 is the most famous among such movements because it led to insurrection over a large part of Tanganyika and was celebrated by later nationalistic ideology. Its leader was Bokero, a priest of a widely revered nature spirit near Rufiji. When the German authorities began to brutally impose compulsory cotton cultivation, he and other priests began to turn out war medicines, which would turn bullets into water (*maji*), in the same way that they had once provided fertility medicines to take on the shape of a fully-fledged religious revival, claiming the power to remove two kinds of evil: witches and Europeans. Maji-Maji unleashed an extremely forceful repression and then died out because it never transcended the making of war charms.

By the 1920s as substantial social tensions had arisen as a result of the wholesale social reorganization imposed by the new authorities, the realization that colonial control was there to stay spawned new religious movements which then spread rapidly, often over large areas. These promised to cleanse local communities from all evil doers and bring back social harmony, fertility and tranquillity. They also had much in common with pre-colonial "witch-finding" movements, a term which is no more accurate than "sin-finding" would be for a Christian millennial movement. A movement began with the visions of a seer. His or her prophetic inspiration, often derived from dreams, convinced a local community, usually after several years of incubation. Once the community accepted the message, it adopted new spectacular and highly emotional rituals of renewal. These ritual innovations were understandable and acceptable because they were usually couched in familiar symbols albeit in new combinations and invested with a new meaning. The first congregation also developed an internal organization of title-holders. Then the movement spread from one place to another, because religious leaders of other communities came to the existing congregations begging to be initiated and willing to pay initiation fees. A new movement diffused very quickly but in an uneven way because the spread depended on the initiative of recipient villages. Initiations were often theatrical. Furthermore, as dreams were considered to be valid sources of revelation, any local seer could further elaborate on the original cult. When the cult reached a cultural boundary its contents could be translated into new sets of symbols familiar to that area just as the organization could easily be adapted to local practices. So flexible were these movements that they could even adopt another name during their expansion and yet remain essentially the same movement.

Many scholars once thought that these religious movements after 1920 were essentially political actions of defiance and protest against colonial domination and that they took this shape because overt political activity was forbidden. Because such movements continued in later periods when the collective expression of political views was possible, this explanation cannot be accepted. Yet in so far as colonial authorities actually tried to suppress religious movements of any kind they became perforce an expression of defiance. The social causes of the movements must be sought in the unbearable tensions wrought within local communities by the wrenching social transformations which resulted from the operation of the new economic and social processes in the new colonial order.

Christian Africans knew similar religious movements in their secessions from the official churches or from each other. A very early secession of Ethiopian type is known from the 1620s in northern Angola while the first Zionist movement was launched in 1694 by Chimpa Vita *alias* Dona Beatrice in the kingdom of Kongo. The earliest ones in modern times seem to have been that of the Tembu national Church of the eastern Cape in 1884 and the so-called Ethiopian church founded in Pretoria in 1892. By the mid-1960s there were an estimated 6000 independent churches in sub-Saharan Africa affecting about 8 million or 14 per cent of all African Christians. Many of these churches just consisted of a few local communities, but some like the Kimbangist church (founded 1921) with its half million followers in Zaire, or the widespread Bapostolo movement (founded 1950s) which extends from South Africa to Zaire and Tanzania have become major and lasting organizations. Nevertheless the total numbers indicate how deeply rooted is the feeling for local autonomy in African societies, for schism affects not just African Christianity, but also the new Islamic brotherhoods and local autonomy is crucial in understanding the spread of tropical African religious movements.

Like its counterparts in the African religious movements, independent Christian movements usually began with a visionary leader, prophecy, an important role for dreams, and the reassessment of existing symbols. A previous connection with an official church was also important, and the majority of leaders seem to have been catechists or evangelists – hence associated with magisterial authority. This constitutes a major difference with other movements, because it preserved the Christian roots both in doctrine and in organization. Preaching remained central and baptism remained the ritual of initiation into the cult.

A great deal also depended on the prophetic and organizational gifts of particular leaders. The African Greek Orthodox Church of Uganda suffered from weak leadership when it emerged in 1929. Its leader wanted autonomy, but also respectability and equality with other major churches. He therefore joined the general communion of the official Greek Orthodox Church in 1946, only to drop out later to form the African Orthodox Autonomous Church in 1966 after Greek technical assistant missionaries had disappointed him. Some independent churches, however, had hardly any visible leadership; the African Independent Pentecostal Church, for instance, was formed in Kenya in 1930 when local mission outposts simply declared their independence from the central mission station and then loosely "agreed" together.

In most cases doctrinal elements were stated early and distinctively. Among the most famous prophets of the colonial period were William Wade Harris of Liberia and the Ivory Coast, active from the 1910s onward, Simon Kimbangu in the lower Belgian Congo, active from 1920 onward, John Maranke, the founder of the Bapostolo in Rhodesia, active from 1932 onward and Elliot Kamwana, the founder of Watchtower in Malawi about 1908. The first three preached a distinct doctrine from the outset. Kamwana's teaching, however, diverged very little from that of Jehovah's Witnesses, its parent body, though the doctrine altered almost beyond recognition c.1920 as the movement spread to Northern Rhodesia and the Belgian Congo under the name Kitawala and was recast by local prophets, especially by Tomo Nyirenda, *Mwana Lesa* or "Son of God". The absence of any church organization in this movement is certainly tied to its considerable doctrinal innovations.

Many founders of new churches were neither unusual, nor impressive personalities; nor were they solitary "voices in the wilderness." Oshitelu, who founded the Nigerian Aladura Church in 1929, was one among several mystics prominent in his day and place. At least one founding figure was a European Franciscan priest, whose followers created the *jamaa* movement in the Belgian Congo and Tanganyika and soon developed it beyond his control. Founders became prophets because their followers chose to see them as such; the message mattered more than the personality. Fervor mattered more than theology, and fueled the movements for a long time, before they became routinized, or withered away.

No single explanation can account for the great variety of these movements. To call them "retaking the initiative" explains nothing; it merely rephrases what the movements did. To call them "religions of the oppressed," to stress that most movements flourished among the underprivileged, and especially in areas of great industrial development is correct. Still such movements were not just expressions of economic unhappiness, collective frustration, or of discontent with European rule. They were deviant movements, but not movements of deviants; they appealed to all levels of the population. Nor was such fission inherent in Christianity itself, although it is true that the very notion of dogma invites dissent. But most African Christians remained within the ecclesiastical framework imported from Europe. They shared the most typical feature common to all of them with the African tropical religious movements of the same period: they involved inspired seers and led to the creation not of large centralized churches, but to congregations in communities where face-to-face relationships among their members were crucial. The refusal of centralization and the urge to address specific concerns tied to a community at a given moment by attributing new meanings to older ritual and belief are the common feature of all movements, Christian or tropical African.

Colonization and African language

One of the immediate concerns of missionaries on founding a station was the question of language. Not only did they have to learn the vernacular language near their stations to be able to preach the gospel, but it was their duty to translate the holy scriptures into the vernacular. That was a problem Muslims never faced because most Muslims hold that the Koran must be learned, understood, and recited in the original Arabic. All over tropical Africa the missionaries found a bewildering kaleidoscope of tongues. It simply was not feasible to translate the Bible or to produce schoolbooks in the speech of almost every single village. Hence before one even began to translate the Bible, one had to choose one among many local languages. Then one had to decide which among the many dialects of the chosen tongue should be picked as a standard to become the basis of the written language. Then a serviceable orthography for that standard language in the chosen script, always Roman, had to be constructed. Only then could one begin to tackle the translation with all its pitfalls. Each of these steps had momentous consequences and the decisions made at each turn were goal oriented, that is political ones.

The choice of language was obvious in cases where speech common at court had to be adopted, as in Buganda or in Zululand, or in cases where variants of the language already had been reduced to writing as was the case for Swahili or Kongo. Elsewhere the choice was often harder and was dictated by an estimate of the number of its speakers and hence the number of potential converts as well as by its political weight and mistaken estimates were sometimes made. Thus in Central Kasai the Presbyterian mission began in Kete and the Catholic mission in Kanyok, but a few years later both found that these communities were too small and adopted the more widespread Tshiluba. The consequences of the choice of language were momentous. The speaker of a chosen language suddenly found themselves at a great advantage over others and soon developed the idea that their language in which one could now become literate was "civilized" and the others were mere *patois*. Schools were founded earlier in their lands than elsewhere, and this lead was never lost. Speakers of languages which were not commited to writing, had to learn a foreign language even as they struggled to become literate. And finally the native speakers of chosen languages found themselves preferred for employment in the missions and in the administration far beyond their territory of origin. Luganda became the regional language for most of Uganda and Tshiluba for instance became the regional language for all of Kasai. Hence Ganda and Luba Kasai people came to dominate large regions. One of the more spectacular consequences of these dynamics can be seen in Barotseland. It was the use of Sotho by the early missions and their reliance on Sotho catechists which explains why the original Luyi was eventually almost ousted by Kololo (a Sotho tongue) and not, as is often thought, the Kololo conquest itself.

The choice of a standard speech also led to major consequences. At first that choice was often made inadvertently. The speech current near the station became the standard. But when more came to be known about the local variants of speech over a wider area problems arose. Well-considered conscious decisions were then made in which linguistic considerations were often minor compared to the interests of competing missions (with different dialect or orthography preferences) and of government which sometimes wanted the widest possible usage in its territory, but differences with foreign territories. These factors are well in evidence for instance in the history of the committees set up to standardize Swahili (from 1925 onwards) and Shona (Zimbabwe) (from 1930 onwards). Technically it was feasible to construct a standard language so as to encompass relatively closely related variants, as in Swahili for instance, or to impose one over variants that were so widely divergent as to be clearly different languages altogether, as in Bambara (Mali) or even more so in Mongo (Zaire). In the latter case the ruthless determination of a single mission succeeded in constructing one standard written language for much of the equatorial province of Zaire. Their known considerations were practical (the need to run schools and missions in the whole area), religious (the desire to ward off Lingala, a "corrupting" trade language) and nationalist (the creation of a single Mongo nation). The consequences of such decisions have been momentous. Thus there exists now a single Shona in Zimbabwe but Rwanda, Rundi and Ha are considered to be three languages, although their spoken variants are so similar that the standard languages sometimes resort to artificial distinctions to emphasize the differences. Consider that standardization would have led to a community of some twenty million speakers! Or consider one Oromo standard (Ethiopia) and one Hausa standard (Nigeria/Niger) serving many millions of people as against Sotho which for political and missionary reasons was never unified, so that today there are at least five written "standards"! (two Tswana, three Sotho) or indeed Fulani in West Africa (four written variants at least). The impact of such decisions on the development of ethnic consciousness is obvious.

The task of standardization itself consisted in approving certain speech patterns, grammatical features, and syntax as correct and labeling others as erroneous. Thus the standard language was a new, artificial and learned construction far removed from the spontaneous and mostly unconscious production of spoken language. The consequence of this feature was to radically dissociate the written and hence learned language from everyday speech. The result was to induce an alienation from one's own language and culture. It placed literacy and book learning in an altogether different world from everyday experience and inherited wisdom. Only this alienation explains how, even in the 1960s, an English academic linguist could berate a Swahili writer for writing "bad" Swahili, who retorted that there were African Swahili speakers and *Wazungu* (European) Swahili speakers! The degree of alienation was stronger for the speakers of aberrant dialects, than for speakers of central dialects but nevertheless both had to interiorize an unfamiliar form (and grammar!) of the language at the very time that they were learning to be literate.

Although a number of languages were committed to writing and standardized during the early colonial period they still constituted only a tiny proportion of African tongues and neither missions nor government could hope to commit all of them to writing. Hence many missionary societies began almost from the outset to impose a written language in schools and churches over wide regions. Thus regional languages arose. The four official African languages in the Belgian Congo (Kongo, Lingala, Tshiluba and Swahili) or the spread of Swahili in East Africa are examples of this process. The problem for speakers of unwritten African languages who had to learn to read and write in a foreign language was both similar and different to the case of native speakers of a written language: similar in the unfamiliarity of the written language, yet different because that language was truly strange. That made it harder at the start of one's studies but easier later on because the barriers between written and spoken language were clear-cut and hence caused less confusion. Foreign speakers did not have the disconcerting impression that the written language was their own tongue, yet that they did not know it, but foreigners did! The case of European languages was merely a more extreme case of the regional language situation, although the added difficulty here was the extreme cultural differences between one's tongue and the written language which induced even more of a culturally split personality in the students. Yet, as we have seen, the elaboration of literary languages led in all cases to profound cultural alienation.

The introduction of writing by itself begat the need for schools and soon led to a sharp divide between the civilized literate who could aspire to some recognition and position in the colonial world, and the ignorant illiterate, who were only good to be ordered about. Africans sensed this quickly enough and soon began to clamor for more schools, even though these institutions had been so foreign to their experience.

Education

A common culture does not imply that everyone who shares it perceives, interprets or evaluates the outside world exactly in the same way as every one else. They obviously do not. Nevertheless, they all share fundamental concepts and insights. To understand this we have only to look at the phenomenon of a common language. Groups of people may share, inherit and transmit a common language, even though different dialects exist and every person has his or her own peculiarities of speech. And so it is with culture of which language is only a part. Education then occurs in all societies as part of the process called "socialization". General education everywhere in the world begins at home as soon as a small child is beginning to learn its own language and advances along with that process. Education beyond the early years was usually quite informal in pre-colonial tropical Africa, although apprenticeship at home or in the workshop of a craftsworker was essential in the acquisition of technical skills. In many societies childhood was formally concluded by the enrollment of adolescents, segregated by gender, in initiation schools where they underwent a last period of intensive and systematic training in the fundamentals of their culture. Ethnographers have reported at length on the initiations for boys, but not about similar initiations for girls which were also quite widespread, mainly because most of them were men and had no access to the feminine realm.

Where writing was used and deemed to be essential to religion, some type of formal schooling was common. Reading and writing were taught in Muslim Africa at village Koranic schools and in Ethiopia by parochial schools. At this elementary level the object was to familiarize the student (usually boys) with the Holy Books, often by making them learn portions of the scriptures by rote. A genuine grasp of the three Rs came only at the next level – the highest normally found in an ordinary village – and affected only a portion of the boys. Thus formal instruction existed wherever literacy was found, but it might not reach very far.

Formal higher education was available only in the *madrasa* of North Africa, or in the higher monastic schools in Ethiopia. Elsewhere West African *'ulamā* or Ethiopian *dabtara* taught such skills on a more informal basis. These stressed disciplines ancillary to religion, such as grammar, literature, music (in Ethiopia) or law (in Muslim countries). Still further advanced were disciplines considered to be culturally valuable, such as medicine, geography, history, and mathematics. Even in formal schools, education was a form of apprenticeship cemented by close personal relations between teachers and pupils; students were often followers of one particular master, though they switched allegiance from one to another. Ethiopian teachers usually were tied to a particular monastery, while Muslim teachers were highly mobile, if not altogether itinerant.

Rudimentary European schools had earlier existed along the West African coasts, but questions about African education in a Western vein were posed seriously only in the nineteenth century. Missionaries were among the first concerned, since they too had a Holy Book to teach. They never questioned the idea that formal schools were essential to education, simply because that was the way education was organized in Europe. For them education took place in schools, where obedient pupils listened to teachers, took examinations, and received diplomas certifying knowledge. Discipline was important, not only to make the children study, but also to mold desirable habits and that was usually considered to be even more important than learning itself.

Education was to be a major tool in the cultural conquest of Africa, and the colonial powers recognized that fact at an early date. France established the first government school in Senegal in 1818 – run by laymen, not missionaries, "out of respect for the Muslim faith." At first Wolof was used as the medium of instruction, but later French became the sole teaching language even in elementary schools everywhere in the French colonies. Vocational training was the main goal throughout the nineteenth century, but conflicting claims soon made their appearance. As early as 1854, the Senegalese authorities established an *école des otages* (literally school for hostages) in Saint Louis, ostensibly for the education of the sons of chiefs or kings from the interior, who were sent there to reside as evidence of their parents' loyalty to France. At this school the object was to train an elite that would afterward be attached to French interests. English language equivalents later developed in British territories, the earliest being a school for sons and nominees of chiefs at Bo in Sierra Leone.

On the British side, the earliest schools were the mission schools of Sierra Leone and the first South African center for instruction in English which was founded in Cape Town in 1803. Most education was left to the missionaries, even when the government paid for it. The aim was to convert and to make the pupils, in the words of an early report, "English in tastes, in opinions, in morals, in intellect." The curriculum encompassed the three Rs, elements of grammar and geography, and a strong emphasis on religion. Authorities paid at least lip service to the ideals of vocational training for African pupils, but the Sierra Leone curriculum was decidedly "clerkly." After 1843, Basel missionaries in the Gold Coast taught more practical subjects as well as manual training, and they began to teach elementary classes in the local vernacular. The main line remained however that a knowledge of English was essential for civilization, so that the English and French educational systems in tropical Africa were remarkably alike, especially when mission schools were established in French-speaking territories. After the European conquest, this pattern was transmitted all over tropical Africa. Only British missionary schools in northern Nigeria stressed practical training more than was done elsewhere, eschewed teaching Christianity, and left free time for Koranic Studies.

The contrast between this policy and that begun in Sierra Leone a century earlier represented a shift in European thought from conversionism to trusteeship. Manual and practical training was deemed appropriate for students who were not expected to rise to posts of command in their own societies. Too much education would only help to produce a disgruntled and overambitious element. In 1910 the first World Missionary Conference adopted the general precedent of northern Nigeria as a goal. But colonial administrations, businesses and the missions themselves still needed clerks and clergymen, and these were the occupations that promised upward mobility for educated Africans. Clerkly education therefore continued to be most in demand, while vocational training remained rudimentary.

Educational policy was not, in any event, wholly set by European wishes. Pressure from the students themselves, backed by their parents, led to a shift toward academic rather than "practical" subjects. Few pupils wanted to undergo the cost and the hardship of study, only to be prepared for a rural life and a low living standard. They knew that good grades in academic subjects meant an opportunity for employment in towns and opened the gate towards secondary education.

Instruction at elementary school was conducted in either the local or a regional language, with the exception of the French and Portuguese colonies where French or Portuguese was the medium of instruction from the very first grade onwards, although Malagasy was used in Madagascar where, as early as 1820, the London Missionary Society had set up a school under close royal supervision.

Once a system of primary education had been created (with a somewhat different timetable for different parts of Africa), the colonial governments followed up by setting up teachers' training schools first, then secondary schools, seminaries and vocational schools and finally universities on a par with institutions in Europe itself. Two general options were available. One was to develop secondary and higher education fairly rapidly, and send some students to European universities at an early date, at the expense of expanding mass education at primary school level. Its effect was to create an elite early on but at the price of creating a chasm between the elite and the general population. The second was to expand primary education first and start offering secondary education only after a large proportion of the youth was enrolled in the elementary schools. This delayed the creation of an elite but maintained continuity between the elite and the general population. Only the Belgian Congo took the second course of action. That choice was to make decolonization very difficult. By 1960 less than one per 10,000 had some higher education, while at the same time 1,500,000 pupils were attending primary school and only 45,000 were in secondary school. At the same moment Senegal, a small country compared to the Congo, had plenty of university educated leaders but far fewer pupils in elementary school. Even as late as 1970 the literacy rate there stood only at 10 per cent compared to 40 per cent in Zaire.

In spite of a few pioneering efforts in Sierra Leone during the nineteenth century, secondary education was not considered in earnest until after the First World War. Between 1922 and 1925, all the colonial powers but Portugal published comprehensive policy documents about the question. All proclaimed the desirability of a secondary education adapted to "African needs," but they also insisted on the preserving of an equivalence between metropolitan and African diplomas, which led them to the almost wholesale adoption of the metropolitan curricula. The diploma soon became the passport to European "civilization" – and, far more significantly, a passport to jobs and an entry into the new colonial elite.

From the outset secondary schools became the strongest agencies of Europeanization. Most were boarding schools, which separated the pupils from their home environment and placed them in surroundings where every facet of their lives could be molded to fit their teachers' mental image of "civilized" behavior. The training also emphasized ethics and groomed pupils for leadership roles. This too was in line with the contemporaneous European schools, where, in the 1920s, only a select minority attended secondary schools. The locations of these schools betrayed European expectations. Where settlers were few, more secondary schools were set up to train Africans for skilled clerical jobs. By 1938, for example, Nigeria boasted of forty-two full secondary schools while Uganda had one and the settler colonies of Kenya, Nyasaland (later Malawi) and Northern Rhodesia (later Zambia) had none at all.

It was also consonant with the contemporary European practice to limit education for women. Girls were only a small proportion of the total school population even in the lower grades of primary school and they were taught domestic rather than academic skills. Only the most exceptionally gifted and determined went on to secondary school. These policies foresaw the creation of educated African families to mirror the European pattern in which men went to the office and women stayed at home.

Several specialized types of secondary education developed to care for special needs. One of these was the preparation of pupils for administrative service. These schools – like Kaduna College in Nigeria, Achimota in Ghana, Fourah Bay in Sierra Leone, William Ponty in Dakar, Gordon College in Khartoum and Kisantu in Zaire – had an impact that can hardly be overrated. They were the nurseries of entire national elites, Europeanized, alienated from the general population, but fervent nationalists whose intention was to seize the leadership for which they had been trained.

The language of instruction in these schools was always the metropolitan one and African public opinion itself strongly supported this policy, because it felt that English or French were world languages that would open doors to more local opportunities and give better access to scientific knowledge. The most violent reaction ever to a policy decision on matters of education was the violent insurrection at Soweto in 1976 when the South African authorities attempted to oust English by Afrikaans in the African schools around Johannesburg. But the African public did not realize that this choice was mortgaging the future ease of communication within Africa by dividing the continent into Arabic-speaking, French-speaking, English-speaking and Portuguese-speaking blocs.

Universities came last. The first full university degrees for South Africans of European descent were only awarded in 1873, and Fort Hare, the first college for Africans, opened in 1916. In North Africa, the first Western-style university of Cairo dates from 1909, almost next door to al Azhar, the oldest university in the world, founded in 969. In tropical Africa universities came after the Second World War with the foundation of four colleges by the British in 1948, followed by others in French speaking colonies and in Ethiopia during the 1950s. It was clear at the time that universities challenged the whole colonial structure by providing an intellectual elite that could take over government, business and church from the colonial powers. In keeping with this potential the curricula were less culture-bound than those of secondary schools, though they still kept equivalence with European degrees and each colonial power followed its own fashions. On British style campuses teachers saw themselves to be more *in loco parentis* than their French-speaking colleagues did. Dakar, the French-run university, was run by the French ministry of higher education in bureaucratic fashion, as just another university, while the autocracy of rectors in the Belgian Congo matched that of rectors at home. Unlike their juniors at secondary schools university students enjoyed enough freedom to mingle with others in town. They easily mixed with both the other African elites and also with some Europeans there especially in the capitals. Although they were deeply involved in nationalist politics, from the very outset, culturally they remained perhaps the most thoroughly alienated Africans at the time. Their views about the future and about nationalism itself were thoroughly Western in origin.

Both rulers and ruled saw education as an instrument of power, either a tool for transforming Africans into black Europeans, or a tool to gain power and wealth through "modernization". But both sides misjudged and overrated the powers of education. Africans did not turn into loyal Europeans and degrees did not solve all problems. Nevertheless, the literate elite became Westernized enough to adopt the patterns of particular European sub-cultures to a remarkable degree, varying from incidental preferences in beverages or types of bread to fundamental approaches concerning the running of government. And although they railed against the metropolis, its capital, especially London or Paris, was still revered as the hub of the universe. Indeed colonial cultural alienation affected these elites so powerfully that even the way in which they denounced its effects was in a European language and through a European mode.

Education in northern and southern Africa ran a different course because school systems had been introduced much earlier in the nineteenth century, an Islamic school system flourished in North Africa, and the settler communities demanded separate education for their own children both in northern and southernmost Africa. As a result education was much more widespread in North and in South Africa than elsewhere. For instance in 1960 North African universities counted almost four times as many university students per unit of population as the rest of Africa did. And South Africa had ten times more university students per unit of population than tropical Africa did. Hence the impact of Western civilization was then greatest in South Africa and it was only due to the strength of Islam and the Muslim school system in North Africa that Islamic civilization held its own there.

The other special features involved were the following. In South Africa segregated education became more rigid over time until the 1950s, when government assumed full control of all education for Africans. It then set up three ethnic colleges for Xhosa, Zulu, and Tswana respectively, as well as separate colleges for the Indians of Natal and the Coloured people of the western Cape. The intention was to isolate all ethnic and racial groups from one another as well as from the outside world. In North Africa the problem of separate schools for settlers was compounded by the prior existence of a Muslim system for training a literate elite. The Egyptian precedent was crucial here because its secular education was modeled specifically on the French system ever since the middle of the nineteenth century. This balanced English influences induced by British rule. And meanwhile al-Azhar continued to flourish in its own way during the whole period of the British protectorate. Secular schools on a French or Italian model were available also to some North Africans in the Maghrib – sometimes alongside the settlers' children, but occasionally segregated. The fundamental ambiguity of education in two different cultural traditions persisted after independence. Thus the Moroccan Faculty of Letters in 1965, still offered three kinds of degree: a Moroccan degree in Arabic, a Moroccan degree in French, and a degree equivalent to the French metropolitan standard. But the gap between secular and religious education was then narrowing. In 1961 al-Azhar was partly reformed along the lines of a Western university, while Egypt began to move towards massive Arabization and an expansion of the elementary school system, a tendency which the countries of the Maghrib later followed.

Political ideologies

Church, written languages, and school brought with them all sorts of Western attitudes outside of the strict realm of religion although some of these, such as the notion of science for instance, were closely linked to the overall worldview. Science dealt with a realm of ultimate reality existing outside religious dogma, which could be discovered by experiment and logic. In this view there were two domains in human life, one governed by religion and the other by scientific reason. The Europeans brought first the marvelous products of science to Africa and later its basic propositions became part of school curricula, especially in secondary school.

   The colonial authorities also brought with them the concepts of distinct secular and religious realms and most colonial powers practiced separation of church and state. Colonial governments regulated and often restricted the influence of particular religious organizations, a fact which did not escape their subjects. The Europeans also introduced secular systems of ideas, or ideologies, which legitimized the authority of the secular realm of government by an appeal to an absolute value, not specifically tied to religion. The most popular absolute value in Europe then was the notion of equality. By the end of the century it had spawned different "radical" political ideologies, including democracy, nationalism, and socialism, all of which were striving to undo older forms of government based on privilege of one sort or another. Democracy denounced elite rule, and proclaimed the equality of all *citizens*, and hence the right to have an equal say in government through elections. Nationalism denounced foreign rule and proclaimed the equality of all *nationalities*, defined by a common territory, a common history and common culture – in practice a common language – and culminated in the right to self-determination, that is to form their own sovereign nation state. Socialism denounced exploitation by the rich and proclaimed the equality of all as *workers*. These three ideologies could be combined but were not necessarily so.

Schools and literacy inevitably brought Africans into contact with all three ideologies. The one which appealed the most to them, because it was the most applicable to their situation, was nationalism, even though the precise *nationality* to which this referred was quite unclear. In North Africa the nationalist movement began in the late nineteenth century. It occurred especially in a pan-Islamic context in Egypt, following the dream of Jamal al-Dīn al-Afghāni to unite all Muslims once more into a single Muslim empire. But Egyptians had other options. They could strive for a greater Arabic-speaking nation, seeking its independence from the Ottoman empire, or more narrowly as Egyptians, stressing their common heritage from Pharaonic times in addition to religion and speech. In their struggle with the British occupiers the last option came to define their nationhood.

South of the Sahara the diversity of experience, language and religion within the boundaries of most colonies was such as to justify a bewildering variety of nationalisms. Moreover the colonial order itself was producing a whole new ethnic map, by sorting out people in recognized "tribes". Such a "recognition" usually led to the subsequent acquisition of a common written language and school system, a history of common experience in a common administrative entity, and the development of a common "customary law", all of which erased much of the previously existing diversity. Such a "recognition" encouraged local people to think that indeed they formed a single ethnic group. In consequence these new ethnic groups acquired all the typical features of nations within a generation of being set up as such by the colonizers.

But the bare fact of colonial rule at first overshadowed all the other options as to what constituted a nation. The earliest nationalism expressed by a Westernized elite in tropical Africa was a pan-African one in opposition to Europe. Edward W. Blyden was one of the earliest to teach a nationalist ideology. He was born in the West Indies but became a teacher in Liberia in the 1860s, was active in Sierra Leone from the 1870s onwards and remained a respected intellectual voice for English-speaking West Africa generally until well into this century. For him Liberia or Sierra Leone were not potential nations, but "Black Africa" was and his main goal was to build that as yet inchoate nation. His first concern was education, especially higher education which could serve as a medium for integrating and preserving African values. J.E. Casely Hayford carried the ideology further in his *Ethiopia Unbound* (1911) and by organizing a National Congress of British West Africa in 1920. His potential nation was no longer all of Africa, but all of the English-speaking territories of West Africa and he strove for a single state which would encompass all of these from the Gambia to Nigeria. An elite united by an English education and the goal of modernization would be the common glue of such a nation. Marcus Garvey's vision in the 1920s called for an African homeland in an unspecified location. It would be independent of European rule and a haven for Africans and their diaspora. In Senegal, meanwhile, Blaise Diagne was a counterpart to Casely Hayford in that he wanted a single French-speaking West

African nation. But in practice he became a deputy to the French National Assembly by campaigning under the slogan "Senegal for the Senegalese". And from the 1930s onwards all practical nationalists equated a colony with a potential nation and strove for independence in the name of self-determination. Only a few leaders equated nation and existing ethnic group, as was the practice in Europe or Asia. In most countries however this view of nationalism was labeled "tribalism" and denounced as a threat to the integrity of the existing territorial order.

Meanwhile however the vision of a pan-African nation continued to develop from the 1930s onwards among African students in France. They found themselves for the first time in close contact with Europeans who knew nothing at all about Africa, yet were thoroughly imbued with the inferiority of Africans. The students also felt homesick and culturally out of place. The result was the growth of the ideology called *négritude* ("blackness"). It was first propounded by Aimé Césaire, a West Indian of African descent, and the ideology crystallized in his *Cahiers d'un retour au pays natal* ("Notebooks of a Return to the Native Land") published in 1939. It held that "Blacks" held a special spiritual mission in the world because of their humane attitude towards the world. To be black was to be warm, human, emotional, ethical, generous, spontaneous; to be white was the contrary. This mixture of ideas about national character and race was very much the fashion in Europe at the time, especially among fascists, but also among their opponents. Thus the proclamation of the ideology ironically shows just how thoroughly Westernized these students were. Léopold Senghor of Senegal, a fellow poet then in France, reoriented Césaire's view and called it *Africanité* (Africanness). He taught that to be "black" was a privilege, that while all people were equal they were also different, and that "blacks" had the virtues sung by Césaire. This message had a wide repercussion among French-speaking African intellectuals and built up their confidence which in turn played a role in the practical struggle for independence. But English-speaking African elites, especially Nigerians, violently rejected it. Only Kwame Nkrumah, the first president of Ghana, espoused the tenets of this ideology and turned it into a cult of the "African personality" to bolster his vision of a single pan-African state. Later the idea of "Africanness" led in 1963 to the creation of the Organization of African Unity and somewhat later still as "authenticity" to an internal justification for many authoritarian regimes in tropical Africa.

The history of nationalist ideologies in South Africa is strikingly different from the above. The Anglo-Boer war opposed two classical European nationalisms, while their common disregard and contempt for Africans provoked the rise of a single African nationalism, which united all southern Africans in a common experience of segregation and exploitation. An African Native Congress was formed in 1907 with the aim of obtaining equal rights for Africans (and other groups) within the South African state. For them the state unit should remain the South African State, and would remain multinational. The equation of nation with ethnic group was made here by the ruling White nationalist South African party whose government began in the 1950s to organize a series of "homelands" (derisively called "Bantustans") for the Xhosa, Zulu, Tswana and others, which were to become nominally independent states.

Socialism spread into North Africa not much later than in Europe itself. It was bitterly opposed by the Muslim establishments, the wealthy landholders and traders, the ruling circles and the colonial authorities, but was espoused by industrial labor unions and later by a fraction among the military. It became an official ideology years after independence as the result of military action in Egypt, Algeria and Libya. In each case it was presented as the "scientific road" to social harmony and rapid modernization. But in each case Muslim movements strenuously continued to oppose it.

Socialism seemed at first sight not to fit the conditions in tropical Africa. The "dictature of the proletariat" made little sense in countries where most people were peasants or farmers, although it appealed to labor union leaders from Senegal to Nigeria and from Zambia to South Africa. The "class struggle" was not welcome to the elites and many disapproved of its hostility towards religion. But the African students who became well acquainted with Marxist doctrines in Europe, especially during the depression of the 1930s and later, were impressed by other features: the experience of the Soviet Union seemed to show that socialism was the road to rapid modernization; the European socialist parties were natural allies in the struggle against colonialism; and in a socialist state ethnicity would wither away. When socialist parties created welfare states in Western Europe after the Second World War, the ideology gained so much prestige that most African leaders now proclaimed to be socialist even though many held Marxist doctrines to be alien to and inapplicable to Africa. Instead they proposed a vague and romantic African socialism which virtually eliminated the whole ideology and reduced socialism to the promise that independence would secure economic equality and material security for all. Socialism as a goal was definitely far less important to them than nationalism. Only a few leaders such as Julius Nyerere in Tanganyika or Sékou Touré in Guinea took the ideology seriously and proposed to make it the cornerstone of the future state. In industrial South Africa socialist and communist ideals were however far more relevant. The ideology was known here since the late nineteenth century and it led to a major insurrection on the Rand in 1922. But at that point most White socialists valued racial segregation more than socialist brotherhood and the socialist movement suffered a severe setback. Opposition to socialism within the African National Congress (ANC) in those years came both from middle-class elites, who also often held strong religious convictions, and from leaders, who wanted the movement to be only open to Africans and were opposed to socialist color blindness. Such tensions between socialist and purely nationalist African leaders eased after 1945 when a younger generation of men sympathetic to socialism captured the leadership of the party.

As to the third ideology, democracy, all African leaders espoused it, but no one had very much to say about it. In practice African leaders used its principles to clamor for elections in the hope of achieving independence via the ballot-box, but remained otherwise quite autocratic, stressing the notions of "chief" or "patron" rather than praising the blessings of multiple parties and parliaments. Colonial governments were also autocratic. Most colonies only organized elections after 1945 as part of the decolonization process, at a time when the nationalist drive towards independence swamped every other consideration. Thus democracy as an ideology was not discussed very much during the colonial period.

Suggestions for further reading

Abernethy, David B., *The Political Dilemma of Popular Education: An African Case*, Stanford, Cal.: Stanford University Press, 1969.

Barrett, David, B., *Schism and Renewal in Africa*, Nairobi: Oxford University Press, 1968.

Hastings, A., *A History of African Christianity: 1950–1975*, London: Cambridge University Press, 1979.

July, Robert W., *The Origins of Modern African Thought: Its Development in West Africa during the Nineteenth and Twentieth Centuries*, New York: Praeger, 1967.

July, Robert W., *An African Voice: The Role of the Humanities in African Independence*, Durham, NC: Duke University Press, 1987.

Lewis, L.J. (ed.), *Phelps Stokes Report on Education in Africa*, London: Oxford University Press, 1962.

Ray, Benjamin C., *African Religions: Symbols, Ritual, and Community*, New York: Prentice-Hall, 1976.

Rotberg, Robert I. and Mazrui, Ali, *Protest and Power in Black Africa*, New York: Oxford University Press, 1970.

Scanlon, David G. (ed.), *Traditions of African Education*, New York: Colombia University, 1964.

Sundkler, Bengt, *Zulu Zion and Some Swazi Zionists*, London: Oxford University Press, 1976.

Van Beek, Walter (ed.), *Religion in Africa*, London: James Currey, 1992.

19

SOCIAL CHANGE IN COLONIAL AFRICA

The process of change within Africa's societies was shaped by the unequal confrontation between African subjects and their colonial rulers. The confrontation was unequal in ways that do not match the preconceptions of those who think that colonizing Europeans were strong and colonized Africans weak. The Europeans, it is true, could usually bring superior force of arms to bear in situations of military conflict. But the colonial period was also shaped by the weaknesses of Europeans and the strengths of Africans. We have already seen how small were the numbers of European administrators in relation to the huge African territories they governed. In southern Nigeria in 1925 there was one British political officer on duty for every 70,000 people. This meant that one administrator might find himself governing over several dozen subchiefs, or (in other parts of the Protectorate) over hundreds of chiefless villages, each with its subtle balance of political and ritual authorities. Under circumstances like these, the Europeans had only the most fragmentary and imperfect knowledge of the daily political struggles among their subjects. The European rulers had the Maxim gun, but early on they gave up hope of developing expertise in all the many hundreds of languages of Africa. It was in these languages that Africans communicated knowledge of politics, of society, and of the natural environment. Detailed knowledge of plants, of soils, of pests, and of diseases, local interpretations of political events and of the relative prestige of competing leaders were all encoded in languages that few (and often none) of Africa's colonial administrators understood.

As the period of colonial rule unfolded, European rulers (even without clear knowledge of African societies) were able to construct a framework of rules and incentives that would shape the decisions Africans took in their daily lives. The need to pay tax forced men to take up labor migration; the European criminal law changed the way people defined individual (as opposed to collective kingroup) responsibility; the economic pressures towards urbanization changed country people into city people. Despite these pressures, Africans succeeded in constructing new ways of life that were different from what Europeans would have wished for them. They created new, yet characteristically African, kinds of kinship association to serve labor migrant families; they constructed new forms of collective responsibility; and they imposed patterns on city life that owed much to indigenous ideas. African culture and European power were still separate and opposed, but now within an intricate process of colonial challenge and creative African synthesis.

Disease and authority in the early colonial period

The separation between the force of European arms and the flow of African knowledge led to disasters of health and survival in the years just after European conquest. Africans had developed substantial bodies of practical knowledge on how to preserve health and how to farm or herd successfully in the varied environments where they lived, but this knowledge did not count with Europeans who imposed their own requirements. For example, some of East Africa's highland peoples who lived in malaria-free areas knew that if they stayed overnight in lowland regions where mosquitos bred, they would be likely to suffer from malaria. Europeans who needed labor in the lowlands either did not know or did not care. They thought of African resistance to lowland labor as motivated by laziness. The Europeans had the armed force to require that African men move to the lowlands – that they take jobs, for example, in the coastal plain. The result, in Kenya, was that workers from the highlands died at annual rates as high as one hundred and forty-five per thousand in Mombasa and nearby coastal regions on the eve of the First World War.

In the first decades of colonial rule, European ignorance of biological hazards contributed to a set of disasters that threatened the population of many of the continent's regions. Sleeping sickness was an enormous killer in eastern Africa in the period just after conquest. Not until decades later, in the period between the two world wars, did colonial scientists learn that if they were to control eastern African sleeping sickness (trypanosomiasis), they would have to adopt African techniques. People (and cattle) contract sleeping sickness when the bites of particular kinds of flies (tsetse flies) inject them with parasites. In the case of the most rapidly virulent form of sleeping sickness (Rhodesian), the parasites survive in the blood of wild animals. Infection occurs when tsetse flies feed first on the animals, and then feed on people or on domestic cattle. In the interwar period colonial scientists began to understand that Africans who were allowed to use the environment in their own preferred way cleared the land near their homes of the brush that tsetse needed to survive. They allowed limited contacts between their livestock and the tsetse, so that the cattle did not die, but instead developed resistance. The scientists who read the record of African history also learned about trypanosomiasis control techniques in a Nguni kingdom in what was later to become the Mozambique-Zimbabwe border area. These people had a complex system for managing contacts between tsetse flies and people or cattle. They made multiple zones, including cleared land, land with brush in which people tried to hunt out wildlife (the reservoirs of infection), and wildlife preserves where people and cattle did not go. By doing this, they controlled trypanosomiasis infections. In the early colonial period, before Europeans learned these techniques, colonial attempts to control the disease were not based on African methods, and in most cases they made the situation worse.

Sleeping sickness in eastern Africa became epidemic in the early 1890s, during the process of colonial conquest. The cause was the enormous loss of wildlife and cattle as a result of a sweeping plague of rinderpest, perhaps introduced by the Italians in Eritrea, perhaps by the British who imported Russian cattle to feed their troops in the Nilotic Sudan. Whatever the source, the losses of wildlife and cattle upset the delicate balance that was at the heart of sleeping sickness control. The decline of herds led to the expansion of bush vegetation, leading, in turn, to the spread of tsetse flies carrying the disease. Colonial administrators, who did not understand the pattern, attempted to control the disease by moving people away from the encroaching bush, leading to still further spread of tsetse flies and sleeping sickness.

The form of sleeping sickness that was carried by wildlife killed its human hosts relatively quickly. A second form, called Gambian, was slower acting. People survived long enough to become reservoirs of the parasite, so that tsetse flies could carry the infection from one person to another, even when wild animals were not present. The way to prevent an epidemic was to stay away from the tsetse flies. Epidemics broke out when colonial requirements forced people to move into settings they had previously avoided. In the northeastern corner of the Congo, for example, Belgian administrators forced people who lived scattered on the upper hillsides above the Semliki Valley to move down to more accessible villages, to make administrative control easier. A large proportion of the valley's population then died of sleeping sickness. In French Equatorial Africa and in some parts of the Belgian King Leopold's Congo, colonial demands that laborers leave their homes, or that they work in the forest, led to the deaths of tens of thousands of people from sleeping sickness. Changes in the ecology of Gambian sleeping sickness led to the deaths of as much as a third of the population of southeastern Uganda in an epidemic that began in 1902.

Smallpox was also a major problem. Epidemics ravaged the population of scattered areas all the way from Kenya to Nigeria. In Kenya, smallpox was the end-product of a process by which conquest led to famine, which in turn led to disease. Under normal conditions a smallpox outbreak in a village affected only a few people at any one time, and after it they were immune. The next outbreak would also be small because it was limited to the villagers who had not yet become immune. Under famine conditions, people moved by the hundreds to places where food was available, and the concentrations of non-immune people were then subject to sweeping epidemics of smallpox.

In the early colonial period much of French Equatorial Africa and of the Congo were given over to private enterprises in which all the administrators were business employees. The concessionary companies often made their profits by compelling Africans to collect wild forest products such as rubber, and by punishing inadequate returns with beatings, rape, or death. Villages were burned and people fled to the forests, where they lived for years. Thousands died.

Even where working conditions were not as brutal as in French Equatorial Africa, labor migration and the increased movement that came with railroads and motor transport led to the spread of old diseases and the introduction of new ones. Smallpox, tuberculosis, gonorrhea, influenza, and many other diseases spread along the lines of rail and the routes most commonly followed by migrants.

In eastern and equatorial Africa a period of demographic decline continued from the time of conquest (or in some cases the period immediately preceding it) until the mid-

1920s. The population patterns of West Africa in this period were more stable, with declines in some places and modest growth in others. The colonial regimes were not as consistently brutal as they were in equatorial Africa, nor in most places were African ecological adaptations as locally specific as on the eastern side of the continent.

What was at stake, in all cases, was a competition between African and European understandings of the causes of health and illness, of the relationship between people and plants, of how the soils ought to be used, of the place held by humans and animals in the world they shared, and of how it is that people live good lives and thrive.

In African societies in the period before conquest, public affairs having to do with health, welfare, and prosperity were often subject to ritual control – by spirit mediums, by senior adepts in healing associations, by diviners, or by oracles. In pre-colonial Malawi, for example, Mbona was a ritual healing association that people joined in time of illness, but it was also "a ritually directed eco-system." Mbona was able to protect fragile resources by restricting farming or grazing, or by prohibiting such land clearing practices as the burning of wild vegetation. Diviners in many places consulted the spirits before advising people on where to locate their villages; in doing so, they decided on places where the water sources appeared clean, and where there were no obvious insect pests. In the kingdom of Bunyoro, senior mediums of the Chwezi spirits (described above in Chapter 5) conveyed advice from the spirits to the king on how to maintain his fertility, to achieve success in warfare, and to promote the fertility of the land. In southern Nigeria the Aro oracle, who spoke to people from inside a cave by a stream, advised on the measures necessary for people to maintain health and fertility, and was also responsible for the maintenance of public order and the regulation of trade. In the Shambaa kingdom of Tanzania, healers and diviners were in charge of the maintenance of irrigation canals.

The Europeans, when they came, found it difficult to imagine how to negotiate with these ritual authorities. They were on familiar terrain when they negotiated with chiefs, but they could not imagine establishing a public order in which they shared authority with spirit mediums or oracles, even if these controlled practical knowledge. In many places Europeans came to think of diviners or mediums as enemies of colonial rule, because they controlled the kind of survival knowledge that became implicated in wars of resistance. In the case of Tanzania's Maji Maji rebellion, for example, Africans who felt their survival threatened by forced cotton cultivation, which was undermining food farming, traveled in great numbers in 1904 to consult a spirit medium named Kinjikitile. They received war medicines from him, and then rebelled. In Zimbabwe, also, leadership for the largest rebellion came from spirit mediums in the great Shona uprising of 1896–7.

Europeans in every colony attacked the ritual authority of African leaders. In Tanzania after Maji Maji many Germans attacked African healers wherever they found them. For the remainder of Tanzania's colonial history, healers who organized public events were likely to be arrested. In Nigeria, a British military force dynamited the cave from which the Aro oracle spoke. In Uganda, the British made Chwezi mediumship illegal. Both the British and the French put laws on the books all across Africa making most forms of local healing illegal. They rarely enforced these laws when a healer treated a private patient. The laws were meant to suppress large-scale ritual authority.

Alongside the government measures were missionary ones. In the early colonial period there were some Christian missionaries who made direct attacks on the ritual authority of Africans – proving their own power by cutting down dangerous sacred forests and attacking shrines. At times they had ritual authorities arrested and detained, and they preached against what they saw as the falseness of African ritual knowledge.

The long-term sustained colonial attack on ritual authority had profound effects. It left ritual leaders weaker than political ones, thus undermining the position of women, who were more likely to hold ritual rather than political authority. Ritual leaders did not disappear entirely, but they were driven underground; their influence was felt more often than it was seen. They learned to be secretive about their skills, so that practical knowledge as expressed through ritual action, much of which had been in the open during the period before conquest, was now invisible. When Germans attacked healers in Tanzania, the healers did not give up their work, but they cut off the hair decoration that was an open mark of their positions, and they exchanged their decorated medicine baskets for ordinary baskets. The healers were part of a more general phenomenon of African life under colonial control, in which the things that Europeans despised or attacked did not go out of existence, but instead became invisible.

Coerced labor

In much of Africa the harshest period of rule was the period before the First World War. Then a transition took place, sooner in some colonies and later in others, from an economy based on the most brutal and naked compulsion, to one based more substantially on economic incentives and constraints. In Kenya, the British system requiring appointed chiefs to recruit laborers by force did not continue for long after the First World War. Elements of coercion continued longer in French, and Belgian, and Portuguese colonies. As late as the 1950s the Portuguese government still gave concessionary companies the legal right to require that peasants cultivate cotton, which the companies bought at low prices administered by the state. Peasants who did not produce the required amount could be whipped, taken off to work in forced labor gangs, or in some cases sent to jail.

One of the reasons for the end of coerced labor (sooner in some places, later in others) was peasant resistance, which undermined the profits of the regimes of coercion. Some Mozambiquan cotton farmers left the territory and moved off to Tanganyika or Nyasaland rather than farm under duress. Others schemed together to convince the authorities that their soil would not support cotton: they met secretly before planting time to cook cotton seeds in boiling water, then carefully planted the seeds according to direction, all to prove to the company that cotton was not a viable crop under local conditions.

The Mozambiquan cotton regime was unusual on the African continent because the coercion continued to 1961, decades after most British colonies had switched to systems of economic incentives as a way of achieving production. In one important respect, however, the early colonial pattern of working by force continued to have profound effects on rural economies right through to the time of independence and beyond. This was in the long-term consequences of the government's seizure of African farmlands for White settlement. Governments gave settlers large tracts of land in colonies all through East, Central, and southern Africa, and in the Maghrib. In Kenya just after the turn of the century, for example, the government gave new settlers 1000–acre tracts of agricultural land or 5000 acres of pastureland. Africans (who in many cases had known the land to be their own before it was taken) became labor tenants on the European farms. In Northern Rhodesia, Nyasaland, Angola, and many other colonies, the labor tenancy system provided Whites with non-wage labor. An African household head worked on a settler's land for a certain number of days a year in return for living, farming, and herding on the land with his family, for their sustenance. In the early days of labor tenancy Africans had substantial bargaining power because land was abundant and labor scarce. In Kenya, in the early years, if a landowner refused to allow tenants to graze their stock, they moved to another farm. In South Africa, moving from one White farmer to another who would let you keep more of your crop was called "jumping the fence." Later in the century, when the economy had expanded, when population had grown, when land was becoming more scarce, the labor tenants lost most of their bargaining power.

Rural society reordered

Typical peasants in most colonies farmed their own land and chose many of their own crops, but did so within a framework of rules and institutions shaped by Europeans. The colonizers took a number of measures to ensure that Africans would produce the export crops that sustained the colonial economy. They imposed high levels of taxation to be paid in cash rather than kind, so that African farmers would have to sell crops for money if they were to meet their obligations, and they built railways to transport crops to the ports. In addition, the colonial governments introduced legal changes that, in subtle ways, made participation in the capitalist economy more likely. For example, in most places they began to tax every adult man, rather than taxing kinship groups. This redefined relations between individuals and the state in most places, removing the lineage or kinship group leader from the position he had occupied as mediator between the individual and formal political authorities. In most pre-colonial states the leader had paid tribute for the group as a whole, and was called on to provide some of his men in war. Now each man, separately, was responsible for his own relationship to the state. Old habits died hard. As late as the 1950s the French, in some places, were prohibiting young men from taking examinations for advanced educational placement unless all members of their lineage had paid tax. Nevertheless, the pressure towards individual legal responsibility was profound, and with it the sense that each man would need to sell crops, or migrate to a work place, if he was to meet his obligations.

Legal individualism showed itself also in the criminal law, which introduced revolutionary principles among the many societies of sub-Saharan Africa that had not imprisoned criminals. Before conquest, incidents of assault or theft were treated as disturbances in the balance between the two kinship groups involved, with harmony to be restored, most often, when the offending group paid some form of compensation.

The introduction of European criminal law, of flogging or imprisonment for criminals, undermined many forms of collective responsibility, and helped to establish the economic individual before the law.

Kinship groupings did not disappear; they remained central to African social organization, but with their character now subtly changed. People could not do without these forms of organization. Kinship or descent groups were insurance associations: they provided support for the sick, the disabled, and the aged. Wealthier members, who often contributed more than their share to serve the needy, benefited from the prestige of their positions, and also from the political support and labor of their poorer kinsfolk.

Land tenure also changed. Tenure systems varied enormously in pre-colonial Africa, but usually enough land was available to those who needed to farm it. People were concerned less with absolute land scarcity than with political rights in land, and with the transfer of improvements that an individual had made in the land. Political rights were held by the local chief, ritual leader, or descent group head, who gave his permission for newcomers to move into a territory, since their arrival would have implications for local political and kinship arrangements. Rights of a different sort were involved if an individual had planted trees or terraced the piece of land on which someone wished to farm. The person who had labored to improve the land might insist on receiving gifts or payment in exchange for the labor invested. Once the investment had been passed on to the next generation it was harder to give away in exchange because an individual's rights were usually passed on to all his heirs as a group. Rights to use the land for a period might be divided among individual heirs, but the right to transfer it to an outsider depended on the entire group's unanimous permission. In practice, this meant that land was not usually sold.

Two major changes came with the colonial period. First, colonial governments worked on the theory that all land had an owner, even when it was unoccupied and unimproved. In many cases the conquest governments laid claim to all land not under cultivation, awarding some of it to settlers, delimiting some of it as forest reserves, and keeping the remainder for government use or sale. This attitude was quite different from a pre-colonial chief's right to welcome or turn away newcomers, based as it had been on the assumption that land was abundant and not to be sold, and that new followers were to be welcomed as contributing to local armed strength and prestige. The idea of owning the right to sell land that neither you nor your ancestors (nor, for that matter, anyone's ancestors) had worked on was completely foreign. The second change resulted from the increasing scarcity of land as a result of population increase, colonial land seizures, and the expansion of land used to grow crops for sale. The increasing competition for crop land created pressures to define individual rights, and this shift made intuitive sense to people who had seen the concept of the individual redefined by criminal law. At the same time, there were powerful counter-pressures for keeping land under collective ownership. We have already seen that people needed and valued their kinship groups, and these often defined their unity in terms of collective land ownership. Moving to individualized tenure therefore carried the threat that people would lose their insurance groups. Another reason for Africans to insist on retaining communal land ownership, especially in settler colonies, was that the emergence of freehold might mean the land would be sold to White settlers.

The individualization of land tenure was at times a matter of government policy. The ruling powers found that collectively held land was hard to buy or sell, and they believed that this immobility of a major factor of production slowed down growth in the settler or export sector. In French Algeria, as far back as the 1850s and 1860s, land ownership was individualized so as to make it available for sale to Europeans, and also to break the solidarity of large lineages whose military power threatened French control. By the time of independence, this policy had not only succeeded in transferring two-fifths of all Algerian farmland to foreign owners; most of the land still held by Algerians also changed from collective to individual ownership. This limited the great majority of Algerian farmers to plots smaller than twenty-five acres, while many others lost their land altogether and became a landless proletariat of agricultural workers on the European farms – or on those of the Algerians who succeeded in putting together sizable holdings under individual control. The French tried this policy south of the Sahara as well, but under different conditions. In these regions the actual individualization of land titles was no greater in French territories than in British ones.

Gender and farm work

The European authorities intervened also to shape rural gender roles and the gender division of farm labor. As in the case of land, their interventions did not impose a new set of practices on African societies, but instead changed the balance of power in preexisting relationships. In societies where positions of authority were divided between men and women, administrators tended to ignore women's authority, and therefore to undermine it. In southeastern Nigeria, for example, the British introduced male warrant chiefs in Igbo-speaking areas where women had previously held some positions of influence. The warrant chiefs were ultimately driven from office after a mass uprising of women in 1929, called the Women's War. In one part of central Africa, small numbers of headwomen lost their positions when the British decided that there were too many local authorities, and began to consolidate administrative units.

The colonial pattern of relying on influential African men in matters of administration meant that it was their opinions that would carry weight, and not the opinions of women. In one part of Nyasaland, for example, female-headed households were having great difficulty paying their taxes during the depression. British administrators exempted many of them from taxes until the economy improved. But the all-male district councils of chiefs, headmen, and rich subjects argued that women on their own should pay tax, and that they should be able to escape taxation only by marrying polygynous men who paid a flat tax no matter how many wives they had. Women who then chose to marry so as to avoid tax spent much of their time farming cotton for their husbands. Colonial rule did not inevitably lead to a loss of autonomy for women. In more prosperous times the cotton-growing women with oppressive husbands had been able to pay back bridewealth with cotton earnings and begin farming for themselves. Elsewhere, oppressed women sought refuge in mission stations, or they gained in independence, as we shall see, by moving to the cities.

The gender division of labor on sub-Saharan farms was extremely varied. In some societies men and women took care of different stages in the farming cycle. Men often cleared the land of brush and then worked together with women to cultivate the soil; the women then took responsibility for weeding. In a second kind of labor division, men did almost all the labor required for growing one crop and women for another. In some parts of the Gambia, for example, work parties of men grew upland millet while women worked on rice. In many African societies, but not all, women contributed the largest share of farming labor. Among the exceptions were the Yoruba of Nigeria, among whom men did most of the farming, while women spent more time on crafts and trade.

Where women performed much of the farm labor, they usually made a clear distinction between their own farm plots and those of their husbands, so that they could keep control of food they grew themselves. This was especially important in times of hunger, when women who were skilled farmers could feed their children and see them thrive, even if other women – perhaps even co-wives in a polygynous household – were short of food. In addition to working on their own farm plots, wives would provide some labor also on their husbands' gardens.

When colonial export crops were introduced, they led husbands and wives to re-arrange farming patterns so as to meet new labor demands. In most but not all cases, cash crops were grown on men's fields. Coffee in most of eastern Africa was a men's crop, as was cocoa in most of West Africa. In a region of the Ivory Coast where cotton had been a pre-colonial women's crop, grown for making clothing, the emergence of a market for the crop led men to insist that cotton for sale would be men's property, grown on their own plots. The reservation of cash crops for men happened for a number of reasons: because Europeans assumed that the commercial sector was meant for men, and also because this fitted gender assumptions in many African societies. Colonial officials distributed seed for new crops to men, organized marketing structures to buy from men, and (late in the colonial period) provided agricultural extension services for men. Women, who did a majority of the farming, and therefore controlled a significant body of technical information, were largely left out of the colonial structure for administering agriculture; women's knowledge was defined as irrelevant.

One of the continuing struggles of the colonial period was over the question of how much labor women would put in on their husbands' farms, and how much they would get back in return. Women's labor had been divided, long before the colonial period, between work on their own plots and work on men's plots, which was seen as labor for the household as a whole. Now, with the rise of the cash economy, husbands and wives had to agree whether women would work on men's cash farms, and whether they would claim part of the profits. In Mazabuka district in Zambia, for example, in the years before colonial conquest women controlled grain crops, while their husbands were concerned with livestock and trade goods. In those days it was the young men who were worst off: they could marry only after providing their in-laws with years of work, as brideservice. Under colonial rule, the division of labor underwent a series of major changes. First, young men withdrew some of their farm labor and began to pay bridewealth instead, using money earned as wages. A second major change came when government officials, worried about the soil erosion caused by men's cash crops, insisted that women interplant their grain crops in men's fields. This innovation shifted the control over some of women's grain crops to men. Later on, after ploughs were introduced for commercial grain cultivation, women began to work at plough cultivation, on men's land, with men claiming the proceeds. In other places, women fought back and won advantages for themselves. When men in the railway region of Zambia reduced the amount of land they allocated to their wives' plots, some women simply left at peak labor periods, refusing to work for their husbands; they went off to the villages of their own kinsfolk, where they had some control over the land.

The division of labor between men and women was shaped also by a second division, between richer and poorer peasant households. Where this division was important, people in poor households often needed to sell their labor to get through a hungry season, or to meet a short-term cash need; wealthier households might hire labor, to ease the wife's burden.

The division between better- and worse-off did not depend everywhere on control over land, or on farming income. Among the earliest rich farmers, in many parts of Africa, were chiefs who could call on the labor of their subjects. They did so in northwestern Tanzania, in Rwanda, in Buganda, and in many other places across the continent. A second source of differentiation between richer and poorer farmers was the wage economy. Men who left home to work at skilled jobs, and who earned high wages, could afford to pay farm workers at home, whereas the wives of low-wage workers were forced to do both men's and women's farm work, without paid help. In central Kenya in the 1930s, carpenters and other skilled artisans were making up to one hundred and fifty shillings a month, at a time when the unskilled wage was between sixteen and twenty shillings. Many of the most prosperous farms were run by the wives of artisans, who used money from their husbands' earnings to hire low-wage workers.

Wage-earners, both skilled and unskilled, and also cash-crop farmers, inevitably invested some of their earnings in kinship relations: in family rituals and celebrations, and in support for relatives who were ill, or moving off to the city, or otherwise in need. The investment in kinsfolk gave life a rich and warm social texture. It also served the most practical of purposes: to insure that the giver would also some day receive help, if it was needed. This was the social security system of colonial Africa, for neither the state nor employers provided health care, disability pay, or support in old age. Households could not survive health crises without help. If a household included a husband, a wife, and two children under five, it could not survive a period when the wife was in the late stages of pregnancy and the husband seriously ill. If it was planting time, there would be no one to plant the seeds which would keep the food supply coming; there was no one to bring water from the stream and wood from the forest for cooking; no one to provide nursing care for the sick; no one to care for the children. The fact that everyone could anticipate a period of need led people to plan for it. The individualization of criminal responsibility or of freehold land ownership might have tempted people to abandon their kinship groups, and did in fact lead to their restructuring, but people who went without support did not survive. It was for this reason (among others) that Yoruba cocoa farmers, Shambaa coffee farmers, Kongo and Shona peasants continued to expend significant proportions of their resources on their wider kin groups throughout the colonial period.

Migrant labor and gender

Investing in kinship relations had special significance for the thousands of peasant farmers (usually men) who left home at some time in their lives to spend periods as migrant workers in mines or plantations, farms or other enterprises. As we have seen in Chapter 17, the male workers who lived away from home for periods that ranged from a few months to many years often left women and children behind. The wives and children of absent workers depended, for their welfare, on the strength and cohesion of a network of kinsfolk.

Migrant labor was important well before most of Africa entered the full colonial period. In the Gambia, "strange farmers" who traveled from their homes to peanut growing areas produced a significant part of the crop by the mid-nineteenth century. In South Africa in the 1840s, Zulu men who had lost their cattle in regional upheavals went by the thousands to Natal, to earn the money to rebuild their herds. They brought forms of association and of mutual assistance with them from Zululand and used them to shape an urban work culture in the town of Durban. Many of South Africa's workers in the late nineteenth century came from parts of southern Africa that had not yet been conquered. They were men from regions that had suffered drought, or some other natural disaster, and who worked to recoup their fortunes by engaging in migrant labor. The rinderpest infection that killed up to 90 per cent of the cattle in numerous regions of eastern, central, and southern Africa in the 1890s impoverished whole regions and sent thousands of men out to seek employment with Europeans. Coming, as it did, at the time when South Africa's gold mines were being built, it contributed to the labor supply at a major time of expansion.

Biological disasters like rinderpest could not ensure a regular labor supply over the years. The gold mines of South Africa, by themselves, employed close to 190,000 people by 1912, and they needed to have workers come every year, not only at disaster times. The forces capable of exerting constant pressure on workers were economic ones. Everywhere in Africa, as we have seen, taxes were meant to push people into export production, but that production might have come in the form of peasant farming, which would have left mines, plantations, and settler farms without workers. Governments that needed migrant workers could ensure a labor supply only by restricting the possibilities for peasant farming. In some places, they did so by limiting the land held by Africans. As we have seen, South Africa severely restricted African land ownership with the Natives' Land Act of 1913; Southern Rhodesia and Kenya took similar measures in the 1920s and 1930s. These governments also restricted African production for sale by keeping most of the land with good transport for Whites. Governments also manipulated duties, marketing, and veterinary services to deprive African farmers of cash income. In Kenya, Africans were not permitted to grow coffee, supposedly because poorly tended African coffee could spread diseases to settler farms, but quite clearly because peasants who earned money from their own crops would not work for low wages. In Southern Rhodesia, a central marketing board paid African farmers much lower maize prices than were paid to Europeans.

Oscillating migrant labor systems, in which men left their rural homes to work for a period and then return, were usually low wage systems. Employers at the mines or plantations did not pay enough to house or feed a worker's family. These expenses were paid for by the people in the farming community back at home, most often by women coping with farm labor on their own, without men's help in clearing or harvesting. Regions that became regular providers of migrant labor often found themselves entrenched in deepening poverty. By the mid-1930s a typical farm household in the Transkei, a labor-source area in South Africa, produced only about 58 per cent of the cereals it needed for basic subsistence, and more than half of all men between the ages of 18 and 54 were away as migrants for at least part of the year.

Oscillating migrant labor systems were considerably less damaging to workers' home areas when the work was seasonal and coordinated with the agricultural cycle at home. This was often the case with migrants from Upper Volta to the Gold Coast, in West Africa, because the farming calendars of the savanna and forest differed substantially. These migrants, who numbered in the tens of thousands by the 1920s, worked on African-owned cocoa farms.

It came to seem natural that men in migrant labor systems would leave home and women would stay, but this was not the inevitable outcome. In East Africa in the late 1890s – the period following famine and rinderpest – rural women appeared in the labor camps and colonial towns, trying to earn money to help their families recover. In South Africa white Afrikaner women, at the turn of the century, migrated to the cities in desperate attempts to save their fathers' farms.

In Southern Rhodesia the early generations of African migrants included women who went into petty trade, selling prepared food or washing clothes for male workers, or selling sexual services. Some women refused to wait for their husbands to return, and took other men in the countryside, or left for the city with other men. Their decisions had subversive consequences, for men who feared losing their wives hesitated to become migrant laborers. Chiefs and headmen also found the loss of women threatening: they were losing women's labor in the countryside, and they were threatened also with the loss of their sons' loyalty. The bridewealth which they received for their daughters, and which was now at risk, could be used to pay for their sons' marriages, thus binding the young men to them. The older men pressed Europeans to tighten laws controlling women. Their pressure led to the passage of the Native Adultery Punishment Ordinance of 1916, which punished married women's adultery with a huge fine or a year in prison with hard labor. District elders also made it illegal for a young woman to marry without her guardian's consent and, by the late 1930s, they made it illegal for a woman to move to the city unless she carried a pass showing that senior men approved. Despite all these legal barriers, some women continued to move to the cities.

The women and children who remained at home in the countryside bore some of the heaviest costs of labor migration. When men's labor was withdrawn from the rural economy, the women left behind had to find a way to construct a new kind of agricultural economy. One way to make do with less labor was to reduce the number of crops, by dropping the crops that had been grown entirely by men, or by choosing to keep a few from among the many crops that had been grown jointly. A reduction in the range of crops meant a reduction in food security. The crops that were kept were the ones that provided the majority of the calories people needed to live. But other crops disappeared, and they might include the ones that had been grown because they were especially resistant to drought or pests, or because they ripened early and supplied hungry season food before the harvest. Levels of infant and child malnutrition were very high in most source areas for migrant labor.

Sometimes new crops were introduced. Cassava became much more popular in a number of labor-source areas. This was a root crop that had two main advantages for labor-migrant families. In places where men cleared new gardens to bring fertile soil into cultivation, women could manage for longer periods without fresh gardens by planting cassava, which grew on poor soils. Another advantage of cassava was that some varieties could be left in the ground, awaiting harvest, for a period of years. Women could therefore rely on it in times of need, when labor was not available for growing grain crops. Cassava was, however, much poorer nutritionally than the grain crops it replaced, and gave children little but empty calories.

Mothers could meet some food needs for their children by purchasing food, or by hiring people to help with farm work, but they could only do this if they received remittances of money from their men at the work place. The very low level of wages made this difficult for all but a very few highly paid workers. Money sent home by men was important for the women and children left behind. In the Ciskei, in South Africa, a medical team did a study of severely malnourished children and found that 70 per cent had fathers who had fallen completely out of touch with their families.

The health situation of women and children was affected in profound ways by infectious diseases like tuberculosis and gonorrhea that men brought with them from the work place. Tuberculosis began to spread in southern Africa by the turn of the century, with the South African mines serving as an originating point of spread. The disease moved into labor-source areas with lightning speed because men who contracted the disease at the mines were sent home. They spread it to their undernourished children in the reserves, who suffered the disease in its active form and so spread it further. By the late 1920s 65–70 per cent of mine recruits from Mozambique were infected with tuberculosis, even though twenty years earlier fewer than 2 per cent of new recruits from Mozambique had tested positive for the disease. A tuberculosis survey in the Transkei in the late 1920s found that 88 per cent of all adult men and women tested positive.

African women in labor-source areas knew that their lives were being damaged. People in Bulozi, in Northern Rhodesia, called some forms of venereal disease *machangane*, named after the Shangaan miners from Mozambique. In Natal and Zululand, in the teens of this century, people began to say that they had illnesses caused by a new kind of spirit called *indiki*. This was the spirit of a dead man, one of many migrants who had come to South Africa to work, but then had died without returning home. The spirits of these lost migrants were wandering the countryside, menacing the local people, entering their chests, and causing them to become deranged and to cry in a deep bellowing voice. In the 1930s some Zulu women thought that their babies were being afflicted by *ipleti*, a malformed placenta that was like an empty plate (hence the name). They were saying that their children were dying because the placenta, normally full of nourishing food, was now an empty plate.

Some women, as we have seen, broke down the barriers of the migrant labor system by moving to cities and mining towns. By the 1930s, mine managers in the Copperbelt of Northern Rhodesia were providing the wives of workers with single-room spaces for married couples, where otherwise a room held four miners. They also provided the women with garden plots to grow some of their own food. The managers accepted the erosion of the migrant system in this case in response to a miners' strike and because they were having difficulty competing for labor with South African mines that paid higher wages.

Some wives at the mines accompanied workers from their home areas, but others were women who came from the countryside near the mines, and who were constructing a new way of life for themselves. They took advantage of the mine garden plots to grow vegetables for sale, or earned large sums by brewing beer, in violation of mine rules. Entrepreneurial mine wives did not always leave when their husbands did: at times they stayed on as "wives" to successive "husbands," or to go into business for themselves. In later periods some of the most prosperous entrepreneurs in the Copperbelt, people who owned retail shops and restaurants, were women who had begun as mine "wives."

In the Copperbelt, in Nairobi, and at other destinations of large numbers of working men without wives, there were some women who lived on their own, and who earned money by selling domestic or sexual services. Some of these women would do laundry, serve meals, provide conversation and possibly also sex, and would be paid according to the services given. They had no male procurers; they decided for themselves on how to spend their earnings. Some sent money home to their rural families, helping in much the way a male migrant would. Others tried to build secure and stable places for themselves in the city. In Nairobi, as in Kano (in Northern Nigeria, in a very different historical setting), women bought real estate with savings from prostitution. They owned urban houses which they rented out by the room. This brought not only a secure income, but also an influential position in the affairs of the town. A landlord acted towards her tenants in much the way a senior relative would, establishing basic social rules, and looking out for their welfare. Women who had bought property were respected and influential urban leaders.

This was not the only possible pattern of African leadership in the towns that attracted migrant labor. These magnet towns were also home to African men who earned their livings in jobs that required mission education: as clerks for trading companies, as school teachers, or as evangelists. Their wives faced conflicts and compromises very different from those of women entrepreneurs. Their churches often taught the value of a very Victorian domesticity for women, but the comforts of middle-class domestic life were rarely available to the wives of African men on colonial pay scales. Small numbers of women were able to live up to the missionaries' domestic ideal. Others found work themselves, sometimes in the houses of White employers, using the domestic skills they had learned.

Post-war changes

During the Second World War, and in the years just before it, and then with increasing rapidity after it, the texture of life in many parts of the continent changed in important ways. Most regions went through a period of quickening population growth along with the increasing commercialization of peasant agriculture, rapid urbanization, and a partial shift from migrant or casual jobs to permanent ones.

Population growth played a role in many of these changes. The great influenza pandemic of 1918–19 was the last of the sweeping population disasters of the early colonial period. By 1930 population in many regions had begun to grow – slowly at first, but then with increasing rapidity after the Second World War. Rough estimates give the continent's population as 164 million in 1930, 219 million in 1950, and 352 million in 1970. Each successive generation since 1930 has had more young people to educate and to feed. In the countryside, children moving to maturity could no longer make do on the land cultivated by their parents: with population growth, some could open up new lands, while others moved to the city. Many colonies experienced urbanization without a reduction in rural numbers.

The causes of population growth are still under debate. For a long time, demographers believed that population in the pre-colonial period was limited by high levels of mortality. According to this argument, Africans always chose to have many babies, but before the colonial period many of them died, and many adults died early. The cause of growth, according to this position, was a reduction in death rates. More recently this view has come under attack by those who argue that birth rates increased in the colonial period, and that it is increasing fertility rather than declining mortality that explains population growth. The evidence on both sides is still accumulating.

The argument for increasing fertility grew in appeal when it became clear that an older explanation – that population growth had resulted from the introduction of biomedical care – was not valid, because this form of health care was unavailable to the majority of the rural population in colonial Africa. The possibility of fertility increase is supported by a general change in birth-spacing practices on the African continent. During the colonial period, all across sub-Saharan Africa, there was a decrease in the length of time that mothers went between births. This appears to have happened when young women became increasingly free from the requirements by older relatives that they wait for a long period after the birth of a child before risking pregnancy again. The decrease may also have grown out of people's perceptions, in the colonial period, of how many children a household needed if it was to send young men out to work and have other children to care for farms at home, and then later to provide for aging parents. The new practice of shortening birth spacing was not good for child health, and so it is not clear whether it led to greater numbers of children surviving, but it might well have done so.

The argument for declining mortality focuses on a number of other changes. Colonial regimes took trouble to control epidemic disease; widespread epidemics of smallpox, for example, became less common as the colonial period continued. The most dramatic population increases came after the Second World War, and they may have been associated, in part, with the introduction of antibiotics and anti-malarials, even in the absence of doctors or medical assistants. Tablets of these drugs could usually be purchased without prescription, or were administered by informal injectionists. Injections administered outside the bounds of medical control probably led at first to a decline in deaths from infectious diseases, but they may also, ultimately, have contributed to the rapidity with which the AIDS epidemic was spreading by the 1980s. Other likely causes of population increase during the colonial period were the increasing availability of famine food, with improvements in the transportation net, and the fact that city people had an easier time getting food, moderately clean water, and medical care than people in the countryside. Hospital care, rarely available in the countryside, reduced the death rate of women in childbirth and of people who had been in accidents. By the late colonial period, urban death rates were consistently lower than rural ones, and this was significant for larger population trends because an increasing proportion of the population lived in cities.

The great social changes of post-war Africa were, in part, responses to population growth. Urbanization, the increasing commercialization of peasant agriculture, and the slow shift towards permanently urbanized labor were all social strategies that Africans adapted at a time of growing population, but they had deep roots also in economic change and in changing colonial policy. At the end of the Second World War the colonizing countries faced difficult dilemmas that called for substantial changes of direction. Britain and France came out of the war weakened, deeply in debt to the United States, and very short of foreign exchange. The solution was to increase imports from colonial Africa that would take the place of others from dollar zones, and also to increase African exports to dollar zones. The way to do this was to invest money in the African colonies, to build infrastructure, and to expand the number of agricultural officers and other technical staff. The total of grants and loans from Britain to the colonies between 1946 and 1960 was more than twice as much (in constant currency) as all grants and loans from 1880 to 1939; French post-war grants and loans were five times as great as all earlier ones.

The building of infrastructure was being done at a time of African political discontent. Africans who had served in the war came back with a wider experience of the world, with an awareness that some colonial peoples, especially in Asia, were moving towards independence, and with a sense of entitlement: they expected personal gain and nationalist political advance. The situation to which they returned was already explosive. Wartime scarcity had led to price increases in imported goods, and coerced wartime production had held down wages and crop prices. The colonial powers saw a need to keep political forces under control while expanding production.

Up until this point Africa's colonial rulers had not placed a great emphasis on raising levels of the productivity of African labor. Workers in mines, docks, and plantations took part in a low-wage, low-skill economy. Migrant laborers and laborers who worked by the day were not expected to build up significant levels of skills, nor were they to be paid for the skills they did develop. In the new era, however, some colonies were to introduce factory production, and this would require skilled workers who did not return to rural homes, or come to work only by the day. Employers who invested in skills expected them to be practiced by permanent workers. This implied a change in society. If increasing numbers of workers were to live permanently at the workplace, they would need urban housing for their families, health care and education for their children, and wages that were adequate to feed a family.

The colonizers hoped that a stable urban work force would also be politically docile. The British and the French had been learning since the 1930s that a work force built on migrant or casual labor was potentially dangerous. They had learned this in strikes by the Mombasa dock-workers in Kenya in 1934, by Copperbelt miners in 1935, by workers in the British West Indies in 1935 and 1938, and in the French West African Dakar general strike of 1946 and railway strike of 1947–8. Workers who moved back and forth between the workplace and other occupations were able to mobilize the help of the wider community in times of trouble. Some of the strikes that began among narrow sets of workers grew into broad-scale unrest among the general population; in others, strikers were able to hold out for long periods because they received material support from non-workers. The way out of this was to transform the basis of urban work: to encourage a permanent urban work force, and to pay workers for their skills.

The colonial authorities faced similar challenges and compromises in the country-side. If farm productivity was to grow sufficiently to meet the need for dollars, then the most able African farmers would increasingly accumulate wealth, and the least able would become more marginal, perhaps ultimately to be driven off the land. The crisis of land scarcity had been clear by the 1930s in eastern, southern, and central Africa, where land in the most densely settled areas appeared to have reached (or in some cases passed) the limits of its carrying capacity. Officials in Kenya in the late 1930s were worried because significant parts of the Kikuyu highlands had reached population densities of five hundred per square mile; soil fertility was declining and fallow periods disappearing. Kenya's White farmers, at the same time, were taking the first steps towards what would later become the wholesale expulsion of labor tenants, who would then need to find land for themselves in the overcrowded reserves. Similar pressures were emerging in the Rhodesias, and South Africa's reserves were already on a downward spiral towards abject poverty, with great numbers of men and women trying to leave.

Even in these land-short places, however, the British worked to increase exports. The question was, where to find the land for this increased production. Both the White settlers, who did not want to give up land to African production, and the new cadres of government agricultural experts, argued that the way out of the crisis was through the strict regulation of African agriculture. This tended to be done in ways that supported the interests of the wealthier African export-crop farmers. In any event, government control of African agriculture was instituted widely in eastern and southern Africa, even though the government's agricultural officers did not fully understand African farming systems. In the Usambara mountains of Tanzania, for example, government erosion control rules had the effect, presumably unknown to the officials, of redefining tenure so that most of the poorer farmers would lose their rights in land, and the richest would benefit. Peasant farmers resisted fiercely, threatening to kill their paramount chief who enforced the rules, destroying government field markers, and holding massive demonstrations at government centers until the plan was abandoned.

Even in land-short parts of eastern Africa, cash crop exports grew very rapidly in the late 1940s and the early 1950s. In West Africa, where the settler presence was minimal, and where land pressure was more unusual, the growth was remarkable. The volume of West African exports in 1955 was four times as great as it had been in 1945. The reasons were simple: rapid rises in world market prices for many of the crops that

African peasants grew, and very rapid improvements in the transportation net, instituted by colonial authorities who placed a priority on exports.

Cash-crop farmers operated in an environment where they could not be certain, from year to year, that prices for their crops would cover costs, where they had no insurance in case of illness, and where their well-being depended on the good will of local traders and of government officials. In these circumstances, they could operate successfully if they had the support of a wide range of relatives, influence with traders and with government officials, and sources of income that were not entirely dependent on their crops. Yoruba cocoa farmers in Nigeria, for example, invested money in their sons' educations, in the hope that they would get good government jobs; they invested in business enterprises, in urban houses, and in family ceremonies. In the Gambia, in a study of a village where commercial peanut farming was being introduced in the early 1950s, young men who headed small households were relatively prosperous among the first generation of peanut farmers. Prices were high and there were few claims on their wealth. Twenty years later, after peanut prices had fallen and risen several times, and the government had changed its way of regulating the economy, the people who were the most secure were men and women in large descent-group compounds. They could count on the support, from within their kin group, of moneylenders and government officials, farmers, traders, and teachers. They were prepared for a much wider range of eventualities than people in isolated households.

It was rare, in most parts of tropical Africa, for farmers to accumulate wealth by the large-scale expansion of farm acreage and of agricultural production. It was much more typical for a pattern of cyclical accumulation to emerge among those who lived by farming: for wealth accumulated in one generation to be dispersed in the next. In places where polygyny was practiced, the wealthiest farmers often tended to have the most wives, but then their holdings were divided among many children in the next generation. Farmers who built their wealth on a single crop were, in any event, vulnerable to the large price swings that would inevitably affect agricultural products. Plant diseases, like the swollen shoot disease that hurt Gold Coast cocoa in the 1940s, could also undermine the prosperity of a farmer. People who wished to see their families accumulate wealth planned ways for them to climb a ladder of occupations. A successful farmer would try to become a trader, then use profits from trade to enter the transport business, and perhaps over the years win a major distributorship from a trading company, or become a building contractor.

The post-war period was a time, in many colonies, when it became easier for Africans to enter trade. Political pressures now made it more difficult for trading companies to exclude Africans: the British West African companies opened the middle level of trade to Africans for the first time. Africans who had controlled only 5 per cent of Nigeria's trade in 1949, controlled 20 per cent by 1963.

Farmers who had substantial earnings from cash crops and trade during the boom years could invest their money in motor vehicles, which were becoming widely available. There were ten times as many motor vehicles in West Africa in 1960 as there had been in 1945. The move from rail transport to motor transport implied a decentralization of control: lorries (trucks) were well-suited to enterprises owned by individual entrepreneurs.

Ambitious African entrepreneurs learned the importance of access to government, and especially to governmental marketing boards, as one of the keys to personal accumulation. These played an important role in British cash-crop colonies. The boards were meant to keep the prices to farmers relatively stable, even though world prices fluctuated widely. When world prices were high the boards would buy at lower prices, hold the difference, and use that money to pay more to farmers in low-price years. In the actual event, they did not pay out when the world market was low. In the Gold Coast the government Cocoa Marketing Board kept 41 per cent of farmers' potential earnings between 1947 and 1961. Marketing board money was actually a heavy tax on African farmers to be used for government development projects. Ambitious African entrepreneurs learned two lessons, both of which remained true in the independence period. One was that in a regulated world, money was to be made by circumventing the official market, either by smuggling or by entering forms of trade the boards did not control. The second was that the path to wealth on a large scale – the way to win major construction jobs or trade contracts – was through personal associations in the government or in the major trading companies. In the Gold Coast, five years before independence, the political party of Kwame Nkrumah, who was to be Ghana's first president, founded the Cocoa Purchasing Company as a subsidiary of the colonial government's Cocoa Marketing Board. The company was able to coordinate its financial dealings so as to serve the needs of the political party.

It was easier for a farmer-trader to gain access to the government bureaucracy, or to a marketing board, if his sons were educated and well-placed. Even before the post-war period, education had been more widely available in the richest cash-cropping parts of the continent. With their wealth growing in the early 1950s people in these places invested in the educations of their children, who were then qualified for the expanding numbers of government jobs. The expansion in education in the 1950s touched most parts of the continent, although young men had better opportunities than young women. In Algeria, between 1950 and 1960, the percentage of children in primary school rose from fifteen to twenty-eight, in Ghana from nineteen to forty, and in Kenya from twenty-six to forty-nine. Chances for secondary education were still very slim: secondary students accounted for less than five per cent of the twelve to eighteen year-old age group in most African countries in 1960. This meant that young people who completed secondary school in the 1950s were likely to have good careers.

Urbanization

The forces for change in post-war Africa all worked to increase the flow of people into the cities. As we have seen, the patterns by which people accumulated wealth in the countryside required that some relatives move to the city. In land-scarce parts of the continent, population growth and the expansion of cash-crop land left people with little choice but to move into the cities. Africa's urban spaces also had a positive appeal, both for their fascinating liveliness, and because they emerged in the 1950s as places where incomes were higher and life expectancy longer. The result was rapid urban growth up to independence, and explosive growth afterwards. Lagos, which had a population of

127,000 in 1931, had grown to 267,000 by 1952, and 665,000 by 1963. Dakar grew from 125,000 in 1943 to 600,000 in 1968. Nairobi held 119,000 people in 1948 and 222,000 in 1957: it had almost doubled in size over nine years.

Cities were not at all new forms of organization: they had histories reaching thousands of years into the pre-colonial past. Alexandria, Carthage, Cairo, and Fez come immediately to mind for North Africa, and urban centers south of the Sahara have also had a distinguished past. Jenne-Jenno, on the inland Niger River, emerged as a trading town more than 1500 years ago, before the rise of Islam. Desert-edge towns like Timbuktu and Gao, and Islamic commercial centers of the savanna like Jenné in a later period attracted merchants and scholars, artisans and nomads. The mosque and the marketplace served as centers of urban life, which had its own characteristic style of architecture built of adobe in desert hues, the horizontal lines of massed flat-roofed houses broken only by the slender round towers of the mosques. Further south, the Yoruba towns of the forest zone, in what is now southwestern Nigeria, held populations in the tens of thousands, most of whom supported themselves through agriculture. The life of these farmer townspeople was a mirror image of commuter life in modern American suburbs. They preferred town life at the expense of commuting to their farms in the countryside. They remained at their farms overnight during the heaviest agricultural seasons, and those with distant farms stayed in the country for weeks; but the city was home.

Some colonial cities grew up around preconquest centers – Ibadan and Lagos in Nigeria, Mombasa in Kenya, Kampala in Uganda. In North Africa, Algiers and Tunis were ancient centers, while Rabat and its twin town Salée were ancient seaports, but other cities had only been tiny villages, even open fields. Casablanca was virtually a new creation in the colonial period, and Oran grew to prominence because the French used it as their main naval base in Algeria. Throughout Africa, many of the new cities were ports or rail junction points. Nairobi began as a shunting point on the rail line from Mombasa to Lake Victoria. Dar es Salaam was a convenient but hitherto insignificant seaport on the Tanganyika coast. As often happened, its choice as the railway terminus meant that it gathered in traffic that had previously flowed through more diverse channels. In mineral regions, the main cities often grew up around the mines, like Lubumbashi in Zaire, the Copperbelt towns in Zambia, or Johannesburg in South Africa.

Because of the extractive nature of the colonial economy, these cities in tropical Africa attracted very little industry before the 1940s; their main function was to serve the export sector. However, the choice of a town as a colonial capital also made it attractive to industry later on, if only because it already had a variety of urban services and transportation links. Kaduna, a new junction point and regional capital in northern Nigeria, became an industrial center in competition with the old Hausa cities. Pretoria in South Africa became a major steel manufacturing city long after its original choice as capital of the independent South African Republic before the Boer War.

Whatever the original reason for being, most African cities grew rather slowly at first, which is an index of the comparatively low level of capital investment. But then after the Second World War, colonial governments and businesses invested in urban ports, docks, housing, and factories. The new industries needed semi-skilled workers who would remain on the job for the long term, living in the city with their families, invested in their jobs. The key to labor control now, from the point of view of employers, was to emphasize divisions between workers and to give permanent workers a stake in stability. The British did this through the legal regulation of trade unions, each of which was required to represent only a small segment of the work force. They did it also by the way they structured rates of pay and benefits for separate sets of workers. The French, who did not fragment the unions in the same way, tried to divide kinds of workers from one another, and to ensure the loyalty of the most skilled workers, by instituting many different levels of pay and privileges. The best-paid African employees working for the government in Dakar, in Senegal, in 1949 made five times as much as ordinary workers in the same enterprises.

The laboring occupations in the service of large enterprises – manufacturing, dock work, railway work, mining – were not the only ones held by Africans in post-war towns. Significant numbers of people held clerical or administrative jobs, either for governments or in commerce. Beyond this, huge numbers of people were self-employed, in what has become known as the informal sector. These people included tailors, carpenters, traders, street vendors, mechanics, and many others. Colonial towns differed widely from one another in the importance of the informal sector, and in the overall structure of occupations. In a town like Jinja, in Uganda, which grew up near a hydroelectric project, the percentage of workers in manufacturing was high, and the mining towns of Zambia and Zaire had high percentages of miners, as one would expect. Administrative jobs were central in capital cities.

In South Africa the same pressures towards urbanization were at work as in tropical Africa, and were if anything more powerful. By the early 1940s the reserves were in severe decline. In many parts of rural southern Africa, 70 per cent of the men were away at work at any given time, and those left behind did not always have land to farm. South African industry went through a boom time during the war, adding the pull of city employment to the push of rural poverty. Conditions in the countryside were so dire, and the needs of industry so great, that in 1942–3 the laws controlling African movement into the city were suspended. During the war thousands of people streamed to the cities, and it seemed likely that migrant labor would become a progressively smaller part of South African life. This outcome was rejected, however, by the country's Whites, who elected the National Party government in 1948 to ensure that the tide of permanent African urbanization would be reversed. The election owed its outcome in part to the position taken by White miners and White farmers, whose prosperity depended on the migrant labor system, and who therefore refused to accept its decline.

Under the National Party's regime of apartheid, strict laws prevented Africans from leaving their rural homes except for brief periods, unless they were employed by Europeans. Enforcing these measures required massive police intervention in the lives of Africans. The severity of the enforcement measures was so great because the forces pushing towards urbanization were so powerful. The country did not, however, move on to a system that depended entirely on migrant labor. Instead, it divided the African population in two: those who had permanent jobs in the urban sector and became city people who could expect to be paid, however inadequately, for the skills they developed, and those who were required to live in poverty in the reserves or on White farms, and to work at low-skill, low-wage jobs. It is the resentments between these two sets of people that led to some of the bitterest fighting by Africans against one another during the period of apartheid's decline and fall.

Southern Africa's cities were unusual among the cities of Africa, not only because of the intensity of government control, but also because the region was one where industrial and commercial employment had an overwhelming importance. Together with public employment and service jobs, they occupied fully 50 per cent of the work force in 1960, as opposed to 5 per cent in West Africa. South African cities were different from West African ones in a second way: the apartheid laws gave the privileges of stable urban residence to Africans who could prove that they had long been city-dwellers and were not rooted in the countryside where, in any event, land was very scarce. In most of tropical Africa people prized their rural roots and rural associations. Ties to kinship groups rooted partly in the countryside and partly in the city were, as we have seen, at the heart of colonial Africa's informal system of social security. Just as farmers in the countryside diversified their sources of support by sending sons to the city, so urban people preserved their rights to assistance in illness or old-age, and their claims to political support, by returning regularly to visit or live with their country relatives, or by sending money. The city-dwellers' rights to assistance were often symbolized by the fact that they retained claims to lineage farm-land. In this respect – in the continuing social links between town and country – African urbanism found its special form, unlike the urbanism of most other regions of the world.

In West Africa, where the ties between city and countryside had been disturbed the least by colonial regulations, a very large proportion of city-dwellers worked for themselves, and not for any of the colonial enterprises. In Kumasi, in Ghana, in 1960, the self-employed were fully 60 per cent of all people in employment. All across West Africa, a significant proportion of the self-employed were women traders. In Kumasi, 91 per cent of employed women were self-employed, whereas in East African towns the numbers would have been very much lower, but still significant. In southwestern Nigeria, among the Yoruba, the great majority of urban women engaged in trade, many of them as street vendors, with some in crafts, and almost none in the farming activities that occupied many husbands. The West African pattern of careers in trade open to women had powerful consequences for gender roles: women in these places had a possible way to accumulate wealth for themselves. If they were in polygynous marriages, they could spend money on their own children, and they had a much easier time functioning in the public world as independent people.

Africans living in colonial cities had a much wider range of ways of being, styles of life, and forms of association than had been planned for them by colonial policy makers. The structures of authority in most city neighborhoods were constructed by African property-owners, men and women, who laid down rules of social behavior in light of lineage practice, in ways that were invisible to the European rulers. The organization of informal trade – the life-blood of many cities – followed paths and practices of which the colonizers were largely unaware. And the organization of social security, and with it the interpretation of life's meaning, depended on links between countryside and city, on inherited forms of kinship association, and often on indigenous forms of religious organization, that Africa's European rulers had not brought into being, and that had grown up just beyond their gaze.

Suggestions for further reading

Berry, Sara, *Fathers Work for Their Sons: Accumulation, Mobility, and Class Formation in an Extended Yoruba Community*, Berkeley, Los Angeles and London: University of California Press, 1985.

Chanock, Martin, *Law, Custom and Social Order: The Colonial Experience in Malawi and Zambia*, Cambridge: Cambridge University Press, 1985.

Coquery-Vidrovitch, Catherine, "The Process of Urbanization in Africa," *African Studies Review*, 34 (1991), pp. 1–98.

Feierman, Steven, and John M. Janzen, *The Social Basis of Health and Healing in Africa*, Berkeley, Los Angeles and Oxford: University of California Press, 1992.

Guyer, Jane, "Household and Community in African Studies," *African Studies Review*, 24 (1981), pp. 87–138.

Iliffe, John, *The African Poor*, Cambridge: Cambridge University Press, 1987.

Isaacman, Allen, "Peasants and Rural Social Protest in Africa," *African Studies Review*, 33 (1990), pp. 1–120.

Mandala, Elias, *Work and Control in a Peasant Economy*, Madison: University of Wisconsin Press, 1990.

Peel, J.D.Y., "Social and Cultural Change," in Michael Crowder (ed.), *The Cambridge History of Africa*, Vol. 8 (from c.1940 to c.1975), Cambridge: Cambridge University Press, 1984, pp. 145–91.

Ranger, T.O., *Peasant Consciousness and Guerilla War in Zimbabwe*, London: James Currey; Berkeley, and Los Angeles: University of California Press, 1985.

Whitehead, Ann, "Rural Women and Food Production in Sub-Saharan Africa," pp. 425–73 in Jean Drèze and Amartya Sen, *The Political Economy of Hunger*, Vol. 1, *Entitlement and Well-Being*, Oxford: Clarendon Press, 1990.

20

AFRICAN RESISTANCE AND THE LIQUIDATION OF EUROPEAN EMPIRE

The liquidation of European empires overseas was not confined to Africa. It involved all continents, just as the European conquest of the non-Western world involved all continents. Local situations were nevertheless often very different and the process differed greatly in detail. The Second World War was certainly the catalyst, but the roots of change lay further back in time. The Government of India Act, passed by the British parliament in 1935, foresaw the independence of the Indian subcontinent, though not in quite the form it actually took. The aftermath of the war, however, gave the European powers a new perspective on the world and their place in it – including their relations with Africa.

As the colonial powers emerged to the shock of victory and devastation in 1945, they did so with good will towards the African colonies for their wartime loyalty and their contribution to the Allied victory. They tended to count on continued loyalty, as well as on African resources in the "cold war" they were just beginning to wage against the Soviet Union and its friends. Anti-colonialism was increasingly popular in European opinion. Britain moved rapidly to accept the independence of India and Pakistan in 1947. France and the Netherlands, meanwhile, decided to fight for their continued rule in southeast Asia, but without success. The Dutch failure to reconquer Indonesia became apparent in 1950, and the French army met its spectacular disaster in Indochina at Dien Bien Phu in 1954. A new configuration of power in the world became obvious, though it had been foreshadowed as far back as the Rif War in the 1920s. Even then it was not quite as obvious as it should have been. The French were to learn the lesson all over again in Algeria of the late 1950s, and the United States was to learn it once more in Vietnam of the 1960s.

In the long perspective of history, the European conquest and the decolonization of Africa took place with amazing rapidity. Only three decades, 1880 to 1910, account for the bulk of the conquest. Only two decades, 1955–75, account for most of the liquidation of that empire. Many underlying causes of the conquest were now reversed. After 1945, colonial territory no longer played an important role in intra-European rivalries. The European powers were now overshadowed by the Soviet Union and the United States, and these superpowers had no African colonies. The ideological justifi-

cation for colonial rule weakened with the decline of the racism and cultural chauvinism that had been so strong in the late nineteenth century. Empire-building was no
longer considered a moral achievement. On the contrary, to hold on to unwilling
colonies was a source of international disrepute in a world where each year more
members of the General Assembly belonged to the group that would later be called the
Third World.

These factors, however, were only incidental compared with the shift in the balance
of military cost. In the late nineteenth century, the known benefit of African empire to a
European state was not very large, but the cost of conquest was exceedingly small. By
the third quarter of the twentieth, the benefit of African empire was better known, and
it was still small; but the cost of holding out against an organized local liberation
movement had become astronomic. European empires and non-European secondary
empires both gained an enormous advantage from the local monopoly on modern
weapons. By the 1950s, the advantage had shifted to guerrilla warfare, where even
small numbers of rival insurgents could tie down many times their own number of
conventional soldiers. The examples of Indonesia, Indochina, and Algeria followed in
short order. No European country could afford that cost for long, though recognition
of that fact was slow to emerge.

Forms and sources of African resistance to colonial rule

Some form of African resistance to colonial rule was present from the beginning – first
of all as military resistance to conquest, sometimes called "primary resistance." This
form was usually organized by the pre-colonial state, however small, and it was brief.
Primary resistance also included a subtype of state-building resistance, where the
leadership had to create a new political structure, and the obvious examples of this
subtype are ʿAbd al-Qādir in Algeria, the Maji-Maji revolt in Tanganyika, and later
phases of the Shona and Ndebele "rebellions" in Rhodesia. The ultimate victory for
African independence, however, had its roots in modern nationalism – a form of
political organization, borrowed from the West or adapted from other non-Western
countries (like India) with the goal of taking over the colonial state as the framework for
a renewed and independent African political life.

Primary resistance had ended in most of Africa before the First World War, and
modern nationalism scored no victories until after the Second. The period between
was dominated by an inconvenient third category, so varied that it hardly deserved to
be called a category. Some resistance was organized around elite political parties like
the West African National Congress or the African National Congress in South Africa.
Other acts of protest were as various as strikes, riots, religious movements, or peaceful
opposition to colonial rule expressed through the press or the political process. The
variety is so great that it is identified most easily by what it was not: it was neither
primary resistance nor modern nationalism.

It is neither possible nor appropriate in a book of this scope to wend our way through
the myriad events of protest and resistance. But it is worth looking for patterns of
organization and ideology to see some of the ways Africans worked together to preserve

an area of autonomy for themselves in the colonial world. A common religion was one source of unity on a scale larger than any local social grouping. This is no doubt one reason why the most successful state-building efforts – from ʿAbd al-Qādir in Algeria, through the Sanusiya, to Muhammad Abdille Hassan in Somalia – were based on a religion with universal claims. Colonial officials therefore paid careful attention to Islam as a potentially unifying force. Especially in North Africa, the French were active in religious politics, suppressing some leaders, but subsidizing others who seemed likely to support European rule.

Appeal to the name of Islam could be a threat even to Muslim governments. The nineteenth-century sweep of religious revolt across the Sudan shows clearly enough that religion could unite people with a variety of different grievances and different goals. Similar movements stopped short of full religious revolt during the colonial period, but such movements as the Hamaliya in the French Sudan (later Mali) and the Muslim Brotherhoods in Egypt of the 1940s onward illustrate the incipient force that might have turned into full-scale rebellion, given the right circumstances.

Christian sects that had broken with the European missionaries and from European versions of Christian orthodoxy, could also turn against the regime. Just before the First World War in Nyasaland (now Malawi) Elliot Kamwana organized the Watchtower movement, based on the American sect of Jehovah's Witnesses. Kamwana, like the parent society, preached the second coming of Christ, and the movement spread to other colonies. It turned anti-European, however, when Kamwana predicted the "second coming" for 1914, when Christ's return would also bring the departure of the Europeans, the end of taxation, and a return to African self-government. The Nyasaland government sent Kamwana into exile and tried to break up his following. It failed; the Watchtower was preached widely through Central Africa, and it kept a strong anti-European flavor until the end of the colonial period.

Further north, in the lower Congo about 1920, another Christian leader, Simon Kimbangu, gained his first following by his power to heal the sick. In 1921, however, some of his adherents predicted that fire from heaven would wipe out the Europeans. Others claimed that Afro-Americans would return to liberate their brothers and sisters. The Belgian authorities put Kimbangu in prison for the rest of his life, but the movement itself went on, with occasional displays of anti-European sentiment. Even the orthodox Christian churches could sometimes serve the cause of resistance. In 1915, John Chilembwe of Nyasaland was a minister who used his congregation as the nucleus of an open revolt, which the government quickly suppressed.

Even gender could sometimes bring people together to protest against colonial rule. The most famous example in 1929–30, was a set of serious riots in southeastern Nigeria, known as the Aba women's war. Many, if not most, women in the region participated. Separate women's action was possible because Ibo society already had separate women's organizations. Some of the women's grievances were against Ibo men, especially those who accepted office as "warrant chiefs" under the colonial government. The women also felt threatened as women, especially in regard to their fertility; and the survival of their children. They were also confident that the colonial troops would not fire on them, as they might have done to male rioters. The women thus felt safe from the kind of force that had defeated the men two decades earlier.

The movement drew on grievances dating as far back as the conquest, and on sharper memories of the terrible mortality suffered during the post-war influenza epidemic. Western cultural penetration from Christian missions or the imposition of warrant chiefs were further disturbing signs. The first women's action came in 1925, when groups of women began to dance and sing their opposition in front of the warrant chiefs' compounds. They told people to return to the old ways, to reject Western dress and colonial currency. Some promised that a rejection of Western culture would force the British to withdraw. Then, in 1928, the British began direct taxation of men for the first time. The next year, they began counting the women as well as the men for census purposes. The women took this to mean that they too were to be taxed. Even more disturbing, local custom allowed the counting of slaves only. At the very least, this implied that both men and women were slaves. To count free people furthermore, was boastful before the spirits, tempting them to kill off the living, as they had apparently done with the influenza epidemic of 1919.

In 1929, the women moved on in a series of riots, destroying Native Courts the British had set up and looting local stores run by British firms. In the largest confrontation, more than 10,000 women converged on an administrative center, their faces covered with blue paint, fern-covered sticks in their hands symbolizing unity and danger. In this case, the soldiers fired, killing more than fifty women. The government then made an effort to allay some of their grievances, and the movement died down, though the women remained bitter far into the next decade.

Still another source of solidarity and common action was a shared economic interest. Consumers could unite against high prices or low quality. Producers could unite in at least two different ways. On one basis, cocoa farm owners, farm workers, and middlemen could all unite in opposition to low cocoa prices. Or one of these groups – wage workers, for example – could unite and strike for higher wages.

In most of colonial Africa, industry was small and scattered. Wage workers were only a small part of the total population, so that united action by workers involved only a few people. Protests against price gauging had a broader base, but they were hard to sustain, though they were important to the rise of independence movements. These protests were especially common in the period of high import prices between 1945 and 1950, often taking the form of urban riots, with some looting of alien-owned shops and trading-company warehouses. Some, however, were more impressive and sustained. In January 1948, the Anti-Inflation Campaign Committee on the Gold Coast organized consumers, who refused to buy cotton prints, canned meat, flour, and alcoholic beverages for almost a month. The campaign finally forced the trading companies to cut their profit margins, and it supported the political parties simultaneously pushing for self-government, helping to bring Kwame Nkrumah into office as premier in 1951.

Common action by producers was harder to organize, and the most successful interwar example also comes from the Gold Coast. In 1937, the world price for cocoa was low in any event, but the major trading companies agreed to divide the market so as to lower still further the price paid producers. The farmers combined under the leadership of the traditional political authorities, with the general support of all people in the cocoa-growing regions, to "hold up" the crop, keeping most Gold Coast cocoa off the market until the big firms consented to raise the price. The effort produced little immediate relief, but it did alarm the government into investigating the monopolistic practices of the trading firms.

Ordinary labor union activity was easier to organize, if only because fewer people had to be reached. African unions were illegal in South Africa, the most industrialized region. After the collapse of Clements Kadalie's ICU in the 1920s, only the "European" unions had an effective voice, and they were powerful instruments for maintaining the industrial color bar and the great gap between European and African wages. In the Maghrib and French-controlled Africa generally, such trade unions as existed tended to affiliate with one or the other of the major trade union federations in France. These in turn were associated with the division of the French left between Socialists on the one hand and Communists on the other. The earliest impressive strike action was mounted by the building trades and dockers of Oran and Algiers in the years 1927–9. The most important protests of the interwar period came in 1936 with the patching up of the Socialist-Communist conflict and the formation of a United Front in France itself. Serious union activity could then move out from the cities into the countryside, not only in Algeria but in Tunisia and Morocco as well. Tropical Africa, on the other hand, had comparatively few wage laborers, but common action in the West African port towns existed from at least the 1890s, just a little later in major East African ports like Mombasa. Even in Rhodesia, workers' action in 1899 managed to bring about the financial failure of an especially badly managed mine, simply because migrant workers refused to sign up, but Rhodesian union activity between the wars was comparatively unimportant.

After 1945, unions took on new significance, often associated with the political parties of the independence movement. But the nationalist leaders and the trade unions tended to part company during the 1950s, partly because the independence movement now had real strength far beyond the urban working class and wanted to avoid such a narrow focus. In addition, government employees had formed some of the most powerful unions, and leaders of the independence movement could already see themselves as a new generation of management. Of the independence elders, only Sékou Touré of Guinea-Conakry rose to power through the trade union movement.

Ethnicity and nationalism

A sense of common culture and shared historical experience was still another basis for common action. The European sense of nationhood had grown from similar roots, but what passed for "nationalism" in Africa was different. The Western-educated elite, who led the early nationalist movements, were united by their common experience as Africans, not that of a particular ethnic group. The pan-African aspect turned up in nationalist demands for the better treatment of all Africans, or the redress of specific grievances. Even national independence or full racial equality under the state were such distant goals they were rarely emphasized until after 1945.

Africans had a sense of solidarity with those who came from the same place, spoke the same language, shared a way of life, and perhaps shared the experience of a particular local form of colonial rule. Ethnic loyalty of this kind was similar to the nationalism of nineteenth-century Poland or Ireland, but where the press writes about Serbian nationalism in Europe, it writes about Ibo "tribalism" in Africa. This usage is a form of cultural chauvinism, and it causes immense confusion. It distorts fundamental similarities among social processes in Africa and elsewhere. The religious conflict in Northern Ireland, language conflict in Quebec, or anti-semitism in Russia would all be labeled "tribalism," if the setting was somewhere in Africa. This is one reason historians today avoid tribe as a term of analysis; it can mean altogether too many things to be useful except for describing deep lineages in nomadic societies.

Press usage also suggests that the African sense of ethnic identity has been there from time immemorial, that ethnic differences are immutable and must necessarily intervene in political life. In fact, people in Africa can change their sense of ethnicity quite rapidly. In Zanzibar in 1924, 33,944 individuals identified themselves as Swahili for census purposes. Only seven years later, the number dropped to 2066. They still spoke Swahili, but it was no longer fashionable to use Swahili for primary self-identification. In the early years of the Belgian Congo, the Belgians recognized the Bangala as one of the great "tribes" along the Congo River. By 1958, Belgian ethnographers decided that no such "tribe" existed, though Lingala remained an important trade language.

The colonial state often tried to manipulate people through their feelings of ethnic identity. Since 1948, the South African state made a conscious attempt to create "homelands" for different "tribes" in an effort to reinforce ethnic feelings and hence to reduce the possibility of united action by Africans, *as Africans*, rather than Xhosa or Zulu. The policy so closely resembled similar efforts in Soviet Central Asia that the "homelands" are often called "Bantustans," after Soviet territories like Kazakhstan or Uzbekistan.

Indirect rule in tropical Africa was designed to produce the same end, and it may well have reinforced local solidarity like the feeling of being Asante, as against loyalty to the Gold Coast. It certainly did so in Uganda, where the Ganda people were allowed to keep a representative assembly. They had a chance to express their discontents in terms of ancient Ganda rights, rather than as a generalized set of African grievances against the colonial state. At independence, the narrower solidarity of the Ganda was a serious block to national unity for the larger Uganda Protectorate.

In the Maghrib, the French tried to use language rivalries in a similar way. They sensed that the Arabic-speaking majority was the most important threat to their rule, provided it could unify the country as a whole. In Morocco, they therefore turned to the Berber-speaking minority. In 1930, the French administration issued the "Berber Dahir" in the sultan's name. It was a decree that favored Berber traditional law over the Muslim *shar'ia*, but it backfired. Rather than rallying Berbers to the French cause, it rallied Muslims of all kinds in opposition to the colonial regime and inspired the first organization that would later turn into an independence movement.

Some instances of increased ethnicity came only directly from government action. Before the colonial impact, the Kikuyu of central Kenya had no deep consciousness of a common identity, probably because they lived on separate mountain ridges, had very local historical traditions, and lacked a unified political system. Colonial rule then brought the building of Nairobi in their midst, the concentrated assault of mission,

Christianity, and the expropriation of much of their land to form the "white high-lands." Their most important common institution was the practice of oath-taking to enforce agreement and unity of action, even though they had no centralized political authority. When they finally reacted to the trauma of the colonial experience in the "Mau Mau" rebellion of 1953, the oath emerged to enforce unity, secrecy, and discipline. Kikuyu feelings of ethnicity were created by the colonial experience, reinforced by new intercommunication in the urban setting, and finally forged in battle through their rising against the British.

But a common culture was not necessarily enough to create an ethnic solidarity all by itself. The colonial experience could also split apart people who were culturally similar. That happened to the Luba Kasai and the Lulua in the Belgian Congo. They still speak the same language, and cultural differences in the pre-colonial period were negligible; yet a violent hostility developed during the colonial era. First, the Luba Kasai were more drastically uprooted in the period of the slave trade and secondary empire after the middle of the nineteenth century. Being shaken out of their local setting, they tended more often than the Lulua to go to the European schools, while the Lulua kept their old pattern of education for farming. As a result, the Luba Kasai got the best jobs at the mines in Katanga. They became more prosperous because the rail line crossed their territory and they could sell their food at the mines as a cash crop. By the 1950s, Lulua land began to be scarce and they too had to go to work in the mines, only to find the Luba Kasai already entrenched in the best positions. The Lulua's response, by 1952, was first to unite in an ethnic association dedicated to improving their competitive position. In 1959, the animosity turned into urban guerrilla warfare of the bloodiest kind, in which the Lulua drove the Luba Kasai out of Lubumbashi. Economic rivalry won out over ethnic similarity, channeled through solidarities created during the colonial period itself, not inherited from the past.

Nor was ethnic unity limited to Africans of long-term African descent. The linguistic divisions between English-speaking and Afrikaans-speaking "European" South Africans was just as much an instance of "tribalism" or ethnic politics as any other. In some ways, it was more bitter than most, because of the animosities of the Anglo-Boer War. In 1948, the electoral victory of the National Party in South Africa made the Afrikaner "tribal" minority dominant over the South African state for more than forty years. But the Afrikaner ethnicity had a curious feature. Its self-identity was based on language and race simultaneously, even though the boundaries of race and language were not the same. Language was used to exclude the English-speakers, even though they were fellow Europeans in physical type. Race was used to exclude the Coloured people, even though Afrikaans was also their mother tongue.

Given the importance of nationality in European politics, it may seem curious that African ethnic feelings were in fact no more divisive than they were. From the first movements toward independence to the recent past, African nations have sought some form of predominance, either within or separate from the colonial states that were moving towards independent status. The National Liberation Movement of the Asante in the Gold Coast in 1954 and 1955 briefly held up Ghanaian independence. A little later, the Krio-speaking people of Freetown and its vicinity wanted separate independence, rather than incorporation in Sierra Leone. More recently the Inkatha Freedom

Party in South Africa has defended separate rights for Zulus, as against the program for a multi-racial, multi-ethnic state envisaged by the African National Congress.

Only Somalia succeeded in uniting two previous colonies – British and Italian Somaliland – in a common state based on linguistic and cultural identity. The unity worked for a time, but by the early 1990s, the Somali ethnic identity had been fragmented and replaced by kin-based subdivisions of the Somali nation. Throughout the rest of Africa, the boundaries of the colonial states became the boundaries of the independent states that succeeded them, in spite of the fact that those boundaries often divided African ethnic groups. In several instances since independence, a secession movement has developed into a real threat to the unity of a particular state. In the early 1960s, Katanga (now Shaba) threatened to make good its secession from Zaire, but it failed. Later, the Ibos of eastern Nigeria fought a civil war for the independence of Biafra as an ethnic state, but that failed too. The mainly non-Muslim peoples of the southern part of the Republic of the Sudan also tried for their independence, but they too failed to make good their claim. Only Eritrea succeeded in gaining its independence from Ethiopia.

No general explanation quite covers all these failures, but it is certainly important that virtually every African state is vulnerable to ethnic secession movements, and therefore all states tend to unite against them. The independence movement was first of all an effort to remove European rule. A common ethnicity was a force for unity in that struggle up to a point; it could be used with Asante to create a unified opposition to colonialism, but, at the same time, the very fact of Asante unity was likely to prevent a greater unity of all Gold Coast people against the British. The political leaders at the time of independence understood this and tried to play down ethnic rivalries that might weaken the common drive for independence.

Political parties and independence movements

Although ethnic, economic and religious solidarity were all to play a role in the independence movements, the actual organizations that carried Africa to independence were political parties, organized on the European model. Parties often played down their association with a particular ethnic group, though such connections could sometimes be strong. Many South Africans associated the African National Congress with the Xhosa people, because Nelson Mandela came from a prominent Xhosa family, and many other prominent ANC leaders were Xhosa. Even so, the Congress tried hard to play down ethnic and racial divisions. The important political fact was that few African ethnic groups could claim a large majority within any colonial state (or its independent successor). To gain power by popular appeal and electoral politics, a party needed to appeal to as many different kinds of people as possible; it also needed to play down its affiliation with an economic force like organized labor. On the other hand, in fact if not in theory, a political party could use ethnicity to build up a quick grass-roots following in rural areas. The three main parties in Nigeria shortly before and after independence stood for Nigerian independence, but each represented a particular region and one or the other of the three major language groups – Ibo, Yoruba, and

Hausa. Like political parties elsewhere in the world, a party could win majority support only by supporters with a variety of different goals and a variety of different grievances.

Political parties existed in Africa, both north and south of the Sahara, even before the main colonial conquests began in the 1880s. They continued through the colonial period, wherever representative politics was allowed, and they could sometimes function as important pressure groups outside formal political life. Political parties appeared in Egypt just before the British takeover in 1882, in the privileged communes of Senegal, and in some British West African towns with elected municipal governments. Among the active pressure groups in South Africa, the African National Congress was founded in 1919, and Clements Kadalie's ICU was active in the 1920s. So was the West African National Congress, and the Graduates' General Congress was founded in the Anglo-Egyptian Sudan in 1938.

By 1940, some kind of political party, pressure group, or informal organization of "nationalists" existed in almost every African colony. But membership was limited in almost every case to Western-educated, middle-class, and urban Africans who understood how the colonial state worked; and who recognized that the best way to achieve independence was to work within the state and ultimately to seize control for themselves, either by force or through negotiation. In the political climate before the Second World War, however, independence seemed so remote that nationalists focused on lesser goals like increased powers of self-government, leaving the claim to independence in the background.

Then came the Second World War, which in Africa served as a major catalyst of the independence movements. It sometimes hardened attitudes, sometimes modified them, but everywhere it sharpened the aspirations for further social, economic, and political change and brought into the open aspirations that had been building since before the First World War. The problem was to find a way to channel and coordinate the demands of so many different groups and ranks within society. In general, the solution was to broaden the existing tiny, middle-class parties so as to reach the urban workers and the rural masses.

The transition came at different times in different colonies. The Algerian experience is indicative for the Maghrib. In Algeria, the first attempt at mass parties began with the Popular Front in France, which allowed relative electoral freedom in Algeria for the first time in 1937, but the real breakthrough was delayed until the end of the war. In 1946, Messali Hadj joined with others to found the Mouvement pour le Triomphe des Libertées Democratiques (MTLD, or Movement for the Triumph of Democratic Liberties). After shifts in leadership and organization, a fraction of the MTLD went on to become the Front de la Libération National (FLN), which fought the war of independence against France from 1954 to 1962 and remained in power long after independence was achieved.

Egypt, of course, had a long tradition of political life in which politics spread gradually to broader sectors of the population, but the first mass parties in the Anglo-Egyptian Sudan appeared only in 1943. One, the Ashiqq' (Brothers), reached the masses through an informal alliance with the religious brotherhood of the Khatmiyya, while the other, the Umma (Nation), worked through the posthumous son of the Mahdi himself. These two parties took up the old rivalries between Sudan's most important religious brotherhoods, each looking ahead to the new kinds of Sudanese relations with Britain and Egypt after the war.

Elsewhere south of the Sahara, mass parties came first in West Africa, where the elite parties had also played a greater role. In the Gold Coast, the main post-war nationalist party was the United Gold Coast Convention (UGCC), the voice both of the Western-educated urban elite and of some of the chiefs in the southern Gold Coast. In 1949, Kwame Nkrumah, a young man returned from his education in America, split off with some of the younger members, formed the Convention People's Party (CPP), and turned it into a mass party. In Nigeria, Nnamdi Azikiwe founded the National Congress of Nigeria and the Cameroons (NCNC) in 1944, with an Ibo base but with the aim to reach out to all Nigerians. Until the early 1950s, however, it lacked the grass-roots support the CPP enjoyed in the Gold Coast.

In French West Africa, the move from relatively elite parties to mass parties came even later. Political activity was possible in all parts of French West Africa only after 1946, and it then included representation in the National Assembly in Paris. The political parties that emerged were actually quasi federations of local parties. The Rassemblement Démocratique Africain (RDA) was the strongest and most broadly based of these early alliances. Broad popular movements emerged unevenly in the different territories. In some, they were barely effective even at the coming of independence, but the general momentum of the independence movement was strong enough to carry whole federations like French West Africa or French Equatorial Africa, in spite of the relative lack of preparation in the colonies that became Chad, Niger, or the Central African Republic.

Mass parties were even slower to develop in parts of East and Central Africa, though the independence of Ghana in 1957 provided an example and an inspiration. Mass parties were in the making almost everywhere by 1958.

The late appearance of mass parties and electoral politics was of the greatest importance for Africa's fortunes after independence. African resistance had been present from the beginning of the colonial period, but the political instrument that was to lead most of North and tropical Africa to independence came into existence only at the very end. Colonial rhetoric made much of the value of European "tutelage" as a preparation for ultimate independence, but this tutelage in the field of electoral politics was slight before the Second World War and uneven thereafter. The contrast between India and the British African colonies is significant. British India began moving toward limited self-government in 1917–19, at least thirty years ahead of the British African colonies. Most Africans adjusted to the world economy, as they had to do. Many had a chance to encounter Western culture and make their own adjustments to its advantages and disadvantages. But the opportunity to practice electoral politics in the democratic tradition was very limited indeed until the 1950s. African leaders learned first of all how to use political organizations so as to gain power; they had little opportunity to practice the harder art of peacefully giving up power after an electoral defeat. This failure was to be an important reason why democratic institutions were to be so weak in post-colonial Africa.

In southern Africa, the settler presence pushed the African nationalist movement in a somewhat different direction, but it was not completely different. There too, a more militant political atmosphere emerged after the Second World War. During the war, the African National Congress (ANC) was still in existence, but it was not very effective. In 1944, a group of young intellectuals, including Walter Sisulu, Anton Lemebede, Oliver Tambo, and Nelson Mandela became active, and they gained control of the ANC in 1949. Their new program included strikes, civil disobedience, and non-cooperation in order to coerce the government into repealing its discriminatory laws. In 1952, they elected Albert J. Luthuli as president-general of the Congress. Similar shifts toward mlitancy came from the South African Indian Congress and a Coloured political organization.

From 1948, however, they were working against the even more deeply entrenched White-power government of the Afrikaner National Party. Through the 1950s, the ANC worked in concert with the other two groups and often with liberal "European" or multiracial organizations as well. It began a series of non-violent campaigns. The main tactic was openly to disobey discriminatory laws, thus courting arrest. In 1952, its first campaign led to more than 8000 arrests. A second campaign in 1955 brought more arrests and more repressive legislation. This time, the National-Party government jailed the leaders of the alliance and charged them with high treason. A long treason trial followed, but the government failed to secure any convictions.

By the mid-1950s, some of the more militant Africans doubted the effectiveness of the multiracial alliance and came out for a purely African movement dedicated to the emancipation of the African majority by any means – violent or otherwise. After the militants failed to gain control of the ANC in 1959, they seceded to form a new pan-Africanist Congress (PAC) under Robert Sobukwe. In 1960, the PAC began a new campaign urging large numbers of Africans to invite arrest by presenting themselves at police stations without their passes, required of all Africans outside the "reserves". At the police station in Sharpeville near Johannesburg, the police opened fire on the crowd, killing sixty-nine African protesters.

The number of deaths was not large by more recent standards, but the "Sharpeville massacre" was part of a major set of political changes over a few years from 1959 onward. It brought out sympathy demonstrations all over the country, and it encouraged expressions of sympathy from the outside world. The government struck back with legislation that outlawed the ANC, the PAC, and even the mild and multiracial Liberal party. On the international scene, South Africa had already begun moving toward secession from the British Commonwealth of Nations, where many of the newly independent members like India were strongly opposed to South African racial policies. In 1961, South Africa became a republic. In the next few years, the United Nations tried to embargo the sale of arms to South Africa, and formally but ineffectually ended the League of Nations mandate that had placed Namibia under South African control. The lines were then drawn, isolating South Africa from the world community, however ineffectively, but ending any hope for open or lawful opposition for the time being. The renewal of African opposition from the mid-1970s and through the 1980s belongs properly to the history of post-colonial Africa.

The liquidation of European empires in northern and central Africa

The first breakthrough toward independence came in the north, precisely where Europeans had maintained at least the fiction of exercising a protectorate over a non-Western government. Egypt, for that matter, was formally independent before 1914 and again after 1922, though the reality of British rule went back at least to 1882 and continued in some respects till the mid-1950s. For thirty years after formal independence, Britain kept, by treaty, a right to control Egyptian defense, foreign, and Sudanese affairs – along with the right of international transit through Egypt by way of the Suez Canal. The newspaper phrase for these continued rights following a period of formal colonization is "neo-colonialism," but the reality was hardly different from the kind of "informal empire" that so often preceded formal annexation.

In Egypt, the parallels between pre-1914 and post-1922 are even more striking. In either period, such parliamentary institutions as existed were ineffective in dealing with the king, who retained substantial power. They were even more ineffective in dealing with the British occupation. The initial "nationalist" opposition to the British occupation in 1882 came from Egyptian army officers who backed 'Urabi Pasha's coup and tried to make a military stand in spite of Egypt's weakness. That effort failed, but the final phase of opposition to Britain began in 1952, when another group of army officers, this time organized by Gamal 'Abd al-Nasser, seized power in another coup that ended the monarchy. The new government reopened negotiations with Britain, which led to a new agreement ending British rule over the Sudan, and gave that country choice between union with Egypt or separate independence. Sudan chose separate independence and became, in 1956, the first of the newly independent states south of the Sahara. Meanwhile another agreement ended the British military presence in the Suez Canal zone as of 1955, and this marked the final end of British informal empire in Egypt.

Ethiopia regained full independence with similar timing. At the beginning of the Second World War, the British navy cut off Italian East Africa from its metropolis. In 1941, British armies began moving in from Kenya and the Sudan, leading to an Italian surrender and the return of Emperor Haile Selassie in 1942. But Ethiopia remained an informal British protectorate until the end of the war and even into the early post-war years. The final steps toward decolonization in the horn of Africa came only in 1949, when the United Nations placed Italian Somaliland under Italian trusteeship for ten more years. At the same time, it gave the former Italian colony of Eritrea to the Empire of Ethiopia, effective in 1952. That ended the decolonization of the Ethiopian highlands, as far as Europe was concerned, but it was only the beginning of a long and drawn-out war for Eritrean independence from Ethiopia.

Libya was still another former Italian colony conquered by the Allies during the Second World War. Their options were to return it to Italy under some form of trusteeship, keep it under their own control, or turn it over to some local equivalent of the Ethiopian emperor. The United Nations decided on independence in 1952. It chose as monarch Muhammad Idris al-Sanūsī, the head of the Sanūsīa, the religious order that had fought Italian conquest most effectively. British and some American troops remained in occupation, so that Libya began its legal independence with a pronounced element of neo-colonialism. It also had oil, which could bring wealth and power to those in charge. In 1969, Captain Mu'amar Qaddafi organized a military coup, deposed the king, made himself dictator and played an important role in African and Middle Eastern politics far into the post-colonial period.

Independence movements in the Maghrib began in the interwar years. The best organized was in Tunisia under Habib Bourguiba and the weakest was in Morocco. Tunisia and Morocco nevertheless came to independence nearly simultaneously, largely because Sultan Muhammad V of Morocco supported the nationalist cause with the power and prestige that remained to his office. French governments tried a variety of maneuvers, such as sending the king into exile for a time and searching for other allies in Moroccan society, but the resistance movements in the countryside continued and grew through the early 1950s. After the beginning of the Algerian war for independence in 1954, France decided to cut its losses in the two protectorates, granting self-government to Tunisia in 1955, followed by independence in 1956, the year Morocco also became independent under Muhammad V.

The French regarded Algeria differently. It was legally part of France, not a mere protectorate, and it had far more European settlers. The first post-war revolt broke out in the region of Constantine in 1945, but it was local, brief, and easily suppressed – at the loss of several thousand Algerian lives. The final war began in 1954 when the diverse independence movements united to form the FLN (National Liberation Front) and to call for general rebellion. Military operations were modest at first, but after 1958 the French were to keep more than a half million troops in Algeria. As time passed, the war became increasingly unpopular with the French public, but the Paris government gradually lost its control over Algerian operations to an informal but effective alliance between the French military and the European colonists.

Finally, in 1958, the French army in Algeria revolted successfully against the Fourth Republic. The constitution of the new, Fifth Republic provided for a strong president, initially Charles de Gaulle, but he was not the diehard imperialist the settlers had counted on. As leader of the Free French in the Second World War, he was a symbol of patriotism; he could therefore give in where others lacked the political courage to do so. He took France out of Algeria by a series of gradual steps, spread over several years, each executed with the danger of renewed military revolt in the background. When independence finally came in 1962, the settlers and extremist military, organized as the Secret Army Organization (OAS), tried one final coup, but it failed. Almost all the settlers fled to France, in fear of reprisals for their final acts of terrorism.

The independence movement south of the Sahara moved in elaborate counterpoint to the independence movements in Egypt and the Maghrib. The first stage, approximately 1951–60, brought generally peaceful agreement on independence for British West Africa, Madagascar, French Africa south of the Sahara, and the Belgian Congo. The second stage, overlapping slightly and located in the early 1960s, brought independence to British East and Central Africa, to Rwanda and Burundi, and to the three still-British territories in southern Africa – Botswana, Lesotho, and Swaziland. After a hiatus of nearly ten years, the third stage came in a rush in 1974–75 with the independence of the former Portuguese territories, leaving Namibia (formerly German

South West Africa), South Africa, and Rhodesia (Zimbabwe) as the only significant remnants of European power.

Because the end of colonial rule came as rapidly and finally as it did, it is easy to forget that the outcome was not what everyone had wanted all along. Britain and France in particular were agreed on the need for colonial reform, but they emerged from their wartime experiences with different objectives. The British were used to the idea of colonies moving toward self-government and then independence within the Commonwealth; the recent examples of India and Pakistan were there for all to see. They expected the process to take a long time in the African colonies but they nevertheless expected it to happen. They tended to distinguish, however, between West Africa, with its comparatively few settlers, and other territories like Kenya and Rhodesia, where settlers, and settlers alone, enjoyed political rights. The problems of European settlement, and of the even larger Indian minorities in Kenya and Tanganyika, suggested that independence there could only follow a long period of gradual preparation and tough bargaining.

In France, independence was not accepted so readily. The post-war period brought a return to the conversionist ideal of the nineteenth century and the hope that African colonies could make steady progress toward equality with France in a wider French Union (later called the French Community), which was similar to the British Commonwealth of Nations, but with more formal ties. As a result, the new political constitutions drawn up for Africa in 1946 began by removing the abuses of the past, like forced labor and some forms of legal inequality. They also brought in new parliamentary bodies to function as embryo legislatures in Madagascar and in each of the colonies that made up the two large federations of French West and French Equatorial Africa.

The most impressive forward movement, however, was the widening of African representation in the French National Assembly itself. African representatives in Paris were only a few dozen, but this handful of African politicians gained a sense of power in a larger setting. They sat in French cabinets, helped to make policy for France as well as for the colonies, not by voting as a colonial bloc but in alliance with several different groups in French political life. That participation paid off in the form of greater equality with France, a gradually broadening franchise, spreading self-government at the municipal level, and other specific gains. It also paid off on the French side, as the Africans voted their support for the war in Indochina, and later for the war in Algeria. In the mid-1950s, many French observers looked back with pride on their achievement in taming the forces of "nationalism" that had brought so much apparent disorder to the political life of nearby British colonies.

Disorder was especially apparent in Nigeria and the Gold Coast during the immediate post-war years, partly because of a vigorous local press, partly because of economic discontents, and partly because of the new mass parties. The British were willing, however, to move toward independence, and the existing elite of chiefs in the countryside and Western-educated leaders in the towns were willing to accept a moderate pace. Not so the young men who gathered around the CPP in the Gold Coast, or Azikiwe's NCNC in Nigeria. They were determined to apply pressure, still short of open revolt, in order to shorten the timetable. The British faced a choice between speeding the march toward independence by giving in gracefully, or facing a period of repression and bitterness. They decided to give in, with an important symbolic gesture in 1951. Kwame Nkrumah was then in jail as a political prisoner, but his CPP won the Gold Coast election. The governor allowed him to leave jail in order to take his place as the newly elected premier. A preparatory period of limited self-government followed, and the Gold Coast became independent under the new name of Ghana in 1957. Nigeria, Sierra Leone, and Gambia followed within the next few years.

Meanwhile, in 1956, French tropical Africa moved a step closer to self-government within the French Community with the passage of a new constitutional, or framework, law (*loi cadre*). It brought in a broad new group of reforms, which had the effect of tying each colony directly to France, but also increasing its representation in Paris. But African acquiescence in a form of self-government that was less than full independence began to be eroded by the independence granted Morocco and Tunisia in 1956, independence for Ghana in 1957, and the army revolt that brought General de Gaulle to power in 1958. Along with his offer of self-determination to Algeria, de Gaulle offered French tropical Africa a choice between immediate independence – with an immediate cut-off of all French aid – or continued movement toward self-government within the French Community. In September 1958, the voters in each colony made the choice in a special referendum, which De Gaulle counted on winning. In fact only Guinea-Conakry voted for immediate independence, but the apparent success of the idea of an Afro-French Community was short-lived.

By 1960, the independence movement was already a visible success in the British and Belgian territories of West and Central Africa, as it was in Algeria. France then gave up its effort to hold colonies south of the Sahara. In 1960 and 1961, the former French territories became independent one by one, with continued aid and France's blessing – and a French hope that good grace would preserve good will and create an informal sphere of French neo-colonial influence.

The second-stage movement toward independence for East and Central Africa began with protests, which became more and more vociferous through the decade of the 1950s. Britain and Belgium, however, still refused the concessions in East and Central Africa that Britain and France had made elsewhere. Before 1955, the Belgian government tried to isolate the Congo from the winds of change and did little to prepare it for the independence that others thought was bound to come sooner or later. Isolation failed; protest movements became better organized and more violent through 1958. By early 1959, it was clear that independence would have to come soon, or Belgium would face a costly war on the Algerian model. The Belgian government then advanced the date and gave the Congo immediate independence in mid-1960. Rwanda and Burundi followed in the next two years.

In British East Africa, unrest among the Kikuyu of Kenya in the years 1952–56 turned into a guerrilla movement that reached open revolt, which the British called "Mau Mau." They suppressed Mau Mau, but the revolt helped highlight the problems facing the overseas Europeans, who were a tiny minority but dominated the economy. One solution was to give up and get out, as the Algerian settlers were finally to do in 1962. Another was for Britain to grant independence on the basis of "one man, one vote" and trust that the future African governments would show forbearance in dealing with their European and Indian minorities. British policy in the late 1950s tried to avoid either course, preferring to set up special constitutional provisions to shield the minorities after independence.

In 1960, however, it became clear that the independence movement was very strong, and no constitutional measures passed before independence could guarantee what would happen once independence was a fact. One by one, the three East African territories became independent on the basis of "one man, one vote," followed by Zambia and Malawi. But that was the end for the time being. In 1965, the Rhodesian government, representing only the overseas European minority, made a unilateral declaration of independence from Britain in order to keep its racial monopoly over power. This time Britain, not France, faced a revolt by its settlers in Africa; the British caved in where France had fought. Great Britain declared its opposition to any Rhodesian independence that was not based on racial equality, but it refused to use force. The Rhodesian "Europeans" remained in power till 1980.

The Rhodesian settlers' unilateral declaration of independence ended the second stage of sub-Saharan decolonization. For the next nine years, until April 1974, the line of advancing African independence stabilized at the northern frontiers of Angola, Mozambique, and Rhodesia. Independence movements were not dead, but neither the Portuguese nor the settler governments of Rhodesia and South Africa would give in without a fight. Guerrilla movements began a long war of liberation against Portuguese rule in Guinea-Bissau, Mozambique, and Angola. The Organization of African Unity (OAU) tried to organize international pressure. The African members of the United Nations secured a UN vote in favor of economic sanctions against Rhodesia; but many members, including the United States, refused to honor their obligation to comply, while South Africa and Portugal supported Rhodesia. The guerrilla movements fared better over the years, with most of Guinea-Bissau and large parts of Mozambique in rebel hands by 1974. Then, in April 1974, the Portuguese army revolted in Portugal itself, overthrew the ruling dictatorship, and began a series of social and economic reforms – including decolonization. First Guinea-Bissau, then Mozambique, the Cape Verde Islands, São Tomé and Principe, and finally Angola became independent before the end of 1975.

The Portuguese defection left the Rhodesian government in a precarious position. An African National Congress had been founded there in 1934, but it was weak until after the Second World War. In 1963, it split into two bitterly hostile factions – the Zimbabwe African People's Union (ZAPU) and the Zimbabwe African National Union (ZANU), which were divided by ideological, personal, and some ethnic differences. From their bases in Zambia and Mozambique, both began to send guerrilla units into Rhodesia with increasing strength and frequency from 1975 onward. The Europeans in Rhodesia were more and more dependent on South African support, but South Africa began to doubt the long-term wisdom of propping up a government supported by only 5 per cent of its own people and recognized by no other nation in the world. The United States government also became alarmed that racial warfare in Rhodesia might encourage Russian or Chinese intervention on the African side. In 1976, South African and American pressure together persuaded Rhodesia to begin the negotiations that led to independence in 1980.

The independence of Angola also put pressure on South Africa, particularly in regard to Namibia, which had been assigned in 1919 to South Africa as a mandated territory under the League of Nations. After the Second World War, it should have moved toward independence like the other mandated territories, but South Africa held on. Meanwhile, the United Nations recognized the South West African People's Organization (SWAPO) as the only legitimate representative of South West Africa, and SWAPO turned to guerrilla campaigns like those in Rhodesia. This and international pressure finally forced South Africa to grant independence in 1989.

The perspective of successive increments of independence may be the correct one for ending a book that ends with the colonial period. One colony after another emerged as a separate state, recognized by international law and membership in the United Nations. We have carried the story in some cases into the 1990s, though the colonial period in general ended about 1960. The final end of the last European domination in Africa came only in 1994 with the electoral victory of the ANC in South Africa.

Independence, however, was probably not the most important thing that happened in Africa over these transitional decades from about 1950 to 1990. This was a period of great hope and of great despair for many of Africa's peoples. Colonial oppressors were going away, but African oppressors often appeared to take their place. Many more people were certainly killed in this period – in places like Idi Amin's Uganda, or by Tutsi or Hutu vengeance in Rwanda and Burundi, or by northern Sudanese aggression against the southern Sudan – than were killed in all the wars of liberation against the Europeans. As things went elsewhere in the world, the colonial period in Africa came to a fairly peaceful end. What followed and still continues is a far more complex interaction among Africans, and between Africans and others who share their world – including the advanced industrial nations some of which, like the United States and Japan, were not direct participants in the colonial period but figure broadly in the new situation that followed.

Suggestions for further reading

Carter, Gendolyn and Patrick O'Meara, *African Independence: The First Twenty-Five Years*, Bloomington: Indiana University Press, 1985.

Gifford, Prosser, and William Roger Lewis (eds), *The Transfer of Power in Africa: Decolonization 1940–60*, New Haven: Yale University Press, 1982.

Gifford, Prosser, and William Roger Lewis (eds), *Decolonization and African Independence: The Transfers of Power, 1960–80*, New Haven: Yale University Press, 1988.

Hargreaves, John D., *Decolonization in Africa*, London: Longman, 1988.

Kepel, Gilles, *Muslim Extremism in Egypt: The Prophet and the Pharaoh*, Berkeley: University of California Press, 1986.

Knapp, Wilfrid, *North West Africa: A Political and Economic Survey*, London: Oxford University Press, 1977.

Lofchie, Michael, *Zanzibar: Background to Revolution*, Princeton: Princeton University Press, 1965.

Manning, Patrick, *Francophone Sub-Saharan Africa 1880–1985*, Cambridge: Cambridge University Press, 1988.

Marcus, Harold G., *Ethiopia, Great Britain, and the United States, 1941–1974*, Berkeley, University of California Press, 1983.

Marks, Shula, and Stanley Trapido (eds), *The Politics of Race, Class, and Nationalism in Twentieth Century South Africa*, London: Longman, 1987.

Peel, J.D.T., and T.O. Ranger, *Past and Present in Zimbabwe*, Manchester: Manchester University Press, 1983.

Rosberg, Carl G. and John Nottingham, *The Myth of "Mau Mau." Nationalism in Kenya*, New York: Praeger, 1966.

Vail, Leroy (ed.), *The Creation of Tribalism in Southern Africa*, London: James Currey, 1989.

Waterbury, John, *The Egypt of Nasser and Sadat*, Princeton: Princeton University Press, 1982.

Young, Crawford, *Politics in the Congo*, Princeton: Princeton University Press, 1965.

INDEX

Italics indicate references to maps